GUARDIAN OF THE GULF

Sydney, Cape Breton, and the Atlantic Wars

GUARDIAN OF THE GULF

Sydney, Cape Breton,
and the Atlantic Wars

Brian Tennyson and Roger Sarty

UNIVERSITY OF TORONTO PRESS
Toronto Buffalo London

ISBN 0-8020-4492-1

Canadian Cataloguing in Publication Data

Tennyson, B.D.
Guardian of the Gulf: Sydney, Cape Breton, and the Atlantic wars

Includes bibliographical references and index.
ISBN 0-8020-4492-1

1. Sydney (N.S.) – History, Military. 2. Sydney (N.S.) – Strategic aspects.
I. Sarty, Roger Flynn, 1952– . II. Title.

FC2349.S93T45 2000   971.696   C99-931116-6
F1039.5.S9T45 2000

University of Toronto Press acknowledges the financial assistance to its
publishing program of the Canada Council for the Arts and the Ontario
Arts Council.

This book has been published with the help of a grant from the Humanities
and Social Sciences Federation of Canada, using funds provided by the
Social Sciences and Humanities Research Council of Canada.

University of Toronto Press acknowledges the financial support for
its publishing activities of the Government of Canada
through the Book Publishing Industry Development Program (BPIDP).

Canadä

Contents

Contents

Maps

Acknowledgments

This book originated in part from a community-based initiative to preserve and restore one or more of the crumbling Second World War fortifications that surround Sydney Harbour. Stéphane Ouellette's fascination with those structures stimulated that initiative, as did Peter Moogk's pioneering work on 'Fortress Sydney,' which provided an excellent introduction to the topic. We have also benefited greatly from the advice and research of Robert Bothwell, Michael Hennessy, Kenneth Mackenzie, and Jay White. Their work on government economic and social policy during the world wars provided context to the story and filled in key details. Robert Caldwell, Michael Hadley, Robert Fisher, Marc Milner, and David Zimmerman gave equally important help concerning military technology and the finer points of submarine warfare, as did John G. Armstrong on home defence during the First World War.

Many others have contributed as well. Alec Douglas, formerly director general history at the Department of National Defence, Olaf Janzen at Sir Wilfred Grenfell College, Memorial University of Newfoundland, and Robert Morgan, director of the Beaton Institute, University College of Cape Breton, and Alex MacQuarrie at the Department of National Defence read chapters and gave excellent advice, as did three anonymous readers. Ken Donovan and Sandy Balcom generously provided access and guidance to the archival collection at the Fortress Louisbourg National Historic Site. The staffs of the National Archives of Canada, the Nova Scotia Archives and Records Management, and the Beaton Institute, as always, went out of their way to be helpful. We were fortunate to have William Constable design and draw the maps.

In a special category are the veterans who agreed to be interviewed and to share their stories with us. We wish we could have met with more of them. Douglas MacLean of Sydney generously made his very extensive Second World War scrapbooks available to us, Leo Kanne of New Waterford let us review his research notes on Fort Petrie, and Joe Joseph of Sydney allowed us to go through his photograph album. Gerard Gouthro was a valued research assistant one summer. Joanne Lachowiez, Brian Tennyson's administrative assistant, provided cheerful support services as always. Henri Pilon, our copy-editor, saved us from many lapses in logic and fact. Leslie Redman and Rachel Poirier of the Canadian War Museum assisted with the final production of the manuscript and Sandra Johnston assembled the index.

Portions of chapters one and seven were published as 'Early Fortifications on Sydney Harbour,' *Nova Scotia Historical Review* 15, no. 1 (1995), 1–32, and 'Sydney, Nova Scotia, and the U-boat War, 1918,' *Canadian Military History*, 7, no. 1 (Winter 1998), 29–41.

This book has been published with the help of a grant from the Humanities and Social Sciences Federation of Canada, using funds provided by the Social Sciences and Humanities Research Council of Canada. It is dedicated to Sandra Atwell and Brenda Donaldson Sarty, who not only indulged the obsession of two otherwise reasonably normal spouses with old fortifications, but also provided invaluable editorial assistance.

Needless to say, the authors accept full responsibility for any errors or oversights in facts and interpretation.

Brian Tennyson, Sydney
Roger Sarty, Ottawa
10 August 1999

GUARDIAN OF THE GULF

Sydney, Cape Breton, and the Atlantic Wars

Introduction

This is the first attempt to tell the story of the full range of military activities at a defended Canadian city from colonial times to the era of the cold war. While the literature of Canadian military history is rich, no one has previously examined the Canadian military experience by focusing on a single community that not only played a significant role during the long sweep of that history but was also largely shaped by it. That this has not yet been done for Halifax, St John's, or Victoria and Esquimalt would seem to be a remarkable oversight on the part of this country's historians.

It may surprise the reader that we have chosen to take the first step towards filling this gap with a volume on the military history of Sydney, Nova Scotia, which does not normally come to mind as one of Canada's great military cities. Yet Sydney, facing the North Atlantic at Nova Scotia's northeastern tip, is closer to Europe than any other port on the North American mainland. It also stands at the entrance to the vast St Lawrence route into the continental interior. For these reasons it became one of the western alliance's vital strategic ports during the two world wars of the twentieth century. Only Halifax was more important as a defended base, and at certain critical junctures Sydney, rather than Halifax, became the foremost bastion for the defence of Canada's Atlantic frontier and of the shipping that sustained the Allied cause. At the same time, and in contrast to Halifax, Sydney was the industrial heartland of eastern Canada: its nearby mines produced enormous quantities of coal, and its steel plant produced a third of the nation's steel; both were vital to the national economy and the war effort alike. Yet the city's place in the great twentieth-century conflicts has only been faintly recognized, and even less is known about the part the city played in British imperial defence policy during the century and a half between the acquisition of Cape Breton by Britain in 1763 and the outbreak of the First World War.

The story we have uncovered is one of consistent awareness over a period of two hundred years of the city's strategic importance among British and, later, Canadian defence authorities, yet persistent reluctance to do anything more than the bare minimum except in moments of dire necessity. The reader of this volume may well conclude that one historian's description of Cape Breton during the early British era as an 'orphan outpost' could be applied to the whole of the island's military history.

Cape Breton's British era began in 1758 with the seizure and subsequent demolition of the fortress at Louisbourg, the centre of France's military power on the Atlantic coast of North America. The conquering forces were based at Halifax, which Britain had founded expressly to counter Louisbourg. With the decisive success of the venture against Louisbourg, the strategic focal point in the Maritime colonies shifted away from Cape Breton, seemingly for all time. Britain's naval strength allowed it the luxury of not having to multiply its fortified stations. In time of crisis, temporary defences and facilities could be set up when and where needed under the cover of squadrons operating from a few substantial permanent establishments – Halifax and Bermuda in the case of the northwestern Atlantic.

It became evident, however, that even regular visits by warships from Halifax could not adequately control access to the splendid Sydney Harbour, then known as Spanish Bay or Spanish River, and the valuable coal seams that lay close to the surface on its shores. After all, it had long been a haven for vessels of the many nations that exploited the rich fishing banks nearby, and its coal had been mined from the 1740s by both the French and the British. When the new colony of Cape Breton was created in 1784, largely as a refuge for Loyalists fleeing the American Revolution, Sydney was founded at the head of the harbour as its capital. This brought a garrison of regular troops, although it operated as an outstation of Halifax and the troops never numbered more than a few hundred. Despite the pleas of local officers and administrators in the face of threats of raids during the wars with France and the United States in the troubled years from 1793 to 1815, there was little reinforcement at Sydney, and the few fortifications built were modest in the extreme. Nevertheless, the garrison was an essential source of security and stability for the small isolated imperial outpost.

By mid century, when the British government was attempting to economize on its imperial defence commitments by shifting the burden increasingly onto the colonies, the outbreak of the Crimean War in 1854 provided the opportunity to remove troops from North America, including Sydney. One outcome of Britain's military withdrawal was Canadian Confederation in 1867, a measure that Britain supported so that the North American colonies could, at least theoretically, protect themselves more effectively. An element of the imperial and colonial politics of defence during the decade before Confederation that has never been known was the protracted consideration given to Sydney's position. This review led to a brief revival of military activity at the port in the early 1860s, when it seemed that Britain and its North American colonies might become embroiled in the American Civil War. Although defence became the responsibility of the new Canadian federal government after 1867, it did not take the subject seriously. The new defensive fortifications at Sydney were allowed to crumble, and proposals over the years by British and Canadian officers to rebuild and modernize the establishment were never pursued. Nevertheless, those proposals demonstrated some awareness on the part of military planners that the port could well become a key position in a future war.

This proved to be the case. The unexpected success of the German submarine fleet in challenging British naval mastery during the First World War brought Sydney into its own as a defended base, albeit only in the eleventh hour and only with facilities improvised frantically. The submarine menace made clear the importance – and vulnerability – of the St Lawrence route, which Sydney directly commanded. The spacious harbour, moreover, was ideally placed at the juncture of the St Lawrence and Great Circle routes across the Atlantic. Here was an extremely convenient gathering spot, where ships coming from ports in eastern Canada and the United States could readily assemble into defended convoys for the dangerous crossing to Britain. In this way, Halifax and Sydney became strategic twins during 1917 and 1918. The Cape Breton port sustained the greater burden of warship patrols and merchant-ship traffic in summer and autumn, while Halifax became predominant when ice closed the St Lawrence. It was a brief flourishing of activity, for after the armistice in November 1918 the distaste of Canadians for military expenditure resulted in the immediate decommissioning of the facilities at Sydney and even those at Halifax were largely mothballed.

Still, the military was better prepared in 1939 than it had been in 1914, with plans in place for development on an unprecedented scale that included facilities at Sydney comparable to those intended for Hali-

fax. Demands on the two ports during the Second World War soon outstripped even the ambitious forecasts of what would be needed, when
the enemy brought the war right to Canada's shores, and both cities
became the centres of much larger and more diverse operations than in
1914–18. Despite the critical role it played in the Battle of the Atlantic
and the desire of military planners to maintain significant operations
there, Sydney was saved from abandonment as a strategic base after
1945 only by the onset of the cold war. It was a temporary respite. As a
result of the increasing emphasis on continental air defence in the
1960s, the naval base was among the first facilities to be closed when the
Canadian government began to trim back the forces it had built up in
the 1950s to meet the Soviet menace.

Boom and bust is the fate of most military towns, especially in Canada, a nation that has for much of its history virtually disarmed in times
of peace. Sydney's experience has been extreme, however, especially
when compared to such other East Coast ports as Halifax, Saint John,
and Quebec City, whose place in peacetime planning and wartime operations was similar. The reason appears to lie in geography. Sydney, more
than any other coastal city, is part of the Atlantic world and removed
from the continental development and integration on which Canada
focused from the time of Confederation. In that sense, its military history is more akin to that of Newfoundland – with which Cape Breton
has had important economic as well as military links – than the main-
stream Canadian experience. Newfoundland and Cape Breton suddenly
became vital when command of that ocean was unexpectedly contested
in the hot and cold wars of the twentieth century, just as they had been
strategically vital when command of the North Atlantic was contested by
the great powers in the seventeenth and eighteenth centuries. Every
time the prospects for peace improved, defence cutbacks quickly removed the military to continental centres (including ports that were
main terminals for continental transportation systems), situated conveniently near the largest concentrations of population, economic activity,
and political influence.

The importance of the military to the early development of Sydney,
and the city's role in the war efforts of 1914–18 and 1939–45 have been
largely forgotten except by the declining numbers of veterans. Some
traces of that role do remain, such as the name Battery Point and the
armed forces reserve base at Victoria Park, which has been occupied by
the military almost continuously for more than two hundred years. The
Point Edward industrial park and Sydney Airport are major legacies of

the two largest projects undertaken by the military in the area, while the recently abandoned radar base in the eastern suburbs bears mute testimony to the community's marginal relevance in the post-war missile era. Most of the low-profile fortifications built around the harbour during the Second World War survive, though they are deteriorating through neglect. However, no prominent military landmark such as the citadel at Halifax exists to serve as a daily reminder to citizens and visitors alike of the city's military heritage.

The great fortress the French constructed at Louisbourg in the early eighteenth century has been rebuilt as a national historic site. It reminds us that Cape Breton once lay not on the remote periphery of a nation but at the strategic heart of the Atlantic mercantile world, where European powers struggled for economic and military supremacy. Similarly, large sums of federal money have rightly been spent at Halifax to preserve the citadel and other harbour fortifications such as York Redoubt that remind us of that city's vital importance to imperial and Canadian defence in the nineteenth and twentieth centuries. This juxtaposition may give the impression that Cape Breton ceased a very long time ago to play a significant role in the Atlantic wars. This book seeks to demonstrate that such was not the case.

Until recently, the world wars of the twentieth century that left the most important mark on Sydney have seemed too recent to merit preservation efforts. The growing interest in the two conflicts in recent years, both as historical events and as important parts of Canada's heritage, has unfortunately coincided with a period of major retrenchment in government spending, which has included drastic cuts to the development of historic sites. Nevertheless, it is reflected in a movement to preserve one or more of the Second World War fortification sites at Sydney, so that Cape Bretoners and visitors alike will not forget the important role Sydney Harbour played over two centuries as a guardian of the gulf and a convoy port. Indeed, this book has its origins in the research done by the authors on behalf of one of the community groups engaged in this effort. This campaign finally resulted, in October 1998, in the recognition by the National Historic Sites and Monuments Board of Fort Petrie as a national site that symbolizes the role of Sydney Harbour in the two world wars.

Most of the material on which this book is based was found in archives. In other nations, detailed official war histories provide a good deal of the basic information concerning such technical subjects as the development of bases. Although Canadian official histories include valuable passages about Sydney, which have been crucial to our work, these accounts are brief and tend to deal with one armed service to the exclusion of the others. The Canadian war history program never included the supporting technical studies and civil histories on industry, construction, manpower, and the economy that in other nations help bring together the many threads that have to be interwoven in order to understand the complex activities at major defended ports. Until the last few years, private and academic authors working in Canadian military history have also tended to focus on national policies and on the forces committed to the main theatres of combat. There have been some notable exceptions, which we have gratefully exploited, and a considerable amount of basic research on the military in Canada and on wartime experience on the home front is now in progress. The scholars engaged in this important work have been generous in sharing information and ideas with us. We therefore offer the present volume in repayment of many debts and as a contribution to what seems to be a new search to understand Canada's military past in fresh contexts and in greater depth.

chapter one

Outpost of Empire,
1696–1802

I have passed a great part of my life in America and been in many unpleasant and disagreeable situations but I do declare without exaggeration that I think Sydney by far the worst.

Anonymous, 1789

Sydney Harbour is the finest on Cape Breton Island, being wide at its mouth and penetrating eight miles inland to where the present city of Sydney sits at the mouth of the river of the same name. Only one hundred miles across Cabot Strait from Newfoundland, Sydney Harbour is geographically at the heart of Atlantic Canada, opening onto the Gulf of St Lawrence, guarding the entrance to the great river and the interior of eastern Canada, abutting the formerly rich fishing grounds of the Grand Banks, and offering the shortest transatlantic passage from North America's East Coast to the British Isles and northern Europe. During the long imperial rivalry between Britain and France, Sydney Harbour was well placed to serve as a trading entrepôt between Europe, Canada, the American colonies, and the West Indies. As well, the only coal seams on the eastern seaboard of North America line the cliffs along its shores. Understandably, possession of Île Royale – as Cape Breton Island was known in the French regime – was long thought to be a matter of considerable significance.

Known in the seventeenth and eighteenth centuries as Baie des Espagnols and then Spanish Bay, the harbour appears in the recorded military history of the European era for the first time in 1692 when, during the War of the League of Augsburg, an English naval squadron

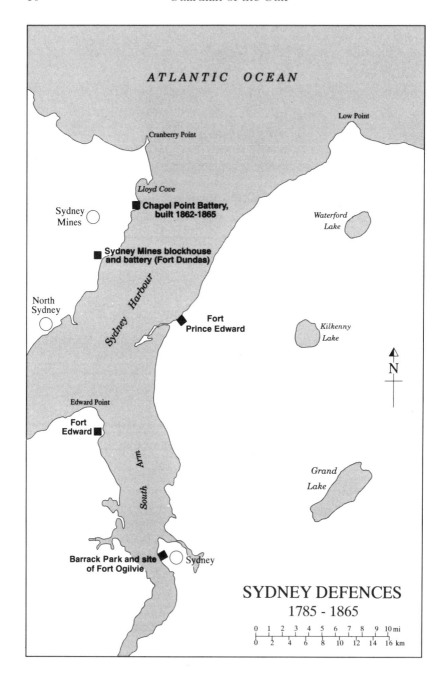

ATLANTIC OCEAN

Low Point

Cranberry Point

Lloyd Cove

Sydney
Mines

Chapel Point Battery,
built 1862-1865

Waterford
Lake

Sydney Mines blockhouse
and battery (Fort Dundas)

Sydney Harbour

North
Sydney

Fort
Prince Edward

Kilkenny
Lake

N

Edward Point

Fort
Edward

South Arm

Grand
Lake

Barrack Park and site
of Fort Ogilvie

Sydney

SYDNEY DEFENCES
1785 - 1865

0 1 2 3 4 5 6 7 8 9 10 mi
0   2   4   6   8   10 12 14 16 km

under Commodore Francis Williams was sent to destroy the fortified French base of operations at Plaisance (later Placentia) on the south coast of Newfoundland. While it was attempting to do so, a French squadron under the command of Camille de Digoine, Chevalier du Palais, was lying at anchor in Baie des Espagnols awaiting the return of a fast-sailing vessel that had been sent out to gain intelligence of English naval movements. This vessel encountered a heavy westerly gale, however, which forced it to return to France, a mishap that saved Williams's squadron from probable annihilation at the hands of du Palais.

Four years later, in 1696, Governor Frontenac of New France sent a naval expedition to drive the English out of Newfoundland, and then to attack either Boston or New York. Two warships, *L'Envieux*, commanded by Pierre Le Moyne d'Iberville, and *Profond*, commanded by Simon-Pierre de Bonaventure, with two companies of soldiers, were sent from Quebec with instructions to call at Baie des Espagnols to collect fifty Mi'kmaq warriors for an assault on Newfoundland. Upon their arrival on 26 June, they 'found there 30 savages who were waiting for us with their families,' according to the Reverend Jean Baudoin, who accompanied the expedition. 'They made their confessions, I baptized some and married others.'[1] D'Iberville received dispatches sent overland by Joseph Robinau de Villebon, the governor of Acadia, urging him to proceed immediately to the mouth of the Saint John River, where three English ships were cruising. He sailed for the Bay of Fundy on 4 July, taking twenty-seven Mi'kmaq with him, and engaged the English vessels in a battle off Saint John on the 14th. According to the Reverend P.-F.-X. de Charlevoix, the Mi'kmaq 'contributed greatly to his victory.'[2] D'Iberville returned them to Île Royale – it is not clear where – before continuing on to Plaisance in September, although at least three apparently elected to remain with the expedition.[3]

In 1711, during the War of the Spanish Succession, the British government sent a fleet of fifteen ships under Rear Admiral Sir Hovenden Walker, accompanied by forty transports carrying some 5,300 troops, to attack Quebec. Having stopped at Boston, the expedition did not reach the mouth of the St Lawrence River until 22 August, when seven transports and one storeship foundered in thick fog on rocks and shoals near Île-aux-Oeufs on the North Shore. Although the warships put about in time, 705 soldiers, 35 women (presumably camp followers), and 150 sailors drowned or died of exposure on the desolate shores of the St Lawrence.[4] Two days later the enterprise was abandoned and the fleet proceeded to Baie des Espagnols, where it arrived on 4 September and anchored in what later became known as Lloyd's Cove. What remained of Walker's fleet, consisting altogether of forty-two ships, was undoubtedly the largest naval armament ever assembled in Sydney Harbour until the wars of the twentieth century.

Walker had been instructed to attack Plaisance after taking Quebec but, having abandoned the attack on the latter, a council of war decided that the secondary objective was also not practicable because of a shortage of provisions, even though Plaisance was only one hundred and fifty miles away and lay almost directly in the fleet's homeward path. This decision was taken despite the fact that the combined force of fifteen warships, mounting nearly nine hundred guns and supported by a land force of four thousand men, was far superior to the defences of Plaisance.[5] Perhaps realizing that he would encounter much criticism on his return home, Walker apparently remarked that 'it would be a pity such a squadron and such a body of land forces should leave America without doing something against the enemy in some part or other.' Accordingly, having been informed

> by several Officers who had been there, that a Cross was erected on the Shoar with the Names of the *French* Sea Officers who had been there, which I look'd upon as a Claim of Right they pretend to for the King their Master, the Island having been always in the times of Peace used in Common, both by the *English* and *French*, for lading Coals, which are extraordinary good here, and taken out of the Clifts with Iron Crows only, and no other Labour: I thought it not amiss therefore to leave something of that kind to declare the Queen's Right to this Place; and having a Board made by the *Carpenter*, and painted, I sent him ashoar to fix it upon a Tree, in some convenient Place where it might most easily be seen.[6]

'This pompous and absurd "monument,"' as Richard Brown, Cape Breton's first historian, rightly described it, claimed Île Royale for Britain, but was 'most likely torn down by the first savage that passed that way, and the sole record of the Admiral's conquest of Cape Breton speedily obliterated.'[7]

In the Treaty of Utrecht (1713), which ended the War of the Spanish Succession, France ceded Acadia, Newfoundland, and the Hudson Bay territories to Britain but retained Île Royale. The severity of these losses had the effect of making the French government recognize the relationship between sea power and overseas commerce, and inspired a greater effort to protect the remaining colonies.[8] This included reconsidering a proposal made in 1706 by Antoine-Denis Raudot, then the intendant of New France, to build a fortress and naval base on Île Royale. Whereas the cost had then seemed excessive, the need to defend France's commerce and fishery, as well as the entrance to the gulf, which was regarded as the gateway to Canada, now made it necessary. Such an establishment could also become an invaluable trading entrepôt linking France with New France and the French islands in the Caribbean.[9]

Consequently, two officers were commissioned to survey the coastline of Île Royale for a suitable site so that the garrison and settlers at Plaisance, the former French military and fishing capital, could be moved there. Although the harbour of Baie des Espagnols was the best on the island, its entrance was too wide to be protected by the artillery then available. The other harbours on the island's eastern coast with sufficient depth of water to admit large vessels were Sainte-Anne and Havre à l'Anglois, and both had narrow entrances that could be defended against enemy ships. Eventually the latter was selected for the French base because it was also ice-free in winter and closer to the fishing grounds and renamed Louisbourg.[10]

It was an instant success. Within a few years of its founding in 1713, the new colony was producing and exporting stocks of cod 'worth about three times as much as Canada's annual beaver exports.'[11] Fleets of vessels had been coming from Europe for two centuries to exploit the fishery, but by this time the competitive advantage was held by resident fishermen, who did not have to endure the risk and expense of the annual transatlantic voyage and who were well positioned to trade with the flourishing West Indian colonies. Britain had a decisive advantage because of its well-established New England colonies and its dominance after 1713 of coastal settlement in Newfoundland. It was Louisbourg that enabled France to remain competitive not only in the fishery but also in the growing transatlantic trade of the eighteenth century. In the words of Sydney's J.S. McLennan, whose pioneering history of Louisbourg anticipated much important modern scholarship, 'more shipping capacity was required to export the fish of Louisbourg than to carry thither the imports of the place. The owners loaded the vessels [bound for Louisbourg] to their capacity [with goods to trade], and this surplus [beyond what Louisbourg could absorb] had to find an outlet. Thus Louisbourg became a trading centre, as it were, a clearing-house, where France, Canada, New England and the West Indies mutually exchanged the commodities their vessels had brought, to avoid making unprofitable the round voyage.'[12] Between 1733 and 1744 an average of

154 vessels went to Louisbourg annually to trade, more than to all but three of the much larger Atlantic ports in the American colonies.[13] Revenues from the fishery and related trade ensured that in most years the balance sheet of government expenditures at Louisbourg showed a surplus, despite complaints from Versailles about the cost of constructing the fortress.

Louisbourg's achievements were part of the general expansion of overseas trade that resulted from the prolonged period of relative peace enjoyed by western Europe after 1713. Competition for commerce sharpened national rivalries, however, not least because of the prevalent mercantilist theory of political economy. By the 1730s, Anglo–French relations were deteriorating again because of British apprehension that France's colonial trade was gaining rapidly at Britain's expense. The British were especially concerned about the flourishing French fishery at Newfoundland and Île Royale, the development of the French East India Company, French competition in the West Indian sugar trade and the West African slave trade, as well as the apparent continuing prosperity of the French fur trade. Fear of French trade competition in these areas increasingly alarmed British merchants and raised talk of a preventive war. The Anglo–Spanish war that broke out in 1739 over the issue of British access to the rich West Indies trade merged with continental conflicts that ultimately involved most of Europe in what was known as the War of the Austrian Succession. When France and Britain finally declared war on each other in 1744, the competition for overseas trade played a much greater role than in their previous wars. In the words of Professor Graham, 'The balance of trade had become part and parcel of the balance of power.'[14] Most of the naval action was along the coast of Europe and in southern waters for the lucrative commerce with the West and East Indies, but the North American colonists themselves thrust their part of the world into the conflict.

The most dramatic event was the capture of Louisbourg, the result of a campaign initiated by the New England colonies, especially Massachusetts governor William Shirley and Commodore Peter Warren, a Royal Navy officer with strong personal ties and business interests in New England.[15] The merchants of the populous and increasingly influential New England colonies had long chafed at the competition from Louisbourg, and their view of the menace posed by the French fortress was confirmed by the swift descent of a hostile force from Île Royale in the spring of 1744 that captured the small, ill-defended British fishing station at Canso, on the Nova Scotian mainland. The French force and its

Mi'kmaq allies continued that summer to make two assaults on the British capital at Annapolis Royal that were only narrowly pushed back by the arrival of reinforcements from the south. Meanwhile, privateers based at Louisbourg – private ships that had been armed to attack enemy shipping – were seizing New England vessels.[16]

Warren persuaded the Admiralty to allow him to come up from the Caribbean with part of his squadron, which, with additional ships from Britain, supported four thousand New England troops in laying siege to Louisbourg in the spring of 1745. This 'Puritan crusade,' as J.B. Brebner called it,[17] captured the fortress, whose garrison included thirteen hundred troops and other men able to bear arms, after forty-seven days. Storms and disease crippled the large French squadron of warships and troop transports that was dispatched to retake Louisbourg in 1746, so that the New Englanders remained in possession of the fortress until the end of the war.[18]

The coal seams on Sydney Harbour were a not insignificant factor in the Anglo–French rivalry in Cape Breton. The French had obtained coal for fuel from the cliffs at Burnt Head on Cow Bay and at Indian Cove on the northern shore of Baie des Espagnols. The British also worked the seams at Burnt Head and mined coal at what would later be known as Point Aconi, at Bras d'Or, to supply fuel to Louisbourg, Halifax, and Boston.[19] Fearing attack by French raiders or their Mi'kmaq allies, Colonel Peregrine Hopson, the lieutenant-governor of Cape Breton, began the construction of a blockhouse at Burnt Head in 1747 and stationed 65 men there from his garrison of 2,046 men.[20] Although no fort was built at Bras d'Or, an officer with a few soldiers were posted there.[21] Hopson appealed to Sir William Shirley, the governor of Massachusetts who had promoted the military expedition to Louisbourg, to provide two vessels to protect the supply route to Louisbourg.[22]

Before anything more could be done, however, a party of 120 French troops and Mi'kmaq warriors led by Joseph Marin de La Malgue attacked the colliery settlement at Burnt Head, seizing nine vessels, burning some two thousand cords of firewood, and capturing seven British soldiers, although the troops who were building the nearby blockhouse were not attacked when they refused to surrender. The mining settlement at Bras d'Or was also attacked.[23] This offensive had no lasting impact; the main effect was that no coal could be shipped to Louisbourg for more than a month because of the loss of the nine vessels. Within two weeks, however, the blockhouse was completed and was

manned by a detachment of 148 officers and men.[24] Named Fort William, it consisted, in fact, of two low wooden blockhouses and an enclosure protecting a number of wooden buildings, including a brewery.[25]
Thomas Pichon, who visited the fort in 1752, described it as 'so strong,
that with fifty men they were able to defend themselves against the
incursions of the savages, and to keep possession of the pit.'[26] Hopson
also allocated makeshift armed vessels to protect the fuel vessels sailing
between Burnt Head and Louisbourg, and began keeping an armed vessel moored constantly in Lingan Bay for protection.[27]

In the Treaty of Aix-la-Chapelle (1748), which ended the War of the
Austrian Succession, Britain returned Île Royale to France, much to the
dismay and anger of the American colonists.[28] The treaty was little more
than a truce, however, and irregular fighting in North America resumed
as early as 1750, although it was not until William Pitt won control of the
government at London that the conquest of Canada became an avowed
object of British strategy. Thus, the Seven Years' War, which began in
1756, was clearly a struggle for empire. One of Pitt's major objectives
was the relief, through the conquest of Canada, of the American colonies from the threat posed by the French and their Indian allies. Pressed
by many American leaders who argued the benefits that would accrue
from the expulsion of the French from Canada, Pitt was determined to
secure Britain's American empire by finally destroying French maritime
and colonial power.[29]

The British had already founded Halifax in 1749 on the magnificent
Chebucto Harbour to protect New England from Louisbourg.[30] Pressed
by colonial leaders, Pitt sent a substantial Royal Navy squadron and British regular forces, which captured Louisbourg in 1758 and Quebec in
the following year. These large operations were mounted from Halifax,
which in the process became a significant naval and army base. When
peace terms were agreed to this time, the British kept all of the French
possessions in North America, including Île Royale, now renamed Cape
Breton, except the small gulf islands of St Pierre and Miquelon as a station for the French fishery. To protect against a possible return by the
French to Cape Breton, British military engineers demolished the fortifications at Louisbourg, securing Halifax's place as the main strategic
port and economic entrepôt in the region.

The British had resumed mining operations at Burnt Head to supply
fuel to their troops at Louisbourg and Halifax, although both the mine
and Fort William had been destroyed in 1752 by a fire that had broken
out during a mutiny among the French troops stationed there.[31] Briga-

dier General Edward Whitmore, the acting governor, had 'a Number of Miners Employed' at the colliery in the winter of 1758–9, and that autumn had had a blockhouse built and had posted an officer and fifty men there 'to Serve not only as a Safe Guard against the Indians should there be any left on the Island, but also as Labourers.'[32] Nova Scotia's lieutenant-governor Michael Francklin described this fort in 1766 as 'a picketed fort 100 feet square, with a Blockhouse, Barracks and Storehouses for lodging the Workmen, Tools and Provisions.'[33]

In 1759 Whitmore was able to report that 'a large quantity' of coal had been produced and shipped to Louisbourg 'in Small Vessels from 60 to 130 Tons which are hired at the Rate of ten shillings per Ton per month.'[34] Some twenty men were employed in the colliery in the 1760s.[35] Despite the fact that coal mining in Cape Breton by private interests was forbidden by the British government after 1763, Lord William Campbell, who had succeeded Francklin as lieutenant-governor, granted an exclusive lease to a Halifax syndicate in 1766 on condition that it not dig coal where the troops were doing so. The syndicate therefore worked the old French seam at Indian Cove on the northern side of Spanish Bay.[36] The British government subsequently repudiated Campbell's attempt to raise public revenue in this way, but illegal mining continued and in 1770 a detachment of troops came to try to control unauthorized coal digging at Cow Bay.[37]

With the outbreak of the American Revolutionary War, Cape Breton and particularly the mines were threatened by American privateers who were operating in the Gulf of St Lawrence and off Canso as early as the winter of 1775. During the late autumn of 1776, privateers destroyed the fishery at Canso and raided harbours all along the coast of Nova Scotia. A British naval vessel had already been sent in July to protect the mines and the ships carrying coal to Louisbourg and Halifax.[38] In the spring of 1778 Placentia, Bay Bulls, Ferryland and St Mary's in Newfoundland were plundered with heavy losses of fishing vessels.[39] This caused the military authorities at Halifax to send a Major Hierlighy to Spanish Bay in April or May 1778, 'with as many of the new raised Independent Companies as he could muster, to protect the Colliery, Boats, Tools & Implements at Spanish River belonging to His Majesty, left there under the care of the Barrack master of Louisburgh.'[40] It is not clear if they reinforced or replaced the forty men belonging to Colonel Frances Legge's 46th Regiment who had been sent to Spanish Bay to dig coal in 1777.[41] Hierlighy's troops worked the mines as well, 'also fortifying a Post which was absolutely necessary for the protection of the people employed in the Mines and to save the Coals prepared for Exportation from being burned by the Rebels in case of an attack.'[42]

The danger seems to have been very real. Major General Eyre Massey reported on 21 April 1778 that only the previous day he had been warned that two privateers were en route to Spanish Bay 'to destroy everything, & fire the Works.' He praised Captain Charles Fielding, who had set out for Spanish Bay within twenty-four hours to protect the mines, 'which may be of so much importance to the further supply of the British Army; and I am certain will be there time enough to prevent the mischief intended.'[43] By this time the mines were supplying fuel to the garrisons in the middle colonies as well as in Louisbourg, Halifax, Newfoundland, and Boston, and more than a dozen ships had been detached for the transport of the coal, along with several naval ships to escort them in convoy.[44] This protection continued throughout the war and after its conclusion, and British troops appear to have remained at Spanish Bay at least until 1781.[45]

The British assumed that France's major effort in the American war would be directed against Newfoundland, Nova Scotia, and Canada, a fear that was reinforced by repeated American threats. British forces therefore seized St Pierre and Miquelon in September 1778 and undertook regular patrols of the Gulf of St Lawrence and the Grand Banks before the end of 1779, with the result that the privateers all but disappeared. In fact, the French had decided to concentrate their forces in the Caribbean, leaving Nova Scotia and Canada to the British. Even so, two French frigates attacked a British convoy off Spanish River on 21 July 1781, 'as they were convoying the coal Ships and some victuallers for the St Lawrence bound to Quebec.'[46] The British squadron consisted of *Charleston*, a frigate of twenty-eight guns, the sloops *Allegiance* and *Vulture*, with fourteen guns each, the armed transport *Vernon* carrying troops of the 70th Regiment going to work at the coal mines, and the cutter *Jack*, with fourteen guns.[47] The convoy had nearly reached its destination when it was discovered and chased by the French frigates. Captain H.F. Evans, commanding *Charleston*, escorted the merchant vessels into Spanish River, then formed his squadron in line of battle. The action began at 8:00 p.m. 'and was fought with little advantage to either side' until dark, when the French sheered off, despite heavy British losses. Evans having been killed in the battle, Captain David Phips of *Allegiance* assumed command of the squadron and sailed eastward. At daylight the next morning, when the French ships were nowhere to be seen, the British squadron sailed for Halifax, 'where it arrived in safety, but in a crippled condition.'[48]

Another smaller battle took place off Petit-de-Grat, in Chedabucto Bay, on 10 October 1782, when *Jack* was pursued by two heavily armed American privateers. R.P. Tonge, *Jack*'s captain, anchored in the harbour and the crew allegedly hauled a nine-pounder cannon ashore and mounted it on a hill in order to bombard the Americans in a crossfire. One of the American ships was captured and the other was driven off.[49]

Because of the influx of thousands of Loyalists at the end of the American war, the imperial government decided to partition Nova Scotia to create the two additional provinces of New Brunswick and Cape Breton. There was, therefore, a need to identify a site for the island's capital. Louisbourg was unsuitable because of its climate and the poor quality of the soil in the surrounding area. As well, the fortress had been destroyed by British military engineers in 1759. Spanish Bay harbour was the finest on the island, as the French had acknowledged in 1713, and Samuel Holland, who had surveyed Cape Breton in 1766, had recommended the peninsula separating the two branches of Spanish River as 'an advantageous situation for a Town; for which Reason, I have laid out Edward Town Lot there; & if thought proper to be fortified, there could not be a better Spot, as it is not commanded by any rising Ground.'[50] Nothing had been done, however, and the imperial government had actually discouraged settlement on the island, preferring to focus development on Halifax, but Cape Breton was now seen as a desirable destination for at least some of the thousands of Loyalist refugees fleeing the new American republic.

J.F.W. DesBarres was appointed the first lieutenant-governor and, having surveyed the coasts of Nova Scotia some years earlier, he decided to establish the capital of the new colony at Spanish River, renaming both the town and the river in honour of Lord Sydney, the secretary of state. Lieutenant Colonel John Yorke arrived from Halifax in the spring of 1785, accompanied by six companies (three hundred men) of the Duke of Wellington's 33rd Regiment, inaugurating Sydney's era as a garrison town, a status it retained until the Crimean War in 1854.[51] What justification can be offered for establishing Sydney as the capital and, more important, for stationing three hundred troops at such an isolated outpost? DesBarres certainly picked the Spanish River location because of its fine harbour, which was well protected from the open ocean, though its entrance was too wide for effective coverage by the artillery then available. As well, it was surrounded by potentially good farmland and rich forest, both of which would support the town. There was, of course, the continuing tension in British relations with France and the new American republic, and France still possessed nearby St Pierre and Miquelon, from which it could threaten the fishery, gulf shipping, and the gateway to Canada.

Although it was taken for granted that another Anglo–French war would take place in the near future, the posting of three hundred troops to the little town seems extraordinary. Robert Morgan, the leading historian for this period in Cape Breton, argues that 'at the root of Cape Breton's problems lay her unimportance to the mother country.' The colony, which he describes as an 'orphan outpost' during its brief existence, 'was born at a critical period in the history of the British Empire, when colonial officials were deeply involved in settling relations with the newly independent United States, when peace with France claimed high priority, and the constitutional problems of India were of the greatest concern. In none of these or other important events before 1820 did Cape Breton play a key role; hence she was ignored.'[52] He goes on to argue that the island's greatest resource, coal, was unnecessary to Britain and even a threat to the mother country's own mining industry, and so it was not encouraged to develop.

The strategic, albeit limited, importance of Sydney Harbour's coal in the recent war has already been demonstrated, however, and when the imperial government established Cape Breton as a Loyalist colony in 1784 it did so on the assurance of DesBarres that the island's coal would supply the garrison cheaply and employ the Loyalists 'without burthen to the Public.'[53] DesBarres opened regular works at the Sydney mines, and among his early instructions from the imperial government was a request that he prepare a report on the 'extent and situation' of the mines, with recommendations on 'the mode to be pursued for rendering them the most beneficial to this Country.'[54] It seems reasonable, therefore, to suggest that the large number of troops were stationed at Sydney to protect the mines, certainly for their strategic importance if not their commercial value, as well as the capital of the little colony. This reasoning does raise the question, however, which was asked by at least one subsequent administrator of the government, of why DesBarres did not locate the town closer to the mines.

It is clear that one of the tasks of the naval forces based at Halifax in this period was to defend the mines. As early as July 1784, having been informed that foreigners were removing coal from Spanish River, Sir Charles Douglas, the fleet commander at Halifax, ordered HMS

Resource there to prevent further removals.[55] When Douglas subsequently learned that residents of St Pierre and Miquelon were taking advantage of the lateness of the season to dig coal, he dispatched HMS *Hermione* to the scene and, to ensure that government policy was fully understood, orders were circulated to all commanding officers explaining that only persons with special permission were allowed to remove coal. Sydney Harbour later became a routine checkpoint for ships cruising the Cape Breton area.[56]

As well, a battery comprising six old four-pounder guns was established 'on the edge of the rock, above the Road'[57] at the mines on the northern side of the harbour, the old operations on the south side having been abandoned. Four-pounders were too small to be of much use for harbour defence, however, and the troops who had been guarding the mines were withdrawn at about the same time, leaving the miners to man the guns themselves in time of emergency.[58] How practical this system was can only be surmised. According to Lieutenant William Booth, who observed the firing of a salute in August 1785, 'tho' these Guns were, seemingly, served by Coal-heavers, and Blacksmiths, and fired with red-hot pokers, yet, the duty was well conducted.'[59] A small battery was also built at Barrack Park in Sydney to protect Sydney Point, and a significant force remained there until 1789.[60]

DesBarres had ambitious plans for his little colony and intended its capital to be a miniature reproduction of the imperial style. He had a town plan designed, and began construction of barracks for the troops at the military grounds, now called Barrack Park, approximately where the present George and DesBarres Streets intersect. The original barracks at Sydney are thought to have been built by John Muggah and Samuel Peters, 'who were sent here for that purpose, and who received grants of land in part payment of their services.'[61] Sydney's development proved to be very slow and uncertain. A 1786 map of Sydney drawn by the assistant surveyor for Cape Breton George Rodgers, shows several buildings at Barrack Park. Those on the western side of the road leading into the park from the Esplanade were probably houses for married soldiers, and the three buildings on the eastern side, near DesBarres Street, look like barracks and perhaps a cookhouse and guard post. The building further north along the road may have been the store, and the two buildings slightly east of the store may have been the prison and infirmary. In the area between Portland and South Charlotte Streets, north of DesBarres Street, were two buildings that may have served as the commanding officer's quarters and the mess house.[62]

It is not clear if all of these buildings were actually built or if some of them were only planned. Certainly those that were built, having been paid for by British money, built by the army, and reflecting European architectural styles, were the most impressive buildings in the town. The lieutenant-governor's residence appears to have been a large classical building, though it seems likely that the depiction of it by John Hames in his 1799 painting, *View of Sydney in the Island of Cape Breton,* exaggerated its size. St George's Church and a few New England-style houses lent some dignity to an otherwise unimpressive village.[63] According to a 1788 visitor, however, the town remained 'surrounded to the very sides of the buildings by an almost impenetrable wood.' There was 'a narrow path from the barracks just to keep up a communication, and that's all the clear country I saw.' The barracks were 'shamefully bad,' but the troops had cleared 'a good parade and made themselves as comfortable as their situation would allow.' There was no room in the barrack building for the officers, who 'were obliged to build huts and log-houses.'[64]

Another military visitor a year later was even more damning. 'What they dignify with the name of a town consists of about 50 Hovels ... There is very little land cleared round the settlement ... and even that [is] not cultivated.' Despite the proximity of the coal mines, the troops, 'who are totally unacquainted with the use of an axe must cut down 1200 cords [of wood] before the winter sets in.' There was 'not the smallest trace of Industry as the Inhabitants live by selling Rum to the Soldiers, and were they to be withdrawn (which God Almighty soon grant) it would be instantly deserted.' Because Sydney 'produces no Earthly article but a few Vegetables,' everything had to be imported 'at a great expense and risk either from Halifax and Boston,' including winter fodder for the livestock. 'Miserable as the place is the price of labour is intolerable as a drunken Rascal who himself an Artificer will not take less than a dollar a day, and the greater part of the materials for work are in proportion.' The military barracks were 'very bad and in danger of falling down.' Indeed, 'those for the few of the officers are so bad as not to be habitable in winter, so that absolutely to shelter my head from the weather, I have been obliged to give the enormous price of sixty guineas to an officer of the 42 Regt for his hut. Twenty are to be paid down and ten paid annually for 4 years to come. My Lodging money amounts to about 10£ per annum. God forbid that I should remain long enough here for my lodging money to amount to the price of this Hut.' He concluded sourly that 'I have passed a great part of my life in America and been in many unpleasant and disagreeable situations but I do declare without exaggeration that I think Sydney by far the worst.'[65]

In 1795, Sydney still consisted of only some eighty-five houses, most of which were in ruins. Only two streets kept to DesBarres's original formal plan for the town. Elsewhere, birch trees covered proposed city blocks, and a cattle track distorted what were to have been straight-lined avenues. There was still little commercial trade and few people were employed in trades or service occupations, so that fifty of the approximately 120 inhabitants had 'only salaries to depend upon for subsistence.'[66] Among these officials were the lieutenant-governor, chief justice, auditor, clerk of the crown, and clerk of the council. A census in 1795 also listed a carpenter, two shoemakers, a butcher, two merchants, two publicans, and a brothel owner. Business was so bad that several were threatening to emigrate to the United States.[67]

This rather pathetic little capital was the political and administrative centre of an equally undeveloped colony. Cape Breton in the 1790s was inhabited by barely 2,500 people, about half of whom were French-speaking Acadians concentrated in Isle Madame and Cheticamp, and most of the rest were Loyalists settled in Sydney and Baddeck. With some 350 inhabitants, Arichat, on Isle Madame, was by far the largest settlement on the island. It was the main fishing port in Cape Breton, one of the colony's two customs ports, and the principal centre for the distribution of imported supplies to the outports and for the collection and export of dried fish.[68] The rest of the population was made up of Irish immigrants and New Englanders settled along the southeastern shore, Gaelic-speaking Scots dispersed along the west coast, and Mi'kmaq in the interior. The economy was dominated by three staples: the cod fishery, which supported about two thirds of the population, shipping and shipbuilding, and coal mining. In 1796 sixty-nine vessels registered at Sydney sailed from that port and Arichat combined, and other vessels not recorded in the shipping returns also worked around the island. This coasting trade earned profits for Cape Breton shipowners and provided considerable local employment: the 152 men who worked on the Cape Breton vessels that sailed from Sydney and Arichat in 1796 comprised a workforce larger than that at the mines. Most of the remaining population was engaged in subsistence farming.[69] There were only two Cape Breton merchants of any importance in 1796: Lawrence Kavanagh at St Peters, and Richard Stout in Sydney.[70] Both were general all-purpose merchants, with fishing as one interest among others. They imported supplies, outfitted fishermen, sold seed and provisions to farmers, and exported fish and country produce. Stout and his partner, the Halifax merchant Jonathan Tremaine, were described by Lieutenant-Governor William Macarmick in 1792 as the principal 'and indeed the only respectable merchants in Sydney.'[71]

Complaining that the mines were a source of great expense to the government, Macarmick strongly recommended that they be leased to private interests. In fact, they had been leased to Thomas Moxley in 1788, but he lacked the capital to develop them very extensively. Sir John Wentworth, then surveyor general of the king's woods, argued in 1790 that coal could now compete favourably with wood on the Nova Scotian market, and, when Moxley died two years later, Macarmick leased the mines to Tremaine and Stout, whom he believed could run them in a more businesslike manner and thus increase exports.[72] At the same time, recognizing that the United States lacked both coal and wood in its developed areas, Lord Dundas, the secretary of state, told Macarmick that 'it follows that the Coal Mines of Cape Breton are increasing in their consequences, and require that particular attention should be paid to them.'[73] James Miller was appointed to evaluate the mines and to recommend a plan for working and exporting the coal in a manner that would be 'most advantageous and beneficial' to the imperial government. More than a year later, he was also asked to report on the feasibility of building 'a durable Wharf or Key of Stone for the purpose of facilitating the shipping of the Coals from that Island.' Macarmick was instructed to 'give him every assistance' in his power, and to 'advance to him from time to time, such Sums as are requisite for his necessary Expenses, during his residence in the Island, out of the Revenues arising from the said Coal Mines.'[74]

Miller subsequently recommended the expansion of coal exports and the construction of a proper stone wharf to facilitate loading, but Lord Portland, the home secretary, thought it would 'be better to wait until the quantity of Coals exported will in some measure provide for the expence of its Erection. At present, the Expence of the Coal Wharf appears to be too disproportionate to the Revenue arising from the Coals themselves.'[75] The imperial government also rejected Macarmick's proposal in 1794 to raise the coal royalty to provide additional revenues for the colonial administration on the ground that 'increasing the price would reduce the Exportation, and consequently both the duties to the Crown and the Profits which those Gentlemen are allowed to receive.'[76]

The mining operations of Tremaine and Stout employed between fifty and one hundred men, who lived in cabins or on nearby farms and worked at the mines during the summer shipping season. Even during the summer months mining was intermittent, dependent upon the arrival of vessels and orders for coal.[77] The colliery agent lived in a framed house, but when it was seriously damaged by underground subsidence in 1795 he was given permission 'to reside in the Guard House, near the Mines ... until it should be required by the Military.'[78] Although Tremaine and Stout succeeded in raising production from a little over two thousand tons to almost nine thousand tons per year, the mine was 'small, primitive, and pre-industrial,'[79] and continued to be unprofitable. Portland displayed little sympathy for Tremaine and Stout, blaming their difficulties on 'the improper manner in which the Mines have heretofore been worked,' and the government took over the operations in 1800.[80]

While it was true that Sydney was a remote outpost of empire, situated some twenty-five hundred miles from Britain and even several days' sailing from Halifax, and hemmed in by forest and winter ice, its military and civil elite struggled to maintain a connection with the values and lifestyle of the empire and society they had left behind them.[81] Documentation on this period is scarce, but the diary of Anna Kearney, the wife of Lieutenant Colonel Frances Kearney, who was stationed at Sydney from 1798 to 1802 with the Royal Nova Scotia Regiment, gives some insight into the lives of the officers and their families stationed there.

New Year's Day in 1802 was celebrated, for example, with a ball hosted by Harriet Despard, wife of the administrator. 'All the Inhabitants of Sydney both civil & military (the Fitzsimmons's excepted)' were there, and 'Ices, Cakes, negus & a variety of refreshments handed about Cold meat for the Gentlemen in adjoining Room & Trays with cold beef pye etc handed about to the Ladies in the Ball Room.' Mrs Weeks, 'to the surprise & disapprobation of many was at the Ball, & danced there but three weeks since she lay in.'[82] Anna Kearney's diary is full of references to such balls, assemblies, teas, and card parties, indicating that the small officer and administrative class at Sydney led very active if restricted social lives. On 18 January, for example, she attended another function at Despard's residence and 'had time to admire Mrs Despard's Elegant taste display'd in the ornaments of the Apartment before the rest of the Company assembled. A beautiful Festoon of the wild Green moss of this Country, intermix'd with artificial Flowers adorn'd the Pillars at the entrance, & had a most lively & elegant effect round the Room. Over every branch of lights were bunches of Evergreen interspers'd with Red and White Roses – the whole the ingenious work of Mrs Despard.' Mrs Despard wore 'a beautiful white Sattin, most of her Guests exhibited new dresses & there were no absentees ... Ices & a variety of other refreshments handed about between the dances, which were succeeded by elegant suppers in the Parlour & drawing Room.' The women went home around 2:00 a.m. 'but most of the Gentlemen K[earney] among the rest sat over the Bottle with the General till past 4 O'Clock.' Meanwhile Captain and Mrs Weeks, whom Anna Kearney clearly regarded as somewhat disreputable, 'did not honor either of the Supper Tables with their presence, as usual they toy'd and kiss'd to the admiration of the Spectators, & return'd early to finish at Home.'[83]

It was not easy to maintain British social manners and a semi-aristocratic lifestyle in the climate and living conditions of Cape Breton. Anna Kearney records that on 28 January a thaw produced 'deep mud [that] much annoy'd those that walk'd to the General's.' She was carried in a sedan chair, '& was better off than any of my neighbours, who however contriv'd to make a considerable muster.'[84] On 24 March Mrs Kearney equipped herself 'with two pr of worsted socks my own shoes & over all a pair of Kearny's [sic] & thus accoutr'd defy'd the mud & sally'd forth. These precautions secur'd my Feet 'tis true from wet but K's shoes sticking almost momently in the mud prov'd nearly as bad & made my Work a *duty* of fatigue. Took some turns on the Parade & then with K proceeded to Wilsons.'[85] Complaints of the cold were more common. On 6 February she reported that it was so cold that her husband's 'drink on a silver Tankard froze near the Fire inside the Fenders & our breath on the sheets.'[86]

Because of the small size and relative isolation of Sydney, it is perhaps not surprising that its political life was exceptionally factional and petty, aggravated by the fact that most of the settlers were Loyalists, while the lieutenant-governors and administrators were military men of limited experience and, sometimes, wisdom. As Anna Kearney put it, Sydney's air seemed 'remarkable for breeding disputes.'[87] Conflicts had started at the very outset and continued with remarkable vigour and pettiness until the island was annexed to Nova Scotia in 1820. DesBarres and Yorke had clashed in 1785 over the role of the military in the colony and the lieutenant-governor's jurisdiction when troops were used to clear the land and build huts and roads. In 1787, 'using as a basis a volunteer militia formed from DesBarres' supporters,' Richard Gibbons, the chief justice and president of the Executive Council, organized the Friendly Society, 'a quasi-military association which he conceived as a protection against any possible tyranny' that might be attempted by Lieutenant-Governor Macarmick and his allies on the council, David Mathews and Abraham Cuyler.[88] When the society attempted to form a select militia company, Macarmick countered by trying to set up a regular militia, which he would have the sole power to organize and call out. The Executive Council insisted that this would give the lieutenant-governor too much power; rather than allow the council to have any control over the militia, Macarmick never organized the militia, at the same time outlawing the Friendly Society as a possible 'Seed of Rebellion.'[89] This led Gibbons to assume the leadership of the movement that pressured the British government to give Cape Breton a representative assembly, at which point, in 1788, Macarmick dismissed him from office.[90] Following Macarmick's return to Britain in 1795, a series of administrators were appointed to govern the island because he retained his post until his death in 1815 but never returned to Cape Breton. So bizarre had the community's politics become that when Major General John Despard arrived as administrator in 1799, his predecessor, Brigadier General John Murray, refused to resign.[91] On 17 September 1800 Despard forced the issue by calling a meeting of the Executive Council to have himself proclaimed. A mob favourable to Murray gathered and violence was prevented only by the presence of the militia, which Despard had taken the precaution to call out.[92]

The substantive issues in Cape Breton politics throughout the colony's brief existence were the related problems of the government's need to raise revenue for public works and general expenses and defence. Although Murray had tried having the government operate the mines, Despard returned to the policy of his predecessors, hoping to raise revenues by leasing them to private interests and collecting a royalty on their production. The mines were, he claimed, in an 'absolute State of Ruin' when he took office.[93] Despard transferred the lease to William Campbell, the attorney-general and a political ally. When Campbell was unable to succeed with the enterprise, Despard gave the lease in 1804 to John Ritchie, a Halifax merchant, who expanded operations and built the extended wharf that had earlier been proposed by James Miller to facilitate the loading of larger vessels. As a result, production increased significantly between 1805 and 1807, and Sydney was now able to supply Halifax and Newfoundland with adequate amounts of coal.[94]

As for the problem of defence, Macarmick had believed that the importance of Cape Breton's commercial and fishing interests dictated that more should be done to protect the island. 'The fertility of the Soil,' he wrote, was 'well known to both the French and to the Americans as well as the consequence it is of to the Trade and Fisheries of Great Britain and her Colonies; therefore it may be provident some preparation for its defence should be made even in time of Peace to prevent the alarm which the loss of an Island containing such advantages would occasion in Europe and the Exultation and spirit it would give the Enemy at the commencement of a War.'[95] He was particularly concerned about the danger posed by the proximity of St Pierre and Miquelon, and, fearing that another war with France was imminent, he surveyed headlands at Low Point, Sydney Mines, and Point Edward, which could be used for signal stations to give advance warning of enemy vessels, noting that guns could be placed on these eminences.[96] He hoped to fortify Sydney and Mount Grenville (at St Peters), obtain arms for the militia, and have a naval ship stationed at Sydney.[97] Meanwhile, he built a military road from Sydney to Bras d'Or and began another to Mira Gut during the winter of 1787–8.[98] He also sent an officer to spy on the French troops at St Pierre and Miquelon; his report confirmed Macarmick in his opinion that in the event of war Cape Breton would be the first place attacked by the French.[99] Macarmick suggested seizing the islands but Grenville vetoed the idea.[100]

Indeed, the continued presence of the garrison itself was hardly assured. As Anglo-French relations continued to deteriorate, Lord Dorchester, the governor-general of British North America, advised the lieutenant-governors of the various colonies that in the event of war all troops were to be withdrawn from outlying posts, such as Sydney, which were instead to mobilize their militias for local defence. In 1789 the 42nd Regiment was removed over Macarmick's objections, reducing the garrison to two companies (approximately one hundred men) of the 21st Regiment under the command of Major Lovell, and even they were under orders to be ready to move on short notice.[101] Macarmick responded by calling a meeting of his Executive Council, which supported his plea to Brigadier General James Ogilvie, the commanding officer at Halifax, to take measures to secure the safety of the island.[102]

Because the harbour remained 'totally destitute' of guns, arms, and ammunition in 1790, Macarmick devised numerous defensive schemes, believing that the only effective defence could be provided by strong works on Sydney Point, Point Edward, and at the north and south bars. The imperial government, however, cautioned him against undertaking any defensive expenditures without having secured prior approval from his military superiors.[103] He therefore presented a defensive plan to Dorchester, proposing that if Cape Breton were attacked in strength, its inhabitants should retire to Mount Grenville at St Peters, which could be fortified to protect them. Vessels could then be alerted by a system of signals so that they could gather at a protected spot, perhaps on the Strait of Canso. He could raise five hundred men from the local population and nearly as many from the crews of the Jersey fishing vessels in the area for the militia, but he had no arms for them. The alarm caused by the removal of the troops was such, he thought, that it was essential that either the militia be called out or provincial troops be provided.[104] Meanwhile, Macarmick armed two large boats with guns from the mines and stationed them at the mouth of the harbour to protect the mines and shipping. Night watches, consisting of a corporal and four men, were established in Sydney and at the mines under the command of Lieutenant Colonel William McKinnon, the commanding officer of the renamed eastern district of the militia.[105] This activity won the approbation of the imperial government, which authorized Macarmick to continue with his defensive works, though no arms or ammunition were forthcoming.[106]

When war with France did break out in February 1793, three of the four British regiments stationed in Nova Scotia and New Brunswick – the 21st, 6th, and 65th – were moved to the West Indies, leaving the 4th and two small detachments of the Royal Artillery as the only regular troops in the colonies. The impact on Sydney was to reduce the garrison to one officer and twenty men, despite the government's protest that many settlers were leaving for other colonies, where they would be better protected, and that the defenceless state of the island would deter the Jersey fishing fleet from coming as usual.[107]

When Henry Dundas, the secretary of state, instructed the colonial governors in February 1793 to call out the provincial militias for home defence purposes, Sir John Wentworth reported that Nova Scotia's militia was 'extremely deficient' in equipment and was 'by no means to be relied on.'[108] Macarmick, who remained convinced that the French at St Pierre and Miquelon and the Americans constituted a very real threat to Cape Breton, promised to raise the militia but again pointed out that there were no artillery, arms, ammunition, or accoutrements for it.[109] He pleaded with Ogilvie for some field pieces, light ordnance, or, failing all else, transport to enable him to retrieve a few dismounted guns from the ruins of Louisbourg. In March, Ogilvie promised that guns would be sent for the defence of Sydney. Notwithstanding Wentworth's description of him as 'so timid and bound up to specific orders, that he declines everything of responsibility,' Ogilvie did eventually send three hundred muskets with accoutrements for the Cape Breton militia.[110]

Macarmick proceeded with the construction of a battery at Point Edward, under the supervision of Captain William Cox, whose difficulties included the high price of labour and the lack of tools for excavation work.[111] Macarmick wanted to move some of the old guns from the cliffs at the mines to Barrack Park, and even conceived a ruse for its accomplishment, requesting permission to borrow one or more guns to fire a salute to the Duke of Kent when he visited Sydney. He was obstructed, however, by a military officer, who argued that a civilian authority could not appropriate military property. Nonetheless, one gun was somehow moved to Barrack Park, where Macarmick built an earthwork battery, which he diplomatically named Fort Ogilvie.[112] When a French privateer was subsequently reported to be in the Sydney area, a few more guns were taken, ostensibly to arm the two gunboats but in fact to place in the empty embrasures of the sod batteries at Barrack Park.

The arrival in 1793 of 360 Acadians from Miquelon and the Magdalen Islands, who settled in various parts of Cape Breton but principally at Isle Madame and Little Bras d'Or, increased Macarmick's fears, even though they offered to take the oath of allegiance. Dundas thought they might 'be a valuable addition' to Cape Breton, 'provided they are well disposed,' but he agreed that 'until their Disposition is thoroughly ascertained, they cannot be watched with too much Care and attention.' If they proved to be unreliable, 'the earliest Opportunity should be taken of sending them to Nova Scotia, where they may be placed in such a Situation as will deprive them of the Power of doing Mischief.'[113] According to Wentworth, this threat, when communicated to the Acadians, had a good effect; they took the required oath and renounced 'all conventional democratic authority now exercised in France.'[114] Nevertheless, Lieutenant Colonel Moore, the commanding officer of the southern district of Cape Breton, was dispatched to occupy the new battery called Fort Dorchester at St Peters. The purpose of this battery was to divert attacks from Sydney, protect local fishermen, and intimidate the Acadians of Isle Madame. How effectively it could have achieved these objectives is questionable, however, in view of the fact that it consisted only of a square redoubt with fifteen embrasures, had been built by volunteers, and was armed with eight or nine very small two-pounder guns.[115]

When in July 1793 France sent several warships to the western Atlantic and gained temporary naval superiority in North American waters, the situation of outlying posts like Sydney became extremely precarious.[116] The lieutenant-governor considered calling out at least part of the militia but held off because it was the middle of the fishing season, although a few men were added to the crew of *Lady Apsley*, a small gunboat that patrolled the harbour area, and as guards for the arms depot at Fort Dorchester.[117] The island 'appears so remarkably bare of Inhabitants,' Dundas observed to Macarmick, 'as to render it highly necessary to concentrate as much as possible the means of its defence and to confine them to the most important Object of Your Government,'[118] namely the mines at Sydney. The arrival from Halifax in October of the schooner *Brothers* with arms and ammunition was greatly welcomed.[119]

In September 1793 it was reported that a French frigate of forty-four guns was at Boston, and that a French fleet lay at New York and many privateers were fitting out for some important expedition.[120] On 17 September great alarm was caused by another report that a French fleet consisting of five warships and several frigates, cruising near St Pierre, had destroyed the fishery at Fortune Bay in Newfoundland and was en route to attack Sydney. Macarmick complained of the British squadron's unwillingness to detach a vessel to protect Cape Breton or to give assistance and support to the civil authorities, and moved *Lady Apsley* to the Bras d'Or Lakes to maintain communication between the most populous parts of the island and assist in the general scheme of defence.[121]

The usefulness of *Lady Apsley* was questionable. It was described in the spring of 1794 as being so leaky as to be useless,[122] and Dundas had in fact authorized Macarmick in September 1793, 'when she shall no longer be equal to the Service required of her,' to purchase 'a proper Vessel for the Service,' although he had inevitably added the proviso that 'no unnecessary Expence will be incurred.'[123] When Macarmick evidently complained that additional funding would be necessary to keep *Lady Apsley* operational, he added, somewhat defensively it seems, that it was 'certainly highly proper that the Government Schooner should at all times be fit for Service,' but that 'the allowance for the said Schooner when settled was thought to be perfectly adequate for the Service, and therefore it would require some very particular explanation of the Causes why any further Expence was incurred before it could be admitted.'[124] The vessel was still officially in service in November 1794, although it had become so leaky by August that the shallop *Nancy* was being used in its place.[125] Lord Portland, who had succeeded Dundas as secretary of state, complained that it 'should long ago have been sent to Halifax' for repairs or replacement.[126]

Macarmick continued to press for large-calibre guns, stressing the importance of building fortifications to defend the coal mines.[127] The government hoped, after an expedition led by Ogilvie in 1793 seized St Pierre and Miquelon, that cannon captured there – and possibly a small detachment of troops – might be sent to Sydney when the islands were evacuated. Nova Scotia's lieutenant-governor Wentworth recommended that a company of troops should be sent to Sydney – he proposed his own unit, the Royal Nova Scotia Regiment – while at the same time advocating Cape Breton's annexation to Nova Scotia.[128] Dundas, recognizing that the island's militia was too small 'to furnish the means for its own defence and Security,' hoped that Ogilvie would be able to send two companies of the Royal Nova Scotia Regiment to Cape Breton in the spring of 1794.[129] Ogilvie promised to send guns,[130] but was unable to spare that many men because the regiment was not up to strength. He would, however, order fifty men 'to hold themselves in readiness to embark for that Island, and take messures [sic] for sending them as soon as I can withdraw the Troops from St Pierre, which I have received Lord Dorchester's Orders to carry into effect as soon as the Season will permit.' Dorchester, he knew, had already reiterated the standard British view that Macarmick should not expect any troops because Cape Breton's best protection lay in the Royal Navy.[131]

Unlike the Seven Years' War and the American Revolutionary War, this conflict focused on Europe, and the North American theatre was of secondary importance. Dorchester was well aware of this, of course, but agreed with the Nova Scotian and New Brunswick governments that the protection being provided to shipping in the Gulf of St Lawrence and along the coasts of the Maritime provinces was inadequate.[132] Still, given the fact that the commanding officer at St John's, the most important port for the Atlantic fishery, believed that that town was 'of no Importance' and its destruction 'of no Consideration,'[133] what hope was there that British forces would protect Sydney?

Macarmick appealed to the Duke of Kent, the major general commanding British forces in Nova Scotia, for assistance in augmenting Cape Breton's meagre defences, and the duke, having consulted Wentworth, agreed that something should be done. He was concerned about the defence of St John's Island (later named Prince Edward Island) as well. While agreeing with Dorchester that the primary defence of the islands depended on the navy, he thought, with respect to Cape Breton, that the mines should be protected. A battery with eight guns 'on the rising ground which commands the Coal mines ... would be extremely advantageous,' he thought, 'as thereby the Shipping of the Coal would be protected, and the buildings belonging to the mines.' The battery could be 'well manned' by the miners themselves until the garrison at Halifax was strong enough to allow for a detachment of one or more companies from the Royal Nova Scotia Regiment to be sent to Sydney. To attempt to defend the entire island 'would be utterly vain,' however, because of its size and small scattered population. Indeed, Cape Breton was 'now almost depopulated,' and, having consulted Wentworth, he too recommended that it be rejoined to Nova Scotia.[134] Portland referred the duke's recommendations to the board of ordnance, but the duke proceeded to order the erection of a blockhouse at the mines anyway.[135]

Meanwhile, Macarmick had employed the crew of *Lady Apsley* during the winter in collecting materials for the construction of coastal batteries, and a guardhouse and magazine were built at South Bar and named Fort Prince Edward in honour of the duke.[136] This initiative drew another reprimand from London, this time from Lord Portland. While pointing out that 'strictly speaking, all Works and Fortifications should not be carried on ... except upon Plans and Estimates previously approved of by the Board of Ordnance,' he acknowledged that 'in cases, however, of great emergency, it may become the Duty of a Governor, or Lieutenant Governor, on communication with the Commander in Chief of the District, and in concurence [*sic*] with his opinion, to erect such Defences for the security of his Government, as may be judged necessary at the moment.' The island's Executive Council, however, 'would, I conceive, be well warranted in examining and giving their opinion' on the expenses incurred, 'altho' they were not concerned in ordering the execution of the Services for which such Bills were drawn.'[137] Accordingly, he regretted 'the want of that cordial co-operation between you and the Council of the Island under your Government which should particularly prevail at the present moment in the adoption of all measures which tend to the general safety.'[138] A few months later he repeated his cautionary remarks, although he acknowledged that Macarmick might sometimes have to ignore his instructions in order to carry out necessary defensive measures. On such occasions, 'it becomes your duty to consult & advise with the Commander in Chief of your district, on the nature of such Works as may be judged necessary, and to receive his approbation of them previous to their execution.'[139]

The Duke of Kent's promised detachment of fifty men from the Royal Nova Scotia Regiment arrived from Halifax during 1795 and erected a four-gun blockhouse and battery, which was named Fort Dundas, at the mines.[140] The site was about midway between Chapel Point and Peck's Head, near Indian Cove on the northern side of the harbour.[141] W.L. Chirgwin claims that the garrison also dug a tunnel from its quarters to the beach to protect the settlers in the event of an invasion. This tunnel 'was named the day tunnel and is known as such to this day. The entrance on the surface is filled in now for safety but the shore end for 20 feet into the cliff is still visible.'[142]

The fortifications that appear on late-eighteenth-century maps of Cape Breton give the impression that Sydney Harbour was protected by substantial defences. In fact, only Fort Dundas, along with Fort Dorchester at St Peters, were worthy of the name, and Fort Dundas had only a handful of troops or often none at all. Fort Prince Edward at South Bar in Sydney Harbour was never more than a guardhouse and magazine.[143] Fort Ogilvie, at Sydney, where most of the troops were stationed, had two gun batteries of sod construction that, although designed for ten heavy guns, had only two or, at most, four small four-pounders taken from the mines.[144] Guns of this size were, of course, largely useless for protecting the harbour, and in 1797 the Cape Breton government even sent two brass three-pounders to Halifax, apparently hoping to obtain bigger guns in return. Four more four-pounders were sent 'for the use and defence of a Blockhouse erected for the Protection of the Coal Mines,' but the authorities at Sydney were told that Halifax was unable to furnish the nine-pounders requested since there were none available that were 'complete with Carriages, and calculated for the Service of a Blockhouse.'[145] This does not seem to have been quite true, because the artificers at Sydney had to make 'Regular Trucks for the Gun Carriages' of the four-pounders, as F.A. Wetherall, the deputy adjutant general, knew.[146] If they could make new mountings for these guns, one assumes that they could have done so for the larger guns as well. The officials at Halifax, it seems, were not inclined to supply larger cannon, dismounted or otherwise.

Macarmick having been granted leave in 1795, David Mathews, the attorney-general and senior councillor, administered the government until Ogilvie was sent from Halifax, no doubt partly to strengthen the defences but also in the misguided hope of putting an end to the extraordinary political squabbling that continued to paralyse the government of the colony.[147] The summer of 1796 was one of crisis. When

French privateers captured some vessels off the coast of Cape Breton in early July, Mathews called out the militia, whose members reportedly responded well.[148] Notwithstanding this alarm and a later warning from the British consul at Norfolk, Virginia, that a strong French fleet had arrived in the West Indies and might be expected to threaten the northern British colonies, Mathews reported in August 1796 that all was quiet.[149] A French squadron of nine ships commanded by Admiral Richery did in fact appear off Bay Bulls, Newfoundland, at the end of the month.[150] In addition to harassing the fishing fleet, it dispatched a force to destroy the mines and burn the town of Sydney. Like others before it, however, this expedition failed as a result of autumn gales, and the French squadron departed in October without having done much harm.[151]

Richery's expedition did have one important result: it emphasized the vital importance of Sydney's coal to the British colonies.[152] Thus, when Mathews reminded the military authorities in Halifax of the exposed position of the mines and how easily they could be destroyed by a small hostile force, the Duke of Kent again responded.[153] Recognizing that the danger posed to the mines by enemy raiders was real, in June 1797 he sent five hundred muskets 'for the use of the inhabitants' and four iron four-pounder guns with carriages and ammunition for the blockhouse at Fort Dundas. Gunner Ian Hayes of the Royal Artillery was sent 'to take charge of the above ordnance and stores.'[154] Two months later, as a result of another alarm caused by French privateers off the coasts, Mathews again called out the militia, and he distributed the arms to the men.[155]

In June 1798, having survived a shipwreck off Scatarie Island, General Ogilvie arrived as administrator of the colony, bringing with him one hundred and fifty men of the Royal Nova Scotia Regiment.[156] In view of the small number of troops at his disposal, Ogilvie reorganized the militia so that it could be called quickly into service, though this achievement appears to have been largely on paper.[157] He also discovered that Government House at Sydney and all of the batteries, with the exception of the newly constructed blockhouse at Fort Dundas, were in ruins.[158] However, the Duke of Kent agreed in September to his request for four nine-pounder guns and ammunition, and a detachment of gunners.[159] These appear to have been in addition to those sent in the previous year at Mathews's request. Ogilvie rightly observed that one problem relating to the defence of the mines was that the town of Sydney, where the main garrison was based, was in the wrong place. Sydney

Point had no particular commercial advantages and was approximately nine miles from the mines, the primary economic staple and strategic interest. He recommended moving the capital to the North Bar area, where North Sydney later developed, but nothing came of this eminently sensible proposal.[160]

Ogilvie soon became embroiled in the continuing political warfare that seemed endemic at Sydney, both between the military and civil authorities and between rival factions on the Executive Council, and he was replaced in 1799 by Brigadier General John Murray, who added military personnel to the council. This resulted in a sharp reprimand from the Duke of Kent, who reminded him that he could not employ military personnel under his command in responsibilities falling under civil jurisdiction. Murray was soon replaced by Major General John Despard, but not before he undertook major repairs and renovations to the military buildings that spring. According to the figures presented by Captain Cox, who supervised the work, the mess house was repaired and had a porch added, 'a Necessary for the Officers' was built, a porch was added onto the hospital, a boathouse and slip were built, and the commanding officer's quarters, then occupied by Captain Weeks, were repaired.[161]

Because of the seemingly interminable Anglo-French war, small detachments of the Nova Scotia Fencibles and the 104th Regiment continued to be stationed at Sydney during the next few years for the defence of the capital and the mines. Although Cape Breton was never attacked, there was privateering off its coasts, and the French had attacked Bay Bulls in Newfoundland in September 1796. The militia was not called out again after 1797, and with the signing of the Treaty of Amiens in 1802 – which proved to be only an armistice – the garrison at Sydney was reduced to its lowest number: a non-commissioned officer and nine men of the Royal Artillery.[162]

chapter two

War and Peace, 1802–1859

The men of my company, with their red coats, sauntering about, as they continually do to kill time, forming the majority of the male kind to be seen, conveyed the idea of a military occupancy of some deserted village.

Lieutenant B.W.A. Sleigh, 1846

The Peace of Amiens of 1802–3 proved to be only a temporary lull, and the European war soon resumed, dragging on until 1815. In 1812 the situation in North America was considerably complicated by the outbreak of war between Britain and the United States as well. Although there was little actual fighting at Britain's imperial outposts between 1803 and 1812, there was 'much dreary watching and arduous patrol work.'[1]

At Sydney some repairs were made to the fortifications in 1804, Captain Cox being appointed to supervise the work. He was by now the barrack master, and, in the opinion of the commanding officer of the Royal Engineers at Halifax, he was 'an Excellent officer perfectly capable to Act as an Assistant Engineer, and ... the only person at that Place qualified for the Duty.'[2] According to Cox, the roof of the blockhouse at the mines was damaged, the whole building required repainting, the platform on the lower floor had to be relaid, and the picketing around the building needed repair. The carriages of the four four-pounder guns were serviceable, as were the traversing carriages of the four twelve-pounder guns at the battery, but the garrison carriages were unusable. At Sydney the two brass six-pounder guns on field carriages were in acceptable condition and work on the recently built magazine was

nearly complete. New picketing, with gates and posts, was needed, however, and the gun shed required a new roof, sills and doors.[3]

Not much seems to have been done, because three years later Cox was
reporting that the blockhouse at the mines was 'very much out of Repair,
particularly the Roof' as the result of a gale which had blown down
'a heavy Flagstaff' and 'carried away [a] great part of the Shingles, so
that the Rain runs thro' the Whole Building.' As well, the battery's platform was 'totally rotten' and the gun carriages were 'unfit for service,'
while the barbette was 'much injured, having been exposed for several
years to Cattle.' The armament consisted of three medium iron twelve-
pounders mounted on traversing carriages and one long twelve-pounder
on a ship carriage. The blockhouse mounted four iron four-pounders
'on very indifferente [sic] made Carriages. This is all the Force at the
Mines.'[4]

If the military authorities wanted to restore the defences at the mines
to a serviceable state, it would be necessary to bring in 'some careful
Artificers' from Halifax because none were available locally, 'all the
Mechanics being Employed in their Harvest,' and even if they were available, 'they would ask Exorbitant Pay.' Cox explained that he was 'making mention of these Circumstances, being so well Acquainted with the
Nature of the People and the manner in which they are situated, as well
as from former Experience.' In fact, he offered to undertake the work
himself and, referring to 'some unpleasant circumstances [that had]
attended my performance of this duty latterly,' assured Captain William
Bennett, the commanding royal engineer at Halifax, that he hoped 'to
Avoid any thing of the same kind in future.'[5] A month later he referred
Bennett to 'my friend, Captain Despard,' who was the son of General
Despard and had served with him in Cape Breton, again asking to be
'reinstated to superintend the Ordnance Works here as Assistant Engineer,' promising to do 'all in my Power to give you every satisfaction.'[6]

Apparently Cox was indeed reinstated, for a few months later he was
predictably reporting to Captain James McLaughlan, Bennett's successor, that the necessary repairs 'will far exceed the sum mentioned in
your letter, as several years ago I had to advertise to get workmen to perform the work in question and could not get it done for less than
upwards of Ninety pounds ... It inevitably at this time will even exceed
that amount considerably.' He recommended that McLaughlan 'pay
this Post a Visit, in order that you may be fully made Acquainted with
the exact situation of the place, and the impossibility of getting any work
done here without the Assistance of some Artificers, unless the most

exorbitant pay is given.'[7] In the meantime, Cox proposed to have the roof of the blockhouse repaired, 'as the rain runs through the Building,' but would await further instructions for the other work.[8]

Evidently, McLaughlan ordered the work to go ahead, and within a year, in the fall of 1808, Cox was able to report that he had 'finished all the Material Repairs of the Publick Works,' consisting of a blockhouse, battery, and cookhouse at the mines, and a magazine and gun shed at Sydney. The blockhouse had undergone 'a thorough Repair,' as had the battery, 'having laid New Platforms, Repaired the Traversing Carriages which were nearly useless, and had a New Fence made round the Blockhouse.' In addition to repairing the magazine and shed at Sydney, Cox had also repaired the fence of the magazine. 'I have still in hand the Repair of the Cook Room & Out Building, the Expence of which will not Exceed Five Pounds, exclusive of any little allowance that may be thought proper to be allowed for my Attendance. The Cause of this Expence not being included in the present Statement is, my being aware that the General Accts of the Ordnance Department are expected to be made up about this time in each Year.' The guns were mounted 'and every thing [was] in as good a State of Defence as the Nature of circumstances of the Place will admit.' What was more, 'the Expense incurred is much within the Sum specified by the Board,' and he hoped that it would not be considered unreasonable, 'particularly when I remind you that many Years back I could not have had the same Work Performed for double the present Amount.'[9]

Four months later Cox was able to report to Colonel Gustavus Nicolls, the newly appointed commanding royal engineer at Halifax, that 'no material repairs' were required at Sydney, 'except the picketing round the magazine which was contracted for and considered last fall amongst the Works completed. ' The person employed to do that work, however, had 'left the place before the Work was done, and it being then so late in the Season as to prevent my Employing any other, No Expence has been incurred on that account.' Pointing out that there was 'no place fit' for the 550 muskets that had been sent for the use of the Cape Breton militia, Cox had, with the approval of Brigadier General Nicholas Nepean, Cape Breton's administrator from 1807 to 1813, 'fitted up one of the vacant Barrack Rooms as an armory & have had them well cleaned and repaired and they are now in exceeding Good Order. The expence answered for this Service was paid by the Revenue of the Island.'[10]

By the spring of 1809 the picketing around the magazine yard was 'in such a state as to make it absolutely necessary to have it repaired without delay.' Cox did so, again with the approval of Nepean but without consulting Halifax. 'This measure I was induced to do,' he explained, 'as the expence was trifling, making use of old Pickets.' He also visited the blockhouse and battery at the mines and found 'some small repairs wanting.' In addition, the flagstaffs at the mines and Sydney, 'both of which have been blown down during [?] some time, being rotten,' needed to be replaced. He proposed to erect new ones, assuring Nicolls that the cost 'shall not exceed the Sum of £50, as mentioned by you.'[11]

When Cox submitted his account for the work done during that summer of 1809, he explained that the cookhouse at the mines was in fact 'a Room Consisting of Seven Births [sic],' which had 'always been Occupied by a non Commissioned Officer and from 12 to 20 Men.' When these troops were 'some time ago ... suddenly withdrawn,' the result was that 'some mischief was done to the Building and every Pane of Glass broke. ' These had been replaced and a signal staff at the mines, 'which is Certainly required,' would be completed within twelve days, but most of the rope required for it was already on hand, so there would be no additional expense. 'You will Observe,' he concluded, that 'I have attended to the extent of the small Pittance allowed for the defence of the Island by the Board of Ordnance.'[12]

Notwithstanding Cox's frequent complaints about the high cost of hiring skilled labour at Sydney, Nicolls instructed him at the end of 1809 to hand over repair work on the fortifications to a civilian contractor, perhaps because most of the troops stationed there had been withdrawn in November. Six months later, he had not yet done so but assured Nicolls that he would 'comply with your directions to the best of my Power.' Again he claimed that 'it is almost impossible to do Business here, in that regular and pleasant manner [in which] it may be performed in other Military Parts of the world,' but if there were 'any Person I could recommend to your Notice capable to carry on what little works requisite to be done here, I would with Pleasure relinquish the Employment.'[13]

Meanwhile, production at the mines was lagging because of mismanagement at a time when the growing number of troops at Halifax was creating greater demand for fuel. To solve the problems of high wages and low production, Nepean put thirty of the New Brunswick Fencibles stationed at Sydney to work at the mines. Output rose until the summer of 1811, when Sir George Prevost, the lieutenant-governor, ordered the troops out of the mines on the grounds that such work should be done by civilian labourers. The mines were not leased to a private company, however, and were virtually abandoned until Brigadier General Hugh Swayne, on his arrival in 1813, leased them to John Ritchie.[14] Although Halifax continued to purchase as much as could be shipped there, the Nova Scotia House of Assembly continued to complain of the high cost of Cape Breton coal.[15]

The troops withdrawn from the blockhouse at the mines early in 1809 were back by the end of the year, though in smaller numbers. At the beginning of 1810, there were a non-commissioned officer and six gunners stationed there who were 'in charge of the Ordnance and Stores.' The guns, carriages, and platforms in the battery were described as being in 'serviceable' condition, while the guns and carriages in the blockhouse were 'in a good state and [there was] a sufficient proportion of ammunition in readiness for each piece. This Station being out of a probable line of Attack (except by a Privateer) it is not necessary to keep a large proportion of Ammunition there.' At Sydney, there were two English light six-pounder field artillery guns. During the course of 1810, the status of the battery at the mines improved from 'serviceable' to 'in good Order,' but sometime during the next six months its ordnance was reduced to four English four-pounder iron guns and the troops stationed there appear to have been withdrawn again.[16]

If the war had come to seem to be remote from Cape Breton, it was soon to approach much more closely. There was mounting frustration in the United States over territorial conflicts with Britain in the northwestern interior of North America and competition for the West Indian trade. These factors finally combined with American outrage over British policy on the high seas to incite the United States to take advantage of the war in Europe, which had reached a critical stage in the spring of 1812, by declaring war on Britain. Because of their location, the Maritime colonies and Newfoundland were especially vulnerable to raids by privateers, hundreds of which were fitting out at U.S. ports. With the exception of the French raid on Bay Bulls, Newfoundland, in 1796, the colonies had thus far escaped attack. Now, fear of American privateers swept through the region, justified by the fact that more than two hundred merchant or fishing vessels were lost in the Bay of Fundy or the waters between Nova Scotia and Newfoundland before the British naval blockade of U.S. ports took effect during 1813.[17]

Swayne, Cape Breton's new administrator, claimed in early 1813 that the crews of enemy privateers had actually landed and established coastal signal stations between Sydney Harbour and Cape North, to the great injury of the Quebec trade. He asked Lord Bathurst, the colonial secretary, for an armed sloop and schooner to repel privateers, since Sydney was 'as perfectly exposed from its situation that any Vessels of the Enemy might easily approach it.'[18] He did not get much relief, but Rear Admiral Edward Griffith at Halifax did agree to send the sloop *Raleigh* to 'vigilantly cruize between the Island of Scatari[e] and Cape North, for the protection of the Coasting Trade, as well as of the Coast itself against any predatory attacks of the Enemy's Privateers,' and he expressed the hope that 'it may soon be in my power to afford protection for the other part of the Coast you have pointed out; at present it is not.'[19]

Batteries, with blockhouses behind them for support, were built at the more important harbours throughout the region. At Sydney the garrison had been increased in 1811 to 168 men, and by January 1812 the four twelve-pounder guns at the mines battery had 'been put in good Order.' The four four-pounder guns at the blockhouse to the rear of the battery were also 'in a good State.' Elsewhere in Cape Breton were eight six-pounder guns that were in serviceable condition.[20] A later report, in June 1812, referred to two six-pounders, situated at Barrack Park at Sydney, as the only other ordnance on the island.[21] When estimates were submitted three weeks later for repairs at Barrack Park, the authorities at Halifax agreed that the barrack building should be reshingled, that its foundation and fireplaces should be repaired, and that the interior of the building should be whitewashed. As for the proposed repainting of the barrack building, 'it is thought that the clap boarding ... can be hardly worth the expence of painting it, and therefore the Lt General defers sanctioning that expence, until it has been thoroughly examined, and a satisfactory report of its actual state transmitted for His Excellency's consideration.' The hospital was 'not considered worth repair.'[22] The authorities at Halifax also wanted to know which tasks were to be performed by military personnel and which by civilian contractors.

Swayne did what he could with the limited means at his disposal to improve the security of the island by repairing the batteries at Sydney and at the mines. During the next six months, the magazine was repaired, new platforms were built, sliding carriages were made for the four twelve-pounders, a small travelling magazine was constructed, and the guns and carriages were painted.[23] This work was paid for, at least in part, with revenue collected by a tax on rum imposed by Despard in 1801, leading inevitably to the later observation that Cape Breton 'faced the War of 1812 fortified with rum.'[24] Nevertheless, the state of Barrack Park at Sydney remained poor. The best that could be said of its provision store was that there was not the 'least danger of it falling this winter,' while the roof of the magazine leaked and the picket fence was 'in danger of falling down from its very decayed state.'[25] The situation was not helped by the fact that the military reserve on Battery Point had been illegally encroached upon by Richard Gibbons, the colony's attorney-general.[26]

Swayne expanded Sydney's defences by building Fort Edward, an earthwork with four bastions, on the northeastern tip of Point Edward, the peninsula that separates the northern and southern branches of the harbour. He was referring to this new fort in November 1813 when he proudly informed Bathurst that 'we have fortified the Capital & river by a strong redoubt & Batteries; the whole has been perfected without incurring the least Expence to Government.'[27] Rather than earning appreciation for this initiative, however, Swayne was reprimanded for having undertaken 'any Public Work however useful' without the express approval of the imperial government.[28] At the same time, however, a company of New Brunswick's 104th Regiment was sent to Sydney, and a non-commissioned officer and five gunners were posted at the mines battery.[29] Shortly afterwards, the lieutenant-governor of Nova Scotia, Sir John Sherbrooke – who had served in Sydney in 1785 and 1786 – sent six eighteen-pounder guns and eight six-pounders, 'Complete with Ammunition and Stores,'[30] followed by five hundred muskets with accoutrements, 'which will I hope enable your brave Militia men to chastise the Crew of any Privateer which may have the temerity to land upon their Coasts.'[31]

There was, in fact, no organized militia, although Nepean, whom Despard had described as 'a remarkably indolent Man,' had made 'a few feeble moves' to raise one.[32] Claiming that 'no steps had been taken before my arrival here towards the formation of a Militia with the exception of the appointment of some Officers,' Swayne 'deemed it necessary to form the Inhabited parts of the Island into Divisions under a Captain and two Lieutenants each.' On the basis of census returns, he calculated that there were thirteen hundred men capable of bearing arms, but some of them, he recognized, could only be called out for permanent duty 'with extreme difficulty, if at all,' because they 'have no other means of supporting their Families but constant labour and Industry.' Many, of course, were fishermen or were employed in the coasting trade, so that they were not always available. Furthermore, the population was 'so extremely scattered and the communication with the several Points so very difficult' that 'no effectual Cooperation could be promptly relied on.' Despite these difficulties Swayne believed that 'unless I am reinforced from Halifax there will be no alternative but to make the experiment.'[33] When no reinforcements arrived, Swayne proceeded to organize the militia into two regiments: the first or northern regiment, and the second or southern regiment, each comprising two battalions. The island was divided into twenty divisions for defensive purposes, and the militia in each division was under the command of a captain and two lieutenants. Understandably, militia organization advanced further in the Sydney area than in the outlying districts.

Swayne's militia ordinance applied to all men between the ages of sixteen and sixty, with certain exceptions. Anyone neglecting to report or avoiding enrolment could be fined the sum of ten shillings, while all persons exempted from drill had to pay an annual charge of twenty shillings.[34] Three months were allowed for those enroled to equip themselves with arms and ammunition, which were supplied by the imperial government and consisted of the old Queen Anne flintlock musket, plus twelve rounds of powder and ball. The regular uniform for officers was a blue jacket, gold epaulettes, black belts, sabre, grey overalls, and a round hat with a feather. According to a later report, the men wore costumes 'of every imaginable style and description,' and when an officer wished to address someone he called out 'the man with the plug hat' or 'the man with the hay foot or straw foot' and so on.[35] Regimental musters were to be held every six months, and company officers were required to muster their men for instruction every three months or face a penalty of five pounds. Any person not appearing for drill might be fined five shillings.[36]

The first parade was held in August 1813 and it was a festive occasion, with many people, including Mi'kmaq, in attendance 'in holiday spirits and dressed in their finest clothes.' The fun began on the evening of Saturday, the 12th, when a salute was fired by the mines artillery to honour its visiting commanding officer, Colonel Thomas Crawley.[37] This was apparently mistaken by some members of the militia for an alarm, and Sunday morning found the regiment under arms and ready to defend the country.[38] North Sydney's *Morning Sun* later drily observed that 'the 1st and 2nd companies received through their colonel the approbation of the commander in chief for the zeal and diligence displayed by them on the occasion.' Two weeks later, on the 24th, when the six guns were fired in earnest 'to test this ancient soldiery,'

Crawley again praised 'the alacrity, steadiness, and general good conduct of the 1st, 2nd, 3rd and 6th companies,' which attributes he
described as 'highly meritorious' and meeting with 'the entire approbation of the commander-in-chief, who considers it a proof of what may be
expected from them when they are called upon to defend any point
which may be attacked.'[39] Nevertheless, Swayne believed that the organization of an effective militia required the appointment of a professional field officer to carry out inspections and generally to supervise its
development. While the members of the militia were displaying 'great
zeal and some of them have offered to extend their service beyond the
Colony if so required,' their scattered disposition meant that 'their discipline must entirely depend upon the exertions of a Staff Officer.'[40] He
therefore applied to Sherbrooke for such an officer and F.E. Armstrong
was appointed brigade major for the duration of the war.[41]

In November 1813 Swayne claimed that 'the Spirit of Loyalty & Courage has already been displayed by the effectual repulsion of the Enemy's
Privateers whenever they have attempted a Landing & great zeal has
been displayed at all the Settlements.' Bathurst commended Swayne for
the zeal that the Cape Breton government had displayed in repelling
'those predatory attacks which the Enemy's Privateers have at different
times ventured to make on the coasts.'[42] In fact, the War of 1812 was
fought primarily in the Canadas, and, while a lively privateering and
naval war was waged on the Atlantic, there were no official reports of
raids on Cape Breton's coasts by privateers. Although the possibility of
invasion was a constant though unlikely threat, the coastal fortifications
were never tested. Indeed, it was known as early as November 1812 that
the commissions being issued to privateers by the American government expressly forbade any attacks on coastal settlements, and 'this prohibition, coupled with the defensive measures financed by the
provincial assembly, combined to make life in the coastal communities
peaceful for the duration of the war.'[43]

The end of the American war in 1814 shortly preceded the long-
awaited end of the war in Europe in 1815, concluding a quarter century
of hostilities. The imperial government immediately sought to reduce
military expenditures, which had soared from £4.5 million in 1792 to
£58 million in 1815. By 1819, defence spending had been slashed to
about £16 million, and 'it remained at or below this figure for decades.'
One obvious area for reductions was in the overseas empire, where the
cost of military garrisons to the imperial government exceeded what the
colonies themselves raised in taxes for their own administrative needs.

The garrisons of the British American provinces soon fell to a total of six thousand personnel or fewer, a small fraction of the nearly thirty thousand troops that had been built up in the Canadas alone during the last months of the war. Still, the British military appreciated that it had been American lack of initiative in concentrating their offensives against strategically crucial centres that had saved the colonies during the conflict. The soldiers therefore recommended a massive program for the building of fortifications at the principal military and naval establishments, and also canals to create an alternative to the vulnerable water transport route along the upper St Lawrence River. Despite the unpopularity in Britain of expenditure on colonial defences, the commanding presence in British politics of the Duke of Wellington, hero of the European war, brought the construction during the 1820s and early 1830s of the Rideau Canal and of fortifications at Kingston, Montreal, Quebec, and Halifax at a cost of well over £1.5 million.[44]

These expenditures did not extend to Sydney. In 1816 the wooden magazine at the mines was 'a good deal out of repair,'[45] while the ordnance at the battery had been reduced to four English four-pounder iron guns; however, the non-commissioned officer and six gunners of the Royal Artillery remained on duty.[46] Another report, written six months later, referred to four English twelve-pounder guns at the battery, suggesting that either the July 1816 report had been inaccurate or the larger guns had been returned to the mines. Elsewhere in Cape Breton, the six eighteen-pounder and six six-pounder guns remained; reference is also made to six four-pounder brass guns, but it is not clear where they were located. Meanwhile, the barrack building at Sydney had recently burnt down.[47]

At this time the longstanding political crisis in Cape Breton finally came to its climax. The question of whether or not the colony should have an elected assembly had plagued Cape Breton since its founding and severely limited the civil government in its activities. Although the imperial government had declared after the American Revolution that colonists would never again be taxed without their consent, it had not granted Cape Breton a representative assembly. Despard's tax on rum had, naturally, proved controversial, and in 1816 Chief Justice A.C. Dodd ruled that it was illegal. The issue was referred to the law officers of the crown in London, who agreed with Dodd, with the result that the imperial government was forced to address Cape Breton's constitutional arrangements. Rather than give the little colony an elected assembly, London opted, because of its size, small population, and relative poverty, to give it representative government by annexing it to Nova Scotia.[48]

The anticipated next crisis in Anglo-American relations occurred in 1825, caused by disagreement over relations with the newly independent Spanish colonies in Latin America, and revealed that annexation had done nothing to improve Sydney's defences. Because of his concern over the security of the British North American colonies, Wellington sent out a commission of military officers headed by Sir James Carmichael Smyth, Royal Engineers, to examine the problem.[49] Its recommendations followed along the lines of Wellington's 1819 memorandum, proposing the construction of very extensive fortifications at Halifax, Montreal, Kingston, and the Niagara frontier, and lesser works for nearly a dozen other points. Much of this work was subsequently carried out.[50] As for Sydney, the Smyth commission said that 'a very trifling Earthen Redoubt, and two Batteries, one for 4 Guns, and the other for 2, have been constructed for the defence of Sydney. Also a Block-house at the Coal-pits, now dismantled. These are all the Fortifications, and they are nearly in ruins. There are Wooden Barracks for 80 men and their Officers, at Sydney, in tolerable repair.' 'In tolerable repair' seems to have meant that the new barrack building, a wooden, one-storeyed, structure on a stone foundation, which had been built some time after the 1817 fire destroyed the earlier structure, suffered only a leaky roof and shrunken doors. The former lieutenant-governor's house, also a wooden structure on a stone foundation, now occupied by the garrison's commanding officer, was in poor repair, however. There were also a small wooden powder magazine and a small wooden shed for gun carriages, both in a bad state of repair, and a commissary store and guardhouse.[51] The militia had not been called out in recent years, but it was thought to number three thousand men from sixteen to sixty years of age, a number that represented a considerable growth over what had been available during the War of 1812. This reflected the fact that Cape Breton's population had grown to approximately twenty thousand as a result of the substantial Scottish immigration that took place in the years immediately following the Napoleonic War. There were 440 muskets at Sydney in the charge of Major C.E. Leonard, the former commanding officer of the militia, and another 235 muskets and bayonets in the possession of one of the battalions.[52]

Rather surprisingly, instead of recommending the improvement of the fortifications at Sydney, the Smyth commission looked to Louisbourg as a potential fortified port. While the strength of the Royal Navy made it unnecessary to rebuild the fortress there, it thought that, should naval superiority be lost in a future war and an invasion of the Canadas by the United States be apprehended, 'Louisbourg may again be a very important point, and require to be fortified in order to shelter the Men of War employed to defend the entrance into the Gulph of St Lawrence. It may also be necessary (should we lose our Naval superiority, even putting an attempt at Canada out of the question) to occupy Louisbourg, to prevent an Enemy from taking possession of it, and establishing his Cruisers at the mouth of the St Lawrence. Should circumstances require it, the Harbour of Louisbourg could easily be placed in a respectable state of Defence, by constructing a Tower and Battery on Light House Point, and another on Goat Island, at the entrance of the Bay.'[53]

Nothing seems to have resulted from this rather startling recommendation, which oddly ignored the long recognized need to protect the coal mines on Sydney Harbour. Instead, a year later, Colonel Nicolls, still commanding the Royal Engineers at Halifax, approved repairs to the magazine at Sydney, including 'New Gate Posts etc.'[54] Two years later, this work had not been done, however, and was again included in the budget for repairs to military property in Sydney.[55] Samuel Rigby, the barrack master, accompanied by the bombardier in charge, inspected the fortifications in April 1828, and after apologizing for the fact that his report 'should have been transmitted ere this, but the snow and frost prevented me from making the necessary inspection of the Batteries until now,' remarked that the magazine was in good condition. The storehouse or gun shed was 'in quite a delapidated [sic] state,' and was not worth repairing, 'being in the first instance but a temporary building.' Two of the batteries 'require facing but the platforms will answer for another season.' However, the four-gun battery, commonly called 'the lower battery,' required immediate repairs as there was 'scarcely a vestige of the platforms remaining, the sleepers etc being in a complete state of decay. The most part of the Works require new facing, the moat round the battery requires to be cleaned and the outside of the work to be trimmed; it also requires to be enclosed, being exposed to the ravage of the Cattle.'[56]

Although T.C. Haliburton thought that Barrack Park added 'much' to the town's appearance,[57] it is unclear whether or not repairs were carried out because no further reports on the state of the fortifications were submitted until 1834, when a select committee of the British House of Commons investigated colonial military expenditures. At that time, the blockhouse at the mines was again described as 'out of repair' and the battery 'in ruins,' and the four twelve-pounder guns were dismounted. The batteries at Sydney's Barrack Park and Point Edward had six eighteen-pounder guns, two dismounted, and six six-pounder guns, one dismounted. The blockhouse was described as being 'in tolerable repair.' The report concluded, apparently referring to the entire Maritime region, by observing that 'the platforms are all in a decayed and unserviceable state,' with the exception of some at Halifax.[58] Oddly, this report does not mention a new barrack building at Sydney, which had been erected in 1833. A photograph taken many years later shows that it was a one-and-a-half-storey rectangular wooden structure with a stone foundation. The large central gable roof had two offset chimneys and two dormer windows. The main entrance was in the centre of the building, with a straight staircase leading to an open porch. There was a small half-round window above the entrance, and four windows on the front or west side of the building had the six-over-six design panes.[59]

Lieutenant Colonel Henry Dundas, commanding the 83rd Regiment, inspected his troops at Sydney in 1834 and, while he thought that the unit was 'in good order,' he found the commanding officer's house still 'excessively out of repair, and in wet weather cannot be kept dry.' Despite their new building, the men were 'in want of every Barrack Utensil,' and there was no hospital, as the old building had been abandoned but not replaced. 'The place made use of as such is a small room, marked off as an Orderly Room, next to and in the same building as the Guard Room. It is not capable of containing more than three bedsteads, and the Asst Surgeon is of opinion that it will be too cold to occupy as a Hospital in winter, and that a Barrack room must be appropriated for that purpose.'[60]

There were at this time 4,720 troops of all ranks stationed in British North America, of whom 1,474 were in Nova Scotia, nearly all of them at Halifax.[61] The 1834 report of the parliamentary committee did not recommend any reduction in these numbers, but it did call for strict economy, particularly with respect to the commissariat, barrack, and ordnance expenditures, and in 1836 some effort was made to achieve this goal by reducing the number of outlying stations. The Sydney garrison was maintained but received minimal support, even for maintenance, which may help to explain why there seems to have been a serious problem with military desertions. The *Spirit of the Times*, a Sydney newspaper, claimed in 1842 that twenty-four men had deserted from the 64th in the previous year, leading it to wonder if Queen Victoria, not having planned to settle Cape Breton with soldiers, might withdraw the garrison.[62]

Anglo-American relations again deteriorated as a result of widespread American sympathy for the rebellions that erupted in Upper and Lower Canada in 1837 and of another flareup of the still unresolved Maine – New Brunswick boundary dispute in 1839. In the opinion of the leading authority on this period, 'from the end of 1838 into the early 1840s the whole northern frontier remained in a dangerous state of excitement and uncertainty. Any incident might have brought war.'[63] In this atmosphere, it was not surprising that in April 1840 the General Mining Association, the British company that controlled the coal-mining operations at Pictou and Sydney from the 1820s, appealed to the imperial government to provide protection for its coal mines at Sydney. Samuel Cunard, the shipping magnate who also served as the GMA's Halifax agent, appealed directly to Lord John Russell, the secretary of state for war and the colonies, pointing out to him that the mines were 'in a very exposed position'; if an American privateer destroyed them, the imperial government would not only lose the income from the royalty being paid by the Association, it would lose the only supply of coal available to Royal Navy ships on the Atlantic seaboard of North America. 'A few Guns and a Small Breast Work would be a sufficient protection,' he thought, 'together with three or four Artillerymen to take charge of the Stores & Instruct the Miners, who would form a Sufficient force to repel any attack.'[64]

Russell sought advice and the question was ultimately referred to Lieutenant Colonel Rice Jones, the commanding royal engineer in Nova Scotia. While Jones thought that 'very extensive Lines or Breastworks would be requisite' to provide effective protection to the mines, defence against 'any sudden attack with an inferior Force' might be achieved by reconstructing the battery at the mines, 'now in ruins,' and repairing the nearby blockhouse, as they were 'well placed below the bar at the entrance of the Spanish River, and command the anchorage in front of the Mines.' It would also be necessary to station a detachment of troops there and to provide barrack accommodation for them within the surrounding enclosure. The garrison at Sydney, being some eight miles away and 'on the opposite bank of the River, over which there is no bridge communication whatever,' was too far distant.[65]

This advice did not lead to any action and two years later Sydney's three batteries were described by the commander of the Royal Artillery in Halifax as 'so much delapidated [sic] that they would require almost to be reconstructed to make them serviceable.' The one nearest to the town 'for six 6 prs' was 'in fact useless, from having had a steam mill constructed between it and the water whereby its range in the most essential direction is obstructed.' As well, this battery's platforms and gun carriages were 'fast decaying,' and four of the five gun carriages were so unserviceable that the recommendation was that they 'be broken up for the Iron Work.'[66] This general neglect of the fortifications and ordnance at Sydney was neither unusual at this period nor unique to this station; it reflected a general policy of ignoring colonial outposts except at times of crisis.[67] Meanwhile, the naval force based at Halifax was reduced from its peak of forty-one vessels in the summer of 1839 to twenty-eight, none of them a battleship, in January 1840.[68] Happily, the latest Anglo-American diplomatic crisis was resolved peacefully, because both governments were involved in other difficulties and wanted to avoid conflict.

Nevertheless, the growing importance of coal to fuel steam-powered naval and commercial ships gave Sydney Harbour a strategic importance it would not otherwise have had to parsimonious imperial authorities in the 1840s. When in 1846 a former member of the Executive Council of Jamaica, who was living in Nova Scotia, reported recent conversations with American naval officers in New York in which they openly 'declared that two of their heavy frigates could in 24 hours so ruin the works and machinery' of the mines at Sydney and Pictou 'as to prevent any considerable supply being derived from those mines for months,' Lieutenant-Governor Falkland took him very seriously and passed on his observations to the War Office. Falkland thought the danger to the Pictou collieries was not great, because they were several miles inland, but the case was 'very different' at Sydney, which was 'utterly defenceless.' He recommended that a large coal depot be established at Halifax to reduce the harm such a raid might do, and that 'a strong Detachment of Troops should be at once sent [to Sydney] in the event of hostilities with the United States becoming imminent.'[69]

Lord Lyttelton, the under-secretary of state for war and the colonies, noted that this was not the first time the defenceless state of the mines had been brought to the department's attention, recalling the 1841 correspondence and that the government had then 'declined to sanction any outlay for works.' This time, however, the master general and Board of Ordnance were instructed 'to consider whether some permanent works should not be constructed with the view of protecting the Mine at Sydney from the Assaults of Privateers,' and the Admiralty was asked to consider the idea of establishing a coal depot at Halifax. At the same time, Major General Sir Jeremiah Dickson, the commanding officer in Nova Scotia, was asked to make use of 'such available means as may be at his disposal for securing these mines from destruction or devastation.'[70]

Meanwhile, Cunard had written to the Admiralty as well, pointing out the unprotected state of the mines at Sydney 'from whence in the event of any difference with the United States, HM Steam Ships would have to secure their supply of Coals,' and reminding their lordships that the mines were situated 'so near to the Sea, that a Privateer could at any time destroy the works without any risk as there is not a single gun mounted.' He recommended, as Rice Jones had done in 1841, that 'a Breast Work or Battery should be thrown up & mounted with a sufficient number of guns, that a non Commissioned Officer and three or four men of the Royal Artillery should be stationed there in charge who should be required to instruct the Miners in working the Guns. This would be a protection against any attack by Sea, and in the event of any Force being landed, a 1000 men could be brought at an hour's notice to repel it.'[71]

When the Board of Ordnance agreed that the mines were at risk, it was asked to recommend measures for their protection against casual attacks by privateers. Picking up on Cunard's suggestion, it proposed that 'after some Work shall have been completed and assured, for the protection of the mines,' half the troops stationed at Sydney might be posted there 'so as to be at hand to direct the Workmen employed there, amounting to about a thousand, who in the event of War will be all armed by the proprietors.' If this were done, the mines 'may be considered as quite secure from any irregular attack.' The Admiralty explained as well that it had already established a coal depot at Halifax three years earlier and that the amount of coal stored there could be increased at any time 'as rapidly as circumstances may require.' Because coal deteriorated in storage and because the mines at Sydney were 'such a short distance from Halifax, it is better not to increase the quantity to be kept there until really requisite.'[72]

The War Office, which was well aware that there was now 'not more than half a company' at Sydney, agreed to inform General Dickson that the Admiralty regarded 'the erection of works for the protection of the coal mines ... to be urgently pressing' and to ask him 'to cause preparations to be made for the accommodation of the men whom he will no doubt eventually station near the mines.'[73] Meanwhile, the Board of Ordnance proceeded immediately to consider the defensive needs of

Sydney. Before it could give any advice to the War Office, however, it had to ask the government of Nova Scotia to provide it with 'an accurate map shewing the locality of the Mines, and the access to them, with a plan of the locale, and a general report describing the nature of attack to which the Mine works could be liable, and the character of defences best calculated for their protection, but keeping always in view of expediency of not constructing fortifications of any kind, if any other defence of a locomotive character (whether vessels or troops) will effect the object in the event of war.'[74]

Lieutenant Colonel Patrick Calder, the commanding royal engineer at Halifax, sent Captain William Molesworth to examine the situation at both Pictou and Sydney and to submit a report 'describing the Nature of attack to which the Mines Works would be liable, and the character of defence he considers best calculated for their protection.' Calder, with Dickson's endorsement, subsequently recommended that the best defence for the mines at Sydney would be provided 'by a Steam Cruiser from the middle of April to the end of December,' the period during which the harbour and the entrance to the Bras d'Or Lake were usually free of ice and open to navigation. Recognizing, however, that 'this mode of protection may be considered expensive and at times inconvenient for the Safety of the Mines in the Event of a Privateer running in,' he also recommended 'either the establishment of the Battery at the old Blockhouse where there is a reserve of two Acres, and arming it with 4 long 32 prs on dwarf traversing Platforms, & the construction of another at one of the places mentioned in Captain Molesworth's Report. To the Battery should be attached a quarter for a Non Commissioned Officer, and a few Gunners of the Royal Artillery, with a sufficient Store. These men could instruct the Miners in the use of the Guns.' This, he thought, would meet the need. And, he added, Cunard agreed – not surprisingly, since these proposals mirrored his own. In the event of an outbreak of war, 'it may be necessary to erect a Barrack in the neighbourhood of the Mines to accommodate a Company of Infantry with its officers, for the purpose of training & cooperating with the Miners; but until then should circumstances render it advisable to quarter a detachment temporarily there, Mr Cunard authorized me to say that the Association will provide the accommodation required.'[75]

William Gladstone, the secretary of state for war and the colonies in the Peel ministry, was less than enthusiastic about overseas expenditures of dubious necessity. 'Considering the many works involving a heavy expense required for the defence of points of much greater national importance,' he responded, 'I do not feel justified in proposing that these works shd now be undertaken at the cost of this country.' He thought that the issue should be referred to the lieutenant-governor of Nova Scotia, who should 'consult his Executive Council as to the expediency of recommending to the Provincial legislature any grant for the purpose.' Lord Grey, who replaced Gladstone shortly afterward, agreed and subsequently did write to Lieutenant-Governor Sir John Harvey to this effect.[76] According to a list of Nova Scotian military installations compiled by the Royal Engineers in 1847, the Sydney battery was 'under the control of the Ordnance and the expenses attending them [were] paid by that Department,' while the battery and blockhouse at the mines, having been constructed by the colony, were 'generally in a state of ruin ... There are however guns at many of them which are in charge of the Militia.'[77]

This was, of course, in accordance with the British government's determination throughout the 1840s to reduce its colonial military expenditures, despite continuing tensions in Anglo-American relations. The abolition of the mercantile system and the related grant of responsible government to Nova Scotia and Canada in 1847 signalled a profound change in the imperial relationship, clearly implying the acceptance of greater responsibility by the colonies for local defence. Thus, the number of regular troops in Nova Scotia was reduced from twenty-five hundred in 1849 to two thousand in 1852, and in Canada from about eight thousand in 1847 to five thousand in 1852.[78] Only the importance of Halifax as an imperial naval base saved the province from cuts as drastic as those imposed on Canada. It was hoped that the provincial legislatures might be persuaded to improve their ineffectual militias, but this did not happen. Similarly, the Nova Scotian government declined to undertake responsibility for building the proposed fortifications at Sydney.

In 1849 the commanding officer there was advising Lieutenant Colonel Henry Savage, the commanding royal engineer at Halifax, that he needed 'a Shed or Storehouse at Sydney for the protection of the 6 Pr field guns & carriages, the latter having been rendered unserviceable by constant exposure to the weather.' New carriages had in fact been approved, but the military authorities had sensibly ordered that they be retained at Halifax 'till there is a Store to deposit them in.'[79] This continuing neglect presumably reflected the determination of the military authorities at Halifax to concentrate capital expenditures on the network of fortifications being built there, while coping with the chronic inadequacy of their budget allocations. Even so, when Lieutenant B.W.A. Sleigh was posted to Sydney with a detachment of the 77th Regiment in 1846, he wrote a very favourable, albeit vague, description of Barrack Park. His residence was 'prettily situated, with the river in the rear, the cottage being perched on an eminence, with the surge rolling on the pebbly shore, directly beneath.' A 'well-kept enclosure of grass lay in our front, while on the left-hand side of the cottage was a nice garden, well planted by our predecessors with vegetables, and on the other side was a large plot devoted to the soldiers who cultivated it with great judgment and horticultural skill.' The barrack building, in addition to housing the men, contained the officers' quarters, the mess, and the orderly room. Nearby were the magazine, stables, the guardhouse, and the engine-house. In all, the site contained about five acres, enclosed by a high stockade, and four sentries kept 'watch and ward' at the corners.[80]

Although physically separated from the town, the garrison was an integral part of Sydney and, indeed, the only real reason for its existence after it had ceased in 1820 to be the capital of Cape Breton. It still did not amount to much, comprising

> two long straggling streets, with four minor intersecting ones, running up from the water. A few grocers' stores, numerous small drinking-shops, an odd cottage here and there, two stories high, the Church of England, Methodist and Catholic chapels, all unpretending wooden edifices, – and you have a full description of this rising spot. The grass grew luxuriantly in the streets, and the cattle were evidently divided in opinion, as to whether the town or country pastures were preferable. Flocks of geese monopolized the roadway, saucily hissing at a stray wayfarer, as if such a human intruder was a novelty. An odd youth, in shooting jacket and slouched sailor's glazed cap, with a fowling-piece, gave occasional token of the place being inhabited; while the men of my company, with their red coats, sauntering about, as they continually do to kill time, forming the majority of the male kind to be seen, conveyed the idea of a military occupancy of some deserted village.[81]

Just how important the little British garrison was to the social life of Sydney is suggested by two incidents related by Sleigh. On the Sunday following his arrival, the troops paraded to church in full-dress uniform. The congregation of St George's, the garrison church, 'presented a vista of young and elderly ladies, very flashily dressed, with airs of considerable pride and conceit. As new comers, we were the observed of all observers.'[82] A few days later, Sleigh's servant, 'in a state of evident excitement,' rushed into his room and reported 'swarms in the streets!'

> As I had heard of nothing remarkable about to occur on this day, my curiosity was excited, and I proceeded to the piazza, to find out what was really the matter. On looking towards the barrack gate, I saw the long street running from it dotted here and there with groups of the masculine and feminine gender, the latter displaying a wonderful variety of colours, pink, green, blue, white and brown, parasols of every shape and size, from the antique to the modern, adding not a little to the gaiety of the scene. To my surprise, the long string of fashionable pedestrians appeared wending their steps towards the Guard-house at the barrack-gate, and passing the sentry and the corporal's guard, who had rushed to the front to scrutinize, with amazed air, the Sydneian exodus of 'manhood, youth, and beauty,' they boldly advanced down the little path leading to my cottage. I looked around to see by what exit they proposed to get out of the field, but a large stockade forbade escape in this direction; while pursuing my military recognizance, I fancied the party leading the advance-group smiled at me in a very friendly manner.[83]

The crowd was in fact coming to meet the new officer and his wife, and Sleigh quickly found his drawing room 'occupied by some couple of dozen ladies and gentlemen, all smiling at us most facetiously.'[84] The room was soon 'crowded to suffocation ... while expectant parties, awaiting the *entrée*, were promenading on the grass before.' Eventually, two hours later, the unplanned levee broke up 'and I learnt that it was the custom of the place, to defer calling upon the military until one week after arrival.'[85]

Despite the somewhat sarcastic and condescending tone of this account, Sleigh found much that pleased him about Sydney. There were, he recalled, 'a few very pleasant families in the town,' and 'the hospitality of the farmers and the gentlemen settled in the Province is proverbial, and deserves grateful mention. They never sent in a waggon to market, but some present was forwarded to our cottage.' Agriculture had clearly progressed since the turn of the century, because Sleigh reported that 'quarters of lamb, poultry, exquisitely-flavoured butter, vegetables and fruit of every kind, and sundry other produce of the farm-yard, or results of the gun, were daily placed in the larder ... I can safely say, that during our entire sojourn in Cape Breton, I had not occasion to spend a single sovereign in marketing, such was the unbounded kindness of the inhabitants to myself and my wife.' What was more, he believed that his experience was not unique, saying that 'I never heard a military man who had been quartered in Cape Breton, but speak kindly and gratefully of the hospitality of the people.'[86] When Sleigh was given a new posting a few months later, he claims that he and his wife left 'our dear little cottage with feelings of sincere regret.'[87]

Sleigh may have been painting a picturesque scene rather than reporting the actual situation, and of course it must be recognized that his published account in *Pine Forests and Hacmatack Clearings* was written for a general reading audience rather than the military authorities. It was also written some years later. There can, however, be little doubt of the close attachment that Sydney felt to its military garrison, and this was reflected in the experience of the 42nd or Black Watch Regiment, which returned to Sydney in June 1851, having served there from 1786 to 1789. On disembarking, led by Captain Daniels, a piper, and a drummer, they marched to the barrack square, where they were loudly cheered by the men of the 38th Regiment, whom they were replacing. The men of the Black Watch apparently became general favourites in Sydney. J.G. MacKinnon, a local historian writing in 1918, cited a newspaper report from the 1850s to claim that 'they were better liked than perhaps any other regiment ever stationed in Sydney.' Not only did they stay out of trouble with the law, 'many of them' were active in the temperance movement and joined the local Sons of Temperance in their processions. 'Some of the older residents,' MacKinnon wrote, 'still remember and speak of hearing the pipes play as these gallant soldiers paraded to and from church on Sunday mornings.'[88]

When a major fire – Sydney's first great fire – broke out in buildings on the Esplanade on 28 November 1851, the soldiers 'were on hand with the military fire engine' and fought the fire alongside the citizens. When the town subsequently tried to buy a fire engine for future needs and proved unable to raise enough money, 'an understanding was arrived at with the military authorities by which the garrison fire engine was donated for the use of the town.' Sydney then organized its first fire brigade, and the old market house at the corner of Amelia and Charlotte Streets became its headquarters, with the market bell serving as the fire alarm as well. According to MacKinnon, 'the old military hand engine was kept in use for a long time. It was easily worked and gave a good stream of water.'[89]

Meanwhile, events in Europe were taking place that were about to disrupt the tranquillity of Sydney and end its role as a minor military outpost of the empire. The relative stability that had prevailed in Europe since 1815 was nearing an end. The Crimean War broke out between Russia and Turkey in 1853 and a year later Britain and France allied themselves with Turkey. Inevitably, this led the imperial government to reduce further its overseas garrisons in order to have as large a force as possible available in Europe. Half the troops still in North America were withdrawn: three battalions of infantry from Canada and one each from Nova Scotia and the West Indies. By the end of 1854 there were fewer than 1,900 troops left in Canada, 1,086 in Nova Scotia, and a mere 311 in Newfoundland.[90] These reductions were facilitated by optimistic assurances given by the Nova Scotian and New Brunswick assemblies, keen to support the war effort, that the defence of their provinces could be safely entrusted to the local militias.[91]

Among the troops withdrawn were those from the 76th Regiment, who were stationed at Sydney. They did not leave much behind. In 1853 Samuel Rigby, still the barrack master, reported to Savage in Halifax that 'the whole of the bottom part' of the commanding officer's residence was 'in a state of decay,' and 'the Kitchen part of this Building (in which the Artillery are quartered) appears to be in a worse state.' He could do nothing, however, because no provision had been made in his budget for repairs. 'This being a very old Building, in my humble opinion, I do think that the Expence necessary to be incurred to put it in a thorough repair would nearly build a new House, containing a Surgery-Hospital as well as a Room for the Artillery, all very much required.'[92] Savage seems to have ignored this advice and authorized Rigby to make repairs; it was not until 22 June 1855 that Lieutenant Colonel Richard Stotherd, the new commanding royal engineer at Halifax, told Rigby that any further work would need to be considered in light of the withdrawal of the garrison.[93]

Within months of that withdrawal, Anglo-American relations deteriorated sharply, as a result, among other things, of the British attempt to recruit troops in the United States for the Crimean War. In the diplomatic crisis, which culminated in May 1856 with the American government's dismissal of the British minister and three consuls, the imperial authorities decided to strengthen their garrisons in North America. General Sir William Eyre was sent out to take command of all the troops in North America, five infantry regiments were dispatched from the Crimea, and the artillery was reinforced, raising the number of troops to about three thousand in Canada and more than two thousand in the Maritimes.[94] Although no troops were sent to Sydney, Rigby was allowed to obtain an estimate 'for the Pointing of the Barrack & Commisariat Store at Sydney.'[95] This latest crisis passed without further incident because of the desire of both countries to avoid confrontation and growing American preoccupation with its internal political difficulties.

The imperial government proceeded to dispose of the buildings and other crown property at stations formerly occupied by its troops in North America but now deemed redundant. In Canada, nearly all the lands and buildings were handed over to the province, the exceptions being chiefly at Quebec, Montreal, and Kingston. At Sydney, the War Office decided to lease its lands around the harbour to local residents. Thus, Douglas G. Rigby, Samuel's younger brother, leased the land and blockhouse at the mines, a property of approximately two acres, for four shillings per acre annually, 'until the said land Etc be required by the War Department, for the use of Her Majesty's Service.'[96] Meanwhile, Stotherd wanted to know what had become of the two guns removed from the blockhouse at the mines. Samuel Rigby discovered that they had been taken 'by the people at that place' to the mines, 'where they are safe. I requested they might be returned to the place from whence they were taken which I was promised would be done.'[97]

The Point Edward site had already been encroached upon by a Donald McDonald, who owned adjacent lands, and Rigby ordered him 'immediately [to] remove his Fences or enter into an Agreement to pay the Sum of 10s per Acre Annually, during the period he may be permitted by the War Department to hold the land in question.'[98] At the same time, Rigby 'ascertained the Cost of a Boundary Stone, to be fixed on the Ordnance Grounds' at Point Edward.[99] He subsequently reported that the elusive McDonald was 'working on the Rail road between Halifax and Windsor. I shall keep him in mind on his return home.'[100] By the spring of 1857 McDonald had formally leased 'a portion' of the Point Edward site, 'say about One Acre, at the rate of One Shilling Sterling annually.' McDonald was to place a proper boundary mark 'and to prevent any encroachment being made' on the land.[101]

Henry G. Bowles of Sydney, a former lieutenant colonel in the British Foreign Legion, applied in 1856 to lease the garrison grounds at Sydney, proposing 'to occupy the Barracks at this place, and to cultivate the land, both inside and outside the fence, which belongs to the Government,' for an annual rent of £20.[102] When the lease agreement was drawn up, however, Bowles objected to its terms. The disagreement seems to have centred on which buildings he would have the use of; he wanted them all, while Rigby argued that at least the ground floor of 'the Barrack Store, which at present is occupied by Two brass six pounders with their Carriages Etc [and] Materials belonging to the Royal Engineer Department,' the 'Engine House, which contains the Fire Engine with Water Buckets etc ... as well as the Powder Magazine,' could not be spared. The remaining buildings – 'viz Cooking House, Right and Left Wings Mens Barracks, Comm[andin]g Officers Quarter, Guard House and Magazine Store House,' as well as the two upper floors of the Barrack Store – were vacant.[103] The dispute went all the way to London, where the secretary of state gave permission in April 1857 to lease the entire grounds at Sydney.[104] It was also decided, however, that tenders should be called for the lease, which was done, whereupon Bowles raised his offer to £25 per annum.[105] There is no evidence that anyone else submitted a tender, and Bowles proceeded to occupy the property even though a formal lease agreement had not yet been signed. Further haggling continued over its terms, as Bowles now did not want to include the commanding officer's quarters in the lease because it was 'in so delapidated a state ... particularly as he does not intend to use it.'[106] In the end, Bowles abruptly announced that he was no longer interested in leasing the property at all, 'in consequence of my having received intelligence which will cause me to proceed immediately to England.'[107]

Tenders were again called with one change in the conditions, namely that 'the Engine House and a store or shed will be reserved for the Fire Engine and Field Guns & Carriages.'[108] Meanwhile, Rigby had shipped the two six-pounder guns 'with their appertenances' to headquarters at Halifax for storage. 'Consequently,' he advised Stotherd, 'I imagine there will be no necessity for reserving the Apartment on the Ground Floor of the Barrack Store ... it now being vacant.'[109] There seemed to be little demand for the garrison grounds, however, a situation that presumably reflected the economic lassitude of the place, and eight months later Stotherd resorted to advertising a public auction of the lease. The hay growing on the land was to be auctioned separately. At the same time, the property at the mines, consisting of approximately two and a half acres, was also to be leased by auction,[110] which suggests that the military authorities thought they could get more than the eight shillings per annum that Douglas Rigby was paying them. This prompted C.E. Leonard, the commanding officer of the 1st Regiment, Cape Breton militia, to remind the authorities that he had more than six hundred muskets and artillery swords belonging to the militia stored in a coach house loft 'adjoining an old building with a very unsafe chimney,' on which the provincial government was paying rent. He suggested that the government rent the garrison storehouse and magazine for this purpose instead, as these facilities would be safer and more appropriate.[111]

When Henry Ince, the land commissioner, held the public auction for the lease of the garrison lands at Sydney and the mines, he divided them into separate lots. As a result, he obtained £57.7 per annum for the lands, as opposed to the £25 to £30 he had anticipated if they had been leased as a unit. He did not offer to lease the lot containing the storehouse and magazine, pending a decision on Leonard's proposal. Ince also reported that 'the Grass [i.e., hay] within the Barrack enclosure' sold for £21.10 and commended Rigby 'for the care which he has taken of it.'[112] Douglas Rigby won the lease for the land and blockhouse at the mines for £1 per annum, which was considerably more than what he had paid in his initial agreement.[113] In subsequent years, Barrack Park was used by the townspeople of Sydney for swimming, picnicking, public functions, races, and cricket matches on a pitch laid there.[114]

Having little reason to exist after the withdrawal of the garrison, Sydney did not prosper. When Joseph Arthur de Gobineau, a French official, visited Sydney in 1859, he saw 'few recent buildings' and 'a number of empty houses. Grass grows everywhere with an exuberance which suffices to show that few feet walk over it.' Much of the town consisted of 'vacant lots fenced with planks while awaiting a purchaser and all that that entails.' He was told that young people were 'eager to emigrate to the United States' and that the population was declining.[115] The Reverend Richard Uniacke, who served at St George's in the 1860s, agreed that 'a remarkably quiet air pervades these streets, – implying what is really the condition of the place, – an absence of mercantile and agricultural enterprise, and the want of Capital liberally expended to give a stimulus to the resources and capabilities of a country deserving a better fate.'[116]

Nevertheless, Sydney Harbour, because it possessed the only coal deposits on the eastern seaboard, was becoming more important as increasing numbers of merchant ships made the transition from sail to steam. In particular, French vessels visiting St Pierre and Miquelon came in for coal and other supplies and to pick up mail. They anchored off the home of John Bourinot, who was the French consul at Sydney. Uniacke recorded that 'their bright flags, the bustling sounds from their decks and the morning and evening bugle quite enliven our otherwise tranquil harbour. Sometimes the band from the Admiral's ship is added to the other gay features of the scene.'[117] Gobineau claimed that British warships seldom visited Sydney and that the town 'would be somewhat abandoned by the rest of the world if the French naval division did not call there every year.' Foreign visitors were 'always sought after,' he believed, because they brought with them 'a breath of the outside world and some of that social activity which would be completely lacking without them.'[118] Henry Archibald of North Sydney seemed to confirm this when he noted in May 1860 that the first French ships of the season had arrived. 'They will be a great God send to the Sydney Ladies & you may be sure that frogs will go cheap.'[119] Gobineau noted that the withdrawal of the British garrison had had a profound impact on Sydney society, producing 'a certain degree of melancholy ... Picture these people, recluses shut off from the world, belonging by their customs, their memories, and especially their reading, to European society, and having available none of the intellectual pastimes that that implies. All of these distractions, great and small, are quite lacking. No theatre, no literary evenings, no cafés, no really stimulating or exciting politics; great stagnation, if not a complete absence of commercial affairs, and everywhere infinite leisure and a kind of uneasiness, of general mediocrity which pre-disposes the mind to sombre thoughts.'[120]

Gobineau notwithstanding, British naval ships did visit Sydney and, understandably, their arrival was an event of considerable social significance in the little port. When the British battleship, HMS *St George*, arrived in July 1861, for example, a French frigate, *Pomone*, was already anchored off Bourinot's home. According to the *Cape Breton News*,

immediately after dropping anchor the band on board the *St George* played the French National Anthem. At eight o'clock next morning, the tri-colour of France was hoisted at the fore, and saluted; and ere the dying echo of the guns had ceased, the band of the *St George* struck up *Partant pour la Syrie*. The effect of the whole was most pleasing. The French National Anthem concluded, up went the Ensign of Old England at the fore on board the French frigate *Pomone*, lying about 300 yards from the *St George*, and which was likewise saluted. Again at twelve o'clock, noon, as J. Bourinot, Esq., who had been on board to pay his respects to the commander, left the side of the *St George*, her guns belched forth a salute due to the rank and dignity of a Consul of *la belle France*.

During the day, 'parties of ladies and gentlemen' were conveyed to *St George*, where they were 'cordially welcomed and conducted throughout her interior, to see and note the wonderful ingenuity that had converted this floating ship into habitations for 800 souls, besides the reserved spaces for implements of war, etc.' Throughout that day and the next, the officers and men of *St George* enjoyed themselves 'as well as the limited capabilities of our town would permit.'[121]

Still, the withdrawal of the Sydney garrison and the leasing of the various military lands around the harbour seemed to end an era in its history. British military strength was now evidently to be concentrated on the imperial naval base at Halifax and the fortress that guarded it, while outlying ports such as Sydney were to be left to their own devices. The fact that the imperial government had leased but not sold its lands at Sydney implied, however, that it foresaw their possible use in a future conflict. Indeed, the military authorities at Halifax were already revisiting the Molesworth recommendations of 1846.

chapter three

Preparing for War, 1859–1867

I should almost expect even Mr. Godley to admit that the safety of the Sydney Coal Mines is a matter of the greatest interest to the Imperial Government and that the case need not be embarrassed by any theories of Colonial defenses.

C.F. Fortescue, 1860

The local military authorities had no sooner disposed of the military lands at Sydney than the War Office began to give serious consideration to building new fortifications there. The growing importance of the area's coal deposits, particularly to the increasingly steam-powered Royal Navy, could not be ignored, and their protection became a significant strategic issue. British naval expenditures increased when France and Austria went to war in the spring of 1859. In the previous year, the General Mining Association had surrendered its monopoly on coal mining in Nova Scotia. Coming four years after the approval of a Canadian-American reciprocity treaty, this immediately resulted in an enormous expansion in the industry all around Sydney Harbour, financed largely by American capital. Thus, in addition to the continuing strong French presence at Sydney, the American influence became a major factor as well.

At the same time, pressure had been mounting in Britain throughout the 1850s to reorganize imperial defence on a more economical and rational basis, and in 1859 the Derby government appointed an interdepartmental committee made up of representatives of the War Office, Colonial Office, and Treasury to consider the matter. Its investigation showed that in the 1857–8 fiscal year the imperial government had spent £3,590,000 on colonial military defence, while the colonies had contributed only £378,000. Furthermore, while some colonies made large contributions to the upkeep of imperial forces, others preferred to spend money on local defence organization, while still others spent nothing at all. In the case of the Maritimes, the imperial government had spent £191,000 in Nova Scotia and New Brunswick, but the only military expenditures that the committee could identify by those colonies amounted to a paltry £432.[1] The committee's report, submitted in 1860, sharply criticized the whole garrison system as being both burdensome and inefficient, and recommended instead one based on 'local efforts and local resources.' Dividing the colonies into two categories, it argued that the imperial government should bear the cost of maintaining stations like Gibraltar that were unquestionably essential to the preservation of British power. As for the rest, the colonial governments should decide the amount of armament that was needed and share the cost with the imperial government.[2]

London was already pressing the British North American colonies to improve their militia organizations, which had become quite ineffective since the War of 1812 as a result of poor organization, patronage, inadequate funding, and inactivity. This demand led to a major political crisis in Canada when a government bill to establish a volunteer militia system with proper equipment and annual training was defeated in the legislature.[3] In Nova Scotia, although all able-bodied men between the ages of sixteen and sixty were liable to military service and could be called out annually for three days' training, the militia had not in fact been called out since 1843. In the view of Nova Scotia's lieutenant-governor, Sir Gaspard LeMarchant, writing in 1857, 'an attempt to enforce, in time of peace, the provisions ... for the annual training of this body, would be a measure charged with difficulty – certainly most distasteful, – probably wholly inoperative.' The militia's weaponry was as derelict as the organization itself, most of its 4,863 muskets and rifles being 'old flint lock muskets that have been upwards of 50 years in the province, and many of them broken and deficient.'[4] Clearly, something had to be done and Sydney became the birthplace of the militia revival in Nova Scotia and a focal point of the debate over imperial defence. Cape Breton had not figured so prominently in defence questions since the days of the great fortress at Louisbourg.

Lord Mulgrave, who had succeeded LeMarchant as lieutenant-governor in 1858, was determined to act, but he was no less a realist than his predecessor. 'In a country like this, where labour is scarce and wages are

high,' the challenge was to find a way of ensuring the efficient training
of the militia 'without rendering the service obnoxious to the people, or
interfering to an injurious extent with the commercial and agricultural
pursuits of the province, which could not fail to be the case were the
Militia called out even for three days' training in the year, under the old
system.' His solution was to appeal to militia commanders to raise units
of volunteers, men who out of interest and commitment would train
regularly to a higher standard than could ever be achieved by compulsory drills. These men would not be paid and would be expected to provide their own uniforms, but they would receive modern rifles from the
government.[5]

This was not a new concept. In the United States, volunteer units
clothed in splendid, even whimsical, uniforms and performing elaborate drills had become popular, combining the attributes of social and
service clubs. Drawing partly on this experience, Canada had created a
force of paid volunteers in 1855 for the very practical purpose of replacing departing British regular troops in the important police functions
they had always carried out in the province's growing urban areas. This
force had become so popular that it was being expanded to include
unpaid units.[6] In Britain, the War Office had begun organizing a volunteer force in the spring of 1859 as a result not only of the profound
alarm generated by the war scare with France but also because of the
fear that steam-powered warships now made it possible for a European
enemy to circumvent the Royal Navy's squadrons and invade the home
islands or attack overseas territories in strength. Steam, it seemed, had
directly exposed the empire to the vast conscript armies of the Continent. By the autumn of 1859 the volunteer movement was sweeping the
nation, and some 120,000 men were enroled by the autumn of 1860. It
was becoming an article of faith on both sides of the Atlantic that enthusiastic citizen soldiers provided a useful line of defence against foreign
invasion, not least because high levels of defence spending and compulsory service were considered un-British, typical of European despotism,
and unlikely to be tolerated by the population.[7]

Being a Nova Scotian himself, Major General Sir William Fenwick Williams, who was appointed commander-in-chief of British forces in North
America in 1859, took a personal interest in the situation in the Maritimes. He was well aware of the hopeless state of the militia and
extremely worried by France's historic and continuing interest in the
region. In the event of war, France's steam-powered navy would be compelled to seize Sydney's coal mines if it intended to undertake major

operations in the northwestern Atlantic, while the loss of the mines would deprive the British fleet of its principal source of coal in North American waters. On his own initiative, therefore, he visited the colonies on his way to Canada in the early summer of 1859 in order to encourage them to follow Mulgrave's lead in organizing volunteer corps. He was also particularly concerned about the need for artillery defences for the region's ports.[8]

One of the places Williams visited was Sydney, where he met with Richard Brown, the manager of the General Mining Association operations there. The two men discussed the need for a shore battery of heavy guns, an earth redoubt on the high ground near the mine workings, and a battery of field artillery that could readily move to the many points outside the immediate entrance of the harbour where the enemy could put troops ashore.[9]

Major General Sir Charles Trollope, the officer commanding British forces in the Maritime colonies, subsequently alerted Colonel Richard Nelson, the commanding royal engineer, in September 1859 'that in all probability immediate orders will be received for the Construction of Works for the Defence of the Mines' at Sydney. What was being contemplated – though the final decision was not made for another two years – was a battery with six thirty-two-pounder guns.[10] Trollope asked Nelson, who was planning a trip to inspect fortifications in Newfoundland, to stop at Sydney 'to look at the ground,' adding that Brown had been directed 'to afford you every facility and assistance.'[11] The intended site for the new battery was not the old one, where the battery and blockhouse lay in ruins, but the Chapel Point site selected by Molesworth in 1846 and approved by Williams during his visit.[12]

The urgency felt by Williams about the defence of the mines at Sydney reinforced that expressed on several occasions by Sir Samuel Cunard on behalf of the GMA. Not surprisingly, the first volunteer units organized under Mulgrave's initiative were two companies, each comprising more than sixty men of all ranks, at Sydney Mines in July 1859, followed in August by two companies at the Albion Mines near Pictou.[13] This swift action was in large measure the result of the 'very liberal and patriotic conduct' of the GMA. 'Not only have I received every possible co-operation and assistance from the local authorities,' Mulgrave declared, 'but the Association in England, generously backing up the exertions of their agents on the spot, have, at their own expense, provided uniforms for the whole of these men.'[14] As well, Brown personally assumed command of the two companies at Sydney Mines.

Among the recommendations made by Williams for the defence of
the Maritimes was the return of small detachments of British regular
troops to instruct the local volunteer and militia units and to maintain
any fortifications that might be built. The War Office was agreeable, but
it insisted that the colonies should bear the expense. Sending experienced, dependable men would cost £7,840 per year, in addition to the
cost of barracks, fortifications, and armament, and the War Office proposed to charge £6,470 of this amount to Nova Scotia.[15] Mulgrave, however, in a classic statement of the North American view of the imperial
defence question, denounced the scheme as so financially unrealistic
that he saw no point in even placing it before his ministers. The province's annual revenue amounted to only £160,000, nearly £60,000 of
which was required to pay the interest on debts incurred to build railways. Virtually all of the remainder was being spent on education and
roads. Even if the financial situation improved in future, there was no
assurance that provincial administrations would vote the necessary
funds in successive years, and so the whole scheme would inevitably collapse as the traditional militia organization had already done. Yet there
was no doubt in Mulgrave's mind about the patriotism of Nova Scotians.
The need was to educate them gradually, like other colonists, to accept
the need for a systematic preparation for wartime needs during times of
peace. That could best be done, he thought, through his intentionally
frugal volunteer movement, which was already attracting considerable
interest. Former members of the British army who had retired in Nova
Scotia, moreover, were willing to help for a small fraction of what the
War Office wanted to charge for its instructors. Already there had been
progress in training the volunteers at the mines at Sydney and Pictou
under the direction of two discharged British army sergeants, 'who fortunately reside on the spot.'[16] Colonial Office officials found Mulgrave's
advice 'sensible' and allowed him to proceed.[17]

Mulgrave proved as good as his word about building on a shoestring
budget. The House of Assembly voted $8,000 for the volunteers in 1860,
which was only about a fifth of what the War Office had demanded for
its instructional detachments. A notable achievement was Mulgrave's
engagement for a moderate salary of Captain R. Bligh Sinclair, a retired
British officer then commanding one of the new volunteer companies
in Halifax, to replace the ineffective and unqualified civilian officials
who had previously presided over the nominal militia organization.
With the local rank of lieutenant colonel, Sinclair became adjutant general of militia and, helped by only one or two other former British offic-

ers, he built a headquarters staff that transformed Mulgrave's personal proselytizing for the volunteer movement into an organized administration. General Williams helped by allocating three thousand Enfield rifles from imperial stocks in Canada at no cost.[18] By the spring of 1860 there were thirty-six companies in existence, nine of them in the Halifax-Dartmouth area and twenty-seven 'rural' companies in the rest of the province, with nearly twenty-three hundred men enroled. In addition to the two original companies at Sydney Mines, the Cape Breton organization included the Mulgrave Rifle Company at Arichat, which dated from the lieutenant-governor's 1859 appeal, and two new units, the Sydney Rifles and the Hawksbury Rifles.[19]

The creation of these units lent some excitement to life in the little communities surrounding Sydney Harbour. Henry Archibald reported in the spring of 1860 from Sydney Mines that 'we have great fun drilling in the mornings.'[20] The men took the activity seriously, however, and there was even some rivalry between the communities. Indeed, a minor mutiny occurred at Sydney Mines in March 1861 when their sergeant major complimented the drill qualities of the Sydney Rifles. According to Archibald, the officers of the Sydney Mines Volunteers had gone to Sydney to observe the Sydney Rifles drilling and

> our Sergeant major took a drop too much and ... declared before the whole multitude, Ladies & all, that he had been drilling the SMV for two years, and they could not do as well as the Sydney fellows. Now, knowing the state the man was in there was nothing said at the time though all of us felt mad enough to knock his brains out on the spot. This all happened on Saturday night. On Monday evening (No 1 Company's Drill) the men would not drill for him, and tried to do every thing as bad as they possibly could. On Wednesday (No 2's Drill) both companys [sic] assembled for the purpose of raising a regular rebellion. The Sergeant Major was called upon to explain himself and ... said that he meant that if the Sydney fellows had only been drilling 3 times with the Rifles (for Read [Lieutenant Colonel Charles Crewe Read, the captain of the Sydney Rifles] presumably told him that his men were only drilled three times with the firelocks) that they do far better than we did in three drills. He also said that if he thought the Sydney fellows understood him in a different light that he would go up the next day and explain himself. The men then became more reconciled and took the above for a suitable excuse.[21]

Partially trained volunteer riflemen were, however, no answer to the threat of bombardment by the heavy guns of a modern steam-powered warship. The central point of the dormant scheme developed by General Williams and the War Office had been to extend to the Maritimes a system of harbour defence that was being developed at non-military ports in Britain, whereby the War Office provided guns and a few Royal Artillery instructors, and local authorities undertook to share the cost of building batteries and raised volunteer artillery units to man them. This was the answer to the GMA's longstanding worries about its mines at Sydney and, having taken such a large interest in Williams's visit, the GMA was determined that his recommendations for the port should be carried out, regardless of the attitude of the provincial government. It therefore lost no opportunity to remind British authorities that it had generously provided uniforms for the volunteer riflemen at Sydney and Pictou in the expectation that the British government would follow through with the construction of fortifications at the Cape Breton port.[22]

Williams was not alone in worrying about the threat posed by the French because of their possession of St Pierre and Miquelon and their presumed influence on the loyalty of the Acadian population. Rear Admiral Sir Alexander Milne, commander-in-chief of the Royal Navy's North America and West Indies station, agreed that the French, in a war with Britain, would attempt to seize Cape Breton to gain control of the coal mines to supply their ships. Aside from the presence of a French consul at Sydney and the frequent visits of French warships to the port, he noted in October 1860 that Napoleon III had sent a gold communion service to the Roman Catholic church at Arichat and made another gift to St Patrick's in Sydney. The recent visit to Cape Breton of Gobineau, 'whose sole occupation appeared to be taking the number and names of all the French inhabitants,' concerned him as well.[23]

In May 1860 the influential and well-informed Cunard stepped up the pressure with a letter to Frederick Elliot, the senior Colonial Office official, whom he knew was resisting the War Office's efforts to establish the principle of colonial financial responsibility for local defence. If the 'practical suggestions' made by Williams were acted upon, Cunard argued, a battery could be erected at Sydney Mines 'at a comparatively small cost, and kept up at a trifling expense,' with only three or four artillerymen stationed there to train the miners to work the guns. The importance of the mines at Sydney as a source of fuel for the Royal Navy, he argued, 'cannot be exaggerated, and when it is borne in mind that these Mines are now open to the aggressive attacks of the Americans, or any other Naval Power, and the Coal they furnish, and the employment and support now afforded to at least 500 Men at once suspended, if not entirely lost, there would appear to be but one opinion as to the paramount necessity for immediately affording such a means of defence as will avert the risk of the loss of that valuable commodity.'[24] Cunard's letter was well targeted, for the Colonial Office was beginning to see the situation at Sydney as a prime example of the futility of attempting to divide imperial defence into areas of British and local concern. Elliot's minute on Cunard's appeal took aim at J.R. Godley, the assistant under-secretary at the War Office and one of the leading advocates of colonial responsibility for local defence. It was all very well to argue that the protection of the mines was a local responsibility, Elliot said, 'but if on the outbreak of a war, Great Britain, in her struggle with her foes, were deprived of this supply of coal for her Steam Fleets from a British Territory, I apprehend that this Country would be practically [felt?] to have had a weighty interest in the matter. This case therefore is one which brings distinctly into view the conflict between the different ideas.'[25] The colonial secretary, the Duke of Newcastle, not only agreed but declared that the defence of the mines was 'a matter to which I attach very considerable importance.' As he was soon to accompany the Prince of Wales on a grand tour of North America, he would 'make a point' of visiting Sydney and Pictou to evaluate the situation for himself. 'I think my recommendation to the War Office ... will be more likely to meet with a satisfactory result when I can lay before them my own personal observations as well as the views and wishes of well informed persons on the spot.'[26]

The visit of the Prince of Wales was the first by a member of the royal family since the Duke of Kent had served at Halifax half a century earlier. The royal party was not scheduled to visit Sydney, but favourable winds put them ahead of schedule, creating the opportunity for Newcastle to inspect the site. The suggestion by one local historian that the royal party visited Sydney Mines because the prince wanted to inspect the Sydney Mines Volunteers, whose fame 'had evidently reached Royal ears,' is obviously incorrect, as the company had only been organized a year and had done nothing to achieve any fame. At the same time, however, Newcastle had been impressed by the GMA's initiative in organizing the unit, and he certainly sent word to Brown that the prince 'had called specially' for the purpose of inspecting the volunteers.[27]

The visit was unexpected and a program had to be hastily arranged. The editor of the *Cape Breton News* reported that he was on the shore

road between North Sydney and Sydney Mines when, 'to the astonishment of all,' the prince's squadron was seen coming into the harbour at
9:30 a.m. He 'hurried [his] steed' and reached the mines just as the vessels were coming to anchor an hour later. Most miners were underground at that time of day, of course, and orders were immediately
given to suspend operations and to muster the volunteers as quickly as
possible. 'This was a work of difficult accomplishment, as many of the
men had to go more than a mile after getting out of the Pits, to dress
and equip themselves. At the Mines a lively scene presented itself, which
place bore all the appearance of a Town besieged by an invading force –
one could in imagination have changed the joy and gladness which
beamed from every countenance around, into the dismay and alarm
which such a state of affairs would have produced; officers in their uniforms passing hither and thither, and Volunteers hastening towards the
Armory for their Enfield Rifles.'

Meanwhile, Richard Brown, accompanied by Captains Robert Bridge
and Yorke Barrington, proceeded to the beach to receive the prince.
Soon 'a beautiful Barge painted white, was seen to shove off from *Hero*,
in the direction of the Cove,' where a large crowd had assembled on the
beach to see the visiting dignitaries. After Brown officially welcomed the
prince, the Duke of Newcastle, and their entourage, the volunteers
formed a guard of honour and presented arms, after which they were
inspected by the prince, who then visited the Mi'kmaq village on Indian
Beach. The royal party then proceeded through North Sydney, where
the ships at the wharves, especially the British surveying steamer *Marga-
retha Stevenson* and the Royal Mail steamer *Merlin*, were gaily decorated.
The prince 'was cheered at various parts during his progress – but especially near Messrs. Archibald & Co.'s shipyard, and the Mining Company's wharves.' Both the prince and the duke reportedly 'expressed
their astonishment at seeing such a large proportion of pretty girls in
every group as they passed through the Bar.' On arrival at Sydney Mines,
the prince inspected the full turnout of volunteers, 126 in number,
including officers, 'after which in response to the Lieutenant Colonel, a
right loyal cheer was given; in which the spectators, now very numerous,
joined heartily.'[28] The officers were then presented to the prince, who
expressed 'his high gratification at the soldier-like appearance and
steadiness of the Corps, and the great pleasure he had derived from the
inspection of so fine a body of men.' The party retired finally to Beech
Hill, Brown's residence, where an official address of welcome was read
by Brown and 'most graciously received by the Prince.' Following

refreshments, the prince and his entourage returned to the beach for their departure. 'At the very last moment,' the prince told Brown 'that he had been much gratified with his reception by the Volunteers, and people of the Mines; and that his only regret was that he could not remain longer with them.' A few minutes later, the squadron set sail for Halifax.[29]

The outbreak of civil war in the United States only eight months later, in April 1861, and the deterioration of Anglo-American relations added considerable urgency to the question of imperial defence. Admiral Milne's squadron was fully occupied in protecting British shipping and could spare nothing for the immediate protection of ports in Nova Scotia and New Brunswick, none of which was adequately fortified. There were fewer than forty-three hundred imperial troops in British North America, approximately nineteen hundred of them in Nova Scotia, and the militia of all the colonies combined could supply only some ten thousand poorly trained volunteers. As for equipment, many of the rifles and much of the ammunition sent out in 1856 had since been withdrawn, and there were only some seven thousand Enfields and ten thousand old smooth-bore muskets in store.[30]

The imperial government agreed to strengthen its land forces in British North America, and, in addition, Milne received six more vessels. Notwithstanding 'the difficulty of obtaining Provincial funds for purposes of Military expenditure in Nova Scotia,' Newcastle pressed the War Office to build a battery at Sydney Mines to protect the coal mines.[31] Recognizing the undeniable seriousness of the situation, the War Office ordered Nelson in Halifax to proceed with the installation at Chapel Point of six thirty-two-pounder guns that would be sent from Britain.[32] Nelson quickly visited the site on 24 May 1861 and 'picketted out what seems to be desirable for the general guidance of Mr Brown,' who was arranging for the purchase of the necessary additional lands, which were adjacent to those of the General Mining Association.[33]

Nelson had reservations about the adequacy of the guns that the War Office was providing, which were thirty-two-pounder smooth-bores of a short light type with barrels weighing forty-two hundredweight. Steam warships and transports were only part of the revolution in technology that was causing concern among the British military. Developments in iron and steel manufacturing had recently brought the introduction of rifled artillery. Spiral grooves cut into the bore allowed the firing of elongated conical projectiles, which were spun on their longitudinal axes much like a football, giving stability in flight and therefore increased range, power, and accuracy. Noting the presence in the area of the French frigate *Pomone*, which carried forty rifled cannon, as well as of three other warships, Nelson cautioned that it might be necessary to place more powerful guns at Chapel Point.

Nelson's visit also made him realize, as General Williams had done two years earlier, that the single heavy-gun battery at the harbour entrance was not sufficient because of the open nature of the country along the coast to the west with its many suitable landing places. No doubt recognizing that there was no chance of obtaining additional guns or of building additional works, as Williams had recommended, he suggested that the thirty-two-pounders be mounted on travelling carriages with large wheels. Although awkward, such equipment would be somewhat mobile and could be moved out to the coast to the west, or at least to a blocking position on the landward approaches to the mines, in case the enemy came from that direction instead of attempting to attack directly in the vicinity of the harbour mouth.[34]

Nelson thus tangled with the profound problems created for defence planners by steam, which seemed to enable an enemy to strike anywhere suddenly and without notice, and by the revolution in weaponry, which allowed an enemy to strike with devastating firepower. Defence resources were already scarce and were likely to become more so because of the high costs of new technology. How much in the way of land defences could be provided, and at which of the few locales that could be defended should they be installed? What use could be made of armament that was available but that was likely soon to become obsolescent and yet unlikely to be replaced by more modern weapons for some time to come? Nelson's suggestions for what might be accomplished at Sydney with the meagre resources available were innovative but, as he himself strongly implied, utterly inadequate. His call for close cooperation between the army and navy was well considered, but it raised even thornier issues. Coordination of land and sea forces was – and remains – one of the most difficult issues in military affairs, and it was especially difficult at the time in which Nelson was writing. No one yet knew how steam would affect naval strategy, except that the effects would be dramatic and of critical importance to imperial defence. The speed of movement at sea was now greatly increased and largely independent of winds; could Britain's admirals still manage to deploy warships in sufficient numbers and at the right time and place, and thereby keep enemies with much more powerful armies than Britain possessed at bay?

As Nelson wrote, the American Civil War was making the question of

British naval strategy in North American waters especially challenging. As a neutral power, Britain insisted on its right to continue its large trade with the southern states. The United States declared a blockade of Confederate ports, but the legality of that blockade depended on the effectiveness of the U.S. Navy in enforcing it. The task of monitoring the blockade and protecting British rights fell to the North America and West Indies squadron, which was thinly stretched from the Caribbean to Newfoundland. An incident anywhere in those waters could easily result in war.[35]

Against the backdrop of these great events, the War Office, the Colonial Office, and the GMA continued to squabble over who should pay for the very limited fortifications at Sydney Mines. In addition to providing the land for the battery, the GMA had agreed to supply free of charge the unskilled labour for construction.[36] In May 1861, as the Royal Engineers were preparing to begin work, the War Office announced that no funds were available for the finishing work on the battery, including masonry revetments for the rear face of the earthworks and construction of the powder magazine and residence for a 'gunner-in-charge' who would serve as caretaker of the site and instruct the volunteers. These were the more costly parts of the project, requiring skilled labour and special materials. In Halifax, Colonel Nelson, aware that no budget had been allocated for this work, had already applied to the GMA's local agent for additional support.[37]

The Colonial Office, however, thought it inappropriate that the imperial government was asking a private company to contribute to the cost of 'a work of really national interest and importance.' Either the battery was needed or it was not, and if it was, then the imperial government should pay for it. At the same time, 'it is not possible, even if it were right,' to seek a contribution from the province. The War Office's view that colonies should contribute to their own defence was understood, 'but the present is not a question exclusively of self defence. It is a case of whether the only mines in British North America, at present available for naval and other purposes, shall receive that military protection which is essential for securing to our Squadron ... the coal of which it may stand in need during war. If a war were to break out between this country and the US or France a dash would be made for the mines of Cape Breton, and, if successful, it would be a very inadequate answer for any Government to allege that protection had not been afforded to the mines on account of difficulties as to the expense.'[38] The Colonial Office's position was strengthened by the concerns being expressed by

Milne about the inordinate interest shown by officers of French warships that were coaling at Sydney in the details of coal production there.
'I cannot but come to the conclusion,' he wrote, 'that in the event of
hostilities breaking out between the two Countries, an early attempt
would be made by the French to possess themselves of Cape Breton.'[39]
Referring to this report, the Colonial Office offered the War Office a
lesson in strategy: 'The Coal Mines at Sydney are not of any political
value to the Government of Nova Scotia. Their public importance consists of the resources which they would afford to our Fleets in time of
War. A large natural supply of coal in a commanding position readily
accessible by sea may be viewed in modern days like a great store of gun-
powder or any other Munition of War, and there are the same motives
for adequately protecting the one as the other.'[40] Newcastle, fuming
that he suspected Godley had got hold of the file, also privately complained to Lord Herbert, the secretary of state for war, about the 'ped-
dling' way his departmental officials were doing business.[41]

For a second time, it seemed the matter had been settled. Then Lord
Herbert personally insisted that the GMA provide a guaranty that it
would 'maintain the Works, when finished, in an efficient state.'[42] The
Colonial Office gently pointed out that a mining company could
scarcely be expected to have the expertise needed to keep up special-
ized·military structures, and it worked out a face-saving compromise
whereby the GMA would 'be expected to afford the same aid towards
the repair of the Earthwork as they have done towards the construction,' to which the War Office agreed.[43] The GMA subsequently agreed
to these terms as well, and construction of the battery was ordered to
proceed.[44]

It was appropriate that the Colonial Office made the effort to bring
the bureaucratic spat over Sydney to an amicable conclusion just as the
British Parliament's select committee on colonial military expenditure
published its findings. This committee, chaired by Arthur Mills, had
been appointed following the 1860 report of the interdepartmental
committee and its task was 'to inquire and report whether any, and
what, alterations may be advantageously adopted in regard to the
Defence of the British Dependencies, and the proportions of cost of
such Defence as now defrayed from Imperial and Colonial funds respectively.'[45] Although the Liberal prime minister, Lord Palmerston, was not
especially sympathetic to radical calls for reform of the administration
of defence in the colonies, opinion was so strong that he had agreed to
the creation of the parliamentary committee. In its hearings, the weight

of testimony, including that from such government members as W.E. Gladstone, the chancellor of the exchequer, and Lord Herbert of the War Office, was for bringing system and greater colonial responsibility to the confused and costly practices that had grown up over the generations.[46] The committee's report, dated 11 July 1861, has been described as 'the most important single document in the long series of events which was to lead at last to the evacuation of the self-governing colonies by the imperial army.'[47] Arguing that 'the tendency of modern warfare is to strike blows at the heart of a hostile power,' the committee concluded that 'it is therefore desirable to concentrate the troops required for the defence of the United Kingdom as much as possible, and to trust mainly to naval supremacy for securing against foreign aggression the distant dependencies of the Empire.'[48] It divided the colonies into two classes, as the interdepartmental committee of 1859 had done, and agreed that responsibility for the purely military stations was imperial, and that the other colonies should bear 'the responsibility and cost' of their own military defence.[49]

The situation of Sydney nicely illustrated the validity of the Colonial Office's insistence on the need for caution in applying principles to particular cases. As has been seen, Newcastle and his staff had always urged British action at Sydney, not because of Nova Scotia's inability and unwillingness to pay, but because the coal supplies were vital to the operations of the Royal Navy. In this sense they were thoroughly modern in their thinking, no matter how much the suggestion of added overseas garrison responsibilities ran against the grain of advanced views of imperial defence in Britain in the 1860s. One of the intriguing aspects of the discussion of the Sydney defences in the years 1859–61 is that it shows the War Office and Colonial Office struggling over the implementation of policies that ministers and senior officials were debating in the interdepartmental and parliamentary committees.[50]

The War Office not only accepted this report, it also set about to reduce the level of expenditures by seeking input from the major colonies themselves in the cost-cutting exercise. Lord Herbert appointed committees in July 1861 'in several of the more important Colonies, for the purpose of considering annually whether any, and what, reductions may be advisable in the Military expenditure incurred for the protection of such Colonies.'[51] At the same time, when General Trollope wondered how the provincial militias were to be armed in the event of an emergency, Newcastle informed Mulgrave that the provision of arms and ammunition for the militia was 'a question which must be decided by the local and not by the Imperial Government, which is not prepared, and could not be expected to bear the expense.'[52]

When the War Office finally approved funds for the Chapel Point battery late in the summer of 1861, the Royal Engineers immediately started work. The unskilled labourers were provided by Richard Brown, the manager of the GMA operations, in whose ability and probity the military authorities had complete confidence.[53] The guns, which did not arrive until the end of the year or early 1862, were mounted on wooden garrison carriages. The plan was to have them fire through embrasures in earth parapets high enough to give cover to the gun crews, a standard design. Before the onset of winter, the parapets had been built up to the level of the bottom of the embrasures, and work was well advanced on the construction of six heavy timber ground platforms on which the gun carriages would be placed. Lieutenant Colonel Spencer Westmacott, who had succeeded Nelson as commanding royal engineer at Halifax, was optimistic that the battery, which would include a 'small magazine,' a shed for artillery stores, and a residence for the gunner in charge, could be completed within the £200 budget provided by the War Office. Only £60 was spent in 1861, mainly for the timber gun platforms.[54]

The American Civil War, it was now evident, would be neither short nor immediately decisive. Both sides had raised vast armies, and the Confederacy had demonstrated its capacity for survival with its victory over Union forces at Bull Run in July 1861. This setback for the federalist cause helped to heighten tensions between the United States and Britain because of the latter's trade with the Confederate states, tensions that the South, hoping for British – and French – intervention in the war, did its best to exacerbate. William Seward, President Lincoln's secretary of state, let it be known that a war with Britain might not be unwelcome, not least because the conquest of the British North American colonies would compensate for the possible loss of the southern states. On 8 November 1861 the USS *San Jacinto* stopped the British mail steamer *Trent* off Cuba with warning shots. The vessel was boarded and two Confederate diplomats en route to France and Britain were taken into custody. When news of this incident became public at the end of the month, *San Jacinto*'s captain, Charles Wilkes, became an overnight hero in the United States, and a tidal wave of anti-Americanism swept over Britain and its North American colonies. War seemed a near certainty.[55]

Lord Palmerston was more interested in the facts of British power and prestige than in theories of imperial defence. During the summer of 1861 he had already sent more than five thousand British troops to Canada, which would bear the brunt of any conflict with the United States. He had wanted to provide more but had been restrained by Cabinet colleagues who warned of the need to avoid provoking the Americans as well as the danger that too large a British military effort would encourage the colonists in bad old habits of dependence on the mother country for defence. In response to the *Trent* incident, however, the imperial government immediately sent more than eleven thousand reinforcements to Canada, almost all of whom had to disembark at Halifax or Saint John, owing to the winter freeze-up of the Gulf of St Lawrence, and trek overland by foot or in sleighs to the railway terminal at Rivière-du-Loup.[56]

The immediate threat of war passed in January 1862 when the American government, emphasizing that Wilkes had acted without authority, released the Confederate diplomats. Any hope that the episode had strengthened defence cooperation between the imperial and colonial governments was short-lived, however. The British Parliament learned in February that the cost of the recent Anglo-American defence scare included £234,000 for the transport of reinforcements and another £40,000 for naval expenditures. The bill for the army added another £609,000, and these figures were not yet complete.[57] It was hardly surprising that a month later the House of Commons adopted without division a motion proposed by Liberal MP Arthur Mills declaring that 'Colonies exercising the rights of self-government ought to undertake the main responsibility of providing for their own internal order and security and ought to assist in their own external defence.'[58] While the approval of this resolution did not result in an immediate reduction in imperial military expenditures in the colonies, it was an important statement of the dissatisfaction in British political circles with the garrison system and an indication that the discontent had become almost universal.[59]

Sir George Cornewall Lewis, the secretary of state for war, now requested a report to say which colonies, apart from Gibraltar and Malta, should have their defences improved and which should have them abandoned or turned over to local governments. The principal method of promoting efficiency and economy was to be through concentration of forces at places such as Halifax, Bermuda, Cape Town, and Hong Kong that gave the Royal Navy the ability to command sea routes whose security was essential to the survival of the empire. No recommendations were made regarding Canada, because a recently appointed Canadian defence commission was then examining its military problems, but in the Atlantic region the report proposed that everything should be abandoned except the fortifications at Halifax, Saint John, Sydney, and St John's.[60] At this point the Canadian government was defeated on a defence bill that proposed to strengthen greatly the volunteers through a compulsory call-up of the militia if that seemed necessary. While unrelated local political issues contributed to the government's defeat, this incident was viewed almost as treason in Britain, further strengthening resentment against colonial defence expenditures among members of Palmerston's own party.

Nova Scotia's loyal response to the *Trent* crisis counted for little on the larger political stage in the face of the seemingly unpatriotic attitude of Canada. Major General Sir Charles Hastings Doyle, who had succeeded Trollope in the Nova Scotia command, was profoundly alarmed at what he found. The Halifax fortifications were out of date or in ruins, as were the very modest and even more neglected batteries at Saint John, which would be the key position for defence of the Maine frontier in the event of war with the United States. Equally worrisome, the only regular troops available were two infantry battalions and two artillery batteries based at Halifax, though with part of their strength detached to St John's and Fredericton. Doyle, who daily expected American filibustering raids from Maine of the sort that had occurred earlier in the century at times of Anglo-American tension, quickly concluded that the time had come to reactivate the militia – that is, to organize and train virtually the entire adult male population of the Maritime provinces. He was, however, extremely pessimistic about the prospects of getting the necessary cooperation from the local governments.[61]

Somewhat to his surprise, Joseph Howe's government proved willing to cooperate. The House of Assembly approved a new militia act on 12 April 1862 and voted $20,000 for defence. A moribund militia structure already existed, under which every county was divided into regimental districts, and officers, some of whose commissions dated back to the 1830s or earlier, retained their nominal appointments. Even if the officers had been more vigorous, the existing regimental districts were too large. This placed an impossible burden on the regimental officers in keeping up with the basic task of maintaining accurate rolls of eligible men, and compelled men to travel long distances when units were mustered, making regular assembly for training impossible. The goal of the 1862 reorganization was to replace these officers with larger numbers of younger, trained leaders from every locality to allow convenient enrolment and training musters at the community level.[62]

In the interests of putting the new organization on a solid basis, there was no attempt at general training and mustering of the militia during 1862. Instead, the staff focused its efforts on training suitable candidates for the commissioned and non-commissioned officer appointments.[63] The staff, which at the beginning of the year included only nine instructors, all former non-commissioned officers from the British army, was very thinly stretched in undertaking this work. As a result of the *Trent* crisis, the War Office sent instructional personnel to each of the British North American colonies, including some twenty commissioned and non-commissioned officers to Nova Scotia. This was virtually what the War Office and General Williams had recommended on a larger scale in 1859 and, as then, the colonies were fully responsible for the costs of these personnel. Nova Scotia, however, was even harder pressed financially than usual, revenues being almost entirely dependent on customs and excise taxes, which had been reduced by the disruption of trade resulting from the American Civil War. The colony therefore retained only Captain Wimburn Laurie and six of the non-commissioned officers. Receiving the local rank of lieutenant colonel, Laurie became the first of the inspecting field officers who assisted Sinclair in overseeing the work of the instructors and inspecting the militia throughout the province. The volunteers, whose members were exempt from compulsory drill, remained separate from the militia. Mulgrave, still convinced that compulsory drill could not produce effective forces in Nova Scotia, hoped that the call-out of the militia would nevertheless inspire interest that would lead to a further expansion of the volunteers from the ranks of the militia.[64]

The *Trent* crisis, the increasing intensity of the American Civil War, and the stepped-up defence preparations throughout British North America had a direct influence on the Chapel Point battery project, as doubts on the part of senior officers at Halifax about the usefulness of the light thirty-two-pounders already being installed deepened. Possibly they were influenced by the dramatic action that took place between the USS *Monitor* and the Confederate *Merrimac* off Hampton Roads, Virginia, on 9 March 1862, the first naval battle between armour-plated steam warships. Although both vessels carried immense modern guns – as much as ten times larger than thirty-two-pounders – neither was able to pierce the other's armour. It was not hard, therefore, to envision the formidable scale of attack that the empire's coastal defences would almost certainly face in the near future. France and Britain had already completed the construction of their first armoured warships, which, unlike the hastily built and unseaworthy Union and Confederate ships, were large vessels fully capable of operations on the high seas and long-distance cruises.

So worried was the British staff in Nova Scotia that it seized a local opportunity to upgrade the Chapel Point battery. The fortifications at Halifax, for which the British government had always accepted responsibility, were being entirely rearmed with massive seven-, twelve-, and eighteen-ton rifled guns. This made available six long-barrelled, long-range, thirty-two-pounders of fifty-six hundredweight at Fort Ogilvie in Point Pleasant Park. Doyle quickly approved the recommendation of his technical officers that they be moved to Chapel Point.[65] This was not a small task. The long thirty-two-pounders were mounted on wooden garrison carriages like the light models, but these carriages in turn were placed on traversing platforms. Atop each platform were two long rails into which the wheels of the block carriages fitted. The platform turned on a low heavy iron pivot at the front; at the rear were large railway-like iron wheels that rolled on a half-moon iron rail or racer set in the ground. This equipment enabled the crew to make fine adjustments in the bearing of the gun for long-range shooting, the rails of the traversing platform all the while keeping the block carriage in line. The upward slope of the rails to the rear controlled and shortened the recoil of the weapon and allowed the crew quickly to return it to firing position simply by rolling it down the slope of the rails. The foundation stones and iron ground rails for the six guns from Fort Ogilvie alone weighed more than thirty tons; setting all of this level in the ground required a considerable excavation and precise masonry.[66]

In September 1862, Lieutenant John Collings of the Royal Engineers, accompanied by a Corporal Flowers, came from Halifax to install the racers from Fort Ogilvie, and by early November the job was done.[67] Richard Brown, as usual, was indispensable. He evidently found the skilled workmen needed, obtained tools that served until a full set of equipment could be hurried from Halifax by the efficient mail steamer service, and helped Collings meet an unanticipated financial crunch resulting from the absence of banks at Sydney.[68] The War Office, in accordance with its agreement with the GMA, was liable for the pay of the skilled workers, for whom the requirement had greatly increased because of the decision to install the long-barrelled guns on traversing platforms. The absence of banks, however, meant Collings had no means of drawing funds. Westmacott, 'apprehensive of workmen in so thinly peopled a locality becoming dissatisfied if deprived of their weekly payments as customary,' arranged to have silver sent to Sydney by mail steamer. In the interim, Brown lent funds to Collings to meet the immediate payroll, a solution that had to be resorted to again on a number of occasions when the money shipments from Halifax were delayed.[69]

During the concerted effort in the autumn of 1862, a good deal more was done than just laying the foundations and racers for the new guns. The light thirty-two-pounders had been moved out of the way, and timber platforms lifted. Two of the light guns were repositioned, together with the ground platforms, on the northern flank of the battery, where their short range would be no impediment in covering Lloyd's Cove and other possible landing places immediately to the north and west. Four long thirty-two-pounders were placed on the centre face of the battery and two to the south to cover the harbour entrance and allow fire down the harbour for prolonged engagement with a ship attempting to run in to smash the loading docks and works at Sydney. There is some evidence to suggest that two separate short earthworks had been built in 1861, each with a portion of the original armament of light thirty-two-pounders, an economical way of dispersing the guns so that they could cover the wide arc of water commanded by Chapel Point. If so, in 1862 the parapets were joined and extended to create the long half-moon work that dominated the point until the ground was levelled during the construction of new fortifications in 1940.[70]

Doyle and his artillery and engineer officers believed, however, that even the strengthened battery would not provide adequate defence. The long thirty-two-pounders, although better than the short guns, were nevertheless 'comparatively useless for the long range required from Chapel Point,' Doyle reported. [71] The enlarged earthworks of the battery left room for additional armament, and Doyle strongly urged that two big sixty-eight-pounder smooth-bores or, better still, modern rifled guns, should be installed. Even if that were done, effective coverage of the wide entrance to the harbour and the mine workings spread out on either side would require additional batteries and infantry fortifications.[72]

In the event, renewed difficulties over funding made completion of even the existing works at Chapel Point a challenge. The work done in 1862, incorporating important improvements as it did, exhausted the

£200 the War Office had originally allocated for completion of the more modest battery of light thirty-two-pounders. Westmacott estimated that it would require another £1,000 to finish the enlarged work. Evidently because the project now went well beyond what the War Office had agreed to and because it had never relented in its view that the defence of Sydney was primarily a local question, the Colonial Office now reversed its earlier position: it now approached the Nova Scotian government, which agreed to contribute £250. That set the limit for construction during 1863.[73]

Richard Brown had recommended that the finishing carpentry and masonry work be done in the spring by private contractors, assuring Westmacott that 'there would be no difficulty in obtaining tenders.' Westmacott had agreed but in June 1863 Brown reported that he had failed in the endeavour.[74] Brown now took the unusual step of making out 'an estimate of the cost ' himself and of asking one of his own sons, David, to submit a bid. 'I would,' he told Westmacott, 'much rather that some one else had taken it but unless you advertize for tenders I fear it will not be done this season.' While the estimate might appear high, he assured Westmacott that it was 'based upon the prices paid here.'[75] The work projected for the 1863 season included the completion of the interior revetment walls of the half-moon embankment with masonry, closing the open landward side of the battery with a wooden fence, and the construction of two stone magazines for each of the northern and southern groups of guns. The magazines were to be banked with earth to form two lateral traverses, banks that would shield the interior of the battery against long-range fire from a ship standing directly out to sea that would otherwise be able to sweep the works end to end. Brown wanted £380 for the job. Westmacott clearly thought this figure inflated and countered with an offer, which had been endorsed by Doyle, of £206.[76]

This offer was agreed to in July and the work was in its final stages by the middle of October when Corporal John Hannon, the Royal Engineers' overseer, submitted David Brown's account.[77] Westmacott appears to have visited the site at this time, and evidently he was not impressed by what he saw, for upon his return to Halifax, he sent a telegram ordering the work stopped, for reasons that remain unclear. Richard Brown, who had already passed complaints to the Colonial Office that lack of funding from the army was hindering the work,[78] nevertheless complied with Westmacott's instructions and had Hannon 'close the works at the Battery.' He could not refrain from asserting that Hannon had completed all the work ordered in a very satisfactory manner – 'the Battery wears a very different aspect from that which it presented when you were here.' He also assured Westmacott that his son had 'kept a rough account of all the men's time which he says agrees with the returns made by the Corporal,' and he proceeded to claim £110.2.0 for 'cash paid by me for Extras on account of the War Department Sterling, also my son's claim for Contract £211.6.11 Sterling.' Westmacott clearly did not care for these claims either, and in the end the War Office paid Richard Brown £38.2.8 and David Brown only the £206 stipulated in his contract.[79] Newcastle thought the colony should pay these costs and Doyle, who was acting lieutenant-governor in Mulgrave's absence, accordingly submitted the bills to the government. Early in 1864 it flatly refused because of the large effort the province was now making to organize and drill the reformed and enlarged militia.[80]

When Collings returned to Sydney in June 1864, he reported that the work done under Hannon's superintendence was indeed 'very satisfactory.' The magazine was 'well built and apparently perfectly dry,' while the retaining wall of the parapet was also 'well built, and considerable care has evidently been taken in its construction.' Promising that 'the work for the present season will commence tomorrow,' he recommended that Hannon be promoted because of 'the able manner in which [he] seems to have superintended the work in his charge last year.'[81]

The War Office provided a further £500, and possibly more, for the work to be done in 1864. Most of it was spent on the construction of a single-storey blockhouse of more than twenty-five feet square consisting of heavy timbers on a masonry foundation, with loopholes in the walls and iron-sheathed doors. In war it would serve as the central defensible barracks of the battery, but it was finished inside for peacetime use as the residence of the artillery sergeant who would watch over the works and instruct the volunteers.[82] Collings having returned again to Halifax, this work was done under the supervision of Lieutenant J.A. MacLean, who quickly realized that the £500 budget would not be sufficient to complete the work. Some £420 had already been spent, and he calculated that he could afford to pay the workmen for only another three weeks, although he would need them for six weeks to complete the project.[83]

It is unclear if the work continued in the next four months. Early in December 1864 Westmacott asked Richard Brown to report on the situation and Brown explained that progress had been slow because 'our

Masons etc were so busy that I could not spare one to do the small walls
till last week, when I had them done; and I now have a Carpenter fitting
the Sashes etc and today they will begin to put in the floors.' He apolo-
gized for not being able to spare more tradesmen 'to hasten on the
work but ours have their hands full, and I cannot find others to hire.'
The job continued to progress well in the next few weeks, and appears
to have been completed by the end of the month.[84]

During 1863 a resident Royal Artillery non-commissioned officer had
arrived in Sydney Mines to begin twice-weekly training of the volunteers
for their duties in manning the battery. Pending completion of the
blockhouse, he lived in a house owned by the GMA at some distance
from the battery.[85] The army refused to mount the long thirty-two-
pounders on the traversing platforms or to supply complete equipment
and ammunition until he could be housed on the site; that was not the
case until the end of 1864 or perhaps the spring of 1865.[86] Prior to the
1865 season, the two light thirty-two-pounders on block carriages that
had been put in place in 1862 would have provided adequate equipment for the training of the volunteers.

By the time the battery was completed, much had changed. Sir Samuel Cunard, the man who had relentlessly cajoled both the British government and his own board of directors to have Sydney defended, died
in London on 28 April 1865. The Duke of Newcastle, the sympathetic
minister who had done so much to help, had died in the previous year,
and Richard Brown, who had carried out Cunard's wishes with such efficiency and enthusiasm, had retired to England at the end of 1864. At
Brown's request, in October 1864 the Sydney Mines Volunteers was disbanded and its members incorporated into the 4th Regiment, Cape Breton County, the militia unit for the Sydney Mines area, which had begun
to organize in 1862.[87]

Brown's request was closely in tune with the policy of the militia staff.
Compulsory drill of the militia, which had begun in 1863, had not stimulated young men to join the volunteers for fuller training, as Mulgrave
had originally hoped it would do. Rather, as the initial enthusiasm for
volunteering flagged, units became inactive and in some cases served as
refuges for men seeking to avoid compulsory militia drill. The militia
staff therefore began in 1864 to enforce strictly the regulations, and disbanded units that did not maintain their strength, failed to provide
themselves with uniforms, or did not carry out regular training; their
members became liable for compulsory militia service. By the end
of 1864 or shortly afterwards, all of the volunteer companies in Cape

Breton had been disbanded.[88] Because the militia staff continued to support active, efficient volunteer units like the Halifax Volunteer Battalion, Brown's recommendation that the Sydney Mines Volunteers be disbanded suggests that he recognized that its existence reflected only his enthusiasm and that he saw no means for continuing the organization after his departure.

The former volunteers, noted by inspecting officers for their knowledge, were prominent in the new 4th Regiment. Robert Bridge, a captain in the volunteers, received the rank of lieutenant colonel in the militia and assumed command of the unit in October 1864.[89] It has been seen that the former volunteers were maintaining the guns at Chapel Point. Presumably they also continued to receive additional training from the Royal Artillery caretaker at the battery, although the otherwise detailed Nova Scotia militia records are silent on this point, possibly because the caretaker served as part of the special arrangement between the GMA and the War Office and not under the provincial government's administration.

By the end of 1864 a total of 56,111 men had been entered on the rolls of 110 county regiments, and during the year nearly 35,000 had come out for the compulsory five days of training. This was too little time to learn anything but the most rudimentary basics, and there were rifles enough only for officers and non-commissioned officers, but the militia staff was providing extended training for key personnel, such as the adjutants of regiments.[90] Although Nova Scotia was the only province to attempt such an ambitious revival of the full militia, its undertakings were typical of increased efforts throughout British North America during the second half of the American Civil War. Union victories in 1863 and the tremendous expansion of the Union land and naval forces, the latter featuring the latest developments in armour plating and heavy artillery, made it clear that a Northern victory was only a matter of time. A series of inflammatory frontier incidents instigated by Confederate agents hoping to trigger British intervention in the war kept alive the fear that the Union might eventually turn its forces northward. Among them was the remarkable *Chesapeake* affair of December 1863, in which Confederate agents seized a New England steamer and took it into Sambro Harbour where, within Nova Scotian territorial waters, the vessel was recaptured by Union warships in hot pursuit. Moderation on the part of both Britain and the United States prevailed, though a hostile mob at Halifax forced the release of three Confederate officers as one of the American captains was handing them over to Nova

Scotian custody for trial. Tests of American patience continued, most notably the raid on St Albans, Vermont, carried out in October 1864 by Confederates based in Canada, who fled back into the colony and were subsequently released by a Canadian magistrate.[91]

All the while, studies and appreciations by British officers emphasized the mammoth effort – new systems of fortifications and special naval forces for the critical St Lawrence and Great Lakes frontiers and thousands of additional regular troops in all of the colonies – that would be necessary for defence against the increasingly powerful Union army. Lieutenant Colonel William Jervois, who had been sent to Canada by the War Office in 1863 and 1864 to review that colony's defences, submitted a supplementary report in January 1865 with recommendations for the Maritime colonies and Bermuda. Having earlier proposed that Britain should contribute £200,000 towards the fortification of Quebec and further sums for armaments both there and at Montreal, he now added £180,000 for Halifax, £250,000 for Saint John, Sydney, and St John's, and £260,000 for Bermuda.[92] Rather surprisingly, the British government at least partially accepted these recommendations, obtaining approval from Parliament in February for £50,000 to be spent in the coming year at Quebec, £190,000 at Halifax, and £260,000 for Bermuda.[93] So serious did the situation appear that the Canadian Parliament actually approved a defence bill calling for the expenditure of $1 million, and a Canadian delegation in London that spring to discuss the proposed union of the North American colonies explored the question of Anglo-Canadian defence cooperation as well.

Although the U.S. army demobilized with unexpected speed following the end of the Civil War in the spring of 1865, a new crisis almost immediately prolonged British North American defence alarms. Throughout late 1865, fear had grown in the colonies that the Fenian Brotherhood, whose goal was the liberation of Ireland and many of whose members were combat-hardened veterans of the Civil War, were preparing an invasion. On 7 March 1866, the Canadian government called out ten thousand volunteers to guard its border with the United States. Ten days later a rumour swept Nova Scotia that a Fenian fleet had sailed from New York to attack Halifax, resulting in a flurry of military preparations throughout the colony, including calling out the militia. In subsequent weeks, although the ephemeral Fenian fleet never materialized, rifles and ammunition were distributed everywhere in the colony, and the militia continued to drill. When a Fenian force did concentrate in Maine near the New Brunswick border in April, Doyle took seven hundred troops to St Andrews to help defend the colony. This crisis evaporated when the Fenians dispersed, and calm was restored at the end of the month. There was renewed panic in June, however, when another Fenian force invaded Canada, but nothing occurred in the Maritime region.

None of this affected Britain's continuing determination to trim its overseas military commitments, which were thought to be draining the treasury and drawing off forces needed closer to home to counter growing French and Prussian military power. This drive for economy, together with a desire to avoid further disputes with the United States, caused the imperial government to support strongly the Canadian proposal in 1864 to unite the British North American colonies in a federation. It was thought that somehow a federation could shoulder better the responsibility for colonial defence, while the British withdrawal that the event signified would reduce American concerns about the presence of a major European power in North America.[94] Although British warships and troops played their traditional role as the principal defence of the Maritimes, the Fenian threat did underscore the fact that the colonies were not safely isolated from the general problem of British North American security. The events of 1866 also drove home the costs of defence. The bill for the mobilization of the militia and volunteers was more than $100,000 in New Brunswick; in Nova Scotia it was more than $40,000, bringing total militia expenditure for the year to $114,460. During the crisis, the British government had sent out an additional 10,000 rifles, for a total of about 17,000 in Nova Scotia, but still more arms and other equipment were needed, and that too would be extremely costly. Meanwhile, as Colonel Sinclair frankly admitted, 'to speak plainly of the result, except the volunteers, the men, as a body, were not fit to meet and manoeuvre against a well disciplined force, although they would probably have repulsed an equal number of raiders of no better trained men than themselves.'[95] In his view, the limits of what could be achieved by compulsory unpaid service had been reached and the time had come to consider paying those members of the militia who were willing to come out for more regular instruction – although he did not say it – along the lines of the Canadian system of paid volunteers.[96]

The Nova Scotia militia mustered for the last time in the summer of 1867. In the case of the 4th Regiment, Cape Breton County, the parade took place on 22 June, only nine days before Confederation was proclaimed. The inspection included the battery at Chapel Point, where all was reported to be in good order.[97] This proved to be the last such event at Sydney Mines for a generation. The 4th Regiment disbanded with the dissolution of the Nova Scotian militia, and Lieutenant Colonel Charles Crewe Read, the inspecting field officer in Cape Breton, now in the employ of the new federal government, failed in his efforts to stir up interest in the formation of a volunteer artillery. In the absence of a militia unit, there was no pressing need to maintain the works, now the responsibility of the Canadian government. The government continued to pay for the sergeant-caretaker, at least until the summer of 1870 (though he was periodically absent on other duties), and Read reported in November 1869 that the battery and buildings at Chapel Point were already 'rapidly being destroyed by the action of the weather and mischievious persons.'[98] Nothing was done to prevent the battery's deterioration, and, across the harbour at Sydney, about an acre of Barrack Park facing the north end of Charlotte Street was relinquished to the county, which erected a courthouse on the site. The remainder of the grounds continued to be a popular gathering place for outdoor activities. A scenic area in the heart of the quiet little town, it provided ideal facilities for picnicking, walking, swimming, and boating.[99]

The achievement of Confederation in 1867, the failure of the Fenians to organize a concerted sustained attack on the colonies, and the subsequent resolution of the most serious Anglo-Canadian-American disputes in the Treaty of Washington in 1871 introduced a period of détente, allowing the British army to complete its withdrawal from Canada. The garrison that pulled out of Quebec City that year was the last, leaving only the imperial naval bases at Halifax and Esquimalt. The only British troops remaining in Canada now were the approximately two thousand men at Halifax, where the imperial government also completed work begun during the Civil War to rebuild the fortifications. Halifax and its sister base at Bermuda were maintained primarily to ensure that the Royal Navy could deploy freely in the crucial Atlantic theatre. The Halifax fortress also provided assurance to Canada of continuing imperial naval support, and it was a secure bastion through which British land forces could return in the event of a crisis.[100]

Although the achievement of Confederation implied greater responsibility for defence, the new Canadian government showed little interest in the matter. Sir John A. Macdonald, the prime minister, continued to put his faith in British foreign policy and the imperial strategic umbrella, as did his successors. In keeping with Macdonald's pragmatic political philosophy, the new dominion would concentrate its energies on developing the physical resources of half a continent. That, rather than squandering money on armed forces that could never be sufficient to resist attack by the only likely enemy, the United States, was the key to securing the future of the federation. The coastal defence of the Maritime provinces did not seem much of a problem because of the strong British presence at Halifax. The new federal government did pass legislation in 1868 creating the Canadian militia, which replaced the former colonial militia systems. Not surprisingly, the new organization was modelled on the volunteer organization that had been developed in the former Province of Canada. Thus, while Macdonald recognized the need for the militia, its primary value until the end of the century was political, because of the extensive opportunities it provided for patronage.[101]

chapter four

Coal and Steel, 1867–1914

I believe the population of Sydney are in receipt of good wages and have constant employment, and therefore, except in case of actual hostilities – when too late – could they only be relied on to turn out.

Major General Edward Selby-Smyth, 1878

Cape Breton did not figure prominently in the military concerns of the new federal government. Nor, on much of the island, does there seem to have been the sort of local commitment needed to raise volunteer units on a substantial scale under the new dominion Militia Act that came into force in 1868. The 718 volunteers who presented themselves for paid drill that year were organized on the basis of the old provincial militia regiments. These included one in the Sydney area but none on the northern side of the harbour.[1] Independent infantry companies, each with an authorized strength of three officers and fifty-five men, were organized in 1869. Two years later these units were combined into the Victoria Provisional Battalion, under the command of Major William Bingham of Englishtown. As its name suggested, the new battalion was concentrated in the southeastern part of the island, with headquarters and two companies at Baddeck, and one each at Middle River and Grand Narrows. In 1872 a fifth company was organized at Sydney.[2] The annual training camp took place at Baddeck and lasted for twelve days, usually in the middle of September when haymaking was done. As one veteran recalled many years later, the annual departure of the Sydney company for Baddeck was a highlight of the year in the little community, one that 'brought a large crowd of admirers to see them off at Harrington's wharf.' The men made the journey by sea, travelling on *Neptune* or *Marion*, and 'were provided with cheese and crackers for a snack going around Cranberry Head, and if the cook was generously inclined a cup of black tea was given for a chaser.' On one occasion, 'as the crowd was waiting ... a young man by the name of Neil McKinnon was drowned after accepting an invitation from Reynolds Harrington to go out for a boat sail. The boat filled with water down near Crawley's Creek ... and Harrington was rescued by J.W. Dobson, who rushed to their aid in his sail boat.'[3]

When Alexander Mackenzie's Liberal Party took office in Ottawa in 1873, it introduced a number of changes that it hoped would make the militia more efficient. One was the creation of the position of general officer commanding the militia, which was to be held by a British officer of at least the rank of colonel. He would receive a Canadian commission and would provide professional leadership to the Canadian militia, as well as military advice to the Canadian government, to which he would be wholly responsible. One of the major concerns of the first incumbent, Major General Edward Selby-Smyth, was to upgrade the artillery in the major fortifications at Quebec, Montreal, and Kingston, and in the much more modest batteries at ports in the Maritimes.[4]

All of these defences, including the recently built battery at Chapel Point, were now obsolescent in the face of two major technical innovations. The first was the development of ironclad steam-powered warships, which were already visiting Sydney Harbour to refuel; the second was the invention of powerful long-range rifled guns, whose missiles could penetrate armour. The smooth-bore cannon of the first half of the nineteenth century were basically iron tubes closed off at one end, that fired simple spherical projectiles, and would have been quite familiar to gunners of the sixteenth and seventeenth centuries. Until the 1860s, the most common heavy gun was the thirty-two-pounder smooth-bore, like those at Sydney, whose two-and-a-half-ton cast-iron barrel fired a thirty-two-pound ball to a maximum range of about twenty-nine hundred yards. By the 1870s, however, the standard gun in British service, including at the forts at Halifax, was the 9-inch rifled muzzle-loader. Its wrought-iron barrel weighed twelve tons and fired a 255-pound elongated projectile to a range of six thousand yards or more. At one thousand yards the projectile could smash through iron plate ten inches thick.[5]

Selby-Smyth believed that it was urgently necessary to defend Canada's ports with these new guns because the change in warships from

sail to steam propulsion was greatly increasing the danger of swift surprise attacks, and a single ship armed with the powerful new artillery
could do immense damage to an inadequately defended coastal city.
Canada could not consider itself safe because of its relative isolation
from the recurrent political problems of Europe. The danger of virtually unprotected coastlines and harbours had already been demonstrated during the brief Franco-Prussian War in 1870, when a Prussian
ship arrived at Sydney with a cargo of rails for the International Railway,
then under construction. It had to remain in port all summer because
French warships cruised offshore, waiting to capture it if it ventured
outside.[6]

Selby-Smyth's warning must have seemed prophetic when, during the
Anglo-Russian war scare of April 1878, a German steamer carrying Russian sailors and heavy guns arrived at Ellsworth, Maine. *Cimbria*'s mission was to arm steamers purchased in the United States so that they
could attack Canadian ports and shipping in Canadian waters in the
event that Britain entered the Russo-Turkish War. The idea that Canada
was vulnerable to attack not only by the United States in its interior but
also by very distant enemies on its coasts seems to have struck Ottawa
like a thunderbolt. Perhaps equally disturbing was the fact that a Canadian appeal to the British government for a 'fleet of fast cruisers' to
meet the threat of *Cimbria*'s privateers brought the chilling response
that steam raiders were nearly impossible to catch and that the Royal
Navy would already have more than enough to do in the event of war.
Canada would be on its own.[7]

Initially, at least, the Mackenzie government was prepared to act. It
authorized the expenditure of $10,000 for precautionary measures and
sent Lieutenant Colonel Thomas Strange, a Royal Artillery officer serving with the Canadian militia, to the Maritimes to put the available
defences in order.[8] Some improvements had already been undertaken
at Saint John before the crisis, in response to Selby-Smyth's advice,
because of that port's proximity to the American border, and the Militia
Department now undertook some work at mainland Nova Scotian ports
to repair existing smooth-bore guns and to mount others. Efforts at Sydney, however, were limited to an unsuccessful attempt to raise an artillery unit at Sydney Mines.

Meanwhile, the government sensibly asked the authorities in London
for advice on what should be done about harbour defences. The sudden
possibility of war with Russia had provoked alarm in Britain as well, with
the result that a special colonial defence committee that included repre-

sentatives of the Colonial Office, Admiralty, and War Office was appointed to advise on emergency measures to protect colonial ports, including those on both coasts of Canada. Its chairman, Admiral Sir Alexander Milne, had served as commander-in-chief of the North America and West Indies Station during much of the American Civil War and knew the Canadian East Coast well. As has been seen, he had already expressed serious concern about the security of Sydney's coal mines.

In addition to improved defences at Saint John and Charlottetown, the committee recommended considerable, and expensive, works at Sydney because of the great size of its harbour. These included two mutually supporting batteries at the harbour mouth, each with two sixty-four-pounder and two 7-inch rifled guns, which fired armour-piercing shells of 90 and 112 pounds respectively. Because the southern side of the harbour approaches was lightly inhabited, the committee suggested that both batteries could be placed on the northern side, in the vicinity of Sydney Mines, where the population existed to supply militia garrisons. Given the width of the harbour entrance, it would still be possible for a determined enemy to push past these defences, however, so the committee recommended that a third battery, with the same armament as the others, be built at Point Edward to protect the International Pier at Sydney. As a somewhat cheaper alternative to this battery, the committee suggested installing underwater mines in the main channel off Sydney Mines. These could be fired electrically by means of cables running to a shore station, a new technology that had proven effective during the American Civil War. Such a minefield, 'under the protection of the ... advanced batteries [at Sydney Mines], and protected at night and in foggy weather by guard boats ... would,' the committee thought, 'afford complete security to the harbour.'[9]

The estimated cost of all this was steep: £16,800 to build and arm the three batteries, or £14,200 for two batteries and the minefield.[10] The total estimated cost of the Milne committee's proposals for the East Coast was approximately £50,000, and for his proposals for Victoria, British Columbia, an additional £13,200. This was far more than the Canadian government was willing to spend. Although Mackenzie had told the governor general that Canada would be 'above shirking her duty in providing for the defence of her own coasts,' some ministers were now even suggesting that it would be cheaper to let the Russians destroy everything.[11] Certainly, the minister of militia decided that the Chapel Point battery had fallen into such disrepair that the cost of renovating it was prohibitive, so that project was terminated.[12]

Selby-Smyth agreed that the Milne recommendations were expensive. In the case of Sydney, he also thought they were hopelessly optimistic with respect to manpower, requiring as they did as many as two hundred artillerymen and an additional one thousand militiamen for the supporting infantry defences. 'I do not rely upon the population of Cape Breton furnishing this quota satisfactorily or reliably,' he wrote. The entire existing militia on the island totalled only two hundred infantrymen, and efforts to raise an artillery unit of forty-two men at Sydney Mines were not meeting with much success. Sydney's importance as a coaling port, however, made it a special case, and he recommended that 'its temporary defence ... should be undertaken by Her Majesty's ships, supplemented, if necessary by a detachment of Royal Artillery from Halifax, to mount and man whatever armament may be deemed necessary, in addition to a gun-boat or small ironclad ship.'[13]

He also had an affordable alternative to the Milne committee's recommendations for the East Coast. A British entrepreneur, Sir William Palliser, had developed a method for improving smooth-bore artillery by enlarging the bore and inserting a rifled wrought-iron tube into the cast-iron gun. In this way, old guns could fire heavy elongated projectiles, though not with the full propelling charges used in guns made completely of wrought iron, which was a much stronger material than brittle cast iron. The Mackenzie government had already, on Selby-Smith's advice, purchased fifteen of these converted guns, which had been used to improve the Saint John and Quebec defences in 1877, prior to the Russian crisis. Now, he persuaded the government to place an urgent order in Britain for additional converted guns, with the intention of allocating as many as eight of them to Sydney.[14]

The Milne committee responded in August 1878 by heaping scorn on Selby-Smyth's proposals, which it declared were 'totally inadequate to meet the defensive requirements of the Dominion.' His suggestion that the Royal Navy might help directly with the defence of Sydney indicated that the general did not understand naval strategy. Ignoring the fact that Selby-Smyth had only made this recommendation for Sydney, which he had carefully identified as a special case, the committee explained that would be 'quite impossible' for the navy to protect 'every port' in the empire. Canadian ports, 'like those of other colonies, must trust to their own resources to secure themselves from the attack of hostile cruisers [sic], deriving from Her Majesty's fleet the great advantage of immunity from attack on a large scale, and such general protection as it is able to afford to all parts of the Empire, but dependent upon their own means for purely local defence.' The committee also poured derision on Selby-Smyth's suggestion that converted guns might be a useful, economical alternative to expensive modern armament. The converted guns lacked the necessary power and, the committee argued, the general had understated their cost. The 7-inch and sixty-four-pounder rifled guns were the smallest and cheapest that could dependably pierce armour.[15] Not surprisingly, the British government supported the committee and shelved the Canadian order for additional converted guns, a decision in which the Canadians acquiesced.[16]

The immediate danger of war with Russia passed during the summer of 1878, and nothing was done at Sydney. In his annual report to Parliament, Selby-Smyth addressed the militia question, observing that, in contrast to the mainland ports in the Maritimes, 'at Sydney ... where perhaps they might have been more needful than elsewhere, the call for Volunteer Artillery has not been responded to with the success that might have been hoped for.' The reason, he speculated, was that 'the population of Sydney are in receipt of good wages and have constant employment, and therefore, except in case of actual hostilities – when too late – could they only be relied on to turn out, and they would, in consequence, have but little knowledge of their duty.'[17]

In Victoria, the similar reluctance of the local citizenry to enlist did not stand in the way of defence efforts because the Royal Navy very much wanted local protection for its undefended base at Esquimalt, a suburb of the provincial capital.[18] Thus, the 1878 crisis proved to be the beginning of cooperation, strained and difficult as it often was, between the imperial and the dominion governments in building batteries and raising garrison troops at the West Coast port. None of these pressures existed at Sydney, apparently despite the coal mines, because Halifax met the essential requirements of both the British and Canadian governments for coastal and gulf defence. The workings of the Canadian patronage system may also have been a factor in the lack of local enthusiasm. In May 1878, Colonel Charles Crewe Read, the permanently employed staff officer at Sydney responsible for the militia in Cape Breton and a hold-over from the pre-Confederation regime, had been dismissed, apparently for political reasons, and in the autumn a successor had still not been appointed.[19]

Growing British pressure for much more far-reaching defence assistance from the self-governing colonies made a policy of rebuilding the close links between the British garrison at Halifax and the local militia that had existed before Confederation politically attractive to the Canadian government, not least because it cost little. From the late 1870s, therefore, the Canadian government responded to British appeals for help by gradually allowing closer integration of the Halifax militia and other units in mainland Nova Scotia with the imperial garrison. This was virtually the full extent of Canadian preparations for the defence of the East Coast until the turn of the century.[20]

Despite its neglect by military and political authorities, Sydney Harbour was becoming an increasingly important commercial port. North Sydney became Canada's fourth busiest port for ocean ships in the 1870s, surpassed only by Quebec, Halifax, and Montreal in gross tonnage. This reflected the growth of steam-powered shipping, the expansion of the coal industry, and the fact that it was strategically located as a refuelling stop for ships travelling between Europe, the American East Coast, and Central and South America. As well, the successful completion of the transatlantic cable in 1866 and the establishment of the Western Union cable office at North Sydney in 1875 resulted in shipping agents cabling their orders there to direct ships' captains to their next assignments. During the 1870s and 1880s, as a result of the demand generated by steamship traffic, railway building, and the development of iron and steel and other coal-consuming industries, all within the framework of the new dominion's so-called National Policy, coal production in Cape Breton grew rapidly. From 98,328 tons in 1872, shipments from North Sydney rose to 108,259 tons in 1879, 128,000 tons in 1881, 913,549 tons in 1891, and over one million tons in 1897. With the completion of the national railway system at the turn of the century, North Sydney became the main entry point in Canada for European mail destined for North America. Because of its strategic location, during the first quarter of the twentieth century the Canadian Pacific mail steamers from Europe dropped their mail at North Sydney, where special trains picked it up for delivery to the mainland. Thus, it reached Canadian and American cities faster than if the steamers had carried it to Quebec or Montreal.[21]

It is not surprising, therefore, that British military officers visiting the East Coast commented on the lack of harbour defences at Sydney. Vice Admiral J.E. Commerell, on completing his tour as commander-in-chief of the North America and West Indies Station in 1885, warned both the British and the Canadian governments of the grave danger posed by the lack of defences at Sydney and Louisbourg. Reiterating the comments of Gobineau in 1859 and the concerns of Admiral Milne in 1860, Commerell warned that 'the French are well aware of the importance of Sydney Harbour as a coaling station; in fact they use it much more than we do.' In the event of war, he predicted that they 'would rendez-vous and seize Louisburg and Sydney Harbours.' He had no doubt that arms and entrenching tools were already stored at St Pierre for this purpose, 'and there is nothing to prevent them seizing Louisburg Har-bour, and by means of earthworks and torpedoes [i.e., mines], holding that place against anything we have to oppose them with. No doubt an expedition from France to sustain them in their possession of Louis-burg and Sydney would arrive before any reinforcement from England could be brought to bear.' The possession of Louisbourg would, in his opinion, 'act most detrimentally to our interests, dealing as the French do so much in sentiment, and the fact of their having taken a coaling station at the mouth of the St Lawrence and by it commanding our trade might have a very disturbing influence on the French Canadians in Lower Canada.' As Selby-Smyth had done seven years earlier, he rec-ommended that 'one of the small ironclads' be kept ready to mine the entrance to Louisbourg Harbour in a crisis in order to block a French attack. It was 'surely time,' he argued, that the Canadian government took measures to protect its coasts with mines. The governor general, he claimed, was 'fully alive to the necessity of some action in this mat-ter, but the Colonial Government are very difficult to move, and unless the Imperial Government take the initiative, nothing will be done but talk.'[22]

This was one of at least three similar unsolicited recommendations made during the middle 1880s on what should be done at Sydney.[23] Continuing tensions with France and Russia, whose navies were pressing forward with the development of new technologies in an effort to neu-tralize British naval superiority, were making the defence of ports a lead-ing issue in both official circles and public debate in Britain and throughout the empire. One result was the creation of a permanent colonial defence committee, modelled on the Milne committee. When the committee reviewed Sydney's defences in 1887, its members strongly endorsed the Milne committee's recommendations and called on Can-ada to implement them. Major General Frederick Middleton, the gen-eral officer commanding the militia, was given the unenviable task of drafting the Canadian government's response. He rather weakly sug-gested that Sydney's needs could not be considered until much more had been done generally to improve the country's underdeveloped forces. 'Should any crisis arise suddenly, doubtlessly the exposed coal sources [at Sydney and Pictou] would be protected or covered by our [i.e., British] fleets, and Saint Johns [*sic*] N.B., like Quebec is not totally unprotected, though far from being properly defended.'[24]

By this time, the militia in Cape Breton was expanding, though not according to any plan of defence for the island. Rather, local interest and influence with federal authorities seem to have provided the impetus. In 1879 the Victoria Provisional Battalion had been converted to a Highland unit and renamed the Victoria Provisional Highland Battalion.[25] This change clearly reflected the Scottish composition of the unit. Following a visit to its summer camp at Baddeck in 1874, the deputy adjutant general, Colonel J.W. Laurie, had commented on the fact that, while the men showed a 'willingness and desire to learn,' many 'only speak Gaelic and do not understand English,' making it necessary 'to interpret all orders and explanations to them, and the progress is, therefore, not so rapid.'[26] The battalion acquired some permanence in 1886, when the term 'provisional' disappeared from the name and it was assigned a number in the roll of Canadian militia infantry, with the designation 94th Victoria Battalion of Infantry, Argyll Highlanders.[27]

In 1883 Dr William McLeod, recently defeated as Conservative member of Parliament for Cape Breton, persuaded the government to establish the Sydney Field Battery, an artillery unit of eighty men.[28] It existed only on paper, however, until January 1887, when McLeod, who was the commanding officer with the rank of major, Captain Walter Crowe, and two sergeants attended the Royal School of Artillery at Quebec for the basic 'short' course. The unit made its first public appearance on 24 May of that year when it paraded at Barrack Park and fired a royal salute in honour of Queen Victoria's birthday.[29] In July it held its first twelve-day training camp, also at Barrack Park, relying for instruction entirely on its own recently and minimally qualified officers and sergeants. Its guns were 'obsolete 9–pr SB [smooth-bore] guns, which are very inaccurate even at ordinary rifle range,' and were fired over the water for practice in the absence of a proper land firing range. The horses, which appear to have been pit ponies leased from the nearby mines, were too small for military harness. Inspecting officers from central Canada thought all these handicaps to be nearly insuperable.[30]

Notwithstanding these difficulties, the Sydney Field Battery's gunners were described by an inspecting officer in 1890 as 'diligent and [they] did their best to become good soldiers.' Their guns were 'well cared for,' and the gun shed and armoury at Sydney were 'in excellent order.' Although the old barracks were dilapidated, a decade would pass before they were repaired. In subsequent years the unit not only survived but became more efficient through the devoted efforts of its personnel, including attendance by still more officers and non-commissioned officers at the artillery school in Quebec. One inspecting officer was clearly impressed by how 'hardy and active' the pit ponies proved to be, and in 1890–1 the unit's old guns were replaced by four nine-pounder rifled muzzle-loading guns, the standard weapon of the Canadian militia artillery.[31] In 1895, when the militia's seventeen field artillery batteries were numbered, the unit became the 17th Sydney Field Battery, still the only field artillery unit in Nova Scotia.[32]

Early in 1896, Captain Walter Crowe of the 17th Battery, who was also a prominent lawyer at Sydney, complained directly to the minister of militia about the state of military affairs in Sydney. The only buildings at Barrack Park were the old officers' quarters and barrack buildings that the departing British troops had left behind in 1854. The 17th was using one of the barrack buildings, and the Sydney company of the 94th Battalion was using the other. Both were too small and in very bad repair. Crowe appealed for the construction of a proper armoury. He also protested the neglect of Sydney's defences generally, and urged that a modern coast artillery battery be built at Chapel Point. In response, Major General Sir William Gascoigne, the general officer commanding the militia, observed that Sydney was just one of many towns wanting a new armoury and that it was not one of the more pressing cases. As for the larger question of harbour defences, 'there is so much of pressing vital importance to do elsewhere' that 'I cannot look upon Cape Breton Island as having the first claim.' Indeed, he thought it 'an extraordinary thing' that the 17th Battery even existed. 'I hear good accounts of the Battery itself, but I should have thought strategically that [Sydney] was the last place in which a Field Battery would have been raised.'[33]

Although Gascoigne's failure to appreciate the need to protect Sydney's coal mines seems remarkable, he was right about the field battery. As hard as the personnel of the unit worked, they had to struggle without proper instruction and training facilities because of Cape Breton's geographical isolation, which created special difficulties for an arm as technical as field artillery. More important, field guns were of marginal use for coastal defence. Given the speed of modern warships, coast artillery needed to be mounted on pedestals that allowed rapid traversing to follow the target. Wheeled field carriages had to be laboriously swung about by lifting and shifting the trail of the mounting, which was adequate for firing against slow-moving or stationary land targets but too slow and inaccurate for use against ships.

Although a modern coast artillery battery was not forthcoming at Sydney, the 17th survived, and a year later a minor crisis occurred that resulted in the more efficient organization of the unit. In the spring of 1897, the district commander, Colonel J.D. Irving, 'wished to have the stores cleaned up for inspection and all losses made good.' McLeod, regarding this as a criticism of his superintendence of Barrack Park, 'would not do it,' and when Irving threatened to remove the stores from Sydney, McLeod resigned his command. He was replaced by Major Crowe, who discovered 'lots of things missing such as axes, picks, shovels, harness, clothing, etc,' but 'had the place in order in five weeks' for Irving's inspection.[34] It was a harbinger of happier days. Barrack Park was renamed Victoria Park in that glorious summer of 1897 in honour of the Queen's Diamond Jubilee, an event that occasioned major celebrations throughout Canada and the empire. The 17th Battery held its summer camp from the 8th to 20th of June, and on the 22nd there was 'a monster procession,' in which the militia and various societies and coal miners marched. As well, four warships visited the harbour.[35]

The late 1890s saw the beginning of important reforms of the Canadian militia. A war scare with the United States in the winter of 1895–6, resulting from British and American sabre-rattling over a settlement of the disputed boundary between British Guiana and Venezuela, caused some brief frantic preparations in Canada that laid bare the weakness of the militia. The final collapse of the Conservative government and the election of the Liberals under Wilfrid Laurier in 1896 combined with a strengthening economy to create a new sense of optimism, symbolized by the new prime minister's subsequent naive but cheerful declaration that the twentieth century would belong to Canada. While the Laurier government had no great interest in military affairs, it was moderately nationalistic and saw the creation of more respectable armed forces as a potentially effective and politically acceptable response to increasing British pressure for greater Canadian participation in imperial defence. The new minister of militia, Frederick Borden, devoted himself during his long tenure to reorganizing and reforming the militia.[36]

For these reasons, and because of the continuing rapid development of naval and military technology, coastal defence again began to receive serious attention in Canada. By the late 1890s, warships were becoming recognizably modern. These large, fast vessels, built of steel, with dependable engines and long steaming ranges, bore little resemblance to the awkward ironclads of the 1870s and 1880s. Artillery weapons, also built of steel, were similarly becoming recognizably modern. Effective fast-operating breech-loading mechanisms had come into service, as had fast-operating compact hydraulic recoil systems. The ponderous labour-intensive effort of loading heavy artillery by the muzzle had been eliminated, and guns could now fire as fast as the breech could be swung open and the ammunition thrust home: several times per minute instead of a minute or two per round. Much longer barrels, made possible with the passing of muzzle loading, and improved ammunition greatly increased range and accuracy. The 6-inch breech-loaders that came into service at the end of the 1890s could fire seven one-hundred-pound rounds per minute to ranges of ten thousand yards and more, with a hitting power equal to that of much larger rifled muzzle-loading guns. These guns formed the backbone of the British empire's coastal defences until well into the Second World War, and many of them remained in service until the 1950s. Beginning in the late 1890s the British army completely re-equipped the Halifax fortress with the new guns and, with the cooperation of the Canadian government, mounted a smaller number of them at Esquimalt.[37]

Lieutenant Colonel F.A. Stone, a British artillery officer seconded to Canadian service, visited Sydney in 1899. There he found the Chapel Point battery in ruins, with the guns dismounted and half-buried. His report virtually reproduced the analysis contained in Vice Admiral Commerell's warning of 1885, although there is no indication that he had seen it. Stone learned that the crews of visiting French warships continued to show interest in Sydney, and he too expressed concern. Recalling the dramatic events of the eighteenth century, he pointed out that the geography had not changed. Cape Breton was still isolated from the rest of the continent, making its reinforcement from the mainland a difficult proposition in time of crisis, and it still commanded the northwest Atlantic, more so than ever now that it was a coaling port and terminus for transatlantic cables. Like Commerell, he feared that an enemy might seize a lodgement in the Sydney area, and therefore recommended that two 6-inch breech-loaders be mounted at Chapel Point and two quick-firing twelve-pounders at Point Edward. The latter guns, each of which could fire as many as twenty twelve-pound shells per minute, were designed to provide a curtain of fire in the immediate confined approaches to docks and other port facilities.[38]

Stone also recommended that the 17th Sydney Field Battery be converted into garrison artillery to man these or any other defences that might be installed. This suggestion especially made sense because the presence of a field battery at Sydney, which was isolated from the training facilities and mobile formations of mainland Nova Scotia and central Canada, had always been an anomaly. Conversion of the unit to a static role would not only be more appropriate, it would also require only half the personnel and no horses, freeing funds to establish a new field battery in Ontario.[39] Borden approved this change, but, as a Nova Scotian, he asked the military staff to expunge any reference to the fact that 'the Field Battery at Sydney has been dispensed with in order to enable a Field Battery to be established at or near Ottawa,' because 'to publish such a reason would be exceedingly awkward for me in the Province of Nova Scotia.'[40] Effective September 1900, the 17th Field Battery was disbanded and its personnel transferred to a newly created Sydney Company of Garrison Artillery.[41]

This proved to be nothing more than a brief change of name, however, because militia headquarters did not pursue Stone's proposal for coastal defences at Sydney. Rather, in 1903 it reconverted the unit back to the 17th Field Battery and subsequently re-equipped it with modern twelve-pounder breech-loading field guns, armament that other batteries had begun to receive in the late 1890s. The twelve-pounders had a range of some five thousand yards, twice that of the nine-pounder rifled muzzle-loaders. These developments were part of a wider expansion of the field artillery. In 1905, Militia Headquarters established the 3rd Brigade, Canadian Field Artillery, with headquarters at Sydney, which consisted of the 17th Battery and a new field battery, the 18th at Antigonish, and, in 1912, the 37th at Souris, Prince Edward Island.[42]

The shuffle of the Sydney battery from field artillery to coastal defence and back between 1900 and 1903 reflected more than administrative vacillation, although that was undoubtedly part of the story. From 1899 to 1902 the British empire was at war in South Africa. What the British had expected would be a short and relatively minor conflict had turned into a prolonged struggle in which the army was hard-pressed to raise massive field forces. Contributions from the empire's self-governing dominions, including infantry and field artillery units from Canada, had become reinforcements much larger and more important than anyone had at first believed would be needed. Accordingly, both during the war and later the British army began to seek economies in static coastal defence forces so that it could more readily raise substantial field forces, and the dominions were encouraged to do the same in case their help was again needed in the future.

The seconded British officers who filled the key positions at militia headquarters in Ottawa needed little persuasion, as they had long been endeavouring to reform the Canadian force from a collection of often isolated small units, like the Sydney battery, into larger organizations, like field artillery brigades that could mobilize in strength for field service when needed. Such sizeable mobile field formations could serve either to resist an attack on Canada or, if the government of the day agreed, to go overseas as part of a British army in the event of another major war somewhere in the world.[43]

The South African War had another, larger, impact on Canada, causing it to assume a much greater share of responsibility for its own coastal defences. Because of its magnitude and its distance from Britain, the war stretched the Royal Navy, the mainstay of imperial defence, as thinly as the army. In addition to protecting the transportation of troops and supplies to South Africa, the Royal Navy sought to ensure that potentially hostile naval powers did not seize the opportunity to attack while such a large portion of imperial military resources was already committed. It quickly became clear that Lord Salisbury's policy of 'splendid isolation' from alliances with other powers was no longer realistic. Accordingly, the British government reached diplomatic settlements with France, Russia, and the United States, and signed a defensive alliance with Japan. These developments enabled it to concentrate its resources, particularly the Royal Navy, closer to home and in the Mediterranean. As a result, the Admiralty closed the naval dockyards at Halifax in December 1904 and announced that British naval commitments in the Western Hemisphere would henceforth be carried out by fast cruisers based in Britain. There was still a need for garrisons and fortifications at Halifax and Esquimalt to ensure that British warships would have secure ports from which to operate in North American waters, however, and the Canadian government – somewhat to the surprise of British authorities – offered to assume full responsibility for both establishments. This decision reflected Laurier's desire to build up armed forces that were clearly committed to the defence of Canada as an alternative to the schemes for imperial military cooperation being strongly promoted by the British. As Laurier well knew from the experience of the South African War, such schemes were highly controversial in Canada. Starting in 1905, the tiny Canadian permanent force nearly trebled in size within a year to provide more than one thousand regular troops at Halifax to replace the departing British troops.[44]

While Canadian coastal defence efforts were being concentrated at Halifax, revolutionary change was taking place in the communities surrounding Sydney Harbour, particularly the sleepy little town of Sydney

itself. At the end of the 1890s, a group of entrepreneurs, led by Henry
Melville Whitney of Boston, undertook to establish a steel plant at Syd-
ney to exploit the abundant coal in the area and the iron ore available at
nearby Bell Island, Newfoundland. The result was the formation of the
Dominion Iron and Steel Company, which was quickly joined by the
Dominion Coal Company, a consolidation of several smaller companies.
Shortly afterwards, a rival steel plant, the Nova Scotia Iron and Steel
Company, was built in Sydney Mines. Sydney Harbour quickly became
an industrial magnet, drawing people not only from outlying parts of
the island but from Newfoundland, the United States, and Europe. Sydney, which for many years had been an insignificant provincial town
struggling to survive, grew rapidly to more than ten thousand people
and became the industrial heart of the Maritime provinces.

Civic leaders like Walter Crowe were understandably thrilled by this
'progress,' but the changes brought problems as well. Among them was
conflict between the large companies and the workers, both miners
and steelworkers, over wages, working conditions, and, inevitably, the
right to bargain collectively through a union. Trouble was not long in
coming: in July 1904 a strike at the Sydney steel plant turned violent.
The local authorities immediately judged the situation to be beyond
the resources of the units in Cape Breton, not least because of the time
that would be required to assemble the men of the widely distributed
companies of the 94th Regiment, and two hundred troops from the
militia infantry at Halifax were rushed to the scene. A week later they
were replaced by 129 troops from Quebec, the nearest garrison of
Canadian regulars. This, no doubt, was a relief to the men of the 17th
Battery and 94th Regiment, who must not have relished being
required to maintain order, and perhaps use force, against people in
their own community.[45]

This was not the first time troops had had to keep peace. The 2nd Battalion, 17th Regiment, of the British garrison at Halifax had been sent
to Sydney Mines in May 1864 during a strike at the General Mining Association operations.[46] Under the new Dominion Militia Act, the Victoria
Provisional Battalion, predecessor of the 94th Regiment, had also been
sent to Sydney Mines for three weeks in 1876, and to Lingan for six
weeks in 1883. One veteran recalled many years later that the Sydney
company of the battalion was conveyed to North Sydney by the GMA
tugboat *Dolphin* in 1876, and then marched to the mines. Because the
1883 strike started in the winter, the four companies based outside of
Sydney marched from their local headquarters to Lingan, and the Bad-

deck and Middle River companies marched across the Bras d'Or Lakes to Little Bras d'Or.[47]

Aside from the obvious difficulty of having to maintain order in a civil dispute, there was a financial problem as well. When a municipal government called on the federal government to send in troops, the latter was obliged to do so, but the municipal authorities were responsible for the costs. In the case of the militia, this service was in addition to the training period paid for by the government and the men had to await settlement of the bills by the municipal government before they received any money. The municipal authorities inevitably baulked. In the 1864 Sydney Mines incident, the British government had insisted on payment for the use of its troops in a purely local matter, and the provincial government eventually complied. In the Lingan incident, the militiamen were not paid until three years later. The 1904 strike resulted in legal action between the city and the federal government over payment of the costs that dragged on for a decade.[48]

Happily for the militiamen, revised legislation in 1904 made the permanent force primarily responsible for providing this necessary but distasteful service. Thus, when a bitter prolonged miners' strike began in July 1909 and the civic authorities again called for military aid, some 535 regular troops were sent from Halifax to occupy the mining communities of Dominion and Glace Bay, while an additional 111 troops went to Inverness. Although the number of troops in the area was reduced in the late summer and autumn, more than one hundred men of the Royal Canadian Regiment, the Canadian permanent force unit that had replaced the British infantry battalion at Halifax, remained in the Glace Bay area until March 1910. That unpleasant experience contributed to the fact that nearly a quarter of the regiment's men deserted or took early discharge during the first half of 1910.[49]

If aid to the civil power was a recurring headache in peacetime defence administration, so too were disputes over real estate with municipal authorities and local businessmen, who sometimes thought that military properties should subsidize urban development. In the 1870s a block of land fronting on Charlotte Street had been cut out of Victoria Park to accommodate a new courthouse for Cape Breton County. In 1913 the county decided to build a larger and more impressive courthouse – one befitting Sydney's significant growth since the turn of the century as a result of the construction of the steel plant – on Charlotte Street near the intersection of Dorchester Street. As a result, it sold the Victoria Park site to J.E. Burchell, a prominent merchant and

financier who owned a wharf on the nearby waterfront and much property in the city.[50] Burchell intended to convert the old courthouse to
commercial use, which involved erecting a fence that would have
blocked the Charlotte Street entrance to Victoria Park. The city wanted
to maintain this public access to the park, and it negotiated a deal with
Burchell whereby he would exchange the site and an additional small
piece of land fronting on Campbell Street for a large rear lot on low
ground. This exchange had to be approved by the federal Department
of Public Works, however, and Burchell called on Senator William
McKay to intervene with the minister, Robert Rogers. McKay impressed
on him the fact that this was the only entrance to the park and that if
Burchell closed it 'the city would be thereby deprived of the advantages
of their only park,' and thought the minister was 'favourably inclined in
the matter.'[51] The difficulty was that the trade appeared to be highly
inequitable: Burchell's land occupied 14,525 square feet, while the land
being demanded of the city was 29,725 square feet in size.

When nothing transpired, Burchell wrote to Rogers himself, only to
be told by his private secretary in July that 'no action was taken by the
Minister before he left for the West early in June.'[52] Later that summer
an official from the department was sent to Sydney to look over the situation, but still nothing happened. By January 1914 Burchell was won-
dering if he should be communicating with the Militia Department
rather than with Public Works. Six months later McKay could only
report that the Militia Department had referred the matter to Colonel
R.W. Rutherford, the commanding officer in the Maritimes, for a recommendation. 'They are very much annoyed,' he claimed, 'that he is so
slow, and their annoyance I suppose is aggravated by me running after
them all the time. They have assured me that they will be in a position to
straighten the matter out by Monday next.'[53]

They weren't. More than a month later Mayor William Richardson
wrote directly to Sam Hughes, the minister of militia, asking for an early
decision. This brought the response that the minister was waiting for a
report from the department's engineers. Burchell now appealed again
to Senator McKay, explaining that the matter was 'just where you left it
sometime ago,' and asking that he intervene, 'as we think that you can
probably bring this matter to a point, better than anyone else.'[54] Notwithstanding continued efforts by local and provincial politicians, the
issue was not resolved when war broke out a few days later and it was
effectively shelved until the return of peace.[55]

Meanwhile, the Canadian military was, for the first time since Confederation, giving some thought to the defence of Sydney Harbour. The government had always been content to leave planning for coastal defence in Nova Scotia to the British garrison at Halifax, much as the Nova Scotia government had done before Confederation. The transfer of the fortress to Canadian control in 1905–6, however, and the resulting expansion of the hitherto small militia headquarters at Halifax brought a change, although it took a few years for the enlarged staff to grasp the wider aspects of their responsibilities.[56] The members of the staff were guided in their efforts by detailed advice from the British armed forces, which, under the terms of the transfer, continued to review the mobilization plans of the fortress. This advice was included in the information on defence planning that the British government provided to all of the dominion governments, as the military departments in London applied the lessons about modern warfare learned from South Africa and the closely observed Russo-Japanese War of 1904–5.

At the same time that British military planners were reducing the number of troops tied down in coastal fortresses, they were recognizing the need to protect vulnerable points outside of fortress areas, such as the transatlantic cable stations at North Sydney. The South African War, fought six thousand miles from Britain with troops and equipment and involving naval forces gathered from British colonies, dominions, and naval stations around the world, had made clear that rapid telegraphic communications were nearly as important as the armed forces themselves. Indeed, the French government went so far as to suggest in 1900 that Britain 'owes her influence in the world perhaps more to her cable communications than to her navy. She controls the news and makes it serve her policy and commerce in a marvellous manner.'[57]

Shortly before the transfer of Halifax, therefore, the British staff stationed there sent Major E.H. Bland, RE, to North Sydney and Canso with instructions to draft plans for the defence of the ocean cable landings that could quickly be executed in an emergency. Bland doubted that enemy naval forces would attempt a bombardment at Canso and therefore recommended infantry defences by a half battalion armed with machine guns or light field guns for protection against subversion or small landings. In the case of Sydney Harbour, however, he argued that the protection of the cable facilities was inseparable from the security of the mining, industrial, and rail facilities, the concentration of which might attract a naval bombardment. He also noted that the large number of foreign nationals among the industrial workforce made subversion a particular concern. He therefore called for defences similar to those suggested by the Milne committee in 1878 and by Stone in 1899, but on a still larger scale. There should, he thought, be four batteries on the northern side of the harbour and one on the southern side, with a total of twelve guns manned by 235 artillerymen, supported by a full battalion of infantry.[58]

These recommendations were not pursued at the time but, when in 1912 the Canadian staff at Halifax began to fine-tune mobilization plans, it assigned half of the 94th Regiment to the Canso area to execute Bland's plan. The other half of the unit was to provide guard detachments in the Sydney area, but only at the communications facilities, which now included the Marconi radio stations at Glace Bay and Louisbourg as well as the cable landing at North Sydney, rather than on the grand scale recommended by Bland. In deference to Bland's warning of the danger of a concerted attack on Sydney Harbour, the 17th Field Battery was assigned, on mobilization, to emplace its guns at Lloyd's Cove in North Sydney.[59]

The efforts by the Canadian staffs in both Ottawa and Halifax to make more comprehensive provisions for the defence of the East Coast soon ran into the roadblock of a bitter political crisis over naval defence. Britain's quest for diplomatic settlements had failed in the case of Germany, and the two powers had entered into a naval arms race. Growing public concern changed to panic in 1909 over the possibility that Germany might actually overtake the Royal Navy in numbers of battleships and threaten Britain's longstanding naval supremacy, the bulwark of imperial defence. This raised the question of the role of the dominions in imperial defence to a new and increasingly emotional level. Having resisted British appeals for assistance for years, the Laurier government now concluded that public opinion in English Canada required that something be done. As in 1904 in the case of the Halifax garrison, it tried to devise a compromise that would satisfy Canadian nationalists and imperialists alike. Accordingly, the government announced that it would expand the civilian fisheries protection service into a navy, which would relieve the Royal Navy of any residual responsibilities in Canadian waters. When this proved insufficient to satisfy either British leaders or Canadian imperialists, Laurier went further than he had originally intended and established a full-fledged naval service, which he promised would acquire seagoing cruisers and destroyers.

The naval question became a major issue in the federal election of 1911, particularly in Quebec, where nationalists condemned what they feared was a commitment to contribute ships and men to future imperial wars. The Conservative Party, led by Robert Borden, exploited this issue in Quebec through its *nationaliste* allies, while at the same time condemning both the government's naval policy and the proposed reciprocal trade agreement with the United States in English Canada as threats to Canadian autonomy and the British connection. Having won the election, Borden stopped development of the Laurier navy, promising to proceed cautiously along the traditional lines of improving the fisheries protection fleet with small warships. At the same time, however, he appeased his imperialist supporters by introducing legislation to give a one-time cash contribution of $35 million to the Royal Navy for the construction of battleships. When this was blocked by the Liberal majority in the Senate in 1913, Borden's naval policy collapsed. Meanwhile, the nascent Canadian navy cooperated with the militia to organize plans for the government's various marine services to carry out very basic coastal defence roles on mobilization, largely at Halifax and Quebec.

Both the naval and militia staffs, however, believed that only the acquisition of proper warships could address the longstanding Atlantic coastal defence problem. The forts at Halifax, despite considerable efforts made by the Canadian forces to keep them modern and efficient, could not defend anything beyond the range of their guns. The civilian government steamers that the navy now planned to use on mobilization could only patrol under the protection of the shore batteries. Although British warships might again operate regularly from the port in the event of war, the Admiralty had made it clear for more than thirty years that there would never be enough of them to provide detailed local coverage. Their mission would be to protect shipping at sea primarily through pursuit of the enemy's main forces. In view of the growth of German naval strength as compared to the Royal Navy, the Canadian staffs worried that the failure of the Canadian naval project would leave the East Coast very vulnerable to raiders. At the end of 1913 they urged the government at least to procure small warships for immediate coastal protection.[60]

Borden sought the Admiralty's advice. While it acknowledged concern about the northwestern Atlantic, port defence by small warships was not an issue, as German raiders would not have to risk approaching the coast. Because much of the vast transatlantic shipping from the Americas to Britain and Europe passed by Nova Scotia and south of Newfoundland, the enemy would have plenty of valuable defenceless targets offshore. The Admiralty therefore recommended that the Canadian navy procure cruisers, as originally planned by Laurier, to protect shipping at sea. To ensure the efficient operation of both these and British warships, the Admiralty also recommended that Halifax be augmented by a second defended port with the capacity for fast refuelling. That port should be Sydney, because of its excellent harbour and coal supply, and it should, therefore, be defended with permanent 6-inch gun coastal batteries.[61] This advice arrived in May 1914, however, and before the Canadian government could consider it, the time for discussion and planning had run out.

chapter five

The Call to Arms, 1914–1916

War fever is sweeping over Sydney.

Sydney Daily Post, 1914

Cape Bretoners enjoyed the summer of 1914, disturbed only slightly by news from Europe of a political assassination that somehow threatened, by the end of July, to engulf the western world in its first major war in a century. As the likelihood of war became more apparent, they shared the general enthusiasm, fuelled by the strident patriotism that had become increasingly popular in recent years and by the promise of overseas adventure in the service of the empire. Early on the afternoon of 1 August, 'hundreds crowded about the bulletin board at the post office till midnight,' as the *Sydney Daily Post* issued the latest news 'hot from the wires.' A special afternoon edition 'was rapidly eaten up,' and an extra edition brought out that evening sold some three thousand copies. War fever was 'sweeping over Sydney,' and the announcement that German forces had been repulsed by the French on that first day of war 'was received with bursts of cheers. Greater even was the enthusiasm when it became known that Britain would undoubtedly declare war within twenty-four hours.'[1] When the *Post* issued the bulletin announcing Britain's declaration of war on the 4th, 'there was an enthusiastic outburst of cheering and a number of people sang the Canadian anthem and "O Canada" with enthusiasm.'[2]

The permanent force at Halifax had already begun to mobilize on receipt of the first 'precautionary' telegram from Britain on 29 July. In accordance with the plans made in 1912, B Company of the Royal Canadian Regiment travelled by train to the Sydney–Glace Bay area and Louisbourg on the 31st, while E Company made for Canso by ship. They were responsible for guarding the communications facilities against a surprise attack until the formal declaration of war, when the militia units designated for this duty, the 94th Regiment and the 17th Field Battery, would mobilize and assume the task.[3]

Between two and three thousand people thronged the Intercolonial Railway station in Sydney that evening to welcome the first detachment of troops from Halifax. According to the *Post*, 'the scene that followed the arrival of the express has not been rivalled for many years in the city,' although 'there were only about ten men in the detachment.' The train was a few minutes late, but when it pulled into the station and the soldiers were spotted by the crowd 'cheers commenced and continued for some little time.' The small number of troops disembarking caused 'a feeling of disappointment ... among the thousands,' but 'a large crowd lingered around and watched the men detraining their ammunition, tents, provisions, and personal effects.' The explanation for the small number lay in the fact that most of the men had left the train at North Sydney to guard the cable station there, while the ten who travelled on to Sydney were headed to Glace Bay to guard the Marconi wireless station.[4]

This precautionary action, as modest as it was, was well-advised. The German cruisers *Dresden* and *Karlsruhe* were loose in the western Atlantic, and many German ocean liners, 'at least 14' of which British intelligence had identified as being fitted for conversion into armed raiders, were at or in the vicinity of ports on the northeastern coast of the United States. For these reasons, the Admiralty took very seriously a report on 3 August from the superintendent of the transatlantic cable station at Heart's Content, Newfoundland, that *Dresden* and *Karlsruhe* were preparing to attack this essential link in imperial communications.[5] Captain E.B. Costin, the officer commanding the detachment of the Royal Canadian Regiment at North Sydney, told the *Sydney Daily Post* that two German cruisers had been sighted off St Pierre, and 'it is surmised that the object of their presence so near Sydney Harbour is to secure coal for a transatlantic voyage,' or that they had been 'detailed to watch this port and the entrance of the St Lawrence.'[6] Three days later, the *Post* reported that HMS *Essex* had captured a German ship that was 'coal laden, not far from the Cape Breton coast and bound south, evidently conveying to German cruisers off the New England coast fuel, of which they were reported short when leaving Mexican waters.'[7] It was also conjectured that the cruisers were 'awaiting word of a formal declaration of war between France and Germany' prior to attacking St Pierre. As the French cruiser *Friant* was thought to be not far away, 'a naval fight seems imminent in these waters.'[8]

There was another report on the 4th, which the British government passed on to the governor general, the Duke of Connaught, that the central powers intended to open hostilities with an attack on strategic communications at Sydney. The Marconi Company, which operated the wireless stations at Table Head and Louisbourg, had learned – on what basis is unknown – 'that several Austrian steamships' were 'meditating an attack' on its wireless station near Glace Bay and asked for 'immediate protection.' In view of 'the great importance of the station,' British authorities regarded this question as 'most urgent' and asked Connaught to 'please suggest to your Ministers that all possible protection should be afforded.'[9] The Halifax garrison sent a further detachment of the Royal Canadian Regiment to Sydney that evening, bringing the total strength in the Sydney–Louisbourg area to about one hundred men. On the night of 4–5 August, as hostilities between the British empire and the central powers were declared, a naval brigade of forty-three personnel from the Halifax Dockyard with two twelve-pounder field guns and two machine guns also entrained for Cape Breton. These naval personnel joined the now thirty troops of the Royal Canadian Regiment already on duty at Glace Bay.[10]

The main excitement, however, was in the pages of the Toronto *News,* which carried a wholly false but nonetheless 'soul-harrowing account of the bombardment of Glace Bay by German cruisers,' allegedly intended 'to destroy the wireless station and the collieries.' The *Post* commented drolly that 'however we may suffer in an economic way from the war, Cape Breton should ultimately benefit from the advertising it is receiving just now.'[11] Nevertheless, when rail cars being shunted at the ferry wharf in North Sydney jumped the tracks and crashed into the post office building on the afternoon of 2 September, the postmaster and his assistant 'naturally' thought that they had been struck by a shell from a German ship.[12]

In view of the enemy's apparent interest in the cable and radio stations, Militia Headquarters in Ottawa authorized the early mobilization of the militia units detailed for guard duty. Even as word arrived on the morning of the 5th that the empire was at war, a special train had set out to collect the rural companies of the 94th Regiment, Argyll Highlanders, and to take them to their war stations.[13] At the same time, it was decided to send a battery of the Prince Edward Island Heavy Brigade, garrison artillery, with four 4.7-inch guns on travelling carriages, to Sydney as well. Under the command of Major J.R. Darke, they travelled on the Black Diamond liner *Cacouna*, which landed half of the unit and two of the guns at Port Hawkesbury for rail transport to North Sydney, and the remaining half of the unit and the other two guns at Canso.[14]

The 94th Regiment, whose headquarters was at Baddeck, mobilized eight companies of men totalling 377 from all ranks under the command of Lieutenant Colonel J.D. McRae. Dan E. MacQuarrie later recalled that he was working in the woods in August 1914 when 'I got this letter, to report to Baddeck,' and 'they sent us down to Marconi Towers in Glace Bay.' 'We were guards. They had about 50 masts there then, and they had – oh, it was foolish, when you come to think of it – ... men hoisted up in them, up in the tower in a kind of a basket, watching, [to] see if the enemy'd be coming. They kept men there all through the war ... Vital to the country, you know, when the war was on. Whether they would be destroyed or not, I don't know.'[15]

By 10 August there were 707 men of all ranks stationed in Cape Breton and at Canso. The garrison at Sydney included three companies and the staff of the 94th Regiment, comprising 169 men. Headquarters for the 94th's detachments in the Sydney, Glace Bay, and Louisbourg area was established at 33 Charlotte Street. At North Sydney and Sydney Mines the 94th had a company of forty-six men, the Royal Canadian Regiment had seventy men, and the Prince Edward Island Heavy Brigade had sixty-six men with two 4.7-inch guns on travelling carriages. The artillery was emplaced to cover the cable landing at Lloyd's Cove, while the infantry's duties included the protection of the old Western Union cable office on the corner of Commercial and Union Streets and, from 1915, the new office on Court Street in North Sydney. Many of the wartime communications from Europe to North America passed through these telegraphic facilities, the staff of which grew to approximately three hundred people. The changing of the guard was accompanied by a piper.[16] The North Sydney company also supplied a detachment at Whitney Pier in Sydney, which was at the disposal of the customs officer to enforce his authority to examine ships and, if they were in any way suspicious, to detain them.[17] At Glace Bay there were two companies of the 94th, comprising eighty-one men, and thirty men from the Royal Canadian Regiment. Another sixty-two men from the 94th were at Louisbourg, while there was a half battery of the Prince Edward Island Heavy Brigade, with seventy-four from all ranks and two

4.7-inch guns on travelling carriages, as well as a company of the 94th, with fifty-nine men, and fifty men from the Royal Canadian Regiment, at Canso.[18]

Meanwhile, perhaps thinking better of the alarm it might have caused, the *Post* reassured its readers that there were 'several' British warships in the western Atlantic, 'and that under present circumstances there need be little fear from any ships of the enemy unless other cruisers make their way across the ocean from the North Sea with a view to sporadic raids on Canadian ports and shipping.'[19] In fact, the Royal Navy had responded promptly to the reports of German cruisers on the heavily travelled shipping routes off Cape Breton and south of Newfoundland by ordering the cruiser HMS *Lancaster*, which had been on patrol in the Caribbean, into the area. Because it had requested that its presence not be reported, its appearance off St Paul Island on 10 August aroused suspicions that it was one of the enemy raiders. Canadian Naval Service Headquarters responded by holding in port all ships due to sail out the St Lawrence, earning a quick rebuke from the Admiralty, as the whole point of the swift reinforcement of the Canadian coast had been to instil confidence in shippers so they would not do the enemy's work by cutting off trade.[20]

It is questionable, however, if confidence was quite what was instilled in the crew of *Beatrice*, a collier returning to Sydney from carrying coal to Bay Roberts, Newfoundland, when it was 'brought to a sudden standstill by the boom of two cannons, fired from a grey battle-colored sea warrior,' about sixty miles off North Sydney. Understandably, Captain Stewart feared that he was being attacked by a German cruiser, but it turned out to be HMCS *Niobe*, the Canadian navy's sole cruiser; after running up the British flag, *Beatrice* was allowed to continue on its way. Stewart was reported to be 'not overjoyed by the experience.'[21]

War fever in Cape Breton showed not only in nervousness about coastal defence but also in enthusiasm to enlist for overseas service. Lieutenant Colonel Harvey McLeod, commanding officer of the 3rd Brigade, Canadian Field Artillery, based at Sydney, offered the services of the 17th Field Battery on the very day that war was declared, and the Militia Department immediately wired its acceptance. No doubt this was the reason why the Prince Edward Island Heavy Brigade was brought in to defend the cable landings instead of the 17th, the unit assigned that role in the pre-war planning. The 17th was, in fact, the only unit in Nova Scotia accepted for overseas service in the first contingent. Recruiting offices were opened at Sydney and Sydney Mines, and men wishing to enlist were asked to report for their medical examination at the Victoria Park armouries or at the residence of Captain J.A. MacDonald, the commanding officer of the 17th Battery, on Beech Street in Sydney Mines. The *Post* predicted on the 8th that 'the number of volunteers will be more than are required,' but it also reassured its readers that 'all possible influences are being used to insure a fair representation from Cape Breton, as it is reported from upper [*sic*] Canada that volunteers are offering in great numbers.'[22] On the 28th, the 17th Battery's 141 officers and men, 4 guns, and 123 horses left Sydney for training at Valcartier, Quebec, and when the thirty thousand men of the First Canadian Division, the first instalment of the half million men Canada would send overseas during the war, sailed from Quebec City in October, the men of the 17th were among them.

In the days leading up to their departure from Sydney, there were a number of enthusiastic patriotic events. On 20 August an informal reception and a procession in which three town bands took part were organized at Sydney Mines to honour Captain MacDonald and the fifteen men of the 17th Battery from that town. The town council 'and all concerned' gathered at the town hall in the evening and marched to the high school grounds where the town clerk, D.C. MacDonald, read a civic address. 'The demonstration was,' according to the *Post*, 'a most hearty one, and certainly spoke volumes for the popular feeling of the mining town for the respect in which the gallant captain, who is an alderman of Sydney Mines, and his associates are held.'[23] On Sunday, the 23rd, 'something in the nature of a great demonstration' took place in Sydney, 'arising out of the enormous crowds of people who congregated for the purpose of watching the movements of the military in various parts of the city, but more especially in connection with the church parades.' The Catholic troops attended Mass at Sacred Heart Church on George Street in the morning and the Protestants attended St George's, the old Anglican garrison church on Charlotte Street, in the afternoon. Following the afternoon service, the troops paraded through downtown Sydney, led by the city band, an event that, as the *Post* observed, had not been seen in Sydney 'for sixty years, for it was in the year 1854 that a similar church parade was accorded a regiment of soldiers stationed in Sydney prior to their leaving for the Crimean war.' There was, it added, 'a tremendous concourse of people at every point' to witness this event, and 'on every hand the highest praise was accorded for the fine soldierlike and well-disciplined appearance of the men.'[24]

On the 28th, crowds began to gather at Victoria Park and along Charlotte Street by noon, although the train taking the troops to Valcartier did not leave until evening. Ferries carried some two thousand people across the harbour from North Sydney and Sydney Mines, and a special half-hour electric tram service from Glace Bay brought thousands more. By 3:00 p.m., when the city's shops closed for the occasion, some ten thousand people lined the streets. 'Everywhere here yesterday, from housetop to button hole, the Union Jack was in evidence. Big flags, little flags, silk flags, cotton flags, all were there. Even the French tricolour was in evidence,' reported the *Post*. The bands of Sydney, Sydney Mines, and the 94th Regiment provided appropriate music. The commanding officers and the mayors of Sydney and the surrounding towns made speeches before the departing battery proceeded to the railway station on Intercolonial Street, where the troop train was gaily decorated with bunting. There, band selections such as 'Auld Lang Syne,' 'Our Old Canadian Home,' 'O Canada,' and 'God Be With You Till We Meet Again' were played, and the enormous crowd cheered the troops off. It seemed a joyous occasion, but, as the *Post* observed,

much of the lightheartedness which prevailed among the tens of thousands who thronged the streets was assumed, for over all there seemed cast a gloom: the realities of the war were being brought home to many as never before. One hundred and fifty of the prime of Cape Breton's manhood going out to do their share towards keeping the old flag flying.

Many were the sad farewells, heart-felt handshakes, and hasty good-byes. Not one of those who so cheerfully wished this one or that one of the battery Godspeed but knew that the other might never return, but find instead a grave beneath the sod of some bloody European battlefield. There was scarce[ly] a dry eye in the vast multitude which swarmed about the station as the troop train slowly pulled away. Even the strongest of those left behind found that unexplainable lump rising in their throats.[25]

Because the Canadian Expeditionary Force did not incorporate the existing unit and higher level formations of the militia, the 17th Field Battery was broken up, part of it joining the 19th Battery from New Brunswick to form the 6th Battery of the 2nd Brigade, Canadian Field Artillery, the other joining the 21st Battery of Westmount, Quebec, to form the new 5th Battery of the 2nd Brigade. Although the 6th Battery identified itself with Sydney's old 17th, it was, as one historian has observed, 'not so much a Cape Breton battery as an artillery unit containing a large number of Cape Bretoners.'[26] In the course of the war, the 6th saw action at Courcelette, Vimy Ridge, and on the Drocourt-Quéant line, and it was the first battery to cross the Canal du Nord. It was also part of the post-war army of occupation in Germany and was not finally demobilized at Halifax until April 1919.

By the time the men of the 17th left Sydney at the end of August 1914, it had become clear that the reports of German cruisers off Newfoundland and Nova Scotia were false. Nevertheless, the danger of a serious surprise raid was real, as fast cruisers could slip past the Royal Navy's main fleet in the North Sea and reach Newfoundland in a few days without being detected. At the same time, fast German liners, which had sought safety in neutral American ports such as New York, could all too easily, with assistance from the large German interests in the United States, secretly mount armaments and make directly for the shipping routes off Nova Scotia and Newfoundland. There was no margin for error in the northwestern Atlantic, as some 30 per cent of Britain's imports, on which its war economy depended, came from North America in ships that passed through these waters. The Royal Navy therefore continued to build up its strength there, expanding the North America and West Indies squadron to about a dozen cruisers, half of them comprising the northern division based at Halifax, which immediately reverted to its historic role as an important strategic naval port.

Colonel Willoughby Gwatkin, chief of the general staff in Ottawa, was keenly aware, however, that the potential menace to shipping at sea was much greater than the immediate danger of serious attack on shore targets. Intelligence confirming that the enemy was in fact nowhere near Newfoundland and Cape Breton therefore sharpened his determination that garrison forces in Canada should be kept to the bare minimum so as not to tie down troops that were needed overseas, where the war would be won or lost. A seasoned hand in Ottawa, he knew how susceptible the government was to local political influences, and this was especially so in the case of the often erratic and emotional minister of militia, Sir Sam Hughes, whom Gwatkin neither liked nor trusted.[27] Nervous citizens wanted a uniformed soldier on every street corner and standing watch at every coastal inlet, and too frequently the politicians agreed. Much of Gwatkin's war, therefore, was a struggle to resist new demands for garrisons and to keep a lid on existing ones, which had a seemingly inexorable tendency to grow.

When Gwatkin attempted in September 1914 to trim the 2,600-man garrison that had been mobilized at Halifax, the new Royal Navy commander on the North America and West Indies Station, Rear Admiral

R.S. Phipps Hornby, complained bitterly that the security of his force's main base was being compromised, and the Admiralty agreed with him. Gwatkin had no choice but to back down, and in fact it proved necessary to build up the Halifax garrison to more than three thousand troops in order to maintain the full harbour defence scheme on a long-term basis. Accordingly, he insisted on economy where he could and that included Cape Breton. There, in his view, the problem was not one of securing a whole harbour as a naval operating base, but merely guarding particular small sites that might attract a few shots, a minor landing party from a warship or disguised merchant vessel, or saboteurs from the United States or possibly recruited from enemy sympathizers among the local population. Thus, when the Royal Canadian Regiment withdrew from the coastal garrisons for service at Bermuda late in August 1914, Gwatkin resisted the suggestion of Colonel R.W. Rutherford, his friend and the commander in the Maritimes, that the 94th Regiment should be authorized to expand considerably.[28] The unit remained at its initial limited establishment of about five hundred men, and the only action taken to replace the Royal Canadian Regiment was to call out a single company of sixty men from the 78th Regiment at Pictou for service at Canso.[29]

At the beginning of October, Gwatkin again pressed Rutherford, suggesting that he was 'employing more men than are necessary' and that he should 'reduce detachments to a minimum.' There was, he thought, 'no cause for alarm,' and he hoped Rutherford could 'keep the sailors in hand.' The situation would, of course, 'change when German vessels break through the Grand Fleet – as some of them, in course of time, are not unlikely to succeed in doing.'[30] Rutherford was ready and willing to cooperate. For reasons that are not clear, when the 94th Regiment had been mobilized, three companies had been deployed in Sydney, even though this had not been contemplated in the defence scheme. Local political influences may have been at work, or perhaps local fears of subversion by the large 'foreign' population in the area. At any rate, Rutherford had already moved one of the three companies to North Sydney and Sydney Mines at the end of August to replace the Royal Canadian Regiment troops at those stations. He now wanted to disband one of the remaining companies in Sydney and to dispatch the other to Canso, where additional men were needed to keep up guard details at the scattered cable facilities. It would be possible, as well, to dispense with the regimental staff in Sydney, as all of the companies would be self-administering detachments.[31]

Canada had been suffering an economic recession since 1913, and
the issue of unemployment and its burden to municipal welfare rolls
inevitably influenced the Militia Department's efforts to trim home garrisons across the country. The issue was also delicate politically, simply
because it involved the militia, a major outlet for patronage. Because of
the 'certainty' that there would be opposition at Sydney to the withdrawal of the two companies, Rutherford proposed to wait a few weeks,
until recruiting began for the second overseas contingent. By allowing
militiamen on garrison duty who met the required standards to volunteer and depart, he could at least carry out the reduction without
removing many men from active service and thereby putting them out
of work.[32]

As expected, when news of the proposed reductions became known,
prominent local Conservatives reacted forcefully. They immediately sent
a telegram to Prime Minister Robert Borden demanding that the rede-
ployment be stopped, and in a subsequent letter they complained that it
was actually a political plot engineered by Colonel W.W. Humphrey, a
member of Rutherford's staff at Halifax, who they alleged was a Liberal.
As evidence of 'the political cloven hoof,' they claimed that Colonel J.D.
McRae of the 94th had been told that very day by Halifax military
authorities to have some of his men sent 'under escort and at the
expense of the Militia' to Baddeck to give evidence in support of D.D.
McKenzie and Premier George Murray[33] in a prosecution they were
conducting to unseat a Conservative member of the House of Assembly.
'The Col[onel] of course is not averse to having the Civil law take its
course, but what do you think of your Halifax Officials acting as political
tools for Murray and D.D. MacKenzie [sic]?' They objected to the
'anomaly' of a regiment 'scattered in so many widely separated locations
as this without a head or executive officers,' especially when Conservative officers, they alleged, 'are to be sent to their homes,' while three
'strong grits ... are to remain on duty.' They warned that neither the
Admiralty nor the Dominion Coal Company would 'stand for' the
removal of the troops guarding the coal supply at Whitney Pier but,
even if they did, 'the people of Sydney can be calculated upon to raise a
very angry howl if at least the Whitney Pier Company is tampered
with.'[34]

Whether or not there were grounds for the charges of political favour-
itism, the surviving records certainly shed doubts on the efficiency of
two of the officers who were to be relieved. Incidents of soldiers from
the 94th, particularly at the North Sydney detachment, being found

drunk while on duty and accosting and even threatening citizens were the subject of not only official reports but scathing comment in the press.[35] On 9 November 1914, for example, the *Sydney Daily Post* reported on a 'decidedly exciting quarter hour' in North Sydney, when two soldiers attacked two residents, Charles Thompson and Archibald McDougall, 'who at the time were making some repairs to Mr. Thompson's house. The soldiers, who were pretty well loaded with bad rum, started the row by removing a ladder which had been used to get to the roof, and when Mr. McDougall protested he was almost knocked senseless by a stone which one of the soldiers hurled at him. At this point Mr. Thompson took part in the proceedings and handled one of the red coats so roughly that his pal drew his bayonet and charged. Before they could do any damage with their weapons, a guard of three men from the barracks arrived on the scene in response to a telephone summons, and after a pretty hard tussle marched the pair off to the guard room. The affair created a good deal of excitement on Court Street while it lasted.' By this time, Major Gillis had already been transferred to the regimental staff in Sydney,[36] but the ultimate responsibility for these and other incidents rested, of course, with Lieutenant Colonel McRae. His explanation – that in the sudden rush to fill the unit on mobilization he had had to accept new men he did not know – drew a rebuke from Rutherford, who concluded that 'he has not fully realized his responsibilities nor used his powers as commanding officer ... and that the general slackness and lack of discipline which has prevailed in connection with his command is deserving of censure.'[37]

The political protest from Sydney appears to have been effective, however, for Hughes intervened to have Gillis returned to the North Sydney Command.[38] As well, when Rutherford implemented the reorganization in late November, the regimental staff at Sydney survived.[39] Although one of the Sydney companies was moved to Canso, the other was not disbanded but transferred to Louisbourg, thus preserving some additional officer positions. With these redeployments, the organization of the Cape Breton garrisons stabilized. As Rutherford had hoped, it proved possible to implement the reductions by allowing men to volunteer for the overseas contingent and by reducing the two Louisbourg companies to forty-two men each from the normal sixty men.[40] In fact, according to the 94th Regiment's historian, fully 311 of the 344 men who had mobilized in August 1914 volunteered for overseas service during the next few months, requiring the unit to recruit and train many new personnel. Like many other home units, it increasingly became a recruiting and basic training depot for the Canadian Expeditionary Force in Europe, and by war's end it had sent 3,362 men overseas.[41]

Meanwhile, during the autumn of 1914 the militia units began to dig in. Nothing remained for their use from the nineteenth century fortifications. All the stone and brick used in the construction of the battery, blockhouse, and magazine at Chapel Point in the 1860s, for example, had been used for the foundation of a nearby church in Sydney Mines.[42] In October 1914 the Bate McMahon Construction Company began building wooden barracks for the soldiers stationed in the industrial area. Up to this point, they were 'sleeping upon the ground [in tents], which they find most uncomfortable.'[43] By the middle of November the buildings at North Sydney, near the new cable office, and at the cable landing at Sydney Mines were completed, a change that 'will be greatly appreciated by the men.' At Louisbourg the troops of the 94th Regiment assisted the contractor with the work, 'with the result that record time in construction has been made.'[44] When Lieutenant Colonel Low, representing Hughes, visited the Cape Breton garrisons in February 1915, he said that it was the minister's wish 'that the men be given all the comfort possible so as to encourage them in the thankless and uncomfortable task they have in keeping guard away from home and home comforts.'[45] Following Low's visit, 'extensive and much needed improvements' were made, including the installation of water, sewer, and electric lights in the barracks that did not yet have these services.[46]

With respect to armament, Militia Headquarters had ordered on 4 August that the defences of the cable-landing places be strengthened by four 4.7-inch quick-firing guns on travelling carriages, two at Sydney Mines and two at Canso. The initial position of the two 4.7-inch guns sent to Sydney Mines, when first emplaced during mobilization, is not certain but may have been on Chapel Point, one of the sites identified in the pre-war defence scheme. In October 1914, on the advice of the staff at Halifax, they were moved to the second site recommended in the scheme, the 120-foot ridge about seven hundred yards behind Chapel Point. There they were mounted in a 'well constructed' earthwork position, with the artillery barracks nearby.[47] Travelling carriages, as has been seen, were of little use for shooting at ships, but the guns provided a deterrent against attacks on the cable facilities and gave confidence to the local population. The military staffs in Halifax and Ottawa regarded the battery as a temporary, emergency measure.[48]

The wireless facilities at Glace Bay and Louisbourg and the cable station at Hazel Hill, immediately southwest of Canso, were more difficult to defend because they were larger and more dispersed than the Sydney Mines and North Sydney sites. The provision of even minimal protection to the most important points required a good deal of manpower, which explains why, although reductions were possible in the Sydneys, it proved necessary to strengthen the outlying garrisons to two companies of the 94th at each place, with a third company from the 78th Regiment and the half battery of the Prince Edward Island artillery at Canso. At each place, the troops strung barbed wire around the main compounds, and Bate McMahon erected what were described as 'blockhouses,' presumably timber structures with rifle loopholes, within the wire. At Louisbourg the garrison built earth-banked firing positions outside the wire, and at Hazel Hill there were extensive trench works behind an outer line of wire around much of the cable company site. The defences also included two blockhouses on the coast east and west of Canso. The location of the 4.7-inch guns has not been determined.[49] In any event, one of them was removed in March 1915 for use in trials by an ammunition manufacturer, and half of the artillery detachment was transferred to Halifax, where there was a pressing shortage of trained gunners. The remaining gun may have been emplaced at one of three advanced positions on the coast, several miles from Hazel Hill, that the garrison had identified to cover the seaward approaches.[50]

Meanwhile, as in other parts of the country, some civilians began to organize themselves into Home Guard units. Motives were undoubtedly mixed: fear of attack, frustration at the evident complacency of distant authorities in Halifax and Ottawa, and a desire by those unable or unwilling to join the forces to participate in the martial fervour. Bridgeport took the lead in September 1914 when about 150 people attended a meeting and sixty-eight men signed the roll. 'It is expected,' the *Post* reported, 'that the neighboring mining towns will join Bridgeport in forming a full battalion.'[51] A month later more than three hundred people attended a meeting at the Empire Theatre in New Waterford to form a home guard. An organizing committee was created and approximately one hundred men signed the roll.[52] It took another six weeks before Sydney joined the movement, but on 20 November a meeting took place that created a committee. It was headed, inevitably, by Walter Crowe, who was described as 'the moving spirit so far as organization and drill are concerned, and he has by popular acclamation become commandant.' Some 120 men signed up, the terms of service obliging them only 'to attend the drills as much as possible commensurate with their business engagements.'[53]

The Sydney Home Guard engaged energetically in squad drills, the men being divided into sections according to whether they were just beginners or more experienced. Special classes were even provided 'for those who wish to have private tuition prior to their taking their place in the ranks.'[54] The lack of rifles was something of a handicap, but it was overcome, to some extent, when a local carpenter made 'a very fair and quite useful imitation of the service rifle.' This dummy rifle allegedly 'called forth the highest praise,' and the *Post* told its readers on 7 December that 'it seems almost an assured fact that about fifty of them, or even more' would soon be available.[55] By this time the Sydney Home Guard, comprising four companies, had been reconstituted as the Sydney Battalion of Home Guard.[56]

Grass-roots initiatives and lobbying had brought some results in keeping up the strength of the coastal defences, but it failed to persuade military authorities in Ottawa of the need to augment Sydney's defences with some form of local naval forces. At the end of October 1914, J.W. Maddin, a Sydney lawyer, appealed to the government to establish a minesweeping flotilla of the type that was operating with small chartered tugs in the Halifax approaches to guard against a quick, silent visit by a disguised German minelayer. 'Considerable anxiety' was being felt in Sydney, he claimed, 'owing to the absolute lack of facilities for Naval Defence,' and 'the very fact that Halifax Harbour is being dragged for Mines adds to the apprehension in this community.' British warships were using Sydney Harbour, 'and with the very large number of Austrians and Germans ... in our midst, a great many people apprehend that some of these might mine our harbour.'[57]

This rather improbable fear elicited no sympathy from Rear Admiral C.E. Kingsmill, the director of the naval service. Sydney Harbour, he thought, 'is one that it is not likely the enemy would take the trouble to mine' because it 'is not a place from which a great deal of trade goes, that is, valuable trade. The coal they ship could be carried by rail another way.' As for the danger from enemy aliens in the local population, that was a matter for the city police but, he added inexplicably, 'if the large number of Austrians and Germans in the place mine the harbour one might also say that the people of Sydney would deserve it.'[58]

Kingsmill notwithstanding, popular fear of German raiders continued in the Sydney area. In February 1915, 'quite a scare was caused' in the Birch Grove area when G.W. Sheppard, a watchman at No. 21 Colliery, saw lights 'away up in the sky' that he thought 'were the searchlights of an aeroplane.' A police officer, John H. MacDonald, claimed to have seen them as well. According to the *Post*, 'the people in the district became quite excited in the belief that, in some way or another, a hostile airship was making some reconnoitering, or had some designs upon the Marconi wireless station near Morien.' Major A.D. MacRae, the officer in command there, reported that 'although they had seen nothing they were taking the story for what it was worth, and every man was out on guard.'[59] When the message was flashed to North Sydney that 'the Sydneys and other parts of Cape Breton were about to be attacked' by German raiders, 'consternation (or was it glee?) was thrown into the rank and file of the soldiers stationed in the Archibald Avenue barracks.' The troops were called out and those on leave hurriedly recalled, as 'throughout the night our brave volunteers experienced their first war fright.'[60] When the *North Sydney Herald* reported a few days later that the lights had been the searchlight of a ship, *Douglas H. Thomas*, that was struggling in the ice off Glace Bay, the *Post* retorted that the ship's captain 'denies that either his or any other boat in the vicinity displayed a searchlight on the evening in question.' Driving home its conviction that the lights had indeed been those of a German airship, the *Post* concluded: 'Birch Grove residents still hold to the aeroplane theory. They point to the fact that the projected invasion of Halifax, as featured in the Birch Grove Times, would be preceded by a reconnoitering force of airmen. That the Germans, who are usually so accurate in topographical details, should mistake Port Morien for Halifax, is the puzzling part of the matter.'[61]

As for the large number of recent immigrants, commonly referred to as 'foreigners,' who had come to the Sydney area in recent years from what were now enemy countries, the *Post* claimed that 'almost three thousand Austrians ... and Hungarians [are] working in the industries there and the authorities anticipate possible trouble from this source.'[62] This number was probably inflated, but certainly there were several hundred such people, and concern about them was not entirely unjustified because the German and Austro–Hungarian governments did not regard British naturalization in Canada as having relieved their former citizens of their allegiance in time of war. Thus, they remained bound by their military obligations as reservists, despite their having immigrated to Canada.[63] As a result, they were required to register with the authorities and sign a document guaranteeing their good behaviour. When three aliens were subsequently charged in June 1918 for failing to register, their explanation 'that they have wives and families in Austria and they are afraid that if they register in Canada they will be arrested as deserters when they return to their own country, and given the penalty provided for deserters,' was rejected. Magistrate W.R. Hearn sentenced them to a month in jail, telling them 'that registering in Canada did not in any way have anything to do with allegiance to their country or military service.'[64]

German and Austrian seamen who were detained by customs authorities at the outbreak of war were subsequently allowed to work on coastal vessels, but they were not permitted to leave Canada until the war was over and were required to report to the authorities at least once a month.[65] In October 1914 it was discovered that the German government had ordered armed forces reservists living overseas to return home for mobilization. This proved, the *Post* concluded, that 'right here in Sydney men, who no doubt felt that they had a duty to their homeland, have nevertheless been traitors to the extreme liberty and freedom to live peaceably and toil profitably which they have enjoyed under the British flag.'[66] Thomas Cantley of the Nova Scotia Steel and Coal Company reported that when he had visited Germany before the war he had been shown detailed maps of his company's operations, as well as those of the Dominion Coal Company, proving – at least in his mind – that spies had been active in the area.[67]

D.A. Noble, the head of the Dominion Coal Company's police, was given responsibility for dealing with the alien issue in Cape Breton, and by the middle of November he was able to report that more than eight hundred 'unnaturalized foreigners' had been registered and given their parole. They were required to report at various stations at regular intervals – weekly, fortnightly, or monthly – or risk prosecution, and they were forbidden to own or carry firearms or ammunition.[68] On the whole, there were no difficulties, although there were a few minor incidents. One Austrian who had refused to register was found in possession of 'a quantity of explosives,' and a rifle was taken from an unparoled man in New Waterford.[69] The local courts appear to have been relatively lenient, as for example when two Germans caught in the woods near Glace Bay, 'having some target practice,' were fined $10 each and had their guns confiscated. The *Post* clearly thought this inadequate, archly pointing out that a similar case in Toronto had resulted in a $300 fine, which 'shows that they are not so quiescent about alien enemies in Toronto as the authorities are in other parts of the Dominion.'[70]

Despite Noble's public statement in November that there had been no incidents of spying in the area,[71] 'a foreigner, apparently an Austrian,' was found in the spring of 1915 near the Nova Scotia Iron and

Steel Company works at Sydney Mines 'with a quantity of explosives on his person.' He was described as being about thirty-three years of age and 'poorly clad' but wearing an iron cross. Whether or not he was a spy or a saboteur, he was taken to Halifax in handcuffs, but it is not known what happened to him.[72] This episode may have caused the authorities to adopt a harder line than had previously been the case. In June, as the *Post* noted with satisfaction, they showed that 'on occasion they can deal with alien enemies in this locality in the manner which some people think can be more generally applied with beneficial results.' When a German who was registered as a resident of New Waterford went to Sydney and sought work at the steel plant, allegedly claiming to be Swiss, he was arrested by Noble's police and sent off to the enemy internment camp at Amherst.[73] It has not been determined if any spies were ever apprehended in the area, but certainly the fear of their presence was so great that as late as August 1918 the *Post* thought it necessary to reassure its readers that 'it is not true that a German captain was seen travelling on a Glace Bay tram car recently.'[74]

As silly as it might seem in retrospect that a newspaper would think it necessary to issue such a reassurance to its readers, it must be remembered that war feeling was very strong and became increasingly so as the conflict dragged on and casualties mounted to appalling levels. The extent of this feeling was suggested by an incident that occurred in August 1915. When a salesman travelling by the electric tram from Sydney to Glace Bay got off at Reserve Junction to purchase some cigarettes, 'he espied a German flag displayed in a prominent place among the goods of the refreshment shop, and he asked the attendant to take it down. He refused, whereupon the knight of the grip went behind the counter, tore down the flag and set fire to it. The attendant said he "would knock his block off" but on being invited to do it, thought that perhaps it was better not to try. The incident attracted a deal of attention, occurring as it did in a public place, and the travelling men are of the opinion that it was the very worst of bad taste that the German flag should have been displayed so flauntingly.'[75]

As can be seen, anxiety about the menace from enemy aliens seems to have sharpened by 1915, once the excitement of mobilization gave way to the stark realization that the war would be neither short nor glorious, and that it would require an unrelenting national commitment. In the spring of 1915 the First Canadian Infantry Division entered combat in the ghastly second battle of Ypres at a cost of some six thousand men killed and wounded. This proved to be only a rite of initiation that foretold three and a half more years of bloody service on the western front. In September 1915, the Second Division went to France and the Canadian Corps was formed. By the end of the year, in response to British appeals for further help, the organization of the Third and Fourth Divisions was under way, and on 1 January 1916 Sir Robert Borden announced that Canada would put 500,000 men in uniform. In an effort to meet the mounting overseas commitments, Gwatkin renewed his campaign during the autumn of 1915 to reduce the militia garrisons at home, which had grown from nine thousand in August 1914 to more than fourteen thousand men in September 1915 despite his efforts. More than a third of these troops were at Halifax, and he admitted he could not cut there because of the Royal Navy's insistence on a high level of security, but that only made him more determined to economize elsewhere.[76]

As always, Rutherford was prepared to cooperate. From September to November 1915 he allowed members of the Prince Edward Island artillery detachments to volunteer for overseas service, and transferred the rest to Halifax to enable gunners there to join the Canadian Expeditionary Force as well. The 4.7-inch guns were withdrawn from Sydney Mines and Canso for use at training camps for overseas artillery drafts.[77] Towards the end of the year, Rutherford reduced all of the 94th Regiment's companies to an establishment of forty-four men (all ranks) and withdrew the company of the 78th that had been on duty at Canso. Guard details were cut to the barest minimum.[78] Again, the reduction appears to have been achieved through personnel volunteering for overseas service, in this case largely for the Nova Scotia Highland Brigade that was then being raised,[79] whose 85th Battalion served at the front with such distinction in 1917–18 as part of the 4th Division.

Expansion of the corps at the front also included another Cape Breton artillery unit, the 36th Battery, which was formed at Sydney in September 1915. The venerable Walter Crowe has been described as 'the organizer and leading spirit in it,' the man to whom 'must be given a great deal of credit for the splendid record which the Battery achieved Overseas.' Crowe commanded the unit, 'supervised nearly all its early training,' and took it overseas in 1916, but then was compelled to give up the command 'on account of being very much over age.'[80] Although the 36th Battery originated in Cape Breton, like the 17th it recruited many men from other areas as well. From the time of the unit's arrival in France in July 1916, it participated in all of the Canadian Corps' major actions before returning to Canada and demobilizing in March 1919.

Even while Canada was increasing its commitment to the western front, coastal defence again became a burning issue, now in a form that placed it squarely on the navy. Warnings from the Admiralty late in 1914 about German success in using disguised merchant ships as long-range minelayers that could sow fields in heavily travelled deep-water channels far offshore had compelled the navy to replace the smallest vessels at Halifax with larger steamers that could keep watch on the outer approaches to the port and at the mouth of the Bay of Fundy, the other main winter shipping route. As the ice cleared from the St Lawrence in the spring of 1915, *Sable I*, an unarmed chartered steamer manned by a civilian crew, began to carry out surveillance duties in the gulf.[81] By that time, a new menace loomed.

Early in 1915 the German navy launched a new type of warfare by unleashing its submarine force with orders to sink on sight all merchant ships approaching the British Isles. Because Britain had imposed a naval blockade on Germany and its allies, Germany now hoped to do the same by using this latest naval technology to destroy the shipping on which Britain depended to feed its population and supply the war effort. Soon the U-boats were inflicting extremely heavy losses. These included ships sailing out of Sydney, such as the Norwegian steamer *Fimreite*, en route from Wabana to Birmingham, under charter to the Nova Scotia Iron and Steel Company with a cargo of iron ore, which was torpedoed off the coast of Scotland in July. Another was *Midland Queen*, a Canadian vessel that sailed from Sydney on 21 July for Glasgow with a cargo of steel and was sunk on 2 August near Queenstown. Although the crew consisted mainly of Newfoundlanders, the master apparently was a Captain Ganeon of Arichat.[82]

As there were no effective means to hunt submarines, the Royal Navy seemed powerless. In the spring of 1915 rumours were circulating in the German community in the northeastern United States that the submarines would soon cross the Atlantic to hunt in North American waters. Indeed, the *New York Times* reported in July that there was 'a strong possibility' that Germany would launch a submarine campaign from a secret base on this side of the Atlantic in an effort to prevent war supplies from the United States (and presumably Canada) from getting to British and French ports. 'It is known,' the unattributed article asserted, 'that Grand Admiral von Tirpitz contemplates a more vigorous campaign against freight ships conveying ammunition and war supplies from this country to the Allies.' Citing 'a very reliable source,' the article claimed that the German navy intended to establish a secret submarine base on an island 'off the New England coast at a point from which German submarines might make sallies to attack munition freighters going from New York and Boston to England and France.' Explaining that the newest submarines were capable of crossing the Atlantic and had a cruising radius of more than five thousand miles, it reminded its readers that the Maine coast 'is within easy striking distance of the Atlantic steamer lanes which run farther north in the summer than in the winter.'[83]

There was good reason to take this warning seriously. While submarines were the most significant technological advance in naval warfare in many years, their effectiveness was limited by their slow speed, especially when submerged. As a result, they were limited to operating against the approaches to ports and in pelagic areas – confined waters in frequent use by enemy shipping – where ship movements can be tracked relatively easily. Information received in London and Ottawa from British and Canadian agents and the Admiralty confirmed that missions such as those predicted by the *New York Times* were indeed possible, if unlikely. In the Admiralty's view, however, any clandestine refuelling arrangements would be vulnerable to attack by a few armed men and, without additional fuel, the submarines would be immobilized. Aside from alerting the military, customs, and other authorities on the coasts, therefore, all that was needed were patrols of isolated areas by small vessels. In the worst scenario, that of a direct confrontation with a submarine, a few fast civilian steamers mounted with some quick-firing guns would suffice. All of this, British naval leaders believed, could be improvised if and when necessary.

Confronted by a major crisis in British home waters, the Admiralty was rightly indisposed to worry much about hypothetical dangers in a distant theatre, but the view from Canada was understandably rather different. Aside from increasingly specific reports from the United States about German plans for transatlantic submarine operations, senior Canadian naval officers knew that their tiny service utterly lacked the resources even for the measures recommended by London, and that the civilian marine community was in no position to help. Following the dramatic sinking of *Lusitania* by *U-20* off the Irish coast in May, Canadians became particularly worried about the virtually unprotected St Lawrence, through which steamed the liners carrying Canadian troops to Europe. Vice Admiral Sir George Patey, the British commander-in-chief, North America and West Indies, who knew how impoverished the Canadian service was, shared these worries and urged Canada to make preparations, warning that his large and unmanoeuvrable cruisers would be sitting ducks in the face of a U-boat attack and could do nothing but run for cover. Under pressure from an alarmed government to do something, the navy issued orders on 6 July 1915 that created the St Lawrence Patrol, with headquarters at Sydney. Its operational area was vast, including the whole gulf from Gaspé in the west to the Strait of Belle Isle in the north, and southeast along the coast of Newfoundland to St Pierre and Miquelon. The mission of this new force was modest, however: to maintain a lookout by single steamers in each of the main areas of the gulf, with particular emphasis on regular visits to isolated bays and on contacts with lighthouse keepers and the local population to detect attempts to establish clandestine refuelling caches.[84]

Newfoundland's coast naturally figured prominently in these plans. The submarine threat, the Royal Navy's inability to help, and the poverty of Newfoundland's military resources had driven home the need for cooperation between the two dominions. With Canada looking after the western and southern shores of the island, Newfoundland did what it could to keep watch on the eastern shore and the coast of Labrador, employing detachments of militia and two or three chartered and government steamers. Modest as these efforts were, they marked the beginning of close defence relations between the two dominions and of the role of Sydney as the key link in Canadian support for Newfoundland. In addition, since the vessels of the St Lawrence Patrol all burned Cape Breton coal, the North Sydney coal piers were kept busy during the remainder of the war supplying fuel to the little fleet.[85]

The new gulf force was inaugurated on 15 July when HMCS *Margaret*, a customs service vessel that had been commissioned into the navy, joined *Sable I* at Sydney to patrol Cabot Strait. While these vessels guarded the principal entrance to the gulf, others from the small flotilla at Halifax and the government marine services rushed in to keep watch on isolated coastlines, such as Quebec's North Shore, and to try to give some support to troop transports proceeding down the St Lawrence from Quebec City.[86] Some additional civilian vessels that had been acquired by the navy went out on patrol immediately, still manned by their civilian crews and even before being armed. So alarming were the reports coming from the German community in the United States and so inadequate the defences available for the St Lawrence that in early August Naval Service Headquarters sent a battalion of troops that had been scheduled to sail from Quebec City for Europe by rail to Halifax instead. The ship proceeded empty down the vulnerable route to pick them up at the Nova Scotian port.[87]

In the end, the American rumours proved to be unfounded, as did reports from the Canadian and Newfoundland coasts of periscopes sighted offshore and of suspicious characters scuttling about in coastal communities. The Admiralty, concerned that panic in Canada might result in a squandering of resources that should be available for the common cause, sent a message to Ottawa advising it that 'exaggerated measures of precaution are to be deprecated.'[88] A similar caution went to Patey, who shared the Canadians' worries and was urging on their defence effort. Admiral Kingsmill (and no doubt Admiral Patey) was irritated by the Admiralty's suggestion that he was overreacting and that adequate defences could be quickly improvised in the event that U-boats actually appeared in Canadian waters. The British officials did not seem to appreciate, he thought, either the paucity of Canada's marine resources or the vastness and inaccessibility of the Canadian coast. So undeveloped were communications on the Atlantic seaboard that it had not even been possible to investigate promptly the recent spate of reports. In the event that the presence of a U-boat was confirmed, virtually no resources existed for any kind of aggressive response, partly because the British government had already requisitioned many of the vessels most suitable for conversion to patrol craft.[89]

Lack of support from the Admiralty was only one of the navy's problems. Canadian ministers blew hot and cold on the patrol scheme. While reacting with alarm to rumoured U-boat activity and demanding quick action, they nevertheless insisted that everything had to be done as cheaply as possible and made no effort to improve the government's ponderous procurement methods.[90] As it was, the navy depended heavily on the charity of its friends to achieve even the limited expansion that took place in the summer of 1915. By late August, when the organization of the St Lawrence Patrol had begun to achieve some stability, there were normally six vessels operating out of Sydney. These included *Margaret* and *Canada*, the best in the Canadian government inventory and the only purpose-built patrol craft, *Sable I*, the tug *Sinmac*, and two yachts.[91] The yachts were charitable donations: *Florence* was the family yacht of John David Eaton, the Toronto department store magnate, and the fast *Grilse* had been purchased in the United States by the Montreal millionaire, J.K.L. (Jack) Ross, and presented to the navy. Indeed, the enthusiastic Ross took a commission and commanded *Grilse* himself. By late August all of these craft had been armed with one or two light guns, while *Grilse* also mounted a torpedo tube.[92] The civilian crews of the vessels were enroled in the Royal Naval Canadian Volunteer

Reserve, and their number augmented by naval officers and a few trained naval ratings.[93]

The force was further strengthened, again as a result of the efforts of the navy's friends. In order to circumvent American neutrality laws, which prohibited the purchase of ships by belligerent governments, Æmelius Jarvis, a Toronto businessman and, like Jack Ross, a leading light of the yacht club set, had posed as a private buyer and purchased two large American yachts. Despite the great value of these substantial vessels for the extended cruising in all weathers required of the St Lawrence Patrol, Kingsmill had to apply pressure to a government worried about costs and expenditure outside the country to close the deal. The ships, which were commissioned as HMCS *Stadacona* and HMCS *Hochelaga* in the Canadian navy, joined the Sydney force in September 1915. They were urgently needed, for three of the force's vessels, *Florence, Sinmac,* and *Sable I,* had proven to be utterly lacking in the necessary sea-keeping qualities, and their crews were living in misery.[94] As well, the navy chartered twelve motor boats to keep close watch on the most isolated areas of Quebec's North Shore and along Newfoundland's gulf coast. These craft were sustained on their remote stations by the patrol steamers, which also serviced lighthouses and radio stations.

The main base for the gulf force at Sydney was no more impressive than its small steamers and motor boats. The navy reopened the radio station at North Sydney, which had been closed at the outbreak of war as part of the censorship scheme to control the broadcast of information that might be useful to the enemy, and used it as the communication link to the vessels at sea.[95] The so-called dockyard consisted of half of a commercial pier rented from the Rhodes and Curry Company, while the gulf patrol headquarters was an office in the Shaver Block on Charlotte Street.[96]

Hard-pressed to maintain the permanent establishments at Halifax and Esquimalt, the navy had to ask the British for help in finding a commanding officer for the gulf force. They recommended Captain Frederick Pasco, who had been serving in Australia at the outbreak of the war. He had resigned from the Royal Navy to join a combat unit in the Australian Expeditionary Force, but had been rejected, apparently because of his age. He accepted the Canadian appointment and took up his post at Sydney in early September 1915. He would remain there, except during the winter freeze-ups, when the ships and personnel moved to Halifax, until the end of the war. Pasco made the ramshackle arrangements in Cape Breton as efficient as possible, and was always a passionate defender of the interests of his rather unusual command. The one description of him that has come to light suggests that he was the archetypal stern, cold British officer, but with a twinkle in his eye that reflected a sense of humour enabling him to get on effectively with the crusty merchant seamen and partially trained youngsters who formed most of the patrol vessel crews.[97] According to one of the few surviving official descriptions of conditions at Sydney, the amenities of the town made particular demands on Pasco's forbearance, which helps to explain the discipline problems encountered by both militia and naval authorities there. Although prohibition was in effect in Sydney, 'more liquor can be obtained at this place than any other port of call,' the commanding officer of *Margaret* wrote in 1916. What was worse, 'the liquor is absolutely poisonous, leaving the men in a drugged state, for many hours, and unfit for duty.'[98]

Rear Admiral L.W. Murray, who went on to command the whole Canadian Northwest Atlantic theatre in the Second World War, was a junior officer on *Margaret* in 1915. Many years later he recorded his memories of the early days of the St Lawrence Patrol. *Margaret* was a new ship, having been built only in 1913. It carried two six-pounder semi-automatic guns, 'the only ones of their kind I believe to have been made,' which meant that ammunition was in short supply. Murray recalled that he 'was given to understand that the one hundred rounds we had onboard were the lot.' Perhaps for this reason, the Customs Service had had no target practice when it operated the vessel, and Murray could find no record of proper gun trials. 'In my time we fired 6 rounds from each gun at an iceberg in the Strait of Belle Isle. We chose a large one so that we could not very well miss. It gave the gun crew a bit of confidence to know both that it would go off and that it would not explode.'[99]

When Parliament reconvened in early 1916, the strong contingent of Liberal members from the Maritimes was quick to pour scorn on these feeble efforts by the Conservative government. W.F. Carroll, the member for Cape Breton South, was especially scathing. J.D. Hazen, the minister of the Naval Service, he charged, had 'allowed the nucleus of the Canadian navy to go to the dogs,' but

> he has not neglected those people along the shores who had motor boats fifteen or twenty feet long; he has sent those boats down to the coast of Newfoundland for what purpose I do not know, unless for the purpose of drawing salaries for the crews and day's wages for the boats, because they

could not be of any benefit in the world for defence or offence unless it be offensive to see them run around our shores, with their crew coming occasionally into the harbours and having a good time. It is current gossip – I do not know how true it is – that the owners of these motor boats are each receiving $75 a day. The people of Nova Scotia are looking at this matter with ridicule. What earthly good could a motor boat be in Newfoundland, of all places? If the minister had allowed those boats to run in and out of Sydney or Halifax or some other harbours, it would not have been so bad. Those boats were not able to cross to Newfoundland under their own steam, but were taken across on the little ship Margaret. Yet, the minister has those vessels on his list for the defence of Canada![100]

One can feel some sympathy for the government. Hazen took pains to explain – accurately – that since the outbreak of war British authorities had repeatedly discouraged Canadian naval undertakings and consistently urged that the dominion could most usefully help with land forces. For this frankness, the government was rewarded with a complaint from London that information of possible use to the enemy was being too freely bandied about in the Canadian Parliament. In any event, given the attitude of the Admiralty and the fact that a substantial improvement in Canadian naval defences had to depend on large-scale British assistance, there was little to be done. Thus, when the flotilla and cadre of base personnel returned to Sydney from Halifax in the spring of 1916, arrangements remained much as they had been in 1915.

chapter six

East Coast Port,
1916–1918

*Much material damage might be done by an attack and under existing conditions
an attack is not impossible.*

Inter-Departmental Committee, Ottawa, 1917

The nightmare of a submarine raid on Canada's ill-protected coast suddenly seemed to be coming true on 7 October 1916 when *U-53* ostenta-
tiously put into Newport, Rhode Island, to show off its powerful
armament and machinery to officers of the U.S. Navy. Its appearance
disproved the British conviction that combat submarines could cross the
Atlantic only on a one-way suicide run, or if followed by a vulnerable
supply ship. *U-53*'s commanding officer boasted to the Americans that
he had no need to top up with fuel, and he put to sea that same evening.
Next morning, it sank five Allied steamers off Nantucket Island; because
of U.S. neutrality, the American destroyers that rushed to the scene
could do no more than carry out rescue work.[1]

Immediately, the British and Canadian authorities were bombarded
with reports, allegedly from German sources, that *U-53* was on its way to
Canadian waters and that other submarines were already or would soon
be on patrol there. Vice Admiral Sir Montague Browning, the newly
appointed British commander-in-chief, North America and West Indies,
made clear the uselessness of his cruisers against this form of attack by
pulling them back into the safety of Bedford Basin, well inside Halifax's
anti-submarine net, and by calling on the Canadian patrol vessels at Sydney to sweep the Halifax approaches. One of them, *Margaret*, dashed off
to St John's, however, as its extremely exposed position was even more

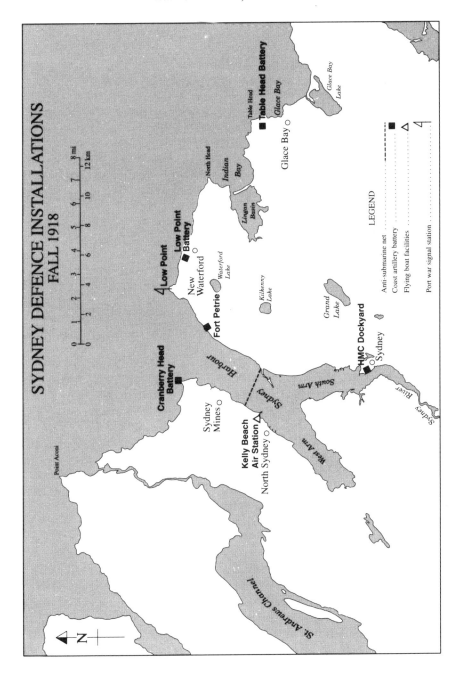

SYDNEY DEFENCE INSTALLATIONS
FALL 1918

weakly defended than the Canadian coast.[2] Captain Pasco's appeal to
Naval Service Headquarters for the return of his ships elicited the less-
than-reassuring response that Browning controlled deployments and he
knew best.[3]

Kingsmill and other Canadian officers shared Pasco's fears about a
German strike against the vulnerable St Lawrence, and this had always
been their darkest worry. Among many warnings that *U-53*'s attacks off
Nantucket were the prelude to such an offensive was an amateurishly
encoded telegram from the British consul in New York: 'Big Fish ranging up stream ... extra large nets quick will make big haul below Montreal.'[4] The danger was not only to shipping. Gwatkin telegraphed Major
General Thomas Benson, who had succeeded Rutherford as general
officer commanding in the Maritimes in November 1915: 'You have no
doubt considered the possibility of attack on Sydney and other
defended points [in] Cape Breton. Submarine carries a gun.'[5] In fact,
U-53 mounted two deck guns, and the Cape Breton and Canso garrisons
had no defences against a surface attack. On 15 October, Benson had
dispatched a 4.7-inch gun on a travelling carriage to Sydney Mines
and another to Canso, each with a detachment of ten gunners from
the coast artillery at Halifax.[6] The precise sites of these guns have not
been determined, but references to the Sydney Mines gun being on a
160-foot ridge called Chapel Hill to the west of the harbour[7] suggest it
was in the same general vicinity as the gun emplaced in 1914–15, but on
higher ground behind Chapel Point. Benson warned that the guns were
of little use other than to boost morale because, 'assuming submarines
did enter these harbours it would be quite impossible for 4.7-inch guns
on travelling carriages to follow their movements, [as] they cannot be
traversed quickly enough.'[8]

Although the reports of a U-boat thrust against Canada proved to be
without substance, during the winter senior militia and naval officers in
Ottawa considered what should be done to protect Sydney better when
navigation reopened in the spring. 'Much material damage might be
done by an attack,' they concluded, 'and under existing conditions an
attack is not impossible.'[9] They decided that the primary defence
against submarines must be warships and aircraft. With their considerable surface speed, heavy torpedoes, and, in some cases, mine armament, U-boats were designed to attack ships, and so the greatest need
was to protect shipping off-shore. The same patrol vessels and aircraft
assigned to that mission could also deploy to cover harbour approaches
should that be necessary. At the same time, the officers heeded Admiral

Browning's insistence on the need for close-in defences, and recommended the installation of an anti-submarine net across the Sydney Harbour entrance to forestall any attempt at a torpedo run against shipping in port. As well, minesweepers should be permanently assigned to the harbour defences, as the Germans were skilled at surreptitiously laying minefields where traffic was heavy, and the only safeguard was meticulous daily sweeps of the shipping channels immediately off the headlands.[10]

Benson also wanted substantial coast artillery defences, including six-inch guns that could be spared from Halifax, to prevent U-boats from attacking shore targets with their deck guns. Because of the growing manpower shortage, coast artillery was limited to two 4.7-inch guns, both on proper coastal defence mounts, which were to be placed at Cranberry Head and Fort Petrie. From these sites, they could fan the surface of the water in order to force a submarine to dive. Once submerged, a U-boat could not attempt to break through the anti-submarine net and, with its slow underwater speed, would be vulnerable to depth-charge-equipped patrol craft.[11]

As a temporary measure, the gun on a travelling carriage at Canso was brought to Fort Petrie early in May 1917.[12] It was probably at this same time that the gun at Sydney Mines was moved out to Cranberry Head. Meanwhile, work began on heavy concrete emplacements for the 4.7-inch guns on coastal defence pedestal mounts, which were sent from stores in Quebec City and which were ready for action in their new positions by the beginning of August 1917. The 4.7-inch guns on travelling carriages were not removed as originally planned but left in position beside the new emplacements to provide some increased firepower. Other construction at the batteries included magazines and shelters for the gun crews, built as semi-permanent bunkers with structural steel and timber and covered back over with earth. Each site also had a battery command post, the fire-control and communications centre of the work. These were wooden huts, with broad view slits covering the full seaward arc. Inside the huts were plotting charts, a coastal defence depression rangefinder, a telescopic instrument that was mounted on a concrete pedestal, and telephones connecting them to the naval establishments and other militia defences. When trained on a target, the depression rangefinder, calibrated to the exact height of the pedestal above sea level, automatically triangulated the ranges, much like a surveying instrument. Inevitably there were delays in the delivery of materials, which slowed the completion of some of the structures until late in the year, while the gun crews lived in tents at these exposed sites and pitched in with much of the heavy labour.[13]

The anti-submarine net, also completed in August, was made of two-inch-thick flexible wire that had been assembled into a twelve-foot mesh and extended from Stubbert's Point on the northside to South Bar. It was suspended from floats on the surface and anchored at intervals along the harbour floor. At mid channel there was a 125-yard gate section, one end of which was fixed to a red spherical hinge buoy. The other end was suspended from the motorized and de-masted schooner *Una*, the gate-opening vessel, which by running forward opened the gate to allow the entry of friendly shipping. Just to the seaward of the gate, the government steamer *Lansdowne*, which had been commissioned into the navy, kept station as a guard ship, having been armed with a six-pounder quick-firing Hotchkiss gun.[14]

At midnight on 7 August all traffic entering and leaving the harbour was placed under strict naval control with the inauguration of an examination service under Captain Pasco's port defence organization to guard against surprise attack by disguised armed merchant ship raiders. No incoming ship could approach past the line between Flat Point and Cranberry Head without first establishing its identity to a naval examination vessel. Because no steamer was available, this duty had to be performed by motor launches. The examination personnel, if satisfied, would order the gate of the anti-submarine net to be opened. Vessels wishing to leave port had to notify the examination staff a day in advance and receive, confidentially, a time when the gate would be briefly opened. Vessels could not enter or leave during darkness or when the weather was thick. One of the primary responsibilities of the coastal batteries at Cranberry Head and Fort Petrie was to be ready at all times to open fire, first with warning shots and then for effect, on instruction from the examination staff. As the *Sydney Daily Post* later put it, obviously impressed, 'no craft – not even the *Marion* or *Aspy* [two well-known local coastal vessels] – could pass in or out without displaying certain prearranged signals set from day to day by the naval authorities.'[15] This endorsement was significant, because the *Post*'s owner, Senator J.S. McLennan, a prominent Sydney businessman and a friend of the prime minister, had made known the community's worries about the state of the harbour defences.[16] The only vessels exempted from the regulations were Canadian, British, and Allied warships and naval transports. These vessels, on the communication of a secret code to the port defences, were given immediate entry at all times in case an enemy submarine or surface raider was lurking offshore. To exchange entry messages with friendly warships and to give advance warning of the approach of suspicious vessels, a naval party was stationed at the Flat Point lighthouse, which was designated the port war signal station.

The system did not operate without incident. On 19 October 1917 the first prosecution under the Defence of Canada Order took place at Sydney when Captain Luke Holmes was fined $10 and $4.76 costs because on 5 September his ship, *Lingan*, had collided with *Lansdowne*. *Lingan* had apparently 'attempted to pass through the gate before it was open,' *Lansdowne* not yet having signalled it to proceed. A claim for damages to *Lansdowne* was subsequently made on the Dominion Coal Company, owner of *Lingan*.[17]

The new defences and security measures were more vital than anyone had previously imagined, for the gravest crisis of the naval war had catapulted Sydney into a crucial strategic role. When the 'sink on sight' offensive against Allied merchant shipping in the spring of 1915 had aroused a storm of criticism, particularly from the still neutral United States, Germany's U-boats had returned to the much less effective 'stop and search' procedure to verify that a merchant ship was indeed carrying war *matériel* and to give its crew the chance to get away safely in lifeboats.[18] In a desperate bid to break the deadlock on the western front in Europe, Germany reinstituted the 'sink on sight' policy in the western approaches to the British Isles on 1 February 1917, gambling that Britain could be brought to its knees before the Americans, if they fulfilled their earlier threats to enter the war, could dispatch decisive aid to the Allies. In the spring of 1917 the gamble appeared to be paying off. Although the United States did indeed come into the war on 6 April, one in four ships sailing from British ports on transatlantic voyages to bring back urgently needed food and war *matériel* could be expected not to return. Given the primitive state of anti-submarine weaponry, U-boats had no difficulty in evading the hundreds of patrol craft with which the Royal Navy saturated the western approaches.[19]

Looking defeat in the face, the Admiralty attempted what had previously seemed administratively and economically impossible: to gather a large portion of the transatlantic shipping into convoys escorted by warships. Trial convoys in the spring of 1917 proved an instant success. A cruiser, or other heavy-gun warship, accompanied the convoy on the high seas to protect it against German surface raiders. When the convoy then neared the U-boats' operating area in British waters, destroyers and other anti-submarine vessels came out to join the escort.

Shipping from North America to Britain had priority when the Admiralty fully implemented the convoy system in the summer of 1917. Aside from the increasing dependence of the British economy and the Allied forces on the industries and vast natural resources of the United States and Canada, British authorities had begun to economize shipping by concentrating on the short North Atlantic routes in preference to the more distant trades in the South Atlantic and Pacific. The ports of assembly initially included Hampton Roads in Virginia, New York City, and – for the Canadian summer traffic, the bulk of which sailed from the St Lawrence – Sydney. Gaspé, where the first Canadian troopship convoy had assembled in 1914, had been another possibility, but Admiral Browning selected Sydney because defences were already being installed and there were ample stocks of the coal, trained labour, and industrial facilities needed to refuel ships quickly and carry out running repairs so that they could meet schedules.[20]

The first Home from Sydney convoy, designated HS 1, included seventeen merchant vessels and sailed on 10 July, escorted by HMS *Highflyer*, a cruiser from the North America and West Indies Station. Thereafter, convoys sailed regularly at intervals of approximately eight days. A month later, to achieve greater efficiency and safety, convoys were divided according to speed, the faster ones sailing from Halifax and the slower ones from Sydney. While awaiting departure, ships containing explosives were anchored in the North West Arm, opposite Upper North Sydney. Frank Jackson, who worked for the customs service at North Sydney during the war, later recalled the vivid image of 'those convoys of multi-coloured ships, with what might be called modernistic designs painted on their sides and funnels to make them less noticeable at sea,' as they 'filed silently out of the harbour starting their long hazardous voyages.'[21]

Jackson was required to board all foreign ships entering the port for inspection.

Foreign ships coming in through the guarded gates of the anti-submarine net, laid across the harbour opposite Centreville, put up an identifying flag seen by the captain of the tugboat on duty. If it were office hours, he phoned me at the Customs House; if outside of hours and before midnight, he notified me at my home. After immediately walking to where the tug was moored, I was taken to the side of the crazily-painted camouflaged ship. Though it was often difficult and perilous, I never refused to climb a rope ladder up the side of a large steamer. I had to do it even in storms.

When he was called, Dr MacLeod [sic] of Sydney, an elderly man, made them lower a companion-ladder.

On board I was taken to where the captain answered the questions I filled in on a sheet for Ottawa's information. At that point the master did not know their destination. For reasons of security, it would not be revealed until sailing orders were given as they were to leave the harbour.[22]

Browning's cruisers continued to put into port every few weeks, according to their places in the escort schedule, but were too few in number to carry the full burden. The gap was filled by fast passenger liners that the Royal Navy had fitted with guns and commissioned as 'armed merchant cruisers.' These ships had previously been employed in the northeastern Atlantic to stop and search merchant vessels suspected of carrying war *matériel* to the enemy. Because much of the contraband had originated in the United States, which had now entered the war, the merchant cruisers were available for convoy duty. These ships became regular visitors to Sydney.[23]

The Canadian navy's shipping intelligence service played a large role in the convoy system. Canadian personnel in Ottawa and at the East Coast ports arranged for the assembly of outbound ships at Sydney. The shipping control staff there, known as the Sydney Naval Transport Office, which was part of Captain Pasco's command, did much of the detailed work. One of their most demanding and important tasks was to plot individual routes for each merchant ship, so that if it became separated from the convoy, or if the convoy had to disperse because of a concerted attack by German surface warships, it could follow the safest possible course.

To ensure effective centralized control and the application of standard procedures, the Admiralty in London dispatched port convoy officers and staffs to each of the convoy assembly ports. Accordingly, Rear Admiral Bertram M. Chambers, a retired Royal Navy officer who had been brought back to active service earlier in the war to help manage shipping at British ports, arrived at Sydney on 3 August 1917, after HS 4 had sailed. He set up his staff in offices at the new *Sydney Daily Post* building on Dorchester Street, which Captain Pasco had arranged. These were conveniently close to the waterfront, although somewhat crowded, and appear to have included a lecture room where merchant ship captains gathered twenty-four hours before sailing to receive their final instructions.[24]

Among the qualities needed in convoy officers was the ability, with a

down-to-earth manner and common sense, to cajole often crusty merchant captains, whose every instinct and habit was for autonomy, into
accepting the procedures and discipline required for group sailings.
Chambers, to judge by his cheerful, practical correspondence and the
efficiency of his organization, was an inspired choice. At war's end, the
commander-in-chief of the North America and West Indies Station
reported that Chambers had 'carried through his work in Canada with
the greatest zeal and ability and the success achieved is in large measure
due to him.'[25]

Chambers, for his part, attributed his success to the 'magnificent'[26]
harbour at Sydney and the unstinting cooperation he had received from
Canadians. 'As a convoy port,' he said, Sydney was 'hard to beat during
the later summer months.' Officials of the Dominion Coal Company
were 'always most accommodating and helpful,' and the coaling
arrangements that they made were 'in the main excellent.'[27] He had
equally high praise for the Canadian navy. When he arrived he found
that the first four convoys had been 'efficiently'[28] dispatched, thanks to
the help provided by Captain Pasco and his staff to the officers of the
escorting cruisers and armed merchant cruisers. Indeed, Chambers was
so impressed that he arranged to have Lieutenant James A. Murray of
the Royal Naval Canadian Volunteer Reserves, the boarding officer at
Sydney who carried out the delicate work of visiting merchant ships to
verify their cargoes and readiness for sea, transferred to his own staff for
the same duties.[29] Lieutenant J.C. Caine, RNCVR, Pasco's routing
officer, virtually became a member of the British admiral's staff, so completely did Chambers rely on him. Similarly, Chambers trusted implicitly
Pasco's communications staff for the encoding and decoding of messages and other services.[30]

Command arrangements for the Canadian and Newfoundland flotillas changed in 1917. With the expansion undertaken in the wake of
U-53's visit, the Canadian government asked the Admiralty for the loan
of an experienced officer to take charge of the forces afloat, and retired
Vice Admiral Sir Charles Coke accepted a considerable demotion to
return to active employment in the new position of commodore of
patrols. Captain Pasco, interpreting the change as a negative reflection
on his management of the patrols and the Sydney establishment,
offered to resign, but was mollified by Admiral Kingsmill's assurances
that he was needed to run the increasingly complex services for both
the navy and merchant marine at Sydney.[31] There was indeed a critical
shortage of experienced officers in the Canadian navy, and the success

of the Sydney convoys, despite the lack of notice and preparation, owed much to Pasco's efforts.

Coke proved incapable of forgetting the fact that substantively he out-ranked Kingsmill, however, and he was not a success. Among the many issues that compelled Kingsmill to have the Admiralty recall him in the summer of 1917 was Coke's reluctance to move the patrols' command from their winter headquarters at Halifax to Sydney for the shipping season.[32] He was replaced by Captain Walter Hose, who took up the appointment as captain of patrols at Sydney in August 1917. A Royal Navy officer of long experience who had become frustrated with the lack of opportunity in the British service, Hose had transferred to the Canadian navy in 1912 to command on the West Coast. He had shown a great deal of initiative in utilizing the meagre resources available there during the naval alarms early in the war. With the virtual disappearance of the German cruiser threat in the Pacific by 1917, Naval Service Head-quarters transferred him, along with many other experienced personnel in British Columbia, to help meet the crisis on the East Coast. Hose repaid the confidence placed in him by providing energetic common-sense leadership to the ragtag anti-submarine patrol.[33]

During the late summer and autumn of 1917 the number of ships reporting for convoy greatly increased. This largely reflected Sydney's convenient location at the eastern extremity of North America, on the short great circle route to Europe. Ships from American ports north of Hampton Roads or New York could save days of backtracking to meet convoys at those ports by making for Sydney; similarly, ships that missed convoys at the American assembly ports could avoid waiting for the next sailing by carrying on to Nova Scotia, a destination that put them a third or more of the way along the voyage to Europe.[34] In mid-October, more than forty vessels were at Sydney, and the crush was cleared only by sending thirty-two of them in HS 14 (some had proven too slow for con-voy and were routed independently), nearly double the number in HS 1.[35] Weather conditions helped greatly in dealing with the expand-ing traffic into and out of the port. 'We were fortunate enough to have on the whole, excellent weather and the way in which a succession of foggy days was invariably broken ... when a convoy was leaving was so remarkable as to cause comment.'[36] Nevertheless, the growing size of convoys at Sydney and other ports caused continual worry. Naval authorities feared that too many ships gathered together would make an easy target, but they underestimated the ability of merchant captains to keep formation. They also did not understand that a large convoy is no easier to find at sea than a small one, or that only a modest increase in the escorts needed for a small convoy could provide an equally effective defence for a much larger number of merchant ships.

Meanwhile, the Canadian navy still had virtually no effective anti-submarine forces. In the wake of *U-53*'s appearance off Nantucket, the Admiralty acknowledged that submarines could now cross the Atlantic and operate there without vulnerable resupply facilities. It therefore recommended that Canada and Newfoundland together assemble a force of thirty-six substantial sea-going steamers with sufficient armament to inflict at least some damage on the powerfully built U-boats. Only five vessels of the existing St Lawrence Patrol met the standard, and the Admiralty warned that it could offer nothing to help out: assistance would be sent only after there were confirmed attacks on the Canadian coast. Canadian Naval Service Headquarters knew that Newfoundland was already doing everything it could by providing three or four patrol vessels. Thus, most of the burden would fall on Canada.[37]

A canvass of available civilian ships eventually turned up another five for ocean patrols. These included three government ships – the Post Office steamer *Lady Evelyn*, and the hydrographic survey ships *Cartier* and *Acadia* – and two from private companies, the whaling ship *Grib* and the steamer *Laurentian*. None was fully adequate: *Lady Evelyn* had good speed but did not handle heavy seas well, the hydrographic ships were slow, and the other two vessels proved more useful in utility jobs such as transporting stores than in patrol work. A further investigation of the American ship market turned up only seven wooden trawlers, which were purchased. These ships were needed for the minesweeping services that Browning insisted on for Halifax and Sydney, however, and were not available for the anti-submarine patrol.

The Canadian government had no choice but to order the construction of twelve 130-foot steel anti-submarine trawlers from Canadian Vickers Ltd in Montreal and Polson's Iron Works in Toronto. The Admiralty made some amends for its inability to help by ordering the construction of a further sixty steel trawlers and one hundred smaller, wooden, anti-submarine drifters from Canadian shipyards along the St Lawrence and on the Great Lakes. All of these vessels were built at British expense and the Admiralty reserved the right to employ them wherever necessary, but promised that some would be assigned to Canadian service if that proved to be necessary. None of the new vessels could be completed until late in the year at the earliest, however, and in fact most were not ready until the spring of 1918.

Meanwhile, a plan to supplement the patrol flotilla with aircraft had come to nothing. The minister of naval services had asked the naval and militia staffs in February 1917 to consider the feasibility of employing maritime aircraft on the East Coast. When they endorsed the idea, the government consulted the Admiralty, which agreed that aircraft would be helpful. Although warning that any aircraft would have to be built in Canada or the United States because of the pressure on British resources, the Admiralty did send some sample machines. It also sent an aviation officer, who visited Halifax and Sydney and made detailed recommendations for the development of air stations and squadrons at the two ports. The government rejected the proposals in April, however, because of the further pressure their creation would put on already scarce industrial resources that, among other things, were urgently needed for the patrol vessel building program, and the long delay that must take place before the air service could be expected to do any useful flying.[38]

The failure to organize the air patrol became another of the complaints levelled at the government by Liberal members of Parliament from the Maritime provinces. Not only had the Borden ministry failed to supply suitable protection against the increasing U-boat menace, they charged, it was also neglecting wartime opportunities to strengthen the economy of the region that would reassert Canada's place as a seagoing nation. W.F. Carroll found it galling that the government, while rejecting aviation development in Cape Breton, was at the same time proceeding with a scheme to build air-training stations in Ontario in order to provide basic instruction to aircrew recruited for service with the British Royal Flying Corps at the fighting fronts. 'The point which I wish to make,' he explained, 'is this: that the present submarine menace does not materially or directly affect the interior of the country.'[39]

Even as the government was ruling the air patrol scheme impracticable, the virtually simultaneous entry of the United States into the war raised the expectation in Ottawa that American reinforcements might become available for the East Coast. It was not to be. So ardently had the American government pursued neutrality since 1914 that its navy had done nothing to prepare for anti-submarine warfare, and the limited number of destroyers and other appropriate available craft were soon committed to European waters in response to British pleas.[40]

The creation of a minesweeping flotilla at Sydney got off to a modest start in the summer of 1917. Two of the wooden trawlers recently purchased in the United States were sent from Halifax in July.[41] Their mis-

sion was to carry out a daily sweep of the main approach channel to a
distance of about ten miles from the headlands, and then, in a different
direction each day, to sweep ten miles further out. They sailed together,
towing a cable between them, which could cut the moorings of any
mine that had been sown, sending it bobbing to the surface where it
could be destroyed by rifle fire. This single pair of minesweepers was
only a token force, however, as the naval staff had concluded that at
least three pairs were needed.[42]

After HS 17 sailed on 13 November 1917, convoy assembly operations
were transferred to Halifax and the anti-submarine net at Sydney was
pulled up on shore for the winter. The naval vessels and all but a skeleton staff migrated to Halifax in what was by now a well-established routine. Canadian naval forces deployed in the gulf during the 1917 season
had been only slightly stronger than in 1915 and 1916. There were eight
or nine patrol vessels, compared to the previous six or seven, as well as
the dozen motor boats that kept watch on the north shore of the St
Lawrence and the western shore of Newfoundland. The Newfoundland
government made a somewhat larger effort, maintaining three steamers
on patrol in the Strait of Belle Isle and the northern approaches. Operations were also much the same as they had been: the patrol ships kept
surveillance in their designated areas throughout the gulf and in the
ocean approaches to Sydney, identifying passing vessels and keeping a
watch inshore for suspicious activity. There were not enough resources
to attempt a systematic escort of convoys as they left Sydney.[43]

Because Canadian defences in 1917 were still incomplete, it was fortunate that German U-boats did not push into the western Atlantic that
year. Senior naval officers were convinced that their good luck would
not continue in 1918, and angry that the Admiralty provided no up-to-
date advice about the threat the Maritimes faced or what Canada should
do to prepare. Naval Service Headquarters therefore dispatched Captain E.H. Martin, superintendent of the Halifax Dockyard, to London to
get straight answers. His mission confirmed Canada's worst fears: the
Admiralty had solid intelligence about Germany's development of large
U-boat cruisers designed especially for long-distance missions. 'It is considered very probable,' the Admiralty acknowledged, that an attack by
one of the new submarine cruisers 'may be expected [in Canadian
waters] at any time after March [1918],' although the prevalence of drift
ice 'may act to a certain extent as a deterrent.' Submarines could go
wherever convoys could go, however, so 'an attack on shipping issuing
from Halifax or other ports on the Atlantic seaboard is to be contem-

plated.'[44] Admiralty officials agreed, therefore, with the Canadians on the need to strengthen the St Lawrence Patrol, but insisted equally on the importance of escorting the convoys as they formed up off Halifax and Sydney and began their transatlantic passage. It was easiest for U-boats to locate convoys when they were close to port, and the merchant ships were especially vulnerable when they were slowly manoeuvring into their sailing formation.[45]

The total requirement in 1918 was for ninety-six patrol vessels, anti-submarine craft, and minesweepers, of which fully two thirds would be assigned to Sydney for the escort of convoys, the St Lawrence Patrol, and minesweeping off the port. Only twenty suitable vessels were available in the existing Canadian naval flotilla, but there were also the twelve trawlers the Canadian government had ordered, half of which were complete or nearly so. To make up the shortfall, the Admiralty assigned thirty of the trawlers and thirty-six of the wooden drifters that it was having built in Canada to the Canadian navy's Atlantic flotilla. As with the Canadian trawlers, however, only a few of these vessels had been able to sail down to the East Coast from the St Lawrence and Great Lakes shipyards before the 1917 freeze-up. Most could only be delivered when the ice broke up in June 1918, by which time a U-boat cruiser might already be operating along the coast. To make matters worse, there were delays in obtaining armament from British sources and the Royal Navy could provide only a few men for the crews. Although the Canadian navy had been beating the bushes since the spring of 1917 to find additional men for the East Coast ships, the overall manpower shortage in Canada resulting from the needs of the army and industry made it a slow process and one that had in particular failed in turning up adequate numbers of experienced seamen.[46]

The Canadian officers had other, more serious, worries. The Admiralty had advised Martin that no number of trawlers and patrol vessels could confidently counter the big U-boats. At least twelve destroyers or equivalent warships, with at least twenty knots of speed and 4-inch guns, were needed to provide the gulf patrol with a fast strike force and lead the escort forces that would shepherd the convoys through the two- to three-hundred-mile danger zone in coastal waters, where U-boats were most likely to attack. The Admiralty initially promised to find these warships for Canada from either British or American sources, but it became clear as spring approached that this was not going to happen. The production of destroyers and equivalent types of ships was behind schedule in both countries, and every vessel available was urgently needed in

European waters, where Germany was inflicting much more damage than it could ever do on the North American coast.[47]

Preparations were being rushed to prepare Sydney for the shipping season. One pressing need was for more coast artillery, the result of intelligence that the new transatlantic 'U-cruisers' carried much heavier deck guns – 5.9-inch calibre – than other U-boats. With their increased firepower, they could well choose to stay surfaced and fight on the approach of patrol vessels rather than diving to escape. If that occurred, the little ships of the Canadian patrol would be hopelessly out-gunned, and their only hope would be to run for safety under the covering fire of long-range coastal batteries, which existed at Halifax but not at Sydney. At the same time, the heavy guns of the U-cruisers made them much more capable than other submarines of inflicting serious damage on shore targets.[48]

In March 1918, therefore, Gwatkin revived Benson's proposal of the previous year that two surplus 6-inch guns from Halifax should be mounted at Sydney. Major General F.L. Lessard, who had succeeded Benson as general officer commanding in the Maritimes in February 1918, recommended that the guns go to two widely separated sites: Low Point, the eastern headland of the port, and ten miles further east at Table Head. The latter position would cover the waters off Glace Bay, from which U-cruisers could bombard the coastal mines or lie in wait for the heavy traffic in and out of Sydney. However, Militia Headquarters in Ottawa directed that both guns should go to Low Point, possibly because a single site would require considerably less manpower than two.[49]

Work at Low Point for the two-gun battery proceeded quickly. The design was similar to that of the Cranberry Head and Fort Petrie batteries, except that the concrete platforms were larger to accommodate the larger guns. By late May the platforms were nearly ready and the guns were on their way from Halifax, when Major General Sir Louis Jackson, a visiting British fortifications and base-development expert, arrived in Sydney at the request of Militia Headquarters to inspect the coastal defences.[50]

Jackson approved of the measures taken to protect the harbour but pointed out that, of the three major targets liable to attack at Sydney – the coastal coal mines, the steel plants at Sydney and Sydney Mines, and ships in the harbour – the mines and steel plants were 'by far the most important, because effective damage to either might result in entire stoppage of output for many months.' Dominion Steel in Sydney was then producing some 30,000 to 34,000 tons of ingots a month; in the past most of that output had been used in the manufacture of shells, but it was now being used for steel rails, which were 'urgently required for the Canadian Railways.' Nova Scotia Steel in Sydney Mines produced 10,000 to 12,000 tons of ingots monthly, which was used mostly for shells. These plants were 'of vital importance,' and both were 'very vulnerable from the fact that there are points where the effect of one shell might stop the work for months.' The Sydney plant, the more important of the two, was 'so far from the mouth of the harbour that [it] could only be bombarded by a vessel that had forced the harbour entrance and come right in; and for this reason, as in the case of the vessels in harbour, [it] may be regarded as comparatively safe' because of the effective harbour defences in place. The Sydney Mines plant lay nearer the ocean, 'but still could only be bombarded by vessels within effective range of the guns at the entrance of the harbour.'[51]

The greatest danger was the exposed position of the coal mines. There were seventeen of them spread around the harbour from Low Point to MacRae Point and within easy reach of a submarine or surface raider coming in from the Atlantic. These mines produced 300,000 tons of coal monthly, about a third of which went to the Dominion Steel plant. Somewhat less exposed were four mines near Cranberry Head, which produced between 50,000 and 60,000 tons monthly, most of which supplied the Sydney Mines steel plant. If these mines suffered serious damage, the steel works would have to shut down because they did not maintain a reserve supply of coal.[52]

Jackson believed that the two-gun battery at Low Point could not protect the main group of mines between Lingan and Glace Bay from bombardment. The guns should be separated, leaving one at Low Point but moving the other to Table Head, as Lessard had earlier recommended. This arrangement 'will suffice to keep any vessels having only medium armament out of bombarding range.' It will be recalled that in the summer of 1917 a 4.7-inch gun on a travelling carriage had been left in place beside each of the newly installed 4.7-inch guns on coastal defence mounts at Cranberry Head and Fort Petrie. Jackson confirmed that two 4.7-inch guns were needed at each of the battery positions, but considered those on wheeled carriages 'practically useless against any but a stationary target.' He therefore recommended that the two guns on travelling carriages be placed on turntables 'or be otherwise made capable of rapid traversing.' With these modifications, Jackson thought that Sydney's harbour defences would be adequate, though they 'will not be more than adequate.'[53]

Militia Headquarters quickly ordered that all of this should be done. A single 6-inch gun was mounted at Low Point in early June, and the other was put in place in a nearly identical battery at Table Head in early August. Later that month the wheeled guns at Cranberry Head and Fort Petrie were remounted on coastal defence pedestals that had been manufactured at the Sydney steel plant. To man the 6-inch guns and bring the 4.7-inch batteries up to strength, 116 gunners were posted to Sydney in July and August, bringing the artillery garrison up to a total of ten officers and 159 other ranks.[54] So great was the shortage of artillerymen that most of these men were diverted from artillery drafts headed overseas from Ontario and British Columbia. Some were conscripted under the Military Service Act but apparently 'were an exceptionally good type and quickly made efficient specialists and gunners. Some were sent for training as officers and would have relieved those officers in the Forts who had been unable to get away' if the war had not ended shortly afterwards.[55] The battery personnel maintained a heavy training schedule designed to enhance their skill at rapidly engaging fast, low-profile targets.

The infantry defences in the Sydney area were also maintained, but reduced at other places in Cape Breton and the Canso area. The 94th Regiment had been having difficulty maintaining its authorized strength of 360 all through 1917. Men had been volunteering to go overseas in preference to the arduous work of manning outposts in Cape Breton's demanding climate, and few new men were coming forward. Gwatkin, as usual, was keen to cut back the garrisons but was resisted by the navy.[56] The global manpower shortage, the government's introduction of conscription, and the especially urgent need for infantry reinforcements in Europe forced the issue in the spring and early summer of 1918. At that time the many militia units on garrison duty in Canada were demobilized and their personnel placed in large new consolidated garrison units. Men from the deactivated militia units who were eligible for the draft were sent overseas, while those not eligible, who had completed the maximum four years of full-time service allowed by law, were released. The resulting shortages in the new garrison units were filled by conscripts and men who had returned from overseas for health or other reasons but who were still fit enough for guard duty. Under this reorganization, the 94th Regiment was replaced by F Company, 6th Battalion, Canadian Garrison Regiment, with a strength of about two hundred men of all ranks. The Glace Bay and Louisbourg garrisons were reduced to detachments of about a dozen men each.

That left a substantial detachment for the cable complex at Canso, and an infantry garrison of one hundred men or more for waterfront security at Sydney, mainly in Whitney Pier, and for the protection of the cable and radio facilities at North Sydney and Sydney Mines.[57]

It appears that Victoria Park, despite the scale of military activities in the area, was not being fully utilized for war purposes. It was being managed at this time by a group known as the Trustees of Victoria Park, which reported annually to Sydney's city council,[58] and was still largely a public park, as it had been since the departure of the British garrison in 1855, despite the presence of the militia. There was a baseball field with seating for spectators, and a playground with swings. As well, visiting circuses set up their operations there each summer, even during the war years. In 1917 the trustees planted potatoes, with the city providing the labour to dig them. A crop of 120 bushels was produced, which was distributed to various charitable institutions in the area. In 1918 hay was grown and sold, yielding a profit of $7.50 for the park.[59]

As significant as the army's activities at Sydney were in 1918, they paled in comparison with the growth of the naval presence. Work to enlarge the base facilities began long before the ice broke up in May and was well advanced or completed by mid-July. The entire Rhodes Curry Wharf at Sydney and the warehouse on it were rented for the shipping season, together with the company's office building on the shore part of the property. Several other buildings were erected at the site, including most notably a large workshop for repairs to the patrol vessels. A block north of the wharf, the navy rented J.E. Burchell's warehouse (110 Esplanade) and converted it into a barracks that accommodated sixty-six sailors. The steamer *Lansdowne* arrived on 31 May and began laying the anti-submarine net, completing the task two weeks later.[60]

Patrol ships began to arrive at Sydney as early as the second week of May, as soon as the ice had cleared sufficiently to allow their passage.[61] The newly built vessels, which had spent the winter at their shipyards, came down the St Lawrence, those most in need of completion work going to Halifax for a few weeks before returning to Sydney. By the middle of July, forty-five new vessels – twenty-two little drifters and twenty-three trawlers – were on station there. As well, five of the wooden trawlers purchased in the United States the previous year for minesweeping duties arrived for service. All six of the veteran government steamers and converted yachts – now termed auxiliary patrol ships – were allocated to the Sydney Patrols Command, but at least one, *Stadacona*, and probably others, were undergoing refits.[62]

As agreed by Canadian and British authorities in discussions during the winter, the auxiliary patrol ships initially carried on much as they had in the wide-ranging gulf patrol of earlier years, responding to reports of suspicious activities, keeping in touch with (and supplying) isolated lighthouses and radio stations, and generally maintaining a presence in areas where submarines might lurk.[63] As the new trawlers became fully operational in July, some were assigned to support the patrol ships to create the Mobile Patrol Flotilla.[64] By early August this flotilla consisted of three divisions, each with a patrol ship and one or two trawlers, the idea being that the two or three ships together could engage one of the big transatlantic U-cruisers with at least some slight chance of success. The Mobile Patrol Flotilla vessels frequently operated from Louisbourg to alleviate the congestion at Sydney and to ensure the quickest possible turnaround when coaling. Arrangements were also made for refuelling in ports as distant as Gaspé to the west and St John's to the east to sustain them in their long-range missions.[65]

Most of the trawlers and drifters were assigned to what was called the Forming-Up Escort and Outer Patrol Flotilla, which operated in divisions that each included one or two vessels of both types. What fragmentary information survives suggests that this flotilla operated like the similar one Hose had organized at Halifax in the spring. The idea was that three divisions of the local force should leave port immediately before a convoy sailed to search for submarines that might be lying in wait. They would take up positions ahead and on either beam of the merchant ships as they came out. After a few hours, one local escort division would return to port for a scheduled rest and replenishment, while the other two remained out for several days conducting patrols in Cabot Strait and the immediate Atlantic approaches, including the east coast of Cape Breton. This patrol system appears to have begun to take shape early in July, before the first convoy of the 1918 season to sail from Sydney, HS 47, departed on the 9th. Certainly, it was functioning when the second convoy, HS 48, formed up on the 19th.[66]

Everything about the expanded naval effort at Sydney was improvised and fell short of what was needed. This was hardly surprising, as the navy was caught in the impossible circumstances created by British warnings of impending U-boat attacks, the non-existence of Canadian resources, and the unavailability of adequate assistance from Britain or the United States. The difficulties – although not the real cause – had long been public knowledge. The Halifax *Herald* published a letter in February 1918 from a writer calling himself 'Sub Rosa,' under the headline:

'Some Reasons for a Spring House Cleaning in the Canadian Navy.' He asked some blunt and awkward questions:

> Who was the official or officials that were responsible for the six 'ships' that were built in Toronto last year ... ? Of what use does the naval department pretend these boats are for war purposes? They are built something like a trawler, equipped with compound engines that are almost obsolete in type ... they can probably make about nine knots an hour in fine weather.
>
> Does the naval department seriously pretend to patrol our coasts with these vessels as protection against German submarines, which we are told are now armed with 6-inch guns and can make 15 knots on the surface? If the money that was spent on these boats had been used in building two or three fast destroyers, heavily armed, there might have been some prospect of the Royal Canadian Navy bagging a few submarines. The boys are anxious and willing enough, but they can't deliver the goods unless they have the tools to do the work with.
>
> There is also the question of the 'CD' boats. Why is it that so many 'skippers' and mates (experienced men most of them) have refused to take these boats out to sea? Are these boats unseaworthy? Surely these men, who have spent their whole lives at sea, would not refuse to sail them and risk imprisonment unless they had good reason.[67]

All of this was true, and the situation in fact was even worse than the author suggested, but for reasons that had more to do with the bitter challenges of submarine warfare than the inefficiency of the Canadian Naval Services Department. The trawlers and drifters, built according to designs borrowed from Britain's emergency anti-submarine program, had never been intended to escort convoys far out to sea or to engage submarines singlehandedly. They were meant only to maintain a presence in coastal waters, where they could readily receive help from proper naval warships, but in Canadian waters no such support was available.[68] The Royal Navy, moreover, had adopted the trawlers and drifters because they were types common in the British fishing fleet, and so there was an abundance of qualified crewmen and ample numbers of commercial shipyards with expertise in servicing such vessels. By contrast, the Canadian fishery still consisted of sailing schooners. It was for that reason that the patrol vessels had had to be built in St Lawrence and Great Lakes shipyards, where the winter freeze-up had delayed their delivery until the spring of 1918, giving their novice crews almost no time to prepare before beginning a full schedule of operations.[69]

As well, when the ships arrived they required a good deal more work to complete their equipment and to correct the inevitable defects in construction, but the facilities on the East Coast were hard pressed to do this work. At Sydney, in addition to the hastily organized naval workshop at the Rhodes Curry Wharf, there were only three small private yards: Sydney Foundry and Machine Works, whose performance on naval work in previous years had been unimpressive,[70] the North Sydney Marine Railway Company, and Robert Musgrave's shops, also in North Sydney. Although the navy used these firms to their capacity, they were unequal to the demand, especially for complicated repairs. Because ships often could not be spared for the weeks required to go to the better-equipped but already overburdened yards at Halifax, Pictou, and Saint John, the condition of the vessels deteriorated.[71] The inexperienced crews were unable to do much repair work themselves, and the miseries caused by leaking decks and constant patrol missions undermined discipline that was already shaky because of the short time and few facilities available for training. Captain Hose was indeed, as 'Sub Rosa' complained, forced to impose harsh punishments when dispirited crewmen deserted; there was no other way to ensure that ships got to sea when they were needed.[72]

These pressures exacted a heavy toll on the senior officers. By late July, Capain Pasco, who was responsible for the shore establishment and harbour defences, had had enough and again asked to be allowed to resign. 'Considerable difficulty has always been experienced owing to the lack of trained Officers and men,' he wrote, 'and more owing to the refusal of the Department to approve of my requests on various matters which I considered were essential and necessary for the efficient conduct of the Naval Service at Sydney.'[73] The final straw had been the rejection of his plea that the unseaworthy motor boats on the examination service had to be replaced by drifters if the port defences were to be effective. Kingsmill persuaded him to stay with soothing words and by winning the agreement of the Admiralty to release two additional drifters for the examination service.[74] Within days, Captain Hose, who was in charge of the flotillas, asked for leave. 'My headaches are increasing,' he wrote, 'and thoughts of Trawlers, Drifters, organization schemes, etc, keep me from getting to sleep till 2 and three in the morning.'[75] Hose did not get to take his leave because, within hours of his request, the Canadian navy faced its greatest challenge of the war, as will be seen in the next chapter.

One of the few bright spots among the many frustrations for the navy in the spring and early summer of 1918 was the provision of limited but timely assistance by the United States Navy. In February and March, when the Admiralty had reneged on its recent promise to find destroyers for Canadian coastal defence, Vice Admiral Sir William Lowther Grant (who had replaced Browning as commander-in-chief, North America and West Indies) supported the Canadians in an appeal to Washington for help. The Americans promised to provide both coastal patrol aircraft and patrol vessels.[76]

There would be difficulties in supplying the aircraft, but six little wooden warships – 110-foot-long submarine chasers – arrived at Halifax on 16 May 1918. Their maximum speed of eighteen knots was only a slight improvement over some of the better Canadian patrol vessels, and their six-pounder-gun armament was considerably weaker. Still, they were much faster than the ten-knot trawlers that made up the bulk of the expanded Canadian force, and they carried good depth-charge equipment, armament that was just beginning to arrive for the Canadian flotilla.[77] The submarine chasers undertook the long-range convoy escort duty at Halifax that should have been performed by destroyers, warships ten times larger and nearly twice as fast. They were organized into two divisions, each of three vessels, one of which accompanied each convoy for the first twenty-four hours of passage, a distance of 150 to 200 miles, before returning to port.

In early July, submarine chasers *SC 51*, *SC 183*, and *SC 241* moved to Sydney, using Dobson's Wharf at Westmount as their base. They arrived in time to escort HS 47, the first Sydney convoy of the season. Unfortunately, the weather was not nearly as cooperative as it had been during the previous summer. In persistent heavy fogs, two merchant ships that were trying to make Sydney to join the convoy ran aground in the approaches. Although the convoy subsequently sailed without mishap, the log of one of the submarine chasers noted that visibility was so bad that the crew could only occasionally catch a glimpse of the merchant ships. It was not an especially auspicious beginning to the season.[78]

chapter seven

Victory, 1918

Glad handshaking and happy individual cheers proclaimed the joy felt on the hun being finally beaten.

Sydney Daily Post, 1918

Suddenly, just three months before the end of the war, Sydney became the most important military port in Canada. At the highest councils of the naval war in London and Washington, this was no great surprise because of the excellent information on the transatlantic U-boat missions that was being obtained as a result of the British penetration of Germany's naval radio codes. Although the German signal traffic identified only general operating zones, senior British and American authorities prepared rapidly to redeploy shipping so that the most valuable merchant vessels could be routed clear as soon as the enemy struck in a particular locality. Canada, always the most junior partner, was, however, not included in the day-to-day planning, and events unfolded in the waters off Nova Scotia in a series of lightning shocks.

The first transatlantic U-cruiser had arrived, as British intelligence had predicted, off Chesapeake Bay in late May, and it confined its operations to those warm waters. It was, as British intelligence knew, a converted freighter submarine that, although heavily armed with 5.9-inch guns, mines, and torpedoes, lacked the structural strength, speed, and manoeuvrability of boats built as combat types. For this reason and because it was so far from friendly bases, it avoided escorted shipping and instead sowed mines in key channels and attacked unprotected merchant and fishing vessels. When it turned back for home in early July, a

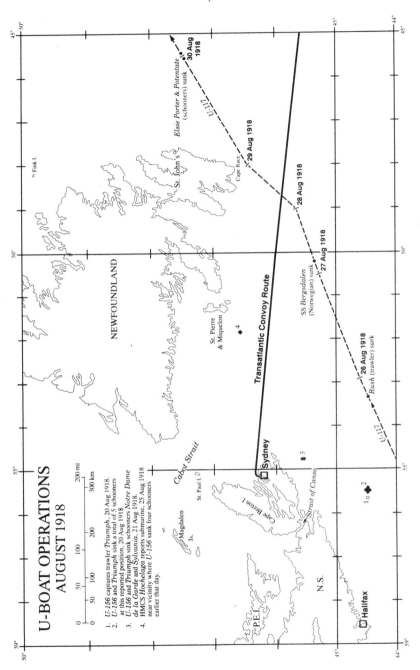

U-BOAT OPERATIONS
AUGUST 1918

1. *U-156* captures trawler *Triumph*, 20 Aug 1918.
2. *U-156* and *Triumph* sink a total of 5 schooners at this reported position, 20 Aug 1918.
3. *U-156* and *Triumph* sink schooners *Notre Dame de la Garde* and *Sylvania*, 21 Aug 1918.
4. HMCS *Hochelaga* reports submarine, 25 Aug 1918 near vicinity where *U-156* sank four schooners earlier that day.

NEWFOUNDLAND

Fink I.

St. John's

Cape Race

Elsie Porter & Potentate (schooners) sunk

30 Aug 1918

U-117

29 Aug 1918

28 Aug 1918

27 Aug 1918

SS *Bergsdalen* (Norwegian) sunk

26 Aug 1918
Rush (trawler) sunk

U-117

St. Pierre & Miquelon

Transatlantic Convoy Route

Cabot Strait

Sydney

St. Paul I.

Cape Breton I.

Strait of Canso

Magdalen Is.

P.E.I.

N.S.

Halifax

200 mi
300 km
0   50   100   200
0   50   100   150

second submarine of the same type, *U-156*, approached on the latitude of New York. Information received from German signals indicated that it would operate in the Gulf of Maine or in waters to the south of it.[1]

The Nova Scotian public learned of *U-156* 's arrival on 17 July when the crew of the Norwegian barque *Marosa* landed in sturdy sea boats on Cranberry Island, near Canso, after a ten-day journey of some seven hundred miles, to report the destruction of their vessel. They also reported that *U-156* had abided by the international law of the time, surfacing and allowing the crew to take to their lifeboats before it sank the ship.[2] Over the next few days, the crew of *U-156* showed both tactical skill and a flair for the dramatic.[3] The American cruiser *San Diego*, well known in Nova Scotia because of its frequent visits while on convoy escort duty, sank after striking a mine that the submarine had laid in the approaches to New York Harbour.[4] On the 22nd, *U-156* attacked a tug and its barges so close to Cape Cod's popular Naussett Beach that shells from the deck guns reportedly flew over the heads of bathers. It then headed north and announced its arrival in Canadian waters on 2 August by sinking *Dornfontein*, a Canadian four-masted schooner, at the mouth of the Bay of Fundy. *Dornfontein*'s crew subsequently reported that they had been taken on board the submarine and treated to dinner before being sent off in a lifeboat.[5] As this attack took place within the Gulf of Maine, the operations area indicated by radio intelligence, there was no reason to think that *U-156* would press further into Canadian waters. In fact, it rapidly rounded the southern tip of Nova Scotia and headed towards Halifax.

The U.S. Navy, which had been assigned responsibility for the defence of the mouth of the Bay of Fundy and the southernmost tip of Nova Scotia as far north as Lockeport on the Atlantic, sent a hunting group made up of the destroyer *Jouett* and eighteen submarine chasers in pursuit of *U-156*. At midday on the 5th, while they were refuelling at Bar Harbor, Maine, the submarine destroyed a tanker, *Luz Blanca*, with torpedoes and gunfire less than thirty miles off the mouth of Halifax Harbour.[6] The tanker had ignored a warning from the navy not to sail in daylight. Although word of the attack got out promptly, there were no fast patrol vessels on hand to respond quickly. All were away at sea, returning from the escort of troopship convoy HC 12, which had sailed on the previous day. While there was great relief that the convoy, carrying some 12,000 Canadian and American troops, had got away safely, it had become abundantly clear that the existing meagre naval flotilla could not secure the Halifax approaches.

Hose dispatched two of the trawler-drifter divisions of the Forming-Up Escort and Outer Patrol Flotilla from Sydney to search the coastal waters between Cape Breton and Halifax. *U-156*, however, had moved back into American waters after its Halifax foray. It was just as well, for more than a third of the principal ships at Sydney – ten of twenty-three trawlers and three of seven auxiliary patrol ships – were out of action. In addition to routine lay-ups, several of the recently arrived trawlers had shown important defects or were awaiting armament whose delivery from Britain had been delayed. Fortunately, a shipment of twelve-pounder guns for the five unarmed trawlers arrived a few days later. These were urgently needed, because the appearance of *U-156* shifted much larger burdens onto Sydney than the short-term reinforcement of the Halifax-based patrols.[7]

Within hours of the attack on *Luz Blanca*, Admiral Grant, the commander-in-chief, who was now almost permanently based in Washington to coordinate operations with the Americans, ordered all merchant shipping bound for Halifax to make for Sydney and to keep east of Sable Island to avoid the coastal waters, where *U-156* would most likely continue its hunt. This change created the largest difficulties in connection with the HC series of medium speed (11–12 knots) convoys that sailed from Halifax. Shipping for these convoys included the better class of cargo vessels, which carried high-value and perishable goods, and troop transports. Prior to the appearance of *U-156*, the vessels allocated to carry American troops had loaded at New York, while most of the cargo carriers and many of the transports carrying Canadian troops had loaded at Montreal. These ships had then gone to Halifax, where they assembled with vessels that had loaded troops and cargo. Henceforth, the Montreal and Halifax ships were to assemble at Sydney and to sail so as to rendezvous with the New York ships on the Grand Banks east of Newfoundland, clear of the coastal danger area. This was an operation that required precision and intimate cooperation between shipping and convoy authorities in Ottawa, Montreal, Halifax, New York, Washington, and, of course, Sydney, which bore the ultimate responsibility for getting the Montreal and Halifax ships to sea in good time, while also maintaining the large HS series convoys.[8] 'It is of utmost importance [that] convoys should not be delayed,' the commander-in-chief directed.[9] Hose responded by reassigning the American submarine chaser division, his fastest group, to the long-range escort of the HC convoys and by giving responsibility for the HS series to the auxiliary patrol ships and trawlers of the Mobile Patrol Flotilla. Of course, both series had additional support in the immediate approaches to the port from the minesweeping flotilla and the Forming-Up Escort and Outer Patrol Flotilla, whose divisions also maintained a constant patrol in Cabot Strait between convoy sailings.[10]

The Sydney section of HC 13 – four merchant vessels and the ocean escort HMS *Victorian* – sailed on 14 August, only two days later than the usual eight-day cycle. This was an impressive demonstration of the efficiency of the shipping control organization after a year's experience with convoys. *Victorian* had arrived at Sydney on the 12th while the thirty-nine ship HS 51 was leaving port, and its captain was impressed by the fact that the file of emerging ships was 'over 20 miles in length' before the vessels began to move into columns for cruising formation.[11] *Lady Evelyn* and at least two trawlers of the Mobile Patrol Flotilla shepherded HS 51 during its first twenty-four hours at sea, although one of the trawlers all too typically suffered a breakdown and had to return early.[12]

The only difficulty encountered by *Victorian* during preparations at Sydney came when the armed liner was boarding the troops that had been brought by train from Halifax, which had been intended as the original embarkation point. Major F.B. Bremner, the transport officer in charge of the troops allegedly 'arrived on board drunk at 8 PM' and 'allowed liquor to be smuggled on board.' When he 'was also drunk and abusive' at 8:30 a.m. the following morning, *Victorian*'s captain ordered him ashore. Soon after the convoy sailed on the morning of the 14th, one of the submarine chasers reported seeing a periscope. Although investigation with hydrophones turned up no confirming evidence, *Victorian*'s captain ordered a sharp turn onto a new course for one hundred miles. The submarine chasers zigzagged on the flanks until after sunset, when, with a gale blowing and the sea getting heavier, they were no longer able to keep up and had to make an early return.[13]

The Sydney section of HC 13 reached the ocean rendezvous east of Newfoundland on time on 16 August, as did the New York group of seven vessels that had sailed on the 11th. Heavy fog and, *Victorian*'s captain claimed, the poor signal procedures of USS *Albany*, the American escort, caused a delay of eleven hours in the joining of the two groups. *Albany* then returned to New York, keeping a radio and visual watch en route for any trace of *U-156*.[14]

The organization and dispatch of two ocean convoys every eight days was only part of Sydney's increased burden. The most important of its other new tasks was the escort of groups of high-value merchant ships between Halifax and Sydney, from Sydney into the Gulf of St Lawrence, and between Sydney and Newfoundland ports. The system was not formally organized, as it would be in the Second World War, with regular schedules and groups of escorts specially designated for each route, but it was comprehensive. And, as in the later war, Sydney served as the central hub. Documentation is unaccountably thin and fragmentary but it is clear that at least thirteen trawlers and auxiliary patrol vessels carried out fifteen local escort missions during the last three weeks of August alone. There is also some evidence that the Newfoundland ferry operating between North Sydney and Port-aux-Basques was regularly escorted, and conclusive evidence that the St John's run had a priority equal to that from Halifax, with groups of two and three escorts being assembled for each voyage. Among the ships shepherded from Sydney to St John's and back were the vessels that supplied the steel plants at Sydney and Sydney Mines with ore from the Wabana mine on Bell Island in Conception Bay, near St John's.[15]

The surprise appearance of *U-156* probably only accelerated far-reaching changes that would have taken place in the shipping and naval operations in Canadian and Newfoundland waters in any event, because British intelligence was learning from German naval signals at the same time of further dangers. *U-117*, a new combat-type minelaying submarine, was known to be approaching American waters to sow mines and hunt along the Halifax–St John's route on its return voyage to Germany. Another converted mercantile submarine would shortly sail from Germany as well, to mine the waters off either Halifax or St John's.[16] Because Halifax is situated adjacent to the wide continental shelf, mines could be laid in shipping channels as far out as one hundred miles from shore. By contrast, the continental shelf off northern Cape Breton quickly drops into the deep trench of Cabot Strait, so that the danger area extended only to about thirty miles. The references to minelaying in the German radio signals indicated that the enemy was well aware of these geographical facts, which further confirmed the wisdom of not assembling convoys at Halifax. To meet the threat to St John's, the Canadian navy sent a trawler and two drifters fitted with minesweeping gear from the Sydney force.[17]

The sailing of the valuable HC convoys in separate Sydney and New York sections with a difficult rendezvous at sea was not satisfactory other than as an emergency measure. The Admiralty therefore began to direct all ships scheduled for HC convoys to make for Montreal, and it asked the Canadian and American governments to concentrate troop embarkations for HC ships at that port. It was intended, when the diversion of ships had taken full effect within about three weeks and all loading was taking place at Montreal, to stop sailing the Sydney and New York sections and have the vessels assemble for convoy at Quebec, a short, safe distance down the St Lawrence River. From there, the HC series could sail north of Newfoundland through the Strait of Belle Isle. Although a difficult route to navigate, it was clear of the potential U-boat operating areas and, lying directly on the great circle route, offered the shortest and quickest passage across the Atlantic.[18] Unfortunately, in making these arrangements the Admiralty had misread a message from Admiral Grant in Washington and believed that the U.S. Army was willing to embark troops at Montreal. In fact, as an exasperated Grant hastened to explain, he had merely suggested the move as a contingency without having consulted the Americans, who were now claiming that they could not use Montreal.[19]

While this tangle was being sorted out, *U-156* announced its return to Nova Scotian waters with its usual panache. On the morning of 21 August the crew of the steam trawler *Triumph*, one of only three vessels of this type in the Canadian East Coast fishing fleet, came ashore in boats at Canso. The day before, some sixty miles offshore, the submarine had surfaced and fired a warning shot, which had hardly been necessary as the fishing vessel was immobilized by its trawls.[20] After allowing the crew to get away in their boats, the Germans took over *Triumph*, mounting one or two light guns and bringing aboard a stock of the explosive charges they used to destroy small unarmed vessels. For a brief period, *Triumph* became an efficient raider; well known on the fishing grounds, it had no difficulty in getting close to other fishing vessels before running up the German naval ensign. On its first day of operations, the trawler destroyed four schooners, while *U-156* sank a fifth. Soon the crews of their victims were arriving at Canso, at least one captain expressing his shock at the outcome of what he had initially taken to be a practical joke on the part of the hitherto friendly trawler.[21] As one of *Triumph*'s former crew declared somewhat unnecessarily on his arrival at Port Hawkesbury, *U-156* was 'plying [*sic*] havoc with the fleet of fishing vessels on the Grand Banks.'[22]

During the night of the 20th the submarine and trawler moved to the northeast, evidently keeping about sixty miles off Cape Breton's Atlantic shore. The next morning, again using the trawler as a decoy, the Germans destroyed the French schooner *Notre-Dame de la Garde* and *Sylvania*, a schooner out of Gloucester, Massachusetts. After twenty-four

hours of rowing, eighteen men from the French vessel landed at
Gabarus, where they were picked up by a small local vessel, *M. O'Toole*,
and taken to Sydney. As it approached Sydney, *M. O'Toole* alerted naval
authorities that it did not have proper facilities and needed help with
the 'starving' survivors. *TR 35*, one of the naval trawlers assigned to the
Cabot Strait patrol, received the signal from the examination service
and rushed to pull *M. O'Toole* into a tow alongside, while its galley personnel hurriedly prepared a hot meal for the French sailors. Part of *Sylvania*'s crew, who had had the good luck to be in a motor-driven boat,
landed at Arichat, reportedly the birthplace of the schooner's captain.
The rest of the crew, in another boat, was picked up twenty miles offshore by a passing vessel, which subsequently transferred them to the
government steamer *Restless*, which in turn took them into Sydney.
Meanwhile, many of the survivors of the previous attacks who had
landed at Canso, including *Triumph*'s original crew, were taken to Sydney for rail transport back to their homes. Government censors were
unable to prevent the spread of newspaper reports of these exciting
events along the coast because reporters had staked out the docks and
train station at Sydney.[23]

The *Sydney Daily Post* claimed that *U-156* had instructions 'to give
steamships a wide berth' and to concentrate on the fishing fleet.[24] An
American crewman from a schooner sunk by the submarine stated that
its commander had said that he had orders to destroy the fishing fleet
and that he had sunk six ships that very day.[25] Indeed, *U-156*'s commander had reportedly told the captain of the *Triumph* that 'he was
going to annihilate the entire fishing fleet.'[26] As alarming as this
seemed, one of the main reasons for the attack on the fishing fleet was
that the submarine could not find more worthwhile targets because
most of the substantial vessels were sailing in convoy. During the period
from 18 to 22 August, when *U-156* was operating off mainland Nova
Scotia and Cape Breton, Sydney-based ships escorted coastal convoys
from Sydney to Halifax and from St John's to Sydney, as well as two
departing transatlantic convoys.[27]

The navy responded to the situation as quickly and fully as its limited
resources allowed. Fortunately, an escort group from Sydney that
included the auxiliary patrol ships *Cartier* and *Hochelaga* and two trawlers had arrived at Halifax on the evening of the 20th with a local convoy.
They immediately returned to sea with *Stadacona*, which had been carrying out coastal escort duties from Halifax, and the submarine chaser
division at Halifax followed later in the day.[28] On the morning of the

22nd, the Sydney submarine chaser division joined the search of the fishing banks, having hastily refuelled after escorting HC 14. Another two trawlers left Sydney on the 23rd for long-range patrols, and the Cabot Strait patrols advanced onto the fishing banks immediately seaward of Cape Breton. As a further precaution, two drifters were also sent from Sydney to escort the Strait of Canso ferry. Many more vessels were likely involved in the patrols as well, but the fragmentary records also suggest that, quite properly, escort duties continued to have priority, as did the surveillance of Cabot Strait.[29]

Naval authorities rightly worried that a second submarine, *U-117*, might be following closely behind *U-156* into Canadian waters, but the concerted coordinated attack they feared did not take place. *U-117* passed 100 to 150 miles offshore between 24 and 30 August, attacking four schooners, one of which was later salvaged, and torpedoing a Norwegian steamer between Sable Island and the waters east of St John's. Because of the length of time it took for the crews to get to shore, however, there was no real opportunity for counteraction.[30] *U-156* meanwhile continued north onto the St Pierre banks, where it destroyed five schooners and a small steamer on 25 and 26 August, just '100 miles from this port,' as the *Sydney Daily Post* later reported in some alarm.[31] The Canadian patrols had anticipated this possible movement by the submarine, but their well-targeted deployment ended in major frustration. On the afternoon of the 25th, *Hochelaga* reported seeing *U-156* in the distance, where it was evidently just finishing the work of setting demolition charges in the last of a group of four schooners it had encountered earlier that day. Instead of attacking, *Hochelaga* turned back to get support from the other ships of the division, *Cartier* and two trawlers, which had been steaming in a dispersed formation. By the time the group returned, however, the submarine had understandably disappeared. The incident resulted in a court martial presided over by Captain Pasco, which dismissed *Hochelaga*'s commanding officer, Captain R.D. Legate, from the service for his failure in the face of the enemy.[32]

This event was not reported at the time, but it is hardly surprising in such a small community that it seems to have been public knowledge. Curiously, the *Post* later displayed some sympathy for Legate. Under the headline, 'A Lost Opportunity,' it suggested that if the facts had been known, they 'might have made the public look more charitably on the man.' Legate had been given the opportunity 'to do a big thing. An opportunity that is given to very few men more than once in a life time. It was within his grasp to bring honor not only to himself but to other

members of the service.' Through 'some weakness in decision' Legate
had done the wrong thing. 'It would have meant a lot to the service to
have brought such a prize into Sydney or to have destroyed it. But hesitate, before you blame too harshly the man who failed. The submarine
was heavily armed and a monster in size compared to the little patrol
vessel. The captain hesitated and – he lost. He waited to call for help
and – he lost. He paid the penalty for his action or let us say lack of
action.'[33]

With clear evidence of the presence of two submarines south of Newfoundland, the biggest concern was for the transatlantic convoys due to
sail from Sydney. On 28 August, HS 53, which included twenty-one merchant vessels and the British cruiser *Highflyer*, departed with long-range
local escort provided by four trawlers. The next day the Sydney section
of HC 15, with five merchant ships and the armed liner HMS *Kilodnan
Castle*, sailed with two submarine chasers and the auxiliary patrol ships
Lady Evelyn and *Acadia* as escorts. The convoys got clear of Newfoundland without incident, and the Sydney section of HC 15 successfully rendezvoused with the New York section on the 31st. It was a few hours late,
but only because of heavy fog on the Grand Banks.[34] *U-156* and *U-117*
were homeward-bound by this time – this was actually reported in the
daily press[35] – but the worries of the shore staffs were by no means
groundless. *U-117* had sunk two schooners on the 30th not much more
than 120 miles northwest of where HC 15 rendezvoused a day later.[36]
Meanwhile, the *Post* had reported on the 27th that it was 'generally
believed by marine men here' that *Triumph* had been scuttled by the
Germans, because it had carried only a week's supply of coal and there
had been no recent reports of attacks by it.[37] That conclusion was
almost certainly correct.

With the naval war being fought so close to Sydney, steps were taken
to tighten up security in the coastal communities surrounding the harbour. Blackout regulations were imposed in September, requiring 'all
seaport towns in Nova Scotia' to show no lights after dark. In fact,
according to Pasco, these regulations had been in effect for two years
but had not been enforced in Sydney because 'they would be obviously
ineffective here because of the Steel Company whose lights are blazing
all the night and as they could not be extinguished it would serve no
good purpose to darken the city.'[38] As one sea captain asked, 'what
would be the use of darkened lights in houses and on automobiles in
this city when the glare from the steel plant, when slag is being poured,
can be observed up to thirty five miles at sea?'[39] At the same time, the

astonishing proclivity of the daily press and the general public to report
and speculate on submarine movements was causing mounting concern
in naval circles. On 3 September the chief press censor at Ottawa notified the telephone companies that 'the transmission of information by
telephone regarding the movements of submarines off the coast, or
efforts taken by the authorities to restrict these activities, is forbidden.'[40]

The arrival of the naval war off the Cape Breton coast had its greatest
impact on the communities surrounding Sydney Harbour through the
comings and goings of hundreds of sailors and merchant seamen. Many
men took advantage of the usual diversions, such as dance halls and
church-sponsored social events. In addition, various organizations and
service clubs undertook to provide badly needed social services to them.
The Navy League, for example, opened tea rooms in the old St George's
Rectory on the Esplanade, opposite the yacht club and near the government wharf, in July 1918. There, the members of the Louisbourg and
Yendys chapters of the Imperial Order Daughters of the Empire
(IODE), assisted by large numbers of volunteers from the city, catered
to anyone who needed a hot meal and comfortable surroundings.[41] The
idea apparently originated 'in the hearts of some kind people who saw
so many homeless young men ... wandering about the streets of our city
far away from their own homes and friends, on shore for a few hours or
a few days, then again away to sea facing danger and bearing hardship
cheerfully for king, country, honour, home and they wished that something might be done to make their hours on land a little brighter.'[42] The
'little green gates' were always open, and 'in the garden, where autumn
flowers still jauntily bloom, are seats where one may sit and smoke and
talk.' Inside, in addition to a dining area, there were three rooms with
newspapers, writing tables, and a piano. On cool days fires burned in
the grates. 'These fires are very cheery and comforting and at times convenient for other purposes than keeping people warm (for instance
when electric toasters go awry in the regions of the kitchen and six people are waiting for toast and tea and seven more for poached eggs on
toast).' When the workload proved too heavy for the members of the
IODE, they appealed for help, and 'the service is rendered voluntarily
by the ladies of the town.' As the *Post* put it in its self-satisfied way, 'There
is a decided sense of satisfaction when some one says "Jolly good cooking they give us here." And when a homesick youngster confides in you
that "This is the brightest spot in Sydney for me." Also when we are told
that this is the best tea rooms of the kind they have ever been in because
of the friendly welcome they receive and the way in which they are made

to feel at home. That is what we want – to give those who come to us a touch of home, a bit of help if need, and cheer and to make them feel that our interest in them is sincere and heartfelt.'[43]

Many servicemen and merchant sailors spent their time at Sydney not on leave but in the local civilian and special military hospitals recovering from wounds or illness. Moxham's Castle – a somewhat grandiose romantic mansion built by a former general manager of the Sydney steel plant – had been converted into a temporary war hospital, as had the less dramatic but substantial Ross mansion.[44] While the Ross Memorial Hospital was on the edge of town, facing Wentworth Park, Moxham was some distance out in the country, and so a bus driven by Tom MacGowan of Westmount was made available several times daily to transport soldiers into town for business or entertainment. Mary Isobel MacNeil, who worked at the Moxham Hospital towards the end of the war, later recalled that the men nevertheless 'always managed to be home for meals prepared for them by a good cook.' She referred particularly to a Mrs Lindsay, for whom the soldiers composed a song entitled, 'Don't bite the hand that feeds you.'[45]

On 11 September 'that busy organization,' the Business Girls' Club, organized an entertainment 'for all the soldier and sailor patients of the Ross and Moxham hospitals.' Enlisting the help of 'nearly every automobile owner in the city,' the women took the staff and patients for a drive 'through the scenic sections of the district.' There were eighteen cars in all, and the tour lasted an hour and a half. By the time they arrived back at the Moxham Hospital, a special dinner had been prepared, which was followed by dancing, pool, and billiards. 'From the third floor, where the "mumps" moaned at his captivity, to the lower floor where the "wall-flower" mentally wailed his incapacity, interest was taken in the merry waltzing and soft syncopating.' The dancing began with a set of lancers, and 'Piper Norman Ross was the man of the hour with his pipes and Sergt-Major E.R. Grant with his calling.'[46] The success of this event encouraged more of the same.[47] Here probably is the origin of the much more ambitious program undertaken by service clubs in Sydney during the Second World War to provide highly popular excursions in the most beautiful and restful parts of the countryside for visiting seamen.

Military authorities did what they could to show their appreciation for the welcoming attitude of the community. On 23 September 1918, for example, a Royal Marines military band from a visiting British warship gave a concert at Wentworth Park in the afternoon and another at the

Lyceum Theatre on George Street in the evening. This was, the *Post* reminded its readers, 'the same orchestra which so richly entertained an audience at the Curling rink upon the ship's previous visit to this port.' On that occasion the proceeds had been donated to the Knights of Columbus and local naval services, and this evening's revenues were to be given to the relief fund for British naval prisoners of war and special naval services. The *Post* not only promised its readers an excellent concert, it even quoted Richard Menzies, a local musician and band leader, as saying that 'if the orchestra and the famous Coldstream Guards Band were giving concerts here the same day, he would unhesitatingly make his choice of attendance the orchestra performance.'[48]

The generally welcoming attitude of the civilian population did not prevent the inevitable difficulties that accompany large numbers of sailors and servicemen on leave in ports, but may explain why there was only one major incidence of violence at Sydney during the war. On the evening of Friday, 30 August, 'a disturbance of some proportions' took place on Charlotte Street when a police officer attempted to quieten down some rowdy sailors. One witness reported that 'the officer knocked the sailor down preparatory to putting the cuffs on him and then the trouble started. Reinforcements were called for and when they arrived the sailors were dispersed.' No arrests were made, but 'some of the sailors were reported to have said that they intend "cleaning up"' the following night.[49] True to their word, a crowd of Canadian and American sailors did indeed gather on Charlotte Street near the YMCA on the following night, apparently looking for trouble. Some carried 'improvised clubs and other weapons ... concealed in their clothes.' When the police were unable to disperse the crowd, they arrested an American sailor and took him off to the jail, then on Pitt Street. The crowd followed and the police felt compelled to draw their guns to keep it at bay. 'Sticks, bottles and stones flew in all directions and a billiard ball thrown from the window of the YMCA went through C.P. Moore's shop window on the opposite side of the street. Women, children and civilians followed every move of the crowd and commented, some more emphatically than elegantly, on the different turns of the affair'. A few arrests were made and leave for all American, British, and Canadian sailors was cancelled on Sunday. The police chief, J.B. McCormack, met with naval officers late on Saturday night and again on Sunday, 'as a result of which the chief believes "there will be little if any trouble of this kind [again],"'[50] and the *Post* observed somewhat hopefully that 'interest in the riot apparently waned early Sunday morning when it had been quelled as there has been little talk of it in the streets during the past three days.'[51]

Captain Pasco set up a committee that included representatives of the naval ships in port to investigate the incident. According to Ensign L.B. Sands, the U.S. Navy's convoy officer at Sydney, the American sailors 'strongly claimed ... that the arrests were largely unjustified,' and he accused the Sydney police of 'extreme violence ... in dealing with our men. All U.S. men who have been arrested are variously bruised and cut, and all claim that this was done at the hands of the police either before actual arrest or during the process of the same.' Sands reported further that several American officers, including Lieutenant Commander Walter May, the commanding officer of the USS *Lake Eckhart*, one of the U.S. Navy vessels in port, spoke to McCormack, 'but were unable to get much satisfaction as to the reason for the start of the trouble or in the manner in which the men were treated after arrest.'[52]

Naval authorities were anxious that this incident not damage relations either among the services or between the services and the community, and when the case went to court a few days later, it was agreed that the payment of damages resulting from the riot and an apology by the American sailors who had caused it would officially end the affair. The *Post* noted that 'war conditions are given as the cause of the decision.'[53] Of the Canadian sailors charged, one was fined $5.75 for his part in the trouble, 'having cleared himself of the most serious charges.' Two others were charged with breaking and entering Travis's music store: 'They are alleged to have broken the window of the store and to have stolen a mandolin. The musical instrument was in the hands of one of the men when arrested.' Other Canadian sailors faced several charges, including participating in a riot and carrying concealed weapons.[54] The crews of the two American ships, *Lake Eckhart* and *Lake Benbow*, were assessed $280 for property damage, which consisted largely of broken plate-glass windows. 'As the four men arrested and held in detention by the police were also under various charges in addition to the rioting, such as carrying concealed weapons, burglary, and assault upon an officer, it was decided that this was the best settlement possible, in that should the men have been further tried and found guilty, outside the damage, heavy fines would have been imposed, and perhaps a jail sentence in addition, to say nothing of their absences from their ships, which are already undermanned.'[55]

Although the American naval officers at Sydney agreed that the matter should be resolved as quickly and simply as possible, they were so outraged at the behaviour of the police that they called for an investigation of the force. Sands, recognizing that 'sentiment is more or less against the Navy,' advised against this, an opinion shared by Pasco. McCormack gave assurances that the two police officers about whom the Americans were complaining would be disciplined, and that 'all of his men' would be 'specially ordered to use no harsh or unnecessary measures' on American sailors in the event of future disturbances.[56] The U.S. Navy subsequently restricted shore leaves in Sydney 'to only a limited number of men at a time, and no liberty [was] to extend beyond twelve o'clock, and patrols must be sent ashore to assist in handling our men.' This applied to the crews of the submarine chasers as well as to the warships and naval transports putting into port for convoy.[57]

If the clash in the streets strained relations between the town and the armed forces, the community's heroic response to the arrival of the Spanish influenza clearly demonstrated that the bonds of affection and mutual interest remained strong. The Spanish influenza epidemic that swept the western world, killing an estimated twenty million people, arrived in Sydney on 22 September 1918 when five hundred infected American sailors were brought ashore. With the hospitals obviously unable to handle such numbers, the Sydney Curling Club's rink on George Street and five church halls were put to use as temporary wards to accommodate them.[58] By the 30th the hockey arena was being cleaned and fitted up as well.[59] On 4 October the *Post* reported that there had been four fatalities among the sailors, but that 'these were men who were practically beyond hope when they landed from the ship.' Major Tefft, a U.S. Army medical officer, was in Sydney by the end of the month, and the American Red Cross headquarters at Halifax sent three nurses, two assistant nurses, and two ambulances to help. As well, two American doctors had come ashore with the sick men, and a quartermaster was brought up from Halifax for a few days to help organize the effort.[60]

Tefft spoke 'in the highest terms' of the treatment that the American sailors received at Sydney, 'and of the consideration shown by the regular staff of doctors and nurses' at the Moxham Hospital. 'Everything was done,' he said, 'that could possibly have been done for their comfort and convenience.' Indeed, he thought it 'a big thing that we should have allowed these sick men to land in Sydney and be cared for in the hospitals at much inconvenience and some danger to the people.' According to the *Post*, 'he mentioned very particularly the kindness received from the ladies of the town, the gracious sympathy shown by the President of the Red Cross Society and the practical help given through the members, as well as from private sources. Soup, custards, ice-cream and other delicacies have been sent to the sick men in abundance. They are without a grievance and all unite in their praise of Sydney hospitality.'[61]

The influenza epidemic quickly infected the general population, though it is unclear whether it was spread by the sailors or arrived by other means. Within two weeks the schools, theatres, and churches in Sydney were closed, and telephone service was reported to have suffered because about half of the operators were ill. 'Poor service makes angry subscribers,' reported the *Post*, 'and biting sarcasm coming on top of the extra work they are doing has caused the nerves of a number of the girls to give way.' Although Glace Bay's Board of Health stated on 10 October that the situation was not serious there, it quickly deteriorated, and a few days later Glace Bay closed its schools as well.[62] The situation continued to worsen in Sydney, especially in the Whitney Pier district, and the home of R.F. Randolph, general superintendent of the steel plant, on St Peter's Road, was requisitioned and equipped as an emergency hospital, capable of accommodating up to thirty patients. Because of the shortage of nurses, women who had studied nursing in first aid classes were urged to volunteer their services. A week later, St Andrew's Church hall was taken over by the Admiralty as a convalescent home for recovering sailors.[63]

By the 28th, however, the situation seemed to be improving. The hospitals reported no deaths from influenza over the weekend, and it was announced that the ban on public gatherings would be lifted in a week's time. By now, theatre owners were complaining about how much money they were losing, and it was reported that 'a dance hall holds sessions, all the blinds being drawn and dancing being on the quiet.' The YMCA was also criticized for remaining open during the epidemic.[64] Pervasive as the influenza epidemic was at Sydney, rather surprisingly it did not hit any of the naval establishments and warships severely enough to interfere with operations, and they continued to work at full intensity.

It was well that this was the case, as the knowledge from radio intercepts that another submarine, *U-155*, would be arriving about the middle of September to attack Halifax and St John's traffic, and that two additional submarines had been assigned to North American waters allowed no respite. At the same time, convoy escort duties became increasingly challenging. The diversion of ships destined for HC convoys to Montreal ordered in early August had taken effect by the end of

the month, and the Admiralty was determined that the assembling of
these convoys at Quebec should begin as soon as possible. It was not
only the U.S. Army that dragged its heels. The Canadian navy, stretched
to its limits on the East Coast, was extremely reluctant to accept the
additional responsibility of protecting convoys of high-value ships in the
Gulf of St Lawrence, where the enemy could lie in wait to ambush ships
·as they filed through confined passages. The Mobile Patrol Flotilla,
which was supposed to have been available for the gulf, was now largely
committed to the escort of local convoys between Halifax and St John's
and patrolling the fishing grounds. It had therefore not been possible in
recent weeks to assign more than one or two auxiliary patrol ships to
escort small groups of the most valuable cargo ships within the gulf.
Senior Canadian officers did not want to sail additional valuable cargo
ships through the gulf unless the Allies could provide substantial numbers of fast well-armed warships like destroyers for escort duty there.
Grant and the Admiralty both insisted, nevertheless, that the full HC
convoys should go through the gulf even though the only help they
could provide was fifteen additional drifters and five more trawlers from
the last batches being completed at Canadian shipyards under the British contracts. They also offered to move some of the patrol vessels at
Halifax to Sydney and the gulf, in view of the fact that use of that port by
high-value shipping would continue to diminish for the foreseeable
future. Hastily undertaken planning soon concluded that there should
be new standing patrols, each of four to six drifters and two trawlers – all
equipped with minesweeping gear – in the passage between Gaspé and
Anticosti Island and in the Strait of Belle Isle. Responsibility for organizing the new gulf patrols and for continuous escort of the HC
convoys within the gulf fell on Sydney, increasing the already enormous
burden being carried by its limited facilities and mostly inexperienced
personnel.[65]

Arrangements for HC 16, the first convoy to assemble at Quebec,
were a compromise. In deference to the Americans, and for the last
time, a separate section sailed from New York to rendezvous with the
Canadian section east of Newfoundland. The Admiralty had intended
that the Quebec section should nevertheless sail north of Newfoundland, but agreed to use the southern route through Cabot Strait because
of Canadian concerns arising from the fact that the first few trawlers and
drifters assigned to establish the standing gulf patrols were just beginning to arrive on station.[66]

The Canadian section of HC 16, comprising nine steamers and the

cruiser HMS *Cumberland*, sailed from Quebec early on 4 September.
Because of the rush and repeated changes, everyone had to scramble.
At Sydney, Captain Hose was sharply criticized by naval headquarters for
his failure to respond more quickly to information about the new sailing
arrangements, when in fact they had not yet been sent to him. The only
vessels available to Hose with the speed, endurance, and sea-keeping
qualities needed for extended escort duty in the gulf were the four fastest auxiliary patrol ships, *Lady Evelyn*, *Margaret*, *Stadacona*, and *Canada*.
The best that could be managed on short notice was to have *Lady Evelyn*,
the sole member of the group at Sydney, conduct a continuous patrol in
the vicinity of Bird Rocks, north of the Magdalen Islands, on the 5th,
while *Margaret* and *Stadacona* came up from Halifax to assist. *Canada* was
undergoing repairs and was therefore unavailable. On the 6th the three
vessels met the convoy near Bird Rocks and stayed with it for about six
hours, breaking off at that early point, it seems, because of stiffening
weather.[67]

Meanwhile, the American submarine chaser division had been waiting all day off St Paul Island to lend further support as HC 16 passed
through Cabot Strait. When it became clear late in the afternoon that
the convoy was behind schedule and that, in any event, there was little
hope of making contact in the building storm, the three little vessels
found themselves unable to get back to port and spent a harrowing
night riding out the gale. *SC 51*'s log recorded that the ship was 'rolling
badly. Crews quarters leaking badly. A heavy "sowester" driving us out to
sea. Our auxiliary engine has gone bad and we have only 125 lbs of air
to start engines with. Lazarette deck has over a foot of water on it damaging our food-stuffs.' 'Feeling our way through the storm,' the submarine chasers finally got into harbour late on the morning of the 7th.[68]
The New York and Quebec sections of HC 16 did successfully rendezvous east of Newfoundland on the 9th, but thirty-two hours late because
of dense fog and the appearance of icebergs. After this harrowing
beginning, the convoy was battered by two more gales during the passage to Britain.[69]

Arrangements – and the weather – were more settled for HC 17, the
next medium-speed convoy. This was the first convoy to assemble at
Quebec, and it included fifteen merchant vessels and the armed liner
HMS *Orvieto*. It departed on the morning of 13 September and, having
had proper notice this time, Hose was able to send out the local escort
vessels *Lady Evelyn*, *Margaret*, and *Stadacona* in time to meet it on the
14th off Gaspé. This was the choke point where any submarine entering

the gulf would most likely try to make its initial attack, and the point at which U-boats would devastate several convoys in 1942. Because one of the merchant ships had not been able to keep up speed, *Stadacona* escorted it to Sydney so that it could join a slow HS convoy. The other two patrol vessels carried on with HC 17 through the Strait of Belle Isle, a journey of nearly four hundred miles, before turning back on the 16th.[70]

In addition to serving as the base for the gulf escort, Sydney also continued as a feeder port for the medium-speed convoys. Ships coming from the south, especially tankers bringing petroleum from the Caribbean, saved sea time by putting into Sydney and departing with the local escort vessels for the rendezvous off Gaspé with the main body from Quebec.[71] In the case of HC 18, which sailed from Quebec on the 21st, four merchant ships joined from Sydney, with one of the submarine chasers assisting the auxiliary patrol vessels as far as Gaspé.[72]

The smoothness with which the HC convoys made the passage through the gulf and out the Strait of Belle Isle was no small achievement. 'I am of the opinion,' wrote Admiral Chambers, 'that the difficulties due to the intricate navigation of the lower reaches of the river are very great, and it is only the very high average standard of seamanship which is possessed by the men who navigate these ships in the North Atlantic, which has made this procedure possible.'[73] The difficulty of the Strait of Belle Isle passage may explain why the HS convoys continued to sail south of Newfoundland. With as many as forty-six ships, as in the case of HS 58, which departed Sydney on 8 October, and seldom fewer than twenty-five, these convoys were two to four times larger than the HC convoys. Moreover, their slow ships crept along at about seven knots and were, therefore, much less manoeuvrable than the eleven to twelve knot medium-speed merchantmen.[74]

The local escort of the HS series was stronger than it had been before, and included one, two, or all three of the slow auxiliary patrol ships *Cartier*, *Acadia*, and *Hochelaga*, two to four trawlers,[75] and the submarine chaser division, which had been freed up by the transfer of the HC series to Quebec. In October, the lightly built submarine chasers began to have an increasingly difficult time in the stormy fall weather, but one of their logs, in language not often found in these dry technical records, does display an appreciation of the occasionally pleasant aspects of their work. *SC 51*, escorting the large HS 58 convoy on 8 October, observed: 'Night clear with myriads of stars in the sky and Northern Lights shining brightly.'[76]

With the auxiliary patrol ships almost entirely committed to the ocean convoys, their previous work in the continuing heavy burden of comprehensive coastal escort and special patrols fell to the trawlers. During September, with the transfers from Halifax and delivery of the last of the first batch of thirty-six steel trawlers being built on Admiralty contract in the St Lawrence yards, the strength of the Sydney trawler force grew to twenty-nine vessels. All were armed, which had not been the case in early August. Still, the force was weaker than had been planned because six of the twelve steel trawlers built on Canadian contract and intended for Sydney required modifications to their machinery and remained at Halifax on limited employment. Admiral Grant allocated five of the second batch of Admiralty trawlers to Sydney, but only two were completed in time to do any service in the autumn of 1918.[77] The drifter force under Sydney Command doubled in September to more than forty vessels, with transfers from Halifax and the allocation of fifteen more drifters by Admiral Grant. As well, Grant temporarily lent eight others, which had been ready to depart from Canadian waters for British service, until all fifteen could be fully outfitted. With this help, it was possible to organize the new standing patrols in the gulf and to strengthen the Cabot Strait patrol – but just barely, as many of the new drifters broke down, and the overburdened maintenance facilities were unable to make quick repairs.[78]

The discovery from German radio signals that another submarine was due to arrive in Canadian waters in the middle of September made it impossible to ease off on operations. When a steamer passing Gaspé on the 15th claimed to have sighted a U-boat, naval authorities took the report very seriously, and two ships entering the gulf were given a strong trawler escort from Sydney, even though the main body of the drifter force for the Gaspé patrol was en route from Quebec at the time.[79] This sighting was soon discounted, however, because of a more dependable one from a steamer that had escaped a U-boat after a running gun battle southeast of Sable Island. This suggested that the anticipated submarine was still approaching the area.[80] Nothing more was heard from it for several days, opening the possibility of danger anywhere in the Canada–Newfoundland area. Actually, the submarine, *U-155*, had been laying mines off Halifax and attempting to cut undersea telegraph cables off Sable Island. It did not betray its presence again until the 20th when it sank a trawler southwest of Sable Island, and then disappeared again. What no one knew, of course, was that its commander had decided to disregard his orders to push north of Halifax. Discouraged by the absence of unprotected traffic off southern Nova Scotia – a tribute to the local and ocean convoy systems – he moved south into American waters instead. There was no hint that *U-155* was not prowling south of Newfoundland as ordered until the 29th, when it made an unsuccessful attack on a steamer well out to sea on the latitude of New York. *U-155* hunted for two and a half weeks longer in northern American waters, not being heard from for days at a time and therefore raising the danger of a surprise reappearance in the Canadian area, as *U-156* had done. Meanwhile, German radio signals indicated that two more submarines had been assigned to North American waters, though neither in fact went that far west. Each false warning of activity in the Canadian area demanded a full and quick response, however, allowing no rest to the hard-pressed patrol flotilla crews and their shore staffs.[81]

In these circumstances, the long-promised U.S. Navy seaplane unit that began to arrive at the end of August was most welcome, even though one of its first acts was to erect a flagpole and run up the Stars and Stripes. The 250 American personnel from the U.S. Naval Reserve Flying Corps under the command of Lieutenant Robert Donahue of the U.S. Coast Guard established a temporary base on Indian Beach at North Sydney, a site that, in the words of the base magazine, 'would never be selected as a pleasure or health resort, even in midsummer,' because the ground was 'bumpy' and 'only a few inches above sea level.'[82] The officers were quartered in the Meech house opposite the beach and the Campbell house on Archibald Avenue, while the men were housed in tents provided by the Canadian army until barracks could be built. Rough sheds were quickly erected to protect the valuable equipment, and wooden runways were built for take-offs.[83] As the base magazine put it, 'Uncle Sam, with his usual confidence in his boys, just unloaded on an old sand bar some big boxes of flying boats and accessories – a bunch of men ready and eager for anything – told them to get up in the air and see that Fritzy kept a respectable distance from these ports. On a Sunday morning, these men came out of their tents, and after a hasty breakfast cooked in tents and served in the open by a faithful galley crew, proceeded to carry out the order of their Uncle Sam.'[84] Poor weather made life on the beach miserable for the Americans, culminating in the gale on 7 September that caused the submarine chasers such a terrifying night in Cabot Strait. It flattened the tents and brought the work crews to hasten the construction of the barracks and mess hall. The latter was considered something of a marvel: 'Whoever, since the world began, saw a mess hall capable of seating over one hundred men at a time, built out of crates, and boxes! This the carpenters did – sides, top and bottom, all out of the wreck of the seaplane crates. They made tables and benches also, out of scrap lumber left on the lot. Anyone who has tried to kid himself into believing that he is enjoying a meal with a hard rain washing deep gullies down both sides of his spine, with cold winds driving it through his pores, would appreciate the luxury of this mess hall made of boxes.'[85]

The storm also damaged the first of the Curtiss HS2L seaplanes that the airmen were then assembling. This setback was quickly overcome, and one machine began test flights on the 11th, causing a local sensation. 'Many people,' the Post reported, were 'suffering from sore necks' after rushing about and straining to keep the aircraft in view.[86] Indeed, it declared proudly but with charming innocence, 'it is almost an everyday sight to witness airplanes and seaplanes flying over the town.' Curious Cape Bretoners in the St Peters area were rewarded in November by seeing two seaplanes make a forced landing near the entrance of the canal when one of them developed engine trouble while returning to North Sydney from Halifax – the first Sydney to Halifax flight ever made.[87]

The first operational flights took place on 22 September when two machines each flew for about two and a half hours, covering HS 56 as it sailed. By early October, four aircraft were operational and two more had been delivered, and coverage was possible on the full scale that had been planned. As HS 58 formed up and sailed on the 8th, three aircraft flew a total of five missions that provided constant air cover from 10:00 a.m. until 6:30 p.m., when the convoy was about sixty miles out to sea. One of the aircraft suffered engine trouble that forced it to put down offshore, but, despite the heavy swell, trawlers of the Canadian flotilla soon rescued the airmen and towed in the aircraft before it had suffered any serious damage. Convoy coverage continued on this scale during the rest of October.

The camp at Indian Beach was only a stopgap while work was carried out on the permanent site at nearby Kelly's Beach, where the water approaches had to be dredged and the ground needed filling and levelling.[88] Construction of the buildings, three three-storey units, had to be quick and of top quality because the U.S. Navy had made the early provision of 'permanent' accommodation for its men a precondition for the dispatch of the air units to a northern climate so late in the season. Indeed, the U.S. Navy Department insisted on the use of its standard designs, which featured full concrete basements and steam heating plants. The beginning of this work was delayed until September because the Canadian Department of Public Works, which was responsible for the project, hesitated to award such expensive contracts when tarpaper huts set on sills on the ground and heated by coal stoves were considered adequate for Canadian personnel.[89] Once started, however, progress was rapid even though, as one weekly report put it, 'the very bad.weather has turned the site into a quagmire.'[90] By late October, one of the two planned hundred-man barracks and a large stores building were nearly complete, and the basements of the mess hall and the second barracks were finished.[91] The performances of both the American aviation personnel and the Canadian building contractor's crews were all the more impressive in view of the fact that the influenza epidemic had hit the camp in late September, causing at least two deaths among the Americans.[92] The Department of the Naval Service responded to this crisis by immediately renting several houses in town to enable the American personnel to move out of the unhealthy tents and sheds at Indian Beach.[93]

Relations between the American servicemen at North Sydney and the townspeople seem to have been generally good but, according to the base magazine, 'there have been various unpleasantnesses.' The problems seem to have arisen from 'convivial meetings with the well known little brown jug on the main streets of our adopted town,' which led to brawling between sailors and civilians. According to the base magazine, on one occasion 'the hard knocks that followed ... were taken in great part by the civilians, another instance of it being more blessed to give than to receive.' By the end of October a ban had been imposed on amusements for the sailors, which was not lifted until 8 November, when a dance – the first to be held at the base – took place. Writing at the end of the month, the editor of the base magazine concluded that it was 'certainly a cause for wonder and pleased surprise that any man or group of men could have held their tempers and retained their dignity under the extreme provocations the men have had and all we have to do is hold on to the few remaining days we are in the town.'[94]

The large and costly undertaking at North Sydney and a similar development at Baker Point, near Dartmouth – the origin of the present Canadian Forces Base Shearwater – were intended to lay the foundations for a still greater effort in 1919, when it seemed certain the U-boats would return in greater numbers and operate more aggressively. Additional planned air defences included both self-propelled dirigible and escort-towed observation balloons, and work began to outfit some of the auxiliary patrol ships with winches. The availability of a pier adjacent to Kelly's Beach, from which to service ships towing the balloons, was one of the features that had recommended the site. The base site selected for the dirigible balloons was 'about a mile away from the seaplane site on the opposite side of the town ... on high land above the railway.'[95]

To extend air coverage along the coast and shipping routes, the new Royal Canadian Naval Air Service was planning, with the encouragement of both the Admiralty and the U.S. Navy, to establish sub-stations at Cape Sable, Canso, Cape North, or the Magdalen Islands, and in the vicinity of the Strait of Belle Isle. Although work had not yet begun on any of these sub-stations or the main dirigible bases at North Sydney and Dartmouth when the war came to an end, much preparatory work had been done. Despite delays caused by outbreaks of influenza among the recruits in the new Canadian air service, groups of them were receiving flying training in Britain and the United States at the time of the armistice.[96]

As with the air patrols the Canadian navy regarded the hastily assembled organization at Sydney as merely a beginning, and not a very satisfactory one. An exhausted, frustrated Hose made it clear that his fleet, its supporting facilities, and the haphazard manner of providing and training personnel would all have to be completely overhauled. Most important, better warships were essential, and during the autumn of 1918 senior officers and the Canadian government pressed the British and Americans hard for the provision of destroyer-type escorts in 1919.[97] Fortunately, U-156's inshore operations and the less destructive cruise offshore by U-117 in August proved to be the worst in 1918. Although U-155 arrived in the Halifax approaches in mid-September, it lay low, unable to find much vulnerable shipping, and moved southward. Two small minefields sown by the submarine did no damage before Canadian forces discovered them. Two submarines that followed it did not approach any closer than the central Atlantic.

Victory celebrations in the Sydney area were held as early as 7 November, four days prior to the armistice of the 11th. This reflected the known facts that Allied forces were at the German frontier and that the government of Austria-Hungary had collapsed on the 4th. In Sydney, the 'premature announcement' that 'the Hun had finally crawled into his hole' caused a demonstration 'equalled only by that held when Sydney's originals left for overseas.' At 3:30 p.m. 'the citizens were first stirred by the blowing of a few whistles,' followed by the ringing of the alarm at the central fire station. 'The vessels in the harbor then took up full cry and the populace were convinced that the chase had ended.' Later, 'dozens of leaders took charge of dozens of parades, but there being no chief, it was a disorganized army of celebrants. It was but a few minutes until apparently every one of the hundreds in Charlotte Street had obtained a flag. Every automobile in the street was commandeered and was a moving piece of bunting. Groups of men each carrying a flag marched behind men carrying a larger flag.'[98]

The impromptu celebrations were premature, but not by much. As the European news arrived through the Western Union cable office in North Sydney, people there tended to have the earliest information, despite the pledge of secrecy taken by the telegraph operators. 'Rumors ran riot' in the town on the morning of the 10th when it was reported that an armistice was near, and, again prematurely, in the afternoon that it had been signed: 'practically everyone went to Commercial Street and waved flags in frenzied excitement as over 20 American servicemen marched down the street singing and beating every pot, pan, and noise-maker they had been able to lay hands on. That evening a huge bonfire was set on the Ballast Ground.'[99]

In fact, the rejoicing of the 10th was not entirely without justification, because the new Austro-Hungarian government had signed an armistice with the Allies that day. This news particularly thrilled the area's Italian community, some eight hundred of whom crowded into the town from the neighbouring communities, the Dominion Coal Company providing a special train for those from New Waterford. Led by police sergeant Rannie MacDonald and the Sydney Mines YMCA band, they 'paraded through crowded streets' with 'gaily decorated horses, carriages, [and] automobiles' in 'a moving panorama of flying flags.' The parade ended with a packed meeting at the Lyceum Theatre, at which patriotic speeches were made. W.F. Carroll, former member of Parliament, reminded the audience that John Cabot was an Italian, while J.W. Maddin, now the provincial president of the Great War Veterans Association, called on the people of Sydney to celebrate the coming victory in a responsible manner. 'Now that the end is coming,' he warned, 'there must be no excesses, no rioting nor breaking of plate glass windows.'[100]

The news 'that the huns had finally caved in' was signalled to the citizens of Sydney at 7:00 a.m. on the 11th 'with the blowing of whistles and ringing of bells.' By 7:05 'the first joyful men, women and children had reached Charlotte Street after having hastily thrown on a few garments, and it was not long after until the whole street was packed.' Compared

with the celebrations of the 7th, however, those of the morning of the
11th were quiet, people being 'content to discuss between themselves
the good news and what it means.' At 10:00 a.m. 'a vast throng' of six
hundred people went to Wentworth Park, where an open-air combined
service was held by the churches of the city.[101] At its conclusion, Captain
Pasco called on the crowd to cheer the king, the Allies, the navy, and the
army, 'and at the conclusion three cheers were given for him' as well.[102]

In North Sydney, the announcement of the armistice was 'uproari-
ously celebrated ... A huge procession in which U.S. sailors, the local
military forces, town firemen, societies and headed by the local band
marched through the streets and the kaiser was burned in effigy.' The
celebration ended with a public meeting addressed by Premier Murray
and other dignitaries.[103] Some two hundred people celebrated that
evening at Coxheath, outside Sydney, 'with a huge bonfire' near Perry
Lewis's corner, which could be seen from the town. Patriotic speeches
were followed by refreshments served by Mr and Mrs Lewis.[104]

The real celebrations took place on the 12th. All stores, offices and
schools were closed in Sydney at the request of Mayor William Fitzgerald, and the streets were

> thronged with people, all laughing and care free, although some of them
> look at times very near to tears. Nearly every car and truck, to say nothing
> of the people, is sporting flags of the Allies. Some of the sailors from the
> ships have brought the mascots ashore and have them decorated out with
> flags and occasionally these dogs get rather wrath at some of the civilian
> dogs and there is [sic] a few moments [of] excitement.
>
> A procession of small boys with two men leading them, all carrying the
> flags of the Allies and trailing the German flag along the street attracted
> quite a lot of attention and some of the comment was not altogether favor-
> able to this proceeding. An auto load of returned soldiers made merry with
> bugles and horns, and aroused the cheering of the people by the sounding
> of the different bugle calls.
>
> There is scarcely a house in the city that has not a flag flying from it
> somewhere and some of them have almost elaborate decorations of flags
> and bunting. J.F. Merchant and Sons, Woolworth's and some of the book
> stores have put stands in front of their stores for the sale of flags and the
> sale all through has been so heavy as almost to tax the capacity of the
> clerks.[105]

The victory parade that day was 'the promised largest parade ever held in Sydney,' the *Post* estimating that 'at least' eight thousand people participated in it. Police chief McCormack led it on horseback, followed by civic officials, sailors, and soldiers. The Sydney Mines band was there, as were the pipers' band, the citizens' band, the band of the 94th Regiment, 'and the colored band.'[106] Because this was the first time in two thousand years that Jews had 'fought for the liberation of Palestine,' according to the *Post*, members of that community took part in the victory parade, 'not only to show that they were grateful but also to show their loyalty to the land of their adoption.'[107] The parade concluded with a large public meeting at Wentworth Park where Mayor Fitzgerald and Major Maddin spoke.[108]

At the Sydney Hotel, the city's finest, the guests entertained themselves at the dinner hour with 'speeches, humorous and patriotic, and then they had a piper come in and play some of the stirring music that the pipes can give.' The guests then 'formed up in line and with the piper at their head gaily marched through the hotel dining room, up stairs and down again. Then they sang some songs, had the piper play some more and then it was all over but the shouting. This was so vociferous that the rafters rattled, but it was for peace and victory and "everybody's doing it."'[109]

The crews of the American submarine chasers gave a dance at Hillcoates' Dancing Academy on Charlotte Street 'that will long be remembered by those who were fortunate enough to attend it.'[110] In addition to dancing, there was musical entertainment. Seaman Jones 'sang the American "Rag" songs in an inimitable manner and was compelled to respond to each solo several times. It was a new thing to most of the people there and they enjoyed it immensely.' The dance music was provided by a jazz band and, in the words of the *Post*, 'they certainly did put some "pep" into it.'[111]

At North Sydney the victory celebrations got a little out of hand. Following thanksgiving services at several of the churches and a parade by school children 'in which the firemen and a number of American naval men and aviators took part,' the festivities concluded in the evening with a large bonfire at the ballast ground, where the kaiser was again burned in effigy. Unfortunately, during the evening there were 'several clashes between returned soldiers and American sailors' on Commercial Street, apparently the only serious incidents of violence. 'Several arrests were made of disturbers on both sides of the argument, and the climax was reached about eleven o'clock when some person set fire to a mattress in the jail, which necessitated the calling out of the firemen. Little damage was done by the fire, but one soldier was nearly overcome by the smoke.'[112] In nearby Sydney Mines, the arrival of peace was celebrated 'with dignity and great joy,' the event being heralded 'by the tooting of the whistles' of the Nova Scotia Steel and Coal Company's engines and 'the ringing of bells' on the morning of the 11th. Following a parade in the afternoon, thanksgiving services were held in town churches at noon on the 12th, and the Protestant denominations joined in a service at the Presbyterian church in the evening.[113]

Sydney's Lebanese community celebrated the armistice 'and particularly the liberation of Syria and Mount Lebanon' with its own parade on the 17th.[114] As the *Post* put it, they were 'celebrating the realization of their object for 575 years, freedom from the unspeakable Turk.'[115] Starting from St Joseph's Hall, then on McKenzie Street, the parade wound its way to St Patrick's Church – then known as the Syrian Church – on the Esplanade, where a service of thanksgiving was held, and then it continued on to Victoria Park and finally to the Lyceum Theatre. Following patriotic speeches, the parade re-formed and returned to St Joseph's Hall.[116]

A thrilling, if brief, epoch in the city's history symbolically came to an end on 25 November when the officers and men of the naval base hosted a farewell dance at Sydney's hockey arena to thank the people of the city for their support and hospitality. More than eleven hundred guests, 'everybody and his wife and a lot of others with other peoples' wives,' as the *Post* put it, were in attendance. Special tram cars ran to Whitney Pier at 1:30 a.m. to take home guests from that area, while a special ferry operated from North Sydney for the occasion. 'There were men in uniforms of all descriptions and ranks of the army and navy, American and Canadian alike allied themselves for the evening's fun and all thought of the war was forgotten. People who had not danced for years forgot that they were too old to dance and after sitting out for a time they were seen to move gingerly, at first, about the floor, and then they danced with all their old time vim.' The arena was transformed for the occasion into 'a fairyland' with streamers of coloured lights, flags, and bunting. At the rear was a huge Union Jack, and across the centre was Nelson's famous signal, 'England expects everyone to do his duty' – and as the *Post* said, 'everybody did ... The affair will long be remembered as one of the most enjoyable ever in the city.' At the close of the evening, 'three cheers were given for Mr Menzies and the bandsmen and the members of the Jazz Band orchestra, who gave their services free for the evening. After these one of the navy men called for cheers for Sydney and these were given with a heartiness which left little doubt as to the warm feeling that Sydney holds in the hearts of the men of the navy of both services. On the other hand they have made friends and they have most of them won the respect and liking of the people of the city.'[117]

With the end of the war the Canadian government, like others, was determined to demobilize as rapidly as possible in an effort to bring expenditures under control. On the morning following the farewell dance, Captain James Turnbull, the acting port convoy officer, officially closed the Sydney convoy office, though not before formally thanking the harbour's pilots for 'the smart way in which they have cooperated with me in the sailing of the convoys.'[118] That same day, the naval patrol organization at Sydney received instructions to discontinue operations, and by the end of December most of the flotilla had moved to Halifax.[119] Most of the American servicemen at the North Sydney air base left almost immediately after the armistice, although a few remained until the spring of 1919.[120] The Canadian army garrison was withdrawn by the end of December as well, leaving only small maintenance parties.[121] Sydney's military usefulness had come to an end, at least for the foreseeable future.

chapter eight

The Years of Neglect, 1919–1939

It would appear, both from the point of view of the steel industry and from that of convoy assembly, that the efficient defence of Sydney is of paramount importance to Canada.

Major B.D. Court Treatt, 1936

There was some local concern about the unseemly haste of the military withdrawal. J.C. Douglas, MP, called on C.C. Ballantyne, minister of marine and fisheries, to keep the patrol vessels at Sydney over the winter because many of them required repair work that could be done 'as satisfactorily in Sydney as elsewhere.' It was not to be. Ballantyne thought this 'would not be practicable,' adding optimistically that the British vessels then at Sydney would remain there for the winter.[1] In a different vein, the mayor of North Sydney 'got the wind up' about bombs and ammunition stored at the nearby naval air base, warning that if guards were not posted he would throw them in the river. In fact, as one officer sardonically observed, such action 'would be convenient to us and save trouble,' except for the fact that the navy was required by its agreement with the U.S. Navy to return the munitions to the United States.[2]

The final cleaning up took somewhat longer. Parties from the Halifax garrison dismantled the coastal batteries in the autumn of 1919 and shipped the equipment back to their home station.[3] While the land at Cranberry Head and Fort Petrie was retained as property of the Department of Militia, the buildings at Table Head and Low Point were disposed of and the leases for the land were allowed to lapse.[4] In 1920 the Dominion Coal Company agreed to the department's request that it reserve 'the extremity' of Table Head and 'endeavour to preserve from damage the existing gun position' there. This meant that the company could not 'carry out any operations on this property that might interfere with the immediate erection of defences or curtail the lines of fire from gun positions which might be constructed.'[5] Victoria Park in Sydney was also retained, although little use was made of it during the 1920s. A band shell was erected between the barracks and the Esplanade entrance, and social events attended by Sydney residents took place there.[6]

The town of North Sydney was allowed to use the accommodation buildings at the former air base as a temporary quarantine hospital during an outbreak of smallpox in the winter of 1919. The Royal Canadian Naval Air Service was disbanded immediately after the armistice, and federal control of both civilian and military aviation passed to a newly created Air Board. In the summer of 1920 it began to ship out the six disassembled flying boats and other equipment that the American government had given to Canada and that were stored in the prefabricated sheet-metal hangar at Kelly's Beach that had been completed at the end of the war. When the hangar was being dismantled, high winds caused the partially disassembled roof to collapse, killing one workman and severely injuring another.[7]

Among the documents concerning the wrapping up of operations at Sydney is an evocative letter written by the former militia engineer who had been transferred from Halifax in 1918 to supervise work on the shore defences. Headquarters in Halifax tracked him down in British Columbia in the autumn of 1919 to warn him that, because of his inadequate accounting procedures, he was being held personally responsible for the rent for a miner's house that had been used for accommodations at the Low Point battery. The poor man could only respond that he was unemployed, living in a log cabin, and 'had nothing coming in and a family to support through the winter.' His accounting may not have been as thorough as it might have been in the summer of 1918, he explained, because he had been 'doing better than two men's work, looking after construction of four different forts widely scattered with very poor transportation facilities ... I gave three years of my time to the service of my country,' he concluded, 'and my family went through the Halifax explosion[,] my wife being killed and three children more or less shaken up and all effects lost.'[8] He could do no more and the government could do what it would. It is not known if any further action was taken against this former officer. Certainly, his letter eloquently made the point, often reiterated by other home-defence veterans, that the country ignored their contribution to the war effort and the hard-ships they had endured, while showering adulation and benefits on those who had served overseas.

Meanwhile, the Admiralty had been giving some thought to post-war defence policy. Despite the evident growth of nationalism in the dominions during the war, it proposed in the summer of 1918 that they should contribute to the support of an imperial fleet. As Sir Robert Borden later wrote, 'I reached the unhesitating conclusion that it could not be accepted, as it did not sufficiently recognize the status of the Dominions.' Borden also recalled: 'It seemed obvious that the acceptance of such a proposal would offend the newly awakened sense of nationhood which pervaded the people of Canada.'[9] When other dominions agreed, the Admiralty proposed that Viscount Jellicoe of Scapa, who had just resigned from his position as first sea lord, should undertake a tour of the dominions to review their post-war naval policies and to make recommendations on how these might be coordinated with those of Britain. All agreed to this, with the exception of Newfoundland. Jellicoe set out on a year-long tour which brought him to Canada in November 1919. He did not confine his recommendations to strictly naval issues, but also considered military and air force coastal defences. With respect to Canada, Jellicoe confirmed the view of the Canadian naval and militia staffs that the Pacific Coast now must have nearly absolute priority over the Atlantic. Given the crushing defeat of Germany and its allies, there was no prospect of a major war in Europe in the foreseeable future, and Jellicoe was quick to dismiss any suggestion of a threat from the United States, as most senior British naval officers and policy-makers had done since at least 1900.[10] Halifax, whatever the shortcomings of its defences and base facilities, provided much of what was needed on the Atlantic, not least because of the Royal Navy's great strength there. The situation in the Far East, however, was looking increasingly dangerous in view of Japan's expansionist policies and large-scale naval construction. Japan's distance from British Columbia and crucial interests on the far side of the Pacific made the danger of attack even on the West Coast somewhat remote, but Canadian defences in British Columbia were almost non-existent. The fact that the Royal Navy would be much less able to provide support there than on the East Coast caused Canadian officers to fear, therefore, that British Columbia offered a good approach route for Japanese raiders to strike at ports in the American Pacific northwest, which might provoke the United States into occupying the Canadian West Coast.[11]

Jellicoe agreed with the recommendations of the Canadian services that the coastal fortification system at British Columbia ports should be completed with permanent defences at Vancouver and Prince Rupert, the principal mainland ports and railheads on the West Coast, and at Saint John and Sydney on the East Coast. He also agreed with the Canadian navy's argument that the fixed artillery must be only the final link in a combined coastal defence system whose primary elements would be fast well-armed patrol vessels and aircraft. On the East Coast, the only danger was from hit-and-run attacks by unarmoured, long-range, Japanese vessels. Clearly taking advice from the Canadian staffs, however, Jellicoe argued that Sydney was a special case because both the coal mines and the steel plant were conspicuously situated at the water's edge, providing 'excellent targets for bombardment.' Similarly, the destruction of the large transatlantic wireless station at Glace Bay would be a very serious matter. He therefore recommended that Sydney be designated a defended commercial port and be provided with defences similar to those that had existed during the war, but more substantial and better equipped. These should include three two-gun batteries of modern, long-range, 6-inch guns on the coastal approaches to the harbour, and a field of shore-controlled, moored, anti-ship mines covered by two shore batteries of 4.7-inch guns just inside the harbour mouth. For local naval protection he recommended a full flotilla of eight trawler-minesweepers armed with both guns and anti-submarine equipment, and other smaller auxiliary vessels. These craft could operate from Louisbourg in winter, where he thought another 6-inch gun battery should be established. He also urged the British government to consider defending the Wabana iron mine in Newfoundland, which supplied the Sydney steel plant with its raw material. It seems likely that Jellicoe had been pressed on this point by the Canadian officers, as the protection of the ore carriers from Conception Bay had been a major commitment for the Sydney patrol flotillas in 1918. These proposals for Sydney and Louisbourg, while substantial, were, however, to rank third in priority after the more significant needs of the West Coast and of improvements required at Halifax.[12]

While no doubt militarily sound, the Jellicoe report was a dead letter from the moment it was completed. Deep post-war cuts in defence spending, and the British government's ruling assumption, which Canada willingly accepted, that there would not be another major war within ten years, prevented any improvements. Canada, as British authorities repeatedly pointed out, was safer than any other part of the empire, and the public mood in the wake of the bloodletting of 1914–18 was for retrenchment in defence. Although Sir Robert Borden, the prime minister, was personally disposed to do something, he was exhausted and about to retire. His successor, Arthur Meighen, agreed to a modest rebuilding of the permanent and reserve militia establishment, but this was severely trimmed when the Liberals came to power in the December 1921 elections, having promised further cuts in the armed forces and a return to pre-war normality.[13]

Canada disarmed to a greater extent than any other industrialized nation, with military spending returning to pre-war levels but with the difference that wartime inflation had greatly reduced purchasing power. The navy's post-war fleet included only two destroyers – gifts from the Royal Navy – one of which was stationed on each coast, together with a few of the wartime trawler minesweepers. There were only five hundred personnel in the permanent navy during most of the 1920s, although the reserves were put on a solid footing with a total strength of about one thousand. A new service, the Royal Canadian Air Force, was committed almost entirely to carrying out civil operations on behalf of the government, such as air photography for mapping. The militia's permanent force included only some three thousand personnel, and fewer than forty thousand of the non-permanent active militia received training each year. In this environment, the army understandably placed coastal fortifications at the bottom of its list of priorities.

In Cape Breton, as in most parts of Canada, military activities soon shifted back to pre-war routines, focused almost exclusively on the non-permanent active militia. Because the militia units that had existed in 1914 had no institutional or legal connection with the units that had been raised for the Canadian Expeditionary Force, the militia was reorganized with its re-establishment in the years from 1920 to 1922 with the view to perpetuate CEF units. Accordingly, the 94th Regiment disappeared and was replaced by a new unit, the Cape Breton Highlanders, which carried on the lineage of the 94th but, more important at the time, was designated as the unit that continued the 85th Battalion, CEF, and carried its battle honours. Although the earlier battalion structure of eight small companies had been replaced during the war by one with four larger companies, the location of the companies of the Cape Breton Highlanders at Baddeck, Sydney, Glace Bay, and Northeast Margaree echoed that of the old 94th.[14]

The restructuring of the artillery units also recognized Cape Breton's contribution to the Canadian Expeditionary Force. The 36th Battery

(Howitzer), Canadian Field Artillery, at Sydney Mines, and the 6th (Sydney) Battery, CFA, received the numbers of Canadian Corps batteries in which many men of the region had served. The 6th also continued the lineage of the old 17th (Sydney) Battery. This was not the case with the new 83rd Battery at Stellarton or the 86th Battery at Antigonish. The former had been a CEF unit with which the long-established Pictou County Artillery had no particular link, and the latter had not been a CEF unit but was selected for consistency with the CEF system of numbering that had essentially been adopted for the post-1919 non-permanent active militia artillery. These four batteries were grouped into the 16th Brigade, another number from the CEF system that had no special association with the region. Each of the batteries received eighteen-pounder field guns from Canadian Corps stocks that had been returned from overseas, with the exception of the 36th, which was equipped with 4.5-inch howitzers.[15] Lieutenant Colonel John Angus MacDonald, who had served with the 17th since 1896, was placed in command of the 16th Brigade.

The Department of Militia and Defence, which was combined with the Department of the Naval Service and the Air Board to create the Department of National Defence in 1923, encouraged the participation of CEF veterans in rebuilding the militia. Although most returned soldiers had no interest in further involvement with the military after their wartime service, this does not seem to have been the case in northeastern Nova Scotia and Cape Breton. Still, the slashing of the defence budget by the government dashed the hopes of the General Staff in Ottawa for a greatly expanded and revitalized militia. Most of the units were skeleton organizations that received pay for no more than forty to fifty men per battery or infantry company and for only a dozen or fewer days of training per year. This included summer camp for concentration with other units at Aldershot, Nova Scotia, on several occasions for the Cape Breton Highlanders, and the artillery firing ranges at Camp Petawawa, Ontario, for the field artillery.[16]

Unfortunately, another pre-1914 tradition also quickly reappeared: military 'aid to the civil power.' The Communist revolution in Russia combined with social and economic dislocation aggravated by the war to produce widespread unrest in the post-war years, not only in Canada but in the United States and Europe as well. A memorandum prepared by the General Staff in 1919 concluded that 'the principal peril confronting us at the present moment is the danger of the overthrow of Law and Order in our own Country.'[17] Following the Winnipeg general strike in

1919, which caused profound concern in Ottawa about the danger of Communist insurrection, the army was called out a number of times to provide aid to the civil power. In the three turbulent strikes that resulted from wage roll-backs and restructuring in the Cape Breton steel and coal industries in 1922, 1923, and 1925, the newly created conglomerate, the British Empire Steel and Coal Company, and local authorities called for massive military intervention. A large portion of the permanent force in eastern Canada, from Halifax to London, was committed – a total of one thousand troops in each instance – for periods of up to ten weeks.[18] Understandably, Cape Breton militia units were not called out for service during these periods of difficulty. Even so, Prime Minister W.L. Mackenzie King found himself 'unable to understand wherein it has been necessary to send to Cape Breton the numbers of troops that are there at the present time.'[19] He subsequently amended the Militia Act so that troops could be called out only on the authority of a provincial attorney-general, rather than a county court judge.

Sydney did continue in a minor way as the guardian of the St Lawrence in the 1920s and 1930s, but the enemy was now demon rum. The adoption of prohibition by eight of the nine provinces and the federal government during the war, then by the United States in 1920, inevitably resulted in a great increase in smuggling, with the nearby islands of St Pierre and Miquelon playing a prominent part. As a result, the Customs Preventive Service of the Department of Customs and Excise (in 1927 renamed the Department of National Revenue) greatly expanded to thirty-eight vessels and nearly 250 personnel, with headquarters at Halifax, and some of the vessels that had served in the wartime anti-submarine flotilla returned to patrol duty in a quite different role. At North Sydney there was a flotilla of four or five small vessels, including at least one rum-runner that had been seized, to keep watch around Cape Breton's northern and eastern coasts, while Canso was the base for the preventive patrols that included the mainland's eastern shore.[20]

In a rationalization of government services, the Customs Preventive Service was transferred to the Royal Canadian Mounted Police in 1932 and became the force's marine section. The service was reformed through improvements in training, the employment of crews year-round instead of a portion being laid off in the winter, the replacement of some of the older craft, the establishment of close links with the navy for ship maintenance services, and the secondment of two naval officers to advise the RCMP commissioner in Ottawa and the officer commanding Maritime Provinces District in marine operations.[21] Virtually to a man, the members of the service enrolled in the Royal Canadian Naval Reserve, the category of the reserve for professional seamen who received courses at Halifax in naval equipment, discipline, and procedures. The vessels were earmarked for transfer to the armed forces in the event of war, some for naval duty and others for rescue and support services for maritime operations by the air force. Thus, the little RCMP-manned anti-smuggling flotilla based at North Sydney would become the first waterborne component of Cape Breton's local defences in 1939.[22]

Another new feature of the reorganized preventive operations on their transfer to the RCMP was the introduction of air patrols by the RCAF. Aircraft could keep tabs on the mother ships that lingered outside the twelve-mile limit of territorial waters, look for evidence that liquor was being off-loaded to small craft for the run in to the coast, and alert the RCMP so that marine section craft and automobile patrols on shore could be deployed where they had the best chance of making arrests. During the 1933–5 navigation seasons, one float-equipped RCAF Fairchild 71 aircraft – a single-engine utility machine of the type that characterized the 'bush pilots in uniform' civil operations of the air force in the 1920s and 1930s – operated from Sydney. There was no question of attempting to refurbish the Kelly's Beach facilities for this small detachment, as the former naval air station at Dartmouth was reopened seasonally to service the aircraft on preventive patrols in the Maritimes. The aircraft assigned to Sydney, therefore, flew from a base established near the bridge at Henry Lewis Point at the mouth of Sydney River, a site that offered sheltered waters, level ground, and proximity to a main road.[23] Shore facilities developed during 1934 included two metal-clad sheds, one of which housed a 100-kilowatt radio transmitter for point-to-point communication with RCAF headquarters in Halifax and RCMP cruisers on patrol.

Meanwhile, smugglers were converting from schooners to powered craft with radio transmitters, and so they could communicate with their colleagues on shore in order to evade the police and move quickly when necessary or when opportunity presented itself.[24] The powered vessels, moreover, enabled the rum runners now to sit some seventy-five miles out to sea, beyond the area that could effectively be covered by the aircraft then available in the RCAF. As J.H. MacBrien, the RCMP commissioner, explained to Air Commodore G.M. Croil, the senior air officer, 'at that distance they are able to get in in a few hours under the cover of darkness and out again before daylight. The air patrols do not cover an area more than twenty-five to forty miles to sea, and, therefore, are usually unable to report the presence of rum runners.'[25] For this reason, and also as an economy measure, the Sydney detachment ceased operations and the little base at Sydney River was not reopened in the spring of 1936, though it remained in existence as an emergency mooring base.[26] Sixty-six patrols had been flown in 1935 and, while smugglers had been 'very active at the first of the season,' the level of activity had declined as the season progressed, and 'during the summer very few boats were spotted.'[27]

Later that year the RCAF withdrew from preventive work to concentrate on military training activities.[28] Although the development of seaward air patrols in cooperation with surface vessels prefigured what the maritime components of the air force would be doing on a large scale in the event of war, much more concerted preparations were needed to convert the air force from civil work into a true military service. As part of the government's works scheme for unemployment relief during the Great Depression, the Department of National Defence renovated the air station at Dartmouth for year-round operation in 1934. Aircraft and personnel from Ottawa that had previously come to the Maritimes for the seasonal operations were then assigned to Dartmouth to create 5 (Flying Boat) Squadron. This, and the creation of a similar unit on the West Coast, was one of the first, very modest, endeavours to rebuild the armed forces in light of the darkening international situation.[29]

Coastal defence was again emerging as a priority for Canada, but the focus was once more on the Pacific. From the time of the Japanese invasion of Manchuria in 1931 until late in the decade, the Far East seemed increasingly the most likely trouble spot that might ignite a general war. Serious differences between the United States and Britain over policy towards Japan, and the continued relative decline of British power in the Pacific since the 1920s, had sharpened Canadian fears about Anglo-American tensions and possible American intervention on Canadian territory if something were not done to secure the British Columbia coast. Thus, the army proposed a modest program to build coastal fortifications, as Jellicoe had recommended, giving priority to the West Coast, but the onset of the depression resulted in further reductions in defence spending that killed the idea for the time being.[30]

Only in the latter part of the decade did the question of military security begin to outweigh financial concerns. By 1935, when King returned to office as prime minister, it was clear that there were dangers in Europe as well as in Asia. Germany, under Adolf Hitler's leadership, was rearming and openly challenging the post-war settlement, while Mussolini's Italy had just invaded Abyssinia (Ethiopia) in defiance of the western powers and the League of Nations. King allowed some small increases in the defence budget in 1936, and that summer asked the armed forces to prepare a five-year rearmament plan, giving priority to coastal defence. The staffs of the three services, who had been planning extensively only for the defence of the Pacific Coast, now addressed the Atlantic in a comprehensive way for the first time since 1919.

In applying British strategic assessments, the Canadian staffs rated the likelihood of a possible attack on the Atlantic Coast as only marginally lower than for the Pacific. Germany's renascent navy, although still small, included powerful, fast warships that had been designed for distant raiding operations, as well as a new generation of submarines. Canadian waters, as experience in the First World War had shown, would be a likely target for German long-range strikes. Specific threats included attacks on shipping and shore bombardment by a single eight-inch gun cruiser, a merchant cruiser mounting 6-inch guns, or by one or two submarines. There might also be attempts by disguised armed merchant ships or small motor torpedo boats of a type that could be carried across the ocean in larger vessels to rush harbours. In addition, there might be bombing of ports by as many as ten ship-carried aircraft, or transatlantic raids by bomb-carrying Zeppelin dirigibles. There was also the possibility of sabotage by agents or of a raid by an armed party that landed from a warship or disguised merchant vessel.[31]

Planning for the defence of the West Coast had already reinforced what had been learned from 1915 to 1918 and in the studies undertaken with Admiral Jellicoe in 1919 about the importance for Canada of being able to mount its own naval and air patrols. The planning had also made clear the hard choices and challenges faced by the fighting services as a result of the country's virtual disarmament since 1919: only token forces were available and the equipment, with few exceptions, was a full generation out of date. Although the navy had acquired two modern fleet-type destroyers in 1932 and would get four more in 1937 and 1938, there was little chance, given the great expense of warships and the length of time needed to train competent crews, that the service could be sufficiently expanded to provide adequate coverage of even one coast. Aircraft, by comparison, could be manufactured in quantity more readily, and their small crews trained more quickly. For this reason, the Royal Canadian Air Force was assigned a leading role in coastal and shipping defence planning, even though the service was just beginning to be converted from civil operations.[32]

Because it would be wasteful to require expensive and scarce aircraft and warships to guard their own bases and other important coastal areas, army garrisons and coast artillery continued to have an important role in the defence thinking of all maritime nations. This was especially the case in Canada, where the naval and maritime air forces were so manifestly unequal to the task of reconnaissance of the country's vast coastlines. Ill-equipped and ill-trained as the Canadian militia was, it was nonetheless the only service that had a comprehensive national command system and the resources to provide at least some military presence at the most important sites on both coasts. That said, the existing coast artillery at Halifax and Esquimalt was short of range and firepower now that heavy naval guns could shoot as far as 32,000 yards and the latest warships could race in to attack at speeds of up to thirty knots.[33]

None of the Canadian services had forgotten the lessons of the First World War about the strategic place of Sydney. Indeed, a navy planning exercise in 1935 concluded that, as the main base for the protection of the heavy steamer traffic from the St Lawrence, the port would again be at least as important as Halifax during the summer and autumn months in the event of another Atlantic war.[34] Later that year, the air force staff expressed the same view with respect to maritime air reconnaissance.[35] For its part, the General Staff prepared an historical study that chronicled why and how coast artillery defences had had to be improvised under difficult circumstances in 1917 and 1918.[36] Having had no significant experience with modern coast artillery, however, the General Staff in Ottawa invited a British specialist, Major B.D. Court Treatt, Royal Artillery, to assist in designing a defence scheme. Treatt visited both coasts in the autumn of 1936 and, using the studies and advice provided by the three Canadian services, drew up detailed recommendations for each defended area. His report, completed in December 1936, after having been reviewed by the Canadian staffs, formed the basis for much of the coast artillery defence development that would take place up to the end of the Second World War.[37]

With respect to Sydney, Treatt argued that there were two reasons to defend it, namely the steel plant and the nearby coal mines, 'and the fact that it is a convoy assembly port.' The steel industry was 'of the utmost importance' because its annual output of some 400,000 tons constituted 35 per cent of total Canadian production, 'and it is not too much to say that, in time of war, an interruption in the Sydney steel supply would completely dislocate the Eastern Canadian munitions industry.' At the same time, 90 per cent of the coal required by the steel plant came from the nearby mines that dotted the coastline from MacRae Point in the east to Little Bras d'Or in the west.[38] The coal was also used to fuel shipping at Sydney, Halifax, and Saint John, for the railways, and for domestic use, in addition to being exported. Meanwhile, the iron ore and limestone used by the steel plant came from Newfoundland, and the power for both the plant and the mines was supplied mainly by three thermal power plants situated along the coast near Glace Bay, New Waterford, and Sydney Mines. Finally, nearly all the steel produced by the plant for use in Canada was shipped by rail to mainland destinations via the ferry at the Strait of Canso. Clearly, then, Sydney was an important industrial centre that required protection in wartime. In addition, Sydney would be 'the main Atlantic convoy assembly port for Canada' during the summer months, 'and will handle the whole of the St Lawrence traffic' in the event of war. As well as shipping that would be destined for Europe in wartime, it would be necessary to protect the ships carrying steel being exported from Sydney and shipping carrying coal to other Canadian ports.[39]

Treatt concluded that 'the efficient defence' of Sydney was 'of paramount importance' to Canada. Indeed, he argued, it was 'doubtful if even the two Naval ports ESQUIMALT and HALIFAX – in the absence of any considerable Naval forces based on them – take precedence.'[40] This seemed a rather substantial qualification, as Halifax at least could surely be expected to have a 'considerable' naval force based there in wartime. Nevertheless, Treatt and the Canadian staffs agreed that Halifax and Sydney should both receive a full layout of modern coast artillery defences. In a major departure from Jellicoe's earlier recommendations, Treatt's report included proposals for two long-range, counter-bombardment batteries at Sydney, one battery with three 9.2-inch guns in the vicinity of Oxford Point, and a second battery with three lighter but faster-firing 6-inch guns near Lingan. All of these weapons were to have the latest high-angle mounts that, by allowing a maximum firing elevation of thirty-five degrees for the 9.2-inch guns and forty-five degrees for the 6-inch guns, nearly doubled their ranges to 29,000 yards and 21,000 yards respectively.[41] Together, these two batteries would be able to keep a modern cruiser beyond effective gun range on a front of nearly fifty miles, from St Ann's Bay in the west to Mira Gut in the east. With the purely visual (i.e., telescopic) fire-control instruments available in the 1930s, however, long-range armament could operate effectively only by day and in clear conditions; hence the danger of an attempt to rush into the harbour under cover of darkness or murky weather by fast-moving surfaced submarines, motor torpedo boats, or armed merchant vessels. To guard against this form of attack, Treatt recommended that Sydney Harbour be ringed by five artillery batteries, whose armament would include fifteen high-powered searchlights.

Three of the proposed works – Chapel Point and Fort Petrie close to the entrance of the harbour, and Point Edward within it – were to be armed with older, low-angle mounted 6-inch and 4.7-inch guns that were available in Canada and that were still efficient for a relatively short-range close-defence role. In addition, there were to be two small anti-torpedo-boat batteries, one on each side of the harbour outside the North and South Bars, the projected location of the anti-submarine nets. One would mount a pair of the older twelve-pounder guns that could fire at a rate of twenty rounds per minute, while the other would have the latest twin-barrelled six-pounder duplex that could pour out seventy rounds per minute. The purpose of these two batteries was to create a killing zone of high-volume fire that would be especially effective in stopping fast craft that attempted to destroy or skim over the anti-submarine boom.[42]

The selection of Chapel Point for a substantial harbour entrance battery requires some explanation. The site is nearly a mile and a half in from Sydney Harbour's western headland, the terrain of which limited the arc on which the guns could fire seaward. Because the Fort Petrie battery's geographical orientation was seaward, it would be able to cover virtually the whole of the outer approach, and particularly the vicinity of the western headland. The value of a battery on Chapel Point was that its guns could bear directly across the harbour entrance, including the 'dead' water under Fort Petrie.[43] What was more, guns at the Chapel Point site, unlike those at Fort Petrie, could also sweep round to fire down into the harbour. This was especially important to Treatt, who was worried about the security of the inner harbour against rush attacks. Approximately two miles across at its most narrow point, the main harbour was too wide for the short-range quick-firing batteries planned for the North and South Bars to give fully effective coverage, and the Point Edward battery site was too far back to catch vessels attempting to rush the anti-submarine nets with fully effective fire. It was Chapel Point's immediate command of the harbour entrance that made it the logical choice for the important task of supporting the unarmed small steamers of the navy's examination service, which, as in 1917–18, would stop each incoming merchant ship to confirm its identity.

Defences planned for the rail ferry and terminals at the Strait of
Canso were on a smaller scale, as it was highly unlikely that a major warship would risk entering those confined waters.[44] There would be two
batteries of 4.7-inch guns, each on the high ground on the western
(mainland) side of the strait, one (Beacon battery) overlooking the
northern entrance, and the other (Melford battery) overlooking the
southern entrance. There would also be a pair of long-range searchlights on the shore beneath each of the batteries, and the navy would
provide an examination vessel at each end of the strait and assign anti-
submarine patrol vessels. Although the Canadian services agreed that it
would be desirable to have anti-submarine nets at each end of the strait,
this ambitious project was considered a low priority after the provision
of nets at Halifax and Sydney.[45]

All of the fortifications were to be permanent structures of reinforced
concrete set into the ground for protection against bombardment.
Thus, these defences were not intended to be an extemporized
response to the immediate international situation but rather to provide
long-term security in a world in which the only constant appeared to be
the emergence of aggressive states armed with ever more powerful long-
range naval and air weaponry. Modern technology and the decline of
British naval supremacy were rapidly eroding Canada's traditional security that resulted from its geographical isolation from the political hot-
beds of Europe and Asia.

In the development of bases, the navy gave priority to its principal –
and inadequate – stations at Halifax and Esquimalt. Thus, its plans for
Cape Breton did not go beyond the installation of anti-submarine nets,
the earmarking of government and civilian ships that would be
equipped for local defence duties, and the designation of officers for
key appointments among those still serving or retired but willing to be
called back in the event of war.[46] The intention – and it was a reasonable one for the modest naval expansion projected until the unher-
alded crisis of 1940 – was to make do with the existing port facilities at
Sydney for running replenishment and repairs. For major refits and
repairs, ships could be dispatched to Halifax and other shipyards in
eastern Canada.[47]

The resources on which the air force could build at Sydney were
much less suitable. The civilian aviation facilities of the Cape Breton Flying Club were typical of what was then available in the Maritime provinces. The club had been formed in 1928 and opened an air strip a year
later.[48] It leased the land from one of its members, Dan MacMillan, a

farmer whose land abutted Grand Lake Road near Reserve, although it is doubtful if MacMillan ever received more than the first year's rent.[49] All the construction work had been done by volunteers, the town of Glace Bay had lent bulldozers to clear the land, and MacMillan lent the club a barn to use as a hangar.[50] There had not been a great deal of activity during the 1930s, aside from flying lessons and occasional landings by visiting aviators, until the government began to be concerned about coastal defence towards the end of the decade.

The existence of such air strips, as primitive as they were, in strategic locations in the Maritimes allowed the Air Staff early in 1936 to decide on the procurement of wheeled planes as the principal type of aircraft for reconnaissance on the Atlantic. These had better airborne performance than flying boats, were much easier to service, and could operate when ice or rough water conditions kept flying boats idle. This was a sound decision, although it seemed scarcely realistic to hope that the latest types of heavy land aircraft could carry out sustained operations from the meagre municipal landing fields. The government's request in the summer of 1936 for rearmament proposals allowed the air force within months to urge what was really needed: the construction of all-weather, hard-surface aerodromes for bomber squadrons at Yarmouth, Dartmouth, and Sydney. There was still an important role for flying boats in areas where the coastal terrain made the construction of aerodromes impossible. On the East Coast, this was the case at the important choke points for shipping in the Gulf of St Lawrence, at Gaspé, and in the Strait of Belle Isle. The intention was to use the existing flying-boat station at Dartmouth and the mothballed station at North Sydney to provide the necessary support for these isolated detachments and any other areas where it might be necessary to send flying boats.[51]

Making plans was one thing; finding the money and the industrial capacity to realize them was another. The military wanted defence spending nearly quadrupled to some $70 million a year to carry out its five-year plan, which included the tri-service programs on both coasts and the organization of a two-division army mobile force, with supporting air force bomber and fighter squadrons. The government, for political reasons, was hardly prepared to go that far and limited the forces to $35 million in each of the 1937–8 and 1938–9 fiscal years. As the prime minister put it, 'it is not what we might wish to do but what we can hope to do, without provoking political and social unrest.'[52] The air force was given top priority for new money, with the navy a distant second, and the militia last, reflecting the government's interest in aviation as an especially flexible military instrument. In addition to providing effective home defence, air forces could also be sent to assist Britain in overseas combat theatres, should the need arise, without incurring the hideous losses suffered by the Canadian Expeditionary Force in the First World War. Wherever squadrons might serve overseas, moreover, much of the Canadian war effort would remain at home, producing the aircraft and training air crews. The government thought this appropriate and useful for a vast continental country that would need a strong aviation sector for future national development.[53] King had no intention of revisiting 1917.

The effect of the ceiling on spending was to limit the naval and militia coastal defence projects to one coast only, which military and political leaders agreed must be the Pacific. Thus, the only important undertaking in the Maritimes was the construction of aerodromes for the air force. At Sydney, surveys undertaken in 1937 selected a site near Reserve close to, but not the same as, the Cape Breton Flying Club's air strip. Work began in the following year to clear and grade the ground for three four-thousand-foot runways.[54]

In the summer of 1938, as German foreign policy became more aggressive, the heads of the three armed services warned the government that the ceiling had to come off defence spending to speed up the army and air force programs and to embark on an ambitious naval expansion to triple the force of six modern destroyers thus far provided for. The government rejected these demands but, following the war scare caused by the Munich crisis in September 1938, it did agree to increase the defence budget in the 1939–40 fiscal year.[55] The $60 million ultimately provided, though impressive by Canadian standards, fell far short of the basic $70 million and additional virtually open-ended allotments for the procurement of weapons and equipment that the military chiefs believed was the base minimum. Once again, the militia bore the brunt of the trimming, including all of the funding requested for the construction of fortifications in the Maritimes. Advice from Britain that three 7.5-inch guns would be available for delivery in 1940 won back some funds for their purchase and for building installations for them, but the guns were allocated to Saint John rather than Sydney because that port's open approaches were more vulnerable to attack.[56]

The major military activity at Sydney during the last year of peace, other than work on the runways at Reserve, was to prepare the militia for coastal defence duties as well as this could be done under the circumstances. The inability to acquire coast artillery posed a particular problem. There was no question of attempting to produce the precision-built, highly specialized equipment in Canada, and British industry, facing rapidly escalating demands from the whole empire, could not begin delivery of even the West Coast armament that had been ordered in 1936 until 1940 or later. American companies could do little better. In late 1937 and early 1938 the militia staff therefore designed a stopgap interim coastal defence plan. Pre-1914 low-angle guns, including those that had been mounted at Sydney in 1917 and 1918, were taken from naval stocks and secondary battery positions at Halifax and Quebec City and allocated to coastal defence positions, with top priority being given to the new fortifications nearing completion on the West Coast. The second priority was for the emergency installation of guns at Sydney and Saint John in the event that war suddenly broke out in Europe. Armament earmarked for Sydney – two naval 6-inch guns for Fort Petrie, a pair of 4.7-inch guns for each of Chapel Point and Point Edward, and a pair of old single-barrelled naval six-pounders for each of the anti-motor-torpedo-boat batteries at North Bar and South Bar – would allow improvisation of the five close-defence batteries proposed by Treatt. Two pairs of naval 4-inch guns were available for the Strait of Canso batteries.[57]

The militia had to undergo another major reorganization and expansion to provide suitable, adequately manned, coastal defence units. Since 1919, based on experience gained on the western front during the First World War, the goal had been to create a framework for the mobilization of large field forces. By the late 1930s the General Staff was convinced, despite the reluctance of the government to agree with the assessment, that it would again be necessary to send a substantial field army overseas in the event of war. Coastal garrisons also had to be raised on a much larger scale than had been projected in 1919, however, and Cape Breton inevitably posed special problems. Because there were two widely separated defended areas to garrison, no economies could be achieved through common services. As well, the expansion of coal and steel production to meet war needs would make many men in the area unavailable to the armed forces. The only solution was to convert existing units from field force to coastal defence roles and to assign additional units from mainland Nova Scotia to help.[58]

Mobilization planning undertaken by the district command in Hali-

fax in 1938 designated the Cape Breton Highlanders as the infantry garrison for Sydney, the Pictou Highlanders for the Strait of Canso, and
elements of the North Nova Scotia Highlanders (Machine Gun) to help
out at both places.[59] Effective 15 June 1938, the 16th Field Brigade,
Royal Canadian Artillery, of northeastern Nova Scotia and Cape Breton,
less the 83rd Field Battery at Stellarton, became the 16th Coast Brigade,
Royal Canadian Artillery. Major J.J. MacKenzie of Pictou County, the
forty-eight-year-old former commander of the 83rd Battery and a decorated veteran of the Canadian Corps artillery of the First World War,
came out of partial retirement to command the new brigade. At the
same time, its constituent units, the 6th (Sydney) Field Battery, the 36th
Field Battery (Howitzer) of Sydney Mines, and the 86th Field Battery of
Antigonish were all reorganized as heavy batteries to man, respectively,
the planned works on both sides of Sydney Harbour and at the Strait of
Canso.[60]

From the middle of June to early August 1938 a permanent force
instructor from Halifax travelled the circuit between Sydney, Sydney
Mines, and Antigonish, teaching basic coast artillery courses to the personnel. Later in August, nearly 180 brigade personnel went to Sandwich
battery at Halifax for fifteen days of training and firing practice.[61] In the
middle of September the district staff at Halifax shipped one of the
6-inch naval guns designated for Fort Petrie to Sydney, where it was set
up in a specially constructed shed near the armouries at Victoria Park to
allow continued training. At the same time, one of the 4-inch naval guns
allocated for the Canso defences was installed in the 86th Battery's
armouries at Antigonish.[62]

At the end of March 1939, utilizing the last of the 1938–9 funds, crews
from the permanent force garrison at Halifax moved a single 4.7-inch
gun to Chapel Point. It was shipped by rail to the Jacob siding,[63] from
which point, with help from the men of the 36th Heavy Battery and
local labour, it was erected by early April on a simple flat concrete platform of the type intended for the emergency installation of interim
armament. In the following weeks, a wooden shed was built over the
gun to protect it from vandalism and to allow the men of the 36th to
train under cover. This modest installation was the first of the new coast
artillery batteries on the Atlantic, and the only new position to be put
into anything like operational condition before the outbreak of hostilities in Europe.[64]

Other specialized coastal defence units were organized from existing
ones. The 9th Field Company, Royal Canadian Engineers, a unit that

supported field forces with bridge construction, field fortification work, and other technical services, had been assigned to Nova Scotia in the early 1920s, but had been dormant for a decade. After a paper transfer from Halifax to Glace Bay, it became active in the early 1930s, presumably because people in that mining community who had suitable engineering experience took an interest.[65] In the summer of 1938, twenty-nine of its members went to Halifax for fifteen days of conversion training in the operation of coastal defence searchlights, fortress construction, and maintenance services.[66] Meanwhile, the organization of British coastal defences, on which Canada's was modelled, was changing. Searchlights were to be turned over to the artillery, which made sense in view of their employment as the eyes of the coastal guns and the simplicity of operation of the new lights compared to the older models, which had required a good deal of specialized skill.[67] Canada followed the British lead, and orders were issued late in the spring of 1939 to convert the 9th Field Company into the 9th (Cape Breton) Searchlight Battery, Royal Canadian Artillery (Coast Defence). At the same time, a small new unit, the 3rd Fortress (Electrical and Mechanical) Company, Royal Canadian Engineers, was created to carry out other engineering work at Sydney and Canso.[68] That summer nearly one hundred men from what was still essentially the old 9th Field Company went to the Halifax fortress for further training, together with nearly 250 from the 16th Coast Brigade.[69]

The militia was much less able to improvise anti-aircraft artillery defences, as interim armament was almost non-existent. In the late spring of 1939, the 83rd Field Battery, RCA, of Stellarton, was converted to the 7th Anti-Aircraft Battery, RCA, and the 84th Field Battery, of Yarmouth, was converted to the 6th Anti-Aircraft Battery, with the intention that they would be assigned to Sydney and Canso in the event of mobilization. Although these units went to Halifax for camp training in their new role in the summer of 1939, the obsolete equipment available allowed them to cover only the barest rudiments.[70]

Meanwhile, the air force planned to station a bomber squadron at the new aerodrome at Sydney.[71] Organization of the unit had not even begun when war broke out, and in August 1939 preliminary grading of the three runways was only about two-thirds complete. The contractor, Standard Paving Maritime Limited, was meeting the schedule laid down according to the availability of funds, and a departmental honorary advisory committee made up of notable former airmen, including Air Marshal W.A. (Billy) Bishop, VC, properly directed its criticism at the government. In their view, such cautious piecemeal contracting methods offered no inducement to firms engaged in defence work to purchase better equipment or to press on quickly.[72] The same could have been said about much of Canada's rearmament effort, and, rather remarkably, the outbreak of war a few weeks later did nothing immediately to change the situation.

chapter nine

Improvising Defences,
1939–1940

*For the time being it is considered that the defence of Halifax and the local sea
area is more important.*

Captain H.E. Reid, 1939

Canadian mobilization for the Second World War began quietly on
22 August 1939. On that date, British authorities responded in part to
Hitler's threats to Poland by sending out the first of a series of short
coded telegrams that activated the war books of the self-governing
dominions and dependencies of the empire. The summer schedules of
the British cruisers *York* and *Berwick* had already brought them to the
vicinity of Nova Scotia, their war station. Memories of the panic about
German raiders that had stopped North Atlantic shipping in 1914 and
of the vital role Nova Scotian ports had played in organizing the
defence of shipping were still fresh. The Canadian government, while
reserving the right to declare war independently, quickly agreed that its
armed forces should follow the script that had already been carefully
prepared in cooperation with British forces. As it happened, the navy
was participating with the Royal Navy in a global radio communications
exercise when the first alerts were sent out from London on the 22nd,
so the earliest measures for passing information on the location of
friendly and potential enemy shipping unfolded almost automatically.

Events moved into high gear on the 25th. Britain responded to the
announcement of Germany's non-aggression pact with the Soviet Union
that freed it to invade Poland by partially mobilizing at the 'precautionary stage,' and Canada followed suit. In Cape Breton, the miners at

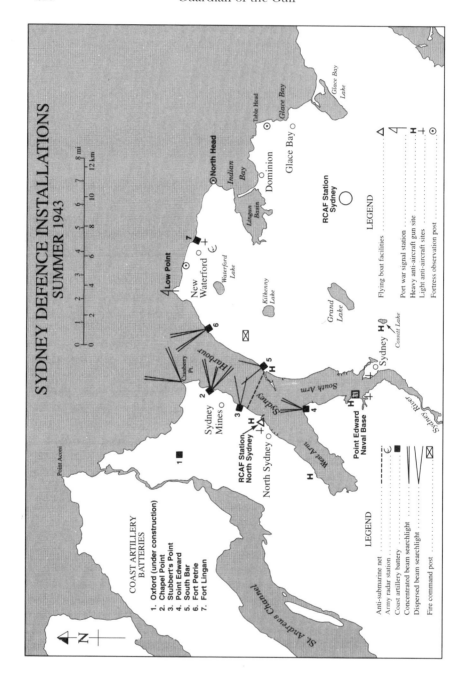

SYDNEY DEFENCE INSTALLATIONS
SUMMER 1943

COAST ARTILLERY
BATTERIES

1. Oxford (under construction)
2. Chapel Point
3. Stubbert's Point
4. Point Edward
5. South Bar
6. Fort Petrie
7. Fort Lingan

LEGEND

Anti-submarine net
Army radar station
Coast artillery battery
Concentrated beam searchlight
Dispersed beam searchlight
Fire command post

LEGEND

Flying boat facilities
Port war signal station
Heavy anti-aircraft gun site
Light anti-aircraft sites
Fortress observation post

seven collieries had just gone on strike and there had seemed a possibility that the militia might have to be called out to maintain public order. Instead, some units were called out on the 26th to prepare for war, and general mobilization began on 1 September, the day Germany invaded Poland. All coastal defence units were placed on active or full-time service, with authority to recruit two or three times more than could be kept on the rolls in the straitened 1930s. When Britain declared war on the 3rd, the Canadian government authorized the coastal defences to adopt what were essentially wartime rules of engagement, that is, freedom to fire on any German forces that approached Canadian shores. Prime Minister W.L. Mackenzie King honoured his promise not to ask King George VI to declare war on behalf of the dominion until Parliament could be reconvened to give its consent, and so Canada did not formally enter the war until the 10th.

As has been seen, the military recognized Sydney's importance in terms of both its industrial capacity and its potential role as a naval base and convoy gathering port. The Sydney area was, as one contemporary observer noted, 'one of the most important industrial areas in the Dominion' because the quantities of coal and steel produced there were 'unequalled anywhere else in Canada.'[1] So valuable, indeed, was Sydney's large, strategically placed harbour that the defences undertaken in the years 1939–40 were, as Leslie Roberts later wrote with only slight exaggeration, 'designed especially' to make it 'the "spare bedroom" (the Navy's own phrase) for the British fleet,' in the event that a German invasion of Britain made it necessary to abandon its home bases. It 'soon became a naval base of world importance, and one of the best equipped.'[2] These developments, however, were exceedingly difficult to imagine in 1939.

It all began for Sydney when Commander Massey Goolden, a retired Royal Navy officer, flew from his home in Vancouver to Ottawa on 28 August, a rare and exciting event in the late 1930s. When the first mobilization messages had arrived from Britain on the 22nd, Goolden, like other retired naval officers, received a telegram from Naval Service Headquarters warning him to be ready. As the crisis deepened, headquarters arranged for Goolden to fly to Ottawa. There, he learned that he had been appointed the naval officer in charge (NOIC) at Sydney, with the temporary rank of captain.[3] After consultations in Ottawa and Halifax, Goolden arrived at Sydney on 4 September. The plan he took with him, which had been roughed out in sketch form only weeks earlier, was for the creation of an organization along the lines of the one

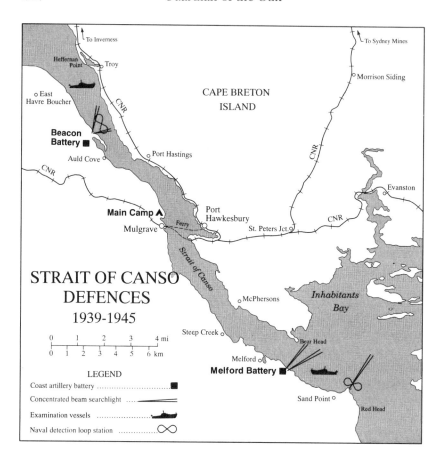

To Inverness

Heffernan
Point   Troy

o East
Havre Boucher

CAPE BRETON
ISLAND

To Sydney Mines

Morrison Siding

CNR

Beacon
Battery ■

Auld Cove o   Port Hastings

CNR

CNR

Evanston

Main Camp ▲

Mulgrave   Ferry

Port
Hawkesbury

St. Peters Jct. o

CNR

STRAIT OF CANSO
DEFENCES
1939-1945

McPhersons o

*Inhabitants
Bay*

| 0 | 1 | 2 | 3 | 4 mi |
| 0 | 1 | 2 | 3 | 4 | 5 | 6 km |

Steep Creek o

Bear Head

LEGEND

Coast artillery battery .... ■

Concentrated beam searchlight .....

Examination vessels ....

Naval detection loop station ....∞

Melford o

Melford Battery ■

Sand Point o

Red Head

that had existed in 1917 and 1918, with an anti-submarine net, mine-sweepers, and anti-submarine patrol vessels.[4]

The difficulty was that no resources existed for this. Commander R.B. Mitchell, a member of the Royal Naval Reserve who was resident in Canada and who had been assigned to Goolden's staff on mobilization, later vividly recalled the harbour in 1939 as 'a company preserve, the most outstanding features [of which] were the coal and ore piers which berthed the small fleet of DOSCO [Dominion Steel and Coal Company] ships engaged in the coal, limestone and iron ore trades and the occasional stranger in for a cargo of steel rails.'[5] Facilities for ship repairs were 'meagre,' consisting only of those of Sydney Foundry, which had a small marine railway for hauling out vessels, Atlantic Spring and Machine Shop, which could handle minor repair work, and the North Sydney Marine Railway. There were only three ships' agents in the area – Dominion Shipping, J.A. Young & Son, and C.R. Lorway – and one tug- boat, which was a converted passenger tender. Harry Kelly operated North Sydney Ship Supply, a ships' chandlery business. While bunker coal was available in quantity, the supply of oil fuel was restricted by the shallow depth of the water at the government wharf and the inaccessi- bility of the storage tanks at Sydney River. There was also a shortage of merchant seamen in the area.[6]

The only patrol craft Goolden had to work with were the half dozen motor launches of the RCMP's marine section at Sydney. Fortunately, most of the RCMP's marine service personnel had joined the Royal Canadian Naval Reserve in the 1920s and 1930s, and virtually all of them volunteered for full-time naval duty. Those who did not went into the RCAF to help organize the Eastern Air Command marine squadron, which would provide essential rescue and service support craft; some of the smaller RCMP launches at Sydney would provide invaluable assis- tance to the flying units based there.[7]

Goolden could do no more than organize the basics: the examination service and naval control of shipping. He rented an office in the *Post- Record* building on Charlotte Street for his headquarters, and here the members of his staff who were assigned to naval control service duties began to assemble and dispatch information about the increasingly heavy shipping traffic through Sydney. This was part of a global shipping intelligence effort, centred in London and with its North American regional headquarters in Ottawa, that would allow the Commonwealth navies to direct vessels away from areas where enemy warships were known to be hunting.[8] The basic local defence measure was the exami- nation service, which Goolden established on 6 September, employing the two largest RCMP vessels, the 112-foot *Adversus* and the 116-foot *Alachasse*. A day later he arranged for them to exercise with Chapel Point battery, which was designated the examination battery for the har- bour. From about this time, navy signallers were stationed at Chapel Point's command post to ensure the intimate cooperation that was essential to port security. Goolden also began construction of a hut at Low Point, which would serve as the port war signal station and which was guarded by troops from the Cape Breton Highlanders. The naval dockyard at Sydney began modestly as well, when the Department of Public Works turned over to the navy a portion of the government wharf and two small sheds for that purpose.[9]

The only armaments on the RCMP patrol craft were small arms. Goolden therefore encouraged one of his staff, who had experience with explosives, to build improvised depth charges using steel barrels and blasting powder obtained from the nearby coal mines. Spurred on by reports of submarines approaching Cabot Strait on 7 September, Goolden's staff quickly produced one of these devices for each of three patrol craft. Meanwhile, he had the patrol craft practise hunting submarines and escorting merchant ships into port. The tactics he worked out with the air force and the army were for aircraft to force a U-boat to dive (or for the coastal batteries to do so if it was close in to the port), immediately alerting the navy so that the RCMP vessels could unload their explosives on the position.

Goolden was a thoroughgoing professional, who was impatient, sometimes cold with outsiders, and utterly devoted to his men.[10] Of the three service commanders at Sydney, he was the most forceful and, appropriately for the representative of the service that had the greatest stake in Sydney, he had the clearest vision of what was needed. More than anyone, he appreciated the inadequacy of the improvised measures, and he pressed the needs of his command so persistently that he ultimately aroused the ire of Captain H.E. Reid, the Atlantic coast's commanding officer, who pleaded with him to 'make the best' of the situation at Sydney. While the importance of Sydney's naval defence was recognized, he explained, it was considered 'for the time being' that the defence of Halifax and its approaches was more important.[11]

Halifax's requirements were all the more pressing because of the British Admiralty's decision in September 1939 to assemble convoys there and to operate stronger naval forces from there than in 1914–18. This reflected a recognition that German strategy had changed. In 1914 Germany had possessed a large battle fleet that it had carefully kept intact in German ports in the hope of finding a favourable moment to smash the British fleet in the North Sea; hence the standoff that had effectively bottled up the German fleet. In 1939, by contrast, with only a few, but very powerful, big ships available, German strategy was to slip these out into the Atlantic to raid Allied shipping. The Allied convoys therefore needed formidable heavy warship protection, and the Admiralty transferred the 3rd Battle Squadron, which operated two battleships and up to a dozen cruisers and armed merchant cruisers, to Halifax. Further raider hunting and shipping protection forces, including additional French and British battleships, aircraft carriers, and other major warships, frequently called at the port as well. It was essential that these valuable squadrons be able to obtain supplies and undergo repairs in safety, a necessity driven home in October 1939 when the submarine *U-47* penetrated the incomplete defences of the Royal Navy's North Sea base at Scapa Flow in Scotland and torpedoed HMS *Royal Oak.*

Although the army was better prepared than the navy to take action in Cape Breton, almost everything had to be improvised. On 24 August, National Defence Headquarters had ordered the army's coastal commanders to begin the construction of the temporary sites for the interim artillery armament, and the next day it made $23,000 available for the five positions planned for Sydney.[12] The telegram ordering the precautionary stage reached district headquarters in Halifax at 1:45 that morning. After a pre-dawn conference by the district staff, Major W.H. Dobbie, DSO, the second most senior permanent force coast artilleryman at Halifax, and Lieutenant Colonel W.D. Simpson, the senior engineer in the district, departed for Cape Breton to supervise the preparation of emergency positions for the interim armament. Dobbie had been appointed in the mobilization plan to command the Sydney defences, including Canso.

Shortly after noon on the 27th a truck left Halifax, arriving at Chapel Point battery at 5:00 p.m. with a cargo of fifty-five rounds of 4.7-inch ammunition that was unloaded into the gun shed by members of the 36th Battery, who had volunteered for active duty on the previous day.[13] The military engineers pressed ahead with work at all of the Sydney sites, making the quickest progress at Chapel Point, where they poured concrete for the second gun platform to the north of the existing position on 31 August.[14] The next day, Major Dobbie brought a 'gun-bucking' party of sixteen permanent force artillery experts from Halifax to mount the armament that began to arrive in Cape Breton from the garrison and naval stores in that city.[15] Meanwhile, volunteers from the Cape Breton Highlanders mounted guards at Sydney Airport, the seaplane base in Sydney River, the cable landing at Lloyd's Cove in Sydney Mines, and Marconi Towers near Glace Bay. Guard detachments from the Pictou Highlanders had begun to arrive at their stations on the Strait of Canso on the 28th.[16]

The 16th Coast Brigade's war diary describes proudly the response of both existing personnel and new recruits to the mobilization order of 1 September. 'Everyone was enthusiastic, inexperienced but very willing.' The 'spirit of 1914–15–16–17 was still very much in evidence,' and 'the new lads showed both in physique, mentality, education and physical appearance that the standard, if anything, had greatly improved.'[17] Volunteers from the 36th Battery, which was based in the northside towns of North Sydney and Sydney Mines, were already helping the permanent force gunners at Chapel Point, and were also responsible for the anti-motor-torpedo-boat battery planned for North Bar. The 6th Battery, which drew its personnel from Sydney and the towns on the southern side of the harbour, was assigned to the batteries planned for Fort Petrie, South Bar, and Point Edward.

George Fraser was working at Dominion Tire and Chemical in Sydney on the morning of 2 September, when Captain Roy Ward of the 6th Battery called him on the telephone: 'he said, "George, we're going to mobilize." Well, I said "fine," so I took the overalls off and I stood them in the corner and said goodbye. And I never intended to come back there if there was going to be a war ... That day ... I went in to Victoria Park. I drew my uniform and I dressed in that uniform right there ... And I was home, here, with my uniform on, by ten o'clock in the morning and my wife pretty near fainted when she saw me in that uniform.' On the following day, the men of the 6th were mustered at Victoria Park. Major Arnel Milburn, their commanding officer, addressed them: 'now, you people who want to stay in the army and want to go on active service, you fall in over here. And you people who want to go back on civvy street, you fall in over there.' Fraser continued: 'There was only one man in our battery that declined to go on active service ... He went into the merchant marine and a very few years after, he was on a ship that was sunk at Wabana and he was one of the casualties. So, he got it in the neck before we did.'[18]

The first major task of the 6th Battery was to move the seven-ton training gun from Victoria Park to Fort Petrie, where it was mounted on 6 September. The next day, assisted by permanent force soldiers, they emplaced a second 6-inch naval gun of 1902 vintage, erected a wooden battery observation post, and installed a depression range finder there. When the ammunition arrived on the 10th, Fort Petrie was ready to perform its duties, and by the middle of the month there were forty-eight personnel there, living in tents borrowed from the Cape Breton Highlanders and the New Waterford boy scout troop.[19] Because of the earlier start at Chapel Point, that fort had come into action on the 7th, with two 4.7-inch guns, and a telephone line had been installed connecting it with Sydney Fortress headquarters, which had been established in the Lyceum Building on George Street in Sydney.[20] The six-pounders were mounted at North and South Bar by the 21st, the mountings of these light guns being bolted to heavy timber baulks set in the ground. Work was slower at the heavily wooded Point Edward site, but by the 23rd the installation of the 4.7-inch guns was nearing completion. At the Strait of Canso, where the 86th Battery from Amherst had begun to arrive in mid-September, both 4-inch guns had been installed at Beacon battery at the northern end by 1 October, and by the 5th two similar guns had been mounted at Melford battery at the southern end.[21]

Searchlight defences took somewhat longer to arrange.[22] While equipment was being purchased from industry sources, the militia engineers from Glace Bay were rushed to Halifax, where they arrived on 1 September, to assist the under-strength units there to man the fortress searchlights and gain practical experience.[23] Plans to convert the Glace Bay engineers into a searchlight unit of the Royal Canadian Artillery were put on hold, and they were now re-styled as the 3rd Fortress Company, Royal Canadian Engineers. During October 1939, when all the equipment was delivered to Sydney, the 3rd Fortress Company returned from Halifax. All nine lights were reported ready for action on the 23rd, rough wooden huts having been built for the equipment rather than the concrete and steel structures called for in the ultimate plan.[24] Two thirty-six-inch searchlights were placed at Fort Petrie and one at Chapel Point. These were quite powerful, with a range on a clear night of about forty-five hundred yards. The purpose of these lights was to search periodically the harbour entrance to guard against vessels approaching stealthily, and to be ready to track targets for the guns at Fort Petrie and Chapel Point. Three of the eighteen-inch lights, which had a range of only about one thousand yards, were mounted at each of the six-pounder anti-motor-torpedo-boat batteries and exposed on fixed bearings across the harbour to create an illuminated zone.[25]

The fire command post, the command centre of the artillery defences, was on the high ground by the Kilkenny Lake Road, about halfway between South Bar and Fort Petrie. By the middle of November a wooden building equipped with a depression position finder had been completed here. Initially the coastal forts were linked with brigade headquarters at Victoria Park by only one telephone and used runners for communication. Eventually, they were provided with a telephone network that converged at the fire command post, and by November 1940 brigade headquarters had moved to the same site, as had the headquarters staff of the searchlight systems and a signals detachment that manned the telephone exchange and radio station there.[26]

In the middle of September 1939, units from the mainland reinforced the infantry defences. The Pictou Highlanders, who were recruiting to a strength of about four hundred, followed the small detachments that had initially gone to the Strait of Canso, and moved the unit's headquarters to Mulgrave, on the mainland side of the strait.[27] Headquarters and two companies of the Prince Edward Island Highlanders – 263 personnel – came to Sydney Mines from Charlottetown to relieve the Cape Breton Highlanders in what was now known as the North Sydney sector.[28] They established additional patrols and defended positions at the headlands and along the coast beyond Sydney Mines, including placing detachments at the entrances to the Little and Great Bras d'Or channels on the western fringes of the fortress area.[29]

With the arrival of the troops from Prince Edward Island, the Cape Breton Highlanders, who had already recruited to their war establishment of 34 officers and 436 men, became responsible only for the Sydney sector,[30] which extended from Port Morien, southeast of Glace Bay, around the coast to the south bank of Sydney River. Headquarters and the main barracks for the unit were in Sacred Heart Parish Hall, one of several commercial and institutional buildings taken over by the military on George Street in Sydney. The Canadian Legion Hall in New Waterford served as the central barracks for the Cape Breton Highlanders in that area.[31] The remaining component of the defences was a detachment of 6 officers and 70 men of the North Nova Scotia Highlanders (Machine Gun), who were dispatched to Sydney on 16 September. They mounted their Vickers machine guns near the South and North Bar batteries to augment those works by providing high density fire for close-in defence of the harbour. The North Novas also sent small detachments to Point Tupper and Mulgrave to provide machine-gun support for the strait defences.[32]

Danger seemed to be everywhere at the beginning of the war. Flickering lights at night were assumed to be the signal lamps of so-called fifth columnists communicating with enemy ships offshore, and soldiers went on more than one fruitless search. Foreign ships were inevitably suspect as well. Thus, when Lieutenant A.W. Rogers of the Prince Edward Island Highlanders stationed at Big Bras d'Or spotted 'a large vessel, equipped with searchlights, coming in ... from the Ocean' on the evening of 14 October, he called out his men, who were off duty at the time, and opened fire on the ship. After several bursts of gunfire, the suspicious vessel 'stopped, turned around and headed out to sea again.' Rogers and his men 'gave chase on the Big Bras d'Or ferry and over-hauled her at sea around 22:30 hrs.' Rogers and two men, 'fully armed,' boarded the ship and interviewed the captain who, not surprisingly, 'was slightly nervous.' The ship was, in fact, a tugboat from Dingwall, a small port on the northeastern shore of Cape Breton, that was towing a dredger up to the Bras d'Or lakes. The captain had been unaware that the lakes had been closed to navigation on the previous evening.[33]

Reassuring as the purposeful activity may have been to the citizens of Cape Breton, perhaps excluding the tugboat captain from Dingwall, the deployments in the autumn of 1939 provided more of a framework for development than an effective defence. There was also no quick solution to these difficulties, which were the result of twenty years of tight-fisted defence budgets. The well-organized mobilization of balanced home defence forces in 1939 was rooted in the lessons that had been learned in 1914–18, but the human and material resources needed to make those forces effective did not exist. The tiny pre-war regular cadre of fewer than four thousand had been barely adequate to sustain a part-time force of forty thousand or fewer, whose most ambitious undertaking was a week or two of annual training at a regional camp. Now that same small group of regulars was confronted with the daunting task of organizing, housing, and training an active service force that numbered more than eighty thousand persons by the end of 1939 and that continued to expand.

The infantry, at least, had a cadre of personnel who had had some training in the inter-war years, however limited and basic, that was directly relevant to their war role. That was not the case with the Sydney coast artillery units, however, which had converted from quite different field-army functions only a year before mobilization. A few technical personnel from the permanent force artillery at Halifax, including an officer and three master gunners – armament specialists of warrant rank – had been assigned to Sydney. There was, however, no expert in coast artillery training and operations other than Lieutenant Colonel Dobbie – he had been promoted on mobilization – the fortress commander, and he had more than enough on his plate. Worried that 'the units manning the defences of Sydney ... are entirely ignorant of their duties,' Lieutenant Colonel C.V. Stockwell, the senior permanent force artillery officer at Halifax,[34] sent two experienced instructors. One of

them, Sergeant Major H. Millen, fifty-nine years of age in 1939, had
transferred from the British garrison artillery at Halifax when Canada
took over the fortress in 1905 and 1906.[35]

In October 1939 the instructors began a series of courses of one to six
weeks' duration, in which the 16th Brigade's most senior officers were
among the students. Thanks to this effort, by early 1940 the situation in
the unit was 'improving,' albeit 'rather slowly.'[36] It was the critically
important technical knowledge of these experienced permanent force
hands that made relations with the often raw non-professionals work.
The regulars held the key to the success of the whole enterprise. These
crusty experts who had come up the hard way with long service and slow
promotion in the peacetime service had a special status within the
expanded wartime army that had nothing to do with their rather junior
rank. At the same time, the permanent force experts had learned
throughout their careers how to nudge young or less knowledgeable
officers in the right direction tactfully and without undermining their
authority. For the senior officers of the 16th Coast Brigade, with experience in business and the professions, it was somewhat like working with
a senior clerk or technician.[37]

One of the great impediments to efficiency in the early months of the
war was the lack of suitable accommodation. During the autumn and
winter of 1939, Dobbie and other garrison officers had found themselves devoting much of their time to haggling over real estate. Funds
were not available for the most logical and efficient course, constructing
buildings at key centres such as Victoria Park so that personnel could be
concentrated to facilitate training, discipline, and *esprit de corps*. Training took place at a former fertilizer plant in Sydney, which was located
on the present L.E. Shaw brickyard site near Ashby Corner. The plant
had not been in use for some time and was like a large empty warehouse. The recruits lived in this building while they went through basic
training, and used an adjacent vacant field, where the Centre Scolaire
Étoile de l'Acadie now stands, for drill practice. Duncan MacDougall
later recalled that the men slept on the concrete floor using pallets
filled with straw, and that the roof leaked.[38]

Construction could not be avoided at the most isolated sites, the
coastal batteries, and the infantry outposts on the headlands. The men
were living in tents that, needless to say, were inadequate protection
against the wind and blowing snow. George Fraser recalled that when
the troops arrived at South Bar, they 'commandeered a couple of summer bungalows that were in the vicinity and we used one for a cook

shack and the OC stayed in the other one.' There was also 'a little shack – a kind of storage shed behind the guns and we used this, kind of, as a gun watch shelter.' One night, 'the weather was very – well, it was downright rotten, you know. It was windy and blowing and we were exposed on that cliff and the men were wet and cold. So my OC said to me, "look, these boys are pretty miserable." He was a veteran of the First War and he knew what it was to be a miserable soldier in poor conditions. "If you can get some of the local brew now," he said, "here's some money, you see what you can do and we'll warm the boys up." So, I knew a bootlegger and I went and I got the quart of liquor and we put a shot into them and we fed them the bacon and eggs, and one thing and another and we toughed the night out.'[39] Dan J. Robertson recalled that a canvas marquee initially served as a cookhouse at Chapel Point at this time. 'We had a little cookhouse built later; you walked in and backed out; it was that small.'[40] At South Bar, Fraser used his own car to drive into Sydney to purchase groceries and cooking utensils. 'I brought it all back into this commandeered bungalow and we set up a cookhouse. And I cooked the first meal for these ten men; we fed them there.'[41]

As early as 23 September 1939, even before the weather deteriorated, district headquarters at Halifax warned National Defence Headquarters that 115 men had reported sick at Sydney 'with colds due to poor living conditions and lack of boots.'[42] On 9 October, with no signs of progress, Major MacKenzie, commanding the 16th Coast Brigade, dispatched a plea to Halifax:

> Practically 100 per cent of the Unit is under canvas in some of the most exposed and bleak positions on this Atlantic Coast. Not much more than half of this personnel is properly clothed and many of them very poorly shod.
>
> If conditions were such that proper accommodation could not be provided, I do not think we would have any complaints but when you consider that the majority of these people are under the close observation of their parents and homes, it is not surprising that adverse criticism of the delay is making considerable headway.
>
> I was able to get a few Marquees to equip with stoves so that the men could get dried out and warmed up but I am held up to procure sufficient stores and have had to raid the junk-piles to provide some heating facilities. There may be some excellent reason for this delay but I fail to see where any advantage could accrue and it is pretty difficult to explain to a father or

mother why their lad should lay around improperly clothed and with no
further covering than a wet tent under conditions with which the other
Coast Brigades do not have to contend, and, in the event of a number of
people developing pleurisy or pneumonia ... we may expect most severe
criticism.[43]

This may have helped to speed up things, as construction got underway
at all of the coastal sites in the area by the end of the month and within
a week or two, walls and roofs were up, allowing the troops to take refuge.[44] Finishing work, however, dragged on for months. Martin Haley, a
young lieutenant with the 36th Battery at Chapel Point, vividly remembered thirty-two years later the wretched months he spent in a tent 'in a
graveyard' – the battery was indeed built around an old cemetery – the
constant wind, the impossibility of getting warm, and seemingly perpet-
ual illness. Haley claimed that Lord Haw Haw, the British turncoat who
broadcast propaganda from Germany, mocked the men at Chapel Point
in the spring of 1940, saying 'you've got the asses out of your pants.'[45]
Whether true or not, the survival of this story certainly evokes the mood
of at least some of the troops.

As much as conditions improved when the huts were finished, they
were still less than comfortable. Purely temporary constructions, they
were light wooden structures covered with roofing tarpaper and lacked
basements. Even Lieutenant Colonel Kendall Partington, the brigade's
commanding officer from 1942 to 1945, remembered his quarters at the
fire command post with anything but fondness. When the wind blew, he
said, 'the calendar lifted off the wall.' The only heat was provided by
coal-fired pot-bellied stoves known as Quebec heaters. On winter nights
he put a sleeping bag on the bed and slid in wearing a sheepskin coat
and fur hat.[46] Needless to say, fire was a constant danger. On 14 April
1943 the barracks at Fort Petrie were destroyed by fire, and on 13 September Bombardier John Favier lost his life while attempting to salvage
a rangefinder when the fire command post was completely destroyed by
fire. The South Bar barracks were also gutted by fire in 1944.[47]

Because the freezing of the harbour put Point Edward battery out of
range of open water in winter, it was abandoned in the middle of February 1940 by all but a maintenance detachment comprising one officer
and a dozen men. Duncan MacDougall later recalled skating across the
harbour from Point Edward to Sydney on at least one occasion. It was so
isolated in those days that once, when he got a twenty-four-hour leave,

he headed for his home in Donkin on foot. A snowstorm struck the area and it took him two days to get there. When he called in he was told that a special train had been hired to return men to their batteries and that he had to leave a couple of hours later. His leave consisted of three days of travelling, mostly on foot.[48]

The emergency-built gun positions that had been installed around Sydney Harbour in 1939 were more primitive than the semi-permanent ones that had been erected in 1917 and 1918. The emplacements were simply flat platforms like the trial one that had been poured at Chapel Point in early 1939, into which the mounting bolts had been embedded. The magazines were made of galvanized metal sheets covered with earth, and the shelters for the duty gun crews were only wooden huts, like the barracks. This did not mean that Ottawa had forgotten the Cape Breton port. Rather, the demand for construction resources by all three services and the uncertainty about when modern coastal defence armament could be delivered from Britain forced National Defence Headquarters to limit the building of permanent fortifications to sites for which the ultimate armament was already on hand. That applied only to Sydney's main close-defence batteries at Point Petrie and Chapel Point, which were the principal gun defences of the port. The Directorate of Engineer Services in Ottawa had drawings ready for Fort Petrie, the more important site because of its seaward command and heavier guns, as early as October 1939. By that time as well, the authorities at National Defence Headquarters had decided that the Chapel Point works would be based on the same plans as those for Fort Petrie. The drawings, like almost all of the designs for new batteries in Canada, were probably standard British type plans, modified in details only for adaptation to the site.[49]

Work on Fort Petrie began at the end of November 1939 and was virtually completed by the end of April 1940, by which time both guns were in action in the new emplacements. The emergency positions had been installed in positions back from the site of the planned permanent fortifications, so that construction interfered as little as possible with the operations of the battery; each gun was left in its old position until the new emplacement was ready.[50] E.G.M. Cape and Company of Montreal, the builders of Fort Petrie, also won the Chapel Point contract for $137,477 on 23 April 1940.[51] The detailed records available for the Chapel Point project show that seventy-three men were employed on the construction work, all but ten of them from the Sydney area. E.G.M.

Cape did its best to meet National Defence's requirement that veterans
of the First World War be given priority for jobs, but when only eleven
men fit for the heavy labour could be found, the company hired the
sons of veterans.[52] Even so, the department received a complaint, evidently from Sydney Mines, when one of the subcontractors brought in
two Montreal truck drivers.[53] When work on the permanent fortifications neared completion in late August, the battery detachment moved
the guns into their emplacements.[54]

The new works were impressive, as can still be seen by a visit to the
Chapel Point or Fort Petrie sites. The gun emplacements featured
sloped semicircular concrete shields some fifteen feet thick that gave
the gun detachment good frontal protection. Dug into the outer flank
of each position were two heavily built concrete rooms, banked with
earth and rock fill to roof level. One was the store for gun equipment
and the other was the shelter for the gun crew on duty. The gun
emplacements at each battery were set one hundred feet apart so that a
hit on one would not disable the other. They were connected, some fifteen feet underground, by a long magazine, at each end of which was
an ammunition hoist shaft running up to the rear of each emplacement.[55] Perhaps the most important modern feature was the heavy
protection for the magazines. Atop the 2.5-foot-thick roof of the ammunition storerooms was three feet of packed sand, and above that a
4.5-foot-thick burster, overlaid by 7.5 feet of soil.[56] The burster and the
intervening layer of sand would diffuse the detonation of a hit on the
battery. To strengthen further the structure, access to the magazines
was not direct, as it had been in earlier works, but through a tunnel at
the base of the staircase from the surface. For this reason, and because
the magazine was more deeply buried than in previous designs, there
were also escape shafts for the magazine crew. To the rear of the gun
positions was a three-storey concrete tower, the battery command post.
On the top two floors there were wide-view windows. The depression
rangefinder was mounted on the upper storey, the battery commander's fighting position; the second storey was for the officer in
charge of the battery's searchlights, and voice tubes allowed the two
commanders to talk directly to one another. All doors in the permanent works were of heavy steel construction and steel blast shutters covered every window.

Meagre as the coast artillery resources were, they were the mainstay of
Sydney's defences. The air force presence at Sydney during the first part
of the war was only a small fraction of that of the army, and it had similar

difficulties. At least the air force had the advantage of larger numbers of professional personnel. The 8 (General Purpose) Squadron of the permanent air force at Ottawa, a unit equipped for civil rather than military operations, had been alerted on 24 August 1939 to prepare for mobilization. Five days later the main body of its ground crew arrived at Sydney by rail. Its five Northrup Delta float planes, none yet fitted with bombs, had already begun to fly in from Ottawa.[57] The squadron's role was to cover friendly shipping and to locate enemy craft in Cabot Strait and its ocean approaches, including the south coast of Newfoundland and the waters southeast of Cape Breton. The southern limits of Sydney's patrol area interlocked with the northern patrol limits of RCAF Station Dartmouth, Eastern Air Command's principal base.[58]

The squadron was not prepared for this large and demanding task, and no facilities yet existed in Cape Breton to support the unit. The Delta was a modern all-metal monoplane, the first ever manufactured in Canada, but this light, single-engine utility machine was in no way comparable to the multi-engine bombers required for maritime reconnaissance.[59] The RCAF had acquired it for photographic survey work and pressed it into the maritime role only because delivery of more suitable aircraft could not be expected for some months. The fact was that the Delta was one of the most capable aircraft the RCAF had, and it was the only machine other than the purpose-built maritime reconnaissance Supermarine Stranraer twin-engine flying boats of 5 Squadron at Dartmouth capable of making extended overwater patrols. Although the Delta could carry only a fraction of the Stranraer's armament, it had similar endurance to and greater speed than the flying boat. Both machines could, with a margin of safety, fly offshore a distance of something over two hundred miles in patrols of five to six hours' duration.[60] At that range, they could linger at the outer limits of the patrol for one and a half to two hours to escort shipping or search in response to any reports of suspicious activities.[61]

Because the military airport at Sydney would not be ready for another year, the squadron hastily removed the Delta's landing gear and installed floats before leaving Ottawa. The unit's temporary station was the site of the dismantled base at the mouth of Sydney River, from which the RCMP's preventive service patrols had been flown.[62] The few houses and cottages in the area were rented for use as the radio and flying control offices. The nearest building that could be found to serve as squadron headquarters and to house the main stores and workshops was near the Sydney Fortress Headquarters at 418 George Street, two kilometres away. Similarly, most of the squadron personnel had to live in hotels and other rented accommodation in town, far from the base.[63] Everything – including a dock on the river, boats for servicing the aircraft, and motor transport to link the dispersed parts of the unit – had to be arranged locally. The one pleasant surprise was the cooperative attitude of the detachment of Cape Breton Highlanders on guard duty in the area, who pitched in with the heavy work.[64]

Notwithstanding these difficulties, the squadron almost immediately began its first mission, a reconnaissance of the Newfoundland coast by two Deltas that took off on 4 September. The aircraft were unarmed, as bombs were not delivered to Sydney until the 10th. With refuelling and rest stops at Port-aux-Basques, Botwood, and St John's, the aircraft circumnavigated the island over the next week.[65] These flights had been requested by Vice Admiral Sir Sidney Meyrick, the Royal Navy's commander-in-chief, North America and West Indies, who was watching for German warships and their supply vessels that might have been prepositioned in the last days of peace for a strike against Atlantic shipping. He also wanted to catch any German merchant vessels that might be following an evasive route home from North America to try to avoid capture by the Royal Navy.[66] In the event, the German raiders limited their initial foray to the central and southern ocean. Still, the squadron's mission was a foretaste of the large responsibilities Canada would subsequently shoulder for Newfoundland's security and of the link Sydney would once again provide in knitting together the defence needs of the island and those of Canada.

Regular patrols over the approaches to the Cabot Strait and to the southeast of Cape Breton began on 7 September. These were simple 'out and back' runs, in which the aircraft took off before first light to reach the sea lanes at dawn to make sure no suspicious vessels had approached under cover of darkness. These missions became more important when, on the 16th, HX 1, the first in the new series of North America to Britain convoys, sailed from Halifax. The squadron was very much learning on the job, and a maritime air pilot was sent from Halifax on 6 September to give courses on overwater flying. It was probably the squadron's lack of experience that delayed its entry into direct convoy escort (as opposed to sweeps over the convoy route), which the seasoned 5 Squadron at Dartmouth had been carrying out from the beginning, until the sailing of HX 5 on 25 October. Early on the morning of the 26th, two Deltas from Sydney flew out to the convoy. They were relieved at midday by a second pair of aircraft, which patrolled through the afternoon until the rows of merchant ships passed out of range. This was a large new commitment, as the convoys sailed every five days. No. 8 Squadron, with only ten Deltas on strength and shoestring service facilities, had also to maintain regular reconnaissance flights,[67] while at the same time responding to alleged U-boat sightings by merchant seamen and the coastal population.[68]

In view of the inadequacy of the organization at Sydney River and the length of time before the airport would be ready, Air Force Headquarters decided to reopen the old seaplane base at Kelly's Beach in North Sydney.[69] Although the hangar had been dismantled, several barrack buildings remained, which the army had been able to repair sufficiently to provide reasonably comfortable accommodation for about 120 troops from the Prince Edward Island Highlander and North Nova detachments in the North Sydney–Sydney Mines area. When the RCAF pressed in November for the early return of the base, leaving only the crowded and ill-maintained former offices of the Nova Scotia Steel and Coal Company at Sydney Mines for army accommodation in the area, district headquarters removed all but one company of the Prince Edward Island Highlanders to Dartmouth for the winter.[70] This reduction in the garrison was not important, as danger of attack during the winter freeze-up was minimal, but the decision showed the seriousness of the accommodation problem in the Sydney area.

When flying ended for the season on 12 December 1939 – it would have been suicidal to try to operate the lightly built Deltas when there was any danger of ice in the water – the whole squadron moved to Kelly's Beach. The aircraft in worst condition were shipped out for major overhauls, and the rest were pulled ashore, where the ground crews faced the challenge of reconditioning them in the open air during the winter, the new hangar would not be ready until the spring of 1940. The unit, living together in a military setting for the first time since the summer, needed a good deal of 'shaking down' to restore the proper discipline and organization, and many new personnel had to be integrated as well. Other personnel came and went from courses at bases across eastern Canada. Disquietingly, many experienced personnel were posted to other units.

In December 1939, the Canadian government agreed to shoulder much of the responsibility for organizing in Canada the huge British Commonwealth Air Training Scheme, which would supply tens of thousands of trained personnel per year, most of them recruited in the dominion. While most would serve in the Royal Air Force, some would be organized into RCAF units, thereby creating a substantial Canadian air force overseas. The units at Sydney soon learned that this effort was being given absolute priority over the home war establishment, as the operational stations and squadrons in Canada were known. Within the home air force, moreover, Sydney took a back seat to Dartmouth.[71]

chapter ten

Building Fortress Sydney, 1940–1941

The grim truth is that, because Sydney is the most easterly city on the North American continent, it is also the Canadian city nearest the war.

Frederick Edwards, 1941

The whole face of the war changed with the electrifying German offensive in the spring of 1940. Norway fell in April, then France in June, when Italy entered the conflict in support of Germany. For Britain the situation was grave, and nowhere more so than in the North Atlantic. German submarines and surface warships had previously had to make the long passage from the Baltic through the North Sea to reach the Atlantic. Now the Germans had direct access to the ocean at Britain's very doorstep through French and Norwegian ports, and their U-boats especially began to inflict grave damage. What was more, at the very moment that British maritime forces lost the vital support of the French fleet, an entirely new theatre opened in the Mediterranean against Italy's considerable maritime strength. British resources were still further divided by the need to maintain a strong guard in the English Channel and along the East Coast against possible invasion from the now entirely hostile continent.

The implications for Canada were profound. The country was suddenly catapulted from being a junior partner with a self-proclaimed limited liability for fighting the war to being Britain's major ally. National interest and the still strong sentimental attachment to Britain of much of the population, including the prime minister, allowed no alternative to an all-out war effort. As a result of the loss of the French fleet and the enormous demands being made on the Royal Navy in European waters, the major British warships that had swept in and out of Halifax disappeared. Convoy protection and the important coverage it also gave to the Canadian coast was largely left to the oldest British cruisers and armed merchant cruisers, none of which was a match for the German heavy units. Moreover, at the end of May 1940 the Canadian government sent four of its seven destroyers to help defend Britain. When one of them was lost off the French coast in June, Canada immediately sent a replacement, leaving only two destroyers based at Halifax. As in the First World War, shipping and coastal defence would depend largely on a motley collection of Canadian armed yachts and other converted civilian craft.

As soon as the first of the new corvette escorts were completed in Canadian shipyards in late 1940 and 1941, they were also sent to Britain, as were the most efficient of the seven old former American destroyers that the navy received in the autumn of 1940 as a result of the Anglo-American destroyers-for-bases deal. Meanwhile, the single army division that was sent to Britain in December 1939 to provide mainly symbolic Canadian representation in the struggle was quickly reinforced with a second division and army corps headquarters in the summer of 1940, a build-up that would continue until there was a full field army of two corps and five divisions overseas in 1942 and 1943.

Military commitments expanded greatly at home as well. Among the most basic requirements was to protect Newfoundland, which was virtually defenceless. In June 1940, 10 (Bomber Reconnaissance) Squadron, which had been equipped with American Douglas B-18 Digby twin-engine bombers that could patrol to a range of 350 to 400 miles, began to move from Dartmouth to Gander Airport, along with a Canadian infantry battalion that would provide local security. During the summer of 1940, work began on defences and naval and air operating facilities at St John's and Botwood, in Newfoundland, and at Shelburne, in Nova Scotia, and at Gaspé, in Quebec.[1] Meanwhile, the Canadian army concentrated the 3rd Division in the Maritimes, with two brigades (six infantry battalions and supporting units) at Debert, Nova Scotia, and one brigade (three infantry battalions and supporting units) at Sussex, New Brunswick. These strong land forces were a mobile reserve, ready to counter-attack in the event of an enemy landing in strength.[2]

These preparations were undertaken in close collaboration with the United States. Although still neutral, the Americans had a vested interest in the security of their northern neighbour and in assisting the Canadians to do their utmost to ensure Britain's survival. In August 1940 Prime Minister W.L. Mackenzie King and President Franklin D.

Roosevelt capped secret missions between their diplomats and military chiefs with the creation of the Permanent Joint Board on Defence, a panel of senior military and civilian officials who, in the first instance, jointly oversaw plans for American reinforcement of Canadian defences in the event of a British collapse.

These developments inevitably increased the importance of Sydney. It was, together with Halifax, the only large defended anchorage available on the Canadian coast from which, in the event Britain were defeated, the remnants of the Royal Navy and the American fleet could carry on the war in the North Atlantic. Still, there was little with which to bring the Cape Breton port to a better standard. Canada embarked upon all-out industrial wartime expansion only with the fall of France, and priority was rightly given to supporting the British forces and Canadian forces overseas. American industry was mobilizing but was still in the process of equipping itself, and Britain had first call on most *matériel*. Canada's home forces were at the end of a very long line-up for very meagre supplies of equipment. Minimal improvements in Sydney's almost non-existent naval defences encountered delays as well. Because of the slow delivery of components from the United States, the anti-submarine net could not be completed until the end of July 1940, when it was strung between Stubbert's Point and Daly Point.[3] The boom depot at the North Bar included a hard-surface working area, two large sheds, and a heavy mobile crane.[4]

In May 1940, as ice cleared from the harbour at Sydney, the authorities at Halifax were able to send only the nucleus of a local defence force to Sydney. This included two trawlers fitted as minesweepers and one of the larger former RCMP patrol vessels, *French*, which in June was replaced by the similar *Laurier*.[5] Not until early August could *Husky* and *Reindeer*, two of the four large converted American yachts intended for convoy escort, take up station. By that time, two tugboats, *Lisgar* and *Bersimis*, were serving as the examination vessels, and a third minesweeping trawler had been added. The third and fourth armed yacht convoy escorts, *Elk* and *Lynx*, came at the end of August and beginning of September.[6]

Only in late September were new buildings completed at the government wharf, and the naval staff at Sydney 'thankfully' moved there from their cramped quarters in the *Post-Record* building and borrowed army facilities at Victoria Park. By this time the navy dockyard area, running about 450 feet along the south end of the quay wall and 250 to 350 feet inland, had been fenced off for security purposes. There were berths for harbour craft and two or three larger vessels along the quay wall, and the substantial administration building included a proper conference room, officers' quarters, and a wardroom (dining room and club). A large warehouse was converted into workshops and quarters for ratings, and there were various small buildings as well.[7] 'We were now,' as Mitchell later recalled, 'our own masters with a tight and compact organization, the Wardroom, of which all ship masters were honorary members during their stay in port.'[8]

The modest naval establishment carried vast responsibilities, which in the summer of 1940 became much larger than anyone had previously anticipated. Halifax, the principal convoy assembly port in the western Atlantic, was not convenient for the heavy summer traffic from the St Lawrence River and gulf, which wasted several days backtracking to Halifax to join convoys before heading overseas. Through the winter of 1939–40 the Admiralty and Canadian naval authorities made plans to have the St Lawrence ships gather at Sydney and sail under escort to join the main convoys from Halifax well out at sea on the Grand Banks. Thus, neither group would lose time by having to alter course away from the route to Britain.[9] On 31 July 1940 the first convoy comprising twenty-five ships sailed from Sydney to link up at sea with HX 62, the main convoy that had departed Halifax on the previous day.

The unanticipated need to protect very large numbers of slow ships had already started preparations for the much fuller employment of Sydney. Convoys had been reserved for ships faster than 9 knots but slower than 15 knots.[10] British authorities would have preferred to keep the slower, older merchant vessels, which the U-boats could most readily find and attack, on safer routes away from the North Atlantic, but they had no choice. Britain was now utterly dependent on North America for a wide range of bulky goods, such as timber and grain, that had previously been available from continental Europe.[11] Accordingly, at the end of July 1940 the Admiralty and the Ministry of Shipping established a new series for ships faster than 7.5 knots and slower than 9, though in practice the actual speed of these convoys was closer to 6 knots.[12] As in 1917, Sydney was selected as the assembly port for the eastbound slow convoys (SC). Because the United States was still neutral, Cape Breton was the gathering point for ships bound for Britain from the whole of the Americas, not just those from north of Virginia.[13]

SC 1 sailed with 40 merchant ships on 15 August, the beginning of sailings on an eight-day cycle. The urgent need for the slow convoys was soon demonstrated by the large numbers of ships presenting themselves to join. The British authorities had hoped to limit the number of merchant vessels to no more than 30 per convoy. In fact, there were 53 in SC 2 and 47 in SC 3, and even when the pace of convoy sailings was increased to a five-day cycle in October more than 30 ships usually presented themselves.[14]

The organization of all this shipping into convoys was a crucial step in limiting the enormous losses of independently sailed vessels, but Allied forces were much too thinly stretched to prevent disasters to some convoys. The early SC convoys suffered losses to U-boats hunting independently in the approaches to Britain, but SC 7, which sailed on 5 October, was the first to be attacked by a group of U-boats massed as a 'wolf pack.' It was savaged, losing 20 of its 34 ships. In November, the German pocket battleship *Admiral Scheer* attacked a Halifax convoy in mid-Atlantic. The convoy turned back to Sydney, bringing the total number of ships in harbour at that time to 127, 'and that in a port where pre-war Canadian Navy appreciation [had] stated that there was safe anchorage for 6 HM ships or 12 Merchant ships!'[15] After SC 15, the last scheduled convoy of the year, sailed on 8 December, the boom defence nets at the mouth of the harbour were lifted. On the 29th, however, 23 ships of a Halifax convoy, HX 98, entered the port after having been forced by enemy action to return to a safe harbour. The departure of that convoy on 2 January 1941 marked the end of Sydney's first convoy season, during which 967 ships sailed from the harbour in forty-eight convoys, 521 in the SC series and 446 in the SHX series.[16]

The hundreds of ships that called at Sydney were, in Commander Mitchell's words, 'a motley crowd, for it was the era of the coal burners [and] maintenance of these ships presented a problem, keeping them manned an even greater one.' Many of the vessels came from the merchant fleets of occupied nations, Britain having taking control of ships that were at sea or in Allied ports; there were also many ships that had been chartered from neutral countries like Sweden and Greece, prior to the occupation of the latter by German and Italian forces in the spring of 1941. The naval control staff at Sydney had early experience of the complexities of the new situation, as more than a dozen French trawlers and merchant ships were either in port or made their way to it after the collapse of France. The British government seized the ships, but many of their crew claimed their right of repatriation in view of the 'neutrality' of the Vichy regime. Mitchell later assigned the credit for keeping the captains and crews of these ships quiet 'until we could get them away to various discharging ports' to Lieutenant J. Carter of the Naval Reserve, 'ex-rum runner and a Geordie.'[17]

Others, whose homelands had been completely occupied or who were employed by ruthless ship owners to operate leaky, ill-founded vessels, did not have the option of repatriation. Worried about their families, whom they might not see in years and who were now living under Axis military authority, and facing apparently certain death in interminable Atlantic crossings with slight protection, many rebelled, either deserting or refusing to sail. The crew of the Norwegian *Ruth 1* took the latter course when the ship arrived from New York, having been promised that it would be armed at Sydney and learning that no defensive weapons were available. The Canadian naval staff did its best, rushing machine guns to Cape Breton to be mounted on merchant ships, but the crews of Norwegian and Dutch vessels were understandably not impressed until stocks of 4-inch guns and other substantial weapons began to arrive in the fall of 1940.[18]

Incidents like the 'sit-down' strike of the crew of *Ruth 1* had the potential to spread panic and unrest that could severely hinder the flow of supplies to Britain. To avoid such a disaster, the Canadian government passed an order in council in September 1940 that empowered immigration officials to place foreign seamen who refused to sail under detention. Still, the Naval Control Service, which dealt directly with the merchant fleets, almost invariably preferred diplomacy, and undertook all-out efforts to address sources of unrest. A report from 1941 typifies the quiet, efficient work that continued until the war's end: 'We had a grand time on one ship especially (SS PARKLAAN, Dutch). Last Sunday Baker and I were on board from 9.00 am until 4:00 pm getting her fixed up to sail that day. At first it was the crew refusing to sail on account of the food situation and other minor things. After the crew was satisfied and willing to sail we had to deal with the Captain for, according to him, he had had trouble in every port with this crew and he was refusing to sail from here with the same lot. However, after a great deal of arguing we were able to swing him around. Personally I think he was so disgusted from having Baker and myself on his neck he thought the only way he would have peace would be by sailing.'[19] In other cases, there was no chance for diplomacy. A 'classic example' was the Polish *Kowatice,* fourteen of whose crew 'filled a lifeboat with provisions and deserted ... before the Convoy was due to sail.' This was only reported at 10:00 a.m., yet new crewmen were on board in time for the ship to sail at 1:30 that afternoon.[20] The surviving records do not mention how the men were so rapidly found, but the task often fell to Ethel Dixon, then a young woman in her twenties, who was Sydney's deputy shipping master, responsible for clearing vessels entering the port and ensuring that outward-bound ships had full crews. The shipping office was at the foot of Dominion Street in Whitney Pier, and 'into our office every day would come the ships' captains. If they were in port any time they had to bring in the ship's articles, list of the crew and rules and regulations that ship is bound by – men and officers all signed it. We had to certify it on the back. And if a man was signing off a ship, we'd have to get his signature, see that his wage was paid and all that.'[21]

Many young Cape Bretoners signed on the merchant ships when these came into port needing replacements. Ethel Dixon joked many years later that men 'were scared to see me coming down the street' because 'they were scared I'd snatch them.' In fact, enlisting was voluntary and 'very few men ever turned her down.' Nevertheless, men had to be found and 'we'd comb the streets,' she said, adding that it was not uncommon for her to be out in a taxi in the early morning hours looking for recruits so vessels could depart on schedule.[22] According to Dixon, 'there was never one ship held up in this port for lack of crew.'[23]

Alec Huntley is also proud of Sydney's record as a convoy port. A local merchant seaman, Huntley became a harbour pilot at Sydney in 1940. There were twenty-one pilots and they had to be available twenty-four hours a day, seven days a week, as every ship coming in and going out had to have a pilot on board. Several would be assigned to each convoy. They would take out the lead ships, and then a navy boat would pick them up and bring them back in to take out the later ships. According to Huntley, Sydney Harbour had the best record on the coast for getting ships out safely and on time.[24]

Huntley and Dixon were guilty of only slight exaggeration. In the words of the historical report assembled in 1946 by the Trade Division, the branch of the naval staff in Ottawa responsible for the shipping control and convoy organization, 'although Sydney never had anything like the shore facilities or staffs which were available at Halifax, the port always worked extremely efficiently and never failed to respond to all the calls made upon it.'[25] Local initiative was largely responsible for this success. In addition to the efficiency of the Dominion Steel and Coal Corporation in refuelling vessels, most of the other, much smaller businesses responded 'very well' to the sudden flood of demand that began in the summer of 1940.[26] Nevertheless, because Sydney had never been properly developed as a port, services for such things as ship repair on anything but a minor scale did not exist. Vessels with special requirements had to be sent to other ports for servicing; at other times, because

of incomplete repairs they broke down after sailing in convoy and had
to return. Either of these regular occurrences imposed long delays that
directly translated into loss of precious shipping capacity. Little had
changed since 1917–18. The naval control staff at Sydney was scathing
in its final report at the end of the war in reference to 'the small amount
of effort or money spent on developing the existing facilities' despite
the 'crying necessity' for improvements. The Canadian government
'may well thank God that the fortunes of war did not force the use of
Sydney as the only Eastern Canadian Port.' Had Halifax been put out of
commission for any reason, 'the Government itself would have been
shaken by the obvious lack of primary preparations at Sydney.'[27] This
was strong condemnation from a staff report. It was also the truth.

Meagre as the port facilities were, defences were thinner still, and it
was fortunate that the Germans did not yet press their attacks on shipping into North American waters. Canada, having rightly committed its
limited main naval force to the anti-submarine campaign in Britain's
western approaches, had almost nothing with which to screen the Sydney convoys as they formed up and began their passage. Initially, a pair
of the armed yachts would remain in their company for about twenty-
four hours, enough time in the case of the SHX joiners to make the link
with the main fast convoys from Halifax. In late October, however, *Husky*
and *Reindeer* were caught by a heavy autumn gale when 180 miles at sea,
the furthest reach of their escort, and did well to survive the return voyage. The storm damage put them out of action for weeks. Thereafter,
the little escorts stayed with the convoys for only eight to ten hours. As
Captain Goolden commented, with no irony evidently intended, 'I consider that vessels of this type which were built for pleasure purposes and
for use in calm waters are unsuitable for convoy escort duties during
winter months.'[28]

Eastern Air Command did its best to fill in for the weak British and
Canadian naval escorts for the Sydney convoys, but the airmen had their
own problems. No. 8 Squadron had initially endured the challenge of
maritime operations with the fragile Deltas at Sydney in the expectation
that better times were around the corner. The unit was scheduled to be
re-equipped with twin-engine Bristol Blenheim bombers that had been
ordered from Britain before the war, or their variant, the Bristol Bolingbroke, which was being produced in Canada. During the winter a large
detachment from the squadron had indeed begun conversion training
on Bolingbrokes in Ottawa.[29] The unit's hopes were dashed, however.
Although the Blenheims arrived by ship at Halifax at the end of May,

the RCAF immediately sent them back in view of Britain's urgent need for aircraft. It was clear by this time that the Sydney aerodrome would not be ready in time for the shipping season in any case, and so 8 Squadron continued with the Deltas at North Sydney. Meanwhile, the Bolingbroke detachment, with 8 Squadron's best personnel, was transferred to 119 Squadron, which was to operate Bolingbrokes from the newly completed aerodrome at Yarmouth, a job for which 8 Squadron had once been designated and that its members had anticipated with enthusiasm. Because so many of the aircrew at North Sydney were new, it was necessary to devote all of June and July to training. [30]

Frustration mounted further when flying began in June. The waters off Kelly's Beach were more exposed than those at Sydney River, and the lightly built Deltas soon began to suffer structural damage in landings and take-offs. This, together with the attrition of the previous season, soon reduced the squadron to only five or six aircraft. In late July, therefore, Eastern Air Command dispatched three Stranraers from 5 Squadron at Dartmouth to North Sydney. The Deltas were only able to provide cover off the harbour mouth and the early escort, and then one of the sturdier Stranraers carried on with the longer-range escort until darkness. [31] On 27 August 1940, the anniversary of the squadron's arrival at Sydney, its diarist reflected bitterly: 'During the last year the movement of personnel has been extraordinary and the unit has lost many officers and NCO tradesmen who formed part of the backbone of the squadron ... The Sydney Aerodrome which is supposed to be our War Station is still under construction and even when it is ready for occupancy, there is no assurance that the equipment Branch will have twin engine Bomber-reconnaissance aircraft available for the Unit ... One officer and eight other ranks have died or are missing as a result of aircraft and other accidents.' [32]

Late in September, as work on the runways at the Sydney aerodrome entered the final stages, some ground personnel began to move there to prepare the station. It was a sea of mud, a situation that nearly had fatal consequences on 24 October. At 11:00 p.m. three shots were heard, and two guards were found 'mired in the mud up to about their waists and were helpless, not being able to extricate themselves. They had fired all their shells, 10 rounds, and only the last three were heard. It was necessary to dig them out and they were put in hospital suffering from shock and exposure.' [33] In December 1940, after convoy operations had closed down for the winter, the squadron completed the move to the airport and began to rebuild itself for the second time, converting to land-based operations with two Bolingbrokes that had just been delivered and three wheel-equipped Deltas.[34]

The greater danger of raids from the summer of 1940 and the weakness of the naval and air forces in the western Atlantic increased the importance of the army defences at Sydney. With the return of warmer weather, the tempo of training increased, climaxing, in the case of the 16th Coast Brigade, with its first firing practice during the last week of July. Halifax's garrison steamer *Alfreda* came to tow targets and Major G.L.W. MacDonald, a senior instructor at the School of Artillery in Halifax, supervised the exercise. The first series were fired from reduced calibre tubes that were inserted inside the bores of the 4.7-inch and 6-inch guns, special settings on the gun instruments allowing for the ballistic properties of the smaller projectiles. This permitted the detachments to fire hundreds of practice shots that would otherwise have emptied the magazines and worn out the gun barrels. At the end of the week, each crew fired a series of ten full-sized rounds in a day shoot, and another series at night in cooperation with the searchlights. A second full-scale firing practice took place in November 1940, again with *Alfreda* towing the targets.[35]

Otherwise, the forts' artillery crews did regular drill on their weapons and instruments, took specialist courses both in the fortress and in Halifax, and carried out rifle and bayonet training and physical fitness training. Part of the routine was 'fatigues' to build entrenchments for local defence, clean up after construction crews, carry out improvements in the accommodation, camouflage the battery sites, and take part in special projects such as levelling areas to make playing fields for the many sports events that were a vital part of army life. To keep the garrison up to the mark, there were periodic alarms, some actually in response to reports of enemy warships approaching the Sydney area, others for practice. In either case, all personnel had to be at their posts immediately with all equipment ready for action and the various communications systems functioning smoothly.

The fort that had to be the most constantly on alert was Chapel Point because of its role as the examination battery. As it happened, Chapel Point had occasion to fire its first full round in July 1940, regrettably three days before its full-calibre practice series, when a Greek freighter ignored the port entry procedures, and the examination vessel called for a stopping shot across the bows. As the brigade's war diary put it, 'at 0815 hrs the stillness of Sunday morning was shattered by the sound of a gun firing.'[36] The freighter stopped but the shell, instead of splashing harmlessly in the water in front of the vessel, ricocheted onto the shore close to the South Bar battery. As a result of this incident, Colonel Dobbie renewed his requests to headquarters for a small-calibre 'stopping gun' of the sort normally issued to examination batteries so that a shell that ricocheted onto shore would not cause serious damage even if it hit a building.[37] He never received one, no doubt because of the shortage of artillery and perhaps because it was normally possible for the examination service at Sydney to intercept ships well to the seaward, where a shot from Chapel Point had no chance of bouncing ashore. Nevertheless, an almost identical incident occurred in 1943, although fortunately the shell once again fell clear of the South Bar buildings.[38]

The construction of modern fortifications at Chapel Point battery, which has already been described, was just one of several projects begun in the spring and summer of 1940 to improve the readiness of Sydney's harbour defences. Victoria Park became a major camp with a fortress headquarters building, officers' quarters, and barracks and dining facilities for more than four hundred men. These buildings, occupied in the autumn of 1940, enabled the army to vacate many, though not all, of its various rented facilities around the city. Other big projects included a 105-bed military hospital and a full-size one-thousand-yard-long rifle range. Perhaps less eagerly awaited by some members of the garrison was a twenty-cell detention barracks that was built at Point Edward in the summer and fall of 1940. Previously, malefactors drawing long sentences of twenty-one or twenty-eight days' confinement had been sent to the grim old cells on Melville Island near Halifax, which had been built by the British garrison in the nineteenth century, and then to the new but scarcely more appealing detention barracks on McNab's Island in Halifax Harbour.[39]

At the Strait of Canso, a large camp like the one at Victoria Park was built at McNair's Point near Mulgrave.[40] Much of this additional accommodation was needed for the Pictou Highlanders, which, like other infantry battalions on the East Coast, recruited during the summer of 1940 to reach a strength of some eight hundred personnel, nearly twice its previous size.[41] The main change in the fixed defences was to move Beacon battery, at the northern end of the strait, onto higher ground during the winter of 1940–1 in order to obtain a better field of fire.[42] The new battery, like the old one, had simple flat concrete platforms for the guns and wooden buildings. Local authorities and senior headquarters agreed that there was no need to improve either these or the similar works at Melford battery to the south, because it was unlikely that the strait, being some distance from open ocean, would be subject to sustained bombardment by heavy warships or aircraft. Even if it did happen, the enemy would have great difficulty in finding the batteries, which were carefully tucked into the heavily wooded terrain.[43]

East Coast harbour defences were further strengthened during 1940 by the arrival of the sixty-inch, eight-hundred-million candlepower U.S.-type searchlights that had been ordered from Canadian General Electric just before the war. Of the first five lights delivered to Sydney, three went into the new fortifications at Chapel Point and two to Fort Petrie, where the concrete and steel light emplacements and engine rooms for the diesel-driven generators had already been built. 'Directing stations' with remote-control equipment for training the lights were on the second floor of the battery command towers, and they were in voice-tube communication with the battery commanders on the upper level. The new lights began operations on 2 November 1940, with crews from the revived 9th Searchlight Battery, RCA, which had begun to organize and recruit in the spring in order to relieve the 3rd (Fortress) Company, RCE, which could then assume its own proper construction and maintenance role.[44] Concentrated-beam lights of the type installed at Chapel Point and Fort Petrie had an effective range on a clear night of at least eight thousand yards, nearly double that of the smaller thirty-six-inch lights of the interim armament.[45]

The remaining ten lights were delivered, and positions built for them, through the winter and spring of 1940–1. These included an additional pair of concentrated-beam lights that were installed at Cranberry Point, the tiny spit of land on the western headland, to extend the long-range coverage of the harbour approaches provided by the Fort Petrie and Chapel Point lights. Architecturally, the Cranberry position was a particularly interesting one, as the searchlight buildings were built in and around the concrete gun positions remaining from the First World War. Location and installation of the two three-light groups of the dispersed-beam version of the sixty-inch lights that were to provide the main illuminated zone required a good deal of rethinking of existing plans and experimentation with a truck-mounted light. During the summer of 1940 the navy had installed the anti-submarine net between Stubbert's Point and Daly Point, further out the harbour than the North Bar–South Bar line originally intended, which had formed the basis of the army's scheme. The little interim battery at South Bar was still suitably placed, but the searchlights had to be dug into bluffs in front of it to get a proper orientation and secure foundations. In April 1941 the North

Bar guns were moved to a new site at Stubbert's Point, about a mile seaward of the original site, behind the newly built searchlight positions there.[46] Design of the innermost group, two concentrated-beam lights at Point Edward that swept the inner harbour to catch fast craft that might push through the illuminated zone, raised questions about the development of permanent gun emplacements, which were planned for higher ground than the interim works. In the end, the fortress command concluded, as in the case of the Strait of Canso batteries, that the heavy forest screening of the interim site provided ample protection and that it would be a waste of money to build concrete and steel works on the more exposed high ground. The permanent searchlight emplacements were sited to serve the interim battery, and the temporary gun positions received only minor improvements to correct the worst defects.

On the night of 5 June 1941 the fortress tested the new nearly completed searchlight system. Two small naval patrol craft, representing U-boats attempting a fast surface attack on the port, approached the outer harbour. No searchlight group was allowed to expose its beams for more than two minutes, in order not to assist the 'enemy' force. The groups had no difficulty in locating the craft, and they handed off one to another effectively, allowing the gun crews to train their weapons on the targets and track their movements.[47]

By this time four of the new lights had also been put in place at the Strait of Canso. There were two on the foreshore below each of the two batteries, Melford and Beacon. Because of the slight danger of sustained naval or air bombardment, they were mounted in wooden huts. A fifth light, one of the older thirty-inch units made available by the delivery of modern lights to other ports, was similarly installed in a wooden hut at Eddy Point to assist the navy in identifying incoming ships.[48]

Much the most important improvement in the Sydney Fortress undertaken in 1940 and 1941 was the construction of a new long-range battery at Lingan. When war broke out with Germany in September 1939, National Defence Headquarters had immediately reallocated its two priority orders in Britain for long-range guns from the West Coast to the East, with a set of 9.2-inch assigned for Halifax and a set of 6-inch for Sydney, the latter being the armament for the planned battery at Lingan on the eastern approaches to the port.[49] J.P. Porter and Sons, a Montreal construction firm that undertook several large fortification projects on the East Coast, began work at Lingan in July 1940, and the battery was largely completed by the beginning of 1941. The standards of construction were similar to those at Chapel and Petrie.[50] The major differ-

ence was that Lingan's three emplacements were widely separated –
some eighty yards from one another – and that each was a self-contained
unit with its own deep magazine. A long-range battery on an exposed
headland was the most likely target for heavy enemy bombardment, and
these design features were intended to ensure that a direct hit on one
position could not disable the others.

There were two fire-control and command positions at Lingan battery. Close to the eastern flank of the gun positions was a two-storey concrete building that still dominates the site. It is a striking structure
because the concrete walls were moulded like lap boarding on the side
of a house and the roofs – now gone – were pitched to complete the
camouflage. On the upper level was a pedestal for a depression rangefinder that directed the guns for close-in fire. Dug into the top of the
high ground some 350 yards behind the gun positions, with only a view
slit showing seaward, was a large flat building. This was the combined
battery observation post and battery plotting room that directed long-
range fire. In the front part of the building was a pedestal for a position
finder, essentially a larger and more complex version of the depression
rangefinder, one that delivered more accurate ranges and bearings. The
rear part of the building, the battery plotting room, was designed to
house the fire-direction table and other instruments necessary for accurate long-range shooting.

The fort included wooden barrack buildings on the low ground
southwest of the gun positions. The infantry barracks were the first to
be completed, and in September the detachment of Cape Breton Highlanders that had been using New Waterford's Legion Hall moved to the
site. Approximately eighty infantrymen were stationed at Fort Lingan,
and they continued to be responsible for the security of the shoreline in
the New Waterford area, in addition to guarding the fort itself. Meanwhile, another 130 men were being recruited for the 6th Heavy Battery,
which would provide the fort's artillery garrison. The plan was to
engage men who were training on a part-time basis with the Pictou
Highlanders at New Glasgow but who had not yet been called out for
active service. Some of the personnel for the fort were recruited in this
way, but the 6th Battery also did local recruiting.[51]

The high-angle gun mountings arrived at Halifax in November 1940
and were dispatched by rail to Sydney. Each mounting, with turret-style
shields enclosing all but the rear, weighed thirty-five tons, but they had
been disassembled for shipment into components of two to eight tons.
As was so often the case on the East Coast, fate conspired to ensure that

the heaviest work had to be done during the least pleasant time of the year, just as the fall rains were beginning to turn to snow. This created especially difficult conditions at the battery site, where the construction work had churned the ground into soft mud. On one occasion the engineers had to be called in to dump slag into the mire to free the big flatbed truck that carried the components from the railhead to the gun positions.[52]

The gun barrels did not arrive from Britain until the latter part of March, and their breech mechanisms were further delayed, reaching Sydney on 16 May. In the following week a thousand rounds of ammunition arrived, and by the end of May the fort was in action. Not everyone greeted the occasion with satisfaction and relief. Three elderly people living in a nearby house had refused to move when construction began, even when a new home was built for them across the road. Before the battery fired for the first time, they were advised once again to move. According to George Fraser, they again refused 'so we fired No 1 gun and the barn fell down and they moved.'[53]

That was not the only problem in making the fort fully operational. Among the fire-control instruments, only the depression rangefinder and position finder were available. These devices triangulated range on the basis of their known height above sea level. In the case of Lingan, that was only about 130 feet, which meant that the data became hopelessly inaccurate at 12,500 yards. However, the guns had a range of 21,000 yards, and would need every inch of that reach if an enemy surface vessel ever hovered off shore. The plan was to erect additional observation posts with bearing-taking instruments at intervals of several miles along the coast to feed data on the bearing of a target electrically to the battery plotting room, where they would be instantly collated and the ranges triangulated on the fire-direction table; bearings simultaneously taken at positions miles apart gave a long base for triangulation and hence extremely accurate firing data. Britain, which was short of all types of fire-control equipment, could not promise early delivery of the fire-direction table and the equipment for the coastal observation posts. These instruments were too complex for speedy manufacture in Canada.[54]

Fortunately, Captain C.H.P.E. Huxford, RA, a British expert who had been sent to Canada to assist with the massive expansion of the coastal defences, was available to help the Royal Canadian Artillery's specialists, none of whom had much experience with the new long-base 'fortress' system of range finding. At his suggestion, the engineers built temporary wooden observation huts at New Victoria, near the harbour mouth, and at North Head, about two miles east of Fort Lingan, during the summer of 1941; both were the sites of permanent 'fortress observation posts' in the ultimate plan. In these huts, pedestal-mounted telescopes stood in for modern bearing-taking instruments. When the position finder at Lingan tracked a target, the crew would warn the hut in that sector by phone, and the crew there would, by phone, call in their bearings on the same target every few seconds. In place of the fire-direction table, Huxford built a large, very rigid table, on the surface of which was a gridded map of the whole seaward area. Mechanical arms pivoted on the exact positions of the Lingan battery observation post and the two remote posts allowed rapid manual calculation of the corrected ranges.[55]

During the spring and summer of 1941 the garrison also worked closely with the air force in developing a second method of range finding and reconnaissance in the further reaches of the approaches to Sydney. The air force was able to provide spotting aircraft for the army's long-range batteries from Canadian production of the Westland Lysander, the standard British army cooperation aircraft. A big, high-wing, single-engine monoplane with a massive unretractable landing gear, the Lysander was fully manoeuvrable at the low speeds and altitudes needed to observe accurately movements on the ground. No. 4 (Coast Artillery Cooperation) Detachment, RCAF, comprising three Lysanders and thirty-three officers and other ranks, was organized at the airport in April 1941 and started flying in May. Missions included air photography of the various sites to assist in the camouflage program, simulated attack runs for the anti-aircraft gunners, and, of course, seaward reconnaissance in cooperation with the coast artillery. The last task was the most difficult one. On the ground, the unit set up and manned radio sets that worked on aircraft frequencies at the fire command post, Fort Petrie, Chapel Point, and Fort Lingan, an effort that encountered the usual problems of slow delivery of equipment and technical start-up difficulties throughout the summer of 1941.[56]

While Captain Huxford was in Sydney helping with long-range fire control, he provided a candid opinion of the coast artillery. He was favourably impressed in some respects, but criticized the officers' weak technical knowledge. They were still too dependent on Sergeant Major Millen and other personnel from the permanent force. This was the kind of criticism often made during the war by professional British officers of Canada's citizen soldiers, sailors and airmen.[57] The Canadian difficulties were the result of the forces having had to expand so greatly and so quickly from the tiny pre-war cadres of regulars. Men with only cursory training themselves and with few competent subordinates to assist them, were suddenly responsible for all aspects of the lives of large numbers of troops, a heavy burden that allowed little time for study. When Huxford visited, moreover, the 16th Coast Brigade was in the midst of an upheaval. Over one hundred persons, including four officers – Lieutenant Colonel MacKenzie among them – and thirteen of the unit's best non-commissioned officers, had been posted in June 1941 to help set up and man the new defences in Newfoundland and at Shelburne and Gaspé.[58]

The frustrations and difficulties facing the infantry in the coastal garrisons as the initial excitement of mobilization gave way to routine were possibly greater than those of the artillery. Aside from the challenges of installing sophisticated equipment and learning to operate it swiftly and precisely, the gunners could take some satisfaction in the knowledge that they were doing the utmost possible within their branch of the service. The same was true for the engineers and signalmen, who were usually busy installing, building, and repairing installations. Garrison duty, however, is at the bottom end of the spectrum for infantry, whose ultimate purpose in war is to prepare for mobile warfare. An infantry battalion on isolated coastal defence duty was an orphan unit. Although everything possible was done to keep the main bodies of the infantry battalions concentrated at central bases like Sydney's Victoria Park to allow sustained training and disciplined community life, a third or more of the men had to be dispersed on outpost duty, with its numbing round-the-clock guard details and patrols. The situation of the garrison infantry became still more difficult in 1940 and 1941 when the best people were periodically posted away from home units to build up the overseas army.

The transfer of some units to Britain, and an army policy of periodically redeploying home defence infantry to help keep battalions from stagnating, produced a shuffle of infantry units into and out of Sydney and Canso. The first change in the garrisons resulted from the selection of the North Nova Scotia Regiment (MG) for the 3rd Canadian Infantry Division in the summer of 1940. The detachments at Sydney and Canso departed in July and were replaced by similar detachments of the Princess Louise Fusiliers (MG) from Halifax. To bring the North Novas up to their full war strength of about nine hundred, more than one hundred and thirty men were transferred to the battalion from each of the Cape Breton Highlanders, Pictou Highlanders, and Prince Edward Island Highlanders.[59]

In January 1941 there was a major turnover in the garrisons. The Pictou Highlanders at the Strait of Canso exchanged with the Halifax Rifles from the Halifax Fortress, and the Cape Breton Highlanders exchanged with the New Brunswick Rangers from Saint John. For the Cape Breton Highlanders, this was the beginning of an odyssey that would take them, after four months of garrison duty at Saint John, to Ottawa and then Camp Borden, where the unit joined a formation that was subsequently organized as the 5th Canadian Armoured Division.[60] The Halifax Rifles received a shock when they arrived at Mulgrave on the Strait of Canso. Although barracks had been built during the summer and fall of 1940, 'the unfinished condition of the buildings left much to be desired.' Only one cold water tap was available, additional water having to be drawn from Mulgrave, which was two miles away, and pumped into barrels by hand. The latrines were outside in unheated huts, there was no ration room, butcher shop, or company quartermaster's stores. On the positive side, the regiment received 125 sets of skis, as well as snowshoes and toboggans, in February for winter training. 'Snow conditions were ideal for this type of training,' their historian recorded, 'and great enthusiasm was engendered in all ranks.'[61] Even so, the unit's officers became deeply concerned about morale during the last weeks before spring. Some needed relief came in June, when units stationed at the big formation camps in Nova Scotia and New Brunswick traded places with Sydney units for the summer so they would have the opportunity to build themselves up with concentrated, higher-level training.[62]

Lieutenant Colonel John Quigley, who spent two and a half years on coastal defence duty with the Halifax Rifles, wrote with some feeling of his unit's experience. Anyone who has not experienced the frustrations and tedium of static defence 'cannot comprehend what the process of waiting does to the human soul; keyed to concert pitch from day to day by numerous rumours of pending change, which does not come, and after a time it loses its charm of novelty.'[63] All levels of command were keenly aware of the problem and, in addition to organizing innovative or adventurous training exercises, lots of sports, entertainment, and social events were arranged. John Quamm recalled that his unit, the 9th Searchlight Battery, had its own orchestra, which included the Lighter brothers from Glace Bay and three other people. They were stationed at the fire command post and went to the various forts playing music for entertainment and dances. Local girls were allowed into the forts for the dances, which took place in the mess halls. The troops also formed baseball and hockey teams that competed in unit, fortress, and inter-service

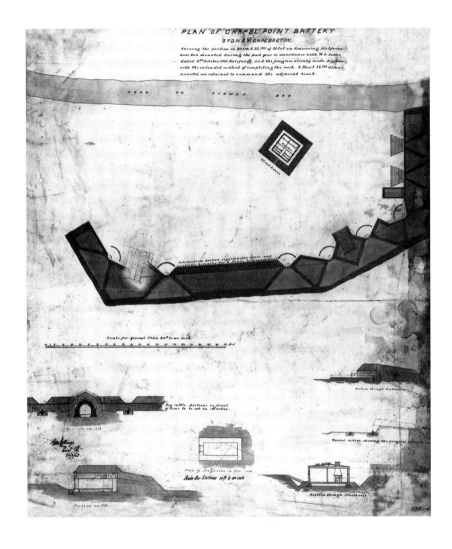

The partially completed battery at Chapel Point, plan by Lieutenant G.M. Collings, Royal Engineers, 26 February 1863.

The former British Army barracks, Victoria Park, c. 1900, with a nine-pounder rifled muzzle-loading gun and ammunition limber of the 17th Field Battery in the foreground.

Argyll Highlanders guarding Marconi Towers, near Glace Bay, 1914.

Commander Walter Hose as commanding officer of the cruiser HMCS *Rainbow*; promoted captain, he commanded the Atlantic Coast patrols in 1917–18.

U.S. Navy air officers at Indian Beach, North Sydney, 1918, with a HS2L flying boat.

HMCS *Lansdowne*, the name given to the rented waterfront facilities that served as the RCN patrol base at Sydney in the 1918 season. Among the vessels at the wharf are the drifter *CD 73*, one of the New England trawler-minesweepers (called PVs in RCN service), and the Admiralty trawler *TR 33*.

U-156, the most aggressive of the German submarines to operate on the coast of Canada and the United States in the summer of 1918.

Installation of a 4.7-inch gun on a temporary flat concrete position at Chapel Point in 1939.

A Northrup Delta of 8 Squadron, RCAF, preparing for departure from Rockliffe, Ontario, for Sydney, August 1939. In the right background is a Supermarine Stranraer flying boat, detachments of which also would operate from Sydney.

A Bristol Bolingbroke bomber.

His Majesty's Canadian Dockyard, Sydney, August 1940.

His Majesty's Canadian Dockyard, Sydney, August 1940.

Captain Massey Goolden, the naval officer in charge, Sydney, 1939–42.

Shipping assembling for convoy in Sydney Harbour during the Second World War. The anti-submarine net and gate vessel are in the foreground.

Royal Canadian Air Force Station Sydney, August 1941.

A Consolidated Catalina flying boat at Royal Canadian Air Force Station Dartmouth in 1941.

Marine railway, Sydney Foundry and Machine Works Limited, with a corvette hauled out for repairs, November 1942.

A 6-inch high-angle gun at Fort Lingan, c. 1945.

The twin six-pounder gun position at Stubberts Point, c. 1945.

The battery command post at Chapel Point battery, c. 1946.

leagues.[64] In addition, there were 'teeming servicemen's clubs and hostels' in Sydney, 'where soldiers and sailors stand in lines for cigarettes, soft drinks and sandwiches, [and] wait hours for a chance at the pool and Ping-pong tables.'[65] The Navy League's Ladies' Auxiliary operated a drop-in centre at the top of Dominion Street, near the shipping office, that included sleeping quarters and a dining room, where many survivors of ship sinkings temporarily stayed. There were regular dances at Hillcoate's Dance Hall on Charlotte Street and at Nelgah Beach Pavilion on King's Road, as well as at the navy canteen on the Esplanade, while street dances were also sometimes held on Sheriff Avenue and in front of Central School on George Street.[66]

In North Sydney, church and community clubs organized socials and dances, while the Canadian Legion War Services hut on Archibald Avenue, assisted by various women's groups in the town, and the Knights of Columbus hostel at the Empire Hall both helped to provide recreational and other facilities for service personnel.[67] More than five hundred people attended the 'gala squadron dance' held at the KOC hostel on 29 September 1943, for example, when the music was provided by the local RCAF band. The 'Kelly Beach Revue,' an evening of skits and music, presented 'one of the most hilarious evenings of entertainment and fun yet witnessed on the Northside for some time' on 7 October 1943, according to the RCAF North Sydney's base magazine. Mart Kenny, a well-known band leader from Toronto, presented a Victory show at Point Edward, which was broadcast by radio across Canada that month as well.[68]

The wholesome amusements organized for the servicemen did not prevent some from seeking entertainment of a less approved kind. Inevitably, prostitution flourished, as did the illicit sale of liquor. Places listed in one unit's orders as out of bounds to personnel included the area commonly known as the coke ovens in Whitney Pier, the KK Taxi Stand, Ida's Lunch Room, the Hole in the Wall on Charlotte Street, the Seaview Hotel, the Mi'kmaq reserve (now the Membertou Reserve), Black Christie's on the Esplanade, and various dance halls and private homes.[69] Men who overstepped the bounds or were drunk and disorderly did penance in the Digger, as the Point Edward detention camp became known. There the inmates dug rocks, drilled with weighted packs, and scrubbed floors endlessly. Duncan MacDougall, who was stationed for a while at the nearby Point Edward battery, later recalled that the prisoners were made to shovel out the road from the camp to the highway during the winter. The guards, in his view, were excessively harsh toward the prisoners, and when they went over to the battery canteen they were ostracized by the troops.[70]

Even though some members of the army garrison feared that the war was passing them by, there was an acute sense among naval and air force personnel and the local population that the community was on the front lines. Frederick Edwards a journalist who visited in the autumn of 1941, observed that, having long boasted of being the most easterly city in North America, 'these days Sydney very often wishes it were not so. The grim truth is that ... it is also the Canadian city nearest the war.'[71] There had been deep alarm over the dramatic events of May 1941, when the German battleship *Bismarck* had evaded British defences, broken out into the North Atlantic, and sunk Britain's own largest battleship, HMS *Hood*, before being hunted down and destroyed by the Royal Navy. 'Newspaper and radio experts may advance all their fancy theories to account for the sudden appearance in the North Atlantic of the German super-dreadnought and her scurrying brood of supply ships. They can talk till they're black in the face about a carefully drawn plan to attack British shipping on a grand scale, to invade Iceland, or to establish a Nazi base in Greenland. Sydney knows better. Sydney is full of people who are absolutely convinced that the *Bismarck*'s real objective was the Cape Breton coast, her errand, the blasting of Sydney and Glace Bay with long-range gunfire. The war comes as close home to them as that.'[72] These fears were exaggerated, but the prime minister shared them. The 1941 incursions into the Atlantic by German battleships caused King to consider recalling the naval forces committed in British waters so they could protect the approaches to Canada's East Coast ports. This idea was abandoned, however, when the chiefs of staff warned him that the Canadian navy's few destroyers could do little against heavy German warships. The best coastal defence was for Canadian ships to reinforce the British fleet, the only Allied force that could safeguard the North Atlantic.[73]

The sense of being on the front line was apparent in many ways. Frederick Edwards remarked on 'the stern admonition printed in black from heavy type, and surrounded by a broad black border, like the announcement of a death,' which he found on the table in his hotel room. This rather forbidding document warned that hotel lights would be extinguished during blackouts, and guests were asked to remain where they were until the blackout ended. All lights were to be turned off when leaving the room at all times, and the elevator would not be in service during blackouts. If this were not enough to remind a visitor that the war was very near, another notice near the telephone reminded him that it was 'FORBIDDEN to mention SHIPS, or SHIP MOVEMENTS, AIRCRAFT, TROOPS, WAR INDUSTRIES or the WEATHER during Long Distance Telephone Conversations.'[74] These warnings evidently were not idle: 'This exhortation, signed by the Maritime Telegraph and Telephone Company, means what it says. If you disregard its advice, even only to the extent of telling your wife in Amherst it is raining in Sydney, the operator will interrupt your chat, reminding you that talk about the weather is taboo. Should you forget twice you are likely to receive a visit from a constable of the RCMP, whose Sydney headquarters are just around the corner. Things like that have happened.'[75] Elva Jackson recalled as well that outgoing mail destined for addresses abroad, for servicemen and servicewomen, for the United States, and sometimes to other parts of Canada was opened, censored, and sometimes cut before being sent on its way.[76]

Air raid precaution (ARP) wardens, under the direction of Chief Warden James Gough, operated throughout the war years with volunteers of all ages responding to periodic air raid drills. Donald MacDonald, who signed up as an ARP warden for his neighbourhood in Sydney's Hardwood Hill district when he was barely sixteen years old, later recalled: 'we were issued a white ARP arm band and a steel helmet and that was about it in the way of equipment, although we were supposed to have gas masks. We did have access to stirrup pumps if they were ever needed.'[77] While total blackouts were not a nightly feature of life in Sydney, practice blackouts were held about every month, and by 1941 'almost one hundred per cent efficiency' was being achieved. It was, a visitor claimed, 'commonplace on Sydney streets after nightfall to see citizens carrying flashlights ready for a surprise blast from the warning sirens.' MacDonald recalled the first blackout particularly well because 'everybody who had a car drove up to Hardwood Hill with the lights off to see the city all blacked out. It sounds funny now, but I guess they came to see the darkness. You couldn't walk on George Street with all the cars.'[78] The first warning of a blackout was for the lights to flicker three times. The 'all clear' was a blast on the city fire horn, known as McConnell's bull in honour of the mayor who had brought it to Sydney. Afterward, the wardens from each area would gather for a debriefing. In MacDonald's case, this took place at Colby School on Cottage Road, near Hardwood Hill.[79] Despite these good efforts, the city's booming steel industry severely limited how much could be accomplished. Elva Jackson, who lived across the harbour at North Sydney, recalled that 'the bright reflections of slag dumped at the Sydney steel plant could be seen for miles in the darkness.'[80]

Duncan MacDougall remembered that one evening in 1940 the blackout siren in Sydney sounded while he and a friend were walking from their training base at the former fertilizer plant at Ashby to South Bar. They turned back and, when an elderly man driving a car offered them a lift, they more or less commandeered the vehicle and ordered him to take them back to the plant. He and his friend stood on the running boards to guide the driver, who couldn't use his headlights because of the blackout. The next day all the men were called out on parade and severely dressed down by the sergeant instructor, who told them that they were never again under any circumstances to commandeer a civilian vehicle. It turned out that the driver of the car had been the sergeant's father, and he had not been amused.[81]

Concern about possible air raids extended into the daylight hours as well. Ms Elsie Walker recalls that children attending her school in the Whitney Pier district during the war 'all wore little cloth bags around our necks containing cotton-batting for our ears, a tongue depressor to bite down on, and some other items that we were supposed to use in the event of a bombing.' There were regular air raid drills as well, for the orderly evacuation of the building.[82]

There was a partial blackout every night in Sydney, but it was part of an effort to save electricity rather than a defensive measure. Sydney's pre-war curfew, intended to keep children off the streets after 9:00 p.m., was now used to signal when commercial electric signs and lighted shop windows should be darkened. Similarly, street lighting was reduced so that walking on the sidewalks was 'like walking along a dimly lit village street that has suddenly become densely populated. People stumble over curbs. They tread on one another's heels. The boys nudge the girls, and the girls giggle by way of acknowledgment of the attention received.'[83]

Naval and military police patrols made regular rounds of the darkened streets, 'marching in twos and threes with a staccato beat of steel-tipped heels on concrete pavements.' There were also daily and nightly first-aid classes, 'one group of prospective rescue workers moving in for instruction as fast as another moves out.' Sydney and Glace Bay were 'especially proud of their first-aid squads. Trained by experts long familiar with rescue work in the mines, the volunteer workers ... achieved an unusually high degree of proficiency.'[84] As well, many women served in the Red Cross Society, sewing hospital supplies and quilts, giving out yarn for knitting, and collecting and packing 'great quantities of knit sweaters, scarves, socks, caps, and such, for the comfort of servicemen.'[85] All of this was in addition to the rapidly rising levels of production at the steel plant and in the nearby coal mines, which were making the industrial area busier than ever before. Helen MacDougall, who lived on the Esplanade near Victoria Park, later recalled the heavy traffic in that area: 'There were staff cars, transport trucks, big trucks with flatbeds carrying military equipment, jeeps and, on special occasions, such as a parade, a couple of tanks [probably light tracked infantry vehicles] would rumble out of the main gate of the park. The north end had to be the busiest place in the city.'[86]

The tempo of the bustle along the waterfront picked up each spring, when preparations began for the shipping season. In 1941 this activity was two or three weeks later than normal because of the slow clearance of ice from the gulf. Only during the latter part of May did merchant ships again begin to assemble, at the same time that the navy reinstalled the anti-submarine net and war vessels assigned to the Sydney local defence and escort flotillas moved up from Halifax. Initially, the naval force at Sydney was no more impressive than the previous year's modest collection of ships. Escort work fell again on the armed yachts *Reindeer* and *Raccoon* and the trawler *Rayon d'Or*, assisted on some trips by the Halifax-based destroyer, HMCS *St Croix*. Late in June the force was strengthened by the arrival of five newly commissioned Canadian-built corvettes, two or three of which provided the escort group for each convoy, while the armed yachts took up station at the new base at Gaspé for patrols in the Gulf of St Lawrence.

Much as the people of Sydney – and government and military authorities – worried about battleship and air bombardment, the Royal Navy's destruction of *Bismarck* in May 1941 largely discouraged German ambitions to challenge Britain's surface fleet. The advocates of major warships and aircraft carriers lost influence within the Nazi Regime, and the U-boat became Germany's principal weapon in the maritime war. As the convoy operations were getting underway again at Sydney, the German U-boat threat was moving closer. Britain's development of bases in Iceland to provide anti-submarine escort well into the mid-ocean area in the winter of 1940–1 caused Admiral Dönitz at the end of May to dispatch a group of submarines to probe the weakly defended focal area of shipping in the vicinity of the Grand Banks. On 13 June, *U-77* sank a steamer only 450 miles southeast of St John's. Familiar with Dönitz's tactic of pressing west in search of concentrated and vulnerable targets, the

Admiralty had already asked Canada to shoulder immediately the major burden of a new escort force, known as the Newfoundland Escort Force, to be based at St John's that would fill the gap in coverage between Newfoundland and Iceland. The Canadian navy hastily dispatched most of its new corvettes to St John's, as well as the destroyers and corvettes that it had previously sent to Britain. The convoys that sailed from Sydney early in June 1941 were among the first to receive 'end to end' anti-submarine escort.

Air support in the Sydney area was somewhat improved in 1941, though not nearly as much as had been intended. No. 8 Squadron was slow to convert to Bolingbrokes because of the primitive conditions at the still only partially completed airport and delays in the delivery of aircraft. Then the squadron's convoy season got off to a bad start. On 2 June a Bolingbroke engaged in one of the first patrols failed to return to base; no trace of the machine or its four-man crew was ever found. The next morning, two other Bolingbrokes crashed on take-off because of mechanical failures, though with no loss of life or injury. By that time, the appearance of U-boats on the Grand Banks had reduced Sydney and the gulf to second priority at Eastern Air Command; the urgent need was to strengthen long-range patrols from Newfoundland. Experienced personnel were once more posted away from 8 Squadron, and some of the available qualified crews periodically departed to ferry new Bolingbrokes from Montreal to both their own and other units. Thus, although 8 Squadron carried out patrols throughout the season, it was equally preoccupied with rebuilding yet again and did not regularly undertake a full slate of operations until September.

The detachment of 5 Squadron Stranraer flying boats that returned to North Sydney from Dartmouth at the end of May 1941 had a busy season until 8 Squadron became fully operational in the autumn. The prospects for fuller long-range coverage of the Sydney and gulf areas brightened in the summer when Consolidated Aircraft in California began delivery on Canadian orders of PBY flying boats, known as Cansos in their RCAF configuration. Personnel for a new flying boat unit, 117 Squadron, began to gather at Sydney Airport, and in August they moved to North Sydney. Shortly thereafter, however, Air Force Headquarters acceded to a British plea for the new flying boats. No. 117 Squadron therefore became dormant and its personnel, together with the Stranraer flying boats it had begun to receive while awaiting the Cansos, moved to Western Air Command.[87]

In view of the evidence that submarines were now patrolling as far west as the Grand Banks, the Admiralty, as in 1918, recommended that convoys should take the northern passage through the Strait of Belle Isle as soon as the ice had cleared sufficiently to allow passage.[88] To make the challenge greater still, all three groups of merchant ships from the Canadian East Coast – the main fast HX convoys from Halifax, the fast SHX joiners from Sydney, and now also the slow SC convoys from Sydney – were joining at sea to form massed convoys, thus allowing a concentration of the limited escort warship strength in order to afford more effective protection. The first convoys to try the Strait of Belle Isle passage were HX 138, which sailed from Halifax on the morning of 11 July, and SHX 138 and SC 37, which sailed from Sydney a day later. The more than ninety merchant ships sailed as three distinct convoys, each under its own local escort, until they were through the Strait of Belle Isle, when they were to combine into a massed group and the Newfoundland Escort Force from St John's would relieve the local escorts. This is in fact what happened, but not without the elements taking their toll.

The Halifax convoy, HX 138, entered the southern Cabot Strait on the evening of 12 July in dense fog. When altering course off Scatarie Island for the run north, one ship evidently made the full change all at once instead of in timed, smaller increments, as laid down in its instructions. Suddenly the crew of *Biafra*, which was turning correctly, saw the bow wave of the rapidly swinging ship loom close out of the foggy darkness. As *Biafra*'s crew shouted over their loud hailer, the other ship's bow sliced deeply into its engine room, which immediately began to flood. A few minutes later a second ship, *Comanchee*, slammed into *Biafra*, and in the mêlée two other ships collided, one of which was seriously damaged. Incredibly, *Biafra* did not sink. *Comanchee* and two others stood by through the night, making fog signals for it, as the stricken vessel had no power. At dawn, *Comanchee* managed to get a towline aboard *Biafra*, and a few hours later two tugs, *Cruizer* and *Foundation Franklin*, groped their way to the scene in the 'murk.' *Biafra*, according to Farley Mowat's famous account of *Foundation Franklin*'s ocean rescues, was an incredible sight. 'Listing fourteen degrees, and so far down by the stern that her after well-deck was almost awash, she seemed to be hanging on in complete defiance of the laws of buoyancy.' *Foundation Franklin*'s crew managed to swing a pump from the tug's deck directly onto the stricken vessel. Even so, the ship just barely survived the tow into Louisbourg Harbour, where it was beached on the evening of the 13th. It took eleven days of patching and reinforcing the shattered hull before it was able to proceed to Halifax, the nearest port with a dry dock. Three of the other ships involved in collisions also proved to be too badly damaged to continue the voyage and returned to Halifax, although they were able to do so under their own power.[89]

Meanwhile, all three convoys had groped their way up the west coast of Newfoundland in heavy fog on the 13th. During a clear spell early on the 14th the fast group from Sydney was able to join the main body of HX 138, but later that day both HX 138 and SC 37 began to encounter ice as they approached the Strait of Belle Isle. The captain of HMCS *St Croix*, one of the destroyers escorting HX 138, described that difficult night: 'Enormous icebergs and innumerable growlers were seen to be in all directions; the ship ahead was going full astern to avoid ramming one and a large tanker was steering 90° to the course, straight for "St Croix," 200 yards off. The convoy was not in recognizable columns but steering various courses and speeds to try and find a way through. A conservative estimate of the largest iceberg's height, judging from the height of the mast of the Commodore's ship, would be 200 feet and they were probably aground in 55 fathoms.'[90] Meanwhile, the British armed merchant cruiser *Aurania*, which had sailed with SC 37 to provide anti-raider protection to both that convoy and HX 138 when they combined beyond the strait, struck an iceberg in the darkness and had to turn back for Halifax. Nevertheless, the two convoys managed to clear the strait after daylight on the 15th and meet their escorts from St John's. They relieved the corvettes from Sydney and destroyers from Halifax, as the ships combined into one large convoy on the 16th and headed for Britain.[91]

The next convoys to attempt the northern passage, HX 140 and SC 38, ran into the same unpleasant combination of heavy fog and ice when they approached the Strait of Belle Isle on 25 July. They were even less successful in maintaining order than their predecessors had been, and six merchant ships had to turn back to St John's or Sydney because of collisions between vessels and with icebergs. This setback, Mitchell declared, 'once more proved the aptness of the title "Newfoundland Navy" as applied to Belle Isle icebergs which are incidentally now being referred to as Hitler's secret weapon.'[92] These losses resulted in the abandonment of the Strait of Belle Isle route for a month, until the sailing of SC 41 from Sydney on 24 August.

Meanwhile, the organization of the transatlantic convoys had been revised. The system inaugurated earlier in 1941 of sailing slow SC convoys every eleven days and of combining them at sea with every second fast HX convoy, which sailed every five to six days, had allowed a stronger mid-ocean escort, but it also had disadvantages. Every second fast convoy was slowed to the rate of the SC ships, which resulted in loss of much-needed carrying capacity and made the fast ships more vulnerable to U-boat attack than they otherwise would have been. The combined SC and HX convoys, moreover, had become very large, eighty to one hundred ships, too large for effective manoeuvring and defence, according to the faulty wisdom of the day.[93]

In August 1941 the Admiralty instituted changes that produced a larger number of more moderately sized convoys. Aside from the problems of combined HX and SC sailings, the HX convoys were becoming too big. The Admiralty therefore raised the slowest speed for a ship's inclusion in the HX series from nine to ten knots, and transferred all the ships slower than ten knots to the SC series. To accommodate these additional ships, the SC convoys now sailed every five to six days, the same as the HX convoys. The SHX series of fast joiners from Sydney was cancelled, and the SC and HX convoys now sailed independently. One immediate result of the change was that larger numbers of ships began to present themselves for convoy at Sydney – 289 in September 1941 compared to 181 in July – and this strained the port's limited service facilities.[94] Another result was increased pressure on the Newfoundland Escort Force. Whereas two eastbound convoys had previously sailed in each eleven-day cycle (one HX and one HX and SC combined), now there were four, two HX and two SC.

As luck would have it, the changes that had both expanded the size of SC convoys and reduced protection for them coincided with another run of very bad times, reminiscent of the ordeal in the summer and autumn of 1940. The transatlantic convoys had had, in fact, a very good summer because, as we now know, British intelligence had penetrated the Enigma cipher, which U-boat headquarters used to communicate with its submarines at sea. This breakthrough allowed the Admiralty to route convoys clear of U-boat concentrations. However, in late August and September, the U-boats, whose numbers had increased with the progress of construction and training programs, launched a fresh and much larger westward offensive.[95] Because of Germany's new ability to deploy simultaneously several groups of submarines to cover possible evasion routes of the convoys, the Allies began to run out of sea room in which to steer the merchant ships clear of danger. As in the German submarine offensive of 1940, the slower SC convoys were especially at risk.

SC 42, which sailed from Sydney on 30 August, tried but could not quite skirt a powerful group of sixteen U-boats that Admiralty intelligence knew to be east of Greenland, and it lost sixteen of its sixty-two merchant vessels in a vicious battle that lasted from 9 to 12 September.[96] SC 44, which sailed from Sydney on the 11th, was attacked by another U-boat group southeast of Greenland from 18 to 20 September, losing five merchant ships and HMCS *Lévis*, the first casualty among the Canadian corvettes.[97] Then the unforgiving elements in the Strait of Belle Isle struck again on the 26th when SC 46, which had left Sydney two days before, became disorganized in heavy fog. One vessel sank after a collision, although the corvette *Shediac* was able to rescue the entire crew. Two other merchant ships ran aground, as did a third after it was damaged in a collision, and three other vessels had to return to Sydney because of damage through collisions.[98]

Misfortune continued to haunt the even-numbered Sydney convoys. In a fierce battle south of Iceland from 15 to 18 October, SC 48 lost nine merchant ships as well as a British destroyer and corvette to a large wolf pack. In addition, the American destroyer *Kearney*, which had come down from Iceland to help, was severely damaged by a torpedo attack, producing the first battle casualties of the still neutral United States.[99] The enemy, meanwhile, was moving closer to Canada. SC 52, which sailed from Sydney on 29 October, followed the route south of Newfoundland because the Admiralty knew that U-boats were probing far to the west to ascertain if convoys were being evasively routed through the Strait of Belle Isle.[100] On finding no traffic there, these boats moved southward and located SC 52 just off Cape Race. Aware from radio intelligence of the great danger to the convoy, the Admiralty ordered it to turn north and return to port by way of the Strait of Belle Isle. The U-boats kept contact, however, and on 3 November sank four ships only eighty miles from the strait.[101] As for the twenty-eight vessels that returned to Sydney, the staff there quickly prepared them again for sea and sent them off with the next convoy. SC 54, which departed on the 10th with seventy-two ships, was the largest convoy to sail from Sydney in the war.[102] The Admiralty succeeded in routing it, as it had so many others, clear of danger. Shortly afterward, the pressure on the North Atlantic temporarily eased when Hitler ordered the submarine fleet to concentrate on the route to Gibraltar and in the Mediterranean to support German forces in North Africa.[103]

The last convoy of the season, SC 64, sailed on 9 January 1942. Total sailings in transatlantic convoys during the 1941 season were 1,582 ships, compared to 967 ships in the shorter 1940 season. The losses to enemy action, the weather, and ice totalled 52 ships, a tiny proportion of what had sailed and a convincing vindication of the convoy system. More disturbing for the naval staff at Sydney, because it was preventable, was the return from convoy of 120 ships because of mechanical defects caused by inadequate maintenance and hard wartime running. These returns resulted in many days or weeks of lost sea time, prompt repairs often proving to be impossible because of Sydney's underdeveloped port facilities and the nature of the local economy.[104]

The Department of Public Works was upgrading the facilities at the largest local ship repair firm, Sydney Foundry, with a three-thousand-ton marine railway and improvements to the wharfage, but Commander Mitchell and Captain Goolden, not the most patient of men, wondered if it was worth the effort in view of some of the business practices they had seen. In one case, Sydney Foundry had refused to supply steel plate to a merchant ship because a competitor was doing the installation work, forcing the other firm to make do with less adequate material.[105] Not that Mitchell was entirely without sympathy: 'The town is primarily a Company town depending on the operations of the Company, The Dominion Steel & Coal Company, for its prosperity. The ramifications of that Company are obvious when one considers that it controls all coal bunkering, the Dominion Shipping Company – one of the Port's three ship agents – and has had one of its Officials appointed as Deputy Representative, [of the British] Ministry of War Transport. By virtue of the work it is able to distribute, the monies it disburses and the business it is able to influence, it practically controls the economic life of the City – a situation which is obviously an unhealthy one.'[106] While problems of this nature were, perhaps, inevitable, given the greatly increased pressure on the port in 1941, the German submarine fleet would not make allowances for inefficiencies at Sydney or elsewhere. The U-boats were headed for Nova Scotia.

chapter eleven

Battle of the St Lawrence, 1942

For all its insignificance to the war's worldwide power balance, in Canada and Newfoundland Caribou *'s loss was the most significant sinking of the war.*

James B. Lamb, 1986

Just as the 1941 shipping season at Sydney was coming to a close, far-distant events were bringing the war even closer to Canada's shores. On 7 December 1941, Japanese carrier-based aircraft attacked and crippled or sank much of the American battleship force at Pearl Harbor in the Hawaiian Islands. Hitler, respecting the terms of the German–Japanese alliance, promptly declared war against the United States. He also lifted a ban on operations close in to the North American coast that he had previously imposed to forestall full-scale American participation in the war. Admiral Dönitz dispatched five big long-range Type IX submarines to the Canadian and American coasts and six smaller and shorter-ranged Type VIIs to hover off Newfoundland.[1]

The opening blow of the German offensive came late on 11 January 1942 when *U-123* torpedoed and sank *Cyclops* about 180 miles south of Halifax. The next morning, a 119 Squadron Bolingbroke, while making a routine harbour entrance patrol about thirty miles north of the mouth of Sydney Harbour, sighted *U-130* on the surface about three miles away. The pilot, Sergeant R.L. Parker, dove from his cruising altitude of seven hundred feet down to two hundred feet and dropped two 250-pound anti-submarine bombs, but he was not quick enough and *U-130* had time to submerge fully. Its commander, Ernst Kals, was shaken that the boat had been taken by surprise, however, and berated the lookout who

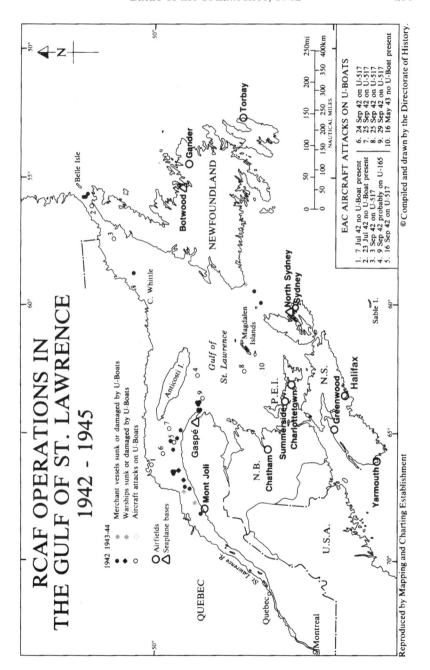

RCAF OPERATIONS IN
THE GULF OF ST. LAWRENCE
1942 - 1945

1942 1943-44
● ◆ ○   Merchant vessels sunk or damaged by U-Boats
● ◆ ○   Warships sunk or damaged by U-Boats
● ◆ ○   Aircraft attacks on U-Boats

○ Airfields
△ Seaplane bases

EAC AIRCRAFT ATTACKS ON U-BOATS

1. 7 Jul 42 no U-Boat present
2. 23 Jul 42 no U-Boat present
3. 3 Sep 42 on U-517
4. 9 Sep 42 probably on U-165
5. 16 Sep 42 on U-517
6. 24 Sep 42 on U-517
7. 25 Sep 42 on U-517
8. 25 Sep 42 on U-517
9. 29 Sep 42 on U-517
10. 16 May 43 no U-Boat present

NAUTICAL MILES
0   50   100   150   200   250   300   350
0   50   100   150   200   250mi
0   100   200   300   400km

© Compiled and drawn by the Directorate of History.

Reproduced by Mapping and Charting Establishment

QUEBEC

Montreal
Quebec
St. Lawrence R.

U.S.A.

Mont Joli
Gaspé
Anticosti I.
Gulf of
St. Lawrence

N.B.
Chatham

P.E.I.
Summerside
Charlottetown

N.S.
Greenwood
Halifax

Yarmouth

Magdalen
Islands

North Sydney
Sydney

Sable I.

NEWFOUNDLAND

Botwood   Gander

Torbay

Belle Isle

C. Whittle

N

had been on watch. Five other flights by 119 Squadron's Bolingbrokes scoured Cabot Strait through the rest of the day until nightfall. None spotted Kals, who was keeping his head down, but he sighted them and warned in his subsequent radio report of the 'heavy air cover' in the area.[2] An experienced unit that had previously been based at Yarmouth, 119 Squadron had only recently arrived at Sydney, taking the place of 8 Squadron, which had gone to reinforce the West Coast's meagre defences in the wake of Pearl Harbor.[3]

Following its run-in with the aircraft, *U-130* slipped out of Cabot Strait. After nightfall on 12 January, some sixty-five miles east of Scatarie Island, it came upon the Norwegian steamer *Frisko* on passage from Savannah, Georgia, which was less than twenty-four hours from its destination, Argentia, Newfoundland. The crew could see nothing in the blackness, when a torpedo slammed into the forward part of the vessel and, a few minutes later, a second exploded amidships, setting it ablaze. Although the captain, second mate, and two seamen were killed in the explosions, the remaining fifteen crew members managed to get away from the flaming hulk in two lifeboats. Distress signals sent out after the first torpedo hit do not appear to have been picked up by anyone, and word of *Frisko*'s fate did not get out until two days later, when a schooner came upon one of the lifeboats, still sailing for Argentia. It delivered the six survivors to North Sydney, where Navy League volunteers cared for them. No trace appears to have been found of the second lifeboat and its nine occupants.[4]

Equally grim was the fate of *Friar Rock*, which had sailed from Sydney early on the 10th, making haste to catch up with its convoy, SC 64, which had departed on the 9th. Kals located the steamer before dawn on 13 January, the same night as his attack on *Frisko*, further out on the shipping route between Nova Scotia and Cape Race. Two torpedoes quickly sank the vessel, and again no word got out to authorities ashore. On the 17th the British destroyer *Montgomery* discovered a single lifeboat with seven survivors and the frozen corpses of twelve others, who had perished of exposure during the nightmarish four days adrift. The survivors said that a second boat with another nineteen survivors had cleared the wreck but capsized; the occupants would not have survived more than a few minutes in the icy water.[5]

U-130 continued to patrol in the approaches to Cabot Strait, cautiously remaining submerged much of the time and not sending radio signals. Unaware that the SC convoys had now shifted to Halifax for the winter and that only a trickle of shipping was entering and leaving Sydney, Kals was puzzled and frustrated by the absence of traffic. He pushed to within twenty miles of the mouth of Sydney Harbour in the hours before dawn on 16 January, intrigued by the bright illumination of the city. Understandably, he took this to be a sign of unpreparedness for war, but in fact the brilliant glow came from the steel plant, about which Canadian military authorities had concluded nothing could be done without disrupting production. Having moved seaward of Scatarie Island, *U-130* now had a terrifying encounter when it was nearly run over by two escorts that seem not to have known of the submarine's presence. This incident persuaded Kals that this barren stretch of paralyzingly cold ocean, bereft of targets and under the watch of active defences, was no longer worthwhile. *U-130* departed for the warmer and more promising waters between Halifax and New York.[6]

The Canadian response to the 'guerrilla' submarines prowling the coast was, as in 1918, immediately to sail as much local shipping as possible under the protection of whatever escort vessel happened to be available at the port of departure.[7] This policy was successful, for the submarines soon had difficulty in finding shipping, and when they did they seldom risked an attack if an escort was present. By contrast, the United States continued to allow its shipping to sail independently in the stubborn belief that weakly escorted convoys merely provided concentrated targets for U-boats. Quite sensibly, the U-boats shifted the focus of the western offensive from Canadian to American waters and further south into the Caribbean.

The main concern in 1942, again as in 1918, was the safety of the big eastbound SC and HX transatlantic convoys during their first few days of passage when they were easiest to locate, still incompletely organized, and, because of the priority for protection on the mid-ocean run east of Newfoundland, weakly screened by naval escorts. There was also a new problem: the security in coastal waters and port approaches of westbound transatlantic convoys when they arrived from Britain. These convoys, which were designated ON, had been started in the spring of 1941, but until now had dispersed off Cape Race; the merchant ships had proceeded independently to their destinations on the Canadian and U.S. coasts when the Newfoundland Escort Force escorts put into St John's or Argentia. In January 1942 the U-boats had found their best targets among these unescorted merchant vessels south and west of Cape Race. Some trimming of the Newfoundland-based escort groups, possible in part because German pressure had shifted from the central Atlantic to the west, freed Canadian and British ships to create the Halifax-based

Western Local Escort Force in February 1942. Its mission was to supply groups of five or six escorts for HX, SC, and ON convoys between Halifax and the rendezvous with the Newfoundland-based groups off Cape Race.[8] Soon, however, the withdrawal of not only all but a handful of American escorts but also of a considerable number of British ones from northern waters to meet the crises on the American Atlantic seaboard and in the Caribbean left the Canadian navy very thinly stretched. These circumstances greatly increased the importance of the air force. For 119 Squadron and RCAF Station Sydney it meant that there was no winter respite from operational flying over the vital route between Halifax and Cape Race. In the dreary routine of endless uneventful hours flying over grey water, the main excitement consisted most often of a gnawing anxiety about safely getting back to base in deteriorating weather. This routine was occasionally punctuated by calls for searches in response to supposedly 'hot' U-boat sightings, though nothing usually turned up.

The sighting frantically broadcast by *Bayou Chico* on the morning of 23 March 1942, however, was absolutely sound. The steamer had fallen behind convoy HX 181, along with the tanker *British Prudence*. *U-754* torpedoed the tanker and then pursued *Bayou Chico*, which proved to be a more difficult prey. It 'zigzagged wildly' and opened fire with its self-defence gun, and eventually succeeded in escaping in the misty weather. Three Bolingbrokes from Sydney took off for the position, some 150 miles to the southeast, and the one piloted by Sergeant W.M. Howes sighted the fully surfaced submarine. Plunging from an altitude of nine hundred feet to just above the surface of the water, the aircraft dropped a 250-pound depth charge, a slightly modified version of the basic naval depth charge just being introduced in Eastern Air Command to replace the ineffective anti-submarine bombs previously carried by Allied maritime aircraft. The depth charge 'dropped just beside the submarine which was partly lifted out of the water bow first by the force of the explosion. It then submerged stern first but reappeared on the surface.' Howes, meanwhile, had come around and dropped another depth charge, whose explosion appeared to cause the submarine to sink.

The British Admiralty's U-boat Assessment Committee disagreed. This panel of professional sceptics, whose task it was to review all reports of attacks on U-boats to guard against inflated claims, had long experience of the difficulties of developing air tactics and weapons capable of splitting open the tough hulls of submarines. In fact, German submarines were so sturdily built that it required a closely spaced 'stick' of several charges, so accurately laid across the hull that at least two exploded within less than eighteen feet of it, to inflict lethal damage. In this case, the committee correctly concluded that the U-boat had suffered only minor damage, although the submarine's commander himself remarked that the depth charges had been 'well placed.'[9]

Winter operations exacted a heavy toll on 119 Squadron. Four Bolingbrokes were lost in serious crashes, two of them with fatalities, among them Sergeant Parker, who had instilled caution in *U-130*'s Kapitänleutnant Kals in January.[10] There was, moreover, no opportunity whatever for either the air force or the navy to gear up for the spring opening of the shipping season as there had been in previous years. As soon as shipping began to sail regularly in May, Sydney became the hub of the coastal convoy system, in addition to having once more to assemble and sail the big SC convoys and the HX feeder groups. As Commander Mitchell put it, Sydney was 'rather in the position of a railway junction as Convoys radiated from us in five directions.'[11]

The pressure on the armed forces in the spring of 1942 was greatly increased by an event that naval officers had feared since 1915: the appearance of a submarine far inside the Gulf of St Lawrence. There was no warning of *U-553*'s passage through Cabot Strait on 8–9 May 1942 because the U-boat fleet had switched in February from the three-rotor Enigma encoding machine to a new four-rotor model that British cryptographers did not succeed in cracking until November. Fortuitously, however, a false submarine sighting from an observer on shore brought out RCAF and U.S. air patrols from Newfoundland. One of the American aircraft unsuccessfully attacked the U-boat near Anticosti Island on the afternoon of the 10th, but there were no warships in the gulf to follow up the contact. The Canadian services, which had carefully and regularly given consideration to the defence of the gulf since before the outbreak of war, had rightly concluded that none of the navy's hard-pressed escorts should be diverted from the critically important ocean routes – where the Atlantic war would be won or lost – until sinkings actually occurred in the gulf. Even then, only the bare minimum number of warships would be transferred; the air force would be the primary defence.[12]

Confirmation from the U.S. command in Newfoundland that the attacks on the 10th were not just another in a series of false claims caused by sightings of floating logs and other flotsam that was so thick in Canadian and Newfoundland coastal waters was slow to reach Halifax. Nevertheless, Eastern Air Command ordered patrols over the gulf on

11 May, although much of the work had to be done by student aircrew
in light training aircraft from the General Reconnaissance School at
Charlottetown because of the shortage of combat units.

On the night of 11–12 May 1942, *U-553* began what became known
as the Battle of the St Lawrence by sinking two ships that were sailing
independently and without escort off the north shore of the Gaspé
Peninsula. As survivors came ashore with the news a few hours later,
Eastern Air Command extracted a handful of aircraft from the mainland Nova Scotia bases and dispatched them to the western gulf for
extended operations.

At Sydney, the RCAF was especially hard pressed. No. 119 Squadron
was flying up to ten four-hour missions per day to maintain coverage of
coastal and ocean convoys outside the gulf, and now, with the assistance
from Coast Artillery Cooperation Lysanders, added a heavy schedule of
patrols over Cabot Strait in case the submarine moved to these heavily
travelled waters.[13] The North Sydney flying boat station was the scene of
frenetic activity as well. Personnel had been posted to the station to re-
establish 117 Squadron, but as yet there were no aircraft. These began
to arrive immediately, together with additional experienced aircrew,
from 116 Squadron at Dartmouth, thus enabling the new unit quickly to
begin operations.[14]

After holding gulf shipping in port following the sinkings, the navy
began sailings in improvised convoys within two days,[15] and on the 17th
started regular scheduled sailings in a new Sydney–Quebec (SQ westbound, QS eastbound) series. Soon afterward, Sydney–Corner Brook
(SB and BS) convoys began to operate to protect the flow of supplies
that sustained both the civilian population and the large American and
Canadian armed forces in the island dominion.[16]

By the end of May, seventy-two merchant ships had sailed in eighteen
coastal convoys to Halifax, St John's, Corner Brook, and Quebec over a
period of only seventeen days. As well, the first transatlantic convoy of
the season, SC 85, sailed on 29 May. During the period from 11 May to
2 June some forty warships cleared port, most of them on escort missions, while the air force flew almost constantly from dawn to dusk to
provide coverage on all routes.

These efforts, though limited, proved effective. *U-553*, reporting
'very, very attentive air cover' in the gulf to U-boat headquarters, kept a
low profile and made no attempt to attack the escorted shipping. By
21 May the submarine had departed through Cabot Strait. Canadian
naval intelligence, using direction-finding bearings on its radio signals,

correctly concluded that *U-553* was homebound, but it incorrectly surmised, from bearings on a westbound submarine's signals, that another U-boat was headed into the gulf to follow up *U-553*'s success.[17]

This false alert increased the pressure on the Atlantic Coast and Sydney Commands to complete preparations for what was already an extremely busy season. The plans for the gulf had allocated Bangor minesweepers, armed yachts, and Fairmile motor launches for escort services. Of these, only the Bangors were fully suitable. Although they were only two thirds the size of a corvette, at six to seven hundred tons displacement, and had less endurance, the original eighteen that had arrived from the shipyards in the latter half of 1941 had proven to be very good coastal escorts when used for that purpose rather than for their designed role as minesweepers. The armed yachts had always been a stopgap compromise with many shortcomings. The 112-foot wooden Fairmile motor launches had good speed – twenty knots – and anti-submarine equipment, but they were light vessels and could not keep the sea in heavy weather.[18]

The Gulf Escort Force for the Sydney–Quebec convoys was based at Gaspé. By 1 July it included five Bangors, one armed yacht, and three Fairmiles. At that time, the Sydney Force included three Bangors, two armed yachts, six Fairmiles, and the three small auxiliary minesweepers *Rayon d'Or*, *Star XVI*, and *Suderoy V*. In addition to the local defence of the Sydney approaches, this force was responsible for escorting the Newfoundland ferry that sailed between North Sydney and Port-aux-Basques and the Corner Brook convoys. In fact, the Gaspé and Sydney Commands acted as one, with ships shuffling from one to the other as needed. The Gaspé ships were constant visitors at Sydney, delivering or picking up Sydney–Quebec convoys. Naturally, the Gulf Escort Force ships availed themselves of the repair and other facilities at Sydney, which were on a larger scale than those at the small Gaspé base. Sydney was also a second home for the destroyers, corvettes, and Bangors of the Western Local Escort Force that now supplied the escorts for the SC convoys, shepherded St Lawrence-bound ships into Sydney from ON convoys, and shuttled coastal convoys between St John's, Sydney, and Halifax.[19]

Given the weakness of the naval escort forces in the gulf, it was fortunate that some resources were available from American aircraft production to strengthen the air forces. By early June 117 Squadron had a complement of seven Canso and Catalina[20] flying boats. A detachment of two or three of these aircraft operated from the recently opened flying boat station at Gaspé, which functioned as a satellite of the bigger, better-equipped North Sydney Station.[21] Although the Cansos and Catalinas were slow, with a cruising speed of one hundred knots or less, they could fly for up to twenty-four hours while carrying a full stick of four depth charges, giving them a formidable patrol range of five hundred miles or more. Also in early June, 119 Squadron at the airport completed its conversion to Lockheed Hudson bombers and had a full slate of fifteen on strength.[22] These sturdy aircraft matched the smaller Bolingbroke's speed of two to two hundred and fifty knots, but they could carry four depth charges to a patrol range of three hundred and fifty miles, which exceeded the Bolingbroke by one hundred miles or more.

The somewhat strengthened air and sea defences at Sydney and elsewhere on the Canadian East Coast were, nevertheless, still utterly inadequate for the tasks at hand. The special difficulties of defending against submarines in the gulf became apparent in July when U-132 followed up U-553's reconnaissance. This U-boat appears to have approached Cabot Strait on 30 June and proceeded to the mouth of the St Lawrence River without the Allies' picking up any hint of its presence. Thus it was able to get in position near Cap-Chat, some ninety miles further than U-553's attacks, and sink three vessels in convoy QS 15 on the dark night of 5–6 July. One of the escorts saw the submarine just as it was diving after the attacks and managed to throw off a quick depth charge salvo that damaged the boat. At no point, however, were the escorts then able to make asdic contact. Although the heavy air patrols in the days following the attack forced U-132 to keep virtually immobile below the water except under the cover of darkness, it was able to torpedo a merchant ship in convoy QS 19 in broad daylight, again in the Cap-Chat area, on 20 July. Once again, the escorts never made asdic contact.[23]

During the summer there were further, unrelated, changes in the convoy system radiating from Sydney. Early in July the port's convoy staff began to organize and sail ships, including troop transports, that sustained large American airbase construction projects in the Canadian Arctic and Greenland. These bases were vital to the ferrying of aircraft across the Atlantic to Britain, as was Gander Airport in Newfoundland and the new northern airfield being built by the Canadian government at Goose Bay, Labrador. Escorts for the American Sydney–Greenland (SG and GS) convoys were provided by the U.S. Navy's Greenland Patrol, a force made up of U.S. Coast Guard cutters and an odd assortment of other craft, President Roosevelt having integrated the coast guard into the navy to meet the crisis in the Atlantic.[24] These vessels became familiar visitors in Sydney as they came in to meet merchant ships that had loaded at American ports and sailed to Cape Breton in the coastal convoys.

Although these convoys were small – there were only three ships in SG 1, which sailed on 6 July – their organization presented many challenges. The coast guard officers were inexperienced in convoy work and therefore needed a good deal of guidance, but the northern operations were so cloaked in secrecy that the Canadians had to struggle to get necessary information, in at least one case ignoring U.S. security regulations and opening sealed classified documents.[25] The tiny U.S. Navy liaison staff in Sydney, which included only two officers and a few support personnel, immediately found itself swamped and deeply dependent on the Canadian services for help with everything from the assembly of detailed navigational information about the Arctic to management of the twelve tons of mail per month and the 'much larger quantities of stores and explosives' that arrived for the ships of the Greenland Patrol. Like so many mariners who visited the Cape Breton port, the Americans were grateful for 'this wholehearted and complete sharing of ... already taxed accommodations and facilities.'[26]

The most significant change in the summer of 1942 was the transfer of the assembly of SC transatlantic convoys from Sydney. With the United States now in the war, an increasing proportion of shipping for the convoys was coming from American ports. The need, because of the heavy scale of the U-boat offensive, to route these vessels northward in coastal convoys every step of the way from U.S. port to U.S. port to Halifax and then on to Cape Breton was causing delays that translated directly into lost capacity at a time when the broadening scope of the war and the heavy demands of the American armed forces for overseas transport were increasing the pressure on shipping available to Britain. Thus, the shipping authorities decided on the more efficient course of having the transatlantic convoys sail directly from New York, the main loading port, with ships that loaded at more northerly ports going out in feeder convoys to join the main body at sea. ON convoys from Britain would similarly terminate at New York, with ships bound for more northerly ports peeling off as the main body passed their destination. SC 94, the last full transatlantic convoy from Sydney, sailed on 31 July. Thereafter, small SSC feeder convoys sailed from Sydney to meet the main body of the SC convoys as they came up from the south.[27] This bid for efficiency was taken when Allied shipping and escorts were coming under still greater pressure. In the summer of 1942, the expanding German submarine fleet was able to take the offensive again at mid-ocean, with packs larger than those available in 1941, while also keeping up the pressure in North American waters. SC 94, continuing the grim saga of the slow convoys, was one of the first to be smashed in the renewed high seas offensive, losing eleven of its thirty-six merchant ships.[28]

Although the new organization of convoys achieved some efficiency in global Allied escort commitments, it did nothing to relieve the extreme demands on the Canadian navy. The Western Local Escort Force was made responsible for escorting the HX, SC, and ON convoys all the way from New York to Newfoundland, a distance of some one thousand miles, and nearly a third of the ocean passage.[29] Traffic in the local convoys on the Canadian coast was somewhat reduced, but none of these series could be eliminated.[30] At the same time, the Canadian navy was providing nearly half of the escorts for the Mid-Ocean Escort Force, as the Newfoundland Escort Force had been renamed earlier in the year, which was responsible for the passage between Newfoundland and Northern Ireland.

Worse still, the U-boats now took full advantage of the conditions that heavily favoured them in the Gulf of St Lawrence. In August Dönitz directed three submarines, *U-517*, *U-513*, and *U-165*, to make another reconnaissance of the Strait of Belle Isle. Because of the continued inability of the Allies to break the four-rotor Enigma cipher, there was no warning and therefore no opportunity to route traffic to the south as there had been in 1941. On 27 and 28 August, *U-517* and *U-165* sank two vessels and severely damaged a third of the six merchant ships in the U.S. Arctic convoy SG 6. One of the ships lost was the American army transport *Chatham* with 562 persons on board, including 145 workers from a Canadian company carrying out construction work on bases in the Arctic. Thanks to the calm weather, the level-headedness of the crew, and effective rescue work by the coast guard escort, assisted by RCAF aircraft from Newfoundland and the Canadian corvette *Trail*, which was in the vicinity, only 13 of those on *Chatham* lost their lives, along with 18 more from the two other ships that were subsequently hit. Most of the survivors returned to Sydney in the coast guard ships that escorted the damaged vessel, *Laramie*, there.[31]

The Canadian navy called on the other two services at Sydney for help, and the army boarded ninety civilian workers at Victoria Park as guests of the garrison units. Some of them remained for a week or more and, 'as most of the men had very little clothing, garments were lent to them and every effort was made to assist them.'[32] The reception given to these men, and especially the care of the injured, reinforced Sydney's reputation as a friendly port. As the U.S. War Department said in thanking the convoy staff, 'your efforts on behalf of these men were largely responsible in reducing the number of casualties and in restoring morale after their trying experience.'[33]

The attacks on SG 6 were the beginning of the most difficult fortnight in Canadian waters during the war. On 5 September, people living around Sydney Harbour were shocked to learn that *U-513* had made a submerged run into the harbour at Bell Island, Newfoundland, and torpedoed two ships, *Lord Strathcona* and *Saganaga*; both went down, the latter with heavy loss of life. The ships were well known in Cape Breton, employed as they were in carrying ore from the Bell Island iron mines to the Sydney steel plant.[34] One immediate result of these losses was the establishment of yet another coastal convoy, the BW–WB series between Sydney and Conception Bay to protect these vital shipments.

By then, *U-165* and *U-517* had passed through the Strait of Belle Isle into the gulf where, between 3 and 16 September, they sank eight merchant ships, damaged a ninth, and destroyed two escorts, the armed yacht *Raccoon* and the corvette *Charlottetown*. These attacks were all classic ambushes, like those in the Strait of Belle Isle and that of *U-132* in the upper St Lawrence in July. In each case, although naval escorts were present and aircraft were either on hand or had recently swept the area, the submarines had managed to get into position, waiting for the shipping on the surface on dark nights or underwater in daylight. These losses were especially bitter because, forewarned by the Strait of Belle Isle attacks and by direction-finding bearings on the submarines' radio messages that correctly placed the boats on southward courses into the gulf, the Canadian air and naval commands had reinforced the gulf at the expense of the hard-pressed escort forces and air squadrons responsible for the higher priority tasks on the ocean routes off Nova Scotia and south of Newfoundland.[35]

The news was not all bad. Although the Canadian forces did not know it at the time, the depth charges dropped by an escort during one of the actions had damaged the torpedoes carried in *U-517*, and this may have contributed to the failure of the boat's subsequent attack on another convoy.[36] More important, there was a good reason why all but one of the submarine attacks in the gulf had taken place in the constricted route west of Gaspé up to the mouth of the St Lawrence River. As *U-165* reported to U-boat headquarters, it was 'difficult to contact [convoys east of Gaspé] because of air patrols.'[37] In other words, east of Gaspé, where the waters of the gulf broadened out and it was therefore necessary for the U-boats to make long runs on the surface to find shipping, the frequent appearance of aircraft made surface runs impossible. In the more constricted waters to the west, however, such searching was not necessary; it was possible to hide beneath the surface for long periods and still be within reach of shipping.

Despite the grim losses to shipping, Eastern Air Command smelled blood. In large-scale searches following submarine attacks north of the Gaspé Peninsula, Hudson bombers had made encouraging depth-charge strikes on 9 and 16 September. These confirmed airmen in their view that what was really needed were more aircraft in order to follow up aggressively every direction-finder bearing and credible sighting report with extensive patrols that continued around the clock for days if possible. Out in the broad central gulf it was sufficient to force the submarines to stay submerged during daylight hours, but in constricted passages, where shipping was more readily within reach, it was essential to so terrorize the submarine crews by the constant appearance of aircraft that they would not dare to make even the short runs needed to get into ambush positions, and would hesitate when there were opportunities for attack. In an unusual step, Eastern Air Command turned the Yarmouth patrol area off southern Nova Scotia over to American forces in order to free up additional reinforcements for the gulf. This, however, only increased the strength at Sydney and the inner gulf stations to about twenty-two Hudsons and ten Catalinas and Cansos, less than half the numbers the staff believed to be necessary.[38]

Modest as they were, the air reinforcements brought results. On 24 and 25 September, *U-517*, the sole submarine remaining after *U-165* turned for home a week before, was attacked three times by Hudsons while attempting to approach a convoy north of the Gaspé Peninsula. It therefore pressed on to Cabot Strait, hoping to attack the convoy in those constricted waters, only to find that conditions were no better there because of the around-the-clock patrols by the Sydney squadrons. On 27 and 28 September, aircraft overflew *U-517* eight times, and on four occasions came so close that it had to crash-dive. Amidst thick fog on the morning of the 28th, the submarine turned back towards the Gaspé Peninsula, where at least the visibility was better. Kapitänleutnant Paul Hartwig, the commanding officer of *U-517*, was nothing if not tenacious. He continued to track shipping and make attacks in the western gulf before departing for home on 7 October, but he was unsuccessful because of the continued air harassment and aggressive tactics of the naval escorts. The air reinforcements and the growing experience on the part of both the air and the naval forces had effectively neutralized the submarine. Had the gulf squadrons been equipped with the latest, most powerful aerial depth charges that were just beginning to reach Eastern Air Command, it is highly likely that *U-517* would have been very severely damaged or destroyed.[39]

The final phase of the September 1942 U-boat offensive in the gulf was laden with irony and, especially for the Sydney area, tragedy. Germany's Admiral Dönitz, who had to make his decisions on deployments before it was clear how effective the Canadian defences were becoming, immediately reinforced the success of *U-165* and *U-517* with three and then two more submarines, much the largest German effort in the gulf of the season. The meagre results in terms of ships destroyed confirmed the success of the methods the Canadians had ultimately employed against *U-517*. Yet Canada had already closed the St Lawrence to most ocean-going shipping, a decision that over time dislocated shipping much more seriously than had the enemy attacks in the gulf. Moreover, heavy loss of life in one of the few U-boat sinkings in the autumn of 1942 obscured the very substantial achievement of the Canadian forces, not just in the public eye, but also within the armed services themselves.

The government approved the closing of the gulf to ocean shipping on 9 September, the moment of greatest pressure on Canada's naval forces during the war. The successes of *U-517* and *U-165* had occurred just when the renewed U-boat wolf-pack attacks in the North Atlantic and the extension of the navy's western ocean escort responsibilities all the way south to New York had stretched the service nearly to its limit. The breaking point was a personal appeal from Britain's prime minister Winston Churchill for Canada to provide immediately seventeen corvettes to support the Allied landings in North Africa planned for early November. In closing the Gulf of St Lawrence in order to provide these ships and ease the strain on the ocean escort forces, the government underestimated how greatly delays to merchant vessels would be increased. Shipping and economic administrators had, in fact, for some months already, been urging that more ships be sent to Halifax and Saint John and fewer to the St Lawrence. During the summer shipping season on the St Lawrence, the East Coast ports were being underused. Thus important parts of their workforce were migrating to central Canada and finding better jobs, and they were not returning to help meet the winter crush of shipping traffic. No one foresaw the extent of the labour shortages at the ports, or the difficulties caused by the need to transport vast additional quantities of cargo over the limited eastern Canadian rail network.[40]

The naval staff at Sydney disagreed with closing the gulf, not least because a significant portion of the traffic in the SQ-QS series supplied important industries in the region. They proved to be right, and the Sydney–Quebec convoys continued, with sailings at intervals of seven or ten days instead of four days. The reduced schedule and the smaller numbers of merchant ships allowed the navy to withdraw the destroyers and corvettes that had been brought in to reinforce the route by the end of September, although the Bangors, Fairmiles, and armed yachts originally allocated to the gulf remained there. The smallness of these vessels and their limited numbers made the forces' achievement in suppressing the U-boats that came in during the autumn all the more impressive.[41]

Admiral Dönitz's headquarters had informed the submarines on their way to the gulf that 'defences proved comparatively weak and were limited to direct convoy escort.'[42] *U-69*, the first to arrive in Cabot Strait, on 30 September, found a different situation. While patrolling in the western strait, not far from St Paul Island, Kapitänleutnant Ulrich Gräf spotted a Sydney-bound convoy on the morning of 2 October. Although he tracked it all day, he was unable to get into attacking position, largely because of the repeated appearance of aircraft. He had to crash-dive four times. Air cover was indeed heavy, for reasons that demonstrated the increased efficiency of the defences. The navy had made direction-finding bearings on *U-69*'s radioed convoy-sighting reports and transmitted them to Sydney, where 119 Squadron flew three special searches, while 117 Squadron kept a Canso over the strait most of the day.[43] Unimpressed with the chances for success off Sydney, Gräf went on in to the gulf. On the night of 8–9 October, *U-69* sank a merchant ship, *Carolus*, well up the St Lawrence River, just short of Rimouski and only 173 miles from Quebec City. This proved to be the most westerly point of the U-boat successes in Canadian waters during the war. Although the naval escorts could not find the submarine in the difficult waters, the air force did its utmost to make the area extremely uncomfortable for it. The airmen saw nothing, but their efforts had an effect. Unable to surface long enough even to recharge its batteries, *U-69* began to slip away back towards Sydney on the 11th, not signalling or giving any indication of its presence.[44]

The Sydney approaches were now menaced as never before, for on

10 October *U-43* and *U-106* had entered Cabot Strait from the Atlantic. Both were operating silently, giving no warning to Allied authorities. Nevertheless, the heightened alert throughout the St Lawrence following the sinking of *Carolus* had a useful result. At Sydney, 119 Squadron was undertaking dawn-to-dusk sweeps of Cabot Strait – a commitment of three Hudson missions, each for four to six hours – in addition to the usual dawn-to-dusk coverage of all convoys in the area, the task in which 117 Squadron's long-endurance flying boats greatly assisted. *U-43* was forced to dive at least three times on the 10th in the face of four warnings of airborne radar and an aircraft sighting, which sufficed to keep it submerged and therefore virtually immobile by day.[45]

U-106 endured the same experience, but when twelve miles southeast of St Paul Island late on the morning of 11 October, it found itself perfectly placed for an ambush. It was running submerged under a rough sea whose waves entirely masked the periscope against radar and the human eye when convoy BS 31 – the armed yacht *Vison* escorting the tanker *Omaha* and the Great Lakes steamer *Waterton* in that order – crossed its track. Flying seven hundred and fifty feet overhead under the heavy, low cloud cover was a 117 Squadron Canso that had been on escort patrol since before dawn. Such was the limited speed of the submerged boat that it could fire only at the last vessel, which it did successfully; the two torpedoes caused an explosion that hurled debris from *Waterton*'s cargo of paper high into the air. The Canso, about half a mile away, dove through the smoke and shredded paper, while *Vison* raced towards the estimated firing position of the submarine and, without making asdic contact, dropped two 'scare' depth charges.

Command authorities on shore later criticized the haphazard counter-attack, the errors in which were partly the result of the technical shortcomings of the armed yacht, but *Vison*'s quick action had the desired effect. *U-106*'s commander, Kapitänleutnant Herman Rasch, who had been aware of the Canso's presence, believed that he was the target of a tightly coordinated, powerful air-sea hunting group. He interpreted *Vison*'s noisy propellers and subsequent more systematic depth-charge attacks as the work of 'two destroyers.' Although Rasch realized that the density layers in the water that were interfering with his manoeuvres were also blinding the asdic, he nevertheless plunged deep – four hundred feet – and hid for eight hours. Above him, *Reindeer*, two Fairmiles, and two 119 Squadron Hudsons, struggling in the poor flying conditions, had come out to support the convoy and continue the hunt. The shattered *Waterton* had gone down in eight minutes, but the navy was able to rescue all of its crew, who were taken into Sydney.[46] In reviewing this incident, Air Vice Marshal N.R. Anderson, a senior officer at Air Force Headquarters in Ottawa and a former commander of Eastern Air Command, rightly commented that it showed how little could be done to stop a U-boat once it was in an ambush position. He reaffirmed the need for the more aggressive tactics that the air force was already adopting: patrolling all areas where the presence of U-boats was suspected rather than merely escorting convoys.[47]

In fact, the Sydney squadrons had done better than Anderson or any other Allied authority knew, having entirely suppressed *U-69* and then *U-43* in their runs through the area, and limiting *U-106* to a single, quite lucky, chance to shoot. Like the rest of Eastern Air Command, the Sydney units were beginning to reach the limits of what aircraft anti-submarine methods could achieve. By compelling U-boats to remain submerged except at night or in poor visibility conditions, the air force had so restricted them that they could no longer make the multiple attacks that had inflicted serious losses in the Gulf of St Lawrence only a month before. In suppressing the submarines so that they seldom dared show themselves or even send out radio signals, however, the air defences also reduced the likelihood of ever locating them. This meant that it was still possible for a U-boat to slip into an area and to make one ambush attack, and Allied anti-submarine doctrine actually accepted that the sinking of a ship would provide the only sure knowledge that a U-boat had arrived in a particular zone. It was this hard reality – and the absence in Canadian waters of the strong specialized naval hunting groups needed to complement air searches – that produced tragedy in the Sydney area at the very time that the U-boats were admitting defeat.

Following the sinking of *Waterton*, the intelligence picture grew hazy, as none of the boats signalled or acted aggressively. The loss of *Carolus* in the river and of *Waterton* in Cabot Strait only a few days apart left no doubt there were two submarines in the gulf. Subsequent sightings – all probably false – suggested that there might be as many as four, possibly in patrol areas extending all the way from St Pierre and Miquelon to the mouth of the St Lawrence River, a distance of about eight hundred miles.[48] Eastern Air Command continued the intense flying program that had been carried out since the sinkings, including dawn-to-dusk sweeps of Cabot Strait by the Sydney units, but it was impossible, given the widely dispersed areas where the submarines might be operating, to concentrate the effort where it would be most effective.[49]

On the evening of the 13th the Newfoundland Railway ferry, *Caribou,* only recently back in service after a long refit, made one of its regular thrice-weekly trips across the strait from North Sydney to Port-aux-Basques.[50] Built in 1925, *Caribou* had been commanded since 1928 by 'big, tough Ben Taverner, a fatherly but no-nonsense man.'[51] He was sixty-two years old and had two sons among the crew of forty-six. Indeed, there were seven pairs of brothers in the crew – Taverner, Hann, Strickland, Dominie, Coffin, Gale, and Thomas. A third Taverner son, Colin, had just recently left the crew.[52] The crew were all men except for Bridget Fitzpatrick, the stewardess. Of the 191 passengers, 118 – many of them Newfoundlanders – 'were members of the Canadian, British, or American armed forces, and most of the seventy-three civilians [had] a direct connection with people in uniform.'[53] *Caribou* was preceded by the Canadian navy's Sydney-based Bangor-class minesweeper *Grandmère*, commanded by Lieutenant James Cuthbert,[54] which made an anti-submarine patrol in the port's near approaches and then fell in behind the ferry about fifteen hundred yards off the starboard quarter, as laid down in standard procedures for the escort of one ship by one warship. This was well-established routine for the SPAB (Sydney–Port-aux-Basques) convoy, as the ferry shuttle was known. The air force had supplied an escort for the ferry following the first attacks in the gulf in May 1942, but this had been only a temporary measure pending the availability of a warship for the task. The navy's Sydney Force had finally been able to take over the job in June, even though the virtually full-time commitment of one of the force's five or six Bangors was a very substantial undertaking.[55]

Although *Caribou* sailed regularly, there clearly was greater than usual concern for its safety on this trip. On the voyage over to North Sydney from Port-aux-Basques on the previous evening, it had been accompanied by the ferry *Burgeo* and a naval escort. According to a later statement by *Burgeo*'s captain Michael Tobin, 'they were dropping depth charges all the way across.'[56] Howard Yorke, a civilian returning to St John's that night, later recalled that when the passengers were all on board, they were 'taken on a tour of the vessel, during which it was explained where to go and what to do should anything unusual happen on the crossing.' Yorke had made the crossing several times since the beginning of the war, and 'had never experienced this sort of concern ... and it should have prepared me for what was to happen later.'[57]

A series of coincidences now put the little convoy at great risk. The success of the Canadian defences in the upper gulf had forced *U-69* back prematurely towards Cabot Strait. The submarine had then lingered on the gulf side of the strait to try to intercept three grain ships that U-boat headquarters had signalled would be passing through the gulf. After daybreak on 13 October, it had been forced to submerge when its radar detection device warned of nearby emissions, almost certainly from RCAF patrols. A few hours later it saw the grain ships but made no attempt to attack, as they turned out to be neutral Swedish ships. *U-69* still fearing the active air defences it was facing, remained almost immobile underwater until evening. Dark, moonless conditions then allowed it to cruise on the surface, as fate would have it, close by the track of the ferry convoy. Visibility was so bad that *Grandmère*'s crew could not discern *Caribou*'s large bulk, even belching smoke as it was on this voyage, at only twenty-five hundred yards distance. The only possible method of locating the tiny profile of the submarine as it stalked the convoy for nearly three hours would have been by radar, which *Grandmère* did not carry because of the supply crisis that had left even the primary ocean escorts ill-equipped in this respect.

At 3:21 on the morning of the 14th, Atlantic Summer Time (3:51 Newfoundland Summer Time),[58] *U-69* fired a torpedo into *Caribou* at a range of only twelve hundred yards about forty miles off Port-aux-Basques. *Grandmère*, sailing on the same side of *Caribou* as *U-69*, saw the explosion and rushed towards the ferry, but at a range of three hundred and fifty yards finally saw the profile of the submarine and altered course to ram it. *U-69* crash-dived, went deep, and stayed there until the next night. *Grandmère* hurled six depth charges into its wake and continued to hunt for the next two hours, but could make no firm asdic contact. An escort's first obligation was to attack a submarine, not least because a warship that stopped for rescue work became an easy target itself. In this case, the two hour delay in the beginning of the search for survivors had ghastly consequences.[59]

The torpedo that struck *Caribou* caused a boiler explosion and the ship sank within five minutes. Most of the passengers had been asleep in the cabins and lounges and, already disoriented, they found there were no lights as they struggled to reach the deck. Worse still, the explosions had destroyed two of the six lifeboats. In the confusion, as the ship rapidly sank, only one of the remaining lifeboats could be properly launched. Most of the survivors were therefore exposed to the bitterly cold water as they clung to overturned boats and bits of wreckage. By the time *Grandmère* began rescue work at 5:20 a.m. AST, the wind and currents had dispersed the survivors, and the minesweeper had difficulty finding them in the dark. The incomplete records suggest that help, in the form of a 117 Squadron Canso from North Sydney, did not arrive until 7:20 a.m., four hours after the sinking. It and a second aircraft, probably a 119 Squadron Hudson, performed invaluable service by locating survivors, dropping flame floats to mark their positions, and directing the minesweeper to them by signal lamp.[60]

The crew of the Canso from 117 Squadron reported in their log what they observed when they arrived on the scene: 'Minesweeper picking up survivors. Signalled asking for air protection. Numerous rafts, lifeboats and wreckage scattered over sea. Commenced search for survivors, dropping flame floats to mark positions. One lifeboat approximately six miles distance was sighted packed with 20 to 30 survivors. Minesweeper slow in responding to Aldis [signalling lamp], making it difficult to indicate position of lifeboat. Dropped flame floats around life-boat to attract attention. Survivors in lifeboat cheered and waved each time aircraft flew over.'[61] Meanwhile, the Newfoundland Railway agent at Port-aux-Basques had been notified and had chartered nine schooners to go out to provide assistance; by 9:20, four navy ships and an air force crash boat were on the scene as well.[62] By this time, however, many of the survivors had been overcome by exposure and carried away by the currents.

Grandmère made for Sydney, where fuller medical facilities were available than in Newfoundland, reaching the dockyard at 3:40 in the afternoon. It brought in 103 survivors, of whom two, one a blond baby boy, died before the vessel reached port. These were the only survivors of the 237 people who had sailed on *Caribou*. Half of the military personnel and two thirds of the civilians (including at least five mothers and the ten children travelling with them) were lost, together with all but fifteen of the crew, including every ship's officer but one. Captain Taverner and his two sons died, as did five other pairs of brothers.[63] Eyewitness accounts suggest that the heavy losses among the ship's crew resulted from their efforts to control the confusion and launch boats as the vessel plunged beneath the surface. There were many examples of heroism that night. Margaret Brooke, a nursing dietitian in the Canadian navy, was made a member of the Military Division of the Order of the British Empire for 'gallantry and courage' in her ultimately unsuccessful efforts over many hours to save her friend, Nursing Sister Agnes Wilkie, as the two of them clung to the side of a capsized lifeboat. Wilkie was the first woman in the navy to lose her life in the Second World War.[64]

When *Grandmère* arrived at Sydney, 'it looked like all the brass in the navy was waiting for us,' according to Petty Officer Ad Stady.[65] The senior air, naval, and army commanders were indeed waiting at dock-side to make sure the survivors received the best possible care.[66] There was also a substantial crowd on the wharf, news of the disaster having preceded the ship despite censorship regulations. Sydney's City Hospital kept eight people overnight for observation and treatment and it was reported that some people staying at the Isle Royale Hotel, the city's finest, gave up their rooms to survivors.[67] Commander Mitchell later paid particular tribute to Roy Young of J.A. Young & Son, ship agents, 'for his care and handling of these people.'[68]

Losses from the Sydney area, although tragic, were fairly light. The five local people identified by the *Post-Record* included twenty-two-year-old Mrs Harriet Burnard of North Sydney and her eight-month-old daughter Shirley, and Hugh Gillis, a mining engineer employed by the Dominion Steel and Coal Corporation. Newfoundland was especially hard hit, suffering what would turn out to be its worst blow of the war because of the heavy losses among the crew, most of whom came from the communities of Port-aux-Basques and Channel. Accounts of the disaster and the names of local victims soon began appearing in newspapers throughout North America. The navy, recognizing the impossibility of silencing survivors, who, devastated by the experience, were talking freely and fuelling speculation, lifted censorship and allowed the publication of all information except tactical details of escort procedure.[69]

When the Battle of the St Lawrence began in May 1942, the German submarine attacks had provoked panic among many people living in the gulf area. But when J.S. Roy, the independent MP for Gaspé – supported by Conservative leader R.B. Hanson and CCF house leader M.J. Coldwell – had demanded action in July, naval services minister Angus L. Macdonald, who understood the need to keep up the main commitment on the transatlantic route to Britain, had bluntly refused 'to change the disposition of one ship of the Canadian Navy for [Roy] or all the questions he may ask from now until doomsday.' The heavy losses in the gulf in September brought Roy to renew his demands for better protection and more government openness about what the forces were doing. 'The people of my constituency want to be assured that the defences along the St Lawrence are adequate and whether the air force's defences against the U-boat menace are directed along the most effective lines.'[70] When Macdonald announced the sinking of *Carolus* on the 15th, he said nothing of *Caribou*, but did promise that there would be 'no abatement ... in our efforts to increase our Navy so that we may cope with the dangers of the trying months that still lie ahead.'[71] When the press reported the sinking on the 17th, he added only that it 'proves the hideousness of Nazi warfare.'[72]

The people of the Sydney area seem to have found some release for their shock and grief in the funeral of the young child, still unidentified, who died aboard *Grandmère*. The navy and community organizations provided a little white coffin, which was heaped with flowers, and 'scores' of mourners and a naval detachment attended the service at Lowden's Funeral Home and the interment at Hardwood Hill cemetery.[73] When the government's $750 million Victory Loan Campaign was launched on the 18th, the Halifax *Herald*'s cartoonist Bob Chambers linked it to the sinking with a sketch of a brutal-looking German naval officer exulting over a sinking ship, with a caption reminding readers that 'Your Victory Loan will help rid the seas of this beast.'[74]

Caribou's sinking had a profound impact on public opinion, and not just on the East Coast. As Douglas How points out, 'of all the ships sunk, the *Caribou*'s loss was the most costly, the only one to claim women and children and to devastate families.'[75] James Lamb believes that it 'brought home to both Canadians and Newfoundlanders the barbarity of the war waged by U-boats against helpless merchant shipping.' Now, 'everyone in Canada realized, probably for the first time, the human tragedies that lay behind those simple statistics ... For all its insignificance to the war's worldwide power balance, in Canada and Newfoundland *Caribou*'s loss was the most significant sinking of the war.'[76]

When *U-69* finally surfaced on the night after the attack on *Caribou*, it crept out of the Cabot Strait towards Scatarie Island. Gräf's intention was to find sheltered waters on the Cape Breton coast in which to transfer his last two remaining torpedoes from the storage locker on the upper deck down into the submarine, then to hunt shipping plying to and from Halifax to the southwest. Around-the-clock air patrols from Sydney, gale force winds, and heavy seas changed his mind, and he headed towards St Pierre and Miquelon. Haunted by aircraft radar warnings, Gräf was finally able to shift the torpedoes on the night of 17–18 October. In the early hours of the 20th he made an unsuccessful attack on *Rose Castle*, a Dosco ore carrier, which had become separated from its Sydney–Wabana convoy (BW 9) in heavy seas south of Placentia Bay. The crew actually heard one of the torpedoes strike the side of the ship, but it did not detonate. Gräf suspected defects in the torpedo pistols, but he had no more weapons to fire, and so headed for home.[77] At this same time, *U-106*, *Waterton*'s attacker, slipped out Cabot Strait after an unproductive eleven days in the gulf. It probed the waters south of eastern Newfoundland, then during the first week of November patrolled the near approaches to the strait, but accomplished nothing before heading towards Halifax. *U-43*, empty-handed after some three weeks in the gulf, passed through Cabot Strait for the central ocean on 7 November.[78]

This was not the end of the U-boat offensive in the Sydney and gulf areas, however. Dönitz had dispatched *U-183* and *U-518* to the Strait of Belle Isle with instructions to hunt there, then to move into the St Lawrence, as *U-517* and *U-165* had so successfully done. The lonely vigil of the submarines in the northern waters proved that major shipping was not moving through the strait, and so the boats searched for coastal shipping off the eastern coast of Newfoundland. On the dark night of 2 November, *U-518*, commanded by Kapitänleutnent Friedrich-Wilhelm Wissmann, repeated *U-513*'s daring feat of two months earlier by attacking the ore carriers anchored at Wabana in the harbour of Bell Island. Wissmann later reported seeing the headlights of cars on shore, and he managed to move in on the surface despite the searchlights. He fired his first torpedo at *Anna T*, a coal boat anchored off the Scotia Pier. It missed, passed under the stern of *Flyingdale*, and destroyed part of the loading pier.[79] The explosion shattered windows and rocked the island. Wissmann then sank *Rose Castle*, whose luck had finally run out, with two torpedoes, killing twenty-eight men, and *PLM 27*, a Free French ship under lease to Dominion Steel and Coal, with a loss of twelve lives, before leaving the harbour.[80]

Following this raid, rumours circulated on Bell Island concerning the allegedly suspicious behaviour of the captain of *PLM 27*. Some thought he had helped or tipped off the enemy prior to the sinking of his ship, because he was ashore when it was torpedoed and had just the previous day sold the ship's piano to a local resident. Naval intelligence investigated the situation and, when the captain and his second officer arrived at Sydney on the 15th and checked into the Isle Royale Hotel, the RCMP kept 'a close watch' on them, even examining their luggage, but no evidence was ever produced to justify the suspicion that had been cast on them.[81] This did not mean that the rampant fears in coastal communities were entirely without merit. After passing through Cabot Strait, *U-518* landed a spy, Leutnant Werner Janowski, near New Carlisle on the Baie des Chaleurs, on the night of 8–9 November. Suspicions among the villagers of the visitor who smoked Belgian cigarettes and appeared at a time of day when there was no bus service into the area resulted in Janowski's arrest by the Quebec provincial police within twenty-four hours.[82] By that time, when Bangors and aircraft began to search the bay and its approaches, *U-518* was safely out in the gulf. It sighted some shipping but was unable to get into attack position, and on the 18th departed through Cabot Strait in search of more profitable hunting grounds.[83]

U-183 never entered the gulf, apparently because of mechanical defects that made its captain leery of taking risks. The boat did close Cabot Strait on 3–4 November, but had to crash-dive when three aircraft suddenly appeared, an event that undoubtedly confirmed the captain's instinct for caution. The submarine then continued along Cape Breton's Atlantic coast, making an unsuccessful attack on a lone freighter about thirty miles off Petit de Grat on the 5th, and then moved across the approaches to Chedabucto Bay to close the mouth of Canso Harbour during the early hours of the 6th. Later that morning, it tracked the Sydney to Halifax coastal convoy SH 59 not far off Canso and made two torpedo attacks, which, like the previous one, were fired at long range and went wide of the mark. The crews of the ships in the convoy heard the torpedoes explode at the end of their runs, and the escorts carried out a search but found nothing. After a long patrol south of Halifax, *U-183* came back along the Cape Breton shore, and on the evening of the 28th, about forty miles southeast of Scatarie Island, fired four torpedoes at the Halifax to St John's coastal convoy HJ 19. These torpedoes exploded close enough to the bows of the escort, the Bangor *Vegreville*, that the ship felt a shock as if it were 'in collision with a large whale,' but did no damage. *Vegreville*'s search came up empty-handed. By this time, naval intelligence in Ottawa had pieced together enough evidence to reconstruct *U-183*'s approximate course, concluding from its record of failed long-range attacks that it was 'apparently a reconnaissance submarine, probably ordered not to attack while on patrol.' That, of course, had not been the intent of the mission, and U-boat headquarters was critical of the captain's lack of aggressiveness.[84]

Although no one knew it at the time, the first round of the Battle of the St Lawrence had ended. Joseph Schull called it 'an almost unmitigated defeat for Canada,' but one 'deliberately and unavoidably accepted' because 'adequate defence of the St Lawrence would have meant recall of many Canadian ships from the Atlantic.' But 'it was in the Atlantic, along the convoy routes, that ... Canada could best serve her own interests and make her greatest contribution to the Allied effort.'[85] As James Lamb has pointed out, 'if public pressure had succeeded in diverting urgently needed warships from the main theatre of the Atlantic battle ... it would have been a victory for the Nazi cause. The trickle of trade down the St Lawrence, however valuable locally, was simply not worth the diversion of forces required to provide efficient escort.'[86] In fact, the Battle of the St Lawrence was a victory for Canada that resulted directly from the efficient defence the Canadian forces had mounted since the latter part of September. During October and November a concerted effort by five German submarines had resulted in the sinking of only three ships within the gulf, a very thin return for such a substantial commitment. The heavy loss of life in *Caribou*, grim as it was for Canadians, was irrelevant to Dönitz's goal: to destroy as many ships as possible to reduce Allied war production and the flow of men and *matériel* to combat theatres. The German admiral sensibly wrote off the gulf as a worthwhile hunting area. As his staff later recorded, the gulf was abandoned because of the 'appearance of a/c [aircraft] and location [anti-submarine radar].' While the naval defences were considered 'relatively slight and unpractised' and 'little to be feared,' the air defences were rated 'medium to strong.'[87] According to Rasch, the veteran commander of *U-106*, the RCAF had created conditions 'exactly like those in the [Bay of] Biscay,' a flattering comparison with the RAF's major offensive against U-boats as they sailed from their French bases. Oberleutnant Hans-Joachim Schwantke, the commander of *U-43*, like Rasch, was alarmed at the manner in which the appearance of aircraft was often soon followed by naval escort sweeps. Both men credited the Canadians with carefully coordinating their strong air resources with their obviously inexperienced surface vessels to make the latter more effective.[88]

The Germans ascribed more system to the Canadian services than was actually possible with the limited resources available. It seems likely that the increasingly aggressive air force policy of saturating an area well before shipping was due to pass through it created the impression that the naval screen of a convoy or a local naval patrol was hunting in response to reports by the air force. The German comments may also be a tribute to the virtually unsung work of the little Fairmiles, which, through a periscope, appeared to be more formidable warships.

A development unsuspected by the Allies had increased the effectiveness of the RCAF operations. The Germans had discovered the secret of 1.5-metre anti-submarine radar, and had built a crude but effective radar search receiver that, as has been seen, warned them when radar was transmitting in the vicinity, thus enabling the submarine to dive before the Allied aircraft or vessel was within detection range.[89] In many instances, however, the German warning equipment actually amplified the effectiveness of the air patrols, even while depriving them of the chance to find submarines, for a U-boat that was compelled to dive repeatedly had much less chance of getting into position to strike at shipping. This is precisely what happened in the gulf and in the approaches to Cabot Strait in October and November 1942. The U-boats seldom surfaced when visibility conditions were at all good, and when they did they were frequently intimidated by the bleating of their radar search receivers.[90]

Sydney, the principal naval and air base in the vast area from the mouth of the St Lawrence River to the waters south of Newfoundland, played a leading role in the suppression of the submarines. Captain C.M.R. Schwerdt, who had succeeded Goolden in the naval command, was consistently optimistic, and doubted, rightly as it turned out, the wisdom of the decision to limit ocean traffic through the gulf. He recommended to Naval Service Headquarters that safety regulations for separating inbound and outbound shipping in the gulf should be waived to allow the fullest possible variation in routes and thereby hinder the submarines in taking up ambush positions. Implementation of this measure by the Sydney staff was one of the changes that made things so much more difficult for the U-boats during the autumn of 1942. Sydney also continued to carry much of the burden of directing the fleet of escorts on the shuttles to Halifax, the St Lawrence ports, and Newfoundland, and of ensuring that they were as effective as possible, despite the pressures of tight, complex schedules and the frailties of vessels that were old and cranky or too new to have been 'shaken down.' As in the 1915–18 period, the shore staffs had continually to exert themselves to help the inexperienced and incompletely trained crews of many of the escorts.

Through the summer and fall of 1942 the Sydney air squadrons were among the most heavily worked on the East Coast because they were responsible for both ocean and gulf patrols. In September and October, 119 Squadron flew more than one thousand hours of operations per month, protecting seventy-six convoys containing 586 merchant ships in September and fifty-seven convoys with 466 merchant ships in October. The North Sydney headquarters of 117 Squadron achieved impressive results as well. With no more than four or five aircraft on strength, it flew more than 450 operational hours each month, while the Gaspé detachment flew nearly 700 hours in September and 367 in October.[91]

The press of operations, often in marginal flying conditions, extracted a cost.[92] On 27 September a Hudson recalled to base in deteriorating weather conditions bounced on the runway, causing one of the landing gear to fail and it punctured a gas tank, which ignited. The flames detonated the depth charges, blasting apart the aircraft and blowing in windows in several of the station buildings. On 16 October another Hudson, taking off in darkness for a night sweep of Cabot Strait, clipped an American aircraft that was parked, unlighted, close by the runway. The Hudson veered out of control and caught fire, and the resulting explosion of the depth charges demolished the Canadian machine and badly damaged the American one. Happily, in both accidents all crew members were able to get clear safely before the explosions. Then, during the dark early hours of Christmas Day, 1942, a Hudson taking off for a dawn patrol lost power and crashed two miles from Sydney airport; none of the crew survived.

To help relieve the burden on the patrol bombers, the Lysanders of No. 4 Coast Artillery Cooperation Detachment had been carrying out the dawn and dusk harbour entrance patrols all through the shipping season. A detachment of three Lysanders from 123 Army Cooperation Training Squadron at Debert, Nova Scotia, moved to Sydney in October to assist with these close-in anti-submarine patrols. Further help came at the end of the month in the form of three Hudsons from 113 Squadron in Yarmouth, which put in a week of intensive flying at the beginning of November.

For the convoy staff and all the local businesses and citizens on whom they depended, 1942 was a year of record achievement. Some 1,800 merchant ships had cleared Sydney in a total of 260 convoys (10 transatlantic SC, 12 joiner SSC, and 235 coastal), compared to about 1,500 ships in 50 convoys (all transatlantic or joiners) in 1941.[93] The convoy system, indeed, was the key to the effective employment of the limited naval and air resources available, and losses had been kept to a minimum notwithstanding considerable attention by U-boats to the area. Despite this success, Sydney's primacy in sustaining the lifeline to Britain faded somewhat in 1942 because the entry of the United States into the war added its mammoth port facilities to the Allied cause. As Mitchell put it in February 1943, 'the Port of Sydney has lost considerable importance as an ocean convoy port but has, owing to intensified submarine activity on the Western Atlantic shores, gained an unchallenged position as the key port of Eastern Canada through its geographical position making it the hub of the coastal convoy system.' This was putting a brave face on the situation, however, and later in the same report he acknowledged that 'the loss of SC Convoys has resulted in a definite loss of interest.'[94]

The convoy staff at Sydney was especially proud of the continuing efforts made in 1942 to extend hospitality to merchant sailors. Because gasoline rationing ruled out the bus trips to pleasant locations in the nearby countryside that had been offered in the 1940 and 1941 seasons – reminiscent of the drives in private cars organized by local business people in the First World War – the convoy staff and the Kennington chapter of the IODE sought a location for a retreat close to the waterfront. The McLennan family, which had already made available the house at its Petersfield estate at Westmount to serve as the residence of the naval officer in charge, now donated its large boathouse, which was converted into a recreation hall and club fitted with a kitchen, games, and sports equipment. A public appeal by the convoy staff brought in more than enough money to fund the project. The entire crews of the incoming merchant vessels that had made the longest voyages were invited and given the run of the place from 4:00 to 8:00 p.m., during which time the women of the IODE prepared and served a meal that, as experience established the seamen's preferences, featured omelettes and such Nova Scotian favourites as fresh baked rolls and fruit desserts, the most popular being strawberry shortcake. Some twelve hundred seamen signed the guest book, but that was by no means the total number of seamen of all nationalities who were entertained there. It was observed that sailors from the Soviet Union seemed to be especially appreciative.

Many volunteer groups in Sydney and from across eastern Canada contributed to the success of this and other ventures, but the officer responsible for merchant navy welfare had particular praise for the IODE. In addition to their work at the boathouse, the women of the Kennington Chapter welcomed into their homes the officers and men arriving at Sydney after having survived torpedoeings and other marine disasters. This meant 'that the majority of Officers were received into homelike surroundings where they could recuperate at ease instead of in a bleak hotel room.' DEMS (defensive equipment of merchant ships) ratings on convalescent leave and officers from Canadian naval ships were similarly accommodated by the women of the IODE and their families.[95]

While establishing still closer links with Sydney society in 1942, the navy gained a more profound sympathy for its boom-and-bust economic conditions, which were controlled by the impersonal distant forces that dominated life on the island. Having lamented the lack of better business practices along Sydney's waterfront, Mitchell had to confess in July 1942 that the bottom had without warning dropped out of the ship-servicing market. Although traffic at the port had increased 'considerably over the same month in 1941,' he reported, the port was 'suffering from an acute shortage of business.' Skilled workers were leaving the repair shops to obtain steady employment at Pictou, some of the recently established ship chandlers were 'contemplating' going out of business, and the more established firms were drastically reducing their staffs. This situation was, he thought, 'probably traceable to the amount of time most ships spend in the United States or larger Canadian ports and while it is understandable, may have serious consequences through the depletion of the port facilities.'[96]

The arrival of Captain Schwerdt as naval officer in charge in August 1942 helped the Sydney Command to endure change, frustration, and disappointment. He fought for the interests of the port no less tenaciously than had Goolden, the tough professional who had literally built the establishment from nothing, but with considerably more diplomacy. Whether because of his personality or by design, Schwerdt seems always to have put the best face on things, as can be seen in a speech he gave to local dignitaries at the Royal Cape Breton Yacht Club on New Year's Day, 1943. Perhaps having in mind the difficulties that had arisen between some sailors and civilians at Sydney during the First World War, he reviewed what the navy was doing in the area to help win the war, and reminded his audience that most of the extraordinary number of sailors who passed through the harbour were transient, 'stopping here only to refuel, revictual and re-arm in order to carry on the Battle of the Atlantic, one of the major fronts of the war and of which Sydney is one of the major western bases.' They spent weeks at a time enduring 'conditions of discomfort and hardship which it is difficult to appreciate,' and he pleaded, therefore, for some tolerance of their behaviour on the part of the civilian population:

> If, then, you should see at odd times one or two of them wending their way unsteadily up Charlotte Street and I disapprove but, I pray you, switch on that light of kindness so proverbial in the people of this Island and think of the weeks at a time during which these same men wend their way unsteadily across the Atlantic in order to ensure that the sinews of war shall reach our soldiers and airmen at the front and that other essentials to help Our Canada's war effort shall reach Canada. In saying this last, I might add

that other essentials include Canadians coming home from time to time to their own country.

And, finally, never forget that these very officers and men in their intense cooperation towards the winning of the Battle of the Atlantic occasionally wend their way, this time, not unsteadily but with high purpose and high promise, from this world to the next.[97]

A talent for diplomacy and administrative competence had shaped much of Schwerdt's career. After service in capital ships during the First World War, he had gained valuable experience in intelligence and planning posts before retiring in 1936 at his own request to become private secretary to Vice Admiral Sir Humphrey Walwyn, governor of Newfoundland. On mobilization in 1939, Schwerdt returned to active service as the naval officer in charge at St John's, in which capacity he virtually singlehandedly looked after almost every aspect of maritime defence so efficiently that he was seconded to the Canadian navy to develop and run its new base at St John's in 1941.When Goolden was transferred in August 1942 to help manage the struggling organization on the West Coast, Schwerdt must have seemed his natural successor. He plunged immediately and enthusiastically into the intense operations of the port and also the large-scale development of its facilities. His energy and enthusiasm were going to be needed.

chapter twelve

Convoy Port, 1942–1943

I am very proud of Sydney ... I am very loath to leave here.
Captain C.M.R. Schwerdt, 1945

During the course of the hectic 1942 season, all three services continued ambitious development in the Sydney area to strengthen local
defences and sustain better their operations at sea. Most important was
the construction of a complete and self-contained new naval base at
Point Edward, an 850-acre site across the South Arm from the Sydney
waterfront.[1] The original intention was to construct modest facilities to
provide basic services – fuel, running repairs, ammunition, and other
stores – for the Sydney Force and visiting warships. The project did not
have a high priority, however, because essential defences and accommodation had been arranged in 1940 and commercial ship services, albeit
limited, already existed at Sydney, whereas at Shelburne and Gaspé, the
navy's other East Coast bases, virtually everything had to be mustered
from scratch. Only late in 1941 was the contract let to Dominion Construction Corporation Limited of Toronto. By early 1942 the estimated
costs had risen to the very substantial figure of approximately $5 mil-
lion.[2] This resulted in part from the entirely undeveloped nature of the
site, without ready access to sewage, water, and power services, but it also
reflected the navy's desire for quality. There seems little doubt that the
naval staff had one eye on the post-war future, building for the long
term to obtain the permanent second base on the East Coast that no
government had been willing to fund in peacetime.[3]

The project grew in importance as construction proceeded. The

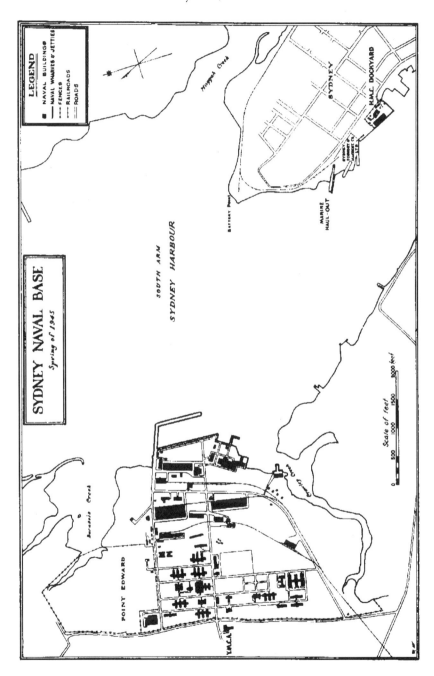

LEGEND

■   NAVAL BUILDINGS
—— NAVAL WHARVES & JETTIES
---- FENCES
++++ RAILROADS
==== ROADS

SYDNEY NAVAL BASE
Spring of 1945

SOUTH ARM
SYDNEY HARBOUR

Muggah Creek

SYDNEY

H.M.C. DOCKYARD

BATTERY POINT

MARINE
HAUL-OUT

Barasois Creek

POINT EDWARD

Wash Brook

YMCA?

Scale of feet
0   500   1000   1500   3000 feet

accelerated expansion of the navy since 1940 had outstripped the growth of support facilities, and the changing shape of the Battle of the Atlantic in 1941 and 1942, which had resulted in most of the fleet operating from Canadian rather than established British bases, exacerbated the problem. Moreover, the hovering of U-boats off Halifax from the beginning of 1942 underscored the danger of the excessive concentration of the existing facilities at only one port. Sydney was the only alternative port with the strategic position and size of harbour that could fully substitute for Halifax in the event of a disaster there. In justifying the Point Edward project to Cabinet in April 1942, the navy declared that 'the Sydney base is now considered as second in importance on the East Coast and, in the case of necessity, all essential naval operations would be carried out from this point.'[4]

The Point Edward base resembled a new town rising up from the harbour. Close to the water were workshops, railways spurs, and fuel storage tanks; inland, towards the highway, were blocks of offices, quarters, a drill hall, and a hospital, all laid out on a grid of streets. On the shoreline was a nine-hundred-foot quay wall, and projecting from it an L-shaped pier some eleven hundred feet in length. Here at last was the berthing space whose absence had so complicated ship servicing at Sydney.[5] On 15 March 1943 the new establishment was commissioned HMCS *Protector II*, the existing facilities on the Sydney waterfront now being known as HMCS *Protector I*. By the end of that month there were 509 officers and men at Point Edward, 216 of them new entries into the navy, who were undergoing their initial training, the necessary buildings at the base having been rushed into service in this role to help ease the pressure on Halifax's facilities. Work to complete the pier area and associated workshops continued into the autumn of 1943.[6] Meanwhile, additional personnel continued to arrive at the new base, so that by late July 1943 there were 1,849 naval personnel at the Sydney shore establishments compared to only 734 in December 1942.[7]

The development of Point Edward in 1942 and 1943 proved to be only the first phase of expansion that continued until the end of the war, the result of circumstances that pushed always in the direction of still more pressure on the Canadian navy. In the summer and especially the autumn and winter of 1942–3, the expanding German U-boat fleet was able to mount wolf-pack operations in mid-ocean on a scale even larger than in 1941. This had devastating effects on the Allied forces that were weakened by the deployments to North American waters and to the support of the invasion of North Africa. Because convoys under the protection of Canadian naval groups suffered some of the heaviest losses, the Canadian service came under close scrutiny and criticism.

The most difficult issues were the related ones of ship equipment and repair. Not only were Canadian ships the most likely to suffer from technical defects because of the lack of regular comprehensive maintenance, they were in many cases a year or more behind their British and American counterparts in receiving the latest weapons and electronic sensors that were proving vital for success in screening convoys. As well, the first sixty-four corvettes Canada had built in 1940 and 1941, which still formed a major part of the navy's escort forces, required extensive reconstruction to make them effective in the open ocean operations for which they had not been designed but were now being used. An early and humiliating result of the these deficiencies was the temporary withdrawal at Britain's request of the Canadian naval groups from the North Atlantic run in early 1943 so that the ships could re-equip and undergo refresher training in Royal Navy establishments while operating on the runs to Gibraltar and the Mediterranean.[8]

The Canadian naval staff had already realized that government policy of assisting the expansion of commercial firms like Sydney Foundry was inadequate. The navy itself would have to get into the costly and complex business of building ship-repair facilities and of finding and training naval personnel for this skilled work. So rapidly were events moving in the first half of 1943 that Schwerdt found himself grappling with a largely new situation when he endeavoured to bring the Point Edward base into operation. His worry was that the substantial new entry training program begun early in the year would create a critical shortage of accommodation as the repair facilities came into operation. When he queried Halifax, however, he learned that the training at Point Edward was only a stopgap measure until the mammoth new training centre at Deep Brook, near Digby, Nova Scotia, came into operation in the summer of 1943. Point Edward and Shelburne, the East Coast bases best located to support Halifax, would concentrate on ship repair.[9]

Meanwhile, the staff in Ottawa was reassessing the Point Edward project to determine what would be needed to carry out the thoroughgoing annual refit of warships. Naval berthing space at Sydney was sufficient to refit simultaneously two destroyers, eight corvettes, and four Fairmiles, while also supporting the operations of the local force and visiting warships. The refit program, however, would require additional workshops and a 250 per cent increase in accommodation in the space built for 975 personnel under the original project to a capacity for more than 2,500 personnel by the time the refit program matured in 1944 and 1945. Even before the existing facilities were completed in the summer of 1943, therefore, construction began on additional accommodation and technical buildings at an estimated cost of $2.8 million.[10]

The phasing out of training for new entrants at Point Edward did not by any means end training activities at Sydney. Aside from attending to the needs of the hundreds of additional personnel being posted to the base, the experienced specialist staffs continued their longstanding practice of providing refresher or additional training for the crews of warships in port. As well, in 1942 headquarters designated Sydney one of the schools for personnel who manned the guns mounted on merchant ships (DEMS). Accordingly, the navy built an over-the-water firing point on the coast just west of Cranberry Head, where anti-aircraft guns of the type fitted in merchant ships were permanently installed. During the period from 1 July to 30 September 1943, 549 Canadian and Allied DEMS personnel on merchant ships passing through Sydney received training from the school.[11]

Because of the efforts undertaken from 1938 to 1941, air force facilities were well developed by 1942. The main project that year was to extend the three runways at the airport from 4,000 feet in length to 5,250 feet so that they could safely accommodate the largest aircraft. The camp at the airport was also considerably expanded with new quarters buildings because the development of more complete services, the expansion of existing units and the addition of others brought the number of personnel at the base from just under seven hundred at the end of January 1942 to more than twelve hundred by the beginning of 1943. Hard surfacing of all roads, the parade square within the base, and the aircraft turning circles on the runways solved the longstanding problem of mud.[12]

The major new air force and army undertakings in Cape Breton during 1942 were part of a program undertaken on both coasts that year to defend against enemy air attack. Canadian production of Hawker Hurricane fighters at Canadian Car and Foundry in Fort William, Ontario, had come on stream by the end of 1940 as a result of contracts let before the war, but Britain had priority for these machines. Early in 1942, Allied allocation authorities agreed that Canada should retain some of them to build up its air defences. At the same time, Canadian industry was beginning to produce in quantity British types of air-defence radar, army anti-aircraft guns and fire-control radar.[13]

At the end of April 1942, personnel for new fighter units began to arrive at the Sydney aerodrome, along with North American Harvard advanced fighter trainer aircraft and Hawker Hurricanes.[14] No. 125 (Fighter) Squadron was formed immediately, and it undertook six weeks of operational flying training before departing for Torbay aerodrome in Newfoundland in early June to provide air defence for St John's.[15] As this unit left, another new squadron, 128 (F), was formed at Sydney. It was soon equipped with a full complement of fifteen Hurricanes, and it remained at the station for a year. The role of these short-range, high-performance fighters demanded split-second speed and precision in getting aircraft into the air and then coordinating them so that they could intercept enemy aircraft within the very few minutes of warning that would be available in the event of an attack. Thus, the unit's flying program focused on constant practice to develop and then hone and maintain pilot skills in fast take-offs ('scrambles'), aerobatics, interceptions, aerial combat, gunnery, and formation flying.

Although the Hurricane's two-hour endurance made it unsuitable for anti-submarine operations, 128 Squadron assisted with routine patrols in the harbour approaches and along the coast. The squadron also assisted the Coast Artillery Cooperation Detachment's Lysanders with flights for the training of the army's anti-aircraft units and, beginning with the spring thaw in April 1943, it dispatched two aircraft on a daily coastal patrol at dusk when enemy aircraft or vessels would be most likely to attempt an approach. At the end of June 1943, 125 Squadron at Torbay and 128 Squadron exchanged stations to give the units more varied operating experience.[16]

The single-engine Hurricane was not a forgiving machine to fly, and, in the event of trouble, the pilot had to react quickly. Engine failure produced some dramatic situations in the skies over Cape Breton on several occasions. Around 4:30 on the afternoon of 6 August 1942, for example, a plane piloted by Pilot Officer C.E. Fairfield (128 Squadron) caught fire when he was about eight miles south of Sydney Airport. Fairfield 'closed his throttle and attempted to reach a runway,' but was forced by the spreading fire to bail out of the aircraft. He landed safely and was uninjured except for slight burns on his legs. The plane crashed in flames about four miles southeast of the airport.[17]

During the summer of 1942, construction was underway on Cape Breton's first radar station, a camp of a half-dozen buildings and a tall lattice-work tower for the big 'mattress' antenna located three miles north of Louisbourg. The strength of this unit, designated 6 Radio Detachment (later 6 Radio Unit), RCAF, was approximately eighty personnel.

The radar, a Canadian-produced version of the British 'chain home low,' which operated on a wavelength of approximately five yards, came into operation early in October 1942. It dependably detected aircraft to a range of one hundred miles, and in favourable atmospheric conditions to ranges of twice that and more. It could also detect surface ships, having been originally developed, in fact, by the British army for employment with coastal defences to locate enemy surface raiders. It had been quickly adopted by the Royal Air Force because it proved able to pick up aircraft flying below the altitudes at which they could be detected by the original 'chain home' radar stations that operated on a longer wave length, hence its 'chain home low' (CHL) designation. The Louisbourg station was one of a network that, together with American-installed stations in Newfoundland, provided overlapping radar coverage from the waters south of Nova Scotia and the Bay of Fundy to the central coast of Labrador.[18]

The display tube of the CHL sets, like all the early radar types, had only a range axis on which a blip appeared when the antenna was directed on the bearing of the aircraft. This was adequate for the job of early warning, but a more sophisticated display, one that showed a plot of all of the contacts in an area in relation to each other, was needed for the challenging task of directing defending fighter aircraft to intercept incoming enemy planes. CHL sets modified with this equipment, the first modern radar 'scopes,' were known as ground control intercept (GCI) radar. Construction of a GCI station began on the clear ground in the vicinity of the runways at Sydney Airport at the end of 1942, but the available evidence suggests it did not begin to operate until the autumn of 1943.[19] By that time the danger of German air attack was receding, but the ground radar systems at Sydney and elsewhere had proven invaluable for the regulation of the increasingly heavy air traffic, the role in which they were, in fact, primarily employed. The Second World War air defences were the origin of Canada's present air navigation and control system.[20]

The job of the army's anti-aircraft artillery was to stand guard within and closely around a city to engage enemy aircraft that evaded the air force's fighters. After the fall of France in 1940, the government made the decision to manufacture anti-aircraft artillery in Canada, Britain obviously net being able to fill Canadian needs. Orders were issued for the British army's standard types: Britain's own 'heavy' 3.7-inch gun and the 40 mm 'light' gun that had been developed by the Swedish Bofors Company and that was being used by both the Axis and the Allied powers. The 3.7-inch gun fired its big twenty-eight-pound shells to a maximum ceiling of forty thousand feet at the rate of seven to eight rounds per minute. These weapons were to be placed in groups of four on the outer ring of a defended area to attack aircraft when they were still flying high and straight on their approach. The 40 mm Bofors gun was something like a large machine gun, and dispatched its two-pound shells at a rate of more than 120 per minute to a maximum altitude of ten thousand feet. These guns were deployed singly in the midst of especially important targets; their hose-like fire and the quick manoeuvrability of their light mounts were designed so that they could engage individual aircraft as they swooped in to drop bombs.

During the first two and a half years of the war, virtually all of Canada's few anti-aircraft resources were concentrated at Halifax. The only anti-aircraft artillery at Sydney were two obsolescent 4-inch guns that had been mounted on emergency-built concrete platforms at Westmount, across the harbour from Sydney, soon after the outbreak of war. Because there was no ammunition for them for some months, their unit, the 6th Anti-Aircraft Battery of Yarmouth, Nova Scotia, spent the autumn on Lawlor's Island in Halifax Harbour – a depressing camp that formerly had been the port's quarantine hospital – undergoing such rudimentary training as was available.[22] Canadian-produced anti-aircraft guns began to be delivered in quantity at the end of 1941 and the first weapons were rushed to the West Coast, where there was profound alarm following the Japanese attack on Pearl Harbor. The East Coast was of no less priority. The sustained U-boat offensive across the full breadth of the Atlantic revived longstanding worries about Germany's ability to make complementary air strikes with long-range aircraft or with machines that could be launched from ships. Although Germany did not have an operational aircraft carrier, a suitably equipped merchant ship could readily establish an improvised base at one of the hundreds of isolated inlets on the northern Labrador coast or in the Arctic.

The first modern anti-aircraft equipment, twelve 40 mm Bofors guns and four 3.7-inch guns, arrived in Sydney in the spring and summer of 1942. The heavy guns went to the 6th AA Battery, which installed them at a new site in the Westmount area, approximately three miles southeast of Point Edward battery. A newly arrived unit, the 24th Light Anti-Aircraft Battery, manned four of the Bofors guns at Sydney Airport, and the others in the waterfront and steel plant areas. One of the barracks buildings at the 6th's original camp in Westmount became a temporary gun operations room, the anti-aircraft artillery's equivalent to the coast gunner's fire command post, to coordinate fire from all the batteries in the Sydney area. [23]

In the fall of 1942, more units and their equipment started to arrive, and by April 1943 Sydney had its full complement of twenty 3.7-inch guns and sixteen 40 mm guns. The additional big guns were manned by the 50th and 51st Heavy Anti-Aircraft Batteries, each twice the size of the 6th AA Battery and each responsible for two four-gun sites. The 50th completed coverage to the east of the city and harbour with a site at Cossit Lake on the outskirts of Sydney and at South Bar, a few hundred yards south of the boom defence battery. The 51st, in the western sector, had a four-gun site at Wireless Hill on the northern outskirts of North Sydney and another at Jacksonville that covered the anchorage in the North West Arm. To administer the growing organization more effectively, the anti-aircraft units in the Sydney area were combined in January 1943 to form the 23rd Anti-Aircraft Regiment, RCA, under the command of Lieutenant Colonel R.F. Capel. The regiment's total strength by the spring of 1943 was 839 personnel, still about three hundred short of full establishment. [24]

The development of these sites was no small job. The detachment for a single Bofors gun was sixteen men, meaning that two buildings – sleeping quarters and a mess hall – had to be provided at most of the widely dispersed positions. A four-gun heavy battery involved some 130 personnel, more if it was also a command and administrative centre. This required a full camp of four or five large buildings, the same as at a coastal fort. The gun mountings were of a mobile type, with removable wheel assemblies and levelling jacks to set the mounting platforms accurately into position. Timber platforms or simple pits sufficed for the Bofors emplacements, while the 3.7-inch guns were put into larger pits, with earth banked against timber or sheet metal revetments into which were built lockers for ready-use ammunition. The gun crews carried out much of this hard labour themselves. The gun pits at the heavy batteries were arranged in an arc around an earth-banked concrete command post, where communications were concentrated, and plots displayed information from the gun operations room and the battery's own fire-control instruments. [25]

Although much of the equipment and many of the personnel were in place by the spring of 1943, a great deal remained to be done. Sydney was only one of ten places in Canada that received full-scale anti-aircraft defences in 1942 and 1943, an ambitious undertaking with new technology that had to be carried out at a time when manpower was drying up.

Inevitably, there were bottlenecks at every level, and much, including basic training and construction, had to be left to the operational units. The 23rd Regiment made good progress, but at the end of 1943 was just beginning to receive the radar fire-control equipment needed for operations at night and in thick weather. Equipment was also needed to complete the permanent gun operations rooms at regimental headquarters on Royal Avenue. Nevertheless, when Major General S.C.M. Archibald, a senior British officer who had been brought to Canada to supervise the development of anti-aircraft defences, visited Sydney in December, he was impressed by what had been achieved.[26]

Development of the coast artillery defences in 1942 concentrated on improving the improvised fire-control arrangements as equipment arrived from Britain. The Department of National Defence had awarded a contract in December 1941 to M.R. Chappell Limited of Sydney to build a permanent fire command post within the compound of temporary buildings on Kilkenny Lake Road, near South Bar. The design was based on that of the Halifax fire command post at York Redoubt.[27] Construction of the Kilkenny Lake post, to the same standards of heavy protection with steel, concrete, and earth as the main works of the principal batteries, was complete by October 1942, when a party of technical experts from Ottawa and Halifax installed the main equipment.[28] In the surface observation post there was a position finder like the one in the temporary post that allowed the fire commander to follow the action and designate targets for the batteries. The most important new feature of the permanent command post was an underground fortress plotting room that was accessed by a staircase from the observation post. In the centre of this room was the fortress fire-direction table, which, with information from the fortress observation posts on the coast, could calculate long-range firing data as a back-up or alternative for the range-finding systems at the forts.[29] During the summer of 1942 the engineers and instrument party also installed a fire-direction table at Fort Lingan and modern observation instruments in the wooden fortress observation posts at North Head and New Victoria. By the end of the year a third fortress observation post had been built of concrete at Table Head.[30]

In 1943 the army, which had the primary responsibility for the defence of ports, received modern shortwave radar sets from Britain that were well suited for detailed coverage of harbour approaches. Known as CD No. 1 Mark Vs, these were essentially the ten-centimetre sets the Royal Navy had hastily developed to detect surfaced submarines, a target that was too small to be dependably located by metric wavelength radar. In May 1943, one of these CD sets, known as the fire command radar, was housed in a trailer on the high ground at Scotchtown with its parabola antenna on the roof. From this position on the southeast fringe of New Waterford, it could sweep the Atlantic approaches. Its crew, from the 16th Coast Brigade, fed information on shipping movements to the fire command post, and thence to the navy and air force. The set was not fitted with the equipment needed to feed precise fire-control data to the guns; rather, it served as a tripwire to alert the defences, especially at night or in foggy weather.[31]

The fast-firing twin six-pounder guns ordered for the ultimate armament at the boom defence batteries at South Bar and Stubbert's Point were expected to be delivered in 1943.[32] In October 1942, therefore, the detachments at these locations shifted several of the temporary installations so that the contractors could begin work on the permanent concrete and steel works for the new armament.[33] These were quite elegant compact structures. Concrete surface buildings, including the magazine, gun crew shelter, gun equipment stores, and an engine house for the searchlights were massed directly behind the semicircular gun emplacements. The new works at South Bar were ready when its gun arrived in August, and it was mounted during the following month, allowing the removal of the venerable single-barrel six-pounders. Progress was slower at Stubbert's Point, because of the need to blast into the bedrock that lay just below the surface. The new armament was mounted there by early December 1943.[34]

The army also launched a new program to improve further the close-in defences of Canada's ports. The pre-1914 4.7-inch and 6-inch guns of the type at Chapel and Petrie were by now barely adequate, and in the fall of 1942 the army ordered replacements from Canadian production of the Royal Navy's splendid twin-barrel 4-inch guns, which could fire as many as thirty thirty-five-pound shells per minute to a range of nearly twenty thousand yards.[35] Chapel Point battery at Sydney Mines was one of the first sites selected for conversion to the new armament, as it was the only one at Sydney positioned to sweep the entire harbour from its entrance back to the inner port.[36] The first of the new guns arrived at the end of May 1943,[37] and on 29 July the garrison shifted the two 4.7-inch guns back onto the temporary emplacements dating from 1939–40 so they could remain in action while the permanent fortifications were modified for the naval equipment. Before the extensive reconstruction could begin, however, headquarters in Ottawa called a halt in view of newly discovered technical problems that would be ironed out in a trial conversion of an emplacement at Partridge Island off Saint John.[38]

Meanwhile, one of the least-known projects for Cape Breton's defence had been undertaken and completed in 1942. During that year R.E. MacDonald, a local contractor, built a complex of magazine buildings in the village of Johnstown on the southeastern shore of the Bras d'Or Lake. A large, heavily built concrete ammunition store and a brick laboratory building for handling and testing explosives still stand on the site and are now in use as summer cottages. The complex held reserves of ammunition that could be transported readily to both the Sydney and the Strait of Canso defences, but that were safely removed from areas that might come under attack. A detachment of approximately twenty troops of the Royal Canadian Ordnance Corps manned the site.[39]

The largest single army construction project at Sydney was the building of Oxford battery. For heavy 9.2-inch guns, this was Sydney's second long-range battery, and it was situated behind Oxford Point, a position west of the harbour entrance that commanded the whole of the approaches. Because Halifax and Sydney had both received equipment for a single long-range battery in 1941 and because other parts of the empire had equally pressing needs for scarce British coast artillery supplies, the guns for Oxford could not be delivered until 1944–5. E.G.M. Cape of Montreal won the contract worth approximately $700,000 for the construction of the fortifications and began work in the spring of 1943. The bulk of the concrete work – three gun positions, magazines, and approximately four hundred yards of trenches that linked them – was largely completed by the fall of 1943. The gun positions at Oxford were laid out like those at Fort Lingan but were on a more massive scale. During that winter the crews built the battery plotting room, which was set more than twenty feet underground and had concrete walls of up to ten feet thick. Nearly two dozen wooden accommodation buildings were scattered about the rear of the gun positions, and they were designed on the advice of camouflage experts to resemble a village. Finishing work continued into the summer of 1944.[40]

Quite aside from the scale of the job, Cape faced special challenges at Oxford. Excavation exposed veins of coal and old 'bootleg' mine tunnels, all of which had to be dug out down to rock or clay and refilled with firmer ground or concrete piers. As well, it soon became apparent that the shale on which the construction was taking place did not absorb rainwater, which meant that flooding was going to be a serious problem. In the end, the underground areas could only be kept dry in wet weather by the continuous operation of sump pumps. A still greater problem, resulting from the demands of war industry and the armed forces on manpower, was the difficulty in finding sufficient numbers of competent construction workers. During the work on Chapel Point in 1940 there had been complaints when the contractors brought in small numbers of outside workers. In 1943, by contrast, when Cape, in desperation, proposed to bring in whole crews of workers, the company was informed by the powerful federal manpower authorities that if it did so the men might well be diverted to work in the coal mines. On another occasion, it had to appeal to the army to have the manpower authorities cancel the call-up for military service of the chief mechanic on the project. When Army Headquarters in Ottawa complained of the slow progress with the battery, the officer at Sydney who was overseeing the work stoutly defended Cape: 'The only explanation for slowness is lack of labor of all kinds to finish [the] job. Apparently Ottawa has no conception of carrying on work. You can't get sixteen year old boys to do anything, and also men available for construction are [the] leavings of army and industry.'[41]

The army's effort ashore was a vital element in the shoestring defence of the gulf and the Atlantic approaches to Cape Breton. Although U-boats, intent upon achieving success at the least possible risk, never attempted to push into Sydney Harbour, the danger of a terror attack – either bombardment by deck guns or by torpedoes at close-range – could never be discounted. If an attack such as the one at Bell Island had taken place at Sydney, then Chapel Point and Fort Petrie, as the principal night-fighting harbour entrance batteries, would have had the main responsibility for stopping it. There was also still the admittedly less likely possibility of a surprise assault by Germany's disguised surface raiders or by one of its major warships. Without the army's defences, the navy and the air force would have had no choice but to dissipate their strength further by assigning the few warships and aircraft available to harbour entrance patrols. It was not simply a matter of military requirements, however. Visible defence preparations ashore gave the government a psychological tool with which to counter political pressure from nervous citizens in the gulf area for the concentration of additional warships and aircraft there.

The pivotal importance of the army's harbour defences did nothing to alleviate the frustration of the garrisons. After the initial flurry of excitement at the beginning of the war, when the men went on fruitless searches for enemy agents suspected of being the cause of blinking lights along the shoreline, or when they rounded up an enemy landing party that turned out to be baffled Portuguese fishermen, life settled into a numbingly dull routine. As George Fraser recalled, 'it was a monotonous job standing there watching the drift ice and looking for mythical submarines who never entered the harbour.'[42] He probably summed up the attitudes of the men in the garrisons well when he concluded that they felt

disgruntled and that we were out of the action ... but then again there was the steel plant, there were the coal mines, there were the convoys in the harbour. The navy seemed to take this thing very seriously; they were in and out of here every day. They had minesweepers sweeping the bottom for mines and I don't know if they ever picked anything up. I know that the air force went out there and they dropped bombs; they dropped depth charges, because we used to have to stand to when there was a military operation of this sort on the move. We wouldn't get the full story, but we were just told to stand to. I've seen us, below the road, at the gun position for ten days without changing our clothes. Another time we got an alarm – these alarms used to come at strange times in the morning, 3 and 4 o'clock – when the navy went out. They thought it was a submarine – but what it was was a table floating bottom up and the legs were above the water – and they thought this was periscopes. There were ships sunk – about four miles from Low Point lighthouse, so if the enemy was on the bottom there, he could very easily sneak in with a convoy that was coming through the gates – so we had to cover these convoys.[43]

Martin Haley, who served at Sydney, Shelburne, and Halifax, was more critical. His conclusion many years later was that 'the men had no idea why they were out there. They were watching for something that would never come. In any event it was futile. They knew it, the enemy knew it ... it was like being in prison but worse, because at least in prison you know why you're there.'[44] Haley's frustration was no doubt heightened by the fact that he had previously served with the coast artillery in Britain. There, despite, or perhaps because of the much greater threat, senior authorities had been less stringent about forcing the men to remain on duty close by the guns hour after hour. On his return to Canada, Haley thought the much stricter discipline artificial and destructive of morale.

The tedium was relieved to some extent by regular firing practice. In the case of the Point Edward detachment, they had to go to Chapel

Point to practise because they were unable to fire their main guns safely so close to the city and anchorage. There were occasional alerts, as well. For example, all forts went on a state of emergency on 17 May 1943 when the RCAF reported spotting a German submarine off Meat Cove. The alarm was sounded again on 29 August when a corvette on inner patrol duty dropped a depth charge some two thousand yards offshore from Fort Petrie; a short time later, the navy reported that a 'large fish and not [a] sub had been attacked.'[45]

In the Sydney garrison, as in the whole of Canada's home army, the worrisome questions from 1942 until the end of the war arose from the government's manpower policies. These grew out of the single most important issue for King's Liberal ministry of 1939–45: keeping the pledge not to impose conscription for overseas service. After the fall of France in 1940, the government had countered conscriptionist agitation with the National Resources Mobilization Act, which introduced compulsory service but only in Canada, a restriction that was later broadened to include the whole of the Western Hemisphere. Compulsory service applied only to the army, which, largely because of the decisions made in 1940–2 to build up overseas land forces to a full field army of five divisions, was twice the size of the other two armed services combined. By the end of the war, some 750,000 men and women had served in the army, compared to 250,000 in the air force and just over 100,000 in the navy.

In 1941 the General Staff had persuaded the government to make the National Resources Mobilization Act an effective instrument for military expansion. Until that time, it had only been applied in a largely symbolic way. Men called up under the legislation did a mere thirty days' training, one quarter of the regular initial basic training, and then returned to civilian life. Army Headquarters now called up fewer men but on full-time service. After completing at least four months' basic training, men were assigned to home-defence units. These men were used to top up the chronically short-handed home units, allowing volunteer members of the units who met the physical criteria to proceed overseas. A bonus for the army in its search for overseas reinforcements was that a considerable proportion of the men called up – initially about 25 per cent – volunteered to 'go active.'[46]

One of the still controversial aspects of Canada's war effort was the extent to which these home-service conscripts, who were meeting their legal obligations in every way, were pressured both within the service and by the general public to go active. As the war continued and casualty lists grew, frustration mounted in many quarters with King's unrelenting stand against overseas conscription. The conscripts sometimes became targets of scorn, at least in English Canada, being described as 'Mackenzie King's cowboys,' the 'zoot-suiters' – a reference to the then fashionable baggy suits with tight trouser cuffs supposedly favoured by lay-abouts, pimps, and worse. Undoubtedly the most popular and lasting epithet applied to them was 'zombies,' which compared them to the victims of voodoo magic in horror films, who had been robbed of their souls and shuffled about with blank dead stares perpetrating the evil will of their controllers. The situation was especially difficult for volunteers remaining in home units, as civilians tended to assume that any soldier still in Canada must have refused service overseas, despite the fact that they wore a red 'GS' – general service, or volunteer – badge on their sleeve. Ironically, many of these volunteers were also frustrated, because they wanted to go overseas but were being kept at home by the army on the grounds that they had expertise in coastal defence work that could not be replaced. One person noted: 'Some of the neighbours, you know, they would make a few snide remarks: "You still here? I see so-and-so's gone overseas. How come you never gone over?" and so on. We had a job to do here and it had to be done. You're subject to military discipline and military discipline it is. Not everybody understood; there were a lot of people didn't care. But some of the people, particularly right in the neighbourhood, when I would come home on leave, there'd be a few remarks. Of course, I would try to put them in their place.'[47]

Within the army, the introduction of home-service conscripts, which took place on a large scale in 1942, had the effect of confirming the second-class status the coastal defence troops had always sensed.[48] The situation was especially difficult for officers and senior non-commissioned officers. All were volunteers and many wanted to go overseas but could not because they were over-age or in too low a physical category, or because they had specialized knowledge. The army, not unreasonably, wanted to keep a core of experienced artillerymen at the forts rather than rely entirely on conscripts. William Molnar, who served with the 16th Coast Regiment at the fire command post, later recalled that when he told his colonel he wanted to go overseas, the colonel replied: 'you go overseas when I do and I'm too old.' He believed that one reason why the colonel did not want him and a few others to leave was because they were able to handle the day-to-day operations at headquarters, allowing the colonel – who was from the northside – to spend a couple of days each week with his family.[49] Some men were so anxious to go overseas that they voluntarily took a reduction in rank. George Fraser was one: 'I thought, sure, I was going to get a transfer into a field unit going overseas. I reverted from WO 2 to a staff sergeant; I dropped one rank. The NCOs in our unit – there [were] only three that got overseas with their rank. The other NCOs, they all reverted to privates or gunners ... When I went to approach my OC for a draft to some unit that was going overseas, he said, "you just step outside the door," he said, "when I need you, I'll send for you and I need you *now*, right *here*, to do your work." So, we were kept here because we were, sort of, the nucleus of the artillery movement here because we had been trained on those coast guns.'[50]

Aside from these frustrations, units were increasingly placed in the unhappy situation in which operational efficiency became secondary to the provision of troops for overseas. As one senior officer in Ottawa had pointed out when home-service conscription was launched, the replacement of experienced volunteers with newly raised conscripts created special difficulties for the artillery and other technical units because 'Gun Detachments, range finding, and PF [position finder] specialists operate as teams, each man depending upon the other. It is precision drill, loading, laying and firing under difficult conditions, without light, with every man fulfilling his particular duties ... One new man on the gun team may upset for a considerable time the working of the whole detachment. If we are to have a constant turnover or flow of changing personnel through these Units, then we must accept and lower the standard of efficiency.'[51] Major General Elkins, the officer commanding Atlantic Command, had reminded headquarters in October 1941 that fully 39 per cent of the non-commissioned personnel in his coast artillery units were in highly specialized tradesmen categories, that units had already recently been thinned out as a result of the expansion required to man the new defended ports in Canada and Newfoundland, and that unit establishments were so closely trimmed to the number of personnel needed to keep essential armament ready on a twenty-four-hour basis that there was little slack for training new specialists.[52]

Despite these difficulties and the evident public disrespect for conscripted soldiers who refused to go overseas, military reports are unanimous in describing the friendly attitude of the civilian population in the Sydney area towards the garrisons. The commanding officer of the Régiment de Joliette, which had the double distinction of being largely made up of conscripts and the first French-speaking unit to serve in the Sydney area, wrote in glowing terms of the unit's stay in Cape Breton:

'Here the Regiment always puts on a good show and we receive only praise from the civilians.'[53] The Régiment de Châteauguay, another French-speaking unit, whose machine-gun companies replaced those from the Saint John Fusiliers early in 1943, reported that morale was 'relatively high ... The men are in good spirits, and are astonished at the very friendly attitude of the civilian population, particularly at Glace Bay.'[54] These reports are confirmed by William Molnar, originally from Ontario, who later recalled that while most of the men in the coastal defence units had been drafted, they were generally well received by most people in the area, 'with the possible exception of soldiers returning from overseas duty.'[55] The 2nd/10th Dragoons of southern Ontario, who relieved the Joliettes, encountered morale problems as a result of their change from active to home-defence status, but again the civilian population was helpful. 'Had it not been for the friendly attitude of the people in the Sydney Area, who are endeavouring to provide the men with entertainment, there is no doubt that the morale and spirit of the men would be considerably lower.'[56]

Although the whole point of introducing conscription had been to eliminate manpower shortages, the dislocations caused by the withdrawal of overseas drafts and the organization of new units often had the opposite effect. In January 1943, for example, the hard-pressed fortress engineers at Sydney were short 73 men, while the two infantry units, the Châteauguays and the 2nd/10th Dragoons, were down by 370 men.[57] Such shortages had a deadening effect, requiring longer hours at dull routine jobs, and allowing no margin for professional development through courses of instruction or variance of duties. What was worse, reinforcement by fresh personnel sometimes brought no early relief. In April 1943 the Fusiliers du Saint-Laurent received a draft of 62 soldiers of a 'very low rating. The men in this group are between 30 and 40 years of age and ... have not yet quite adapted themselves to army life.'[58] Some weeks previously, the Régiment de Châteauguay had been burdened by an even greater challenge. On the arrival of a draft of 27 men, 'it was found that none of them had had basic training. Some of them had been in the Army for only a few weeks, others only a few days and most of them were inadequately equipped.' Even worse, 'on several of their documents was a notation that they should be examined by a psychiatrist before being trained, but this was not carried out.'[59]

This documented incident gives credence to Colonel Partington's recollection that some conscripts arrived at his unit untrained and poorly equipped because, he suspected, of prejudice against them by one or two key personnel at training establishments. Some were also profoundly worried and distracted because government support payments had not yet reached their dependents. Many years later, Partington remembered spending a good deal of time straightening out these lapses and being richly rewarded. 'If you treat a man like a soldier, then maybe he'll be a soldier. If you treat him like an animal the same is true.' Partington also found that many of the conscripts had understandable reasons for not going active, including, among some of the French Canadians, admonitions by the extremely influential small-town clergy against shedding Canadian blood on foreign shores. One of his cherished memories was of a small, French Canadian member of his unit who was attacked by a group of young toughs who had been preying on conscripts. This particular soldier was in fact a volunteer but was not wearing his badge; he was also an expert in unarmed combat, and gave the youths a severe beating.[60] Even if apocryphal, this story suggests the level of sympathy that at least some of the unit officers felt for the conscripts in their charge.

Aside from addressing the problems and pressures of long-term development and expansion in the winter of 1942, the forces in Cape Breton had also to make additional preparations for the coming shipping season, when there was every reason to expect the U-boats would renew the offensive. *U-518*'s successful attack at Wabana in November 1942 underscored the very real danger of close-in attacks on incompletely protected harbours. Thus, as soon as the anti-submarine boom at Sydney was lifted for the winter season at the end of that month, it was loaded onto freighters and rushed to Bell Island for installation around the ore-loading piers. Meanwhile, the personnel at the boom depot at North Sydney began the assembly of new nets for Sydney for the 1943 season.[61] Naval Service Headquarters also gave approval that month for the previously low-priority project to install anti-submarine nets at each end of the Strait of Canso to protect the train ferry that operated between Mulgrave and Point Tupper. The naval staff made this decision despite warnings from boom defence experts that, because of the tides in the strait, the job would be expensive and, even with the installation of large gates in the nets, pose a hazard to shipping. One officer was bold enough to suggest that the real solution, both in terms of military security and efficient transport between Cape Breton and the mainland, was to build a causeway. Not surprisingly, this proposal was dismissed as impracticable in view of its magnitude and expense, but a decade later the causeway would be built.[62]

As predicted, the installation of nets at the strait encountered difficulties that ultimately caused the project to be cancelled. A related scheme to provide indicator loops proved to be more successful.[63] These were heavy cables laid on the sea floor across the breadth of a channel. An electric current through the cables created an electromagnetic field; the passage of a ship or submerged submarine across the field caused a disturbance that registered on instruments in the control station on shore, allowing the dispatch of anti-submarine vessels to the position of the contact, the alerting of the shore defences, and a warning to the train ferry either to stay in port or, if it were in transit, to hurry to safety. Loop systems at both entrances to the strait, with control stations at Eddy Point in the south and in the vicinity of the beacon on the mainland shore of the north entrance, began operations in the spring of 1943.[64]

The U-boat attacks on Wabana in 1942 also brought Louisbourg, Sydney's ice-free alternative port, into the network of East Coast defences.[65] Its ice-free harbour was especially important in winter, when it became the assembly point for coastal convoys that maintained essential shipping services between the mainland, Cape Breton, and Newfoundland while Sydney was closed for the season. Accordingly, the Wolfe battery – named after General James Wolfe in honour of his successful siege of the old fortress in 1758 – was established west of the lighthouse to be used during the winter months. Its armament consisted of two eighteen-pounder field guns mounted on concrete platforms and two dispersed-beam sixty-inch searchlights brought from the boom-defence batteries at Sydney. They were installed in wooden huts disguised as fishing shacks on the shoreline. The battery was intended to surprise a surfaced submarine after it pushed through the harbour mouth and rounded the point to attack vessels moored at the railway and coal-loading pier. 'Any submarine,' wrote Partington, 'would have to come through the channel on the surface due to [the shallow] depth of water, and our guns commanded the channel.' In mid-January 1943, fifty-two personnel of the 86th Battery at the Strait of Canso, freed by the reduced manning of Beacon battery when the freeze-up closed the northern entrance to the strait, moved to Louisbourg, where they occupied fourteen Nissen huts, and brought Wolfe battery into action.[66] A unit from Quebec subsequently manned the battery during one winter, becoming, as Peter Moogk has pointed out, the first French-speaking gunners stationed at Louisbourg since 1758.[67]

Efforts by personnel from the navy's boom-defence depot at North

Sydney to lay anti-torpedo nets at the mouth of Louisbourg Harbour were defeated by heavy ice conditions until spring. Ice conditions also made it impossible for two Bangor minesweepers that were based at Louisbourg to escort the Newfoundland railway ferries – whose hulls were strengthened for ice – between North Sydney and Port-aux-Basques. In February the Bangors were relieved by two British-manned Western Isles anti-submarine trawlers that had recently been built in Canada for the Royal Navy but were lent to the Canadian navy because of the shortage of coastal escorts. Even these tough trawlers had difficulties with the ice and limited their operations to the clear waters between the ice fields off Cape Breton and southwestern Newfoundland.[68]

The bitter winter conditions nearly produced a disaster right at the entrance to Louisbourg Harbour. Just before midnight on 21 January 1943, authorities ashore got word that the American submarine chaser *SC 709* had gone aground in a snowstorm about three-quarters of a mile southwest of Lighthouse Point while en route from Portland to Argentia. Two navy harbour craft rushed out but could not get close because of the heavy swell, shallow water, and nearly blind visibility. They returned to port and the Canadian government ship *Laurier* immediately offered its surf boat and crew. Towed out by the navy craft, the surf boat was also unable to get to the wreck but did fire rocket lifelines all through the night. None of these took hold because the American vessel was so encrusted with ice that the exposure-weakened crew members could not reach the lines before they slid into the surf. Finally, when conditions eased on the morning of the 22nd, the American seamen succeeded in securing two lines. Then, two dories from a local schooner and a cargo barquentine, *Angelus*, managed to get close to the wreck and bring off the ten most seriously injured crewmen. Soon after, tugs broke the ice in the harbour to clear the way for a privately owned, shallow-hulled motor boat, which brought off the other sixteen crewmen. Captain Schwerdt and Commander (Engineer) A.V. Wells, the base engineering officer, had come out on one of the tugs to oversee the rescue. Ashore, navy doctors, members of the Sydney Navy League, and especially the ladies' auxiliary of the Louisbourg Navy League, were waiting with blankets, clothes, food, and drink. They revived and stabilized the half-frozen men, who were then whisked to the army hospital in Sydney. In his report on the incident, Schwerdt paid tribute to the courage of both the rescued and the rescuers and to the selfless efficient response of the townspeople.[69]

The ferocity of the convoy battles east of Newfoundland during the winter of 1942–3 seemed to leave no doubt that with the arrival of warmer weather the Germans would again strike in those coastal areas that had been most profitable in 1942. The armed forces had to take account of more than purely military considerations, however, as they were coming under scathing criticism as members of Parliament and the press probed the events in the gulf in 1942. Much of the information, allegations, and sometimes wild speculation came from people living around the gulf who had witnessed the events and felt both endangered and powerless. One problem that could be addressed was the primitive and incomplete civilian telephone system, which hindered the military's own communications and also made it difficult for civilians to report quickly suspicious events or to call for assistance. A new crown corporation, Defence Communications Limited, was created to assist the military to upgrade and fill the large gaps in the land-line system along the shores around the gulf. At the same time, civilians were co-opted into the coastal defence program by the air force through the civilian Aircraft Detection Corps, a scheme in which volunteers living in strategic areas received instruction in aircraft identification and on the proper method of making quick reports to the nearest operational headquarters. In close cooperation with provincial and municipal authorities, police forces, and churches, air force teams recruited thousands of new observers around the gulf, supplied them with pamphlets on submarine identification, and ran training sessions with slide presentations.[70]

These measures were urgently necessary, but they did not resolve the main problem for gulf operations: the shortage of long-endurance, all-weather escort warships. The solution worked out by the staffs in Ottawa and on the East Coast was to continue to restrict merchant-ship traffic in order to limit demands on the navy's most capable escorts, while at the same time using everything else available to hunt more aggressively for U-boats throughout the gulf. The Fairmiles, which were not suited for extended escort duty, were to be pooled into offensive forces that, operating mainly from the central position at Gaspé, could come rapidly to the help of any convoy in trouble or make a determined hunt of the sort that had not been possible in 1942 in response to sightings, direction-finding fixes, or other contacts. The navy once more appealed to the air force to lead the offensive. The air force, having done just that in the fall of 1942 and having come within a hair's breadth of actually sinking a U-boat, needed no persuasion. Joint service training exercises began at St Margaret's Bay near Halifax during the winter to improve the level of cooperation between aircraft and the Fairmiles.[71] There was, of course, a good deal of irony in all of this, because the Canadian forces were endeavouring to build the air–sea hunting capability in the gulf that their improvised efforts of the previous autumn had convinced the U-boat force they already had. For that reason, as has been seen, Dönitz had no intention of renewing the gulf campaign for which the Canadian forces were preparing themselves.

Canadian naval and air deployments to the gulf took place sooner than anticipated in the spring of 1943. Although the ice was heavy at Louisbourg, it was somewhat lighter than normal at Sydney and in the gulf, and it began to clear early. The action started on 24 April, when a shore watcher on the Baie des Chaleurs made the season's first submarine report. Although the armed forces did not take it very seriously, they nevertheless rushed their plans into effect. That same day, 119 Squadron at Sydney began to deploy its entire strength to stations in the western and central gulf, while 113 Squadron moved from Yarmouth to take over at Sydney Airport. This unit was re-equipping with fifteen new Lockheed Vega Venturas, an aircraft that resembled the Hudson but was faster, heavier, and could carry six depth charges instead of four. The assignment of the more capable Venturas to Sydney made good sense in light of the heavy demands on that station. In mid May, 117 Squadron returned to North Sydney and Gaspé from its winter station at Dart-mouth with fifteen Canso and Catalina flying boats, as compared to seven in 1942. The assignment of three full-strength bomber squadrons to Sydney and the gulf in 1943 provided twice the number of aircraft that had normally been deployed in 1942, and equalled the greatest strength achieved by emergency detachments from Nova Scotia late in the 1942 season.[72]

In late April the coastal convoys shifted from Louisbourg to Sydney, and warships assigned to the Sydney Force began to arrive from their winter stations. The force was larger than in previous years, as all gulf convoy escorts were now based at Sydney, Gaspé being reserved for the support force. Among the early arrivals were two of the Western Isles trawlers and six additional anti-submarine trawlers – converted British commercial fishing vessels comparable to the Western Isles type – that the Royal Navy had lent to Canada. As in 1942, there were also five Bangors, although some of them did not arrive until early July. One of the four Fairmile flotillas assigned to the support role in the gulf arrived at Sydney in mid May and stayed there. Some of these craft operated from Ingonish, sixty miles northwest of Sydney, from which point they could more readily reach the inner Cabot Strait and eastern gulf. The build-up at Gaspé in May and June for support operations in the central and western gulf included five Bangors, the Fairmile depot ship *Provider*, and the other three Fairmile flotillas, each with six vessels.[73]

These efforts were spurred on by reports of U-boat sightings throughout the gulf, including several attacks on supposed submarines by escorts and aircraft. All the contacts were in fact false, but on 29 April Naval Service Headquarters sent firm intelligence that a U-boat was coming, 'presumably to land or pick up enemy agents. May four is most likely date but there is no indication of place operations will take place.'[74] Britain's code-breakers had succeeded in decrypting U-boat signals again late in 1942, and the form of this warning strongly suggests that it was based on a message that U-boat headquarters had sent to *U-262*, then in mid-Atlantic, on 15 April. However, the vagueness of the alert that could be provided, even with this very high-grade intelligence, revealed the limitations of what could be learned from German communications on many occasions, especially when submarines were assigned to penetrate coastal waters. One difficulty was that the coastal destination was referred to only generally, partly for security reasons and partly to allow the U-boat commander the necessary freedom of action. The problem was compounded by the fact that, expert as Allied intelligence had become at estimating the progress of a U-boat moving across the Atlantic, arrival dates could only be predicted within a range of several possible days. Given the vast expanse of the approaches to the St Lawrence and the fact that the best radar could only detect a submarine at up to a few miles, and sonar at little more than one mile, the submarine was still as hard to find as the proverbial needle in a haystack. These difficulties, as will be seen, would continue to bedevil the Allied forces in trying to counter U-boats lurking in coastal waters until the war's end.

U-262 was not running agents. Nor, as things turned out, did it pose any threat to shipping in Canadian waters. Its mission was to rescue the captured crews of German submarines being held in a prisoner-of-war camp near Fredericton. The plan, worked out through messages encoded as innocuous passages in letters between the prisoners and their friends and families in Europe, was for the prisoners to break out of the camp and meet *U-262* on the shore at North Point, Prince Edward Island. In a feat that can only be described as heroic in view of the limited underwater endurance of Second World War submarines, *U-262* pushed under the ice floes that still blocked the western approach to Cabot Strait, and came through on the night of 26–7 April, a week earlier than expected. Within the gulf, the waters were clear and, despite severe ice damage, the submarine stood off North Point from 2 to 6 May, surfacing several miles offshore at night to watch for a signal from the escaped prisoners. Ironically, false U-boat sightings in the area had triggered a thorough air search a couple of days before its arrival. Although the appearance of aircraft on exercise from the Prince Edward Island training bases caused *U-262* to take extra precautions, it had the advantage that poor weather hindered or stopped flying on several days during its sojourn in the gulf. The prisoners, however, had not succeeded in escaping from the camp. After failing to make contact, *U-262* slipped out of the gulf as quietly as it had come in, and by the 10th had safely passed through Cabot Strait again. Again ironically, aircraft and shore watchers then made a series of false U-boat sighting reports from the very areas through which the submarine had passed some days earlier.[75]

Pushing hard to follow up thoroughly each sighting report, the experienced aircrew of 119 Squadron patrolled the entire gulf for thirty-six hours and reported finding 'nothing ... except schools of porpoises.' That, they were sure, was the source of the excitement, as 'porpoises diving ... presented a very realistic picture of a submarine' to people unfamiliar with submarine silhouettes.[76] Nevertheless, command authorities could scarcely disregard sighting reports, given the firm intelligence about *U-262*'s mission and the well-known capacity of U-boats to linger in the gulf for weeks at a time. There was also evidence of other submarines heading towards the Canadian coast, and the continued German interest in the area was confirmed when *U-119* laid sixty-six mines off Halifax on 1 June 1943.[77]

Meanwhile, much larger and entirely unanticipated events were unfolding on the transatlantic routes between Newfoundland and Greenland. The Germans had massively reinforced the wolf packs there since the autumn of 1942, and in the early months of 1943 seemed on the brink of victory, intercepting many convoys and smashing several of them. Then, in a series of pitched battles during April and May, the tide suddenly turned as the Allied escorts, reinforced and fitted with improved weapons and detection equipment, began to strike back. The submarines still inflicted substantial losses, but began to suffer unsustainable losses themselves, with the result that Dönitz pulled them back from the North Atlantic convoy routes at the end of May to regroup. The U-boat force had by no means been destroyed. Lost vessels were being replaced, morale was unbroken, and tactical and technical innovation would bring renewed if limited successes right through to the end of the war, so that the Allied anti-submarine forces would never be able to let down their guard. That guard, however, finally existed on an adequate scale, and that, combined with the flood of new merchant ships coming from American and Canadian shipyards, made possible the buildup of Allied forces in Britain for the eventual invasion and liberation of Europe.

As the summer passed with no fresh evidence that the Germans intended a new campaign in the St Lawrence, the Admiralty pressed Naval Service Headquarters to accelerate the passage of merchant ships supplying Britain by allowing them to sail independently through the gulf. The British supply departments had not accepted the Canadian intention to continue closing the St Lawrence to ocean shipping in the 1943 season, because bulk shipments of timber and grain could not be efficiently moved by rail and loaded onto ships at Halifax and Saint John. Early in the 1943 season, therefore, the Canadians agreed that twenty-two ships per month might enter the gulf, and traffic soon began to exceed this number despite the navy's fear that its limited escort force could not supply adequate protection should the Germans manage to repeat their ambush tactics of 1942.[78]

Following the British request to allow ships to sail independently, Naval Service Headquarters terminated the Sydney–Quebec and Sydney–Corner Brook convoy series on 11 September 1943, as they were now almost entirely made up of British grain and timber vessels. Nevertheless, the services retained on station in the gulf all of the aircraft and escorts that had previously been assigned there, and carried out frequent patrols in areas the U-boats were known to prefer, in order to avoid any unpleasant surprises. The shipping changes made little difference at Sydney, whose responsibility for the organization and close protection of convoys for the SSC joiner ocean convoys and the coastal convoys to St John's–Wabana and to Halifax continued, together with the air and sea escort of the Newfoundland ferries at the full level instituted after the loss of *Caribou*.[79]

Another U-boat did in fact come into the gulf in 1943. *U-536*, like *U-262*, entered quietly to pick up escaped prisoners of war with a rendezvous on 27–8 September in the Baie des Chaleurs. By this time, naval intelligence had deciphered the codes through which the prisoners were communicating with Germany. In an elaborate scheme organized at Halifax, a boarding party waited at the rendezvous in order to capture the submarine. *U-536*'s captain, however, detected the warships in support of the boarding party that were lurking in the distance and fled the scene.[80] There also seemed to be danger of a fresh strike through the Strait of Belle Isle at the end of October 1943, when deciphered German signals revealed that *U-537* was off the Labrador coast. The naval authorities at Sydney promptly resumed the Quebec and Corner Brook convoys, but reverted to independent sailings again within two weeks when it became clear that the submarine had continued down the Atlantic coast of Newfoundland.[81]

In the absence of aggressive enemy action, the cruel elements of the North Atlantic continued to test ships, aircraft, and men to their limits, and sometimes beyond. One of the most dramatic incidents to occur at Sydney was the salvage of a new American Liberty merchant ship, *J. Pinckney Henderson*, which on the night of 19 August collided with a tanker in heavy fog while sailing in convoy off Cape Race. The ship, which was carrying drums of oil on deck and an unpalatable combination of lumber, bales of cotton, and chemically unstable magnesium ingots in its holds, quickly caught fire, and only three of its sixty-seven man crew survived.[82] Six days after the collision, the hull was still white hot, though the ship remained structurally sound. When the tugs *Griper* and *Cruizer* towed it into Sydney Harbour on the 31st, rainstorms had cooled the deck but the magnesium in the holds was still burning. Captain Milton MacKenzie, a harbour pilot, boarded the stricken ship outside the anti-submarine net, accompanied by personnel from the Sydney convoy and medical and technical staffs. A grisly sight awaited them – the 'charred remains' of several bodies, 'some on deck, some in their bunks amidship, some in obvious running positions in the alleyway, others in the showers and many in the Gunners quarters aft ... flash blasts and/or asphyxiation had struck them down instantly.' MacKenzie counted twenty-eight bodies, and these could be identified only from their positions in relation to the identity tags normally worn around the neck that were scattered on the decks. The tugs brought the ship through the boom gate and moored it at the entrance to the West Arm, while the tug *Security* came alongside and rigged a hose that wetted down the still smouldering cargo. The grim work of removing the human remains and live ammunition had just begun when there was 'a fairly heavy puff with a burst of flame and showers of ashes ... from no. 2 hold.' Personnel on board quickly got clear, with two of the men who were manning the hoses jumping into the harbour. The tugs then moved the hulk further up into the North West Arm, grounding it at Watson's Creek, the area furthest removed from settlements, in case further explosions opened the hull. 'During all this time internal explosions were taking place and as darkness fell the scene was one to strike awe even to the most experienced.'[83]

The next day, 1 September, Lieutenant (E) P.F. Squibb, RCNR, a professional ship salvager, and two naval fire-fighting specialists, arrived from Halifax to take over the operation. This was the sight that greeted them: 'All holds were still burning, hatch covers had blown or burnt off, burnt out motor trucks and motor tank trucks were hanging from coamings [i.e., around the open cargo hatch openings], twisted and coiled AND Nets [i.e., Admiralty net defence anti-torpedo equipment] covered the decks, along with burned over debris and bits of charred [human] remains.' The decks had 'bulged up and buckled' or even 'blown out,' bulkheads had shattered, and no. 2 hold 'was half full of water and gave off gas from the magnesium which burnt freely on the water's surface.' Because the oil storage tanks were in the forward part of no. 4 hold, 'there was danger of them bursting with the heat, or if an explosion took place in this hold thousands of gallons of oil would have been released.' The Halifax crew had brought with them fog hose equipment that had proven effective in battling electrical and fuel fires in ships. Days of saturation eventually solved the problem in most of the holds but not in the critical no. 4. Squibb, always in terror of the fuel tanks blowing, had large holes cut in the sides of the hold at low tide and had the holes sealed with wooden patches. At high tide boats alongside the wreck pulled off the patches to allow an inundation of water into the burning hold. This helped, but still the burning gases were bubbling to the surface. He noticed that, contrary to any other fire he had experienced, gusts of wind seemed to smother it. He therefore had other holes opened in the sides of the ship and brought alongside it steam equipment on a barge to pour in jets of steam under high pressure. That did the trick: on 25 September, after twenty-four days of continuous firefighting, the blaze was extinguished. For the next month, naval and civilian crews trans-shipped the gutted and salvageable cargo to other vessels and patched and pumped out the hull. Even then, the magnesium gave off gas that sickened the men, and steam equipment had to be kept in operation constantly to control the problem. Finally, at the end of October, the vessel was pulled free, and on 4 November the Naval Control Service handed it over to American authorities, who had it towed to Halifax.[84]

Squibb rightly received a commendation from the U.S. War Shipping Administration, one of whose officials described him publicly as a 'cool devil.' This had been a rare instance of a magnesium fire having been fought successfully and, aside from the feat itself, the technical knowledge gained was of great importance.[85] Lieutenant Commander W.E. Simpson, who had replaced Mitchell as naval control shipping officer at Sydney, while regretting the failure of the press to mention his unit, which had actually been responsible for the hulk, the safety of the port, and providing much of the support to Squibb, confirmed that the salvage officer richly deserved recognition. Squibb had frequently been 'obliged to enter the holds at great personal risk and often penetrated where he could not ask a subordinate to go.' Further, he had done 'a very fine job under conditions which, at times, were heartbreaking. Lack of equipment in the port and inexperienced help left him, at times, very discouraged – but he nevertheless persevered.'[86]

Reflecting back at the end of the war, Simpson was less restrained about the frustrations he and Squibb had had to endure. *J. Pinckney Henderson*'s presence in Sydney had 'made the port's lack of equipment so very obvious that one could do little more than hope that World War III would not find this fine assembly port so "schooner rigged."' Nevertheless, the port and its naval and civilian facilities and personnel had saved a ship still worth nearly $2 million despite the appalling damage it had suffered. The incident, and especially the emotional mass burial of the remains of crewmen in Sydney's Hardwood Hill Cemetery, 'could not fail in bringing home to all that the war in the North Atlantic was far from over.'[87] That an 'Eastern Canadian Port' – the press censor's usual term for Halifax – received credit for this brilliant operation was noted at Sydney without much enthusiasm, however.[88]

Fire was indeed one of the most dangerous enemies to seamen in the age of oil-stoked steamships. On 11 October, days after the long fight with the fire in *J. Pinckney Henderson*, a fuelling accident touched off a blaze that destroyed the new pier at the Point Edward naval base. Thanks to the efficiency of the base personnel and of the crews of the vessels alongside, no lives were lost, but the incident set back the full development of Point Edward as a refit base by nearly nine months. Reconstruction of the pier was not completed until July 1944.[89]

Point Edward had carried out its first refit, that of the borrowed Royal Navy Western Isles anti-submarine trawler *Liscomb*, in the summer of 1943. It next refitted the armed yacht *Reindeer*. Subsequent records are thin but show that in late October and early November 1943 the base repaired the Royal Navy submarine *L-27*. Once its repairs were completed, the submarine carried out training exercises with the forces based at Sydney.[90] The Point Edward engineering staff was also busy with running repairs to warships based at or visiting Sydney and in supporting commercial firms, for which the navy's refit and repair crisis created a bonanza. The first big job, begun in May 1943, was the refit and modernization of the corvette *New Westminster* by Sydney Foundry. This entailed much more than a normal refit, as large parts of the upper hull and superstructure had to be torn apart and rebuilt. The fact that the work, begun in May 1943, was not completed until early December, twice the expected time, showed the difficulties of bringing local firms up to speed for this kind of large-scale project.[91] In 1944 the naval establishment at Sydney would face the triple challenge of making the port into an efficient refit centre, while also hastening the passage of an increasing flood of merchant shipping and facing, against all odds, a renewed U-boat offensive.

chapter thirteen

The End, 1943–1945

After six years of war during which we supported Canada's war effort to the hilt by buying Victory Bonds and sending our sons and daughters overseas what do we find? Some big shot in Halifax decides to close the liquor store before the official announcement of V-E Day.

Unidentified citizen, 9 May 1945

While the Point Edward base and commercial repair firms continued to expand, the army and air force presence at Sydney – and elsewhere on the Atlantic coast – began to contract in late 1943 and early 1944. The successful invasion of Sicily on 10 July 1943 marked the initial step in the liberation of western Europe, and Lieutenant General Kenneth Stuart, chief of the General Staff, advised the government that home defences could safely be reduced because Germany and Italy were now so thoroughly on the defensive that it was inconceivable that they could attempt large-scale raids on the North American coast. The Allied forces that had invaded Sicily included the 1st Infantry Division, the first Canadian army formation to go into sustained action, and this was another reason to reduce the home forces: they still included thousands of general-service men who would be needed to build up the reinforcement pool for the overseas army.

Among the reductions, the largest was the disbandment of the 7th Infantry Division, the formation that had been raised with mostly conscript-manned units for the mobile reserve role in the Maritimes in 1942 when the last of the overseas divisions had departed from the big East Coast camps for Britain.[1] The infantry in the defended ports was also further trimmed. In the case of Sydney, the 2nd/10th Dragoons, the single infantry battalion then in garrison, detached a company of about 150 men in August 1943 to the Strait of Canso defences, where they replaced the 3rd Battalion, Royal Winnipeg Rifles, which was disbanded.[2] No anti-aircraft gun sites were shut down, but units were reduced in strength by up to 20 per cent. During the summer of 1943 headquarters staff in Ottawa decided that there was no longer a need to retain both Chapel Point and Fort Petrie for the defence of the 'small entrance' to Sydney Harbour.[3] Chapel Point and also the Point Edward battery were struck from their operational roles on 25 September and 5 October 1943 respectively, and Fort Petrie became the examination battery.[4] Fort Petrie was retained in preference to Chapel Point, because it had a greater command over the outer approaches and its 6-inch guns were more powerful than Chapel Point's 4.7-inch armament. The garrison at the Point Edward battery departed, but at Chapel Point more than one hundred men – almost the entire detachment – remained. Because of its location near the railhead closest to Oxford battery, Chapel Point became the staging camp for the installation of the equipment and armament scheduled to arrive soon for the new fort. Colonel Dobbie sensibly arranged for the Chapel Point detachment to provide the work crews and to man the new fort when it was completed.[5]

Eastern Air Command was making reductions in its strength at this time as well. The coastal artillery cooperation detachments were the first to go, including 4 Detachment at Sydney, which disbanded on 31 October 1943.[6] No. 125 (Fighter) Squadron, which closed down operations at Sydney on 22 December, went overseas. Redesignated 441 (Fighter) Squadron, it formed part of the large RCAF component of the RAF's 2nd Tactical Air Force, providing close air support for the Allied invasion of Normandy in June 1944.[7] No. 117 Squadron, the flying boat unit that had moved from its summer home at North Sydney to winter quarters on the ice-free waters of Shelburne at the end of November 1943, was disbanded on 15 December. Its Canso and Catalina aircraft were sent to Western Air Command, where such modern machines were still in short supply. Adequate numbers of the more flexible wheeled amphibious version of the Canso, which could operate from water or landing fields, were now available from Canadian production, and were much better suited to East Coast conditions. The North Sydney flying boat station closed in March 1944. No. 119 Squadron, one of the two medium-range squadrons based at Sydney Airport since gulf operations ended for the season in December (the other was 113 Squadron), was also disbanded in March.[8]

Despite these reductions, Canada's home forces and particularly those at Sydney faced large challenges in 1944, even as news from the main combat fronts improved. More shipping than ever had to cross the North Atlantic to mount and sustain the Allied invasion of France that began on 6 June 1944, but the means for defending it were greatly reduced by Britain's demands on Canada for help in carrying out the Commonwealth's share in the liberation of northwestern Europe. In the early months of 1944, Canada assumed full responsibility for escorting convoys between Newfoundland and Northern Ireland to enable the Royal Navy's escorts to support the invasion. That was not enough, however, and the Canadian destroyers that had always formed the backbone of the mid-ocean force also left the convoy routes to form special submarine hunting groups for the invasion. Some of the frigates now coming out of Canadian shipyards replaced them on the North Atlantic run, while others joined the Canadian submarine hunting groups for the invasion. The navy also dispatched sixteen Bangor escorts, reconverted to their original minesweeper design, to help clear the English Channel for the invasion force, as well as a further nineteen corvettes for escort duties in the channel. These last contributions cut into the Western Escort Force, which, nevertheless, continued to be entirely responsible for escorting the transatlantic convoys between New York and Newfoundland.[9]

The key to doing more with less in the defence of shipping was superb signals intelligence. The renewed ability of the British government's Code and Cypher School at Bletchley Park to decipher German submarine radio communications had contributed greatly to the Allied victories over the submarines in 1943. In 1944, as the enemy developed new equipment and tactics, it became increasingly difficult for the Allies to find and sink U-boats, but Bletchley Park's timely decryptions were an enormous help in suppressing the submarines and in keeping them away from shipping. Beginning with the cruise of *U-537*, whose passage past the Strait of Belle Isle had brought the reintroduction of convoys in the St Lawrence in October 1943, the Germans kept one or two U-boats constantly on patrol in Canadian waters, but they were not aggressive. Like the submarines that had come in October and November 1942, they remained submerged and virtually immobile by day, seeking ambush positions from which they could strike with impunity at shipping unlucky enough to pass close by. As in the autumn of 1942, the regular appearance of RCAF aircraft left them no alternative but to exercise extreme caution. What was unknown to the U-boat command – and indeed to any but the most senior Allied commanders – was that the RCAF achieved these results more economically than in 1942 because of decryption intelligence. Since mid 1943, decryptions had been immediately dispatched by secure cable from Washington and London to the submarine tracking room at Naval Service Headquarters in Ottawa. There, the submarine tracking experts used this and other information to design patrol areas that were transmitted to Admiral Murray's big new naval and air force Area Combined Headquarters, on South Street in Halifax. It, in turn, used the improved East Coast communications system to dispatch quickly specific and coordinated orders to the naval and air bases.[10]

Although the Germans did not realize that their radio codes had been broken, they did know that the Allies had an efficient radio direction-finding system. Therefore, the submarines that came to Canada during 1944 increasingly observed radio silence from the time they approached from the mid-Atlantic until their departure back to the central ocean several weeks later. This silence, and the fact that the boats seldom surfaced when visibility was at all good, denied Allied forces any means of locating them reliably, as decrypted messages usually revealed only the very general orders issued to the submarines. These orders allowed the U-boat captains wide latitude to attack in broad areas, such as the waters off Nova Scotia or the whole of the approaches to St John's. Knowledge of these orders was, however, often sufficient for the submarine trackers to define air patrol areas that assured that the U-boats regularly saw aircraft and stayed submerged.

Still, no matter how well organized, harassing patrols could never guarantee complete security. It was always possible for submarine commanders to ignore or modify their orders. Bold commanders might bring their submarines into Canadian waters days before they were expected, and cautious commanders might arrive days later. False but convincing radar and sonar contacts by aircraft and escorts could also put the limited defence forces on the wrong trail. As a result, several boats were able to make a single attack on shipping, but it was a measure of the defence that they were seldom able to repeat their success. Thus, their returns were very meagre compared to the multiple sinkings achieved by each submarine in 1942. The Allied commands were willing to tolerate these small losses in North American waters at a time when the main weight of anti-submarine forces was urgently required in European waters to support the invasion of France.

Another winter of light ice conditions allowed shipping operations to begin at Sydney during the last week of April 1944. Although the Sydney–Quebec convoys were again suspended because of the apparent absence of U-boats, the navy wanted to limit the entry of ocean-going shipping to forty-eight ships per month, the number that could, in the event of an attack, be adequately escorted by the forces available. Because of the incapacity of the rail system and the Atlantic ports to handle grain and timber shipments, however, the British schedules alone called for sixty-nine ships per month, over and above Canada's own ocean-going shipping requirements in the gulf. The build-up of British trade was initially slow, but it soon rose to the anticipated high levels.[11] Meanwhile, the naval forces assigned to the gulf in late April and May were smaller than in 1943. At Gaspé there were only two flotillas of Fairmile launches, which, as in 1943, carried out patrols of the choke points where U-boats could take up ambush positions. All escorts with sea-going capabilities – eight Bangors, three British trawlers, and the Free Norwegian escort ship *King Haakon VII* – were concentrated at Sydney. The three venerable minesweepers, *Rayon d'Or, Suderoy V,* and *Star XVI,* were also at Sydney, as well as a Fairmile flotilla, which, as in 1943, usually worked out of Ingonish.[12]

None of the submarines that hunted in Canadian waters during the first seven months of 1944 pushed towards Cabot Strait. Nevertheless, the Sydney air squadrons saw periods of intense activity during most months when they joined in harassment sweeps off Halifax, the preferred destination of the submarines. The Sydney air base was especially busy in May because the spring thaw caused the runways at Gander to heave, and five or more of 10 Squadron's big four-engine Consolidated Liberator bombers shifted to the Cape Breton Airport for the month.[13] Initially, these fast, very long-range aircraft swept the waters around Cape Race where *U-548* was known to be lurking. They were unable to help the Canadian frigate *Valleyfield,* however, which passed through the danger area on the night 6–7 May. Rushing back to port after a transatlantic convoy, it failed to take adequate precautions and had the bad luck to stumble into the sights of the submerged U-boat. The torpedo attack quickly sank the warship, which went down with the loss of more than 130 lives.[14] A few days later, the survivors passed through Sydney, where personnel at the naval base, shocked by this stark reminder that the Battle of the Atlantic was far from over, did their utmost to assemble new kits for them.[15]

To enable the Canadian navy's reduced escort forces to cope, British authorities revised the transatlantic convoy system for the spring, summer, and autumn of 1944, the period of peak demand for the invasion of France. Previously, four fast HX convoys had sailed from New York every month, and two slow SC convoys from Halifax. Now four much larger convoys per month all sailed from New York, two of them fast (over ten knots, designated HXF), one medium speed (ten knots, designated HXM), and one slow (less than ten knots, designated HXS). These were all fed along the way by joiners from Halifax, Sydney, and St John's. Convoys from Britain were similarly rearranged, now sailing in ONF, ONM, and ONS series, with ships peeling off in groups to the convoy port closest to their destination.[16]

The effect of this reorganization was to double the monthly sailings of joiner convoys from Sydney from two to four. This was an important commitment for the Sydney Force, which assigned two to four escorts to take each of the joiners out to the Sydney Ocean Meeting Point, about twenty-four hours' sailing (some 225 to 250 miles) southeast of the port. Commander Simpson recalled that 'invasion was in the air and any ship sailing was liable to see the beach heads before returning to Canada – a fact which was not lost on masters and crews.' Nor did the port staff escape the tension. On 6 July 1944, for example, the Sydney portion of HXM 298 sailed three hours early, at 2:00 a.m. local time, even though this meant that some ships coming into Sydney could not join in time. According to Simpson, the naval control boarding boat 'proceeded to sea with the convoy and picked up 2 incoming vessels and turned them 'round to save five days delay [i.e., until they could join the next transatlantic convoy] ... On arriving back ashore at 0700 Naval Control felt that a good job had been done and hope[d] Eisenhower would do as well!'[17]

The naval and merchant shipping authorities had wanted to make Sydney the main assembly port for the joiner convoys to relieve pressure on Halifax. After a trial with HXS 291, which sailed from New York on 10 May 1944, this idea was abandoned, as many ships originating from points south of Halifax had to load there or make other use of that port's facilities and could not get to Sydney in time to meet the transatlantic schedules.[18] According to Simpson, Sydney businessmen had been sceptical all along and 'no great expenditure was incurred by local interests in preparing for an event which had remote chance of becoming established practice. The big sister port to the South had all the advantages of being in full running order at no inconsiderable expense, shipping companies had practically moved their head offices there during the war years and the servicing of escorts, Mac ships and Rescue ships was a smoothly functioning operation tested and proved. The expression "Manifest destiny" ... was no figure of speech.'[19]

To speed up the flow of shipping and reduce demand for escorts further, Naval Service Headquarters introduced the Cancon system of shipping control. The coastal area was divided into zones, within each of which requirements for merchant vessels to sail in convoy could be relaxed by various degrees when the good intelligence that was now available indicated that there was little or no threat of submarine attack in the area.[20] After nearly five years of war, the communications and shipping control systems were so well organized that the status of each zone could be reviewed and, if necessary, revised daily. This was essentially a refinement and general application of the practice that had begun in the gulf in 1943. In the Canada–Newfoundland area, the destruction of *Valleyfield* was the last loss for some months, and U-boats proved to be almost no hindrance to shipping operations.

When it became clear at the close of May 1944 that southern Nova Scotia had replaced the St John's and Halifax areas as the targets of the submarines,[21] Admiral Murray's headquarters in Halifax suspended the Sydney–Wabana iron ore convoys and the Halifax–Sydney series. Especially vulnerable or high-value ships on coastal routes, however, were escorted in the Halifax–St John's series, which now made a stop at Sydney. Similarly, because of the importance of the Newfoundland ferries, the Sydney–Port-aux-Basques series continued with full-scale naval and air escort. The navy relaxed restrictions more than at any time since 1942 on the passage of ocean shipping through the Strait of Belle Isle. Ships in the ON series from Britain bound for gulf ports now began to break off near the strait to follow independently the short route into the St Lawrence, thereby easing Britain's difficulties in moving bulk cargoes of grain and timber quickly. Aside from the large task of sailing the transatlantic HX series joiners, the work of Sydney's naval control staff now was to hurry vessels on their way by ensuring the fast servicing of vessels that came into port, particularly by stepping up the unloading and turn-around of the ore ships from Wabana. At the same time, the NCS staff continued meticulously to track all shipping so that increased precautions could be quickly implemented if needed.[22]

The air force also made changes in the spring of 1944. The Cansos of 161 Squadron, the unit assigned to the interior of the gulf for the season, took up station at Summerside and Gaspé at the end of April and beginning of May. In early July, as work progressed on the new air strip at Sept-Îles on Quebec's North Shore, the Gaspé detachment shifted a unit to that station. In June, 113 Squadron was transferred from Sydney Airport to Torbay, and was replaced by 116 Squadron, a Canso unit.[23] Like all the East Coast units, 116 had a busy time supporting both Canadian and U.S. Navy groups in their anti-submarine work. On 4 July, Cansos from 116 Squadron helped search for *U-233* south of Sable Island. On the following day, American warships destroyed the submarine, which had been en route to Halifax to lay mines.[24]

As busy as the forces at Sydney were on the Atlantic front, life for units within the gulf was relatively dull. 'Nothing seen but miles and miles of waves and whales,' was how the diarist of 161 Squadron described the results of his unit's patrols in July.[25] It was, however, the proverbial calm before the storm. Within weeks, the Cape Breton approaches and the gulf became the target of a U-boat offensive on a scale that matched the 1942 Battle of the St Lawrence.[26]

By 21 July 1944 the Allies knew from German naval communications that *U-802*, under the command of Kapitänleutnant Helmut Schmoeckel, had recently sailed from France, bound for the gulf on a course that would bring it about one hundred miles south of Cape Race. The submarine trackers also knew that this U-boat was equipped with a snorkel breathing tube, a device that was being fitted in an increasing number of submarines since early in the year to protect them against the omnipresent Allied aircraft. With a snorkel tube, the underwater endurance of submarines was no longer limited by the charge in the batteries for electric propulsion and the deteriorating quality of the air in the submarine. Submarines could now cruise almost indefinitely about twenty-five feet below the surface, running their powerful main diesel engines, all the while recharging the batteries that powered their electric motors for emergency deep dives. While doing so, nothing showed above the surface of the water except the small snorkel masthead, which, especially in the rough waters of the North Atlantic, was all but invisible to both the human eye and the best Allied radar. The snorkel tube had made U-boats almost impossible to detect in the English Channel during the recent invasion of Normandy, despite the saturation of the area with hundreds of anti-submarine vessels and aircraft, demonstrating that it gave them considerable security against both warships and aircraft in coastal waters.

Sonar for underwater searching in the Second World War had a range of only about a mile, and for that reason warships usually depended on visual or radar contact on a surfaced submarine – albeit rapidly plunging beneath the surface – to narrow the search area to practical limits. The snorkel tube now gave little opportunity for that crucial initial contact. Moreover, even when Allied escort crews did succeed in spotting the masthead, or were close by when a submarine gave away its position by firing a torpedo, they found sonar to be of very limited effectiveness in shallow waters. The returns from U-boat hulls were hopelessly muddled by returns from rocks, old shipwrecks, and innumerable other objects cluttering the bottom. As well, experience in the gulf in 1942 had revealed that the mixing of ocean currents of different temperatures in coastal areas and the flow of fresh water from rivers often created layers of water of different densities that deflected sonar pulses and completely hid a submerged U-boat.

In their effort to catch *U-802* and the U-boats that followed, both Canadian and American forces discovered the full extent to which the snorkel tube had made submarines virtually undetectable. On 9 August, when intelligence estimates placed *U-802* about five hundred miles east of Newfoundland, Admiral Murray launched Operation Perch, a large, well-organized air and sea hunt. His forces now included a specialized anti-submarine hunting support unit called EG 16, made up of newly built frigates that were bigger than corvettes, several knots faster, and carried a heavier armament. While they searched the expected course of the submarine, aircraft constantly swept a vast area, all around the warships, day and night. The universal fitting of radar and other electronic aids to navigation made night flying much less of a challenge than it had been in 1942, and several of the aircraft carried Leigh searchlights that enabled them to attack even in total darkness. Sydney and the gulf stations sent Cansos to Newfoundland to help with this effort. Meanwhile, the most successful anti-submarine group in the U.S. Navy, the escort aircraft carrier *Bogue* and its destroyer escorts, was chasing *U-802* in from the central ocean.

A series of events now demonstrated that even the best information could not pinpoint submarines operating evasively. Schmoeckel arrived 250 miles south of his assigned course, and ran submerged so much of the time that he arrived four days later than the date estimated by both the German and Allied naval staffs. When he finally signalled his arrival on the night of 12–13 August and Allied intelligence was able to determine his approximate position, Murray adjusted the air-sea hunt to cover the southerly rather than easterly approaches to Cabot Strait. *Bogue* was still on the hunt as well, and on the night of 18–19 August its aircraft caught the U-boat on the surface about three hundred miles south of St John's. The attack was unsuccessful, but on the 20th, somewhat to the west, the American pilots were startled to see what they thought was the same submarine fully surfaced in broad daylight. It was quickly destroyed, Allied intelligence declared the Canadian area clear, and Murray cancelled the coastal convoys that had already resumed sailing again between Sydney and Halifax and Sydney and Wabana.[27]

There was a further surprise in store when interrogation of the survivors of the boat destroyed by *Bogue*'s aircraft revealed that it was not *U-802*, the submarine assigned to the gulf, but *U-1229*. It had sailed from France on a mission to land agents on the American coast in the Gulf of Maine and stumbled into the search area. Because of the secrecy of its mission, no reference had been made to it in German naval radio communications, so that Allied intelligence had not been aware of its presence in the area. This meant that *U-802* was still making for Cabot Street, and on 22 August Murray reinstituted all of the measures that had been cancelled two days earlier. The frigates again began to sweep the estimated track into the strait, supported once more by dense air coverage from Sydney, where 116 Squadron was reinforced by Cansos from other stations and two Liberator bombers from Gander. This hunt fell back towards Cabot Strait, where it focused from the night of 25–6 August to the night of 28–9, when it was expected that *U-802* would make its entry. During this time the Fairmiles at Sydney and Ingonish, reinforced to two flotillas of eight craft each, joined in a continuous search between St Paul Island and Cape Ray. Thereafter, the frigate and air searches began to pull back into the gulf. The full strength of 116 Squadron remained at Sydney, together with the two Fairmile flotillas, to keep watch over the strait area, while 161 Squadron began to fly in the gulf from its home stations, with assistance by aircraft from other stations. In conjunction with the westward-moving air patrols, the Gaspé Fairmiles began constant sweeps of the choke points in the western gulf.[28]

Direct protection of shipping had to be strengthened as well. Admiral Murray assigned six corvettes to Sydney, and these, with the Bangors and trawlers of the Sydney Force, resumed the suspended coastal convoys, including the Sydney–Quebec series, during the last week of August.[29] That by no means solved the problem, as the arrival of *U-802* unhappily coincided with the increase in British shipping to the St Lawrence. The slow start of transatlantic trade to the gulf in the spring had been the result of merchant ships being held in British waters to carry the invasion force to Normandy. As these ships were released back to trade during the summer, activity on the St Lawrence had grown to the point where there were sixty ocean cargo ships in the river by the end of August, with comparable numbers en route to load. Naval Service Headquarters warned that this was far more ships than could be protected in the difficult conditions of the gulf, but both British and Canadian transport officials responded that there was no choice; the railways could not carry extra cargo between Montreal and the East Coast without transferring so much rolling stock from the Prairies that the collection of the 1944 grain harvest would be severely hindered.[30] As in 1942, the burden of organizing the extra shipping in convoy and of keeping the overstretched escort and air forces up to the demanding schedules fell to the bases and staffs at Sydney.[31]

The pressure was in no way diminished by reports that a second U-boat, *U-541*, was on its way to the gulf. To make matters worse, both submarines had so deviated from normal operating patterns that intelligence estimates of their locations were way off the mark, although Allied estimates were more accurate than those of U-boat headquarters itself. Terrorized by the air attack on the night of 18–19 August, *U-802* had crawled towards Cabot Strait, not daring even to raise its snorkel tube except at night. It finally passed through on the 31st, three days after the main search had shifted westward into the gulf. Meanwhile, *Bogue* and its destroyer escorts, supported by the RCAF in Newfoundland, began to hunt for *U-541* as it came in five hundred miles east of Cape Race, but the weather soon closed in. Encouraged by the poor visibility and lack of air activity, Oberleutnant Kurt Petersen made long fast runs on the surface and was soon a day or more ahead of the 'furthest on' point in the Allied estimate.

In the early hours of 3 September, *U-541* surfaced about one hundred miles off Scatarie Island, where it spotted the small steamer *Livingstone*, on its way from Halifax to the American naval base at Argentia. Too slow for convoy, the ship sailed alone but, according to both Allied and German estimates, it should have safely traversed the approaches to Cabot Strait long before *U-541* reached the area. During what must have been a frustrating half hour, the submarine fired five torpedoes as the steamer, alerted by the flame and 'huge column of water' caused by one of the misses, took desperate evasive action. The last shot ran true, causing an explosion in the engine room that broke up the ship at about 4:15 a.m. Crewmen in the forward part of the ship managed to launch a lifeboat and pick up men who had been thrown overboard by the blast, but there were only fourteen survivors, several of them badly injured, from the crew of twenty-eight.[32]

Livingstone had broadcast distress signals but they appear not to have been picked up by anyone. Thus, word of the attack did not get out until noon, when a fast convoy – the troop transport *Lady Rodney* escorted by the corvettes *Barrie* and *Shawinigan* – came upon the lifeboat in the now heavy seas. While *Barrie*'s crew carried out courageous and successful small boat work to bring in the survivors, Admiral Murray's staff hastily switched the U-boat hunt in the St Lawrence back to the Sydney area. *Livingstone* had been attacked so far to the west of *U-541*'s probable track that the submarine trackers believed that it was the work of *U-802*, which had apparently lingered outside Cabot Strait rather than entering the gulf.

At Sydney the base staff rushed the frigates, which had come into port late on 1 September, back out to sea to establish a barrier patrol in Cabot Strait. This was intended to prevent *Livingstone*'s attacker from entering the gulf. Meanwhile, Murray's headquarters diverted a New-foundland-based Mid-Ocean Escort Force Group, C 6, to patrol east of the position where *Livingstone* had been attacked, to intercept the sub-marine if it was trying to move back out to sea. At the same time, further out to sea, *Bogue*'s group continued the hunt for *U-541*, which intelli-gence incorrectly believed was still making its transatlantic passage. The RCAF supported all three naval hunting groups, although the initial flight from Sydney on the 3rd was delayed by foul weather, and then lim-ited to a crawl at an attitude of only a few hundred feet.

These were well-conceived operations that focused the maximum forces available but, as the Allies were learning at the same time in Euro-pean waters, they were not enough to catch a snorkel-equipped subma-rine in coastal waters. More ships with better equipment and training than were ever available in Murray's command would have been needed to throw an effective barrier across Cabot Strait. With its great breadth, wide open approaches, sinuous shores, and deep waters, the strait pre-sents many of the most difficult challenges of both coastal and open-ocean underwater warfare.

After attacking *Livingstone*, *U-541* ran submerged, snorkelling only at night, and had no difficulty in making its way through Cabot Strait on 4 and 5 September. The weather continued to favour Petersen, curtailing and then shutting down air patrols from Sydney as he made his passage. Emboldened by the lack of opposition, *U-541* surfaced on the night of the 7–8th, southeast of Anticosti Island, to attack an apparently un-escorted freighter, *Fort Rémy*, which had just detached from convoy QS 89 to hurry ahead to Sydney 'at best speed.' As the submarine closed in for the kill, however, the sky was suddenly lit up by star shells as the corvette *Norsyd*, which had also left the convoy to escort the freighter, charged into view, pouring 20 mm cannon fire into the conning tower of the hastily diving *U-541*. As was usual in these waters, the corvette was unable to get a firm sonar contact. The situation was, however, right for a 'hunt to exhaustion,' a combined air-sea tactic employed when forces were immediately available and the exact position of a submarine was known. The key was to get aircraft to the scene quickly to perform a constant sweep around the position of the dive to prevent the submarine from making a hasty escape on the surface. The gulf stations were fogged in, but a Canso from Sydney reached the scene within hours, while the frigates of EG 16 rushed up from Cabot Strait.[33]

The hunt to exhaustion near Anticosti continued for thirty-six hours, with five Cansos at a time scouring the probability zone. *U-541*, meanwhile, had gone deep and hidden on the bottom, safe from sonar detection, as the crew discovered to its relief, where it waited for more than twenty-four hours before creeping away and beginning to snorkel. That, of course, was the great advantage of the snorkel tube, as a conventional U-boat would have had to come to the surface where it almost certainly would have been detected by sight or radar by the warships and aircraft. When the search failed to produce a contact, the aircraft, frigates, and Fairmiles based at Gaspé shifted to barrier patrols across the choke points in the central gulf, particularly the Gaspé Passage, with the aircraft also undertaking round-the-clock area sweeps.[34]

Although the hunt for *U-541* was unsuccessful, the Canadian airmen and seamen accomplished more than they realized. Schmoeckel, in *U-802*, which had by now reached the mouth of the St Lawrence River, did not know that *U-541* had also been coming into the gulf, and he naturally assumed that the increased air activity was directed at him. He therefore began to creep back out of the gulf, and Petersen, who also became demoralized by the constant appearance of naval vessels and aircraft, soon followed. They moved through Cabot Strait on 23–4 September, but neither Allied nor German intelligence had confirmation of their departure until they were once again safely out on the high seas and began to send signals.

At this stage in the war, Admiral Dönitz regarded as promising any area where submarines could make even one or two attacks and survive. He therefore dispatched three more submarines to the gulf: *U-1223*, which operated there in October and early November, and *U-1228* and *U-1231*, which arrived in Cabot Strait at the end of November, with the latter patrolling the gulf for much of December. The new boats accomplished little more than the meagre score of *U-802* and *U-541*, although, in a worrying display of what a snorkel boat could do if it found a good ambush position, *U-1223* blew the stern off *Magog*, an EG 16 frigate, while the support group was screening a convoy that had air cover. The submarine also eluded the ensuing forty-eight-hour air-sea hunt. Still, its only other success was to damage a freighter that had been allowed to sail independently after the submarine trackers mistakenly declared the gulf clear. *U-1228* destroyed HMCS *Shawinigan*, a Western Escort Force corvette that had come to help at Sydney for much of the season, while *U-1231*'s attacks were all unsuccessful.

The defensive operations against *U-1223*, *U-1228*, and *U-1231* followed the pattern established in dealing with *U-541* and *U-802*.[35] As well, in every case the Allies had excellent information from radio interceptions about their orders to enter the gulf, their general approach courses, and their actual progress across the central ocean. In every case the picture began to lose focus as the submarines neared Newfoundland, because they ran silently and submerged. There was no way of finding out to what extent they were following or disregarding their instructions or maintaining their expected rates of advance. As always, false sonar contacts further confused the situation. The numbers of U-boats now entering, patrolling, or leaving Canadian waters caused further difficulties for the trackers, as did advisory signals from German headquarters that gave submarines already on station the option of moving to other areas of the coast where hunting might be better. In these circumstances, Murray maintained the defences in the gulf and the approaches to Cabot Strait at the same high level they had reached in September. Sydney remained the focus of activity, both for supporting gulf operations and for covering the waters seaward of Cape Breton.

The Canadian forces in fact achieved from the beginning of the 1944 campaign what they had finally accomplished in the autumn of 1942. The constant presence of patrol vessels and aircraft made it impossible for the submarines to press concerted attacks. More impressively, this was done while a very large volume of shipping moved through the gulf, whereas shipping had been cut to a trickle in the autumn of 1942. In contrast to the slaughter of several convoys that had occurred in the summer of 1942, the only successful attack on a convoy in 1944 was *U-1223*'s one shot at *Magog*. Sadly, however, there was major loss of life in the attack on HMCS *Shawinigan*. This late-season tragedy on the ill-fated North Sydney–Port-aux-Basques ferry run uncannily echoed the ghastly events that had taken place in those same waters twenty-five months earlier with *Caribou*. The submarine trackers estimated – extremely accurately – that *U-1228* would arrive south of St Pierre, in the outer approaches to Cabot Strait, on 14 November. Knowing of U-boat headquarters' interest in that area, they also correctly allowed for the possibility that the submarine might linger there for several days before moving on to carry out its assigned mission in the gulf. The situation was complicated, however, by the fact that *U-1231* was known to be following *U-1228* by several days. This inevitably thinned out the searching forces, especially because convoys were proceeding through the danger areas and the frigates periodically had to give up the hunt to reinforce the escorts.

To compound the difficulty, the weather was especially miserable that November, and on many days aircraft could not fly. Then, *U-1228*, although encountering little opposition, did the entirely unexpected: on 22 November it headed up close to the southern shore of Newfoundland, clear of the shipping lanes and well out of the Canadian search areas, to lie low because its snorkel tube was malfunctioning. Over the next few days, it began to run better, and *U-1228* therefore headed into Cabot Strait, still hugging the Newfoundland coast.

On the night of 24–5, in a nightmarish coincidence, the boat made hydrophone contact with *Shawinigan* only seventy minutes after Oberleutnant Friedrich-Wilhelm Marienfeld had decided to turn back from the strait because of renewed problems with the snorkel tube. The corvette passed so close by that the submarine was able to attack without even surfacing for fast pursuit, a rare occurrence. Marienfeld recorded the destruction of the corvette as follows: 'Tube VI fired ... Torpedo and [corvette] screw noises merge. A hit after 4 min 0 secs. High, 50 m, large explosion column with heavy shower of sparks, after collapse of explosion column, only 10 m high now, then smoke cloud, destroyer disappeared. On hydrophone set screw noises disappeared with hit, great roaring and crackling sounds.'[36] There were no survivors among the ninety-one personnel on board.

Shawinigan had been carrying out the most routine of duties. Having escorted the Newfoundland ferry *Burgeo* and a U.S. Coast Guard transport from North Sydney to Port-aux-Basques on the 24th, it had proceeded to carry out a night patrol along the first part of the return track, as laid down in standing procedures to guard against a U-boat lying in wait for *Burgeo*'s return trip to North Sydney the next day. Other than Marienfeld, *Burgeo*'s captain was the last person to see the corvette, and his account is chilling in showing how the destruction of ninety-one men could be scarcely noticed immediately in the humdrum routine and daily worries of wartime:

> The Escort K-136 [*Shawinigan*] left us close by Channel Head at approximately 3:10 Nfld time Friday evening, Nov 24th, after calling us and asking what time we would be sailing, we gave him 7:15 ADT [Atlantic Daylight Time]. He thanked me and said will see you outside in the morning. I sailed from Port aux Basques 7:45 Nfld time Nov 25th ... It was a fine morning, just getting dawning – I expected to see Escort any moment or for him to call me on R/T [radio telephone]. After ten or fifteen minutes passed I called him on R/T but got no reply. I kept on my course expecting to see him any time as it was getting lighter. But when morning broke I could not see him or pick him up on R/T. It was about 11 miles from Channel Head at 8:45 Nfld time and every appearance of a heavy North East wind coming.

Worrying about the safety of his ship in the threatening weather, *Burgeo*'s captain hurried on to North Sydney, continuing to call *Shawinigan* on his short-range radio telephone but not reporting the corvette's absence to shore authorities with his main transmitter.[37] No one suspected anything was amiss until *Burgeo* arrived alone at North Sydney that afternoon. Sydney naval radio then broadcast, asking the corvette to report. As the signal went out – twenty-three times – into the silent grey skies over the strait, the horrible truth became apparent. In fact, a civilian volunteer shore watcher a few miles west of Port-aux-Basques had reported the previous night a 'loud explosion followed by 3 mins silence followed by roar like thunder.' This report had gone through to headquarters at St John's and Halifax but the staffs had had a ready explanation: American armed forces' construction crews were known to be working in the vicinity at a project that involved 'blasting operations ... day and night.'[38] As valuable as the information from civilian shore watchers could be, they were obviously not kept informed about military activities and frequently called in alarms about incidents that proved to be innocuous. Because of *Shawinigan*'s disappearance, the staffs made further inquiries that day and learned that there had been no blasting at the American construction site during the night.[39]

As usual, the weather was wretched, preventing aircraft from getting into the air at Sydney to search the strait until the morning of the 26th. Meanwhile, Admiral Murray's headquarters called in EG 16, which had been carrying out a search south of St Pierre, to support Bangors and

Fairmiles from Sydney in scouring the area. That day the British trawler *Anticosti*, while escorting *Burgeo* on its next trip, discovered an empty Carley lifesaving float. A day later, aircraft from Sydney sighted an oil slick and homed in the warships, which found a fragment of the ship's bridge structure and six bodies. 'Each body was wearing a life belt when recovered, and appeared to be floating upright in the water, the face submerged.'[40] Marienfeld had long since escaped into the ocean east of Cape Breton. Continuing equipment malfunctions and close approaches by a Canso and an escort group persuaded him, on 6 December, to abandon the mission and head for home.[41]

The loss of *Shawinigan* exacerbated the bad feeling between the navy and the Newfoundland Railway Company that had simmered since the destruction of *Caribou*. Commander Simpson, who took evidence from *Burgeo*'s captain after *Shawinigan*'s loss, linked the two tragedies in his final report. The Newfoundland government's representatives had objected, he claimed, to 'the delays which would necessarily follow' when the ferry convoy was first organized in June 1942, and this reluctance to cooperate plagued Sydney Command until the end of the war. '"Misunderstandings" were very frequent and the plain fact was that uncertain railway schedules were balanced against human lives and it was by the Grace of God and the earnest endeavours of the Sydney escort force that a further tragedy to civilian life was averted. The fact that in 1944 the loss of one of the escorts, HMCS "SHAWINIGAN," was reported late due to the ignoring of orders by the "BURGEO" is something that could never be satisfactorily explained or dealt with.'[42]

While Simpson's anger was understandable, German records show that there was little ground for recrimination. In the cases of both *U-69* in 1942 and *U-1228* two years later, the submarine captains had come to Cabot Strait after abandoning their main operating area, while observing radio silence and employing cautious submerged running tactics. Both had stumbled on their victims by pure chance under extremely favourable conditions in the dead of night. Even the strongest anti-submarine forces proved incapable throughout the war of guarding against such chance attacks. In view of the fact that *U-1228* was already beating a retreat and scrupulously employing evasive tactics when it sank *Shawinigan*, it seems unlikely that earlier notice by *Burgeo* of the corvette's disappearance would have increased the likelihood that the hunting forces would have been able to find the submarine.

During 1944, Sydney's development as a major refit centre for warships continued. By the middle of the year, the reconstruction of the pier at Point Edward was completed, as were most of the new facilities that had been decided on late in 1943 as a result of the refit crisis, including a steel plate shop and foundry. Openings in American ship-yards and on the Canadian West Coast had overcome the immediate shortfall of refit berths for the Canadian fleet, but over the winter of 1943–4 the navy allocated two corvettes to Sydney Foundry to help that firm retain its workforce and thereby develop the East Coast facilities that would be needed for the expanding fleet in 1944.[43] During the first part of the 1944 season, however, the demands of the Normandy inva-sion and the increased responsibilities that the navy shouldered in the North Atlantic forced delays in the withdrawals of ships from operations for refit. Although Point Edward was busy with running repairs and sup-port to the commercial firms, officers began to worry that the technical staffs in Ottawa and Halifax lacked confidence in the new and still incomplete establishment.[44]

Somewhat paradoxically, just when the success of the Normandy inva-sion allowed the scheduling of refits, there was also an increase in run-ning repairs because of the large additional forces assigned to Sydney to counter the snorkel submarine offensive. Although services to the hunt-ing and escort groups consumed some 60 per cent of Point Edward's resources,[45] from September 1944 to early January 1945 the base refit-ted four Bangor and Algerine escorts and minesweepers, each refit requiring six to eight weeks. In December two corvettes arrived, fol-lowed by another corvette and the destroyer *Chaudière* in January and February 1945. Although the personnel in the Sydney Naval Command grew by nearly a third during 1944 to 2,612 men of all ranks by the end of the year,[46] the crush of work beginning in the late summer and autumn – especially the unpredictable and urgent demands of running repairs – ran the staffs ragged. It was especially frustrating because such a large-scale industrial effort was new to the navy, and the service had no clear idea of precisely how many personnel were needed, so that post-ings of additional manpower lagged behind demand. As always, part of the pressure came from the base's responsibility to provide technical services to private firms. These were busy at both Sydney and Louis-bourg, completing refits of nine corvettes and Bangors between August 1944 and early January 1945, and two more corvettes that arrived in December, followed by a frigate and a Bangor in January and February 1945.[47]

There were also important army projects at Sydney in 1944. Like some aspects of development at the Point Edward naval base, these looked towards the creation of permanent modern defences for the post-war future, so that Canada would not again be caught as unprepared as it had been in 1939. The biggest new army undertaking was the construction of concrete and steel towers at all major defended ports for the CDX coast artillery fire-control radar that had been developed by the National Research Council. This state-of-the-art equipment, which operated on a wavelength of ten centimetres, automatically converted contacts into firing data for a battery's guns. The initial plans for Sydney included four stations, three long-range slow-scanning sets at Lingan, Oxford, and Point Aconi to the west of Oxford, and a fast-scanning close-defence model for shorter range targets at Fort Petrie.[48] Work began on the Petrie and Oxford installations, which had priority, during the first part of 1944, and they were the only ones actually built at Sydney. Meanwhile, the project to convert the emplacements at Petrie and Chapel Point continued, but only slowly owing to fresh difficulties encountered in the prototype installation at Saint John. In July 1944 Petrie's old 6-inch guns were moved back onto the temporary platforms that had been built in 1939 to allow the battery to carry out its important responsibilities as the key inner defence battery while the conversion of the permanent emplacements dragged on.[49]

The task that involved the most back-breaking labour was the installation of the armament at Oxford battery. The first of the enormous 9.2-inch guns – a Mark XV barrel on a Mark IX mounting, the most modern installed at any site in Canada – arrived at Halifax from Britain on 1 February 1944 and was shipped by rail to Sydney Mines. The load filled seven railway cars and weighed more than 125 tons, including the twenty-eight-ton barrel, the mounting, circular armour plates to cover the pit of the emplacement, and a full turret-like armoured housing that enclosed the entire top of the mounting. The one-hundred-man detachment of the 36th Coast Battery that remained at Chapel Point undertook the work of trans-shipping each massive component onto flatbed trucks, moving it out to the site, and hoisting and levering it into place. Expert artificers were installing the last of small parts and making adjustments when the second gun arrived at the end of May. The third gun would not arrive until the spring of 1945.[50]

The project lost its urgency while the second gun was being installed, and none of the Oxford guns was in fact ever brought into action during the war. As German defences stiffened in Normandy during the summer of 1944, the 1st Canadian Army's casualties soared, and the General Staff began a desperate search for additional manpower. The destruction of the last elements of Germany's surface fleet and much of its air force ended the threat of a major raid on Canada's East Coast, and so the army shut down much of the home-defence organization. The strength of the Sydney and Canso garrisons fell from more than 3,300 personnel in June 1944 to 2,400 by late September, and 1,500 or fewer in early 1945. By that time, all of the anti-aircraft defences had been removed from action, and the infantry had been reduced to a single company at Victoria Park in Sydney and one at Mulgrave. In early February 1945 Fort Lingan and South Bar battery were shut down. This left in operation at Sydney only Fort Petrie, Stubbert's Point battery, and the searchlights at Cranberry Head, the bare minimum required to support the navy in the event that a snorkel-equipped submarine was forced to the surface or attempted a fast surface run into the harbour. Because Louisbourg and the Strait of Canso presented just the sort of heavily travelled confined waters where snorkel-equipped submarines could make ambush attacks, Melford battery at the Atlantic end of the strait remained in action. The personnel from Beacon battery, closed during the winter freeze-up, manned Wolfe battery at Louisbourg for its third season.[51]

Despite the fact that Germany was obviously near collapse, the snorkel submarine threat continued to cause deep concern, which was heightened by the knowledge that Germany had completed the construction of several vessels of a new type, designed for high underwater speeds, that enabled them to pursue shipping while submerged, which conventional U-boats could not do. In January 1945 the Anglo–American Combined Chiefs of Staff issued a disturbing report that declared that the number of sinkings by submarines had 'recently been steadily increasing' and that the new submarine technology had '*considerably reduced the effectiveness of our present naval and air counter-measures, especially in shallow coastal waters.*'[52] It was a remarkable testimony to the spirit of the U-boat fleet and to Admiral Dönitz's leadership.

One of the most successful conventional snorkel-equipped submarines operated in Nova Scotian waters. In January 1945, *U-1232* sank five ships within sight of the Halifax headlands and, in the abysmal sonar conditions, was able to escape mammoth air-sea searches in which the Canadian forces were reinforced by U.S. destroyer groups. It was the beginning of a busy winter. From late January to April, intelligence revealed eight, possibly nine, U-boats entering Canadian waters. Most were headed for American ports but two were assigned to Halifax. The U.S. Navy responded by putting a full destroyer escort group to the task

of hunting each submarine as it came in from the central ocean, while
Admiral Murray's more limited naval forces guarded the Halifax
approaches and escorted convoys; his stronger air forces provided support to both the Canadian and American naval search groups.[53]

Sydney's Cansos had a busy winter as well, joining in many of these
operations. There was a substantial force of nineteen aircraft based at
Sydney Airport, made up of 116 Squadron and, after the freeze-up in
the gulf, half of 161 Squadron.[54] On 15 February a hangar accident,
always a danger because of the presence of high-octane gasoline fumes,
explosives, and electrical equipment, resulted in the worst losses of the
war at the station. At 9:05 that morning, 'suddenly with no warning, the
Station was rocked by a heavy blast and a wall of flame and smoke arose
from No 4 hangar. The shock had barely subsided when the Fire Department, hospital staff and all sections sprang to immediate action to dis-
cover the hangar completely engulfed in flames and a hail of lead from
exploding .303s and other calibre ammunition. Thick black smoke
filled the area. Through this periodically darted various coloured flares
accentuating the blackness. From all sides of the doomed building came
the injured, the more seriously being carried or assisted, others struggling as if in a daze, touching or holding the injured portions of their
anatomy.' The fast response of the emergency teams and other personnel saved the surrounding buildings and aircraft parked in the vicinity,
but three Cansos in the hangar were destroyed. More significantly, four
members of the ground crew died and sixteen were injured, three of
them seriously.[55] The mishap did not, however, interfere with operational schedules.

The American hunting forces destroyed one of the two submarines
headed for Halifax in the early spring of 1945, but the second one
escaped detection and on 16 April sank the Bangor minesweeper HMCS
Esquimalt in the near approaches. Although Canadian naval authorities
worried that the submarines would find much greater opportunities in
the gulf, especially because it was known from radio interceptions that
U-boat headquarters continued to regard the St Lawrence as a prime
hunting area, there was no alternative to accepting the risk and using
the gulf route more fully in 1945 than in 1944 because Halifax and Saint
John were already swamped with traffic.[56]

The gulf season opened early, at the beginning of April, after another
year of unusually moderate ice conditions. Murray began to assign corvettes from the ocean forces to Sydney and Gaspé to strengthen the
usual complement of Bangors, trawlers, and Fairmiles. Canso aircraft,

this time from 5 Squadron, also returned to the gulf stations. Perhaps the most striking evidence of the concern felt for the St Lawrence situation was the demand by Naval Service Headquarters, to which the Admiralty quickly agreed, that one of the Canadian frigate groups serving in British waters should immediately return to Canada. In the event of a renewal of the submarine offensive in the gulf, this would permit the operation of two frigate groups there, one based at Gaspé and the other at Sydney.[57] The continued gravity of the U-boat threat at the same time that the Allied armies and air forces were smashing Germany's last-ditch defences created a certain air of unreality. As Simpson subsequently recalled, 'the season was propitious for the 90 ships a month scheduled for the River and everything was off to a flying start with the hope and expectation, it must be claimed, that we no sooner would get started than the end would come ... However, much optimism had been misplaced since "D" day, [and] masters and crews, as all the world, were waiting for the happy release.'[58]

The end did in fact come quickly. Despite the continuing efforts of the U-boats, the war in Europe had been grinding to its inevitable conclusion since D-Day, and on 8 May Germany surrendered. The giddy celebrations that broke out in the cities, town, and villages of the Allied nations had a darker side in the rioting and looting that marred the occasion in Nova Scotia. The riots that ripped apart downtown Halifax are notorious; less well known is the serious and prolonged rioting that took place in Sydney and New Waterford. The spark, as at Halifax, may have been the fact that, although the day was declared a public holiday, no civic victory celebrations were organized. More important, in the hope of keeping public celebrations under control, all dances and other entertainments were cancelled, and restaurants and stores were closed. Perhaps still more ill-advised, the liquor stores were closed as well. As a result, according to the Sydney's *Post-Record*, 'crowds hundreds in number roamed the streets aimlessly,' although 'comparative quiet' prevailed until about 11:15 p.m. 'when a crowd of civilians and naval men' broke into a liquor store on George Street. They were cheerfully looting the place when city police, the RCMP, and the Naval Shore Patrol arrived. Remarkably, they managed to move the crowd across the street and away from the liquor store without having to use force. Meanwhile, a large bonfire had been started in the middle of Charlotte Street opposite Dave Epstein's clothing shop. 'Doorsteps, planks and wood of all description' had been piled on the fire, but the situation began to get serious only when 'several civilian youths wheeled up a delivery wagon which was placed on the flames.' A fire engine was then called to extinguish the fire, an action the crowd 'strongly disapproved.' Some of them, 'by this time made bolder with stolen liquor,' attempted to argue with the firemen. Then a sailor who was standing in the doorway of the Epstein store when the hose was turned on was driven by the force of the water through the plate glass window.

At this hotheads in the crowd began an orgy of window smashing which continued for over three hours and saw more than a score of business establishments suffer damage.

First place to go was Dave Epstein's where all plate glass windows were broken. Clothing displayed in the window was seized by various civilians and made off with. Police, Mounties and naval police were standing by but in the milling throng, most of them were sight-seers, they were unable to stem the tide.

Several attempts were made to turn over a small fire truck owned by the Navy which was parked near the scene but these petered out when attention was diverted to window breaking in other shops.

The crowd continued down the street in the direction of Wentworth Street, Pollett's, National Shoe Store, Michael's and others on this side of the street being the targets for flasks, by this time completely emptied.

For a time the milling people returned and crossed Pitt Street into the next block. Moraff's poolroom, Victory Grill, Oak Hall Ltd, and others lost their windows before the vandalism outbreaks began again in the Prince–Wentworth Street block.

MacDonald's Shoe Store, Woolworth's, Agnew-Surpass and more than a dozen more stores on this side of the street were targets. Individuals were seen walking off with as many as half a dozen pairs of shoes, jackets, topcoats and other articles which had been left on display in shop windows.

Few injuries were reported although several in the crowd suffered bad hand gashes from broken glass. Glass littered the streets along with paint, shoe polish and other articles removed from windows. The street was in spots covered with water following the hose incident ...

With the effects of the pillaged liquor wearing off the tempo of vandalism began to slow down. However, the crowd continued to mill about and stores near Wentworth Street received damage. Macaulay's Men Store received a broken window and several large windows in Bonnell's Ltd were the targets for a can of paint stolen from another establishment. A beautiful chesterfield on display in the window of the latter place was ruined when it became splattered with aluminum paint.

McLeod's Bookstore suffered considerable loss of window stock when baseballs, gloves and other articles were removed.

A small group of civilians wended their way to Johnston Street where the Ideal Sausage Factory was the target for the night. This place was looted considerably ...

Many incidents of a humorous nature were observed such as the lamentations of a civilian who had stolen a case of whiskey from the liquor store only to have it in turn stolen from him. A sailor wandered aimlessly around trying to recover two bottles of rum which were stolen from him.

At Michael's store a sailor was seen trying on several pairs of shoes before he obtained his size. At Agnew-Surpass three civilians were reported to have made off with over a dozen pairs of shoes, tucking them inside their jackets and coats.

While all of this was going on, plainclothes RCMP officers were in the crowd, 'and picked up several of the ring-leaders and escorted them quietly off to the city lockup.' Around 2:30 a.m. Lieutenant Commander Payne of the Naval Shore Patrol ordered all naval personnel to be rounded up and taken to the base. The crowd began to disperse around 3:00, and by 3:30 the excitement was nearly over. However, 'two or three more windows were broken by small groups who were mischief bent.' By four o'clock there was little activity on the street with the exception of carpenters boarding up windows. Eleven civilians arrested during the mêlée were charged with intoxication, breaking windows, and wilful damage. A taxi driver, who 'is reported to have tied the stolen delivery wagon to his car and raced up and down Charlotte Street at a high speed at four o'clock this morning,' was charged with reckless driving. Sydney police chief R.J. MacDonald, 'who along with most of his force was on the scene all night,' reported the next day that further charges would be laid within a short time.[59]

On the next night, the 9th, the trouble spread out from downtown Sydney. 'Hundreds of curiosity seekers lined the business section of the city to view anything out of the ordinary that might occur,' but early in the evening Mayor Jack MacLean proclaimed a 9:00 curfew, and at a few minutes after nine 'a large body' of city police, more than a dozen Mounties armed with batons, and forty Shore Patrol and Provost Corps on motorbikes and in vans cleared Charlotte Street. By 9:20 the police had arrived at the corner of Charlotte and Dorchester Streets, 'where several hundred civilians along with a smattering of sailors had gathered. The crowd was quickly herded ahead of the police down Dorchester St and with a few exceptions all obeyed.' By 9:30 Charlotte Street 'presented the appearance of a ghost town.'[60]

In the Whitney Pier district, however, a mob had collected near the subway, the narrow roadway through the grounds of the steel plant that then connected that part of the city with the main area. According to the *Post-Record*, windows were smashed in a number of stores on Victoria Road, including the liquor store, but there was no looting. When city police arrived with the RCMP, the Provost Corps, and the Shore Patrol, their cars were stoned by the crowd, which had collected in an open field opposite the subway and near the liquor store. In a scene which the *Post-Record* described as 'reminiscent of the steel plant strike of 1925 as stones and bottles were hurled at police,' several city police and Mounties 'rushed the crowd in the open field and they quickly scattered to spread all over the Pier area ... For hours bands of them roamed through the Coke Ovens district but by 12 o'clock many of the streets were deserted.'[61]

Trouble broke out in New Waterford that evening as well when a mob broke into the liquor store and started to clean out its contents, 'beginning, at the same time, an orgy of window smashing.' The navy radio telephone located at the police station 'was kept busy sending and receiving calls,' and within a short time Commander Payne had dispatched twenty-five men from the Shore Patrol to New Waterford. Members of the Provost Corps were also hurriedly sent there.[62] The *Post-Record* claimed that tension had been mounting in the town since early afternoon, 'as word was received via the grapevine that an attempt would be made to invade this Cape Breton mining town with a view to cleaning out the Commission store.' Members of the local detachment of the RCMP as well as local and service police received orders to stand by, and everything remained quiet on Plummer Avenue until about 10 o'clock. 'Shortly after this hour the first rock was fired at the window of the local Commission store. It caused little damage. Within a few minutes another flurry of rocks followed. The wooden windows withstood the attack. Meanwhile Plummer Ave became crowded as citizens gathered attracted by the sounds of the rocks.' Realizing that throwing rocks was getting them nowhere, the gang rushed the liquor store, at the same time breaking windows in the nearby stores of Sam Epstein, Schwartz and Company, and Glustein's, also situated on Plummer Avenue. According to the *Post-Record*, police officer Joseph Campbell 'was hit by one of the flying stones and sustained injuries with [*sic*] fortunately were not serious.' The police now retreated, and the front door of the liquor store was broken in. 'During the next 15 minutes liquor flowed on the streets of New Waterford. The best of brands were going for as low as 25 cents a quart.' Cases of beer and hard liquor were being carried away from the back door of the store. Plummer Avenue remained crowded until about two o'clock in the morning, but there was no trouble aside from the window breaking and the raid on the liquor store. The *Post-Record* reported that 'on being ordered by police to move along citizens carried out the wish of the officers.' Remarkably, no arrests were made.[63]

Some in the town blamed the authorities for the riot. One man undoubtedly spoke for many people in the area when he declared that the Nova Scotia Liquor Commission had got 'just what they asked for' when it closed its stores on V-E day. As another put it, 'After six years of war during which we supported Canada's war effort to the hilt by buying Victory Bonds and sending our sons and daughters overseas what do we find? Some big shot in Halifax decides to close the liquor store before the official announcement of V-E Day. The sooner they get clear of this crazy provincial law and get this liquor business down to a sane basis the better.' Another man said that he was working in the mine when he heard the news that the war was over. 'I expected to be able to come up town and buy a bottle of liquor with my permit. I arrived up town about three o'clock. The liquor store was closed. I have been waiting for this occasion for six years. During the past two days I notice bootleggers apparently have all the liquor they require. At least they are getting a dollar a bottle for beer and as high as $15 a quart for hard liquor. My permit was legally due on Monday. I wish I had the money to fight the case. I would make a test case of it! I am not a drinking man. I have two sons overseas.' Another New Waterford citizen suggested that the rioters were not even from the town. 'Look around you,' he demanded. 'Where did all these strangers come from? I have been a resident here for the past 25 years. I did not recognize any New Waterford citizen carrying away liquor tonight.'[64]

The next day, the 10th, the mines were idle, 'as a feeling of unrest gripped the population' of New Waterford. The town council held an emergency meeting in the afternoon to prepare plans to cope with further trouble, but rioting broke out before these plans could be put in effect. In the words of the *Post-Record*, 'a shrieking mad mob of over 200 youths ranging in age from 13 to 18 years ran amok on this town's main business thoroughfare tonight, wrecking two business firms and smashing practically every window on Plummer Avenue. Damage will run into thousands of dollars.' The trouble started around 10:00 p.m. when large numbers of youths gathered in the vicinity of No. 12 district.

They made their way to the center of the business section. With methodic thoroughness they began to smash glass windows. By midnight there was hardly a single window left in the main business district. Looting had begun. First the mob entered the premises of the New Era Cafe. Within fifteen minutes the interior of the restaurant was a shambles. Fixtures were smashed, dishes, cooking utensils and food thrown out through the open door. The mob continued down Plummer Avenue accompanied by several hundred adults who stood idly by, unable to interfere.

After a preliminary warming up by smashing windows along the route, the mob whipped itself into a fury. The premises of the Nova Scotia Liquor Commission was [*sic*] again entered. Boarded up windows were torn down and thrown out on the street. A number of youths entered the liquor store and secured ale which had been overlooked in Wednesday night's raid.

As they continued down Plummer Avenue practically every window was a target for rocks. Huge plate glass windows crashed to the sidewalks.

Upon arrival at King's Fountain Service, a combined restaurant and soft drink establishment, the youths broke the large windows and entered the premises. The entire contents of the store were thrown out on the street. The Post Office on the opposite side of the street was the next target. A number of windows were broken. The premises of the Exchange Grill, a Chinese restaurant, was next. Windows were broken and the premises entered.

Town police, who had been on duty 'continuously for the past forty-eight hours were unable to control the actions of the mob which for five hours carried out the depredations.' The Reverend Raymond Campbell, the priest of St Agnes parish, appeared on the scene and pleaded with the mob to control themselves, but with little or no effect. Meanwhile, Mayor W.J. Hinchey contacted the Attorney-General's Department in Halifax and Colonel Dobbie, asking for assistance. The arrival of the RCMP and naval and army police patrols from Sydney soon brought the situation under control, but not before acting chief of police William Poirier and police officer Len McNeil received minor injuries when they were struck by rocks hurled by the youths. The mob eventually began to disperse, and at about 3:00 on Friday morning the situation was reported to be under control.[65]

That same evening in nearby Dominion, rioters including men, women, and children 'stormed into the liquor store after they were held at bay more than an hour' by town police and RCMP officers. The 'unequal battle ended when a rock smashed the street light in front of the store and the mob rushed through police lines in the darkness with someone yelling: "They wouldn't sell us the liquor on V-E Day, now let's take it." Joining the mad rush was a woman, with two small children in tow, who made three trips into the store to lay in a supply. Cars were parked nearby, ready to carry the stolen liquor and beer home.'[66]

Glace Bay was declared out of bounds to naval personnel, and it remained quiet that evening. When seven men – four of whom were from New Waterford, it was claimed – 'threatened trouble,' they were arrested. Nevertheless, the liquor store trucked its supplies out of town for safe-keeping, and a number of merchants 'stayed on guard in their stores until late at night.' North Sydney was similarly quiet, although town police 'were on the alert last night after they said they had been tipped off that the liquor store was due to be raided. Patrols were strengthened, but the threatened raid wasn't made.' At midnight, as the *Post-Record* put it, 'there wasn't [*sic*] enough people around to raid a cherry tree.' A mid-night curfew was in effect for service personnel, and 'civilians out after that hour were questioned by town police.' Sydney Mines too was quiet. Despite 'ugly rumours ... the crowds gathered in Main Street ... thinned out as the hours passed by,' and no disturbances took place.[67]

In Sydney the 9:00 p.m. curfew was 'rigidly enforced,' and the city remained uneasily quiet. The curfew was expected to remain in effect for at least one more night to prevent further trouble. The *Post-Record* credited the Naval Shore Patrol for preventing the rioting in Sydney from being worse than it was because of its prompt action in stopping the looting of the George Street liquor store and Charlotte Street busi-nesses. The Naval Shore Patrol had also effectively dispersed the crowds after the curfew hour on the 9th and responded promptly to urgent calls for help from the surrounding towns, thereby succeeded in break-ing up threatening demonstrations. By the 11th, eighty extra naval police had arrived from Halifax and, in the view of the *Post-Record*, there was now 'a sufficient force here to curb a disaster of major proportions, should it threaten. But it is unlikely, since the "celebrations" have now passed their peak, that any further incidents will take place. The chief danger now, and it should be one easily taken care of, is from vicious local hoodlums who are seeking liquor and loot. Sailors who figured largely in Monday and Tuesday night's disturbances are not expected to give further trouble.'[68]

Fifty additional RCMP officers also arrived on the 11th, flown in from Halifax, to patrol the streets of New Waterford, where a 7:00 p.m. curfew was imposed to prevent further outbreaks. 'As an extra precaution 100 soldiers, stationed at nearby forts, are also standing ready tonight to come to the assistance of the RCMP and naval police, should further trouble break out.' Business in the town was suspended for the day, 'as merchants, assisted by their staffs and carpenters boarded up their windows and cleaned up the debris. There was plenty of work to do. With the possible exception of five large windows which escaped damage during Thursday night's melee, the entire business section of this town's main thoroughfare, Plummer Avenue, was in a shambles today.'[69] J.T. McMillan, who operated a jewelry store, reported that $600 worth of merchandise had been looted from his store, while the liquor store's losses were estimated at $25,000.[70]

Twenty-three youths were arrested by police and taken to the county jail at Sydney to be held for one week without bail as authorities continued their investigation into all phases of the riot. The youths were charged with destroying property, but police 'intimated that a more serious charge of attempted arson may be laid against several youths if investigations now underway by authorities warrant the charges. Additional information received by police today indicated that attempts were made to burn the Central school and the building containing the Nova Scotia Liquor Commission store during the height of Thursday night's out-breaks.'[71]

Eventually, things settled down, a number of rioters were charged with various offences, and people in the area began the transition to peace. Although the war with Japan continued until its sudden termination in August, it was remote. The communities surrounding the harbour had endured six stressful though exciting years of hard work, disruption, sacrifice, and bloodshed. The rioting of 9–11 May seemed a curious way to celebrate the triumph of democracy over Fascism, and it left a stain on the hard-earned reputation that the communities surrounding Sydney Harbour had achieved in the war. It involved only a minority of the population, of course, but at the same time it reflected the profound stress imposed on the coastal community by the nearness of the war and the magnitude of the emotional liberation felt by its conclusion.

Epilogue

Although the army and air force establishments at Sydney were quickly scaled down in the late spring and summer of 1945, the Point Edward naval base was busier than ever. With its large and still expanding blocks of warehouses, it was one of the principal depots for the stores and equipment removed from the scores of now surplus warships. Meanwhile, both the naval and private refit facilities in the Sydney area were fully employed 'tropicalizing' warships selected for service in the Pacific in the final offensive against Japan.[1] The unexpectedly abrupt end of the war as a result of the use of atomic bombs in August soon brought sharp reductions in the refit work, however, and both companies and unions were quick to complain about the allocation of the remaining work both among the various East Coast ports and among particular local concerns. In an area that had suffered higher than average unemployment in the pre-war years and that feared its recurrence with the return of peace, this was a highly political situation. As Acting Captain J. McCulloch, the commanding officer at Point Edward and overall commander in the Sydney area after Captain Schwerdt's return to Britain shortly following the defeat of Germany, wearily explained to his superiors in December 1945, 'the practice in Cape Breton is for anyone who imagines he has an interest in government work to make application direct to his local member or other friends in power and never approach the Naval Service authorities in Sydney.'[2]

Whether or not Sydney was getting its fair share of work, the military withdrawal from the area was nearly as rapid and complete as it had been after the armistice in 1918. In December 1945 the air force turned the airport over to the Department of Transport for development as a civilian facility.[3] Army forces on full-time service had already been cut back to an artillery detachment for caretaking duties, and in April 1946 the unit headquarters vacated Victoria Park to take up residence at the fire command post, which now became known as Kilkenny Barracks. The intention was to preserve all of the forts at Sydney in a mothballed state, with the exception of the temporary battery at Point Edward, which had been closed in 1943.

The 'ultimate' coast artillery program of the late 1930s had, of course, been designed not merely as an emergency war program but as a permanent system to provide the necessary minimal protection for ports. Accordingly, work continued until early 1947, with the assistance of technical parties from Ottawa and Halifax, to complete the most important parts of the program: installation of Oxford battery's third 9.2-inch gun, and completion of the modernization of the Chapel and Petrie batteries with 4-inch twin naval guns and improved fire-control systems, including the fast-scanning close-defence CDX radar station at Fort Petrie.[4]

Meanwhile, it had become obvious that the regular army, which the government had trimmed to fewer than twenty thousand personnel as opposed to the fifty thousand the General Staff had recommended, could not efficiently maintain the large number of widely dispersed, isolated coast artillery sites at Sydney and elsewhere. Nor did it need to. Despite the onset of the cold war following the collapse of the Axis powers, intelligence assessments suggested that the Soviet Union, the only potentially hostile major power, had been so exhausted by the war that it was incapable of aggression without preparations that would give at least a year's warning. In 1947 and 1948, therefore, the army stripped the coastal fortifications and placed the equipment in central ordnance depots where it could be properly preserved, ready for quick reinstallation should war again seem likely. At Sydney, only the main components of the heavy guns at Lingan and Oxford were left in place under the charge of a few caretakers.

The navy had to make do with about seven thousand regular personnel, compared to the twenty thousand it had recommended to the government. Although many bases were closed, the Naval Staff never considered giving up Point Edward, no doubt because its wartime development had been undertaken with an eye to the longstanding need for a second operating base on the East Coast to supplement Halifax. To economize in the use of service personnel, it ceased to be commanded by a naval officer and was run by a civilian manager with a largely civilian staff purely as a support facility. The fuel tank farm was leased for a time to commercial interests and the magazines were closed, but the warehouses and some of the workshops continued to be fully employed. In addition to the receipt, storage, and reissue of vast amounts of clothing, furniture, kitchen equipment, and other such domestic *matériel*, the base served several specialized functions. The workshops of the Naval Armament Depot repaired and preserved guns and mountings, while a large boom-defence depot looked after the heavy buoys, miles of cable, and tons of hardware for anti-submarine nets from the now vacated boom-defence yards at North Sydney, Halifax, and other East Coast ports. Point Edward was also the home of the Naval Records Centre, the archive for thousands of files from across the country going back to the founding of the service.[5]

The assessment that the Soviet Union and its allies were incapable of early, surprise, offensive action was quickly proven wrong in the autumn of 1948 when they blockaded the ground routes to West Berlin in a confrontation that continued until the spring of 1949. This crisis, coming on the heels of the Communist takeover of Czechoslovakia, raised the spectre of a third world war and led to the formation of the North Atlantic Treaty Organization, a military alliance of which Canada was a founding member. The North Korean invasion of South Korea in June 1950, following upon the triumph of the Communist revolution in China, was interpreted in western capitals as an attempt by the Soviet Union not only to gain more territory but also to divert attention from the crucial European situation. As the world entered the 1950s, another war seemed imminent, and western nations began to rearm. Defence spending in Canada soared from $196 million in 1947 to $1.5 billion in 1951 as it dispatched forces to Korea, joined with the United States in unprecedented continental defence projects, and contributed substantial forces for service with NATO in Europe.

With rearmament, Sydney's role as the second strategic port on the East Coast and alternative to Halifax assumed a somewhat more definite shape, although it remained very much a 'shadow' facility. The Soviet emphasis on submarine development, based on the powerful types that Germany had been building in 1945, underscored the need for very large numbers of escort vessels. To fill the gap while new warships were built and the best of those in the existing fleet were modernized, the Canadian government bought back dozens of frigates and Bangor and Algerine escorts that had been sold as surplus soon after the war.[6] These ships were then laid up at Sydney and elsewhere and kept in a state of readiness for swift reactivation in a crisis.

In 1952 work began on reopening and renovating the facilities at Point Edward for the Reserve Fleet, Sydney Group, which began operations a year later when eighteen Bangors arrived after refit at shipyards on the St Lawrence. This unit, which soon expanded to nearly forty naval personnel and seventy-three civilians, completed the hasty basic refits, packed all sensitive equipment in preservatives, sealed and dehumidified the ships' hulls, and installed anti-corrosion equipment. The ships were tied alongside the protected, shoreward side of the big Point Edward pier.[7]

There was also a brief small-scale revival of the coast artillery at Sydney. The Berlin crisis had caused not only an immediate reversal of the policy of virtually abandoning the East Coast forts, but had also led to a lot of hard thinking about the high cost of maintaining them in a ready or near-ready state, given the Soviet Union's emphasis on submarines rather than major surface warships. As well, the advances being achieved in long-range missile technology seemed to make heavy artillery redundant for the defence of North America's coastlines. Thus, the navy and the RCAF's maritime bomber group were assigned full responsibility for defence against surface attack, and the army scaled back coast artillery to the modest level needed to support the navy in protecting harbour entrances against assaults by submarines. The army's long-range batteries, including Lingan and Oxford at Sydney, were stricken from the war plans, leaving only close-in, quick-fire batteries. In 1951 regular artillery troops from Halifax reinstalled the two twin 4-inch guns at Fort Petrie and the single twin six-pounder at South Bar, as well as the searchlights and fire-control systems, including the radar, at Petrie. All of the equipment from Stubbert's battery was moved into immediate reserve at Fort Petrie and Kilkenny Barracks, where a maintenance detachment of no more than twelve regular army personnel from Halifax took up residence.[8]

When the forts had been dismantled in 1948, the militia's coast artillery units, including the 16th Coast Regiment at Sydney, had been converted to anti-aircraft artillery, as a transpolar attack by Soviet bombers then seemed the most likely danger for the foreseeable future. After the removal of the wartime anti-aircraft defences in 1945, there was no full-scale training facility in Cape Breton so that, as in the 1920s and 1930s, militia gunners travelled to the artillery schools at Halifax and in Ontario for summer training camps.

The reinstallation of the coast artillery brought the establishment of new units, among them the Sydney Coast Regiment, which began to organize in 1949 and which by early 1951 had some 135 personnel on strength. The unit shared Victoria Park with the 16th Anti-Aircraft Regiment, and included old hands from the latter's days as a coast artillery unit. The Sydney Coast Regiment trained with instructors from the regular force gunners at Sydney, but also sent detachments for summer camp at the Halifax forts.[9]

As the navy and the RCAF's Maritime Air Group built up their capabilities in 1953 and 1954, the coast artillery was trimmed back yet again. South Bar was dismantled and its equipment, together with that in storage for Stubbert's, was removed. Fort Petrie's equipment remained in place – it was now the only site at Sydney that would be manned in case of war – but in long-term maintenance, and the regular force detachment was reduced to a handful of caretakers. The militia coast artillery regiments in the Maritimes were amalgamated and reduced to a single battery with units at Halifax, Sydney, and Saint John. The personnel attended annual camps at Halifax until the end of 1956, when the entire Canadian coast artillery, aside from a small detachment and one fort at Halifax, was shut down. Fort Petrie was again dismantled that year; the heavy guns at Oxford and Lingan had already been removed and shipped with Canada's other 6-inch and 9.2-inch armament to NATO partners in Europe, including Turkey, that still apprehended close-in naval assault on their shores.[10]

In the reorganization of the militia artillery in 1954, the 16th Heavy Anti-Aircraft Regiment disappeared, as aerial defence of Canadian cities became an air force responsibility in the new age of high-altitude jet aircraft and nuclear weapons. An advance party of 221 Air Warning Squadron, RCAF, had already arrived in Sydney in March 1953 to assist in the preparation of a modern long-range air defence radar station that was under construction on a hilltop on Lingan Road in Whitney Pier. Its most prominent feature was three towers topped by semi-spherical radomes that housed the antennae of the equipment. In April 1954 the new RCAF Station Sydney began what would be a thirty-six-year round-the-clock surveillance of the skies on the Atlantic seaboard. It was one of a chain of similar radar stations across southern Canada known as the Pinetree Line, which was built in close cooperation with the United States to provide early warning and ground control for American and Canadian fighter aircraft so that they could intercept Soviet bombers before they reached major North American cities.

At this stage, the system was an improved version of the chain of Canadian and American air-defence radar stations and fighter squadrons that had protected the East and West Coasts during the Second World War. The Sydney Station had its closest dealings with the RCAF base at Chatham, New Brunswick, where there was an advanced-training unit of North American F-86 Sabre jets, and with the large American air force base at Stephenville on the West Coast of Newfoundland. The Canadian and American air stations in the Atlantic provinces were fully integrated with the American air-defence organization in New England.[11]

During the later 1950s, additional construction transformed the station from 'a collection of huts with dirt roads'[12] into a substantial, tidy community. Aside from the expansion of the administrative and operational buildings, there was a housing development that provided quarters for those among the more than two hundred RCAF personnel who had families. The station was important not only for its military role but also because it contributed significantly to the local economy through expenditures by the air force and its personnel and the employment of about one hundred local civilians for food services, cleaning, and grounds maintenance.

Early on, the remoteness of the station from the main centres of service life in the country caused the personnel stationed at Sydney to identify themselves as members of the Royal Cape Breton Air Force, an organization that they claimed was much superior to the RCAF.[13] This new air force soon took on formal trappings, with the adoption of a station crest featuring a deer surrounded by spruce trees over water to symbolize the special character of Cape Breton and a Gaelic motto, *sior fhurachas* (ever vigilant). Membership certificates were presented to departing personnel and honorary membership certificates to visitors.

The mid 1950s also saw the continued growth of activities at Point Edward and at Sydney's civilian marine engineering firms, as expansion of the fleet hit full stride. In addition to the lay-up of vessels in short- or long-term reserve – there were as many as twenty-four warships in Point Edward's hands – work was also undertaken to reactivate and refit vessels for service with the Canadian fleet or for transfer to European Allies. By April 1956 the workforce at Point Edward had grown to 649 civilian employees under the direction of thirty naval personnel.[14]

Most of this activity, like that in the years immediately after the war, was an ad hoc response to very specific needs. The demands for substantial labour, moreover, were rather short-term in nature. The creation of the reserve fleet had been the result of the unique circumstances of the early cold war years, when there had been a large stock of Second World War vessels available. During 1956 the strength of the mothballed fleet began to shrink as ships were returned to service, and it was never replenished with similar numbers of vessels. Although Point Edward had gained some organizational stability with the appointment of a naval officer as base superintendent in April 1954, the further step of defining a long-term operational role for the establishment was a vexing problem.[15]

The navy's view of Sydney as the alternative to Halifax never changed. Indeed, the Cape Breton port's strategic importance increased in the early 1950s with the development of nuclear weapons that were many times more powerful than the bombs dropped on Japan in 1945.[16] The fact that a single one of these weapons could devastate a large city underlined the vulnerability of the dockyard at Halifax, a likely target for a Soviet first strike. Thus, the need to disperse operating facilities seemed greater than ever, and Sydney, though possessing a large port and good location, was considered to be a low priority target for an initial attack.[17]

The navy had a vested interest in maintaining a skilled workforce at Sydney, but this, more than ever in the mid 1950s, required a steady stream of ship-repair projects. The Point Edward base had become a major employer, ranking second only to the Dominion Steel and Coal Corporation, but Dosco itself was shrinking because of the declining demand for Cape Breton steel and coal. Thus, if the base laid off any of its tradesmen, even temporarily, they would have no choice but to leave the island. Understandably, workers and the community generally were in a state of constant anxiety about the prospects for assignment of warships for lay-up or reactivation work to Point Edward. There was an emotional roller-coaster ride every few months as rumours circulated that there might not be a new project to follow one nearing completion. This strained atmosphere became a leitmotif in the naval commander's monthly reports. In August 1955, for example, he reported that the unemployment rate in the area was 17 per cent, so that any reduction in personnel at the base 'would at this point increase the tenseness of the situation.'[18] A year later, he reported that the Sydney area was 'still considered a depressed area' and that 'the morale of the civilian personnel is affected by the air of insecurity for the future.'[19]

The solution preferred by the East Coast naval authorities was to turn Point Edward into a complete operating base with a squadron of frigates permanently based there. The fundamental difficulty, of course, was money. From a peak of $1.8 billion during the Korean War in 1953, Canadian defence spending had been gradually trimmed to $1.4 billion in 1958. The services were left to struggle with the problem of funding the increased permanent establishments built up earlier in the decade while somehow absorbing the rapidly escalating costs of essential new technology. The permanent deployment of a squadron of frigates at Sydney would entail millions in additional expenditure, including the construction of quarters for a thousand or more personnel and their families.[20]

The crunch came in the spring of 1958. Employment had been not only sustained but increased in 1957 by reactivation of the frigates and full refits of ten of the Bangors for transfer to the Turkish navy. Only a dozen ships remained at Sydney, the bulk of them scheduled to be sold for scrap. According to the base commanding officer, reports of drastic reductions brought a sense of betrayal and gloom to the community. Hopes on the island that new work and roles would be found for the base had been raised by the upheaval in the 1957 general election that had ended the long tenure of the Liberal Party and unexpectedly brought John Diefenbaker's Progressive Conservatives into office. The sense of excitement generated by this event, which was increased by the new government's re-election in the spring of 1958 with an unprecedented majority, was profound, especially in the Maritimes, where it was believed that Diefenbaker's New National Policy would be reflected in a serious effort to address the region's high rate of unemployment. The fact that the new minister of national defence, George Pearkes, was a retired general who had won the Victoria Cross in his youth no doubt also encouraged the belief that cutbacks in the military budget might be reversed. Instead, Point Edward's establishment was slashed by 50 per cent, a decision that, according to the base commander, 'especially after all the political assurances that this would not happen has, of course, caused a great deal of bitterness amongst the Civilian employees. The behaviour of all Civilian personnel has been exemplary. No incidents of any kind whatsoever have occurred ... the impact on the economy of the area will be serious and is exaggerated by the fact that over two thousand employees of Dosco are presently out of work.'[21]

In the event, large-scale lay-offs did not take place. Instead, as a result of concerted protests from the island and of parliamentary questions, the navy assigned additional reactivation and repair work to Point Edward.[22] Frigates were to be rotated one at a time for periodic refit there. The naval staff again rejected the proposal to base a squadron of frigates at Sydney permanently because of the high costs, but decided that ships would use the port more regularly. The renovation and expansion of facilities that had begun in the early 1950s was to continue and to be broadened to provide all that was needed to support warships that might be dispersed to Sydney in time of war. The effect of these decisions was to stabilize civilian employment at the base at approximately six hundred, while ship refitting and the improvement of the base facilities provided a boost to local firms.[23] All of this was in accordance with what the navy had long thought desirable for Sydney, but there can be no doubt that Nova Scotia's strong representation in the new government was decisive in raising the priority of these projects at a time of constrained defence budgets.[24]

The base's new role brought greater and more diverse naval activity to the Sydney area. Indeed, the naval commander reported in September 1959 that activity there had 'reached the highest peak since the conclusion of the Second World War.' The frigate *Victoriaville* was undergoing refit, and the base was playing a major role in a NATO exercise. As well, a 'considerable proportion of the fleet' operated out of Sydney during that month, and three naval air units operated from the Point Edward naval base and facilities established at Sydney Airport.[25]

According to E.C. Russell, the naval historian who visited the base two years later, Point Edward 'appeared to be in peacetime in almost every respect ready for an emergency.' The various buildings on the base were 'in very good repair and while little landscaping has been effected the roads are in very good condition.' The base was largely manned by civilians, but was headed by Commander J.V. Steele and a staff of some seven or eight naval officers who, with their families, lived there in converted married quarters. Their children attended a school operated by the federal government, 'complete with a well outfitted playground, located just inside the main gate.' 'The repair facilities ... are in good condition and all are working. The administration building is completely fitted out for a Commander-in-Chief to take over at a moment's notice having full communication facilities even to the pencil and paper on the desk. Sufficient plots are in readiness and, in fact, shortly after the Naval Historian left the Senior Officer Afloat, Commodore [M.G.] Sterling, was able to move in and conduct fleet exercises in the Gulf Area directly from the base.'[26]

One problem that Russell noted was the 'condemned status' of the main jetty, of which the decking and even some of the basic structure had decayed. Heavy repairs were required, 'particularly because this jetty supports a stationary crane which if left very much longer could topple into the sea.'[27] This was already slated to be corrected. Early in

1961 the boards of trade of Sydney and Glace Bay had launched a campaign for further development of the base as a measure to help bolster the industrial economy. Robert Stanfield, the influential Progressive Conservative premier of Nova Scotia, and Donald MacInnis, the member of Parliament for Cape Breton South, lent their full support. In a hopeful editorial, the *Cape Breton Post* suggested that 'we should be frank in avowing our appreciation of the augmented use of this base since the Diefenbaker Government came to power, indeed since Cape Breton became represented in the House of Commons by the Members who do Cape Breton credit.'[28] Despite the fact that another election was not far off, however, Douglas Harkness, who had succeeded Pearkes as minister of national defence in October 1960, informed the boards of trade that the prohibitive cost made it impossible to station warships permanently at the base. He was, however, able to announce a $2 million program to renovate the pier and improve the ammunition handling and fuelling facilities.[29]

Some of this work was still in progress when the death-knell sounded for the base in December 1963. The Diefenbaker government had lost its majority in the 1962 federal election, but it had clung uncertainly to power until it collapsed ignominiously in another hard-fought election a year later that brought the Liberals back to power under the leadership of Lester Pearson. This was a rare if not unique Canadian election because defence policy – specifically Diefenbaker's equivocation over the acquisition of defensive nuclear weapons – figured prominently in the result. Although that large and very important issue had no direct bearing on Sydney, Pearson's appointment of a strong minister, Paul Hellyer, to reform the defence establishment almost immediately had an impact. To bring escalating costs throughout the armed forces more closely into line with the funds actually available, Hellyer soon announced sweeping cuts that included many secondary support facilities. Among the programs to get the axe was the ship-repair facility at Point Edward, the main source of civilian employment at the base.[30]

In a minor concession to the area's economic difficulties, the government promised that the winding down would be a gradual process. New projects, including the refit of frigates and the deactivation of some of the fleet's oldest vessels for disposal, kept the ship-repair unit occupied until the end of 1964, while lay-offs proceeded and federal employment officials tried to help displaced workers find new positions wherever available across the country. The decision of the Department of Transport to establish a new college at Point Edward to train personnel for its expanding coast guard fleet offered some hope, and in 1965 it acquired many of the buildings for that purpose. By this time, plans to continue in operation the naval stores and records sections had been scrapped as well, however, and in the spring of 1966 the last of the navy employees were laid off.[31]

Federal involvement in Cape Breton's economic development shifted to other channels, among them the partial reconstruction of the eighteenth century fortress at Louisbourg – initiated by the Diefenbaker government – to stimulate the tourist industry. It is ironic that these demolished ramparts began to rise again precisely when the Point Edward naval base, the most important continuing element of Cape Breton's strategic role during the two world wars and the early cold war, disappeared. Interestingly, Senator J.S. McLennan, who had lobbied hard for the development of Sydney as a defended port during the First World War and whose former Petersfield Estate formed part of the Point Edward property, was also the godfather of the Louisbourg restoration. His excellent history of the old fortress, published in 1918, and his campaign for its recognition as a national historic site, which had been carried on into the 1960s by his daughter Katharine, had planted the seed for the reconstruction.[32]

The story of Point Edward summons up other parallels. Its closing had come after two decades during which there had been no war in the Atlantic and, inevitably, the sense of urgency had declined. Retrenchment resulted in the concentration of resources at the traditional military centres that had close ties to the North American continent. This was precisely the same cycle that had always dictated military developments at Sydney. At the beginning of the nineteenth century, in the 1850s and 1860s, and again in the two world wars of this century, Cape Breton's strategic importance had been recognized. Every time, when the immediate danger passed, drastic reductions were introduced as economy took precedence over preparedness.

Aside from budgetary considerations, the reductions in the support elements of the Canadian forces that began in the early 1960s also reflected the transformation of war, or at least informed assessments of what a future war might be like.[33] As both the western Allies and the Eastern Bloc multiplied their arsenals of nuclear weapons and long-range missile delivery systems, it seemed that victory, if it could be called that, would come within days or weeks – not years as in previous major conflicts – after nuclear exchanges wiped out much of civilization as we know it. Policy makers and military planners were convinced that there would be no time or need for the organization of the resources and lines of supply that had made Sydney an important centre during the two world wars and in the early part of the cold war.

'Mutually Assured Destruction' enhanced the importance of air defence. In the North American context it became the shield that would assure the survival of sufficient American strategic forces to strike back in the face of surprise attack. The 'survivability' of those forces was considered to be a crucial element in deterring the enemy from considering a general offensive. The earliest possible detection of an enemy attack became vital, therefore, and during the late 1950s Canada and the United States cooperated in extending the detection system northward with the installation of the Mid-Canada Line, and then the Arctic stations of the Distant Early Warning (DEW) Line. In 1958 Canadian and American air defences were still more closely integrated, with the creation of the North American Air Defence Command (NORAD). Information and control systems, meanwhile, were being increasingly centralized through the use of computers. Data from stations could now be transmitted almost instantly for automated collation and analysis at regional command centres and at NORAD headquarters in Colorado. The digested data could then be relayed quickly through the regional centres to fighter air bases. Precise navigational information about the tracks of unidentified contacts was transmitted directly to airborne aircraft that were dispatched to intercept them.[34]

In 1963 Sydney's radar base joined this system, known as the Semi-Automatic Ground Environment (SAGE), a change that all but eliminated its role in fighter control and made it primarily an information-gathering facility.[35] More than ever it was a very small cog in the immense North American air defence system. This evolution in technology resulted in only small and gradual reductions in manning strength, and does not appear to have affected the community life of the Royal Cape Breton Air Force. The station remained fully operational until it was finally closed down in 1991,[36] by which time progress with the joint Canada–United States North Warning System in the Arctic and associated radar modernization projects had rendered the southern stations redundant.[37]

The closing of the Sydney station closely followed the demolition of the infamous Berlin Wall in 1989, an event that signalled the end of the cold war and that was soon followed by the collapse of the Soviet Union and the breakup of the Eastern Bloc. Once again, when the prospect of peace on the Atlantic seemed assured, Sydney was stripped of its last element as a military strategic centre. Today, all that remains of Sydney's important military tradition is the armouries for Canadian Forces reserve units at Victoria Park. In 1999 the local staff named the newest building Fort Ogilvie, recalling the British garrison of two centuries earlier. There are also the many veterans of all three armed forces who served overseas or at home, and the survivors of the merchant marine, many of whom sailed out of Sydney. Finally, there are the crumbling remains of the coastal fortifications that ring Sydney Harbour, silent yet eloquent reminders of a time when Cape Breton was strategically central to the North Atlantic world and Sydney guarded the Gulf of St Lawrence, the gateway to Canada.

Notes

1: Outpost of Empire, 1696–1802

1 Quoted in Alan F. Williams, *Father Baudoin's War: D'Iberville's Campaigns in Acadia and Newfoundland, 1696, 1697* (St John's 1987), 15.

2 P.F.X. Charlevoix, *History and General Description of New France* (Chicago 1871), 5: 24. The work was first published as *Histoire et description générale de la Nouvelle-France* (1744).

3 Richard Brown, *A History of the Island of Cape Breton* (London 1869), 126.

4 Gerald S. Graham, 'Sir Hovenden Walker,' *Dictionary of Canadian Biography*, vol. 2, *1701–1740* (Toronto 1969), 661. While briefly acknowledging his appalling losses, Walker optimistically reported that 'by God's good Providence, all the men of War, tho' with extreme Hazards and Difficulty escaped ... and had I not made the Signal as I did, but continued sailing, 'tis a great question whether any Ships or Men had been saved.' Walker to Josiah Burchett, secretary to the Admiralty, 12 September 1711, quoted in Gerald S. Graham, ed., *The Walker Expedition to Quebec, 1711* (Toronto 1953), 87–8.

5 Brown, *History*, 137.

6 Quoted in Graham, *Walker Expedition*, 153–4.

7 Brown, *History*, 139. The final ignominy occurred when Walker, having arrived back in Britain, went to London to report to the Admiralty. His flagship, *Edgar*, blew up in Plymouth Harbour, killing the maintenance crew and destroying most of Walker's public papers, books, journals, and charts. When the ministry changed in 1715, he was dismissed from the service and denied his pension, despite having held a commission for twenty-eight years. He subsequently settled in South Carolina, then 'moved about restlessly between Ireland and the continent' until his death in 1725. Graham, *Walker Expedition*, 661–2. Charlevoix, *History*, 253n.

8 See also Dale Miquelon, *New France, 1701–1744* (Toronto 1987), chap. 5.
9 On Raudot's proposal, see Donald J. Horton, 'Antoine-Denis Raudot,' *Dictionary of Canadian Biography*, vol. 2: 551. Horton argues that Raudot's idea, 'at once brilliant and original,' was 'actually a project for the future commercial development of France's entire Atlantic empire.'
10 On the selection of Louisbourg, see Andrew Hill Clark, *Acadia: The Geography of Early Nova Scotia to 1760* (Madison 1968), 269–71.
11 Christopher Moore, 'The Other Louisbourg: Trade and Merchant Enterprise in Île Royale, 1713–58,' *Histoire sociale/Social History* 12 (May 1979), 79; see also Jean-François Brière, *La pêche française en Amérique du Nord au XVIIe siècle* (n.p. 1990), and B.A. Balcom, *The Cod Fishery of Isle Royale, 1713–58* (Ottawa 1984).
12 J.S. McLennan, *Louisbourg: From Its Foundation to Its Fall, 1713–1758* (London 1918; republished Halifax 1979), 223.
13 For detailed figures, see ibid., 221–2.
14 Gerald S. Graham. *Empire of the North Atlantic* (Toronto 1958), 113, 114.
15 On Warren's role and financial interests, see Julian Gwyn, 'Sir Peter Warren,' *Dictionary of Canadian Biography*, vol. 3, 1741–1770 (Toronto 1974), 655–8. See also H.W. Richmond, *The Navy in the War of 1739–48* (Cambridge 1918–20).
16 Julian Gwyn, 'War and Economic Change: Louisbourg and the New England Economy in the 1740s,' in Pierre Savard, ed., *Mélange d'histoire* (Ottawa 1978), 114–31.
17 J.B. Brebner, *New England's Outpost: Acadia Before the Conquest of Canada* (New York 1927), 104.
18 Julian Gwyn, 'The Royal Navy in North America, 1712–1776,' in Jeremy Black and Philip Woodfine, eds., *The British Navy and the Use of Naval Power in the Eighteenth Century* (Atlantic Highlands 1989), 130–7.
19 In 1766 British surveyor Samuel Holland described 'several Coal Veins, one of which the French formerly used,' on the northern side of the harbour, 'but the supporters of the Shafts are decayed & fallen in.' Quoted in D.C. Harvey, ed., *Holland's Description of Cape Breton and Other Documents* (Halifax 1935), reprinted in Brian Douglas Tennyson, ed., *Impressions of Cape Breton* (Sydney 1986), 31.
20 Fortress Louisbourg National Historic Site (FLNHS), CO 217/NS/B, ser. 4, Minutes of Council of War, 15 March 1747/8. Hopson had arrived at Louisbourg as senior officer in the 29th Foot Regiment and was appointed lieutenant-governor, succeeding Charles Knowles, in September 1747. In July 1748, following the Treaty of Aix-la-Chapelle, he handed Île Royale over to the French and removed his troops to Halifax. He subsequently served as lieutenant-governor of Nova Scotia from 1752 to 1755.

21 Writing in 1871, Richard Brown claimed that 'the ruins of an old building which still goes by the name of the "King's Store"' could still be seen at Bras d'Or. See Richard Brown, *The Coal Fields and Coal Trade of the Island of Cape Breton* (London 1871), 49. The discovery of a cannon ball during excavation work in October 1995 suggests that there may in fact have been a small fort as well. A blockhouse had already been built at Grassy Island, near Canso, in 1743 to protect the valuable fishery there and another would be built at Louisbourg in 1761. Richard J. Young, *Blockhouses in Canada, 1749–1841: A Comparative Report and Catalogue* (Ottawa 1980), 74, 81.

22 FLNHS, CO 217/A32: 48–58, Hopson to Newcastle, 12 April 1748.

23 Minutes of Council of War, 15 March 1747/8. On Marin's colourful career, see W.J. Eccles, 'Paul Marin de La Malgue,' *Dictionary of Canadian Biography*, 3:431–2. The miners were mostly French settlers who had remained after the fall of Louisbourg and taken the oath of allegiance. Brown, *History*, 259.

24 FLNHS, CO 217/A32:228, Hopson to Bedford, 28 October 1748. Professor Moogk claims that there were a lieutenant and fifty troops there but he may be confusing the situation in 1748 with that of 1758. See Peter Moogk, 'From Fortress Louisbourg to Fortress Sydney: Artillery and Gunners on Cape Breton, 1743–1964,' in Kenneth Donovan, ed., *Cape Breton at 200* (Sydney 1985), 131.

25 A description of Fort William by Desherbiers in 1749 is in FLNHS, Archives des Colonies, Série C[11B], 28: ff. 76–6v. It also appears as Fort Guillaume on map ND-37 in the FLNHS map collection. Richard Brown, writing in 1871, said that the remains of a ditch that surrounded the blockhouse could still be seen. Brown, *Coal Trade*, 49.

26 Thomas Pichon, *Genuine Letters and Memoirs, Relating to the Natural, Civil, and Commercial History of the Islands of Cape Breton, and Saint John* (London 1760), 59.

27 FLNHS, CO 217/A32:150–2, 180–6, Hopson report, 3 June 1748; see also ibid., CO 217/A32:180–6, Hopson to Bedford, 12 July 1748.

28 Chauncy Townsend, the contractor who supplied coal to the garrison at Louisbourg, succeeded in having a clause included in the treaty that allowed him time to remove his stockpile before the fortress changed hands. See FLNHS, State Papers 78/232, Townsend memorial to Duke of Bedford, n.d.; Bedford to Lieutenant Colonel John Yorke, 16 February 1748.

29 Richard Middleton, *The Bells of Victory* (Cambridge 1985), gives the Duke of Newcastle much of the credit for Britain's successful war policy and criticizes historians who have built up Pitt's image rather too handsomely. See Jeremy Black, 'Naval power and British foreign policy,' in Black and Woodfine, eds., *British Navy*, which points out that Britain's navy was spread too thin to meet

all the demands made upon it, so that Pitt could have done no more than his predecessors to concentrate on North America before 1758, and Julian Gwyn's 'The Royal Navy in North America, 1712–1776' in the same volume.

30 On the founding of Halifax and its early development, see W.A.B. Douglas, 'Halifax as an Element of Sea Power, 1749 to 1766' (unpublished MA thesis, Dalhousie University 1962).

31 'The pit took fire in the summer of 1752, and intirely [*sic*] consumed the fort.' Pichon, *Genuine Letters*, 28. See also Holland to Shelburne, 10 November 1766, cited in Dilys Francis, 'The Mines and Quarries of Cape Breton Island' (1965), 50 (copy at FLNHS). According to Brown, *History*, 271, the fire did not burn out until 1764.

32 National Archives of Canada (NA), MG 12, WO 34/B69:17 (mfm 2646), Edward Whitmore to Lords of Treasury, 25 April 1759.

33 FLNHS, CO 217/21/A78:112–9, Francklin to Board of Trade, 30 September 1766. Writing in 1868, Richard Brown, in *History*, 258, claimed that 'the ruins of this fort may still be seen.'

34 Whitmore to Lords of Treasury, 25 April 1759.

35 Francklin to Board of Trade, 30 September 1766.

36 The syndicate's local agent was William Lloyd, after whom Lloyd's Cove at Sydney Mines, adjacent to the Chapel Point battery, is named.

37 C.W. Vernon, *Cape Breton, Canada, at the Beginning of the Twentieth Century* (Toronto 1903), 166. According to Brown, *Coal Trade*, 57n, 'the coal smugglers, as they were styled, had not only dug a large quantity of coal, but had coolly taken up their quarters in the old barracks, where they resided without molestation.'

38 FLNHS, Adm. 1/484:578–80, Vice Admiral Molyneux Shuldham to Philip Stephens, 8 July 1776; Brown, *History*, 380. Shuldham (c. 1717–98) was commander-in-chief on the Newfoundland station in 1772–5. In March 1775 he was promoted to rear admiral. He was again promoted to vice admiral and became commander-in-chief on the North American coast later that year. He was superseded by Lord Howe in June 1776, was raised to the Irish peerage in July, and returned to Britain early in 1777.

39 Graham, *Empire*, 209.

40 FLNHS, CO 218/19:40–1, Major General Eyre Massey to Lord ?, 21 April 1778.

41 Brown, *History*, 380.

42 Hierlighy to General Clinton, 6 December 1778, quoted in Young, *Blockhouses*, 98.

43 Massey to Lord ?, 21 April 1778.

44 FLNHS, Adm. 1/487:133–6, Admiral Howe to Stephens, 27 November 1776; Adm.1./488:407–9, Howe to Captain Charles Fielding, 12 May 1778; 417–21, Fielding to Howe, 21 August 1778. When Ensign Walter Prenties of the 84th Regiment was shipwrecked off Margaree Harbour in November 1780, he and a few fellow survivors eventually, with the aid of Mi'kmaq guides, made their way in April 1781 to Spanish River. There, 'Captn Thomas Green who commanded at this place treated myself and the rest of the people with the greatest humanity. He informed me he expected Your Excellency [Governor Haldimand] would send a vessel from Quebec this summer for coals.' Quoted in G.G. Campbell, ed., *Ensign Prenties's Narrative: A Castaway on Cape Breton* (Toronto 1968), 67. Messrs Frazer, McDonald, Green, 'and other Contractors' were paid £2,054 for supplying 3,081 chaldrons of coal to the garrison at Halifax between July 1780 and March 1783. At the same time, Green received £259.4.3½ for 240 chaldrons of coal destined for the Halifax garrison that had been lost at sea. John Ley received £8 for freight and other expenses incurred in transporting bedding and other supplies from Halifax to Spanish River for the service of the troops employed at the mines. FLNHS, AO 1/147:356, accounts for 1 July 1780 to 31 March 1783.

45 The ship logs record frequent arrivals at and departures from Sydney of Royal Navy vessels during the war years. For example, when *Assurance* arrived at Sydney on 12 August 1778, accompanied by *Danae* and *Surprize*, it found *Allegiance* already there. Similarly, when *Assistance* arrived on 10 July 1785, it found *Hermione* and *Resource* already there, and *Ariadne* arrived on the following day. FLNHS, Adm. 51/72, Journal of Captain Swiney, *Assurance*, 12 August 1781; Adm. 51/73, Journal of Captain William Bentinck, *Assistance*, 10 July 1785. Many other examples could be given as well.

46 FLNHS, Adm. 1/489:442–3, Thomas Graves to Philip Stephens, 26 September 1781.

47 William Laird Clowes, *The Royal Navy: A History from the Earliest Times to the Present* (London 1899), 4:71. C. Bruce Fergusson says the convoy included sixteen vessels employed in the coal traffic; Fergusson, ed., *Uniacke's Sketches of Cape Breton and Other Papers Relating to Cape Breton Island* (Halifax 1958), Introduction, 28.

48 Brown, *History*, 383.

49 Ibid., 384. There is some confusion about this incident. It appears that *Jack* had been captured by the French during the July naval battle off Sydney and its crew taken to Boston as prisoners. They were subsequently exchanged for American prisoners held by the British. Upon his return to Halifax, Tonge was given another smaller vessel, which he named *Little Jack*, and it was this ship that won the battle at Petit de Grat. Beamish Murdoch, *A History of Nova*

Scotia or Acadie (Halifax 1866), 2:617–20; see also Claribel Gesner, *Cape Breton Anthology* (Windsor 1972) 19–21.

50 Harvey, *Holland's Description*, 31.

51 The troops were barely settled in at Sydney when a remarkable event took place, involving two young officers. On 15 October 1785, around four o'clock in the afternoon, Captain John Cope Sherbrooke and Lieutenant George Wynyard were sitting in the latter's rooms in the barracks. Sherbrooke happened to look up, 'and there, at the door to the passage, stood a tall young man, about twenty years of age, with sunken cheeks and wasted frame, and dressed in a light indoor costume.' Wynyard saw him as well and recognized his brother John, who was serving with the 3rd Regiment in India at the time. Wynyard interpreted the apparition to mean that his brother had died, and in fact when the first overseas mails arrived in the spring, on 6 June 1786, they learned that John Wynyard had indeed died in India on 15 October at the very hour of his appearance in Sydney. This story is reported in J.G. MacKinnon, *Old Sydney* (1918; Belleville 1973), 33–8. So seriously was the story of the apparition taken at the time, according to MacKinnon, that the grand jury of Cape Breton's Supreme Court undertook an investigation and even proposed in February 1786 to haul Sherbrooke and Wynyard before the court because of their refusal to allow the jury 'to examine the floor' in Wynyard's room. Sherbrooke, of course, went on to a distinguished career as a lieutenant-governor of Nova Scotia and governor-general of British North America. E.A. Cruikshank, 'The Military History of the Island of Cape Breton, 1785–1815' (Sydney, n.d.), 5.

52 R.J. Morgan, 'Orphan Outpost: Cape Breton Colony, 1784–1820' (unpublished PhD thesis, University of Ottawa 1972), vi.

53 Remarks by DesBarres on copy of a letter from Evean Nepean to DesBarres, 2 July 1784, quoted in ibid., 19.

54 FLNHS, CO 218/12:9–10, Sydney to DesBarres, 19 April 1786.

55 Douglas to Captain Paul Minchin, 31 July 1784, cited in Roger A. Evans, 'The Army and Navy at Halifax in Peace-Time, 1783–1793' (unpublished MA thesis, Dalhousie University, 1970), 48. At about the same time, a French naval vessel's request at Halifax for permission to have coal conveyed from Sydney to St Pierre and Miquelon was refused on the grounds that such trade would violate the navigation laws. Not only French and American subjects were prohibited from removing Cape Breton coal, but unauthorized British subjects as well. See Admiralty to Douglas, 1 October 1784, cited in ibid., 49.

56 Douglas to Stephens, 24 November 1784, and Douglas to commanding officers, 1 April 1785, cited in ibid.

57 'Lieut W[illiam] Booth's Description of Sydney, August 1785,' in Fergusson, *Uniacke's Sketches*, 144.

58 Brown, *History*, 404. There had been thirty-two men posted at the mines in 1783. See Evans, 'The Army,' 81.

59 'Booth's Description,' 144.

60 Yorke's 33rd Regiment returned to Britain in 1786 and was replaced by six companies of the 42nd, or Black Watch, Regiment under the command of Lieutenant Colonel Graham. Yorke was not unhappy to leave, reporting in December 1785 that his men were 'in the half-finished barracks but the officers are still in tents, which are almost rotten.' CO, A & WI/407:31, Yorke to Major General Campbell, 4 December 1785, cited in Public Archives of Canada, *Annual Report 1895*, 'State Papers – Cape Breton' (Ottawa 1896), 6.

61 MacKinnon, *Old Sydney*, 26. He added that 'both made their homes here, and are today represented by a large number of descendants.'

62 Diane Chisholm, 'The Evolution of Victoria Park' (1994), 3.

63 Stephen Hornsby, *Nineteenth-Century Cape Breton* (Montreal and Kingston 1992), 28.

64 'Lieut (later General) William Dyott's Description of Sydney, 1788,' in Fergusson, *Uniacke's Sketches*, 145. Dyott (1761–1847) was adjutant of the 4th Regiment, which went to Nova Scotia in 1787. There he became a personal friend of Prince William, later William IV, who was commanding *Andromeda* at Halifax. He saw service in Britain, the West Indies, Egypt, and Europe, retiring in 1810 as a lieutenant general.

65 'A Letter Written at Sydney in 1789,' in Fergusson, *Uniacke's Sketches*, 147.

66 James Miller to J. King, 17 July 1795, and W. Smith, 'State of the Island of Cape Breton, from the Year 1784 to the Present Time,' quoted in ibid., 25. A mining engineer, Miller had been sent out by the British government in 1793 and served as superintendent of mines until his death in 1799. See Brown, *Coal Trade*, 62.

67 Hornsby, *Nineteenth-Century*, 26–8.

68 In 1796 81 per cent of Cape Breton's dried fish exports passed through Arichat. See ibid., 5.

69 Ibid., 19.

70 Richard Stout (c. 1756–1820) was a Loyalist who went to Sydney around 1788 as the local agent of Jonathan Tremaine, also a Loyalist, who had settled in Halifax. The most important merchant and creditor in Cape Breton, Stout served on the Executive Council from 1797 to 1800, from 1810 to 1812, and from 1813 to 1817.

71 Macarmick to Henry Dundas, 6 October 1792, quoted in ibid., 7. William Macarmick (1742–1815) had raised the 93rd Regiment at his own expense

and was appointed its colonel in 1780. He served in the House of Commons from 1784 to 1787, resigning to become lieutenant-governor of Cape Breton. He returned to Britain on leave in 1795, but retained his position until his death. He also continued in the army, being promoted to lieutenant general in 1803 and general in 1813.

72 R.J. Morgan, 'Richard Stout,' *Dictionary of Canadian Biography*, vol. 5, *1801–20* (Toronto 1983), 780.

73 Dundas to Macarmick, 4 July 1792, quoted in Morgan, 'Orphan Outpost,' 72.

74 FLNHS, CO 218/12:75, Dundas to Miller, 27 June 1792; 74, Dundas to Miller, 22 September 1793.

75 Ibid., 96, Portland to Macarmick, 4 November 1794. Stout actually acknowledged in 1794 that he and Tremaine made more money from selling food and supplies to their miners than they did from the sale of coal. See Morgan, 'Orphan Outpost,' 72.

76 Ibid., 92. Portland to Miller, 4 November 1794.

77 Hornsby, *Nineteenth-Century*, 16.

78 FLNHS, CO 218/12:99–100, Portland to Macarmick, 1 June 1795.

79 Hornsby, *Nineteenth-Century*, 16.

80 Ibid., 100, Portland to Macarmick, 1 June 1795. Hornsby, *Nineteenth-Century*, 15–16.

81 Hornsby, *Nineteenth-Century*, 28. This included the possession of slaves, according to the records of St George's, the garrison church, which mention the baptism on 10 May 1787 of 'James, a negro, his parents belonging to the 42 regiment.' Quoted in MacKinnon, *Old Sydney*, 27. Slavery was not uncommon in Cape Breton in the eighteenth century, as Ken Donovan has documented in 'Slaves and Their Owners in Île Royale, 1713–1760,' *Acadiensis* 25, no. 1 (1995), 3–32, and 'A Nominal List of Slaves and Their Owners in Île Royale, 1713–1760,' *Nova Scotia Historical Review* 16, no. 1 (1996).

82 Nova Scotia Archives and Records Management (NSARM), MG 1/526A, Anna Kearney diary, 1–2. We are indebted to Dr Robert J. Morgan, director of the Beaton Institute at the University College of Cape Breton, for making available a copy of this document.

83 Ibid., 7–8. Captain and Mrs Weekes 'disgraced' themselves again at an assembly held on the 25th, when they 'chose to give *public* proofs of their contempt "of *fix'd* & *settle'd rules*" by being partners in the Dance, as well as for Life & were as well in this, as in other parts of their conduct ridiculous to a degree. She honor'd poor Charlotte with the most malignant glances & refus'd her *fair* hand to the Dr [Clarke] in the course of the dance.' Ibid., 11.

84 Ibid., 12.

85 Ibid., 37.

86 Ibid., 16.

87 Ibid., 17. An indication of how bad relations could be between the military and civil authorities is the duel that took place in Sydney on 28 February 1801 between an officer and a member of the government. The site was George Street, where the Cape Breton Victoria District School Board offices are now located. Both men reportedly paced out thirty feet, turned, and fired, and both fell to the ground, apparently wounded. In fact, however, their seconds had loaded their pistols with cranberries rather than shot, and the only harm incurred was to their pride. Pam Newton, *The Cape Breton Book of Days* (Sydney 1984).

88 For the history of this conflict, see Morgan, 'Orphan Outpost.'

89 R.J. Morgan, 'Richard Gibbons,' *Dictionary of Canadian Biography*, vol. 4, *1771–1800* (Toronto 1979), 292.

90 Ibid., 293. See also Morgan, 'Orphan Outpost,' 82–3. Gibbons travelled to Halifax, Quebec, and London in his campaign to be reinstated in office. He succeeded in 1791, but did not attempt to return to Cape Breton until 1794. The ship on which he and his family were travelling was captured by the French and he died in prison that year. His family was released and returned to Cape Breton, where his son, also named Richard, subsequently served as attorney-general.

91 Major General John Despard (1745–1829) was administrator of Cape Breton from 1799 to 1807. He had served in the army during the colonial and the American Revolutionary Wars, and was appointed commanding officer of the forces in the Maritime colonies in 1793.

92 Despard denied that there was any armed force involved: he said there was only one sentry from the militia at Government House, and the inhabitants generally rejoiced at his accession to office. He acknowleged, however, that 'a few windows were broken by boys.' Despard to Portland, 19 September 1800, cited in PAC, *Annual Report*, 92. The Reverend Ranna Cossit, rector of St George's and a supporter of Murray, claimed that there had been 'an armed party outside' Government House, that he was afraid to leave his house because of 'the tumult in the streets,' and that his windows were broken; see ibid., Cossit to Despard, 16 September 1800. When Bishop Charles Inglis visited Sydney in 1805, he concluded that Cossit should be sent elsewhere. 'All the officers of Government and people of any property and distinction are violently prejudiced against him. Nor can it be other-wise; for he wages incessant war against them. Were he continued here, the Church of England would probably sink entirely.' NA, MG 23/C616, Charles Inglis journal, 7 July 1805, (typed copy in Beaton Institute). Cossit resigned on 18 July and was sent to Yarmouth.

93 NA, MG 11, CO 218/120:73 (mfm 2646), Despard to Lord Hobart, 15 February 1802.

94 R.J. Morgan, 'John Despard,' *Dictionary of Canadian Biography*, vol. 6, *1821–1835* (Toronto 1987), 203.

95 Quoted in Ian Macintyre, 'Victoria Park and the Army: The First Two Centuries' (1984), 8. The report of an agent who had been sent to ascertain the resources of St Pierre confirmed Macarmick in the opinion that in the event of war Cape Breton would be the first point of attack by the French.

96 Macarmick to Grenville, 24 August 1789, cited in PAC, *Annual Report*, 24.

97 Macarmick to Grenville, 16 February 1790, cited in ibid., 26.

98 Macintyre, 'Victoria Park,' 5.

99 The ship carrying the spy became trapped in the ice and he was forced to spend the winter on the islands. When he returned to Sydney in the spring, he brought two cases of Bordeaux wine to Macarmick, a gift from the French commandant. This provoked a minor crisis, as the Executive Council debated whether the wine was intended as a gift or a bribe. Eventually, it was decided that it was merely a gift and Macarmick was allowed to keep it. Newton, *Book of Days*.

100 Macarmick to Grenville, 16 February, 18 June 1790, cited in PAC, *Annual Report*, 29.

101 Macintyre, 'Victoria Park,' 5.

102 Macarmick to Grenville, 30 April 1790, cited in PAC, *Annual Report*, 27.

103 Ibid., Macarmick to Grenville, 18 June 1790.

104 Ibid., Macarmick to Dorchester, 25 August 1790, 30–1.

105 Moogk, 'From Fortress Louisbourg,' 131.

106 Macarmick to Grenville, 11 October 1790, cited in PAC, *Annual Report*, 32.

107 Mrs Roderick Bain, 'History of Sydney Mines' [1951], 10; Cruikshank, 'Military History,' 8.

108 Dundas to Wentworth, 8 February 1793, quoted in G.F.G. Stanley, 'The Royal Nova Scotia Regiment, 1793–1802,' *Journal of the Royal Army Historical Society* 21 (1942), 157–8; Wentworth to secretary of state, 22 March 1793, quoted in G.F.G. Stanley, 'The Defence of the Maritime Provinces During the Wars of the French Revolution,' *Canadian Defence Quarterly* 14 (1936–1937), 438. Stanley described Nova Scotia's militia as 'little more than a Falstaffian array, lacking arms, ammunition and accoutrements.'

109 Macarmick to Dundas, 16 April 1793, cited in PAC, *Annual Report*, 43–4. He also noted that with the population declining, he could hope to raise only 423 men for the militia.

110 Wentworth went on to say that Ogilvie, who was offering little cooperation with Wentworth in his efforts to organize the Nova Scotia militia, 'ventures

nothing that is not specifically commanded, which of course renders the service dilatory and difficult to a dangerous degree.' Quoted in Stanley, 'The Defence,' 440. James Ogilvie (1740–1813) joined the army at an early age and served in the West Indies from 1759 to 1762. He saw extensive service during the American Revolution and was captured by the French in 1778, not being freed until 1780. He was appointed brigadier general commanding the Nova Scotia District in 1787, then lieutenant general and administrator of Cape Breton, 1798–9. He retired in 1799 and was promoted to a general in 1802.

111 He did so after being so instructed by Lord Dundas. FLNHS, CO 218/ 12:72, Dundas to Macarmick, 7 August 1793.

112 Cox to Macarmick, 12, 14 August 1793, cited in PAC, *Annual Report*, 45. Cox, then a lieutenant in the Royal Artillery, had been posted to Sydney in 1790, when he was granted one thousand acres at Sydney River, where he established a substantial farm in the area that later became known as Coxheath. Beaton Institute, Cox File, John Payne, surveyor of lands, Sydney, to Sir John Wentworth, 1 September 1790. He seems to have returned to Halifax, as he was sent back to Sydney as an assistant engineer in 1796. See NSARM, MG 12, Ordnance Department letter-books, 1794–1800:34 (mfm 12347), J. Vesey, aide-de-camp to Duke of Kent, to Clement Horton, ordnance storekeeper (Halifax), 22 May 1796; ibid., 67, John Vigden, Board of Ordnance, to Horton, 8 December 1796. Cox subsequently became a captain in the Nova Scotia Fencibles stationed there. See NA, WO 55/857 (mfm B2805), commanding royal engineer (Halifax) to Lieutenant General Morse, inspector general of works and fortifications (London), 18 June 1804 (copy in Beaton Institute, Cox file). Cox served on the Executive Council from 1801 to 1803, replacing James Miller upon the latter's death. See NA, MG 11, CO 217/120:44–5 (mfm 2646), John Despard to Lord Hobart, 15 February 1802. When Bishop Charles Inglis visited Cox's farm in 1805 during a pastoral tour of Cape Breton, he described it as 'the best [farm] I have visited. More than 100 acres are cleared. The dwelling house is small, but convenient. The barns, stables for cows and sheep are extensive, neat and very convenient. As is also the Dairy, where I first saw a barrel churn, which appears to be much more convenient and more easily worked than the common churn. Here we had field strawberries of an uncommon size.' Charles Inglis journal, 13 July 1805. Those familiar with Cape Breton's unpredictable weather will not be surprised by Inglis's report that 'Captain Cox told me they had frost that morning, and he thought the frost injured the grass [hay] this summer more than the drought.' Cox sold potatoes and possibly other foodstuffs to the government for consumption by the min-

ers. See NA, MG 11, CO 217/120:103 (mfm 2646), Cox receipt, 5 December 1801.

113 FLNHS, CO 218/12:72–3, Dundas to Macarmick, 4 September 1793.

114 NA, MG 11, CO 218, Nova Scotia A/120:80 (mfm C9136), Wentworth to Dundas, 25 March 1794. See also 69:65, Macarmick to Dorchester, n.d., enclosed in Macarmick to Dundas, 12 December 1793.

115 Cruikshank says that nine small cannon were purchased from local merchants for the battery, while Moogk says eight two-pounders were bought from an island merchant. Cruikshank, 'Military History,' 8; Moogk, 'From Fortress Louisbourg,' 133.

116 In July it was reported that two seventy-four-gun ships and five frigates were en route to Boston and Rhode Island for repairs; these vessels remained in American ports throughout the summer. Stanley, 'The Royal,' 167.

117 Macarmick to Dundas, 26 August 1793, cited in PAC, *Annual Report*, 46. Dundas thought Macarmick 'should embody the Militia' if it seemed necessary to do so, though he should 'do so in as economical a manner and for as short a period as possible.' FLNHS, CO 218/12:76, Dundas to Macarmick, 3 October 1793.

118 Ibid., Dundas to Macarmick, 8 November 1793.

119 Macarmick to Dundas, 25 October 1793, cited in PAC, *Annual Report*, 47.

120 This report was later thought to have been unfounded. FLNHS, CO 218/12:77, Dundas to Macarmick, 8 November 1793.

121 Cruikshank, 'Military History,' 8.

122 Tremaine to Miller, 13 August 1794, cited in Morgan, 'Orphan Outpost,' 77.

123 FLNHS, CO 218/12:72–3, Dundas to Macarmick, 4 September 1793.

124 Ibid., 77, Dundas to Macarmick, 8 November 1793.

125 Macarmick to Dundas, 18 August 1794, cited in PAC, *Annual Report*, 51–2.

126 FLNHS, CO 218/12:91, Portland to Macarmick, 4 November 1794. It was sold in the spring of 1795 and replaced by the schooner *Hope*. See ibid., 102, Portland to Macarmick, 1 July 1795.

127 Macarmick to Dorchester, 20 December 1793, cited in PAC, *Annual Report*, 48–9.

128 Nova Scotia A, 120:50, Wentworth to John King, 11 February 1794.

129 FLNHS, CO 218/12:57, Dundas to Ogilvie, 14 February 1794.

130 Macarmick to Dundas, 17 March 1794, cited in PAC, *Annual Report*, 49.

131 FLNHS, CO 218/12:91–2, Ogilvie to Dundas, 5 May 1794. On French and American naval activity in the coastal waters of the Maritimes at this time, see Stanley, 'The Defence,' 444–6. Macarmick didn't get the guns from St Pierre either. When the French islands were evacuated in September, 'the Commanding Officer of Artillery conceiving that it was not worth the

expense to remove the heavy Guns, I ordered him to render them unserviceable.' See Nova Scotia A, 120:290, Kent to Portland, 11 November 1794. Believing that the French prisoners from St Pierre and Miquelon, 'who were violent democrats to a man,' were 'poison[ing] with democracy' the minds of the Acadians in the Arichat area, Wentworth sent them to Guernsey for imprisonment. See David Allison, *History of Nova Scotia* (Halifax 1916), 603.

132 According to Gerald Graham, only one frigate was cruising in the Gulf of St Lawrence in the summer of 1798. In 1800, when ninety-five warships protected British possessions in the Caribbean, Halifax and Newfoundland had to be content with only six each. Graham, *Empire*, 219, 223–4.

133 Major Peregrine Thorne to admiral commanding his majesty's ships, 3 August 1793, quoted in ibid., 226n.

134 Nova Scotia A, 120/376–8, Kent to Portland, 31 December 1794. Dundas informed Macarmick that he approved of his 'communicating to Lord Dorchester your Ideas respecting the Works of Defence you allude to, previous to your commencing the execution of them, & in the meantime I expect that you will incur as little expence as possible, in preparing the Materials you mention.' See FLNHS, CO 218/12:83, Dundas to Macarmick, 2 April 1794.

135 Nova Scotia A, 120:83, 235–6, Portland to Kent, 2 April 1795; Kent to Portland, 26 June 1795. See also Kent to Portland, 26 June 1795, cited in Young, *Blockhouses*, 98.

136 This outpost was also known locally as Fort Gow or Fort Guion. It may have been named after Jean-Baptiste Guyon, who lived in Louisbourg through the two sieges until at least 1760 and may have subsequently settled in the South Bar area. We are indebted to Kenneth Donovan, Fortress of Louisbourg National Historic Site, for providing this information. Guyon may have been a son of François Guyon (1666–1701?), a Canadian who became a notorious freebooter, raiding vessels and outposts in New England. He became a close friend of Antoine de Laumet de la Mothe Cadillac (1648–1730), who married his sister, Marie-Thérèse, and eventually became governor of Louisiana (1712). Guyon was captured by the English off Boston and taken prisoner in April 1695 but was subsequently released and arrived in Plaisance in 1696 just before d'Iberville sailed to attack the English settlements in Newfoundland. He died before 12 July 1701. Williams, *Father Baudoin's War*, 149–51. According to W.L. Chirgwin, the peninsula on which the fort was built washed away in later years but the blockhouse was still standing until 1862. 'Harbour Forts of 200 Years Ago Recalled,' *Cape Breton Post* (undated clipping, c. 1961).

137 Macarmick had acknowledged that he was facing criticism because he had undertaken defensive measures and expenditures without first consulting his Executive Council. See Macarmick to Dundas, 17 March 1794, cited in PAC, *Annual Report*, 49. The Executive Council minutes, with Macarmick's accounts and vouchers for expenditures, may be found in Macarmick to Dundas, 18 July 1794, ibid., 51.

138 FLNHS, CO 218/12:83-5, Portland to Macarmick, 31 July 1794.

139 Ibid., 91, Portland to Macarmick, 4 November 1794.

140 Brown, *History*, 409. Cruikshank, 'Military History,' claims that the guns did not in fact arrive from Halifax until the summer of 1797. Moogk, 'From Fortress Louisbourg,' 133, suggests that these guns were in addition to those already installed.

141 Bain, 'Sydney Mines,' 21, says it was situated 'between E.A. MacDonald's house and the harbour.' Richard Brown claimed that there were two batteries, one in front of the blockhouse and the other on Peck's Head. See Brown, *Coal Trade*, 63.

142 Chirgwin, 'Harbour Forts.' Although he had left in 1864, Brown, writing in 1871, said that the blockhouse was still standing. *Coal Trade*, 63.

143 Moogk, 'From Fortress Louisbourg,' 133.

144 Ibid., 135. Moogk speculates that 'a gun outside the headquarters building at Victoria Park barracks, on the right hand side as one enters, could be one of these pieces.'

145 Beaton Institute, MG 1/D3:4, F.A. Wetherall, deputy adjutant general at Halifax, to David Matthews, 27 June 1797.

146 Ibid., 6, Wetherall to Mathews, 6 August 1797.

147 David Mathews (d. 1800) was a key player in the ongoing political crisis at Sydney in these years. A Loyalist who had served as mayor of New York, he went first to Halifax, then to Sydney where he was appointed attorney-general and to the Executive Council in 1785. When Macarmick left in 1795, Mathews became administrator and appointed one of his two sons acting attorney-general and the other provost marshal. He also appointed Richard Stout, to whom he was deeply in debt, to the Executive Council. He fought with William McKinnon, the colony's secretary and registrar, as well as with Ranna Cossit and James Miller, the superintendent of mines, all of whom he imprisoned at different times. When General Murray dismissed him from office in January 1800, Mathews aligned himself with the Duke of Kent; the latter was also in conflict with the general, and Murray was replaced by John Despard in June. This final triumph did Mathews no good, as he died a month later. See R.J. Morgan, 'David Mathews,' *Dictionary of Canadian Biography*, 4:522; 'James Ogilvie,' *Dictionary of Canadian*

Biography, 5:634. Macarmick, who had been promoted to the rank of major general, offered to raise a regiment for the defence of Cape Breton but his proposal was declined.

148 Mathews to Portland, 7 July 1796, cited in PAC, *Annual Report*, 64.

149 Mathews to Portland, 29 August 1796, cited in ibid.

150 Wallace to Wentworth, 5 September 1796, cited in Stanley, 'The Royal,' 168.

151 Stanley, 'The Royal,' 168.

152 Ibid.

153 Tremaine and Stout to Mathews, 1 December 1796; Mathews to Duke of Kent, 6 December 1796, cited in PAC, *Annual Report*, 65. This was the only occasion on which the government suggested that a fortification might also be built at Arichat, where Cape Breton's principal fishery was carried on.

154 NSARM, MG 12, Ordnance Department letter-books, 1794–1800:83 (mfm 12347), J. Hale, military secretary, to Clement Horton, 16 June 1797; Wetherall to Horton, 24 June 1797.

155 Mathews to Portland, 2 August 1797, cited in PAC, *Annual Report*, 70.

156 Ibid., 74, Ogilvie to Portland, 10 April 1798. When the Royal Nova Scotia Regiment was disbanded in 1802, these men were replaced at Sydney by troops from the 7th Royal Fusiliers.

157 Morgan, 'Ogilvie,' 634. Portland agreed that he should call out the militia 'at the shortest possible notice in case any attempts of a predatory nature should be made by the Enemy upon the Coast.' FLNHS, CO 218/12:131–2, Portland to Ogilvie, 1 July 1798.

158 Ogilvie to Portland, 10 May 1798, and Portland to Ogilvie, 1 July 1798, cited in PAC, *Annual Report*, 74.

159 NSARM, MG 12, Ordnance Department letter-books, 1794–1800, 118–19 (mfm 12347), J. Vesey to Horton, 23 September 1798. In the event, twelve-pounders were sent instead of the proposed nine-pounders. See ibid., Lieutenant Colonel Thomas Desbrisay to Horton, [September 1798].

160 Ogilvie to Portland, 10 January 1799, cited in PAC, *Annual Report*, 77.

161 NSARM, MG 2/10, Cox, 'Estimate of the Expence of Sundry Necessary Works & Repairs as Here Undermentioned,' 17 October 1800 (copy in Beaton Institute, Cox file).

162 NA, MG 11, CO 217/120:267 (mfm 2646), Despard to Hobart, 31 August 1802.

2: War and Peace, 1802–1859

1 Graham, *Empire*, 234.

2 NA, WO 55/857 (mfm B2805), Captain W. Fenwick, commanding Royal

Engineer (Halifax) to Lieutenant General Morse, 18 June 1804 (copy in Beaton Institute, Cox file). It is noteworthy that all references henceforth are simply to the blockhouse or battery at the mines or to both, and not to Fort Dundas. For whatever reason, that name had been abandoned.

3 NA, RG 8, C series, 1432:174–5, Cox to Fenwick, 5 July 1804.

4 NSARM, MG 12/RE 14, Cox to Captain Bennett, commanding royal engineer, 24 June 1807. There were at this time forty-three men of the Royal Newfoundland Fencibles at Sydney, led by a captain, as well as three men from the Royal Artillery, plus a barrack master, a town adjutant, a commissary, and a hospital mate. See NSARM, WO 17, 2356–9 'Monthly Return,' 1 June 1807 (mfm 21431). The Royal Newfoundland Fencibles appear to have left Sydney in September 1807, and they were replaced by a company of seventy-four men from the New Brunswick Fencibles in August 1808. There were also seven men from the Royal Artillery, under the command of a sergeant. See 'Monthly Return,' 1 September 1808. The New Brunswick Fencibles appear to have been withdrawn in November 1809. See ibid., 25 November 1809.

5 Cox to Bennett, 24 June 1807. This reference may have been to a claim for £15 that Cox had submitted in 1796 'for travelling to the Island of Cape Breton' when he was assistant engineer. The Board of Ordnance had declined to pay the bill, 'as Lt Cox does not appear to have been appointed by the Master Genrl or Board and as the under receipts are not produced.' NSARM, MG 12, Ordnance Department letter-books, 1794–1800, 67 (mfm 12347), John Vigden to Clement Horton, 8 December 1796.

6 NSARM MG 12/RE 14, Cox to Bennett, 20 July 1807.

7 Largely because of the shortage of labour and the high cost of living, workers at the coal mines were well paid, wage costs comprising 80 per cent of total production costs. See James Miller to Duke of Portland, 31 October 1794, cited in Hornsby, *Nineteenth-Century*, 15. In 1794 the wages of a common labourer were $8 per month, and those of a coal cutter between $8 and $10, sometimes $12. The truck system operated by the company left few miners with much money, however, because wages were paid irregularly and were usually credited at the company store, where the miners were allowed to have a running account. The large premium Tremaine and Stout charged on imported goods recouped much of the money paid out in wages. See ibid., 18.

8 NSARM, MG 12/RE 14, Cox to McLaughlan, 12 October 1807.

9 Ibid., Cox to commanding royal engineer, 26 September 1808.

10 Ibid., Cox to Nicolls, 8 January 1809. Nicolls had enlisted in the Royal Artillery in 1794 but transferred to the Royal Engineers a year later. He became a

lieutenant colonel in 1813 but, serving most of his career in the colonies, was still a colonel in 1825. He was largely responsible for the design of the Halifax Citadel before being transferred to Quebec in 1831. He eventually achieved the rank of general in 1854 and died in 1860.

11 Ibid., Cox to Nicolls, 6 June 1809.

12 Ibid., Cox to Nicolls, 2 October 1809.

13 Ibid., Cox to Nicolls, 6 June 1810.

14 Morgan suggests that Ritchie may also have been influenced by his desire to open the Pictou coalfield in his own colony. R.J. Morgan, 'Nicholas Nepean,' *Dictionary of Canadian Biography*, 6: 538.

15 Morgan, 'Hugh Swayne,' *Dictionary of Canadian Biography*, vol. 7, *1836–1850* (Toronto 1988), 840. Hugh Swayne (d. 1836) served in the Royal Irish Artillery from 1782, retiring in 1801. He was appointed brigadier general and administrator of Cape Breton in 1812, and served until forced to return to Britain because of poor health in 1815.

16 NSARM, MG 12/RE 52, Lieutenant Colonel William Dixon, commanding Royal Artillery, and Gustavus Nicolls, 'Report of the State and Strength of the Forts and Batteries Etc Composing the Ordnance Establishment in the Provinces of Nova Scotia and New Brunswick and the Islands of Cape Breton and Prince Edwards' (Halifax, 1 January 1810).

17 Graham, *Empire*, 250.

18 Swayne to Lord Bathurst, January 1813, cited in Brown, *History*, 404.

19 Beaton Institute, MG 9/38/5/496, Swayne Papers, Griffith to Swayne, 28 August 1813.

20 NA, MG 12, WO 44/144:98 (mfm B1328), Gustavus Nicolls, 'Report of the State of the Forts, Batteries, Ordnance, Ammunition, Etc composing the Ordnance Establishment in the Island of Cape Breton' (Halifax, 1 January 1812).

21 Dixon and Nicolls, 'Report' (Halifax, 1 July 1812).

22 Beaton Institute, MG 9/38/4, T.F. Addison, military secretary, Halifax, to Nepean, 20 July 1812.

23 Nicolls, 'Report' (Halifax, 1 January 1813).

24 Moogk, 'From Fortress Louisbourg,' 135.

25 Beaton Institute, MG 9/38/5/500, Swayne to Addison, 14 September 1813.

26 Beaton Institute, MG 1/D3, 1, Swayne to Bathurst, draft letter, c. 1814. According to James A. Crowdy, who was clerk of the Executive Council and registrar of records, 'the Point of Land at the head of the Town of Sydney' claimed by Gibbons 'never appears by the Books of my Office to have been leased or granted but is reserved for Government purposes.' Gibbons had received grants of eighteen town lots and one thousand acres of farm land.

He also held 651 acres of farm land and a town lot 'by Lease from the Crown.' See Beaton Institute, MG 9/38/1, Crowdy to Swayne, 12 May 1815. This Richard Gibbons was the son of Richard Gibbons (c. 1734–94), who had served as chief justice of Cape Breton and president of the Executive Council from 1785 to 1788.

27 Beaton Institute, MG 9/38/1, Swayne to Bathurst, 30 November 1813.

28 Ibid., MG 9/38/5, Swayne to Addison, 14 September 1813.

29 Nicolls, 'Report' (Halifax, 1 January 1813); Nicolls, 'Report' (1 January 1814). The Sydney garrison remained at this strength until its removal in 1854.

30 Nicolls, 'Report' (1 July 1813).

31 Beaton Institute, MG 9/38/5, Sherbrooke to Swayne, 22 December 1813. Sherbrooke was acting on instructions from Bathurst. See FLNHS, CO 218/13:55, Bathurst to Swayne, 10 July 1813.

32 Quoted in Morgan, 'Nepean,' 538. See also Morgan, 'Swayne,' 839.

33 Beaton Institute. MG 9/38/1, Swayne to Bathurst, 15 April 1813. In the same letter, Swayne also proposed to raise a fencible corps, largely from Cape Breton, 'for the Service of North America'; recruits would have been offered future land grants on the island. C.E. Leonard subsequently supported Swayne's claim that 'there was no Militia formed in this Colony previous to the arrival of M General Swayne.' See ibid., Leonard to Lieutenant Colonel Cooper, adjutant general, militia, 10 April 1816.

34 NSARM, RGH 11/2/343, *An Ordinance for the Establishment and Government of the Militia Forces, of the Island of Cape Breton* (1814).

35 'With Sword and Rifle,' *Morning Sun* (North Sydney), 1 October 1892.

36 Ibid.

37 Thomas Crawley (1757–1851) had served in the Royal Navy for several years, attaining the rank of captain. He arrived in Cape Breton in the 1780s and was appointed to the Executive Council in 1788. He was also an officer in the militia and a justice of the peace. He was appointed surveyor general in 1803 and superintendent of mines around the same time. He owned extensive land holdings in the Point Aconi area and in Westmount. His home, Point Amelia, was situated on the present site of the Canadian Coast Guard College.

38 The firing of six guns in quick succession was the alarm signal, which alerted all members of the militia in the immediate vicinity to repair to their respective headquarters armed and accoutred.

39 'With Sword and Rifle.'

40 Beaton Institute, MG 9/38/4, Swayne to Sir George Prevost, 25 March 1814.

41 Ibid., MG 9/38/5, Military secretary, Montreal, to Swayne, 28 May 1814; Armstrong to Swayne, 9 July 1814.

42 Ibid., Swayne to Bathurst, 30 November 1813. See also FLNHS, CO 218/13:60, Bathurst to Swayne, 6 March 1814.

43 Young, *Blockhouses*, 28. Richard Brown acknowledged that, while the men of the 104th Regiment stationed at Sydney were sometimes called upon to oppose imagined attacks by the dreaded privateers, 'fortunately, there was no real cause for alarm, as neither the French nor the Americans visited Sydney.' See Brown, *History*, 404.

44 John Joseph Greenough, *The Halifax Citadel 1825–60* (Ottawa 1977), 14; Kenneth Bourne, *Britain and the Balance of Power in North America, 1815–1908*, (Berkeley 1967), 33–44.

45 PANS, MG 12/RE 53, 'Report of the State of the Forts & Batteries and Field Ordnance Etc Etc Etc composing the Ordnance Establishment in the Provinces of Nova Scotia, New Brunswick and their Dependencies' (Halifax, 1 January 1816).

46 Ibid., 'Report' (1 July 1816).

47 Ibid., 'Report' (1 January 1817).

48 Brigadier General George Ainslie (1776–1839), who arrived as governor in 1816, supported this decision. He thought the people of Cape Breton were 'the refuse of 3 Kingdoms' and too poor and illiterate to support an assembly. He was a dubious authority, however. After a singularly undistinguished military career, he obtained the governorships of St Eustatius, Grenada and Dominica, from which he was recalled in the wake of his brutal suppression of an uprising. See also R.J. Morgan, 'George Robert Ainslie,' *Dictionary of Canadian Biography*, 7:10.

49 Smyth was a protégé of the Iron Duke, who had recommended him for his baronetcy four years earlier. Smyth had served as Wellington's chief engineer at Waterloo and had already headed a similar commission in the West Indies. See Greenough, *Halifax Citadel*, 16.

50 On the report and British military policy in British North America at this time, see C.P. Stacey, *Canada and the British Army, 1846–1871* (Toronto 1963), 14–15.

51 NSARM, MG 20, United Kingdom, Ordnance Department, *Report on Fortifications, 1825* (London 1825), 132–3. Also cited in Elizabeth Vincent, 'The British Garrison at Sydney, Cape Breton Island, 1785–1854' (Ottawa, 1984), 159.

52 Vincent, 'British Garrison,' 132; Stacey, *Canada*, 16.

53 Ibid., 134.

54 NSARM, MG 12/RE 34, Richard Creed, clerk of works, to Samuel Rigby, barrack master at Sydney, 24 May 1826.

55 Ibid., Creed to Rigby, 19 March 1828.

56 Ibid., Samuel Rigby to Nicolls, 18 April 1828. Rigby, son of Isaac Rigby, who
    had come to Nova Scotia as private secretary to the Duke of Kent, appears to
    have been at Sydney since at least 1796, when he was sent there as a master
    carpenter in the Royal Artillery. NSARM, MG 12, Ordnance Department
    letter-books, 1794–1800, p. 55. (mfm 12347), J. Hale to Clement Horton
    storekeeper, 8 October 1796. He was commissioned a lieutenant in 1811 and
    appointed barrack master in 1824. See NSARM, MG 100/213:39, Samuel
    Rigby file. Sheriff John Ferguson of Sydney wrote of Rigby in 1889 that 'he
    was undoubtedly the most popular officer ever known in Sydney – a gener-
    ous, kind, warm-hearted, hospitable gentleman – ever ready with an open
    hand, an open pocket and an open purse, to help the poor, to feed the hun-
    gry, and whenever in his power to relieve sickness, misery and want.' Quoted
    in MacKinnon, *Old Sydney*, 69–70. Rigby seems to have served as barrack mas-
    ter for some thirty years, to the 1850s.
57 T.C. Haliburton, *An Historical and Statistical Account of Nova Scotia* (Halifax
    1829), quoted in Tennyson, *Impressions*, 91. Haliburton did not actually visit
    Sydney, however, but relied on Herbert Crawley and John G. Marshall for his
    information on Cape Breton.
58 NSARM, MG 12/RE 53, 'Return of the Defences in the Provinces of Nova
    Scotia, New Brunswick and Prince Edwards Island' (Halifax, 13 August
    1834). This report is signed by Lieutenant Colonel Rice Jones, the com-
    manding royal engineer.
59 Chisholm, 'Victoria Park,' 23.
60 NSARM, MG 12/RE 47, Dundas to brigade major, 1 October 1834. A new
    fuel depot was built at Sydney in the autumn of 1835, apparently without the
    prior approval of the commissary at Halifax. See ibid., J.W. Keen, commissar-
    iat issuer at Sydney, to G.G. Slade, 3 November 1835; W. Hewetson to Rice
    Jones, 12 November 1835. With respect to the hospital, there is one report of
    surgery being performed around this time, c. 1830, by Dr Inglis of the Syd-
    ney garrison on a Mr MacVicar of Clark's Road for a strangulated hernia.
    MacVicar was sedated with opium and rum and strapped onto a barn door
    with ropes. The operation was reported to be a success. The marine hospital
    at Barrack Park was the only hospital in Cape Breton. Hanging on the walls
    of its convalescent ward were two mottoes: 'All Men Must Die' and 'Prepare
    to Meet Your Maker.' Newton, *Book of Days*. This building burned down on
    8 January 1959. Henry Dundas (1801–76), 3rd Viscount Melville, earned dis-
    tinction when serving with his regiment during the Upper Canadian rebel-
    lion in 1837.
61 Stacey, *Canada*, 16.
62 Cited in Newton, *Book of Days*. The problem of desertions was 'a constant vex-

ation to the military authorities in Canada, particularly at border stations.' In 1840–1 a special regiment, the Royal Canadian Rifles, was raised 'from solid old soldiers, many of them married, who were allowed to volunteer into it from other regiments' to man border posts in an effort to check this problem. Stacey, *Canada*, 20.

63 Bourne, *Britain*, 76. See also Stacey, *Canada*, 19.

64 NSARM, RE 51, Cunard to Russell, 13 March 1841.

65 Ibid., Jones to Captain O'Malaley, assistant military secretary, 9 July 1841.

66 Ibid., RE 21, commanding Royal Artillery, Halifax, to director general of artillery, 31 August 1843. The reference presumably is to the grist mill built at this time on the Sydney waterfront by James Anderson.

67 In 1841, for example, the commanding officer in the Windward and Leeward Islands reported that of 109 pieces of ordnance at St Lucia and Dominica, fifty were 'quite unserviceable.' See Lord Vivian, master general, to Sir Frederick Mulcaster, inspector general of fortifications, 25 February 1841, quoted in Bourne, *Britain*, 87.

68 Bourne, *Britain*, 88.

69 FLNHS, WO 1/543:39–41. Falkland to Gladstone, 2 March 1846, enclosing John Campbell (Guysborough) to Falkland, 26 January 1846.

70 Ibid., Lyttelton note to James Stephen, 17 March 1846. 'Much of the unpopularity of the Colonial Office can be attributed to its association with James Stephen, the stiff and upright under-secretary from 1836 to 1847, Charles Buller's "Mr Mother Country." Even Russell, whom Stephen admired, could privately joke that Stephen's great fault was that "instead of being Under-Secretary *for* the Colonies, he was Under-Secretary *against* the Colonies."' See Ged Martin, *Britain and the Origins of Canadian Confederation, 1837–67* (Vancouver 1995), 120.

71 FLNHS, WO 1/543:501–3, Cunard to H.T.L. Corry, secretary to the Admiralty, 11 March 1846.

72 Ibid., 57, Gladstone to Falkland, 3 April 1846.

73 Ibid., 576, Robert Smith, under-secretary of state for war, note, 28 March, initialled by Lyttelton and Gladstone, appended to ibid., 513, Corry to Stephen, 27 March 1846.

74 Ibid., 605–7, Richard Byham, secretary to the Board of Ordnance, to Stephen, 11 April 1846.

75 Ibid., 771–7, Calder to inspector general of fortifications, 28 October 1846. Two maps drawn of the harbour and the mines are included with Calder's report. Both show the sites of the old batteries, as well as Molesworth's proposed site for a new fortification on Chapel Point. A sketch of Sydney Harbour made by Edward Walker two years later shows these three sites as well.

See NSARM, Map Collection, REO S.4, Edward Walker, 'Sketch of the Harbour of Sydney,' 30 November 1848.

76 FLNHS, WO 1/543:701–2, 768–70, Byham to Stephen, 30 November 1846; Gladstone minute, 4 December 1846; Grey to Harvey, 14 December 1846.

77 NSARM, MG 12/RE 32, 'Return of Military Works and Posts in the Province of Nova Scotia' (Halifax, 29 January 1847).

78 Bourne, *Britain*, 173.

79 NSARM, MG 12/RE 32, William McLeod to Savage, 16 August 1849.

80 B.W.A. Sleigh, *Pine Forests and Hacmatack Clearings* (London 1853), reprinted in Tennyson, *Impressions*, 128–9.

81 Ibid., 130.

82 The service was dominated by a 'long, uninteresting sermon,' during which Sleigh claims that his thoughts 'were far more impressed with the wondrous works of God, and my senses were more prompted to religious contemplation' by viewing the countryside through an open door 'than in listening to the vague, soulless, vapid nonsense issuing from the pulpit, which consumed above an hour and a half in its delivery.' See ibid., 129.

83 Ibid., 130.

84 In the course of many introductions and much small talk, Sleigh (ibid., 132) met 'one old Provincial' who claimed to 'have travelled in my time pretty well over the world, seen a good deal in the different colonies, and I am satisfied, after all, there's no place like Sydney.' It transpired that his travels had taken him around the Maritime colonies. His daughters, whom he thought 'very fashionable,' Sleigh described as 'two huge, fat ungraceful women, who playfully considered themselves "children of nature." Vulgar specimens, I must confess.' The failure to impress worked both ways. Sydney's sheriff John Ferguson later recalled the wife of a military officer stationed in the town in 1849 who was 'passably fair, and ruddy; of medium size; very aristocratic, looking down with unfeigned disdain on such of our Sydney "quality" as presumed to be thought ladies. This dainty gentlewoman was a walking perfumer's shop, using musk and other mysterious cosmetics to a most offensive extent. The church, the shop, the market, and even the public highway, felt and acknowledged her presence.' Quoted in MacKinnon, *Old Sydney*, 70–1.

85 Sleigh, *Pine Forests*, 133.

86 Ibid., 134.

87 Ibid., 135.

88 MacKinnon, *Old Sydney*, 29.

89 Ibid., 118. It is on view today in St Patrick's Museum in Sydney.

90 Bourne, *Britain*, 186.

91 Stacey, *Canada*, 90–1.

92 NSARM, MG 12/RE 38, Rigby to Savage, 22 April 1853.

93 Ibid., Rigby to Savage, 11 April 1853, 23 June 1854. See also NSARM, MG 12/RE 50:237–8, Stotherd to Rigby, 27 July 1854; MG 12/RE 59:231, Stotherd to Rigby, 9 September 1854; MG 12/RE 50:234–5, Stotherd to Rigby, 22 June 1855.

94 At the same time, there were nearly fifteen hundred troops in Bermuda and the Bahamas and more than two thousand in each of the West Indies and the Windward and Leeward Islands commands. British forces in North America remained above four thousand until the end of the decade. Bourne, *Britain*, 207. Sir William Eyre (1805–59) served with the 73rd Regiment in Canada, Argentina, and South Africa, and with the 3rd Division, which he rose to command, in the Crimean war. He was knighted in 1855 and given the command of British forces in Canada in 1856. He returned to Britain in failing health in 1859.

95 NSARM, MG 12, C series, 443:78, Rigby to Stotherd, 23 August 1856.

96 NSARM, MG 12/RE 57:51, Douglas G. Rigby to War Office, 1 September 1856. See also Samuel Rigby to Stotherd, 23 August 1856. Douglas Rigby (1813–95) was the first postmaster on the northside, the post office being in his home on Shore Road in Sydney Mines.

97 NSARM, MG 12, C series, 1443/79, Samuel Rigby to Stotherd, 2 September 1856.

98 Rigby to Stotherd, 23 August 1856.

99 Rigby to Stotherd, 2 September 1856.

100 Ibid.

101 NSARM, MG 12/RE 38:113, Lease signed by Donald McDonald, 2 March 1857.

102 Ibid., 53–4, Bowles to Stotherd, 13 November 1856.

103 Ibid., 59–60, Draft agreement signed by Stotherd, 26 November 1856. Ibid., 61, Bowles to Stotherd, 1 December 1856, telegram; ibid., 57–8. Samuel Rigby to Stotherd, 2 December 1856; ibid., 87, Samuel Rigby to Herbert Pringle, storekeeper, 19 January 1857.

104 Ibid., 117, Lieutenant Colonel Thomas Le Marchant, military secretary, to Stotherd, 12 March 1857. Thomas Le Marchant was the brother of Major General Sir John Gaspard Le Marchant, lieutenant-governor and general officer commanding in Nova Scotia. See also ibid., 157, B. Hawes to Major General Le Marchant, 11 April 1857; ibid., 163–4. Wilford Brett, acting assistant military secretary, Halifax, to Stotherd, 10 May 1857. Samuel Rigby, 'A Report of Proceeds of the War Department Lands, Brought to the Public Account, During the Year Ending 31st March 1857, at Sydney, Cape Breton, Pursuant to the Honorable Board's General Order of 5th Decem-

ber 1848' (1 April 1857), describes the land leased by Bowles as 'at the Sydney Mines lot' but this appears to be an error. See ibid., RE 38:119.

105 Ibid., 226–8.

106 Ibid., 281–3, Bowles to Stotherd, 1 October 1857; Ibid., 287–8, Rigby to Stotherd, 7 October 1857.

107 Ibid., 289–91, Bowles to Stotherd, 15 October 1857.

108 Ibid., 313–4, Stotherd to Rigby, 25 November 1857.

109 Ibid., 317, Rigby to Stotherd, 30 November 1857.

110 Ibid., 577, 580, Stotherd to Henry Ince, land commissioner, 18 June 1858.

111 Ibid., 581–2, Leonard to Ince, 19 July 1858.

112 The lands at Sydney were leased by Edmund Outram, who obtained the barrack square with three buildings and the commissariat store, by Charles Crewe Read, who obtained the guardhouse, engine house, and hospital, and by Donald McLean (Lot no. 1), Philip Ormand (Lot no. 2), Donald MacQueen (Lot no. 3), Alexander McInnes (Lot no. 4), and W.G. Ouseley (Lot no. 5). Ibid., 574–6, Ince to Colonel Fordyce, quartermaster general, 26 July 1858. P.H. Clarke, the auctioneer, when forwarding his account to Stotherd, said that after deducting 'the expences from the amount of the grass sold, the nett proceeds' amounted to £13.13.4, which was considerably less than the amount that was claimed by Ince. Ibid., 465, Clarke to Stotherd, 27 July 1858.

113 Ibid., 467, Report, 'Leased at Public Auction the Following Lots of Military Ground and Buildings at Sydney Cape Breton on 22nd July 1858 Agreeable to Advertisement and Hand Bills,' by P.H. Clarke, Sydney, 22 July 1858; Clarke to Stotherd, 27 July 1858.

114 Dr William McK. McLeod, *Memoirs* (Sydney n.d.), 13. In 1910 the second annual Cape Breton Farmers' Association agricultural fair was held in temporary buildings at Barrack Park, since renamed Victoria Park. Although the first fair had been held at North Sydney, it would remain in Sydney, though not at Victoria Park, until it returned to North Sydney in 1930.

115 Quoted in Michael Wilkshire, ed., *A Gentleman in the Outports: Gobineau and Newfoundland* (Ottawa 1993), 35.

116 Richard Uniacke, quoted in Tennyson, *Impressions*, 151. See also Brian Tennyson, 'Economic Nationalism and Confederation: A Case Study in Cape Breton,' *Acadiensis* 2 (1972), 39–53.

117 Tennyson, *Impressions*, 149.

118 Quoted in Wilkshire, *A Gentleman*, 49.

119 NSARM, MG 1/151:305, Archibald to Richard Brown Jr, 14 May 1860.

120 Quoted in Wilkshire, *A Gentleman*, 49–50.

121 *Cape Breton News*, 6 July 1861, quoted in Tennyson, *Impressions*, 139. The

men may have enjoyed themselves in Sydney but they evidently did not enjoy serving on *St George.* Lord Palmerston, the British prime minister, claimed that seventy of them had deserted the battleship during its recent visit to Halifax. Cited in Bourne, *Britain,* 215n.

3: Preparing for War, 1859–1867

1 *Report of Committee on Expense of Military Defences in the Colonies* (London 1860), cited in Stacey, *Canada,* 112.
2 Ibid., 113. There was another view, especially strong in the Colonial Office, that was more sensitive to the colonial perspective and the difficulties involved with putting sweeping principles into practice. See Bruce Knox, 'The Concept of Empire in the Mid-Nineteenth Century: Idea in the Colonial Defence Inquiries of 1859–61,' *Journal of Imperial and Commonwealth History* 15 (May 1987), 243–63.
3 Stacey, *Canada,* 132–6. The Macdonald–Sicotte government did succeed in amending the 1859 Militia Act to authorize the raising of ten thousand volunteers and allocating $250,000 for defence, compared to the thirty thousand volunteers and $500,000 proposed by the Cartier–Macdonald government.
4 Quoted in Moogk, 'From Fortress Louisbourg,' 136.
5 Mulgrave to Sir Edward Bulwer-Lytton, 20 January 1859, quoted in *Journals and Proceedings of the House of Assembly of the Province of Nova Scotia, Session 1860* (Halifax 1860), 173. Bulwer-Lytton (1831–91) was a popular poet and novelist who also pursued a successful diplomatic and political career. In addition to serving as British minister at Lisbon, viceroy of India, and ambassador at Paris, he was a member of Parliament, and colonial secretary from 1858 to 1859. One commentator said of his poetry that 'Browning has never been reproduced so well, but reproduction it is.' See *Dictionary of National Biography* (Oxford 1917), 12:387.
6 Marcus Cunliffe, *Soldiers and Civilians: The Martial Spirit in America, 1775–1865* (New York and London 1968), chap. seven; Stacey, *Canada,* 91–4, 101–2; Elinor Kyte Senior, *Roots of the Canadian Army: Montreal District, 1846–1870* (Montreal 1981), 11–18.
7 Hugh Cunningham, *The Volunteer Force: A Social and Political History, 1859–1908* (Hamden 1975), 5–15.
8 NA, CO 217/225:191–3, Williams to commander in chief, 14 May 1859. See also J.M. Hitsman, *Safeguarding Canada, 1763–1871* (Toronto 1968), 163, and David Facey-Crowther, *The New Brunswick Militia, 1787–1867* (n.p. 1990), 88.
9 NA, CO 217/225:247, Sir Samuel Cunard to Newcastle, 26 July 1859. See also

the digest of Williams's report in NA, CO 217/227:598–600, Elliot minute, 2 June 1860. Frederick Elliot (1825–68) was a rare Colonial Office official who had visited the colonies when he was secretary to the Gosford Commission in the 1830s. He supported Maritime union but opposed Confederation. Martin, *Confederation*, 110. Richard Brown (1805–82) immigrated to Cape Breton in 1827 to manage the GMA operations. He retired in 1864 and was succeeded by his son, also named Richard.

10 NSARM, MG 12, C series, 1650:122–3, Fordyce to Nelson, 8 September 1859; ibid., 1436:162–2a, Nelson to Colonel Chapman, deputy adjutant general, 24 July 1861. Nelson has been described as 'in many ways the most singular Commanding Royal Engineer ever to serve in Halifax. He was a specimen of that peculiarly Victorian type – the insatiably curious amateur scientist. Humourless, righteous and pedantic,' he had written and illustrated 'the definitive study of Bermudan geology,' and was one of the editors of *The Aide-Memoire to the Military Sciences*, 'the standard dictionary on the subject for all his fellow military engineers.' See Greenough, *Halifax Citadel*, 119.

11 NSARM, MG12, C series, 1650:122–3, Fordyce to Nelson, 8 September 1859.

12 *Cape Breton News*, 4 August 1860. The site of the new battery was known as Chapel Point because a Roman Catholic log church and cemetery had been built there by the French as part of a settlement known as French Village. Chirgwin, 'Harbour Forts,' claims that the church foundation was built of cut stone brought out from France and that when Immaculate Conception Church was being built in Sydney Mines, the priest, a Mr MacKinnon, used the foundation stones from the log church in the new structure. Elva Jackson, in *Windows on the Past* (Windsor 1974), 87, says the first Catholic church was built in 1844–5 on what became known as Convent Street, opposite Stella Maris residence, near the top of the hill. It was constructed under the direction of the Reverend James Drummond, the second priest at Sydney, who also had charge of the parishes of North Sydney, Sydney Mines, Florence, and Bras d'Or.

13 NA, CO 217/230:341ff, Mulgrave to Newcastle, 10 July 1862, forwarding R. Bligh Sinclair, 'Abstract A. Effective and Non Effective Return of Nova Scotia Volunteers for the Year June 1862.' This return gives 19 July 1859 as the date of the formation of the 2nd Sydney Mines Volunteers and 18 July 1860 as the date of the formation of the 1st Sydney Mines Volunteers. All other evidence, including that cited in the following note, makes clear that the latter date is incorrect and should be 18 July 1859.

14 Mulgrave to Newcastle, 22 September 1859, quoted in *Journals and Proceedings*, 1860, 179.

15 Newcastle to Mulgrave, 18 November 1859, with enclosures, cited in ibid.,

1860: 180–2. See also NA, CO 217/224:322–3, Mulgrave to Newcastle, 29 December 1859; 227:602–5, Jadis to Elliot, 29 May 1860.

16 Ibid., 224:319–34, Mulgrave to Newcastle, 29 December 1859.

17 Ibid., 334, Chichester Fortescue minute, 14 January 1860. Fortescue (1823–98) was parliamentary under-secretary at the Colonial Office.

18 Newcastle to Mulgrave, 30 June 1858; Mulgrave to Newcastle, 20 July 1859; Mulgrave to Newcastle, 22 September 1859 and 2 November 1859, in *Journals and Proceedings*, 1860, 76–9.

19 NA, CO 217/227:539–41, Trollope to secretary of state for war, 12 June 1860, enclosing Sinclair, volunteers return for 16 April 1860. Sinclair, 'Abstract A,' gives the dates of organization. The name of the Hawksbury Rifles was spelled without the 'e' that appears in the later name of the community, Port Hawkesbury. At this time, Port Hawkesbury was still called Ship Harbour.

20 NSARM, MG 1/151:305, Brown Papers, Archibald to Richard Brown Jr, 14 May 1860.

21 Ibid., 310, Archibald to Richard Brown Jr, 6 March 1861. See also ibid., 311, Archibald to Richard Brown Jr, 8 May 1861.

22 See, for example, NA, CO 217/224:242–3, Secretary, GMA, to Herman Merivale, 25 October 1859. The company's directors subsequently agreed that batteries were less urgently needed at Pictou because of the inland location of the mines there. See ibid., 229:235–6, Cunard to Fortescue, 21 March 1861.

23 Régis Courtemanche, *No Need of Glory: The British Navy in American Waters, 1860–1864* (Annapolis 1977), 46. As was seen in the previous chapter, Gobineau also commented on the strong French presence at Sydney. Milne would have been even more concerned if he had known that the director of naval construction had had a cargo of Sydney coal shipped to Brest in 1860 for trial in French warships. The director subsequently reported to the minister of marine that 'in steam power it was little inferior to the Cardiff and quite equal to the Newcastle coal.' Quoted in Brown, *Coal Trade*, 81.

24 NA, CO 217/227:591–2, Cunard to Elliot, 21 May 1860. The Americans had always worried Cunard more than the French.

25 Ibid., 598–600, Elliot minute, 2 June 1860. John Robert Godley (1814–61) was an Irish-born colonial reformer who served as assistant under-secretary at the War Office from 1852 until his death.

26 Ibid., 601, Newcastle minute, 5 July 1860.

27 Bain, 'Sydney Mines,' 21. See also W.L. Chirgwin, 'The Sydney Mines Volunteer Rifles,' *Cape Breton Post*, 13 June 1959. The editor of the *Cape Breton News* suggested that the Sydney Mines unit was deliberately honoured as 'the first in the Province to receive their Prince' because it had been 'the first organi-

zation in the Province, in response to the Lieutenant Governor's suggestion to form Volunteer Corps.' See *Cape Breton News*, 4 August 1860.

28 The officers of the Sydney Mines Volunteers were Richard Brown (lieutenant colonel), Robert Bridge (captain, 1st company), D.G. Rigby (1st lieutenant), Edward Robson (2nd lieutenant), T.E. Jeans, Jr (2nd lieutenant), C.B. Brown (adjutant), Yorke Barrington (captain, 2nd Company), J. Barrington (1st lieutenant), W. McQueen (2nd lieutenant), R.H. Brown (2nd lieutenant), H.W. Archibald (2nd lieutenant), and T.E. Jeans (surgeon). See *Cape Breton News*, 4 August 1860.

29 Ibid.

30 Bourne, *Britain*, 211.

31 FLNHS, CO 218/36:203, Newcastle to Mulgrave, 1 April 1861, confidential.

32 NA, CO 217/229:171–2, Sir Edward Lugard to Elliot, 13 May 1861.

33 NSARM, MG 12, C series, 435:133–6, Nelson to J.F. Burgoyne, inspector general of fortifications, 24 May 1861. Nelson also thought that the Albion mines at Pictou should be included in the defence plan because their coal 'is in far greater abundance, more accessible, of a superior quality, and equally open to easy attack from Merigomish harbor.'

34 Ibid.

35 Courtemanche, *No Need of Glory*, chap. 2.

36 NA, CO 217/229:167–8, Fortescue to Sir Samuel Cunard, 19 March 1861, and an unsigned minute referring to a personal meeting with Cunard, undated; ibid., 235–6, Cunard to Fortescue, 21 March 1861.

37 Ibid., 179–80, Lugard to Elliot, 25 May 1861; NSARM, MG 12, C series, 1650:240, William Cunard to Nelson, 1 May 1861. See also ibid., 436:162–2a, Nelson to Chapman, 24 July 1861.

38 NA, CO 217/229:180, 184–5, Blackwood to Elliot, 29 May 1861.

39 Ibid., 10, Milne to Secretary of Admiralty, 23 April 1861.

40 Ibid., 181–3, Elliot to Lugard, 20 June 1861. The reference in another part of this letter to Admiral Milne's report of 23 April 1861 about French designs on Sydney was inserted in Newcastle's own hand.

41 Ibid., 186–7, unsigned undated minute in Newcastle's hand. See also ibid., 181, Newcastle undated minute on Elliot to under-secretary, War Office, 20 June 1861.

42 NSARM, RG 1/105/53:259–61, Lugard to Elliot, 16 July 1861.

43 NA, CO 217/229:180, 191–2, Lugard to Elliot, 16 July 1861; Elliot to Fortescue, 18 July 1861. See also NSARM, RG 1/105/53:262–5 (mfm 15258), Elliot to Lugard, 29 July 1861; ibid., 266–7, Lugard to Elliot, 8 August 1861; NA, CO 217/229:209, Rogers to Cunard, 16 August 1861; ibid., 215, Fortescue to Cunard, 2 September 1861.

44 NSARM, MG 12, C series, 1650:272–3, William Cunard to Nelson, 27 June 1861; RG 1/105/53:268–70 (mfm 15258), Frederic Rogers to Samuel Cunard, 16 August 1862; ibid., 53:256–8, Cunard to Rogers, 20 August 1861; ibid., 53:254–5, Newcastle to Mulgrave, 21 August 1861; ibid., 55:285–6 (mfm 15258), Newcastle to Mulgrave, 1 September 1862.

45 Quoted in Stacey, *Canada*, 113–14.

46 For a summary, see Donald C. Gordon, *The Dominion Partnership in Imperial Defence* (Baltimore 1965), 12–23.

47 Stacey, *Canada*, 123–4.

48 Quoted in ibid., 127–8.

49 Ibid., 127.

50 Lieutenant Colonel Spencer Westmacott, who succeeded Nelson as the commanding royal engineer at Halifax, agreed with the Colonial Office point of view. He told Sir John Burgoyne, the inspector general of fortifications, that 'apart from any Provincial Question, Sydney Harbour as a Coal Port has a close reference to Halifax Harbour in its important supply of Coal for the use of HM Navy on the N American Station.' He thought they should send 'a further Armament of 68 pd guns' because the old thirty-two-pounders lacked the range needed to cover the mouth of Sydney harbour. NSARM, MG 12, C series, 1436:266–7, Westmacott to Burgoyne, 4 September 1862.

51 These committees included the governor, the commanding officer, the commanding royal engineer, and the senior commissariat officer. NSARM, RG 1/105/42:20304, Newcastle to Mulgrave, 4 July 1861, enclosing Herbert to officer commanding his majesty's troops, June 1861 (circular).

52 Ibid., 51:242–8, Trollope to general commander in charge, 24 June 1861; Newcastle to Mulgrave, 20 August 1861.

53 See, for example, NA, RG 8, C series, 1431:55, Hastings Doyle minute [July 1863], which refers to Brown's 'irreproachable character.'

54 NSARM, MG 12, C series, 1/1436:177–8, Westmacott to Burgoyne, 15 October 1861. NA, RG 8, C series, 1430:283–4, Westmacott to acting military secretary, 18 August 1862.

55 For a detailed discussion, see Brian Jenkins, *Britain and the War for the Union* (Montreal and Kingston 1974), vol. 1, chapters 7–9.

56 The British North American provinces, with Joseph Howe, premier of Nova Scotia, playing a prominent role, took this opportunity to press the imperial government to underwrite the completion of the railway from Rivière-du-Loup to an Atlantic port.

57 Bourne, *Britain*, 257–8.

58 Quoted in Stacey, *Canada*, 129. See also Bourne, *Britain*, 257–8.

59 Stacey, *Canada*, 130.

60 *Report of the Defence Committee*, 6 August 1862, cited in Bourne, *Britain*, 260–1.

61 NA, RG 8, C series, 1671:12–18, Doyle to secretary of state for war, 28 November 1861. See Ronald H. McDonald, 'The Public Career of Major-General Sir Hastings Doyle, 1861–1873' (unpublished MA thesis, Dalhousie University, 1969), 1–20, for a full discussion of Doyle's role in the reorganization of the Nova Scotia militia.

62 NA, CO 217/230:67–76, Mulgrave to Newcastle, 19 March 1862; the adjutant general of militia's report for 1862, Nova Scotia, House of Assembly, *Journals and Proceedings*, 1863, app. 4; and Joseph Plimsoll Edwards, 'The Militia of Nova Scotia, 1749–1867,' *Collections of the Nova Scotia Historical Society* 17 (1913), 99–100.

63 Among the earliest steps in training officers was a program at Halifax in the spring of 1862. Although most of the candidates were from the Halifax–Dartmouth area, there were three from Cape Breton, including one member of the House of Assembly, William Ross (1825–1912), the Liberal member for Victoria County from 1859 to 1867. Elected to the House of Commons in 1867, he served as minister of militia in 1873 and 1874, when he founded the Royal Military College at Kingston. NA, CO 217/230:348, R. Bligh Sinclair, 'Abstract B Metropolitan and County of Halifax Regiments of Militia. Return of Militia Officers and Gentlemen Cadets attending Drill from March 10th to May 3rd Halifax, NS, 1862.'

64 NA, CO 217/230:70, Mulgrave to Newcastle, 19 March 1862.

65 NSARM, MG 12, C series, 651:8–9, Nugent, assistant quartermaster general, Halifax, to Westmacott, 21 August 1862. For this and the following two paragraphs, see the printed correspondence in Nova Scotia, Legislative Council, *Journals and Proceedings* (Halifax), 1864, app 39. See also NA, National Map Collection, 0034614, 'Plan of Chapel Point Battery,' 26 February 1863.

66 NSARM, MG 12, C series, 1430:292, Westmacott to acting military secretary, 13 September 1862.

67 Ibid., 287–8, Westmacott memorandum, 2 September 1862, forwarded to Collings. Chirgwin claimed that both the old Fort Dundas blockhouse and the one built by the Duke of Kent were burned down by the engineers sometime in 1863. Brown, however, claimed that Fort Dundas was still standing in 1871. Chirgwin, 'Harbour Forts'; Brown, *Coal Fields*, 63; NA, RG 8, C series, 1430:306, Westmacott to acting military secretary, 27 October 1862.

68 NSARM, MG 12, C series, 1562:82–5, Collings to Westmacott, 8 September 1862. Collings received a shipment of thirty picks, thirty shovels, twelve wheelbarrows, a spirit level, a mason's level, four crowbars, two handsaws, two axes, and a pot and ladle for melting lead. See ibid., 1652:110, Collings

note, 22 September 1862; NA, RG 8, C series, 1430:294, Westmacott to
Cunard, 18 September 1862, and minutes.

69 NA, RG 8, C series, 1430:295, Westmacott to acting military secretary, 19 September 1862. The problem was aggravated when, despite Westmacott's promise to send regular supplies of cash to pay the workmen, the money failed to arrive. On the 16th Collings complained to Westmacott that 'no money whatever is in my hands for the payment of men and materials ... The total amount of payments coming due next Saturday is about £40. I would beg to suggest that the amount be forwarded in 2s pieces by the mail steamer Osprey, which will arrive at Sydney next Saturday morning. The money is most urgently required.' Westmacott authorized him to borrow £50 from Richard Brown so that he could pay his accounts while awaiting transfers of cash from Halifax, a procedure that was repeated on subsequent occasions. Archibald & Co., the North Sydney ship agent for the mail steamer *Osprey*, took on this unofficial banking role in November. See NSARM, MG 12, C series, 1652:89–90, Collings to Westmacott, 16 September 1862. See also ibid., 104, 106, 108–9, Collings notes, 24 September 1862, 6 October 1862, 4, 20 November 1862.

70 Ibid., 98–101, Collings to Westmacott, 24 September 1862; NA, National Map Collection, 0034614, 'Plan of Chapel Point Battery,' 26 February 1863.

71 NA, RG 8, C series, 1430:283–4, Westmacott to acting military secretary, 18 August 1862; Doyle to Milne, 6 June 1863, quoted in Nova Scotia, House of Assembly, *Journals and Proceedings*, 1864.

72 NA, RG 8, C series, 1431:100–1, Westmacott to Doyle, 31 October 1863. This was the ultimate version of various previous recommendations, for which see, for example, NSARM, RE 8/1436:308–9, Westmacott to Burgoyne, 19 March 1863.

73 NA, RG 8, C series, 1653A:306, 312, Royal Engineers estimates, Nova Scotia, 1863–4. These show the original estimate of £1,000 for Chapel Point stroked out and replaced by £250. See also ibid., 1431:100–1, Westmacott to acting military secretary, 17 July 1863; Doyle to Milne, 6 June 1863, quoted in *Journals and Proceedings*, 1864.

74 NSARM, MG 12, C series, 1653:93–5, Collings to Westmacott, 23 September 1862; ibid., 130–1, Richard Brown to Westmacott, 4 June 1863.

75 Ibid., 132–3, Brown to Westmacott, 23 June 1863.

76 Ibid., 134–6.

77 NA, RG 8, C series, 1431:55, Westmacott to acting military secretary, 17 July 1863, with Doyle's undated minute; NSARM, MG12, C series, 1563:174–8, Hannon to Westmacott, 14 October 1863; ibid., 179, same to same, 13 November 1863; ibid., 158, Brown to Westmacott, 20 October 1863.

78 Foord to Fortescue, 1 September 1863, in Nova Scotia, House of Assembly, *Journals and Proceedings*, 1864, app. 39.
79 NSARM, MG 12, C series, 1563:173, Brown to Westmacott, 13 November 1863. According to Moogk, 'From Fortress Louisbourg,' 127, the old block-house on Peck's Head was also torn down in 1863.
80 The correspondence is printed in Nova Scotia, House of Assembly, *Journals and Proceedings*, 1864, app. 39 and 61.
81 NSARM, MG 12, C series, 1563: 216–17, Collings to Westmacott, 13 June 1864.
82 NA, RG 8, 1653A:363, Westmacott, Royal Engineers estimates for 1864–5, 4 January 1864, which includes a plan of the same date for the block-house.
83 NSARM, MG 12, C series, 1563: 234–6, MacLean to Westmacott, 23 August 1864.
84 Ibid., 278, 283, Brown to Westmacott, 6 December 1864; Brown to Westmacott, 20 December 1864.
85 Brown to J.B. Foord, 14 August 1863, printed in Nova Scotia, House of Assembly, *Journals and Proceedings*, 1864, app. 39.
86 NA, RG 8, C series, 1431:150, 168, 187, 196, Westmacott correspondence, 9 June–26 October 1864; ibid., 1671:580, Westmacott, 'Report on the Lower Provinces British North America,' 1 May 1865: NSARM, Cambridge Library MSS, vol. 3, A4:652–3, Nova Scotia Militia letter-book, 1864–1866, Sinclair to Read, 12 January 1866.
87 Nova Scotia, House of Assembly, *Journals and Proceedings*, 1865, app. 5: 10, 22–3.
88 See, for example, the comments by the adjutant general of the militia in ibid., 1864, app. 7: 16–18, and in ibid., 1865, app. 5: 3–5, 22.
89 Ibid., 10; *The Army List of the Local Forces of Nova Scotia ... January 1866* (Halifax 1866), 147.
90 Edwards, 'Militia,' 102–3; *Journals and Proceedings*, 1864, app. 7.
91 See Robin Winks, *Canada and the United States: The Civil War Years* (Baltimore 1960), chap. 12 and 14 for the most detailed and entertaining account of these events.
92 Martin, *Britain*, 244; W.F.D. Jervois, *Report on the Defence of Canada and of the British Naval Stations in the North Atlantic*, WO 33/35, Confidential Print, January 1865, cited in Bourne, *Britain*, 277–8.
93 Bourne, *Britain*, 285.
94 On the politics of this period and the role of the defence crisis in the achievement of Confederation, see Peter B. Waite, *The Life and Times of Confederation* (Toronto 1962), Kenneth G. Pryke, *Nova Scotia and Confederation* (Toronto 1979), Philip A. Buckner, 'The 1860s: An End and a Beginning,' in

Philip A. Buckner and John G. Reid, eds., *The Atlantic Region to Confederation: A History* (Toronto 1994), and Martin, *Britain*. There is some evidence to suggest that imperial officials and military commanders in the region somewhat exaggerated the gravity of the crisis to help assure the result. See McDonald, 'Doyle,' 61–2.

95 Quoted in James M. Cameron, 'Fenian Times in Nova Scotia,' *Collections of the Nova Scotia Historical Society* 37 (1970), 135.

96 Adjutant general of militia report, 12 December 1866, *Journal 1867*, app. 3, 18–21.

97 R. Bligh Sinclair, 'Militia. Adjutant General's Report 1867, Nova Scotia,' 31 December 1867, 13, 24, copy at Royal Canadian Military Institute, Toronto.

98 NA, RG 9, IIA1/12/1776, Read to deputy adjutant general, Halifax, 16 November 1869.

99 Cape Breton's first golf course was established there in 1895 by Walter Crowe, the Rev. E.B. Rankin, J.J. Hearn, and F.I. Stewart. It moved to Lingan in 1908 because of competition for space with baseball and cricket teams. Claribel Gesner, *Cape Breton Vignettes* (Windsor, NS 1974), 5–7.

100 On British military policy and activities concerning both Canadian coasts, see C.S. Mackinnon, 'The Imperial Fortresses in Canada: Halifax and Esquimalt, 1871–1906' (unpublished PhD thesis, University of Toronto 1965), a superb piece of scholarship that still commands the field despite the large number of books and articles on Canada and imperial defence that have since appeared.

101 On the relationship between Canadian politicians and the militia, see Desmond Morton, *Ministers and Generals: Politics and the Canadian Militia, 1868–1914* (Toronto 1970). Sir Wilfrid Laurier reportedly told Lord Dundonald at the turn of the century that he 'must not take the militia too seriously, for though it is useful for suppressing internal disturbances, it will not be required for the defence of the country, as the Monroe doctrine protects us from enemy aggression.' Quoted in Don Macgillivray, 'Military Aid to the Civil Power: The Cape Breton Experience in the 1920s,' *Acadiensis* (spring 1974), 45.

4: Coal and Steel, 1867–1914

1 Canada, Department of Militia and Defence, *Report on the State of the Militia for the Year 1868* (Ottawa 1869), 72, 79.

2 Ibid., *1870* (Ottawa 1871), 212–3; *The Militia List of the Dominion of Canada ... 1870* (Ottawa 1870), 74–7; ibid., *1873* (Ottawa 1873), 79–80. The officers were Captain Norman MacRae (1st Company, Middle River), Captain

Charles MacRae (2nd Company, Middle River), Captain J.S. MacNeil (3rd Company, Grand Narrows), Captain D.S. MacRae (4th Company, Baddeck), and Captain William Hill (5th Company, Sydney).

3 W.L. Chirgwin, 'The 94th Argyll Highland Regiment,' *Cape Breton Post,* undated clipping [1958].

4 Roger Sarty, 'Silent Sentry: A Military and Political History of Canadian Coast Defence, 1860–1945' (unpublished PhD thesis, University of Toronto, 1983), 48–51. On Selby-Smyth's appointment and service in Canada, see Morton, *Ministers,* chap. 1 and 2.

5 Roger Sarty, *Coast Artillery, 1815–1914* (Bloomfield 1988), 11–26.

6 Colin MacKinnon, 'Old and New Sydney; Notes by Mr M'Kinnon,' *Sydney Daily Post,* 21 March 1919. The International Railway ran from Bridgeport Mines to the International Pier, which then extended into Sydney Harbour from the Esplanade, across from the later site of the YMCA. Colin MacKinnon worked at the pier, and from 1891 to 1893 was mayor of Sydney.

7 NA, RG 9, IIA1/611/04630, Admiralty to Colonial Office, 10 June 1878.

8 Morton, *Ministers,* 43. Despite its appeal to Britain for assistance, the government was not sufficiently concerned to agree to contribute troops to an imperial reserve force proposed at this time. See Adrian Preston, 'Canada and the Russian Crisis of 1878: A Proposed Contingent for Imperial Defence,' *Dalhousie Review* 48 (1968–9), 185–99.

9 Parks Canada, CAB 7-1, Colonial Office Misc. 35F, Milne to Colonial Office, 18 May 1878, enclosing 'Report on Defences of the Principal Canadian Atlantic Ports,' May 1878.

10 Ibid.

11 Mackenzie to Lord Dufferin, 11 June 1878; Dufferin to Sir Michael Hicks Beach, colonial secretary, n.d., both cited in Morton, *Ministers,* 43.

12 NA, RG 9, IIA1/611/04630, Laurie to adjutant general, 14 June 1878. The minister was A.G. Jones (1824–1906), a Halifax businessman who had commanded the Halifax garrison artillery militia. He served in Parliament for many years, (1867–72, 1874–8, and 1887–91), and was lieutenant-governor of Nova Scotia from 1900 until his death.

13 Parks Canada, CO 885/4, Colonial Office Misc. E, February 1879, Selby-Smyth to Mackenzie, 8 June 1878.

14 Ibid.

15 Sarty, 'Silent Sentry,' 48–51; Parks Canada, CAB 7-1, Colonial Office Misc. 35E, February 1879, Selby-Smyth, memorandum, 2 July 1878.

16 Parks Canada, CO 885/4, Colonial Office Misc. E, February 1879, Simmons and Barkly, 'Report,' 10 August 1878. See also Sarty, 'Silent Sentry,' 53–4;

ibid., 55–7, on Selby-Smyth's ultimately unproductive efforts to organize artillery manufacturing and a naval reserve for coastal defence.

17 Quoted in Canada, Department of Militia and Defence, *Report on the State of the Militia for the Year 1878* (Ottawa 1879), xxvi.

18 One may have been the fact that the prime minister, Sir John A. Macdonald, represented Victoria in the House of Commons from 1878 to 1882.

19 Beaton Institute, MG 9/23, William MacDonald Papers, Hugh MacLeod to William MacDonald, 22 October 1878, private; Crewe Read to MacDonald, 28 October 1878, private and confidential. William MacDonald (1837–1916) was a Glace Bay merchant and postmaster. He was Conservative member of Parliament for Cape Breton from 1872 to 1884, when he was appointed to the Senate. Although the Conservatives had been returned to office in the 1878 federal election, Crewe Read was still waiting for his appointment four years later. See ibid., Crewe Read to MacDonald, 5 April 1882.

20 Sarty, 'Silent Sentry,' 58–91.

21 Jackson, *Windows*, 28. For a valuable account of the rise and fall of the shipping industry in Sydney Harbour during the nineteenth century and its relationship to the coal industry, see Rosemary Langhout, 'Alternative Opportunities: The Development of Shipping at Sydney Harbour 1842–1889,' in Donovan, *Cape Breton at 200*, 53–69.

22 NA, RG 7, G21/76/165/4c, Commerell to secretary of Admiralty, 27 July 1885, copy enclosed with Commerell to Lord Lansdowne, 13 August 1885.

23 See NA, RG 9, IIA1/611/A3959 and /A7564.

24 Ibid., A3959, Middleton memorandum, 29 November 1886.

25 W.L. Chirgwin, 'The 94th Argyll Highland Regiment,' *Cape Breton Post*, undated clipping [1958]

26 *Report on the State of the Militia for the Year 1874* (Ottawa 1874), 49, quoted in Alex Morrison and Ted Slaney, *The Breed of Manly Men: The History of the Cape Breton Highlanders* (Toronto 1994), 52–3.

27 *Report on the State of the Militia for the Year 1886* (Ottawa 1886), 215. It is possible that this particular name was adopted because of the influence of Charles Campbell, the Conservative member of Parliament for Victoria County, who played an active role in organizing the battalion. He had formerly served in the Argyll Highland Regiment in Britain. Chirgwin, 'The 94th.' Charles Campbell (1819–1906) emigrated from Scotland to Cape Breton in 1830. He became a prominent merchant, mine owner, and shipbuilder at Baddeck. He was Conservative member of the Assembly (1855–9, 1860–1, 1863–7, 1871–3), the Legislative Council (1873–4), and the House of Commons (1874–5, 1876–8, and 1882–7). He also served as a lieutenant

in the 1st Regiment, Victoria Militia, from 1840 to 1869. The Duke of Argyll was, of course, a Campbell.

28 William McKenzie McLeod (1854–1932) was born in Sydney and practised medicine there. He won election to the House of Commons as a Conservative in a by-election in October 1879 but was defeated in the 1882 general election.

29 Chirgwin, 'The 94th Argyll Highland Regiment.'

30 *Report on the State of the Militia for the Year 1887* (Ottawa 1888), 153. See also Moogk, 'From Fortress Louisbourg,' 137–9.

31 *Report on the State of the Militia for the Year 1890* (Ottawa 1891), 143.

32 G.W.L. Nicholson, *The Gunners of Canada: The History of the Royal Regiment of Canadian Artillery* (Toronto 1967), 1:131.

33 NA, RG 9, IIA1/391/14692, Crowe to minister, 7 February 1896, enclosing 'Memorandum as to the Defence of Cape Breton Island'; Gascoigne to minister, n.d. Sydney's town council may have agreed on the pointlessness of its local militia unit. In September 1895 it appears to have attempted to take over Barrack Park or at least to obtain some form of joint tenure of the site. Dr McLeod, who remained active in militia affairs and seems to have been the officer in charge of the property, vigorously resisted this move, apparently with success. See Beaton Institute, MG 9/23, McLeod to MacDonald, 23 September 1895.

34 Ibid., D.L. MacDonald to William MacDonald, 7 May 1897. D.L. MacDonald was the senator's son. Walter Crowe (1862–1934) settled in Sydney in 1886, where he practised law. As mayor from 1897 to 1903, he played a major role in bringing the steel plant to Sydney and his firm became the most important in town, representing Dominion Iron and Steel and the Dominion Coal Company.

35 Moogk, 'From Fortress Louisbourg,' 141.

36 A cousin of Robert Borden, who became leader of the Conservative party in 1900 and served as prime minister from 1911 to 1920, Frederick Borden (1847–1917) was a physician at Canning, Nova Scotia. Active in the militia for many years, he served in the House of Commons from 1874 to 1882, from 1887 to 1891, and from 1892 to 1911, and was minister of militia and defence throughout the Laurier government's term of office.

37 Sarty, *Coast Artillery*, 27–36.

38 NA, RG 9, IIC2/4, Stone, 'Report on Sydney Harbour,' 9 October 1899.

39 Ibid., IIB1/660, Cotton to quartermaster general (QMG), 1 June 1900.

40 NSARM, MG 2/98:640–1, Borden to O'Grady-Haly, 16 March 1901.

41 DHH, Militia general order 79, September 1900.

42 Ibid., Militia general order 82, May 1903. See also Moogk, 'From Fortress Louisbourg,' 141–2; Nicholson, *Gunners*, 1:132, 179–80.

43 Sarty, 'Silent Sentry,' 203–5. Stephen J. Harris, *Canadian Brass: The Making of a Professional Army, 1860–1939* (Toronto 1988), 73–81.

44 Sarty, 'Silent Sentry,' chap. 3.

45 Jean Pariseau, 'Forces armées et maintien de l'ordre au Canada, 1867–1967: un siècle d'aide au pouvoir civil' (unpublished PhD thesis, Université Paul Valéry III 1981), tome 3, étude 78. The documents assembled by Dr Pariseau can be found in DHH, 79/90.

46 The justice of the peace who accompanied the troops, Samuel Macdonnell, later reported to the provincial secretary that 'it was quite necessary to have sent down the troops and I have no doubt the strike would be persisted in and acts of violence committed, were not the means pursued adopted to quash the proceeding.' See Macdonnell to Charles Tupper, 24 May 1864, quoted in C. Bruce Fergusson, *The Labour Movement in Nova Scotia Before Confederation* (Halifax 1964), 27.

47 Chirgwin, 'The 94th Argyll Highland Regiment.' In 1876 Richard Brown, by this time retired in England, grumbled to his son, who was then managing the GMA operations, that 'the county of course will have to pay the expense of the Militia though a large portion no doubt will fall on the Association or the sum will have to be raised on the assessment.' See NSARM, MG 1/151/ 260, Richard Brown to Richard Brown Jr, 21 August 1876.

48 Fergusson, *Labour Movement*, 28; Pariseau, 'Forces armées,' études 21, 49, and 78.

49 Ibid., étude 85; Sarty, 'Silent Sentry,' 172.

50 John E. Burchell founded the Sydney branch of the Merchants Bank in 1871 and managed it until his retirement in 1910. President of the Sydney Land and Loan Company, he was also a director of the Cape Breton Coal, Iron and Railroad Company, president of the Board of Trade for twenty years, and vice consul for the United States, Norway, and Sweden. His son, Charles J. Burchell, became a prominent lawyer and director of the Dominion Iron and Steel Company and the Dominion Coal Company. Charles moved to Halifax in 1911, where he practised law with J.L. Ralston, and was Canadian high commissioner to Newfoundland when that dominion joined Canada in 1949.

51 William McKay (1847–1915) was the physician for several mines in the area and established a system of local boards of health in 1878. A Conservative, he served in the House of Assembly from 1886 to 1890 and again from 1894 to 1897, when he was also leader of the Opposition. He was appointed to the Senate in 1912.

52 Beaton Institute, MG 12/170/2, J.E. Burchell Papers, George Buskard, private secretary to minister of public works, to Burchell, 8 July 1913.

53 Ibid., Burchell to McKay, 27 January 1914; McKay to Burchell, 12 June 1914.

54 Ibid., Richardson to Hughes, 17 July 1914; Lieutenant Colonel Charles Winter, military secretary to the minister, to Richardson, 28 July 1914. Richardson was mayor of Sydney in the years 1903–5, 1908–10, and 1914–17.

55 Ibid., Burchell to McKay, 1 August 1914; Burchell to Lieutenant Colonel Robert Lowe, 12 February 1915; Gunn to J.C. Douglas, 23 March 1915. Burchell's lawyer, Gunn was mayor of Sydney from 1910 to 1914, when this whole affair started. A former mayor of Glace Bay, Douglas was the Conservative member of the House of Assembly for Cape Breton County from 1911 to 1917. He later became attorney-general and minister of lands and forests. He also served in the House of Commons from 1917 to 1921 and in 1926. See ibid., Gunn to Burchell, 21 May 1915, enclosing Rutherford to Douglas, 8 May 1915; W.A. Richardson to Burchell, 21 July 1915; Mayor Fitzgerald to Major L.G. Van Tyne, 28 March 1918; Fitzgerald to Burchell, 15 April 1918, enclosing copy of Van Tyne to Fitzgerald, 9 April 1918. In the end, the new courthouse was built further up Charlotte Street in 1915, and the public entrance to the park from Charlotte Street remains in existence today.

56 Sarty, 'Silent Sentry,' 192–5. Under the Dominion Militia Act of 1868, Nova Scotia became Military District 9, with headquarters at Halifax. This headquarters was, of course, entirely distinct from the British command at Halifax and essentially continued the previous Nova Scotia militia headquarters. In 1905, shortly before the Halifax garrison passed to Canadian control, the militia districts in the Maritime Provinces were combined into a single new Maritime Provinces Command under Colonel (later Brigadier General) C.W. Drury, Royal Canadian Artillery, with headquarters at Halifax. From 1906 the command's responsibilities included the Halifax Fortress. In 1911 the name of Maritime Provinces Command was changed to the 6th Division. In a further reorganization in 1917 Nova Scotia and Prince Edward Island became Military District 6, and New Brunswick became a separate command, Military District 7, at this time. This structure continued until the end of the Second World War, although in the period from 1940 to 1944 a separate umbrella Atlantic Command existed at Halifax to coordinate the overall land defence of the East Coast. It did not supersede the district commands, however, which continued to carry out most of the daily administration. For the sake of clarity and convenience, we refer simply to Halifax Command or Maritime Provinces Command, meaning the headquarters at Halifax that always had responsibility for Nova Scotia, whatever its name or other responsibilities at any given time.

57 Quoted in Paul M. Kennedy, 'Imperial Cable Communications and Strategy 1870–1914,' *English Historical Review* 86 (October 1971), 748.

58 DHH, 340.003 (D13), Bland, 'Report on Cable Stations and Cable Landing Places at Canso NS, Dated about 1904.' Other evidence indicates that this report was written in 1903. See DHH, 340.003 (D15), 'Report on Cable Stations and Cable Landing Places, Chap II – North Sydney. Dated about 1904.'

59 DHH, 340.003(D1), 'Halifax Defence Scheme: Revised to June 1912,' 90; ibid., 340.004 (D15), Hayter, 'Defence of Cable Stations – Cable Landing Places and Wireless Station North Sydney – Glace Bay – Louisburg, Cape Breton, NS' (1912). R. Hayter, 'Report on Marconi Wireless Station: Glace Bay and Louisburg – CB' (9 August 1912); DHH, 340.003 (D13), Hayter, 'Defence of Cable Station and Cable Landing Places: Part 1, Canso NS' [1912 or 1913].

60 NA, RG 24, 2509/HQC 1440, 'Memorandum on the Defence of Halifax in View of Recent Developments in Naval Warfare,' 11 December 1913.

61 NA, MG 26, H/126:68026–30, 'Admiralty Comments on Memorandum "Remarks on Naval Defence on the Atlantic Coast," Prepared by the Department of Naval Service,' 5 May 1914.

5: The Call to Arms, 1914–1916

1 *Sydney Daily Post*, 3 August 1914.

2 Ibid., 5 August 1914.

3 Ibid.; R.C. Fetherstonhaugh, *The Royal Canadian Regiment, 1883–1933* (Fredericton 1981), 198; NA, RG 24, 3966/NSC 1047-2-1, 'War Diary: Measures Adopted by Divisions ... since 29 July 1914, 6th Division.'

4 *Sydney Daily Post*, 1 August 1914.

5 United Kingdom, Admiralty Naval Staff, *The Atlantic Ocean, 1914–1915* (Naval Staff Monographs [Historical]), Fleet Issue, vol. 9 (London 1923), 10.

6 *Sydney Daily Post*, 3 August 1914. Fetherstonhaugh, *Royal Canadian Regiment*, 198.

7 *Sydney Daily Post*, 6 August 1914.

8 Ibid., 3 August 1914.

9 DHH, Canada, 'European War, 1914,' no. 1:18. Colonial secretary to governor-general, 4 August 1914.The threat of coastal bombardment by battleships was not unrealistic. As the *Sydney Daily Post* showed in a map published on its front page on 15 April 1915, HMS *Queen Elizabeth*, a British dreadnought, could shell Sydney while lying off Scatarie Island. 'But to destroy the town, she would lie off Glace Bay, bringing her range down to twelve miles, which is the distance at which her fire begins to be effective.'

10 NA, RG 24, 2510/HQC 1509/1, telegrams between officer commanding
    (OC) 6th Division and chief of the general staff (CGS), 4 August 1914; ibid.,
    3966/NSC1047-2-1, 'War Diary'; ibid., 1198/HQC 95/4, OC 6 to adjutant
    general, telegram R78, 10 August 1914; A Fortescue Duguid, *Official History
    of the Canadian Forces, 1914–1919* (Ottawa 1938), 1:17–18.
11 *Sydney Daily Post*, 11 August 1914.
12 Ibid., 4 September 1914.
13 Ibid., 5 August 1914.
14 Ibid., The Black Diamond ships belonged to the Dominion Coal Company.
15 'Cape Bretoners in World War One,' *Cape Breton's Magazine*, no. 33:3. On the
    development of the Marconi station, see Mary K. MacLeod, *Whisper in the Air*
    (Hantsport 1992). Hunt describes this militia regiment as 'perhaps the most
    distinctively Highland Battalion in the forces of the Empire, inasmuch as the
    Gaelic language was the mother tongue of eighty per cent of its personnel.'
    He adds that 'as a rural Battalion it is recognized as having sent more officers
    and men Overseas than any other similar Unit in Eastern Canada. All its
    original members, excepting those over age or physically unfit, were trans-
    ferred to CEF Units.' See M.S. Hunt, *Nova Scotia's Part in the Great War* (Hali-
    fax 1920), 263.
16 'Cape Bretoners,' 3. According to Bain, 72 per cent of the available men in
    Sydney Mines enlisted during the First World War. Eventually the military
    authorities refused to accept those employed in the collieries. See Bain, 'Syd-
    ney Mines,' 22; Elva Jackson, quoted in 'With Frank Jackson at 99,' *Cape Bre-
    ton's Magazine*, no. 34. Coded telegrams were transmitted between Europe
    and North America through the Table Head and Louisbourg wireless sta-
    tions as well.
17 NA, RG 24, 2533/HQC 1723/1, OC 6 to CGS, 1 September 1915, enclosing
    'Report on the Measures Taken for the Defence of the Cable Landings at
    Sydney, CB,' which makes clear that the defences had been fully developed
    by the end of 1914 and were not substantially altered subsequently. See also
    NA, RG 24, 1199/HQC 95/6, OC 6 to secretary of Militia Council (SMC),
    26 November 1914.
18 Ibid., 1194/HQC 95/4, OC 6 to adjutant general, telegram R. 78, 10 August
    1914. Strengths of the militia units are very rough, derived from returns
    dated 8 and 13 August 1914 in NA, RG 24, 451/HQ 54-21-4-1/2.
19 *Sydney Daily Post*, 4 August 1914.
20 *The Atlantic Ocean*, 15-6, 24–5; NA, RG 24, 3966/NSC 1047-2-1, Reports for
    deputy minister of the naval service, 'East Coast: Synopses of instructions
    issued by Navy Department'; DHH, European War, no. 2: 75, Colonial secre-
    tary to governor-general, 11 August 1914.

21 *Sydney Daily Post*, 16 September 1914.

22 Ibid., 8 August 1914.

23 Ibid., 21 August 1914. The town clerk represented the mayor, Angus Stewart, who was ill and soon died.

24 Ibid., 24 August 1914.

25 Ibid., 29 August 1914.

26 Moogk, 'From Fortress Louisbourg,' 142.

27 Professor Eayrs describes Gwatkin as an intellectual who 'relaxed by writing Latin poetry and macaronic verse, half Latin, half English, or half English and half French; his fugitive writings included studies in Canadian ornithology and on the traces left in Canada by the Basques, and he was awarded an honorary Doctor of Laws degree by the University of Toronto.' See James Eayrs, *In Defence of Canada: From the Great War to the Great Depression* (Toronto 1964), 103.

28 NA, MG 30, E51, Rutherford to Gwatkin, 24 August 1914; Gwatkin to Rutherford, 28 August 1914.

29 NA, RG 24, 1198/HQC 95/4, OC 6 to adjutant general, telegram, 29 August 1914.

30 NA, MG 30, E51, Gwatkin to Rutherford, 1 October 1914.

31 Ibid., Rutherford to Gwatkin, 17 October 1914.

32 Ibid.

33 D.D. McKenzie (1859–1927) was a North Sydney lawyer and the Liberal member of Parliament for Cape Breton North–Victoria from 1904 to 1906 and from 1908 to 1923. He served as Liberal house leader from 1917 to 1919 and as solicitor general from 1921 to 1923. George H. Murray (1861–1929) was a North Sydney lawyer, Liberal member of the Legislative Council from 1889 to 1896, member of the House of Assembly from 1896 to 1923, and premier from 1896 to 1923.

34 NA, RG 24, 5884/HQ 7-96-26, John C. Douglas, D. Hayes, and W.J. Egan to A.E. Blount, 2 November 1914. A Glace Bay lawyer and former mayor, Douglas was a member of the Assembly from 1911 to 1917 and from 1925 to 1926, and president of the Liberal-Conservative Association of Nova Scotia from 1914 to 1915. He represented Cape Breton South and Richmond in the House of Commons (1917–21), and Antigonish-Guysborough (1926). Dr Joseph Hayes was secretary of the Liberal-Conservative Association of Nova Scotia and a party organizer. Dr W.J. Egan was a Sydney physician and the president of the Cape Breton County Liberal-Conservative Association. See also RG 24, 1198/HQC 95/4, Protest by William Gallant, an Inverness lawyer, to Lieutenant Colonel Charles Winter, 22 October 1914.

35 Ibid., 5884/HQ 7-96-26.

36 Ibid., Colonel, assistant adjutant general, 'Re 94th Regiment ...,' [October 1914].

37 Ibid., McRae to deputy assistant adjutant and quartermaster general, 6th Division, 26 October 1914; OC 6 to SMC, 30 October 1914.

38 He was posted to North Sydney, while McRae was moved to Glace Bay. See *Sydney Daily Post*, 20 November 1914; NA, RG 24, 5884/HQ 7-96-26, Colonel, assistant adjutant general, minute, [November 1914], added to his 'Re 94th Regiment.'

39 This is not discussed in the surviving contemporary records but subsequent correspondence shows that the Sydney staff was retained. See, for example, NA, RG 24, 847/HQ 54-21-11-60/1, OC 6, 'Daily Statement Showing Disposition of Troops ...,' 18 August 1915.

40 NA, RG 24, 1198/HQC 95/5, OC 6 to CGS, 29 October 1914, telegram R280; Ibid. 1199/HQC 95/6, OC 6 to SMC, 26 November 1914.

41 Hunt, *Nova Scotia*, 265.

42 DHH, 345.009 (D4), 'Report on Chapel Point, Sydney, NS,' 12 May 1927.

43 *Sydney Daily Post*, 23 October 1914.

44 Ibid., 10 November 1914; NA, RG 24, 471/HQ 54-21-4-2/2, OC 6 to SMC, 21 November 1914.

45 *Sydney Daily Post*, 8 February 1915.

46 Ibid., 10 February 1915.

47 NA, RG 24, 2533/HQC 1723/1, OC 6 to CGS, 1 September 1915.

48 Sarty, 'Silent Sentry,' 278–9.

49 NA, RG 24, 847/HQ 54-21-11-60/3, General officer commanding, 6th Division (GOC 6), to SMC, 5 November 1915, forwarding 'Present and Proposed Strengths of Detachments.' This report on proposed reductions in the Cape Breton and Canso defences fortunately includes detailed descriptions of the Louisbourg, Glace Bay, and Hazel Hill sites as they had been developed by the end of 1914 and maintained until late 1915. It is the only such account that has yet come to light.

50 NA, RG 24, HQC 843 (mfm C5055), GOC 6 to SMC, 2 March 1915; ibid., 1199/HQC 95/8, GOC 6 to CGS, 20 April 1915, telegram.

51 *Sydney Daily Post*, 12 September 1914.

52 Ibid., 7 October 1914.

53 Ibid., 21 November 1914.

54 Ibid., 24 November 1914.

55 Ibid., 7 December 1914.

56 Ibid., 12 December 1914.

57 NA, RG 24, 3970/NSC 1047-30-2/1, Maddin to Hazen, 29 October 1914. A Sydney lawyer, James Maddin (1874–1961) was elected to the House of Com-

mons in 1908 as a Conservative but was defeated in 1911. He was not considered a good party man because he supported the Liberals provincially. He joined the army at the outbreak of war and eventually went overseas with the 85th Highlanders, rising to the rank of major. He became president of the Nova Scotian branch of the Great War Veterans Association in 1918, and also acted in the first two movies made in Cape Breton, in the 1920s. Writing in 1950, Cyril Robinson said of Maddin that 'he can today look back on an at times madcap career which included the varied roles of machinist, lawyer, politician, Hell-raising Cape Breton Highlander, movie actor, and inveterate prankster ... He once facetiously campaigned for the Sydney mayoralty on a platform which included free beer in automatic drinking fountains at every street corner, street reform, moral reform, police reform, park reform, and chloroform.' See Cyril Robinson, 'It's Difficult to Hang Jim Maddin's Clients,' *Montreal Standard*, 2 December 1950.

58 NA, RG24, 3970/NSC 1047-30-2/1, Kingsmill to deputy minister of naval service, 2 November 1914.

59 Quoted in *Sydney Daily Post*, 6 February 1915.

60 *Sydney Daily Post*, 11 February 1915. The alarm caused in North Sydney may have been heightened by the reported discovery on that same day of several sticks of dynamite beneath the barracks of the 94th Regiment on Archibald Avenue. Although 'enquiries made at military headquarters elicited nothing but denials,' the *Post* claimed that leaves appeared to have been curtailed and 'there was also a rumor of some difficulty with the German "colony" at Centreville' (6 February 1915).

61 Ibid., 11 February 1915.

62 Ibid., 31 July 1914.

63 NA, RG24/3970/NSC 1047-30-2/1, Maddin to Hazen, 29 October 1914.

64 *Sydney Daily Post*, 2 July 1918. Following the war the republican governments of Austria and Germany were quick to acknowledge that naturalization in Canada ended both original citizenship and allegiance. See Robert Keyserlingk, '"Agents within the Gates": The Search for Nazi Subversives in Canada during World War II,' *Canadian Historical Review* 66 (1985), 215.

65 *Sydney Daily Post*, 12 September 1914. It should be noted that other governments adopted similar policies.

66 Ibid., 23 October 1914.

67 Ibid.

68 Ibid., 16, 17 November 1914.

69 Ibid., 19 September 1914, 7 November 1914.

70 Ibid., 17 November 1914.

71 Cited in ibid., 7 November 1914.

72 Ibid., 22 April 1915.

73 Ibid., 7 June 1915.

74 Ibid., 23 August 1918. The fear of enemy spies in Canada was not entirely fanciful. See Martin Kitchen, 'The German Invasion of Canada in the First World War,' *International History Review* 7 (May 1985), 245–60.

75 *Sydney Daily Post*, 2 August 1915.

76 NA, RG 24, 847/HQ 54-21-11-60/2, CGS minute to adjutant general, 25 November 1915.

77 Ibid., 2510/HQC 1509/3, Rutherford to Gwatkin, 30 September 1915. See also ibid., 847/HQ 54-21-11-60/1, GOC 6 to CGS, 9 October 1915, and following correspondence.

78 Ibid., 847/HQ 54-21-11-60/3, GOC 6 to SMC, 5 November 1915, forwarding 'Present and Proposed Strengths of Detachments'; Acting adjutant general to GOC 6, 27 November 1915.

79 Hunt, *Nova Scotia's Part*, 122–9.

80 Hunt, *Nova Scotia's Part*, 43.

81 NA, RG 24, NSC 1062-13-4, Kingsmill, 'Memo for Information of Minister,' 11 August 1915; Kingsmill, 'Memorandum for the Deputy Minister,' 28 September 1915; DHH, Naval Historical Section files (NHS), 8000 'Niobe,' 'Notes of 47-5-11 ... Defensive Measures – 1914: Reports on Situation ...' This is an important set of notes at DHH because the original file was subsequently destroyed. See also Michael Hadley and Roger Sarty, *Tin-Pots & Pirate Ships* (Montreal and Kingston 1991). These references also provide a detailed account of naval developments in 1915; only additional sources for particular points will be noted in the following pages.

82 *Sydney Daily Post*, 27 July, 9 August 1915.

83 Quoted in ibid., 5 July 1915.

84 NA, RG 24, 4030/NSC 1065-4-1, Naval secretary to captain in charge, HMC Dockyard, Halifax, 6 July 1915.

85 Jackson, *Windows*, 132. The local mines and coal piers benefitted as well from the decision of the Admiralty in 1916 that all transports that could do so should take on enough coal at Canadian ports for their return voyage.

86 NA, RG 24, 4022/NS 1062-13-4, Kingsmill to commander in chief North America and West Indies (CinC, NAWI), 23 July 1915. The only reasonably full and accurate records of the allocation of ships to the St Lawrence Patrol and their movements in 1915 are in DHH, NHS 8000, 'Niobe,' 'Notes of 47-5-11 ...'; and the signals and reports in NA, RG 24/4030/NSC 1065-2-1.

87 NA, RG 24/4022/NS1062-13-4, Kingsmill, 'Memorandum for the Deputy Minister,' 25 September 1915.

88 Ibid. Graham Greene to Borden, 15 August 1915.

89 See, for example, ibid., Kingsmill 'Memorandum for the Deputy Minister,' 25 September 1915.

90 Hadley and Sarty, *Tin-Pots*, 118–19.

91 NA, RG 24, 4030/NSC 1065-2-1, 'Report of Patrols. Sydney. From 10th August to 10th September 1915.'

92 F.M. McKee, *The Armed Yachts of Canada*, (Erin, Ont. 1983), chap. 2; DHH, NHS, 'Ships and Vessels of the RCN on the Atlantic Coast in the Great War, 1914–1918,' 17 July 1963.

93 DHH, 81/520/1440-6, 'Halifax NS, 1906–1920,' Director of naval service to secretary of the Admiralty, 1 September 1915.

94 McKee, *Armed Yachts*, chap. 2; Hadley and Sarty, *Tin-Pots*, 119, 123.

95 DHH, Naval Service orders in council, PC 1299, 1 June 1916, 137–8.

96 NA, RG 24, 4030/NSC 1065-2-1, Naval Service Headquarters (NSHQ) to Navyard Halifax, telegram 460, 27 July 1915.

97 National Personnel Records Centre (NPRC), file 60-P-30; Hadley and Sarty, *Tin-Pots*, 122–3.

98 NA, RG 24, 5659/NS 58-16-1, May to director of naval service, 14 August 1916. Our thanks to John G. Armstrong for providing this reference.

100 DHist, NHS 8000, 'Protector (Shore Establishment),' Murray to Russell, 6 September 1964.

101 Canada, House of Commons Debates, 13 March 1916, 1696. William Carroll (1877–1964) was a Glace Bay lawyer who was elected to the House of Commons in 1911. He joined the army in 1916 and served overseas. Defeated in the 1917 election, he was re-elected in 1921, then was appointed to the Supreme Court of Nova Scotia in 1925. He chaired a provincial royal commission on mining in 1936–7, and was also appointed an Admiralty court judge in 1937. He resigned from the bench in 1949 and was re-elected to the House of Commons in 1949, retiring in 1953.

6: East Coast Port, 1916–1918

1 For a full account of *U-53*'s operation and the Canadian response, see Hadley and Sarty, *Tin-Pots*, Chapters 6–7.

2 NA, RG 24, 7493, *Margaret* log, 10–14 October 1916.

3 Ibid., 4026/62-13-13/1, Patrols Sydney to Naval Ottawa, signal 1230, 15 October 1916; Naval Ottawa to Patrols Sydney, signal 492, 1745, 16 October 1916.

4 Quoted in Hadley and Sarty, *Tin-Pots*, 159.

5 NA, RG 24, 2523/HQS 1624/1, quoted in Gwatkin to Kingsmill, 9 October 1916.

6 Ibid., GOC 6 to master general of ordnance (MGO), 17 October 1916, telegram. GOC 6 to CGS, 29 November 1916.

7 Ibid., 2533/HQS 1723/1, GOC 6 to CGS, 10 February 1917; GOC 6 to SMC, 23 April 1917, and enclosed blueprints.

8 Ibid., 2523/HQS 1624/1, Benson to CGS, 29 November 1916. Kingsmill fully supported the deployment of the gun, in a complete reversal of his earlier dismissive attitude. He was 'certain,' he told Gwatkin, that the Germans had 'good information and know the absence of any means of offence or defence at Sydney.' With the gun emplaced there, 'if the submarines think it desirable to expend a few shells into the steel works at Sydney, they would not do it twice.' Ibid., Kingsmill to Gwatkin, 11 October 1916.

9 Ibid., 2533/HQS 1723/1, 'Extract from Report of Proceedings of 43rd Meeting of Inter-Departmental Committee,' 26 January 1917.

10 Ibid., Gwatkin to naval secretary, Inter-Departmental Committee (IDC), 16 March 1917; proceedings of 48th meeting, IDC, 17 March 1917; naval secretary, IDC, to military secretary, IDC, 20 March 1917; proceedings of 49th meeting, IDC, 28 March 1917.

11 Ibid., Benson to Gwatkin, 28 February 1917; Gwatkin to Benson, 6 April 1917.

12 Ibid., GOC 6 to SMC, 5 May 1917.

13 Ibid., 2534/HQS 1723/1, correspondence, 12 June–7 August 1917.

14 NA, RG 24, 3809/NS 1010-11-1/1, 'Information Regarding Marine Defences of Defended Ports ... in Canada,' 1 July 1917; DHH 322.009 (D280), 'Summary Regarding Guns ...,' 25 September 1919, describes the net as being between North West and South East Bars, but all editions of 'Information Regarding Marine Defences ...,' which were distributed as aids to navigation, give the Stubbert's–South Bar location. See DHH, J.O.B. LeBlanc, 'Historical Synopsis of Organization and Development of the Royal Canadian Navy,' 46, 67, identifies *Una* and *Lansdowne* as the gate vessels. See also DHH, *Naval Intelligence Report*, 16 (16 April 1917), 165; 26 (25 June 1917), 272; 29 (16 July 1917).

15 *Sydney Daily Post*, 23 November 1918.

16 NA, RG 24, HQS 1723/1, McLennan to Kemp, 5 February 1917.

17 *Naval Intelligence Report* 46 (12 November 1917), 512.

18 Captain Hans Rose of *U-53* had scrupulously followed 'stop and search' procedures during his operations off Nantucket in October 1916.

19 The literature on the events in the naval war in the Atlantic in the first part of 1917 is large and complex, as were the events themselves. Recent accounts with wide-ranging references include Hadley and Sarty, *Tin-Pots*, and Paul G. Halpern, *A Naval History of World War I* (Annapolis 1994), chap. 11.

20 United Kingdom, Admiralty, Technical History Section, *The Atlantic Convoy System, 1917–18*, vol. 3, pt. 14, *The Technical History and Index* (London 1919), 125.

21 Jackson, *Windows*, 133.

22 Jackson, *Fivescore*, 92. This is the same William McKenzie McLeod (1854–1932) referred to in Chapter four, who had served in the House of Commons as a Conservative from 1879 to 1882 and had been active in the militia into the 1890s.

23 DHH, Adm. 137/2658/264, 'Abstract of HS Convoys.'

24 *Naval Intelligence Report* 29 (16 July 1917), 303; DHH, Adm. 137, 1435/354, Chambers to Admiralty, 7 August 1917; ibid., 2658/106. Chambers to CinC, NAWI, 2 December 1918; Admiralty, *Navy List (Corrected to 18 June 1917)* (London 1917), 395h, 635; NA, RG 24, 3981/NSC 1049-2-40, Unwin to secretary, Department of Naval Service, 5 December 1918.

25 DHH, Adm. 137/2658/102, 'Remarks on Report from Rear Admiral Chambers, Halifax,' December 1918.

26 Ibid., 1435/355. Chambers to Admiralty, 7 August 1917.

27 Ibid., 108, Chambers to CinC, NAWI, 2 December 1918.

28 Ibid., 354, Chambers to Admiralty, 7 August 1917.

29 Murray was subsequently killed in the Halifax explosion on 6 December 1917.

30 DHH, Adm. 137/2658/105-6, CinC, NAWI, 2 December 1918.

31 NPRC, NS 60-P-30, Pasco to Kingsmill, 15 January 1917; Kingsmill to Pasco, 7 March 1917.

32 Hadley and Sarty, *Tin-Pots*, 190–1.

33 NPRC, NS 0-34178. When Admiral Kingsmill retired in 1920, Hose succeeded him as director of the naval service, an appointment he held (from 1928 under the new title, chief of the naval staff) until his own retirement in 1933.

34 Hadley and Sarty, *Tin-Pots*, 201.

35 DHH, Adm. 137/1620/26-7, Chambers to Admiralty, 19 October 1917.

36 DHH, Adm. 137/2658/108, Chambers to CinC, NAWI, 2 December 1918.

37 On Canadian warship construction and acquisition, see Hadley and Sarty, *Tin-Pots*, 187–90. See also DHH, NHS, Ships and Vessels; Daniel G. Harris, 'Canadian Warship Construction, 1917–19: The Great Lakes and Upper St Lawrence River Areas,' *Mariner's Mirror* 75 (May 1989), 149–53.

38 J.D.F. Kealy and E.C. Russell, *A History of Canadian Naval Aviation, 1918–1962* (Ottawa 1967), 1–2. See also S.F. Wise, *Canadian Airmen and the First World War: The Official History of the Royal Canadian Air Force*, vol. 1 (Toronto 1980), 603.

39 Canada, House of Commons, *Debates*, 11 May 1917, 1332–9.

40 Hadley and Sarty, *Tin-Pots*, 197–8.

41 DHH, NSS 1057-1-1/1, Navyard Halifax to Naval Ottawa, signal 940, 18 July 1917, reporting the dispatch of trawlers *PV 1* and *PV 2* to Sydney; Transports Sydney to Naval Ottawa, signal 181, 18 September 1917, complaining about the absence of additional minesweepers to replace *PV 1* and *PV 2* while they carried out boiler cleaning.

42 NA, RG 24, 6197, NS 1001-19-4, Stephens to director of naval staff, 5 April 1917.

43 Summaries of the service of patrol vessels in the summer and autumn of 1917, extracted from NS 1047- 5-7, a file that no longer exists, are in DHH, NHS 8000, files for *Margaret, Lady Evelyn, Laurentian, Acadia, Cartier, Grib*, and *Hochelaga*. See also *Stadacona* logs for 1917 in NA, RG 24, 7870, and for *Margaret* in NA, RG 24, 7493.

44 NA, RG 24, 3831, NS 1017-10-1/1, Admiralty memorandum M-015744, 3 January 1918.

45 Ibid.

46 Hadley and Sarty, *Tin-Pots*, 222–3.

47 Ibid., 212–4.

48 NA, RG 24, 11122/501-1-1/1, Admiral superintendent Halifax Dockyard to GOC 6, 22 February 1918.

49 This account of army developments at Sydney in 1918 is, except where noted, drawn from NA, RG 24, 2534-5/HQS 1723/3-5, and NA, RG 9, IIID3/5062/978, MD 6, war diary, March–October 1918.

50 He was accompanied by General Lessard, Captain Willis, Colonel Deroche, Major Pringle, Captain Hose, Captain Pasco, Commander Attwood, RCN, and Mr MacDougall from the Dominion Steel Company.

51 NA, RG 24, HQS 1723/3, Jackson to CGS, 21 May 1918.

52 Ibid.

53 Ibid.

54 NA, RG 24, 4557/MD 6, 131-45-1, Lang, 'Artillery Defences, Halifax and Sydney,' 9 October 1918.

55 Hunt, *Nova Scotia's Part*, 239.

56 NA, RG 24, 853/HQ 54-21-11-124/1, Gwatkin to naval secretary, IDC, 30 August 1917; naval secretary, IDC, to military secretary, IDC, 1 September 1917.

57 NA, RG 24, 4567/MD 6, 133-111-1/1, June–August 1918 correspondence; ibid., 4547/MD 6, 79-1-1/3, 'Monthly Distribution of Troops CEF,' 31 October 1918; ibid., 854/HQ 54-21-11-124/3, GOC 6 to SMC, 26 November 1918.

58 The secretary of the trustees was J.E. Burchell.

59 *City of Sydney Annual Report, 1917* (Sydney 1917), 37–8; ibid., *1918* (Sydney 1919), 28–9 (copies at Beaton Institute).

60 NA, RG 24, 5662/NS 58-53-19/1-2; naval historians' notes and correspondence in the following NHS 8000 files: 'Lansdowne,' 'Seagull,' and 'Protector (Shore Establishment).' This material is especially useful because it includes notes on files that no longer exist and correspondence with veterans who served at Sydney. See also Canada, *Auditor General's Report for the Year Ending 31 March 1919* (Ottawa 1919), ZZ269–70.

61 *TR 32*, one of the trawlers built for the Admiralty and released to the Canadian navy, nevertheless found itself trapped in pack ice off Glace Bay from 21 April to 2 May, suffering damage that caused its hold to flood to a depth of two feet. See NA, RG 24, 7953, *TR 32* log, 21 April–2 May 1918.

62 DHH, NHS 8000, 'Trawlers and Drifters,' pt 2, NHS notes from NS 1057-4-31/2; NA, RG 24, 4031/NS 1065-7-6, Kingsmill to secretary of the Admiralty, 18 July 1918; DHH, NSS 1057-1-1/1, Navyard Halifax to Naval Ottawa, signal 847, 8 May 1918; ibid., Patrols Sydney to Naval Ottawa, signals 396 and 401, both 17 June 1918; *The Canadian Navy List for August 1918 (Corrected to 20 July 1918)* (Ottawa 1918), 79–108. NA, RG 24, 7871, *Stadacona* log, July 1918.

63 NA, RG 24, 7493, *Margaret* log, July 1918; ibid., 7444, *Lady Evelyn* log, July 1918.

64 As early as 5 July *Armentières*, one of the trawlers assigned to the mobile patrol, and the auxiliary patrol ship *Acadia* were operating together. See DHH, NHS 8000, 'Trawlers and Drifters,' pt 2, NHS notes on NS 1057-4-31/2.

65 NA, RG 24, 3831/NSS 1017-10-1/1, Hose to director of the naval service n.d., forwarded by Kingsmill to minister, 21 February 1918; DHH, NHS 1440–6, 'Halifax 1905–20,' NHS notes from NS 1047-5-25.

66 Ibid.; Roger Sarty, 'Hard Luck Flotilla: The RCN's Atlantic Coast Patrol, 1914–18,' in W.A.B. Douglas, ed., *The RCN in Transition, 1910–1985* (Vancouver 1988), 115; Hadley and Sarty, *Tin-Pots*, 235–6; DHH, NHS 8000, 'Trawlers and Drifters,' pt 2, NHS notes from NS 1057-4-31/2, entries for 1, 5, 11, 19 July 1918; NA, RG 24, 7953, *TR 30* log, 1 July–12 August 1918. *TR 30* was part of the Forming-Up Escort and Outer Patrol Flotilla.

67 Halifax *Herald*, 19 February 1918 (clipping in NA, RG 24, 5605/NS 29-16-1).

68 Sarty, 'Hard Luck Flotilla,' 113.

69 NA, RG 24, 5604/NS 29-16-1/2, Desbarats to Canadian Vickers, 6 December 1917; Lynch, Canadian Vickers, to Desbarats, 11 December 1917; ibid., 5605/NS 29-16-1/3, Norcross to Ballantyne, 12 January 1918; ibid., 5, Director of ship construction to Desbarats, 31 July 1918; ibid., 6, Wright to Desbarats, 18 September 1918. See also Hadley and Sarty, *Tin-Pots*, 220–1, 224.

70 NA, RG 24, 3832/NS 1017-10-4, Kingsmill to minister, [March 1918].

71 Ibid., 5657/NS 58-9-4, Hose to secretary, Department of Naval Service, 19 August 1918. The accounts for HMCS *Seagull*, the depot ship of the Sydney flotillas, show a total expenditure of $202,296 for ship repair and refit, of which about $54,000 was spent at Sydney Foundry, the North Sydney Marine Railway, and the Musgrave works. The accounts for HMCS *Lansdowne*, depot ship of the shore establishment, show payment of another $11,000 to these firms for marine hardware and work on the anti-submarine net. These figures may well not be complete, as the accounting system for the East Coast naval activities was divided under many headings and is not fully clear, but they demonstrate both the extensive use the navy made of these firms and the fact that they were far from equal to the full demands of the greatly expanded naval establishment. See *Auditor General's Report*, 1919, ZZ270–1, ZZ287, ZZ289, ZZ291.

72 Hadley and Sarty, *Tin-Pots*, 222–3.

73 NRPC, NS 60-P-30, Pasco to secretary, Department of Naval Service, 20 July 1918.

74 NA, RG 24, 4031/NS 1065-7-6, Naval Ottawa to Admiralty, signal, 3 August 1918; Naval Ottawa to Britannia (CinC, NAWI) Washington, signal, 7 August 1918; Haggarty to Britannia, Washington, signal, 14 August 1918; Department of Naval Service, 'Drifters Built in Canada,' 3 March 1919, shows that the two drifters were *CD 84* and *CD 91*, which sailed from Quebec on 23 August 1918 for Sydney.

75 NPRC, file 0-34178/1, Hose to Kingsmill, 4 August 1918.

76 Hadley and Sarty, *Tin-Pots*, 212–16.

77 Kealy and Russell, *Canadian Naval Aviation*, 3; Wise, *Canadian Airmen*, 603–4; Hadley and Sarty, *Tin-Pots*, 212–16.

78 National Archives and Records Administration (NARA), RG 24, USS *SC 51* log, 16 May–10 July 1918; DHH, Adm. 137/2658/123-4, 'History of Canadian Convoy Organization,' 2 December 1918.

7: Victory, 1918

1 Transcripts of the deciphered radio traffic concerning the converted mercantile submarines to the end of July 1918 are in DHH, Adm. 137, 4155. The U-boat headquarters signal of 22 July 1918 mentioning that *U-156* was to operate in the Gulf of Maine, with the approaches to the Delaware as an alternative, is on pages 432 and 451. See also Office of Naval Records and Library, *German Submarine Activities on the Atlantic Coast of the United States and Canada* (Washington 1920), 10–11.

2 *Sydney Daily Post*, 18 July 1918. This proved, in fact, to be the practice of all of the U-cruisers that came to North America in this final campaign of the war.

3 On *U-156*'s early operations in American and Canadian waters, see *German Submarine Activities*, 52–9; Roger Sarty, 'Hard Luck Flotilla,' 114–16; Hadley and Sarty, *Tin-Pots*, 248–57.

4 *Sydney Daily Post*, 5 August 1918.

5 Ibid. *Dornfontein* had been launched at Saint John only a few weeks earlier.

6 Ibid., 6 August 1918.

7 The precise number of patrol vessels available at Sydney (or Halifax) at any given time is difficult to determine because of the incompleteness of the records. NA, RG 24, 4031/NS 1065-7-6, Hose to secretary of Naval Service, 1 August 1918, one of the few reasonably full returns to have survived, shows that seventeen of the numbered trawlers were present, in addition to six of the named trawlers built by the Canadian government, for a total of twenty-three. This figure does not include the former New England trawlers employed on mine-sweeping duties. Ibid., Patrols Sydney to Naval Ottawa, signal 5 August 1918, mentions that two Sydney-based auxiliary patrol vessels were laid up or about to be docked for repairs, that two recently arrived trawlers lacked guns, and that five other trawlers had defects or were undergoing routine lay-up. *Stadacona*'s log, 1 July–11 August 1918 (NA, RG24, 7871), shows that this vessel, whose status was not specifically mentioned in Hose's report, was also undergoing repairs, making a total of three auxiliary patrol vessels out of action. NA, RG 24, 7450, *Laurentian*'s log, 11 August 1918, shows that newly arrived twelve-pounder guns were delivered on that date to five, not two, trawlers at Sydney, suggesting that the total number of trawlers that had been unarmed or were otherwise not operational was ten.

8 DHH, Adm. 137, 903, Britannia, 'war warning' signal 418, 0225, 6 August 1918; NA, RG 24, 3773/NSS 48-48-1/4. Britannia to Naval Ottawa, signal 101, 0359, 5 [actually 6] August 1918; Naval Ottawa to Britannia, signal 1735, 6 August 1918; Britannia to Naval Ottawa, signal 104, 1908, 6 August 1918.

9 NA, RG 24, 4031/NSS 48-48-1/4, Britannia to Naval Ottawa, signal 110, 0225, 8 August 1918.

10 Ibid., 3775/NSS 1048-48-12, Patrols Sydney to Naval Ottawa, signal 839, 1530, 9 August 1918; 3773/NSS 1048-48-1/4, same to same, signal 863, 2145, 11 August 1918. The activities of the Forming-Up Escort and Outer Patrol Flotilla can be followed in the log of *TR 30* at NA, RG 24, 7953.

11 DHH, Adm. 137, 2566, Walter, 'Letter of Proceedings,' HMS *Victorian*, 25 August 1918.

12 NA, RG 24, 7444, *Lady Evelyn* log, 12–13 August 1918; 7040, *Armentières* log, 12–13 August 1918; 7953, *TR 30* log, 12–13 August 1918.

13 NA, RG 24, 4021/NSS 1062-13-2/3, Hanck to senior officer patrols, 16 August 1918; NARA, RG 24, *SC 51* log, 14 August 1918.

14 NARA, RG 45, subject file 1911–27, 185, file JA 2, CO USS *Albany* to commander, Cruiser and Transport Force, 20 August 1918.

15 The *Sydney Daily Post* later reported (on 23 November 1918) that the ferries 'made their trips under strong convoy' during 1917–18. See also NA, RG 24, 7493, logs of *Margaret*; ibid., 7871, *Stadacona*; ibid., 7040, *Armentières*; 4031/ NSS 1065-7-1, Hose to secretary, Department of Naval Service, 30 August 1918. DHH, Notes from file 1057-4-31/2 in NHS 8000, 'Armentières,' and from file 1057-4-30 in NHS 8000, 'Trawlers and Drifters,' pt 2.

16 Robert M. Grant, *U-boat Intelligence, 1914–1918* (London 1969), 154–5; *German Submarine Activities*, 11; NA, RG 24, 3970/NSC 1047-30-2/1, Britannia to NSHQ, telegrams 115 and 118, 10 August 1918.

17 DHH, Adm. 137/903, Admiralty to Britannia, signal 326, 9 August 1918; ibid., 504: 410. Britannia general letter, 3 September 1918; Entry for 23 August 1918 in notes on NSS 1057-4-30, NHS 8000, 'Trawlers and Drifters,' pt 2.

18 NA, RG 24, 3773/NSS 1048-48-1/4, Admiralty to Naval Ottawa, signal 42, 2035, 8 August 1918.

19 DHH, Adm. 137/903/777, 799, Britannia to Admiralty, signal 447, 13 August 1918; signal 458, 14 August 1918. See also 504/409, Britannia general letter, 3 September 1918.

20 NA, RG 24, 4023/NSS 1062-13-10/4, Report form, 'Particulars of Attacks on Merchant Vessels by Enemy Submarines,' for the capture of *Triumph*, forwarded by Gibbs to secretary of the Admiralty, 5 September 1918.

21 NA, RG 24, 4021/NSS 1062-13-2/4, Navinet Halifax to Naval Ottawa, signal 335, 21 August 1918; *German Submarine Activities*, 66–7. This account incorrectly states that the American schooner *Sylvania* was sunk off Canso on 20 August; in fact, it was sunk on the following morning off Cape Breton. The crew of *Una P. Saunders*, which was sunk about sixty miles off Canso, claimed to have watched *Triumph* operating in conjunction with the submarine; see *Sydney Daily Post*, 23 August 1918.

22 Quoted in *Sydney Daily Post*, 22 August 1918.

23 Published and archival reports of the sinking of *Notre Dame de la Garde* and *Sylvania* are contradictory and incomplete compared to those for most other encounters with U-boats. The following sources are the most accurate, although they contain some obvious errors and contradictions: NA, RG 24, 4021/NSS 1062-13-2/4, Transports Sydney to Naval Ottawa, signal 996,

22 August 1918; Sydney Transports to Naval Ottawa, signal 4, 23 August 1918; Captain-in-charge Sydney to Naval Ottawa, signal 17, 24 August 1918; Captain-in-charge Sydney to secretary, Department of Naval Service, memorandum, 24 August 1918; DHH, NHS 1440–6, 'Halifax, NS, 1905–20,' notes from file 1045-5-25; *Record* (Sydney), 23–24 August 1918; *Sydney Daily Post*, 23–24 August 1918; *Yarmouth Herald*, 27 August 1918.

24 *Sydney Daily Post*, 28 August 1918.

25 Ibid., 6 August 1918.

26 Ibid., 23 August 1918.

27 DHH, NHS 8000, 'Trawlers and Drifters,' pt 2, entries for 18–20 August 1918 in NHS notes from file 1057-4-30; NA, RG 24, 7953, *TR 32* log, 18–20 August 1918; ibid., 7040, *Armentières* log, 20–22 August 1918; NARA, RG 24, *SC 51* log, 20–21 August 1918; NA, RG 24, 7953, *TR 30* log, 20–21 August 1918.

28 NA, RG 24, 7871, *Stadacona* log, 20–23 August 1918; 7953, *TR 32 log*, 20–23 August 1918; NARA, RG 24, *SC 240* log, 21–23 August 1918.

29 NA, RG 24, 7953, *TR 30* log, 23–26 August 1918; 7040, *Armentières* log, 23–29 August 1918; DHH, NHS 8000, 'Trawlers and Drifters,' pt 2, entry for 23 August 1918, in NHS notes on file 1057-4-30.

30 Hadley and Sarty, *Tin-Pots*, 276–7.

31 *Sydney Daily Post*, 28 August 1918.

32 Hadley and Sarty, *Tin-Pots*, 268–9.

33 Unaccountably, the *Sydney Daily Post*, 25 November 1918, identified the disgraced captain as W.G. Tudor, a ship's captain employed by the Dominion Iron and Steel Company; no explanation has been found for this discrepancy. The newspaper also claimed, on 23 November 1918, that *Hochelaga* had been the first Canadian vessel to sink a submarine during the war, which it allegedly did on 23 April 1918 some seven hundred miles from Britain. *Hochelaga*, however, had never left Canadian coastal waters and never sank a submarine.

34 NA, RG 24, 4031/NSS 1065-7-1, Hose to secretary, Department of Naval Service, 30 August 1918; DHH, Adm. 137/2567, Warton, letter of proceedings HC 15, 8 September 1918; NA, RG 24, 7444, *Lady Evelyn* log, 20–30 August 1918; NARA, RG 45, *Jouett* war diary, 28 August 1918.

35 *Sydney Daily Post*, 23 November 1918, citing the St John's *Herald*.

36 *U-117* log, 30–31 August 1918, copy courtesy of Professor Michael Hadley. On the 31st the submarine passed through position 48° 6′ N, 48° 3′ W. HC 15's rendezvous that same day was at 45° 5′ N, 48° 35′ W. DHH, Adm. 137/2567, Blacklin, 'Report of Proceedings HC 15,' 9 September 1918.

37 *Sydney Daily Post*, 27 August 1918.

38 Quoted in ibid., 23 November 1918.

39 Quoted in ibid., 30 September 1918.

40 Quoted in ibid., 4 September 1918.

41 Ibid., 31 July 1918.

42 Ibid., 21 September 1918. The organizing committee comprised Mrs L.X. MacDonald, a Miss DeWolfe, Mrs W. McK. McLeod, and Mr John Young, chairman of the Navy League in Sydney.

43 Ibid.

44 The Moxham Military Convalescent Home, as it was properly known, was housed in 'Kinsack,' the former residence of Arthur J. Moxham, the first general manager of the Dominion Iron and Steel Company from April 1917 to May 1920. This house, popularly known in Sydney as Moxham Castle, burned down on 27 April 1966. The Ross Memorial Hospital was in the mansion of the late James Ross, one of the founders of the Dominion Iron and Steel Company. His son Jack equipped it and lent it to the government shortly after the outbreak of war. It was taken over by the Sisters of Saint Martha after the war and operated as a maternity hospital until St Rita's Hospital was built some thirty years later. Ross was the general manager of the Dominion Steel and Dominion Coal Companies, but, as seen in chapter 5, he purchased the American yacht that was fitted out as HMCS *Grilse*, and commanded that vessel during the war. A celebrated tuna fisherman in later years, he was also the first Canadian to own a horse that won the Kentucky Derby, in 1919.

45 Quoted in 'Magnificent Moxham's Castle in Sydney Used as a Convalescent Hospital in WWI,' *Cape Breton Post*, 9 November 1985.

46 *Sydney Daily Post*, 12 September 1918.

47 Ibid., 14, 21 September 1918.

48 Ibid., 23 September 1918.

49 Ibid., 31 August 1918.

50 Ibid., 3 September 1918.

51 Ibid., 5 September 1918.

52 NARA, RG 38, 198/R-3/1, Sands to Hines, 1 September 1918.

53 *Sydney Daily Post*, 5 September 1918.

54 Ibid. The same issue also reported that there was a 'race riot' in Glace Bay on the Monday as a result of an alleged attack by blacks from Sydney on an Italian during a bicycle race taking place during the Labour Day celebrations. According to the *Post*, 'it is stated in Glace Bay that [the] Sydney negroes were the cause of the riot and it is reported that many of them are carrying wounds as a result.' This incident does not, however, appear to have had any connection with the presence of the soldiers and sailors in the area.

55 NARA, RG 38, 198/R-3/1, Sands to Hines, 5 September 1918. The ships'

officers were subsequently ordered to charge the $280 'against the men who damaged the property, and also to take proper disciplinary measures against them, as this point may not have been impressed upon them owing to the departure of the convoy from Sydney.' See NARA, RG 38/198/R-3/1, Hines to director of naval intelligence, Navy Department, Washington, 7 September 1918.

56 Ibid., Sands to Hines, 6 September 1918.
57 Ibid., Hines to Sands, 9 September 1918.
58 *Sydney Daily Post*, 23 September 1918.
59 Ibid., 30 September 1918.
60 Ibid., 4 October 1918.
61 Ibid., Actually, there was one 'complaint.' It seems that the sailors did not really appreciate the frequent cups of tea lavished on them, being accustomed to coffee. This situation 'did not last long, however. It soon leaked out, and before long the change was made. Major Tefft says that coffee is not made quite strong enough in Canada, but in everything else we are just right.'
62 Ibid., 11, 28 October 1918.
63 Ibid., 15, 26 October 1918.
64 Ibid., 28 October 1918.
65 Hadley and Sarty, *Tin-Pots*, 282, and especially 363, note 62.
66 NA, RG 24, 3775/NSS 1048-48-10, CinC, NAWI to Naval Ottawa, signal 182, 23 August 1918; same to same, signal 188, 24 August 1918. DHH, Adm. 137/1620, Chambers to CinC, NAWI, 2 September 1918; ibid., 2658: 124–5, 'History of Canadian Convoy Organization,' 2 December 1918.
67 NA, RG 24, 4031/NSS 1065-7-6, Signals between Naval Ottawa and Patrols Sydney, 3–5 September 1918, especially Patrols to Naval, signal 179, 5 September 1918; 7871, *Stadacona* log, 4–6 September; ibid., 7493, *Margaret* log, 4–6 September 1918; 7444, *Lady Evelyn* log, 4–6 September 1918.
68 NARA, RG 24, *SC 51* log, 6–7 September 1918.
69 DHH, Adm. 137/2567, Blackett, 'Letter of Proceedings HMS *Cumberland*,' 16 September 1918, and Chambers to CinC, NAWI, 12 September 1918.
70 Ibid., England, 'HC 17 Report of Proceedings,' n.d., incorrectly states that it was *Margaret* that shepherded the straggler to Sydney. See NA, RG 24, 7871, *Stadacona* log, 13–16 September 1918; 7493, *Margaret* log, 13–17 September 1918.
71 DHH, Adm. 137/2658/126, 'History of Canadian Convoy Organization,' 2 December 1918.
72 DHH, Adm. 137, 267, Vivian, 'HC 18 Report of Proceedings,' 2 October 1918; NARA, RG 24, *SC 51* log, 22 August–3 September 1918.

73 DHH, Adm. 137/2658/126, 'History of Canadian Convoy Organization,' 2 December 1918.

74 In 1941, when the U-boat menace off Cape Race was greater than in 1918, the navy sailed large slow convoys through the Strait of Belle Isle but at a heavy cost. See Chapter 10 below.

75 HS convoy letters of proceedings are in DHH, Adm. 137, 2544; NA, RG 24, 7040, *Armentières* log, 13–15 September 1918; DHH, NHS 8000, 'Trawlers and Drifters,' pt 2, notes from NSS 1057-4-30/2, 15, 29–30 September, 8, 23 October 1918.

76 NARA, RG 24, *SC 51* log, 8 October–8 November 1918.

77 NA, RG 24, 4031/NSS 1065-7-6, information compiled from Hose to secretary, Department of Naval Service, 1 August 1918; same to same, 13 September 1918; DHH, NHS notes from file 1047-5-25, in NHS 1440-6, 'Halifax NS 1905–20'; notes from file 1057-4-30 in NHS 8000, 'Trawlers and Drifters,' pt 2.

78 In addition to the sources in the preceding note, see NA, RG 24, 4031/NSS 1065-7-6, NSHQ to captain of patrols, Sydney, and admiral superintendent Halifax, memorandum 'by command,' 3 September 1918; Hose to secretary, Department of Naval Service, 22 October 1918; Department of Naval Service, 'Drifters Built in Canada,' 3 March 1919.

79 Ibid., 4021, NSS 1062-13-2/5, Fame Point to Naval Ottawa, signal, 15 September 1918; Patrols Sydney to Naval Ottawa, signal 328, 15 September 1918; DHH, notes for 15–17 September 1918 from NS 1047-4-30 in NHS 8000, 'Trawlers and Drifters,' pt 2; NA, RG24, 7040, *Armentières* log, 16–21 September 1918.

80 Ibid., 4021, NSS 1062-13-2/5, Navinet Halifax to Naval Ottawa, signal 732, 14 September 1918.

81 Hadley and Sarty, *Tin-Pots*, 283–8; *German Submarine Activities*, 11–12, 101–19.

82 *North Sydney Flight*, 1 December 1918.

83 Jackson, *Fivescore*, 32.

84 *North Sydney Flight*, 1 December 1918.

85 Ibid.

86 *Sydney Daily Post*, 17 September 1918. The account in this and the following paragraph is based on NARA, RG 24, US Naval Air Station, North Sydney, log; DHH, RCNAS weekly reports, copies in NHS 1700–219, 'RCNAS 1918–20'; and DHH, notes on NSS 1047-2-4/3, in NHS 1440-6, 'Halifax NS, 1905–20.'

87 *Sydney Daily Post*, 12 November 1918.

88 In the spring of 1918 a reconnaissance party that included a U.S. Navy aviation officer had selected Keating Cove on the south arm of Point Edward as the permanent site. Although it featured waters that were better protected

than those at North Sydney, the undeveloped state of Point Edward meant that access roads would have to be built at great expense before work could begin on the station. Wing Commander J.T. Cull, the British officer lent to Canada to oversee development of the station and to command the new Royal Canadian Naval Air Service, selected Kelly's Beach because of its proximity to roads and town services. In his view, the North Bar provided adequate if less than perfect protection against ocean swells that might, he admitted, on some occasions interfere with flying operations. See DHH, NHS 1700–219, 'RCNAS 1918–1920,' Cull to director of naval service, 11 July 1918. On the original selection of Keating Cove, see DHH, 77/58/20, Fuller to deputy minister of public works, 23 May 1918.

89 The American insistence on top quality accommodation and the resistance of the Department of Public Works is fully documented in DHH, 77/58/20; see esp. 106–9, 123, 130–1, 134–6.

90 Ibid., NHS 1700–219, 'RCNAS 1918–1920'; 'Royal Canadian Naval Air Service events for week ending 12 October 1918.'

91 Ibid., for weeks ending 12–26 October 1918. Only the two buildings were completed by war's end.

92 Ibid., for weeks ending 30 September, 5, 19 October 1918. John Crilly, a quartermaster, died on 28 September, and William Schaffert, a carpenter, died on 30 September, both at the North Sydney hospital. See the *North Sydney Flight*, 1 December 1918.

93 DHH, 77/58/14, Desbarats to deputy minister of public works, 1 October 1918; Norrington to director of stores, 18 December 1918; Campbell to Ballantyne, 21 January 1919.

94 *North Sydney Flight*, 1 December 1918.

95 DHH, NHS 1700–219, 'RCNAS 1918–1920'; Cull to director of naval service, 11 July 1918 (copy).

96 Kealy and Russell, *Canadian Naval Aviation*, 5–6.

97 Hadley and Sarty, *Tin-Pots*, 292–7.

98 *Sydney Daily Post*, 8 November 1918.

99 Jackson, *Windows*, 133–4.

100 *Sydney Daily Post*, 11 November 1918.

101 Ibid., 11, 12 November 1918.

102 Ibid., 12 November 1918.

103 Ibid.

104 Ibid.

105 Ibid., 11 November 1918.

106 Ibid., 13 November 1918.

107 Ibid., 14 November 1918.

108 Ibid., 13 November 1918.
109 Ibid., 14 November 1918.
110 Located at 336 Charlotte Street, this popular school and dance hall was operated by 'Professor' C.H.B. Hillcoates.
111 *Sydney Daily Post*, 14 November 1918.
112 Ibid.
113 Ibid., 15 November 1918. For accounts of the celebrations at Port Morien, Baddeck, and St Peters, see ibid., 13 November 1918.
114 Ibid., 16 November 1918.
115 Ibid., 18 November 1918.
116 Ibid., 16 November 1918.
117 Ibid., 26 November 1918.
118 James Turnbull to F.C. Kimber, 26 November 1918, quoted in *Sydney Daily Post*, 27 November 1918.
119 *Sydney Daily Post*, 27 November 1918; DHH, NHS notes on file 1057-4-31/2, in NHS 8000, 'Trawlers and Drifters,' pt 2.
120 DHH, NHS 1700–219, 'Royal Canadian Naval Air Service 1918–1920'; RCNAS events for week ending 14 December 1918.
121 NA, RG 24, 2324/HQS 66/11, DOC 6 to SMC, 8 January 1919.

8: The Years of Neglect, 1919–1939

1 Douglas to Ballantyne, telegram; Ballantyne to Douglas, telegram; both quoted in *Sydney Daily Post*, 29 November 1918.
2 DHH, 77/58/14, Norrington to director of stores, 21 December 1918.
3 NA, RG 24, 2535/HQC 1723/5, DOC 6 to SMC, 24 November 1919.
4 DHH, 420.009 (D4), HQS 1723, FD 637, Macklin, 'Memorandum. Joint Staff Sub-Committee on Coast Defence,' 10 February 1937, 3.
5 Ibid., 4.
6 Chisholm, 'Victoria Park,' 22.
7 DHH, 77/58/14, Mitchell to commander in charge, HMC Dockyard, Halifax, 11 June 1920. Case to civil engineer, HMC Dockyard, Halifax, 5 January 1921.
8 NA, RG 24, 473/HQ 54-21-4-2, Rice to commanding officer, Royal Canadian Engineers, Halifax, 1 December 1919.
9 Quoted in Henry Borden, ed., *Robert Laird Borden: His Memoirs* (Toronto 1938), 2:841.
10 Nonetheless, Canadian defence planning through the 1920s gave priority to the possibility of an American attack. See Eayrs, *In Defence of Canada*, 70–8.

11 Roger Sarty, *'Entirely in the Hands of the Friendly Neighbour': The Canadian Armed Forces and the Defence of the Pacific Coast, 1909–1939* (Victoria 1995).

12 NA, RG 7, G21/235/343/9, 'Report of Admiral of the Fleet Viscount Jellicoe of Scapa on Naval Mission to the Dominion of Canada (November–December 1919),' 2:47–8.

13 The ruling Conservatives, or Unionists as they now styled themselves, came third in the elections. The strong Liberal contingent from Quebec and the wave of Progressives from Ontario and the western provinces agreed on withdrawal from international entanglements and reductions in military spending, if on nothing else.

14 Morrison and Slaney, *Manly Men*, 56–61.

15 Nicholson, *Gunners of Canada*, 2:3–8; James M. Cameron, *Pictonians in Arms* (New Glasgow 1969), 186–9; Moogk, 'From Fortress Louisbourg,' 145–7.

16 Morrison and Slaney, *Manly Men*, 61–6; Moogk, 'From Fortress Louisbourg,' 147–51. Cameron, *Pictonians*, 187–203, provides a splendid account of events in which the author participated. See also DHH, 321.009 (D259) and 321.009 (D262). According to Macintyre, 'Victoria Park,' 14, both officers and men often trained without pay.

17 Quoted in Eayrs, *In Defence of Canada*, 62.

18 Pariseau, 'Forces armées,' vol. 4, études 119, 120, 122, synthesizes the military records of these events and includes full critical bibliographies of the published literature, including the excellent studies produced by historians in Atlantic Canada during the 1970s. See, for example, Macgillivray, 'Military Aid,' and David Frank, 'The Cape Breton Coal Industry and the Rise and Fall of the British Empire Steel Corporation,' *Acadiensis* 7 (1977), 3–34. Brereton Greenhous, *Dragoon: The Centennial History of the Royal Canadian Dragoons, 1883–1983* (Ottawa 1983), perhaps the finest regimental history ever produced in this country, contains a detailed, balanced, and humane account.

19 King to George P. Graham, 20 July 1923, quoted in Eayrs, *In Defence of Canada*, 67.

20 David J. McDougall, 'The Origins and Growth of the Canadian Customs Preventive Service Fleet in the Maritime Provinces and Quebec, 1892–1932,' *Northern Mariner*, 5 (October 1995), 37–57.

21 *Report of the Royal Canadian Mounted Police for the Year Ended September 30, 1932* (Ottawa 1932), 9–10; see also Donovan T. Saul, ed., *Red Serge and Stetsons* (London 1993), 135–6. The equipment operating out of Sydney comprised one RCAF Fairchild 71 seaplane, two RCMP cruisers, *No. 4* and *Scatarie*, based in North Sydney, and three RCMP motor boats, *Tenacity*, based in North Sydney, *Stalwart* based at Little Bras d'Or, and *No 10* based at Big Bras

d'Or. See DHH, 004-74/57/5, unsigned, 'Annual Report, 1933, RCAF Maritime Preventive Operations for RCM Police,' n.d., apps. D and E.

22 NA, RG 24, 3849/NSC 1018-1-10, Naval secretary to commander in charge, Halifax, 24 August 1939.

23 DHH, 004-74/57/3, Higgins to CO, RCAF Station Ottawa, 4 January 1934. Notwithstanding 'the scarcity of any suitable locations elsewhere in the vicinity,' Higgins referred to 'the excellence of this site' and recommended that it be purchased from its owner or negotiated for a long-term lease. The air force attempted to negotiate a lease in 1935 but the owner refused, with the result that the rental agreement was cancelled. Negotiations were under way to lease a piece of land adjacent to the base when the decision was taken to close the Sydney operation. See DHH, 004-79/57/7, Edwards, 'Annual Report 1935 Maritime Preventive Operations for the Royal Canadian Mounted Police,' 9 December 1935.

24 Douglas Spettigue, The Friendly Force (Toronto [1955]), 101–3.

25 DHH, 004-74/57/7, MacBrien to deputy minister of National Defence, 12 October 1935.

26 Ibid., Edwards to secretary, Department of National Defence (DND), 2 March 1936; DHH, 74/2, 'History of Eastern Air Command,' 1:47. The equipment at the Sydney River base, comprising two metal-clad buildings, the wireless transmitter, a floating dock, and a rowboat, were subsequently removed. See ibid., 1:51.

27 DHH, 004-74/57/7, Fleming, 'Annual Report of the Season's Operations 1935,' 15 November 1935. Nineteen rum runners were identified by the Sydney base during the 1935 season, while three other vessels were classified as 'unidentified suspicious craft.' For reports of successful captures of rum-running vessels and seizures of illegal liquor onshore in Cape Breton during this period, see Report of the Royal Canadian Mounted Police for the Year Ended March 31, 1936 (Ottawa 1936), 81–2; ibid., 1937 (Ottawa 1937), 91–2; ibid. 1938 (Ottawa 1938), 105, 108.

28 DHH, 74/2, 'Eastern Air Command,' 1:54–7. The RCMP subsequently acquired its own aircraft for offshore surveillance. For an interesting and useful account of liquor smuggling by a smuggler who went on to become chief of police in Lunenburg, see Hugh H. Corkum, On Both Sides of the Law (Hantsport 1989).

29 DHH, 74/2, 'Eastern Air Command,' 1:38–55.

30 Sarty, 'Entirely in the Hands.'

31 NA, RG 24, 2535/HQS 1723/6, 'Summary of Forms and Scales of Attack on Sydney, Confirmed by JSC [Joint Staff Committee], 10 December 1936.' In 1938 the estimated risk of attack on the Canadian East Coast was expanded

to include a possible raid by one of the new German heavy ships with 11-inch guns. See NA, RG 24, 2689/HQS 5199, JSC, 'A Review of Canada's Position with respect to Defence,' 22 July 1938, extract.

32 Roger Sarty, *The Maritime Defence of Canada, 1892–1945* (Toronto 1996), 111–13, 147.

33 Ibid., 139. The best guns in the Canadian service could fire only about 15,000 yards.

34 NA, RG 24, 11,124/501-5-7, Murray to chief of Naval Staff, 15 July 1935.

35 Ibid., 2506/HQS 1066/3, Croil to CGS, 4 December 1935.

36 Ibid., 2535/HQS 1723/6, General Staff, 'Memorandum on the Defences of Sydney, NS,' 21 October 1936.

37 Staff tables which list each of Treatt's recommendations, the Canadian staff's comments, and their final recommendations, are in ibid., 2693-4/HQC 5199C/1–2.

38 Ibid., 2535/HQS 1723/6, Treatt, 'Sydney,' 14 December 1936. The analysis in the following pages is derived from this seventeen-page, closely typed, report. See also the 'consolidated summary' of the Canadian Joint Staff Committee's review of the Treatt report, 2 September 1937, in ibid., 2694/ HQS 5199C/2, which essentially gave it blanket approval.

39 Treatt, 'Sydney.'

40 Ibid.

41 United Kingdom, War Office, *Handbook for the Ordnance, BL, 6-inch, Marks VII and VIIv on Mountings, BL 6-inch, Marks II, IIA, IV and V Land Service, 1938* (London 1938), 46, 74–104.

42 Treatt, 'Sydney.'

43 Coastal guns mounted on a height of land could not be depressed sufficiently to fire into the waters immediately below the site and for some hundreds of yards out from the shore. Such areas, which were within the range of a battery's armament but could not be covered because of geography or the technical limitations of the guns, were known as 'dead' zones.

44 NA, RG 24, 2693/HQS 5199C/1, 'Strait of Canso; Scales of Attack' [March–April 1937].

45 Ibid., 2, 'Summary of Proposals for the Defence of the Strait of Canso,' enclosed with 'Report of Joint Staff Committee on the Defences of Halifax, Sydney, Strait of Canso, Saint John, NB,' 2 September 1937. Melford battery was near Melford Point, while Beacon battery seems to have been named for the flashing light beacon that marked the northern entrance of the strait.

46 See DHH, 78/461, for mobilization action for Sydney in 'Halifax Defence Scheme. Chapter III [Naval],' 1 June 1937, amended to 21 July 1939. See also the 1939 correspondence concerning Sydney in NA, RG 24, 11124/501-

6-1; 11129, 'COAC [Commanding Officer Atlantic Coast] Secret and Personal'; [NSHQ], 'Action in an Emergency [on the East Coast],' 16 September 1938.

47 See, for example, ibid., 3840/NSS 1017-10-18/1, Nelles to deputy minister, 31 May 1938, and NA, MG 27, IIIB5/32, file X-51, same to same, 30 September 1938. NA, RG 24, 2685/HQS 5199/6, Chiefs of Staff Committee to minister, 17 September 1939, 'Appendix "A." Participation by RCN Instructed to Work in Closest Co-operation with HM Forces,' forecast a requirement of only $100,000 in fiscal 1940–1 for the development of storehouse accommodation and repair base at Sydney.

48 The founding of the club resulted from the federal government's decision in 1927 to place all civil government flying operations, along with the control and supervision of civil aviation, in civilian hands.

49 L.B. Stevenson, 'A Summary of the Activities of the Cape Breton Flying Club from its Organization in 1928 to 1949' (Sydney 1977), 10. This was, in fact, the first flying field in Nova Scotia, because the Halifax Flying Club, which was a year older, operated off floats. Ibid., 2.

50 Craig MacSween, 'YQY History Sydney Airport' (Sydney 1994), 2.

51 NA, RG 24, 5198/S15-24-11/1, Croil to CGS, 2 April 1936, 'Report of a Meeting Assembled by Authority of the Senior Air Officer at NDHQ on the 23rd and 24th March 1936 to Consider, Further, the Type of Aircraft Most Suited for Coastal Reconnaissance Duties on the Canadian Atlantic Coast'; NA, MG 27, IIIB/37, file D-19, senior air officer to deputy minister, 22 September 1936.

52 King to Canon B. Heeney, 20 November 1936, quoted in James Eayrs, *In Defence of Canada: Appeasement and Rearmament* (Toronto 1965), 140.

53 See Roger Sarty, 'Mr King and the Armed Forces,' in Norman Hillmer et al., eds., *A Country of Limitations: Canada and the World in 1939* (Ottawa 1996), 220.

54 DHH, Air 2/1/585/4581, Ashton to Sir Cyril Newall, 21 December 1937; Same to same, 11 April 1939; NA, RG 25, D-1/721, file 47, senior air officer to minister, 15 September 1938.

55 Sarty, 'Mr King,' 221–9.

56 NA, RG 24, 2695/HQS 5199C/5, master general of ordnance to CGS, 24 July 1939.

57 Ibid., 2, 'Proposed Interim Allotment of Existing Armament, and Method of Procurement ...,' amended to 8 November 1937, forwarded by CGS to prime minister, 1 December 1937. The intention in this early draft of the interim plan was to mount two 6-inch naval guns at Point Edward, but this was changed to 4.7-inch guns as a result of subsequent changes in allocations to

other ports. Nothing remained of the fortifications built at Chapel Point in the 1860s except 'traces of the battery parapet,' and the site was 'being rapidly lessened by erosion so that the line of the cliff is now within ten feet of the line of the parapet.' DHH, 345.009 (D4), 'Report on Chapel Point, Sydney, NS,' 12 May 1927.

58 See, especially, NA, RG 24, 2742/HQS 5902/5, DOC 6 to secretary, DND, 27 January 1938; ibid., 2744/HQS 5902-2, same to same, 27 June 1939.

59 Ibid., HQS 7362/1 (mfm C8340), correspondence, March–June 1938.

60 DHH, Sketch history series, '6th Independent Field Battery, RCA and 15th Harbour Defence Troop, RCA. Organization,' 29 March 1959; Cameron, *Pictonians*, 246–7.

61 DHH, 321.009 (D259), Macdonald to MD 6 headquarters, 11 January 1939.

62 NA, RG 24, 2742/HQS 5902/5, CGS to quartermaster general, 8 June 1938, Director of engineer services to DOC 6, 13 July 1938; DOC 6 to secretary, DND, 20 September 1938; DHH, 345.009 (D89)/1, Blake to Vince, 3 December 1938; Vince to Blake, 14 December 1938.

63 The Jacob siding was an old disused rail line which had formerly linked Jacob's Pit, a coal mine situated close to Chapel Point, to another rail line running to the shipping pier at North Sydney. Jacob's Pit was worked only from 1834 to 1853 but its railway siding survived into the 1950s. Indeed, the old ties can still be seen protruding through the asphalt of what is now Jacob Street in Sydney Mines. We are indebted to Kate Currie of the Beaton Institute for providing this information.

64 DHH, 345.009 (D89), Correspondence, 28 March–9 August 1939.

65 A.J. Kerry and W.A. McDill, *The History of the Corps of Royal Canadian Engineers* (Ottawa 1962–6), 1:288–9. The unit began to train in 1932. See *Report of the Department of National Defence for the Fiscal Year Ending 31 March 1933* (Ottawa 1933), 11. For additional detail, see DHH, 321.009 (D261), annual returns of non-permanent active militia units trained in MD 6, 1927–40.

66 DHH, 321.009 (D159), DOC 6 to secretary, DND, 'Short Annual Report; Military District No 6,' 1 February 1939.

67 DHH, 142.009 (D66), adjutant general to officer administering Royal Canadian Artillery, 15 August 1938.

68 *Report of the Department of National Defence for the Fiscal Year Ending 31 March 1940* (Ottawa 1940), 60. See also NA, RG 24, 2744/HQS 5902-2, CGS to adjutant general et al., 12 April 1939, forwarding staff table, 'Proposals for the Formation of Additional Coast Defence ... Units Required in Military District No 6,' and following correspondence.

69 The anomalies in DHH, 321.009 (D261), 'Numbers Trained NPAM, Year

Ending 31st March 1940,' and DHH, 321.009 (D262), 'Military District No 6 Half-Yearly Return of Strength,' for 1 January to 30 June 1939 and for 1 July to 31 December 1939, and the published training returns in *Report, 1940*, 37, show that the organization was in flux. These anomalies suggest that the 9th Field Company expanded, and then divided in the early summer of 1939 into the 3rd Fortress Company and the 9th Searchlight Battery, the latter unit taking the majority of the personnel. In fact, Military District 6 headquarters in Halifax trusted mainly in the existing engineer units at Halifax and Sydney to man the searchlights until, sometime in the future, the new artillery searchlight units were fully and properly organized. See, for example, NA, RG 24, 2744/HQS 5902-2, DOC 6 to secretary, DND, 27 March 1939. This is what happened when war broke out, only a few weeks after the nominal creation of the 9th Searchlight Battery. Although general orders for active service called out both the large new 9th Searchlight Battery and the smaller 3rd Fortress Company, personnel who had been transferred to the 9th came out with the 3rd, which carried out both searchlight and fortress engineering duties at Sydney. The 9th was left dormant until the spring of 1940. This is the account given, in less detail, in Kerry and McDill, *Royal Canadian Engineers*, 2:2–7, and the archival sources suggest it is the only correct published source. See, in addition to the sources mentioned earlier, DHH, General Order 135, 1 September 1939, and NA, RG 24, HQS 7362/1 (mfm C8340), director of military operations and intelligence to director of engineer services, 3 September 1939.

70 NA, RG 24, 2744/HQS 5902-2, CGS to adjutant general et al., 12 April 1939, forwarding staff table 'Proposals for the Formation of Additional Coast Defence ... Units Required in Military District No 6,' and following correspondence; *Report, 1940*, 60; Cameron, *Pictonians*, 203–4.

71 DHH, Air 2/1584/4044, Croil to Newall, 29 November 1938.

72 NA, RG 24, 2695/HQS 5199-C/5, chief of air staff to deputy minister, 2 August 1939; DHH, 114.1 (D181), Vince to Schmidlin, 3 February 1939; DHH, 74/628, folder A25, McGill to Maclachlan, 12 October 1939, enclosing 'Memorandum for Air Marshal W.A. Bishop, VC, regarding Inspection Trip to the Eastern Air Command – July 10th to 13th, 1939.'

9: Improvising Defences, 1939–1940

1 Frederick Edwards, 'Farthest East,' *Maclean's*, 1 November 1941, reprinted in Tennyson, *Impressions of Cape Breton*, 257. In 1941 there were twelve thousand miners working in fourteen collieries in Cape Breton County and five thousand men at the Sydney steel plant.

2 Leslie Roberts, *Canada and the War at Sea* (Montreal 1944), 31.

3 NPRC, O-27840/1, NSHQ to Goolden, 22, 28 August 1939; command appointment certificate, 29 August 1939; DHH, Nelles biographical file, Folder A, Nelles diary, 29–30 August 1939.

4 NA, RG 24, 11124/501-6-1, commander-in-charge HMC Dockyard Halifax to naval secretary, DND, 18 July, 3 August 1939; commander-in-charge HMC Dockyard Halifax to Goolden, [end August or beginning September].

5 R.B. Mitchell, 'Sydney Harbour – the War Years, 1939–1945,' in R.J. Morgan, ed., *More Essays in Cape Breton History* (Windsor 1977), 42.

6 Ibid., 44.

7 NA, RG 24, 11063/31-1-2, commanding officer Atlantic coast (COAC) to naval secretary, 12 September 1939; DHH, No. 8 Squadron operations record book, 30 September, 7, 9, 23, 30 October 1939.

8 Mitchell, 'Sydney Harbour,' 42.

9 NA, RG 24, 11063/36-1-8/1, Goolden to COAC, 8 September 1939.

10 NPRC, O-27840/2.

11 NA, RG 24, 11063/36-1-8/1, Reid to Goolden, 12 September 1939.

12 Ibid., 2775/HQS 6756/2, director of engineer services (DES) to DOC MDs 6 and 11, telegram engineers 548, 24 August 1939; DES to DOC 6, telegram, 25 August 1939.

13 Ibid., 13972, MD No. 6, MD and war diary, September 1939, Appendix 167; ibid., 14870, No. 6 Detachment, Royal Canadian Engineers, war diary, 26 August 1939.

14 Ibid., 2775/HQS 6756/2, DOC 6 to secretary, DND, 31 August 1939. Little remained of the old fort built in the 1860s. According to Chirgwin, 'when the fort was of no further use all the guns but two were broken up by a scrap dealer. The two remaining had fallen over the cliff to the shore. These were broken up by another junk dealer in 1904.' See Chirgwin, 'Harbour Forts.'

15 NA, RG 24, Defended Port of Sydney war diary, 1 September 1939 (mfm T10895).

16 Ibid., RG 24, HQS 7362/1, DOC 6 to secretary, DND, 21 February 1939 (mfm C8340), contains a plan for the precautionary mobilization of guards for 'vulnerable points.' See also Morrison and Slaney, *Manly Men*, 4; Moogk, 'From Fortress Louisbourg,' 152. These included Ottawa Brook and Grand Narrows Bridges, St Peters Canal, and the cable landings at Fox Cove and Dover Cove. In addition, small detachments began to guard the cable stations at Canso and Hazel Hill on 31 August. See Cameron, *Pictonians*, 120–1.

17 NA, RG 24, 14353, 16th Coast Brigade war diary, 1–5 September 1939 (1 September 1939 quoted).

18 According to Fraser, 'active service offered excitement and it offered an

'out" from the "rat-race." There was an awful lot of fellows joined the service, particularly the miners, I think, that this was the incentive to get away from the mines, to get into action, to get into something that was different.' Quoted in Moogk, 'From Fortress Louisbourg,' 152.

19 Ibid., 153.

20 NA, RG 24, 13972, MD 6 war diary, September 1939, app. 75, DOC 6 to secretary, DND, telegram 65, 7 September 1939; ibid., HQS 7362/1 (mfm C8340), same to same, telegram 71, 7 September 1939.

21 See progress report telegrams in NA, RG 24, HQS 7362/1–2 (mfm C8340), DOC 6 to secretary, DND, September–October 1939. See also Moogk, 'From Fortress Louisbourg,' 152.

22 NA, RG 24, 2647/HQS 3498/13, 'Report from Engineer Services Branch on situation existing at 23rd Aug, 1939.' DHH, 345.009 (D36), Smith to DOC 6, 25 August 1939. Macdonald to Anson, 31 August 1939.

23 Kerry and McDill, *Royal Canadian Engineers*, 2:16; NA, RG 24, HQS 7362/1 (mfm C8340), Anderson to director of military operations and intelligence (DMO and I), 2 September 1939. See also the account of the militia reorganization in the spring of 1939 in chap. 8.

24 NA, RG 24, 2645/HQS 3498/6, 'Interim Plan, Progress Report,' 14 October 1939; 14882/1, 3rd Fortress, Electrical and Mechanical (E and M) Company, RCE, war diary, 23 October 1939.

25 DHH, 345.009 (D36), Boak to secretary, DND, 23 December 1938, reports on tests of the lights carried out at Halifax shortly before they were purchased.

26 Moogk, 'From Fortress Louisbourg,' 156.

27 Cameron, *Pictonians*, 121–2.

28 The defence scheme, which fleshed out details of the outline scheme of 1938, was issued as 'Headquarters MD No 6 Operation Order No 1' on 6 September 1939; see NA, RG 24, 13972, MD 6 war diary, September 1939, Appendix 74. Actual deployments were generally in accordance with this scheme but varied in some particulars.

29 NA, RG 24, 15144, Prince Edward Island Highlanders war diary, 14–16 September 1939; RG 24, Defended Port of Sydney war diary, October 1939, app. 4 (mfm T10895), Desroches to MD 6 headquarters, 'Dispositions as at Noon 30th October 1939.'

30 Morrison and Slaney, *Manly Men*, 8, 14.

31 NA, RG 24, Defended Port of Sydney war diary, October 1939, app. 4 (mfm T10895), Desroches to MD 6 headquarters, 'Dispositions as at noon 30th October 1939.'

32 Will R. Bird, *No Retreating Footsteps: The Story of the North Nova Scotia High-*

landers (Kentville, n.d.), 7–8; NA, RG 24, HQS 7362/1 (mfm C8340), DOC 6 to secretary, DND, telegram 159, received 14 September 1939.

33 NA, RG 24, Defended Port of Sydney war diary, October 1939, app. 1 (mfm T10895), Rogers to Major R.E. Howard, OC Prince Edward Island Highlanders, n.d.

34 DHH, 142.009 (D66), Stockwell to secretary, DND, 24 September 1939.

35 Canada, *Defence Forces List* (Ottawa 1931) April 1931, 477, shows that Millen served 7 years and 238 days in the British army before joining the Canadian permanent force in 1905. 'Pay-Sheet, NCO 6 Men,' No. 1 Company, RCGA, September 1906. NA, RG 9, IIF8/140 confirms that Millen served in the coast artillery at Halifax from the time of his enlistment in the Canadian service.

36 NA, RG 24, HQC 8328-105/1 (mfm C4979), Ashton to CGS, 25 March 1940.

37 Interview with G.E. Avery, Halifax, January 1973. Avery was a member of the permanent force of about the same age and background as Millen.

38 Interview with Duncan MacDougall, 11 May 1994.

39 Quoted in Peter N. Moogk, 'Remembering Cape Breton Gunners,' *Canadian Gunner,* 13 (December 1979), 131.

40 Quoted in Moogk, 'From Fortress Louisbourg,' 158.

41 Quoted in Moogk, 'Remembering,' 131.

42 NA, RG 24, HQS 7362/2 (mfm C8340), DOC 6 to NDHQ, telegram 248, 23 September 1939.

43 DHH, 321.009 (D264), MacKenzie to MD 6 headquarters, 9 October 1939.

44 NA, RG24, Defended Port of Sydney war diary (mfm T10895), November 1939, app. 2, Des Roches to MD6 Headquarters, 'Disposition as at 1200 hrs 15 Nov 1939.'

45 Telephone interview with Martin Haley, 29 December 1971.

46 Interview with K.J.B. Partington, 27 December 1971. The son of an American mining engineer, Partington (1903–86) grew up in Halifax, where he became active in the militia. At the outbreak of war he was a major commanding the 9th Heavy Battery at Halifax. He subsequently served at Lawrencetown, Shelburne, and in New Brunswick before being transferred to Sydney to command the 16th Coast Regiment. Following the war, Partington served in the Reserves until his retirement in 1969. He also became provincial fire marshal in 1954, a post which he retained until his retirement. See Lorna Inness, 'Lt.-Col. Kendall J.R. Partington ... Soldier, Firefighter,' *Novascotian,* 8 March 1986.

47 Moogk, 'Remembering,' 134; 'From Fortress Louisbourg,' 170, 173.

48 Duncan MacDougall interview.

49 DHH, 345.009 (D89)/3, QMG to DOC 6, 23 August 1940.

50 NA, RG 24, 13139, Fort Petrie record book; 14353; 16th Coast Brigade war diary, 15, 20 March, 18–20, 29–30 April 1940.

51 DHH, 345.009 (D89)/2, QMG to DOC 6, 29 April 1940.

52 Ibid., 3, DOC 6 to secretary, DND, 30 May 1940.

53 Ibid., 2, QMG to DOC 6, 23 May 1940.

54 NA, RG 24, 14353, 16th Coast Brigade war diary, 12, 13–21 August 1940.

55 Ibid., 13148, Chapel Point battery record book.

56 NA, RG 24, 14353, 16th Coast Brigade war diary, 30 April 1940.

57 DHH, 74/2, 'Eastern Air Command,' 1:104–5. See also NA, MG 26, J1/ 262:230475-8, Croil to minister, 31 August 1939, with appendices on aircraft deployments updated to 5 September 1939.

58 NA, RG 24, 2517/S19-6-5/1, Anderson to secretary, DND, 'EAC Emergency Defence Plan,' 29 August 1939.

59 K.M. Molson and H.A. Taylor, *Canadian Aircraft Since 1909* (Stittsville 1982), 415–18.

60 NA, RG 24, 11123/501-1-13, 'Aircraft Performance Data,' Appendix C to EAC operation order 3, 25 May 1940.

61 W.A.B. Douglas, *The Creation of a National Air Force* (Toronto 1986), 378–9. The rule of thumb that aircraft should be able to devote about one third of their total flight time to tasks at the outer limit of the patrol would dictate the practical ranges of maritime air operations among all Allied air forces throughout the war.

62 It had been mothballed in 1936 and its equipment long since removed. DHH, 74/2, 'Eastern Air Command,' 1:41.

63 Discussions had been taking place early in 1936 to house the RCAF personnel at Sydney in the building being used for that purpose by the RCMP personnel, which was the old marine hospital at Victoria Park, when it was decided not to reopen the Sydney base. See DHH, 004-74/ 57/7, Edwards to secretary, DND, 8 February 1936; 2 March 1936. The RCAF personnel at Sydney from 1933 to 1935 had stayed at the Vidal Hotel, which then stood on the present site of the Bank of Nova Scotia at the corner of Charlotte and Pitt Streets. See DHH, 004-74/57/7, Fleming, 'Annual Report of the Season's Operations–1935,' 15 November 1935.

64 DHH, 74/2, 'Eastern Air Command,' 1:105–7.

65 DHH, 8 Squadron operations record book, 4, 9, 11, 13 September 1939.

66 DHH, Adm. 199/36, America and West Indies war diary, 29 August 1939.

67 DHH, 8 Squadron operations record book, September–October 1939.

68 See for example, DHH, NSS 1000-5-7/1, Naval Service weekly reports, week ending 3 November 1939. The report from the master of a British merchant

ship of what he took to be a U-boat on 29 October 1939 resulted in a long patrol to Anticosti Island by two Deltas.

69 DHH, 74/2, 'Eastern Air Command,' 1:107. Kelly's Beach was named after Frank Kelly, a former mayor of North Sydney and father of Harry Kelly, who operated North Sydney Ship Supply during the war.

70 DHH, 321.009 (D264), 'Report from Major J Jeffrey ...,' 20 September 1939. Dunbar to general staff officer, MD 6, 24 October 1939.

71 DHH, 74/2, 'Eastern Air Command,' 1:108–10, 131–3, 149–52; Douglas, *Creation*, 343–7.

10: Building Fortress Sydney, 1940–1941

1 There was already a civilian flying boat station at Botwood, Newfoundland.

2 Although this grim eventuality never occurred, the camps in the Maritimes did serve as a useful staging area, where formations could organize and train before going overseas.

3 DHH, NSS 1000-5-7/1, Naval Weekly Report, nos. 40 (20 June 1940), 46 (1 August 1940); DHH, NHS convoy signal cabinet, 'Convoy General,' NSHQ to COAC, signal 1629, 11 July 1940, 1 June to 15 July 1940.

4 NA, RG 24, 11063/36-1-8/2, 'Information Relative to Sydney Harbour,' forwarded by Goolden to COAC, 28 January 1941.

5 *Alachasse* and *Adversus* had originally come back to Sydney, but in early July were assigned as the examination vessels for the Strait of Canso defences.

6 DHH, NSS 1000-5-13/1. 'Auxiliary Vessels Monthly Report–May [1940]'; NSS 1000-5-13/2, June [1940], and NSS 1000-5-13/3, September [1940]. For further details, see the weekly reports in NA, RG 24, 11124/501-11-11/1.

7 NA, RG 24, 11063/36-1-8/2, 'Information Relative to Sydney Harbour,' forwarded by Goolden to COAC, 28 January 1941; 11685/1-3-1, Plan, 'HMCS Protector, Sydney, NS' [summer 1944].

8 Mitchell, 'Sydney Harbour,' 46.

9 NA, RG 24, 11079/48-1-11/2, COAC to naval secretary, 18 January 1940; Naval secretary to COAC, 13 March 1940; Nelles to Burrough, 5 April 1940; DHH, Adm 199/2078, Oland to Morey, 13 March 1940; Morey to Oland, 20 April 1940.

10 Ships of fifteen knots or faster did not need much protection as they had a good chance of evading submarines or of outrunning them.

11 C.B.A. Behrens, *Merchant Shipping and the Demands of War* (London and Nendeln 1978), 108–10.

12 DHH, 81/520/1440-127, Simpson, 'A History of Naval Control Service at Sydney, Nova Scotia' (Ottawa, n.d.), 7.

13 DHH, NHS convoy signal cabinet, 'Convoy General,' Admiralty to NSHQ, signal 2013, 30 July 1940.
14 DHH, NSS 1000-5-13/3, Mitchell to naval officer in charge (NOIC), Sydney, 4 September 1940, 3 October 1940.
15 Mitchell, 'Sydney Harbour,' 46.
16 DHH, 81/520/1440-127, Simpson, 'History of NCS,' 8.
17 Mitchell, 'Sydney Harbour,' 45.
18 Frederick B. Watt, *In All Respects Ready* (Scarborough 1985), 72–3. A similar incident occurred at Halifax, involving the crew of the Norwegian tanker *Marit*; see ibid., 71–80. See also NA, RG 24, 3942/NSS 1037-28-6/1, Beatty to chief of naval staff, 24 August 1940; Nelles to Beatty, 28 August 1940.
19 NA, RG 24, 3942, NSS 1037-28-6/1, Brown to Watt, 5 June 1941.
20 DHH, NSS 1000-5-21/1, Mitchell to NOIC Sydney, 3 October 1940.
21 Quoted in 'Sydney Harbour in World War 2,' *Cape Breton's Magazine*, No 13: 37.
22 Julie Zatsman, 'War Years in Sydney Recalled,' *Cape Breton Post*, 10 November 1989. This account is confirmed by the official records, which indicate that a merchant manning pool was never established at Sydney. According to Simpson, 'Cape Breton Island was combed to exhaustion to find seamen to fill vacancies on ships assembled for convoy.' See Simpson, 'History of NCS,' 4.
23 Quoted in 'Sydney Harbour,' 37.
24 Interview with Alec Huntley, 9 June 1994.
25 DHH, 81/520/8280/1/8280B/2, 'Outline History of Trade Division NSHQ Ottawa,' March 1946, 18.
26 DHH, NSS 1000-5-13/3, Mitchell to NOIC Sydney, 4 September 1940.
27 DHH, 81/520/1440-127, Simpson, 'History,' 2, 4.
28 NA, RG 24, 11685, file 27-R-1, Goolden to COAC, 25 October 1940. Reports of proceedings for the Sydney escorts are in DHH, NHS, Sydney file 48-2-2/4.
29 Separate operations record books for the Bolingbroke detachment are annexed to the 8 Squadron operations record book at DHH.
30 DHH, 74/2, 'Eastern Air Command,' 1:136–9.
31 8 Squadron operations record book, 31 July–30 September 1940.
32 Ibid., 27 August 1940. Some levity was added to the situation a couple of weeks later when a Stranraer dropped 60,000 leaflets urging people to 'Buy Bonds to Best Barbarism' over the communities surrounding the harbour. As the plane flew at an altitude of only about 250 feet above the main streets of the towns, the flood of leaflets looked 'like a smoke barrage from the tail of the plane.' However, they landed 'in the desired spots' and the event generated considerable excitement, and so the mission was deemed a success. See ibid., 9 September 1940.

33 RCAF Station Sydney operations record book, 24 October 1940, quoted in Douglas, *Creation*, 384.

34 DHH, 74/2, 'Eastern Air Command,' 1:209–14.

35 NA, RG 24, 14353, 16th Coast Brigade war diary, 22–27, 29, 31 July, 4–18 November 1940; DHH, 321.009(D366)/1, Arnett, 'Artillery Gun Practice,' [November 1940].

36 NA, RG24, 14353, 16th Coast Brigade war diary, 28 July 1940.

37 DHH, 321.009 (D366)/1, GOC Atlantic Command to commander, Sydney–Canso defences, 13 June 1941, Dobbie to Atlantic Command, 14 June 1941; Sydney and Canso defences weekly situation reports, August–September 1940.

38 For accounts of this incident by Dan Robertson, who fired the shell from Chapel Point, and George Fraser, who was serving at South Bar, see Moogk, 'Remembering,' 134, and Moogk, 'Fortress,' 160.

39 DHH, 321.009 (D366)/1, Sydney and Canso defences weekly situation reports, week ending 11 August 1940, Morris to DEO, 30 November 1940; NA, RG 24, 14353/16th Coast Brigade war diary, 2 April, 24 June, 13 September 1940.

40 DHH, 321.009 (D366)/2, Sydney and Canso defences weekly situation reports, week ending 22 March 1941, app. B; 345.009 (D43), Elderkin, 'McNair Point Mulgrave,' plan W-616-1, 26 October 1943.

41 DHH, 321.009 (D366)/1, 'Operational Location Statement [Sydney and Canso],' 28 August 1940.

42 DHH, 321.009 (D365)/1, Wilkins to Colonel General Staff Atlantic Command, 26 November 1940; ibid., 321.009 (D366)/2, Situation report, week ending 29 March 1941; 142.61B86009 (D8), Trotter, 'Site Plan New Beacon Battery,' 5 July 1941; 321.009 (D374), 'Table of Angles New Beacon Battery,' 25 September 1941; 'Report of Colonel C.S. Craig, 7 July 1940. Pending construction of the new battery, the garrison placed an eighteen-pounder field gun on the shoreline near the light beacon at the northern entrance to the gut to serve as the examination gun. It remained in position after completion of the new battery to provide coverage of the 'dead water' immediately below the site. See DHH, 142.61B86009 (D4), Partington to area commander, Sydney and Canso Area, 23 October 1942.

43 DHH, 345.009 (D48), Elkins to secretary, DND, 14 April 1941; 321.009 (D374), Smith for DES to GOC Atlantic Command, 9 February 1941. At Melford battery the temporary magazine, an arched corrugated iron structure covered with sandbags, proved fully adequate.

44 DHH, 321.009 (D365)/1, Dobbie to Atlantic Command, MD 6, armament officer, Halifax, and district ordnance officer, 2 November 1940; NA, RG 24,

14630, 9th Searchlight Battery (Coast Defence) war diary, April–October 1940.

45 Shortly after the new searchlight equipment had been installed, one of the personnel at Petrie or Chapel let fly with some choice phrases close by the tube, unaware that the brigade commanding officer, Lieutenant Colonel MacKenzie, was near the other end on the next floor. MacKenzie was a tolerant man and 'no comment made' was how the war diary concluded the incident. See NA, RG24/14353, 16th Coast Brigade war diary, 17 November 1940.

46 In April 1941 the infantry detachments in the North Sydney area moved into the North Bar barracks. They had been housed in bell tents in the fields next to St John's Anglican Church, whose kitchen facilities they had used. See DHH, 321.009 (D366)/2, Dobbie to Atlantic Command, 12 April 1941; Julie Collins, 'Historical Group to Show Northside as a War Port,' Cape Breton Post, 30 January 1997.

47 DHH, 321.009 (D366)/2, Dobbie to Atlantic Command, 10 June 1941, progress reports for weeks ending 7, 21 June 1941; NA, RG24, 14353, 16th Coast Brigade war diary, 5 June 1941. All these sources give different dates for the exercise, ranging from 2 to 6 June. We have taken the 16th Coast Brigade's daily diary as most likely to be accurate.

48 DHH, 345.009 (D37)/3, DOC 6 to secretary, DND, 17 July 1941. As a result of the navy's calls for stronger illumination, one of the 60-inch lights was brought to this position from Melford battery in the winter of 1943–4, while that work was shut down for the freeze-up at the northern end of the strait. See DHH, 321.009 (D111), Pipes memorandum, 23 November 1943.

49 NA, RG 24, 2695/HQS 5199C/5, CGS to minister, 7 September 1939.

50 On the construction of Lingan, see the excellent MD 6 file in DHH, 345.009 (D78). For plans and photographs, see DHH, 340.019 (D17).

51 DHH, 321.009 (D366)/1, Morris to MD 6, 24 September 1940, progress report for week ending 20 September 1940, which shows the infantry barracks at Lingan as 85 per cent completed. See also ibid., 321.009 (D365)/1, King, to commanding Royal Canadian Artillery, Halifax, officer commanding Sydney and Canso et al., 15 November 1940; NA, RG24/14353, 16th Coast Brigade war diary, 15–17, 21, 22, 26, 27 November, 1, 11, 12 December 1940.

52 NA, RG 24, 2579/HQS 3338/4, DOC 6 to NDHQ, telegram 55, 9 November 1940; ibid., 14353, 16th Coast Brigade war diary, 8 November 1940–27 January 1941; DHH, 321.009 (D366)/1, Arnett, 'Move of 6-inch Mark V Mountings to Lingan Battery, 2nd Report,' [c. 18 November 1940].

53 DHH, 321.009 (D366)/2, app. A to situation reports for weeks ending 29 March to 5 July 1941; Fraser quoted in Moogk, 'Fortress,' 16.

54 DHH, 321.009 (D365)/2, Huxford, 'Temporary Range-Finding System Using Cross Observation for Lingan Battery, Sydney, NS' [July 1941]; 321.009 (D366)/2, Goodeve to Huxford, 7 June 1941; 321.009 (D365)/2, Morres, Canadian Military Headquarters, London, to secretary, DND, 11 June 1941.

55 Ibid., (D365)/2, Huxford, 'Report on Visit to Sydney–Canso Defences,' June 1941; Huxford, 'Temporary Range-Finding,' [July 1941]. In 345.009 (D11)/1, Dickson to DEO, 9 August 1941, reported the New Victoria observation post complete and the North Head post would be completed by 21 August 1941.

56 DHH, 4 Coast Artillery (CAC) Detachment operations record book, May–August 1941.

57 Huxford, 'Report on Visit to Sydney–Canso Defences, June 1941.' John English, *The Canadian Army in Normandy* (New York 1991), focuses on the overseas army, but has much to say about military professionalism in Canada in general. Marc Milner, *North Atlantic Run* (Toronto 1985), and Douglas, *Creation*, feature comments by British officers on the Canadian naval escort force and Eastern Air Command that virtually replicate what Huxford said about the coast artillery at Sydney.

58 NA, RG 24/14353, 16th Coast Brigade war diary, 10, 28 April, 8, 21, 31 May, 2, 8, 18, 27 June 1941.

59 Cameron, *Pictonians*, 123; Bird, *No Retreating Footsteps*, 8–11; Morrison and Slaney, *Manly Men*, 15.

60 Cameron, *Pictonians*, 124; Morrison and Slaney, *Manly Men*, 28–48; DHH, 321.009 (D166)/1, Morris to Atlantic Command, 23 January 1941.

61 John Gordon Quigley, *A Century of Rifles, 1860–1960: The Halifax Rifles* (Halifax 1960), 122.

62 DHH, 321.009 (D366)/2, Sydney and Canso situation reports for weeks ending 31 May to 9 August 1941. The Elgin Regiment replaced the New Brunswick Rangers at Sydney, and the Grey and Simcoe Foresters relieved the Halifax Rifles at the Strait of Canso. The Saint John Fusiliers (MG) had just taken over the machine-gun detachment duties at Sydney from the Princess Louise Fusiliers (MG) in early June, allowing that unit to concentrate at Halifax. In late June a detachment from the Lake Superior Regiment provided summer relief for the Saint John Fusiliers at Sydney, while a detachment from the Irish Regiment of Canada stood in for the Princess Louise Fusiliers detachment at the strait.

63 Quigley, *Century*, 127.

64 Interview with John Quamm, 12 May 1994.

65 Edwards, 'Farthest East,' 257.

66 'Sydney Harbour,' 39. For an interesting account of wartime life in Halifax,

which was not dissimilar from that at Sydney, see Jay White, '"Sleepless and Veiled Am I": An East Coast Canadian Port Revisited,' *Nova Scotia Historical Review* 5 (1985), 15–29.

67 Jackson, *Windows*, 137.

68 *Pitch* (October 1943).

69 Moogk, 'Fortress,' 175.

70 Ibid.; interview with Duncan MacDougall, 11 May 1994.

71 Edwards, 'Farthest East,' 255.

72 Ibid., 257.

73 David R. Murray, ed., *Documents on Canadian External Relations*, vol. 7, *1939–1941*, Part 1 (Ottawa 1974), 939–47.

74 Edwards, 'Farthest East,' 255–6.

75 Ibid., 256.

76 Jackson, *Windows*, 136–7.

77 Quoted in John Campbell, 'Blackouts Remembered,' *Cape Breton Post*, 5 November 1994.

78 Ibid.

79 Ibid.

80 Jackson, *Windows*, 136–7.

81 Interview with Duncan MacDougall, 11 May 1994.

82 Noreen Marsh, 'Cape Breton Prospered While War Raged,' *Cape Breton Post*, 8 May 1990.

83 Edwards, 'Farthest East,' 256–7.

84 Ibid., 257.

85 Ibid.

86 Quoted in Marsh, 'Cape Breton.'

87 DHH, EAC headquarters operations record book, 1 June–30 October 1941, provides the most convenient listing of all missions carried out by the command in this period. See also DHH, 74/2, 'Eastern Air Command,' 2:289–90, 323; Douglas, *Creation*, 390.

88 DHH, Adm. 1/11338, Schofield, director of trade division, minute, 16 April 1941; Director operations division (home), minute, 19 April 1941; DHH, NHS, Sydney file 48-2-2/6, Admiralty to COAC, 1950B/20 June 1941, COAC to Admiralty, 1206Z/23 June 1941.

89 Farley Mowat, *The Grey Seas Under* (Toronto 1958), 205–13. This colourful account, although generally accurate, must be treated with caution. The claim that *Biafra* was rammed as a result of panic caused by a submarine contact is, according to the official records, not true, and neither is the statement that all the other merchant ships had swept away, leaving the stricken vessel alone. See DHH, NHS, Sydney file 48-2-2/5, Kingsley, 'Report of Pro-

ceedings – Convoy HX 138 HMCS "St Croix" ..., 18 July 1941'; Mackay, 'Damaging of S/S "Biafra," 14 July 1941.'

90 Kingsley, 'Report.'

91 DHH, 81/520/8280-SC 37, Herman, 'Convoy 37' (report of proceedings of HMCS *Matapedia*), 16 July 1941; NA, RG 24, 11311/8280-HX 138, Stevens, report of proceedings of HMS *Broadwater* with HX 138/SC 37, 29 July 1941.

92 DHH, NSS 1000-5-21/1, Mitchell to NOIC Sydney, 8 August 1941; Sydney file 48-2-2/6, Dobson, 'Report on Convoy Duty with SC 38,' 28 July 1941; Davis, 'Report of Proceedings 24th July to August 2nd, 1941' (HMCS *Columbia* with HX 140/SC 38), 4 August 1941.

93 United Kingdom, Admiralty Naval Staff, *Home Waters and the Atlantic*, vol. 2, *9th April 1940–6th December 1941* (London 1961), 313–14. When scientists began operations research for the Admiralty in 1942, they proved that a large convoy with an increased escort was more secure than a smaller one with a smaller escort. That, however, was not appreciated in 1941.

94 DHH, NSS 1000-5-21/1, Mitchell to NOIC Sydney, 8 August 1941; same to same, 3 October 1941.

95 United Kingdom, Admiralty, *The U-Boat War in the Atlantic*, vol. 1, *1939–1941*, German Naval History Series (London 1950), 80–4.

96 W.A.B. Douglas and Jurgen Rohwer, '"The Most Thankless Task" Revisited: Convoys, Escorts and Radio Intelligence in the Western Atlantic, 1941–43,' in James A. Boutilier, ed., *RCN in Retrospect, 1910–1968* (Vancouver 1982), 193–207.

97 DHH, NHS 81/520/8280/SC-44, 'Loss of HMCS Lévis (Corvette).'

98 DHH, 8280-SC 46 (mfm 88/1/31), Taylor (commodore SC 46), 'Convoy Form D Mercantile Convoy No SC 46,' 9 October 1941, and attached 'Report of Proceedings while Approaching the Belle Isle Straits,' 27 September 1941.

99 Jurgen Rohwer, 'Special Intelligence und die Geleitzugsteuerung im Herbst 1941,' *Marine Rundschau*, no. 11 (November 1978), 711–19 (translation in DHH, SGR II 224).

100 DHH, Adm. 237/188, Admiralty, 'Estimated U-boat Disposition,' 1328A, 28 October 1941; NA, RG 24, 6788/NSS 8280–166/16/2, Nelles to minister, 27 October 1941; United Kingdom, *U-boat War in the Atlantic*, 1: 83–4.

101 Marc Milner, *North Atlantic Run: The Royal Canadian Navy and the Battle for the Convoys* (Toronto 1985), 83; Michael L. Hadley, *U-boats against Canada* (Montreal and Kingston 1985), 25–6; DHH, Adm. 237/188, White, 'Report of Convoy SC 52,' 6 November 1941.

102 DHH, NSS 1000-5-21/1, Mitchell to NOIC Sydney, 6 December 1941; DHH, 81/520/1440-127, Simpson, 'History of NCS.'

103 United Kingdom, *U-Boat War in the Atlantic*, 1: 84–5, 90.
104 DHH, NSS 1000-5-21/1, Mitchell to NOIC Sydney, 6 December 1941; 81/
    520/1440-127, Simpson, 'History of the NCS.'
105 NA, RG 24, 11,683/File 24-9-1, Goolden to secretary of Naval Board, 11 May
    1942.
106 DHH, NSS 1000-5-21/1, Mitchell to NOIC Sydney, 6 December 1941. More
    details are in same to same, 6 January 1942.

11: Battle of the St Lawrence, 1942

1 United Kingdom, *U-Boat War in the Atlantic*, 2: 1–6. This states that seven
  Type VII U-boats were sent to Newfoundland, but Robert Fisher's detailed
  analysis, primarily in the Befehlshaber der Unterseeboote (BdU) [German
  submarine headquarters], war diary, DHH, 79/446, could identify only six.
2 Hadley, *U-Boats*, 62–5; Douglas, *Creation*, 486-7.
3 DHH, 181.003 (D43), Sydney intelligence report, week ending 2 January
  1942, which corrects some of the details in DHH, 74/2, 'Eastern Air Command,' 2: 321–2.
4 NA, RG 24, 4023, NSC 1062-13-10/6, Whitehead, 'Particulars of Attacks on
  Merchant Vessels ... FRISKO,' n.d; Whitehead to NOIC Sydney, 16 January
  1942.
5 Hadley, *U-Boats*, 64. This good account errs in stating that the attack took
  place in the Cabot Strait. See DHH, mfm, NSS 8280-SC 64, COAC to Admiralty, signal 2244Z, 18 January 1942; Simpson to NOIC Sydney, 14 December 1943.
6 Hadley, *U-Boats*, 66–8.
7 DHH, NSS 1000-5-20/1, Flag Officer Newfoundland Force, report of proceedings for January 1942; S.C.R. Tremblay, 'Chronology of RCN North
  Atlantic Convoy Operations, May 1941–January 1942'; NSS 1000-5-13/9,
  COAC, 'Report of Proceedings Staff Officer Operations January, 1942.'
8 DHH, 81/520/8280A, Plans Division, 'History of North Atlantic Convoy
  Escort Organization ...,' 1 May 1942.
9 DHH, 74/2, 'Eastern Air Command,' 3: 357–8; 119 Squadron operations
  record book, 23 March 1942; Hadley, *U-Boats*, 78–9.
10 DHH, 74/2, 'Eastern Air Command,' 3: 358.
11 DHH, NSS 1000-5-21/1, Mitchell, NCSO, to NOIC Sydney, 29 May 1942;
   NSS 1000-5-7/3, Warship sailings from Naval Weekly Reports, nos. 139 to
   142, 14 May–4 June 1942; DHH, NSS 1000-5-20/1, Flag Officer Newfoundland Force (FONF) reports of proceedings for March–May 1942.

12 NA, RG 24, 11692/H 1002-1-8/1, Secretary, Naval Board, 'Defence of Shipping–Gulf of St Lawrence–1942 (Short Title–Plan GL2),' 1 April 1942.

13 DHH, EAC war diary, 12–15 May 1942; 181.003 (D624)/2, EAC weekly intelligence report, week ending 16 May 1942.

14 DHH, 116 Squadron operations record book, 12–25 May 1942; NA, RG 24, 5217/S19-6-5/4, Operations summary signals for 13 to 21 May 1942.

15 DHH, NSS 8280-ON 90, CO *Arrowhead* to Captain D Halifax, 22 May 1942, Report of proceedings for convoy SQS 1, which 'Sailed from Sydney at 2055/14 with seven ships from ON 90.'

16 DHH, NHS 48-2-2 (C)/1, CO *Arrowhead* to Captain D, Halifax, 'Report of proceedings QS 1 and SH 2,' 22 May 1942; NHS 48-2-2(C)/2, 'HMCS Medicine Hat Report of Proceedings,' 9–20 May 1942; Gilbert Tucker, *The Naval Service of Canada: Its Official History* (2 vols., Ottawa 1952), 2: 538–9.

17 Hadley, *U-Boats*, 92–3.

18 NA, RG 24, 3976, NSS 1048-48-32/1, Loy, 'Appreciation of Situation in River & Gulf of St Lawrence,' 21 March 1942; 'Defence of Sydney–Gulf of St Lawrence–1942.'

19 DHH, 81/520/1650-DS, 'Daily States, I-HMC Ships & HM & Allied Ships Operated by RCN Authorities,' 1 July 1942.

20 The Canso was the Canadian variant of the U.S. Navy's PBY 5 flying boat, and the Catalina was the British variant. Britain had allowed the RCAF to take delivery of nine of its Catalina versions from Consolidated Aircraft in California in the spring of 1941, and the RCAF had subsequently begun to receive its own Canso version. The Canso and the Catalina both strongly resembled the original PBY 5, the changes being mainly internal ones to improve cold weather performance and to accommodate the types of machine guns and bombs or depth charges used by the RCAF and RAF.

21 DHH, 117 Squadron operations record book, June 1942.

22 Ibid., 119 Squadron operations record book, June 1942.

23 Ibid., 79/446, BdU war diary, 20 July 1942 (*U-132*'s report); Hadley, *U-Boats*, 100–3, 105–6; Douglas, *Creation*, 498–500; DHH, 181.003 (D43), RCAF Station Sydney weekly intelligence reports, weeks ending 10, 17, 24 July 1942; 117 Squadron operations record book, 6–22 July 1942; mfm, NSS 8280-QS 19, CO HMCS *Weyburn* to NOIC Gaspé, 23 July 1942.

24 Samuel Eliot Morison, *The Battle of the Atlantic, September 1939–May 1943* (Boston 1947), 58–62, 330.

25 DHH, 81/520/1440-127, 'A History of Naval Control Service at Sydney, Nova Scotia.'

26 NARA, National Records Center, RG 313, Red, 1942 confidential, box 8811, file A4-2, Representative commander, Greenland Patrol, Sydney to U.S. naval

observer, Halifax, 14 October 1942; Brainard to Schwerdt, 7 November 1942.

27 DHH, 81/520/8280B/3, Secretary, Naval Board, 'Rearrangement Convoys East Coast of North America,' 3 August 1942; Brand to director of merchant seamen, commissioner of immigration, et al., 8 August 1942; 'History of Naval Control Service at Sydney.'

28 See Milner, *North Atlantic*, 142–7, on SC 94. The Canadian navy's part during the renewed U-boat offensive at mid-ocean in 1942–3 is the focus of much of this important book.

29 This is an important point, made by Milner on many occasions. See, for example, ibid., 97.

30 DHH, 81/520/8280B/3, 'Outline History of the Trade Division,' 38.

31 NARA, RG 313, Red, Box 8702, CTF 24 convoy file SG 6; DHH, 181.003 (D304), 1 Group RCAF to AOC EAC, signal 0300 GMT, 29 August 1942.

32 DHH, 321.009 (D124), Dobbie, situation report for weeks ending 29 August 1942 and 5 September 1942.

33 Ibid., NSS 1000-5-20/2, Mitchell to NOIC, Sydney, 29 September 1942.

34 For an account of this incident, see Steve Neary, *The Enemy on Our Doorstep* (St John's 1994).

35 Hadley, *U-Boats*, 115–27; Douglas, *Creation*, 501–3.

36 Admiralty, Naval Staff, Anti-Submarine Warfare Division, *Monthly Anti-Submarine Report* (January 1943), 20–1.

37 DHH, 79/446, BdU war diary, 17 September 1942.

38 Douglas, *Creation*, 504–5.

39 DHH, *U-517* log, 24 September–8 October 1942.

40 See 1941 and 1942 correspondence in DHH, MT 59/940.

41 NA, RG 24, 6789/NSS 8280-166/16/3, NSHQ to Admiralty, signal 2223Z, 9 September 1942; 11504, file Misc. 2, NOIC Sydney to COAC, 15 September 1942; DHH, NSS 1000-5-21/2, Mitchell to NOIC Sydney, 29 September 1942; NSHQ Coastal Convoy Cabinet, SQ-QS file; Douglas, *Creation*, 503.

42 DHH, 79/446, BdU war diary, 19 September 1942, and 'Submarine Situation and Intended Operations,' memorandum filed after 30 September 1942 entry.

43 DHH, mfm, *U-69* log, 2 October 1942; 181.003 (D43), RCAF Sydney intelligence report, week ending 2 October 1942; 181.003 (D423), EAC intelligence report, week ending 2 October 1942.

44 Ibid., 181.003 (D423), EAC intelligence report, week ending 16 October 1942. 113 Squadron's operations record book, Chatham and Mont-Joli detachments, 9–13 October 1942, suggests there were even more flights; see

DHH, 181.003 (D304), AOC EAC to AFHQ, signal 0435 GMT, 13 October 1942; Hadley, *U-Boats*, 132, 137.

45 DHH, mfm, *U-43* log, 10 October 1943; 181.003 (D43), RCAF Station Sydney intelligence report, week ending 16 October 1942; 117 Squadron operations record book, 10 October 1942.

46 DHH, mfm, *U-106* log, 10–11 October 1942; NHS 8000 'Vison,' CO *Vison* to NOIC Sydney, 13 October 1942, Staff officer (operations) (Sydney) to NOIC Sydney, 20 November 1942; NA, RG 24, 5217/S19-6-5/5, AOC EAC to AFHQ, signal A413, 11 October 1942; same to same, signal A451, 19 October 1942; Hadley, *U-Boats*, 135.

47 NA, RG 24, 5217/S19-6-5-/5, Anderson to deputy air member air staff (plans) and director of operations, 23 October 1942.

48 DHH, NHS, NSHQ Operations Division daily summaries for 9–14 October 1942; 181.003 (D43), RCAF Station Sydney intelligence report for week ending 16 October 1942; *Royal Canadian Navy Monthly Review* 10 (October 1942), 39; DHH, NSS 1000-5-7/4, Naval weekly reports as at 8 October 1942 and 15 October 1942.

49 DHH, 181.003 (D43), RCAF Station Sydney intelligence report for week ending 16 October 1942; 113 Squadron operations record book, Mont-Joli and Chatham detachments, October 1942; 181.003 (D304), AOC EAC to AFHQ, signal 0435 GMT 13 October 1942.

50 The following narrative depends primarily on NA, RG 24, 11939/ 8871-3986, CO HMCS *Grandmère* to NOIC Sydney, 'Report of Proceedings, Sydney–Port aux Basques Convoy,' 15 October 1942; Dalton, marine superintendent to Russell, general manager, Newfoundland Railways, 23 October 1942, enclosing evidence of survivors of *Caribou*. Dalton's final report, which contains much of this evidence, was published in the *St John's Daily News*, 14 November 1942 (copy in NA, RG 24, 6892/8871-3986); DHH, mfm, *U-69* war diary, 13–15 October 1942.

51 Douglas How, *Night of the Caribou* (Hantsport 1988).

52 Ibid., 32.

53 Ibid., 24.

54 *Grandmère* had been commissioned only in December 1941 and completed trials in May. A Scottish-born merchant seaman, Cuthbert had joined the Canadian navy in June 1941. See ibid., 40–1.

55 NA, RG 24, 11503/1-14-2, Correspondence, 24 April 1942–5 June 1942, and NCSO, Sydney, to Long, Newfoundland Railways agent, 20 October 1942.

56 Quoted in How, *Caribou*, 19.

57 Howard K. Yorke, 'A Saga of the *Caribou*,' *Nova Scotia Historical Review* 5 (1985), 32.

58 *U-69*'s log states that the attack took place at 0821 German standard time, which was two hours ahead of Greenwich Mean Time. This matches well with *Grandmère*'s initial report of the attack. See NA, RG 24, 6892/NSS 8871-3986, *Grandmère* to Sydney W/T signal timed 0625 Greenwich mean time, 14 October 1942. NA, RG 24, 11939/8871-3986, Dalton to Russell, 23 October 1942, reporting on the survivors' evidence, states that 'they all pretty well agree as to the actual time of torpedoing about 3:45 am October 14th.' Because *Caribou* was keeping Newfoundland Summer Time (confirmed by the published version of Dalton's report in the *St John's Daily News*, 14 November 1942), that matches well with *Grandmère*'s signal. Thus, the statement in *Grandmère*'s report of proceedings, 15 October 1942, that the torpedoing took place at 0640 Greenwich mean time is incorrect.

59 How, *Caribou*, 95, 147–8.

60 DHH, 117 and 119 Squadrons operations record books, 14 October 1942.

61 Quoted in How, *Caribou*, 100. In fact, the people in the boat thought the plane had not seen them and were cheering and waving to attract its attention.

62 Ibid., 101, 106.

63 Ibid., 108–9.

64 DHH, NHS 8001, 'Merchant Shipping,' Russell to director of naval information, 17 February 1959; 81/520/1440-166/25, vol. 2/1, Gilhooly, naval information officer, to J.J. Connolly, 16 October 1942. For survivor accounts, see 'Caribou Sinking, & Grandmère: 1942,' *Cape Breton's Magazine*, no. 46:37–49; 'The Sinking of the "Caribou" Ferry,' *Cape Breton's Magazine*, no. 10:20–8; Yorke, 'Saga'; How, *Caribou*.

65 Quoted in How, *Caribou*, 111.

66 The senior air force officer, Group Captain A.D. Ross, would subsequently experience tragedy in 1944 when he was commanding a Canadian bomber base in Britain. When a returning bomber crashed, he rushed into the blazing wreckage and saved crewmen amid exploding bombs. One of his arms was 'nearly severed' by the blasts, but 'he calmly walked to the ambulance and an emergency amputation was performed on arrival at station sick quarters.' See Brereton Greenhous et al., *The Official History of the Royal Canadian Air Force*, vol. 3, *The Crucible of War 1939–1945* (Toronto 1994), 827.

67 How, *Caribou*, 111.

68 Mitchell, 'Sydney Harbour,' 48.

69 On the release of full information to the press, see NA, RG 24/11015/5-2-3-D, staff officer (intelligence), St John's, to director of naval intelligence, Ottawa, signal 2104Z, 14 Oct. 1942.

70 Quoted in How, *Caribou*, 28. A native of Dunvegan, Cape Breton, Angus L.

Macdonald (1890–1954) served in the First World War with the 25th Battalion, then taught at Dalhousie University's law school. From 1933 to 1940 and again from 1945 to 1954 he was Liberal premier of Nova Scotia. From 1940 to 1945 he was minister of national defence for naval services in the King government.

71 Quoted in ibid., 114.

72 Quoted in ibid., 117.

73 *Sydney Post-Record*, 17 October 1942. See also clippings in NA, RG 24, 6892/ NSS 8871–3986.

74 How, *Caribou*, 117–18.

75 Ibid., 123.

76 James B. Lamb, *On the Triangle Run* (Toronto 1986), 134.

77 DHH, mfm, *U-69* log, 14–22 October 1942; 117 and 119 Squadrons operations record books, 15–17 October 1942; 181.003 (D304), AOC EAC to AFHQ, signal A430, 16 October 1942.

78 DHH, mfm, *U-43* and *U-106* logs, 20 October–11 November 1942.

79 Neary, *Enemy*, 55–6.

80 Among those killed on *Rose Castle* was eighteen-year-old Michael MacPherson of New Waterford; see Greg Hines, 'Survivor Helps Remember Sinking,' *Cape Breton Post*, 11 December 1993. Gordon Hardy of Ingonish, then seventeen, survived the attack. He was pulled out of the water after the sinking by another crewman, who turned out to be George Hardy, a cousin from Newfoundland whom he had not yet even met. Hardy's previous ship, *Lord Strathcona*, had been sunk two months earlier. He was not yet old enough to join the army, but his father and four brothers were in the services. See Maureen Scobie, 'Ingonish Native Gordon Hardy Recalls Night Rose Castle Torpedoed Off Newfoundland,' *Cape Breton Post*, 10 November 1993.

81 Neary, *Enemy*, 70–1, 74.

82 On Jankowski's mission, see Dean Beeby, *Cargo of Lies: The True Story of a Nazi Double Agent in Canada* (Toronto 1966). See also Neary, *Enemy*, 55–6.

83 DHH, 79/446, BdU war diary, 27, 29, 30 October, 10, 20 November 1942, and 'Submarine Situation on 19 October,' filed after entry for 31 October 1942; Hadley, *U-Boats*, 149–62; DHH, mfm, *U-518* log, 8–18 November 1942.

84 DHH, mfm, *U-183* log, 2–30 November 1942; NSS 8280–SH 59, NSS 8280–HJ 19, CO *Vegreville* to Captain D Newfoundland, 1 December 1942, and de Marbois, memorandum, 22 January 1943.

85 Joseph Schull, *The Far Distant Ships* (Ottawa 1961), 122.

86 Lamb, *Triangle*, 126.

87 DHH, DEFE 3/756, Bletchley Park to IDG 8 (Admiralty), message ZTPGU 31873, 1755Z, 27 September 1944; Decryption of multipart BdU signal

1339/1459/1855/2005/2058 (Central European Time), 23 September 1944.

88 Hadley, *U-Boats*, 135–7.

89 United Kingdom, *U-Boat War in the Atlantic*, 2: 42–3.

90 Hadley, *U-Boats*, 137.

91 DHH, 181.003 (D25), 'EAC [Monthly] Anti-Submarine Reports,' 1942.

92 This account is drawn from DHH, 181.003 (D43), RCAF Station Sydney's weekly intelligence reports; DHH, 74/2 'Eastern Air Command, pt 3: 444–7, 450–1, 489–94, and RCAF Station Sydney and 119 Squadron operations record books.

93 NA, RG 24, 11079/48-1-11/2, Mitchell, 'Summary of Convoy Season 1942,' 2 February 1943.

94 Ibid.

95 NA, RG 24, 11079/48-1-11/2, [Lieutenant J.S. O'Neal], 'Entertainment of Merchant Seamen Season 1942,' enclosure to Mitchell, 'Summary of Convoy Season 1942,' 2 February 1942. Prior to the opening of the naval base at Point Edward, many naval personnel were boarded in private homes throughout the community. Laureen (Black) Szewczok recalls that her mother once had twenty-three sailors boarding at their home on the Esplanade. 'They were all over the place, even in the attic. They usually worked shifts. One would be getting out of bed and another would be getting in.' Marsh, 'Cape Breton.'

96 DHH, NSS 1000-5-21/1, Mitchell to NOIC Sydney, 1 July 1942.

97 NA, RG 24, 11685/2-6-1/2, 'Speech 1 January 1943 to the Royal Cape Breton Yacht Club,' Sydney, NS. Edna de Sanctis later recalled that her family entertained many sailors at their home on Trinity Avenue. One night, 'it was as if they just couldn't bring themselves to leave. Looking back, it was almost as if they sensed something was going to go wrong. It was obvious, they didn't want the evening to end and prolonged their good-byes as long as they could.' The next day, 'while having lunch at the Dome Grill,' she heard the news that their ship had been torpedoed. See Marsh, 'Cape Breton.'

12: Convoy Port, 1942–1943

1 The following account draws on Tucker, *Naval Service*, 2: 170–3, with additional sources as noted. Tucker's account of the Point Edward base is less complete than the treatment of other Second World War bases. Certainly the present authors had particular difficulty in locating specific material on Point Edward in archives. A complete history of the development of Point Edward, and of ship repair by commercial firms in the Cape Breton area,

would require a substantial specialized research effort. The present account, like Tucker's, must be treated as a preliminary survey.

2 DHH, NSS 1000-5-8/3, 'Summary of Naval War Effort,' 1 January–31 March 1942, 25.

3 See, for example, DHH, NHS 1650-1/2, Todd, 'The Post-War Canadian Navy,' 17 November 1943, p. 12.

4 Quoted in Tucker, *Naval Service*, 2: 171.

5 Ibid., plate V, includes a sketch of the Point Edward base as fully developed in the spring of 1945. Compare with the more detailed sketch, 'HMCS Protector 2, Point Edward Naval Base,' 7 [?] October 1943, in NA, RG 24, 11064/36-1-8/3. There are also helpful plans in DHH, NHS 8000, 'Protector (Shore Establishment).'

6 DHH, NSS 1000-5-21/2, NOIC Sydney, reports of proceedings, and especially the attached base engineer officer, reports of proceedings, January–September 1943.

7 Ibid., NSS 1000-5-7/4, Naval weekly reports, 10 December 1942, 22 July 1943.

8 Milner, *North Atlantic Run*, chapters 6–8; David Zimmerman, *The Great Naval Battle of Ottawa* (Toronto 1989); Tucker, *Naval Service*, 2: 456–60.

9 NA, RG 24, 11064/36-1-8/3, Schwerdt to COAC, 15 February 1943 et seq.

10 DHH, Minutes, 124th meeting of the Naval Board, 5 July 1943, and appendix A, DeWolf to ACNS, 'Expansion Programme Point Edward, Sydney, NS,' 3 July 1943; NSS 1000-5-8/4, Summary of naval war effort, 1 July–31 October 1943.

11 DHH, NSS 1000-5-8/3, Summary of naval war effort, 1 January–31 March 1942, 35; 1 April–30 June 1942, 45; 1 July–30 September 1942, 34; ibid., 4, 1 January–31 March 1943, 46; 1 April–30 June 1943, 47; 1 July–30 September 1943, 28. See also NA, RG 24, 11685/1-3-1, Drawing no. B-86, 'HMCS Protector, Point Edward NS Naval Anti-Aircraft Range,' 10 August 1944.

12 DHH, 181.003 (D43), RCAF Station Sydney weekly intelligence reports for weeks ending 12 June, 18 September, 16 October, 5 November 1942, 28 January 1943; RCAF Station Sydney operations record book, 31 January 1942, 1 January 1943.

13 Molson and Taylor, *Canadian Aircraft*, 378–9; Douglas, *Creation*, 361–5.

14 RCAF Station Sydney operations record book, 25–6 April 1942.

15 DHH, 441 Squadron operations record book, 7 May–9 June 1942.

16 Ibid., 128 Squadron operations record book, 7 June 1942–26 June 1943.

17 DHH, 181.003 (D43), RCAF Station Sydney weekly intelligence report, week ending 7 August 1942. The actual site of the crash was in a field on McGuire's farm, at what is now the corner of Cow Bay Road and Industrial Drive in Sydney. Sydney Slaven, then a boy, recalls seeing the wreckage

strewn all over the field. Interview with Sydney Slaven, 21 January 1997. For an account of a similar incident in 1943, see 128 Squadron operations record book, 17 February 1943.

18 Douglas, *Creation*, 377, 397. W.E. Knowles Middleton, *Radar Development in Canada: The Radio Branch of the National Research Council of Canada, 1939–1946* (Waterloo 1981), 97–8; A.P. Sayer, *Army Radar,* The Second World War 1939–1945, Army (Confidential History Series) (London 1950), 116–25; DHH, 6 Radio Unit operations record book, August–December 1942, regular reports on the ranges achieved by the set appear in the entries for 1944.

19 DHH, 181.003 (D43), RCAF Station Sydney weekly intelligence reports, weeks ending 10 December 1942 and 28 January 1943, report that construction had started but was progressing very slowly. The 20 Radio Unit operations record book opens only on 1 October 1943.

20 DHH, 80/395, A.H. Cristey, 'Narrative History of the Formation and Development of the Fighter and Filter Control System,' September 1944; 20 Radio Unit operations record book, 13, 19 January 1944, 19, 21–2 June 1944, mentions specific late improvements in the communications and other facilities at Sydney.

21 The following account draws on two excellent studies in army records: DHH, 321.009 (D433), General Staff, 'Review of AA Defence Plan,' 30 July 1946; 112.3M2 (D58), 'Narrative of Directorates, NDHQ: Director General of Coast and Anti-Aircraft Defences,' n.d.

22 DHH, 345.003 (D3), 'Record of Anti-Aircraft Units Halifax Fortress from Sept 1939 to date,' (December 1944). See the pointed comments regarding the 7th AA Battery of Stellarton, which shared many of the same experiences as the 6th on mobilization, in Cameron, *Pictonians*, 206–7. As a member of the 7th who was seconded to the artillery at Sydney, Cameron was writing from personal knowledge.

23 DHH, 321.009 (D124), Defended Port of Sydney weekly situation reports, May–June 1942; 321.009 (D346)/14, [Sydney–Canso] 'Operational Location Statement,' 1 September 1942.

24 The 24th Light Anti-Aircraft Battery expanded to serve the four additional Bofors, two of which went to the new naval base at Point Edward, and two to cover the RCAF flying boat station at Kelly's Beach, North Sydney. There were two additional Bofors that went to Fort Lingan for local air defence, but they were manned by the artillery detachment at the fort. See ibid., 321.009 (D124)/2–3, Defended Port of Sydney weekly situation reports, October 1942–April 1943; DHH, 142.81A23 (D1), Colonel G.W.L. Nicholson's notes on anti-aircraft developments at Sydney for the Army Historical Section,

1943–4; 321.009 (D346)/19, 'Operational Location Statement Sydney and Canso Defences,' 15 April 1943.

25 See, for example, NA, RG 24, HQC 8828-1-1 (mfm C8377), DEO, MD 6, plan W-1253, 'Site Plan C Battery H/AA ... Westmount,' 22 October 1942; DEO, MD 6, plan W-1255, 'Site Plan No 2 L/AA ... Crawley Creek,' 22 October 194[3?]; HQC 8828-1 (mfm C8837), DEO, MD 6, plan W-1258, 'Site Plan D Battery H/AA ... Jacksonville,' 17 November 1943; DEO MD 6, plan W-1260, 'Site Plan A Battery C Heavy AA South Bar,' 10 September 1943.

26 DHH, 142.83B5009 (D2), Archibald, 'DGAA Tour Notes, Sydney AA Defences – 2/4 December 1943,' 5 December 1943.

27 It has been preserved as part of the York Redoubt National Historic Site and is open to visitors, although, unfortunately, most of the instruments have been removed. See DHH, 345.009 (D24); 345.009 (D11).

28 DHH, 321.009 (D124)/2, Defended Port of Sydney weekly situation reports, 3, 10, 17, 24, 31 October 1942.

29 A fortress plotting room, together with much of the equipment, including the fortress plotter, has been preserved at the Ford Rodd National Historic Site in Victoria, BC.

30 DHH, 321.009 (D124)/2, Defended Port of Sydney situation reports, weeks ending 27 June, 15 August–10 October, 19 December 1942. Major Huxford's misleadingly entitled 'Report on Reconnaissance at Oxford Battery Site, Sydney, NS' (August 1942), includes a good description of the work in the battery plotting room and at the gun positions at Lingan. See ibid., (D111).

31 F.A. Kingsley, *The Development of Radar Equipments for the Royal Navy, 1935–45* (Basingstoke 1995), 206–8; DHH, 312.003 (D24), Canadian Military Headquarters, London, 'Radar Equipments,' 23 July 1945, 86; ibid., 321.009 (D346)/22, 'Operational Location Statement, Sydney and Canso Defences,' 20 August 1943.

32 NA, RG 24, 2580/HQS 3338/8, Canmilitry to NDHQ, telegram GS 3857, 13 November 1942.

33 DHH, 321.009 (D124)/2, Defended Port of Sydney situation reports, 17, 24 October 1942.

34 DHH, 321.009 (D112)/9, Jenkins to CGS, 'Progress Report – C and AA Defences Month Ending 31 Aug,' 7 September 1943; NA, RG 24, 2696/HQC 5199-C/6, Operations, 'Canadian Coast Artillery ...,' 13 October 1943; DHH, 321.009 (D124)/3, Defended Port of Sydney situation reports, 26 December 1942, 20, 27 March 1943, Jenkins to CGS, 5 May 1943; 321.009 (D112)/10, Jenkins to CGS, 'Progress Report – C and AA Defences Ending 31 Dec 43,' 10 January 1944. A complete restored six-pounder duplex position, Belmont battery, may be seen at Ford Rodd Hill in Victoria, BC. Although the battery

buildings are laid out differently to those at Sydney because they integrated earlier structures, the gun emplacement is virtually identical. Interestingly, the six-pounder duplex mounted there – a rare and fascinating piece – is the one originally installed at South Bar.

35 NA, RG 24, 2580/HQS 3338/7, Director of artillery memorandum, 29 September 1942; DHH, 322.009 (D656), Coast Defence Construction Committee minutes, 19 January 1943.

36 DHH, 193.009 (D22), Director of military operations and plans (DMO & P) to CGS, 24 July 1943.

37 Ibid., 321.009 (D124)/3, Sydney and Canso Defences situation report, week ending 29 May 1943, appendix B. The second 4-inch twin did not arrive at Chapel Point until June 1944. See NA, RG 24, HQS 8224-2/1(mfm C8359). 'Monthly Return of Installation of Coast Artillery and Associated Instruments and Transmission Systems, Sydney ...,' 20 June 1944.

38 NA, RG 24, 13148, Chapel Point fort record book, section G; DHH, 345.009 (D89)/4, 'Alterations to Exis. No 3 (Six Inch) Empl., drawing no S-2118-37, 24 May 1943. This was the type design for Partridge Island at Saint John that was also used at Chapel Point and Fort Petrie; see DHH, 345.009 (D117), QMG to DOC 6, 13 August 1943.

39 NA, RG 24, HQC 8835-1-1, pt. 1 (mfm C5276), 'Progress Report MD 6, 31 July 1942' for Financial Encumbrance 23174. The considerable sum of $33,780 allocated for the project indicates the substantial scope of the construction. See DHH, 321.009 (D346)/22, 'Operational Location Statement Sydney and Canso Defences,' 20 August 1943.

40 The construction of the battery is well recorded in the seven-volume project file of the district engineer officer for MD 6, which survives in DHH, 345.009 (D79) and 345.009 (D10).

41 DHH, 345.009 (D10)/6, Simpkins to DEO 6, 21 June 1944.

42 Quoted in Peter Moogk, 'Fortress Sydney: Manning the Guns on the Cape Breton Coast,' *Cape Breton's Magazine*, no. 33.

43 Quoted in Moogk, 'Remembering,' 132.

44 Interview with Martin Haley, 29 December 1971. Although the language is strong, the sentiments are not far from comments digested from returns from many units in DHH, 113.3R4003(D1)/2, 'Special Report Number 105: Home War Establishment Personnel (21 January 1944),' p. 5.

45 Moogk, 'Remembering,' 134.

46 C.P. Stacey, *Six Years of War: The Army in Canada, Britain and the Pacific* (Ottawa 1955), 120–2. On the intentions of the General Staff as the scheme came into place, see especially NA, MG 27, IIIB11, vol. 38, 'Army Programme 1940–1,' Maurice Pope to CGS, 'Army Organization' (a survey as of Septem-

ber 1941), 23 September 1941. Ibid., vol. 68, Crerar to minister, 26 January
1941, mentions that 25 per cent went active, although three fifths of these
opted for the navy or air force and only two fifths for the army.

47 Quoted in Moogk, 'Fortress Sydney.'

48 The question of morale in the citizen army was of such importance that Army
Headquarters established the Research and Information Section in the Adjutant General Branch to make periodic surveys of opinion. A good selection of
these reports is in DHH, 113.3R4003 (D1). This was one of the principal
sources of R.H. Roy's useful 'Morale in the Canadian Army in Canada during
the Second World War,' *Canadian Defence Quarterly* 16 (autumn 1986), 40–5.

49 Dan MacGillivray, 'Many Who Protected CB Coasts Died Overseas,' *Cape Breton Post*, 28 September 1990.

50 Quoted in Moogk, 'Remembering,' 135. George Slaven was one of the
'lucky' ones. A veteran of the First World War, he was a pharmacist and the
mayor of Sydney. He was also second in command of the 16th Coast Brigade
at the outbreak of war. In 1941 he was given the command of the 108th Artillery Battery, which was sent to Goose Bay, Labrador to protect the airfield
being built there. He went overseas in 1944, and became commanding
officer of the 6th Coast Defence Artillery Brigade after the war, retiring with
the rank of lieutenant colonel. Slaven interview.

51 DHH, 112.3S2009 (D223), Director of staff duties to DCGS, 11 January 1941.

52 Ibid., 112.3M3009 (D109), Elkins to secretary, DND, 26 and 27 October
1941.

53 Ibid., 324.009 (D188)/1, Bellefeuille to Brigadier General E. de B. Panet,
DOC MD 4, 18 December 1942.

54 NA, RG 24, Defended Port of Sydney Headquarters war diary, February
1943, appendix 4, Intelligence and security report week ending 2 February
1943 (mfm T 10895).

55 MacGillivray, 'Many.' Indeed, Molnar met his future wife while on duty at
Sydney. Although she lived in Toronto, she was visiting her family in the
Whitney Pier area, which is near the fire command post at South Bar.

56 NA, RG 24, Defended Port of Sydney Headquarters war diary, Intelligence
and security report week ending 15 February 1943 (mfm T 10895). One of
the few complaints among the overwhelmingly favourable comments on
relations with the civilian population at Sydney is to be found in the results
of a survey of morale carried out by Army Headquarters in January 1944.
Several units commented that civilians had begun to make sarcastic comments about active personnel, not the conscripts, who had done long home-
defence service and become familiar faces in the community. See DHH,
113.3R4003 (D1)/2, Research and Information Section, Adjutant General

Branch, 'Special Report Number 134: Civilian–Army Relations (30 June 1944).'

57 DHH, 321.009(D124)/3, Defended Port of Sydney situation report, week ending 9 January 1943.

58 NA, Defended Port of Sydney Headquarters war diary, April 1943, Appendix 3, Intelligence and security report, week ending 13 April 1943 (mfm T 10895).

59 DHH, 321.009(D124)/3, Defended Port of Sydney situation report, week ending 20 February 1943.

60 Partington interview.

61 DHH, NSS 1000-5-21/2, Schwerdt to COAC, 9 December 1942; Hamilton to NOIC Sydney, 28 November 1942.

62 Ibid., Naval staff minutes, 133rd meeting, 12 November 1942.

63 Ibid., 233rd meeting, 10 April 1944; 240th meeting, 29 May 1944; Naval Board minutes, 153rd meeting, 17 April 1944.

64 Ibid., NSS 1000-5-7/3, Naval weekly report, 16 April 1943, 7; 1000-5-8/4, summary of the naval war effort, 1 July–30 September 1943, 47; NSS 1000-5-8/5, summary of the naval war effort, 1 April–30 June 1944, 29.

65 On 6 November 1942, immediately after *U-518*'s attack on Wabana, the Joint Service Committee Atlantic Coast ruled that Louisbourg should be defended. See DHH, 323.009 (D160), minutes of 95th meeting, 6 November 1942. That same day Schwerdt, Dobbie, and their staffs went to Louisbourg to select sites for emergency defences. See ibid., NSS 1000-5-21/2, Schwerdt to COAC, 9 December 1942.

66 Ibid., 321.009 (D111). Goodeve, 'Visit ... to Sydney–Canso and Louisburg, 12–14 November, 1942'; ibid., 321.009(D124)/3, Defended Port of Sydney situation report, weeks ending 7, 16 January 1943.

67 Moogk, 'From Fortress Louisbourg,' 15.

68 DHH, NSS 1000-5-21/2, Schwerdt to COAC, 4 February, 6 March, 12 April 1943.

69 NA, RG 24, 11686, file 11-10-1-SC 709, Schwerdt to COAC, 25 January 1943. These sailors were honoured on 24 August 1996 when a plaque was erected at Louisbourg to commemorate their courage. In attendance were the only two survivors, Walter Boudreau, who had served on *Angelus*, and Ed Levy, one of the local fishermen. Boudreau was one of only two of the *Angelus* crew who survived when it was subsequently sunk by a U-boat in March 1943. See *Cape Breton Post*, 26 August 1996.

70 Douglas, *Creation*, 509–13.

71 NA, RG 24, 6789/NSS 8280-166/16/3, Murray to secretary, Naval Board, 17 February 1943; DHH, NHS 1650-239/16B/1, Secretary, Naval Board, to COAC and FONF, 27 February 1943; Douglas, *Creation*, 509–10.

72 Douglas, *Creation*, 513–4.

73 DHH, 81/520/1650-DS, RCN weekly states, 15, 31 May, 15 June 1943; NSS 1000-5-21/2, NOIC Sydney to CinC Canadian Northwest Atlantic, 17 June, 10 August 1943.

74 Ibid., 181.002 (D68A), NSHQ to CinC CNA, signal 2258Z, 29 April 1943.

75 Hadley, *U-Boats*, 168–75. Unaware of the information that the navy had received about *U-262*'s mission, Hadley believed the Canadians were ignorant of the submarine's presence and was therefore somewhat puzzled by the earnestness with which the gulf forces pursued doubtful U-boat contacts. On weather conditions, see DHH, 181.000 (D1556), and 181.003 (D423), EAC intelligence report, weeks ending 7 May 1943, para. 18, and 14 May 1943, para. 19.

76 DHH, 181.003 (D423), EAC intelligence report, week ending 21 May 1943, para. 18.

77 Thanks to the fact that several of them broke free of their moorings and were spotted by alert escort crews, only one ship was lost in the minefield. See Hadley, *U-Boats*, 172, 187–9.

78 NA, RG 24, 6789/NSS 8280-166/16/4, Hurcomb to Huband, Montreal (British Ministry of War Transport [MWT] representative in Canada), 10 March 1943. See also the internal British correspondence behind this and other communications to Canada about the importance of the St Lawrence for ocean shipping: DHH, MT 59/940, Lees to Snow, 8 February 1943; Huband to Shipminder (London), signal 55484, 24 March 1943; Huband to Shipminder, signal 57126, 18 May 1943; MWT London to Huband, signal MAST 15208, 15 July 1943.

79 DHH, Minutes, 200th meeting of Naval Staff, 13 September 1943; NA, RG 24, 6789/NSS 8280-166/16/4, NSHQ to CinC CNA, signal 2125Z, 9 September 1943; CinC CNA to NSHQ, signal 2031Z, 10 September 1943; CinC CNA to secretary, Naval Board, 16 September 1943.

80 Hadley, *U-Boats*, 176–84; Douglas, *Creation*, 514–5. *U-536* was subsequently destroyed by a Canadian ocean escort group in the eastern Atlantic two months later.

81 One measure of the improved Canadian defences is that Newfoundland-based aircraft so terrorized the submarine that it did not dare attempt to attack shipping or even come in close to the coast. See Jurgen Rohwer and Roger Sarty, 'Intelligence and the Air Forces in the Battle of the Atlantic 1943–1945,' International Commission of Military History *Acta*, 13 (1991), pt 2: 151–2; DHH, 181.003 (D423), EAC intelligence report, week ending 25 October 1943, para. 3; DHH, NSS 1000-5-21/2, NOIC Sydney to CinC CNA, 9 May 1943; Simpson, to NOIC Sydney, 6 December 1943.

82 DHH, NSS 1000-5-20/3, Flag Officer Newfoundland, operational war diary for August 1943; NA, RG 24, 11686/11-10-1- 'J. Pinckney Henderson,' unsigned, 'Reports from survivors ...,' 7 September 1943.

83 Ibid., Simpson to NOIC Sydney, 'Report of proceedings arrival of burned out "J. Pinckney Henderson" ...,' 2 September 1943. See also Moogk, 'Remembering,' 136. Mackenzie's wife Moira gave birth to their youngest daughter at the Hamilton Memorial Hospital in North Sydney that same night. He was subsequently awarded the MBE for his actions. One of the first men to board the ship was George Prosser, a naval shore patrolman who had formerly served as boatswain on *Rose Castle*. He was also a member of the naval guard that participated in the burial service. See John Campbell, 'Ill-fated Crews Remembered in Battle of Atlantic Services,' *Cape Breton Post*, 3 May 1997.

84 NA, RG 24, 11686/11-10-1- 'J. Pinckney Henderson,' P.F. Squibb, 'Salvage Report US Liberty Ship "J. Pinckney Henderson,"' n.d., but forwarded by Hibbard to CinC CNA, 10 November 1943.

85 NA, R6 24, 11686/11-10-1- 'J. Pinckney Henderson,' secretary, Naval Board, to NOIC Sydney, 24 December 1943, enclosing unidentified press clipping.

86 Ibid., Simpson, 31 December 1943.

87 They were later removed to the United States for permanent interment. See Moogk, 'Remembering,' 136.

88 DHH 81/520/1440-127, 'History of Naval Control Service at Sydney.'

89 DHH, NSS 1000-5-21/2, NOIC Sydney to CinC CNA, 9 November 1943; Tucker, *Naval Service*, 2: 173.

90 DHH, NSS 1000-5-21/2, Wells to NOIC Sydney, 30 August 1943; NOIC Sydney to CinC CNA, 9 December 1943.

91 Ibid., HMCS *New Westminster* movement card, May–December 1943.

13: The End, 1943–1945

1 The following account is largely based on NA, MG 27, IIIB11/38/'Army in Canada General'; Stuart to minister, 'Reduction in Operational Troops in Canada,' 30 August 1943, includes detailed appendices on cuts already made and proposed cuts that were in fact shortly carried out. See also Stacey, *Six Years*, 183–6.

2 DHH, 321.009 (D352)/1, Page to DOC 6, 28 July 1943; 321.009 (D346)/22, 'Operational Location statement Sydney & Canso Defences,' 20 August 1943.

3 Ibid., 193.009 (D22), DMO&P to CGS, 24 July 1943.

4 Ibid., 321.009 (D433), 'Review of the Development of the Canadian Coast Artillery Plan 1937–1945,' 11 June 1946.

5 NA, RG 24, 14355, 16th Coast Regiment war diary, October 1943, January 1944; DHH, 321.009 (D346)/25, 'Operational Location Statement Sydney and Canso Defences,' 29 February 1944; 321.009 (D125)/2, Dobbie to headquarters, MD 6, 27 September 1943.

6 DHH, 4(CAC) Detachment operations record book, 31 October 1943.

7 Ibid., 441 Squadron operations record book, 14 October–22 December 1943.

8 Ibid., S.096-105/4, Chief of air staff to minister, 'Air Defence of Canada Plan – 1944,' 24 September 1943; S.096-105/5, Acting chief of air staff to minister, 27 November 1943; Douglas, *Creation*, 394–5, 581, 656.

9 DHH, 81/520/8280A/1, Hodgson, 'The First Year of Canadian Operational Control in the Northwest Atlantic,' 18 August 1944, 3.

10 This and the following paragraphs are based on Douglas, *Creation*, 568–71; Rohwer and Sarty, 'Intelligence and the Air Forces,' 135–61.

11 NA, RG 24, 6789/NSS 8280-166/16/4, Brand to Ropner, 15 March 1944; DHH, MT 59/940, January–May correspondence; 81/520/8280/1, Annual report of director of trade division, 1944; 77/554, Staff Officer (Trade), 'Convoy Cycles,' SQ and QS convoy summaries.

12 These are the vessels that actually reported to Sydney. See DHH, NSS 1000-5-21/2, NOIC Sydney to CinC CNA, 3 March, 10 April, 9 May, 8 June 1944.

13 Ibid., 10 Squadron operations record book, 4–25 May 1944.

14 Douglas, *Creation*, 579–80.

15 DHH, NSS 1000-5-21/2, Schwerdt to CinC CNA, 8 June 1944.

16 Hodgson, 'The First Year'; DHH, 77/554, Staff officer (trade), 'Convoy Cycles,' summaries for HX, ON, and SC series; NA, RG 24, 11684, file 30-7-1/4, NCSO Sydney to NOIC Sydney, 10 July 1944.

17 DHH, 81/520/1440-127, Simpson, 'History of NCS.' Simpson recalled that the SHXM 198 incident occurred in June but see DHH, NSS 8280-SHXM 298 (mfm 89/34, reel 31).

18 NA, RG 24, 11053/30-1-10/32, CinC CNA war diary, May 1944.

19 DHH, 81/520/1440-127, Simpson, 'History of NCS.' 'Mac' or merchant aircraft carrier ships were large merchant vessels, usually grain carriers, on which a wooden flight deck was built. A few single-engine aircraft were serviced in the open on these primitive facilities, which nevertheless gave convoys some air protection to supplement or stand in for coverage from naval aircraft carriers and shore-based aviation.

20 Tucker, *Naval Service*, 2: 387.

21 NA, RG 24, 6896/NSS 8910-20/1, Otter, 'U-boat estimates signals for 20–31 May 1944.'

22 DHH, 77/554, staff officer (trade), 'Convoy Cycles,' BS-SB, BW-WB, HS-SH convoy summaries; NA, RG 24, 11053, file 30-1-10/34, CinC CNA war diary, July 1944; DHH, 81/520/1440-127, Simpson, 'History of NCS.'

23 DHH, 161 Squadron operations record book, 30 April–7 July 1944; 74/2, 'History of Eastern Air Command,' pt 4:804–6, 812–13, 822–3.

24 DHH, 181.003 (D354), EAC operations summary signals, 4–5 July 1944; *United States Fleet Anti-Submarine Bulletin* 2 (August 1944), 22–3.

25 DHH, 161 Squadron operations record book, July 1944.

26 The account in the following pages is based on Douglas, *Creation*, 597–9, and Roger Sarty, 'Ultra, Air Power, and the Second Battle of the St Lawrence, 1944,' in Timothy J. Runyan and Jan M. Copes, eds., *To Die Gallantly: The Battle of the Atlantic* (Boulder 1994), 186–209.

27 NA, RG 24, 11054/30-1-10/35, CinC CNA war diary, August 1944.

28 NA, RG 24, 6901/NSS 8910-166/10, CinC CNA to NOIC Sydney, signal 1701Z, 24 August 1944, and signal 1222Z, 28 August 1944; DHH, 181.003 (D4863), EAC weekly intelligence reports, week ending 31 August 1944; 181.003 (D3254), EAC proposed operations and operations summary signals, 22–31 August 1944; 10 Squadron operations record book, 22–31 August 1944. The strength and deployment of the Fairmile flotillas can be followed in DHH, 81/520/1650-DS/6/40, RCN weekly and daily states, 16–31 August 1944.

29 DHH, 81/520/1650-DS/6/40, RCN weekly and daily states, 16–31 August 1944, add important details to NA, RG 24, 11684/file 30-7-1/4, NOIC Sydney to CinC CNA, 12 September 1944. See also DHH, 77/554, staff officer (trade), 'Convoy Cycles.'

30 NA, RG 24, 6789/NSS 8280-166/16/4, Brand to ACNS and CNS, 27 and 31 August 1944.

31 DHH, 77/554, staff officer (trade), 'Convoy Cycles,' QS-SQ convoy summaries; NA, RG 24, 11684/30-7-1/4, NOIC Sydney to CinC CNA, 12 September 1944, 17 October 1944, 7 November 1944; 11054/30-1-10/37, CinC CNA war diary, September 1944.

32 DHH, *U-541* log, 3 September 1944. In addition to Sarty, 'Ultra,' 197–8, see Joseph Prim and Mike McCarthy, *Those in Peril: The U-Boat Menace to Allied Shipping in Newfoundland and Labrador Waters, World War I and World War II* (St John's 1995), 70–2, which includes important reminiscences by Captain Norman Hinks, second officer in *Livingstone* at the time of the sinking. See also DHH, NSS 8280-HJF 28 (mfm 83/34, reel 7), which includes accounts of the rescue.

33 DHH, 181.005 (D1555), Gulf controller's log, 7–8 September 1944; 181.003 (D3254), EAC operations summary signal for 8 September 1944; 81/520/1650-DS/41; RCN weekly and daily states, 5–12 September 1944.

34 NA, RG 24, 11054/30-1-10/37, CinC CNA war diary, September 1944; DHH, 81/520/1650-DS/41, RCN weekly and daily states, 12–21 September 1944.

35 See Roger Sarty, 'The Limits of Ultra: The Schnorkel Boat Offensive against North America, November 1944–January 1945,' *Journal of Intelligence and National Security* 12 (April 1997), 44–68; Douglas, *Creation*, 599, 602.

36 DHH, *U-1228* log, 25 November 1944, translation by David Wiens.

37 NA, RG 24, 4108/NSS 1156-331/93, Cullage to Simpson, 29 November 1944.

38 Ibid., 6897/NSS 8910-23/3, NSHQ submarine contacts log, 25 November 1944.

39 Ibid., 4108/NSS 1156-331/93, 'Findings of the Board of Enquiry regarding circumstances surrounding the loss of HMCS *Shawinigan*, 24th–25th November, 1944.'

40 NA, RG 24, 4108/NSS 1156-331/93, Halliday to NOIC Sydney, 2 December 1944; EAC operations record book, November–December 1944; 'A/S Ops Intelligence Summar[ies],' 133, week ending 26 November 1944, and 134, week ending 3 December 1944.

41 DHH, *U-1228* log, 28 November–6 December 1944.

42 Ibid., 81/520/1440-127, Simpson, 'History of NCS,' entry for October 1942. See also NA, RG 24, 4108/NSS 1156-331/93, Simpson to NOIC Sydney, 29 November 1944.

43 DHH, Minutes, 217th meeting of the Naval Staff, 27 December 1943; Ken Macpherson and John Burgess, *The Ships of Canada's Naval Forces, 1910–1981* (Toronto 1981), 71, 78; DHH, NSS 1000-5-8/5, 'Summary of Naval War Effort,' January–March 1944, 32; April–June 1944, 43; July–December 1944, 46; NSS 1000-5-21/2, Schwerdt to CinC CNA, 5 February 1944. The authors are grateful to Dr Michael Hennessy for sharing his research on refits.

44 NA, RG 24, 11686/CSS 1-2-1, McCulloch to NOIC Sydney, 22 March 1944.

45 Ibid., Acc. 83/4-167/4011/NSS 8785-166/10/1, Merry to ACNS, 6 March 1945.

46 DHH, NSS 1000-5-7/6. 'Summary of Information ... for the month ending 31st December 1944.'

47 The refit figures are approximations based upon DHH, 95/2, HSHQ, Fighting Equipment Coordinating Authority refit plots, 29 August 1944–6 March 1945; NA, RG 24, 3855/NSS 1021-2-1/2, 'Ships allocated for refit, East Coast ports, 1944,' table annexed to Raymond to ACNS, 4 November 1944; Acc. 83/4-167/4011/NSS 8785-166/10/1, Raymond to ACNS, 'Appreciation of the refitting situation,' 15 January 1945. On manpower and workload problems, see NA, RG 24, 11686/CSS 1-2-1, McCulloch to base engineer superintendent, 27 April 1945, and attached 'Notes on CSSO to Cdr Killop, Deputy Superintendent.'

48 Roger Sarty, 'A Narrative and Structural History of Fort McNab, 1939–1963' (unpublished manuscript commissioned by the Halifax Defence Complex, 1988); DHH, 321.009 (D15), director of signals to chief signal officer, Atlantic Command, 8 January 1944.

49 DHH, 345.009 (D117), QMG to DOC 6, 4 April 1944; QMG to DOC 6, telegram Engineers F110, 12 April 1944, 18 April 1944; Coast Defence Construction Committee minutes, 11 October 1944; 321.009(D421), Sydney and Canso situation reports, weeks ending 29 July, 2 September 1944; 345.009 (D261), Engineer progress reports, week ending 7 July 1945

50 NA, RG 24, HQS 3338-25-1 (mfm C-8272). The detailed reports on the gun installation are summarized in DHH, 321.009 (D421), which also provides information on other work at the battery. For Frank Robertson's colourful account, see Moogk, 'Fortress Sydney.'

51 DHH, 321.009 (D421), Sydney and Canso Defences situation reports, weeks ending 17 June 1944–21 April 1945; 321.009(D346) Sydney and Canso operational location state, 15 July 1944; 193.009 (D42), DMO & P to CGS, 11 November 1944; 193.009 (D39), CGS to minister, 21 January 1945; 112.21009 (D74), Morrissey to DOC 6, 29 January 1945; 'LMC' to DOC 6, 14 February 1945.

52 Ibid., 112.21009 (D74), Combined Chiefs of Staff, 'Estimate of the Enemy Situation – Europe (as of 23 January 1945): Report by the Combined Intelligence Committee' (emphasis in the original).

53 Ibid., NSS 1926-102/1, CinC CNA war diaries, January–April 1945; Douglas, *Creation*, 604–9; Hadley, *U-Boats*, 275–94.

54 DHH, 181.003 (D267), RCAF Station Sydney weekly intelligence reports, January–April 1945.

55 Ibid., RCAF Station Sydney operations record book, 15 February 1945.

56 Ibid., DHH, 193.009 (D53), Minutes, 317th meeting, Chiefs of Staff Committee, 9 March 1945.

57 NA, RG 24, 11684/30-7-1/4, Schwerdt to CinC CNA, 4 May, 8 June 1945; DHH, 1650-239/16B/2, NSHQ to Admiralty, 1720Z, 6 April 1945; NHS 8440-'Support Groups,' Admiralty to NSHQ and CinC Western Approaches, signal received 0610 hours, 13 April 1945.

58 DHH, 81/520/1440-127, Simpson, 'History of NCS.'

59 *Sydney Post-Record*, 9–10 May 1945. The eleven civilians appeared in police court the next day on various charges. One of them was fined and had his driver's licence revoked, six were remanded until Saturday, and two were let off with a warning. The taxi operator, A. Lewis, was fined $50 and costs.

60 Ibid., 10 May 1945.

61 Ibid.
62 Ibid.
63 Ibid.
64 Ibid.
65 Ibid., 11 May 1945.
66 Ibid.
67 Ibid.
68 Ibid., 12 May 1945. This proved to be a correct assessment. Sydney lifted its curfew on the 14th, by which time forty people had been charged and convicted of curfew violations during the five days it was in effect. See ibid., 15 May 1945.
69 Ibid., 12 May 1945.
70 Ibid., 14 May 1945.
71 Ibid., 12 May 1945.

Epilogue

1 DHH, 95/2 Large,'FECA [Fighting Equipment Coordinating Authority] Plot: Refitting Situation,' 7 August 1945.
2 NA, RG 24, Acc. 83-4/167/4011, file 8785-166/10/1, McCulloch to commodore superintendent, Halifax, 27 December 1945. Telegrams and letters of complaint are also in this file.
3 DHH, RCAF Sydney operations record book, June–December 1945.
4 Sarty, 'Fort McNab,' 31–9; 'A Structural and Narrative History of Chapel Point Battery, Sydney Mines, NS, 1861–1950' (unpublished study prepared for Chapel Point Historical Society, 1991), 80–6.
5 DHH, Naval Staff minutes, 353-2, 11 November 1946; 409-5, 20 April 1948; 415-10, 10 June 1948; NHS 8000, Point Edward Naval Base, reports of proceedings, 1948–51.
6 Roger Sarty, *The Maritime Defence of Canada* (Toronto 1997), 207–10, includes a summary account and references to important recent publications.
7 DHH, NHS 8000, Point Edward Naval Base, Reserve Fleet, Sydney Group, reports of proceedings, February–November 1953.
8 Sarty, 'Fort McNab,' 39–47; DHH, 1326-0390/49, 49th Coast Battery, RCA, annual unit historical reports, 1950–1, 1951–2.
9 Ibid., 1326-0390/1, Sydney Coast Regiment, RCA, annual unit historical reports, 1949–53; Moogk, 'From Fortress Louisbourg,' 178–9.
10 DHH, 1326-0390/49, 49th Coast Battery, RCA (from 3 September 1954 49th Harbour Defence Battery, RCA), annual unit historical reports, 1953–6; Sarty, 'Fort McNab,' 47–51. DHH, 112/3M2 (D561), DMO&P to director of

weapons and development, 21 May 1954, refers to preparations to send Oxford's 9.2-inch guns to Turkey.

11 This account is drawn from Dan Fraser, ed., *CFS Sydney Jubilee Booklet, 1953– 1978* (Sydney 1978), with further details from DHH, 1326-2373, daily operations record book, 1953–62, and the annual unit historical reports, 1963–89. On the development of Canadian and American air defences, see Joseph T. Jockel, *No Boundaries Upstairs: Canada, the United States and the Origins of North American Air Defence, 1945–1958* (Vancouver 1987). There is additional useful information on the air defence of the Atlantic provinces in A.M. Lee, *Chatham: An Airfield History* (Fredericton 1989).

12 Fraser, *Sydney Jubilee*, 3.

13 DHH, 1326-2373/1, RCAF Station Sydney operations record book, 31 May 1956.

14 Ibid., 79/246, file Q5, Base Planning Committee minutes, 3 April 1956.

15 The *Canadian Navy List, July 1955* (Ottawa 1955), 436, shows that Captain (E) Alfred B. Arnison was appointed base superintendent at Sydney with effect from 20 April 1954.

16 DHH, 79/246, file Q5, Policy and Projects Coordinating Committee minutes, 30 April 1956.

17 Ibid., 73/1347, 'Base Development Plan, Point Edward Naval Base,' tab 6, includes a detailed discussion of 'dispersal' plans for the East Coast. Internal evidence suggests these documents are from the period 1960–2.

18 Ibid., NHS 8000, Point Edward Naval Base, report of proceedings, August 1955.

19 Ibid., report of proceedings, September 1956.

20 Ibid., 79/246, file Q5, Policy and Project Coordinating Committee minutes, 30 April 1956.

21 Ibid., NHS 8000, Point Edward Naval Base, report of proceedings, April 1958.

22 Ibid., Point Edward Naval Base, Clippings from the *Chronicle-Herald* (Halifax), 20 April–28 May 1958.

23 DHH, Naval Board minutes, 12 August 1959, 6 January 1960. The navy was somewhat embarrassed by press reports in Nova Scotia suggesting that the base was to be considerably increased in size. DHH, NHS 8000, Point Edward Naval Base, Senior naval officer Sydney to Canflaglant, signal 1905z, February 1959; staff officer (information) to 'Mac,' 13 February 1959; See *Chronicle-Herald*, 9 January 1959.

24 On the Diefenbaker government and economic assistance to the province, see James P. Bickerton, *Nova Scotia, Ottawa, and the Politics of Regional Development* (Toronto 1990), chapter 5.

25 DHH, NHS 8000, Point Edward Naval Base, report of proceedings, September 1959.

26 Ibid., Naval Historian, 'Notes on Point Edward Naval Base – 1961,' 10 October 1961.

27 Ibid.

28 Ibid., clipping, 20 February 1961.

29 Ibid., 79/246, file Q5, Harkness to Reeves, 16 March 1961. For a description of the pier and quay wall renovation project, see 'Reconstruction of Berthing Facilities at Point Edward Naval Base, Sydney, NS,' *Naval Technical Review* 2 (2nd quarter 1963), 14–15.

30 DHH, NHS 8000, Point Edward Naval Base, Canavhed (Canadian Naval Headquarters) to Cangen (general message to the forces), signal 2145z, 5 December 1963; Canavhed to Comsuptlant (commodore superintendent Atlantic), signal 1438z, 6 December 1963.

31 Ibid., report of proceedings, December 1963–November 1965; Comsuplant to RCCWC/Canforcehed, signals 1918z, 6 January 1966, 1859z, 7 February 1966.

32 C.J. Taylor, *Negotiating the Past: The Making of Canada's National Historic Parks and Sites* (Montreal and Kingston 1990), 19–20, 56, 80–1, 107, 175–88.

33 See, for example, Paul Hellyer, *White Paper on Defence* (Ottawa 1964), especially 10–12.

34 Jockel, *No Boundaries*, Chapters 3–6; Jon B. McLin, *Canada's Changing Defense Policy, 1957–1963* (Baltimore 1967), especially Chapters 3–4.

35 DHH, RCAF organization order 2.19/22 November 1963 changed the station's role to feed data to the SAGE system.

36 Ibid., National Defence Headquarters to Address Information Group 1879, signal 1600z, 17 January 1991.

37 Department of National Defence, *Challenge and Commitment: A Defence Policy for Canada* (Ottawa 1987), 55; Department of National Defence, *Defence 1990* (Ottawa 1991), 90–1.

Bibliography

This book is largely based on the very extensive twentieth-century records of the Directorate of History and Heritage (DHH), National Defence Headquarters, Ottawa. Much use was also made of British Colonial Office, Admiralty, and other records, copies of which are available at DHH, the National Archives of Canada (NA), and the Fortress Louisbourg National Historic Site (FLNHS). The records of the British army in North America, particularly the Royal Engineers, which are available at the Nova Scotia Archives and Records Management (NSARM), were an invaluable source for the nineteenth-century fortifications. The Beaton Institute at the University College of Cape Breton has collected specialized local records, which are also important. The North Sydney Historical Society allowed us to consult copies of rare publications from the air force bases situated in that town during the two world wars, as well as photographs in their possession. We were fortunate to locate very useful materials on the role of American forces at Sydney in the two world wars at the National Archives and Records Administration and the Naval Historical Center in Washington, DC. A general list of the major sources is given below. For detailed information, the reader should consult the Notes.

Primary Sources

Beaton Institute, University College of Cape Breton, Sydney
MG 1. Hugh Swayne Correspondence
MG 2. William Cox Correspondence
MG 3. Anna Kearney Diary
MG 9. William MacDonald Papers
MG 9. Hugh Swayne Papers

MG 23. Charles Inglis Papers

MG 73. David Mathews Papers

Public Record Office. War Office 55/857, Correspondence, 1804

Bain, Mrs Roderick. 'History of Sydney Mines.' Unpublished manuscript.
[1951]

Beaton, Kevin. 'Captain Thomas Crawley (1757–1851): A Brief Sketch.' Unpublished undergraduate essay. 1978

Canada. Department of the Naval Service. *Naval Intelligence Reports.* 1917

Chisholm, Diane. 'The Evolution of Victoria Park.' Unpublished manuscript.
Sydney 1994

Cruikshank, E.A. 'The Military History of the Island of Cape Breton, 1785–1815.' Unpublished manuscript. Sydney nd

Handspiker, Todd. 'The Military History of Victoria Park.' Unpublished undergraduate essay. 1992

Kanne, Leo, and Blair McIsaac. 'Research Study of Fort Petrie, New Victoria, Nova Scotia.' Unpublished manuscript prepared for Sydney Harbour Fortifications Society. 1991

Keagan, Cheryl. 'The Northside Militia – 1800–1950 – with an Emphasis on Sydney Mines.' Unpublished undergraduate essay. 1990

Macintyre, Ian. 'Victoria Park and the Army: The First Two Centuries.' Unpublished manuscript. 1984

McSween, Craig. 'YQY History Sydney Airport.' Unpublished undergraduate essay. 1994

Stevenson, L.B. 'A Summary of the Activities of the Cape Breton Flying Club from Its Organization in 1928 to 1949.' Unpublished manuscript. 20 July 1977

Directorate of History and Heritage, National Defence Headquarters, Ottawa
Army and Air Force kardex

Document collection (materials collected since 1970)

Naval Historians' files

Public Record Office. Admiralty 116, Secretariat 'Cases'

– Admiralty 137, First World War Records

– Admiralty 199, Second World War Records

– Ministry of Defence 3, Ultra signals intelligence

– Ministry of Transport, Records

Royal Canadian Air Force, daily operations record books

Fortress Louisbourg National Historic Site, Louisbourg, Nova Scotia
Archives nationales de France. Archives des Colonies, Série C^{11B}, 28/76–6v. Map of Fort William

Public Record Office. Admiralty 1/484–9, Correspondence
- Admiralty 51, Journals of Ship Captains
- Audit Office 1/147/356, Accounts for 1 July 1780 to 31 March 1783
- Colonial Office 217, Correspondence and Minutes of Council
  of War
- Colonial Office 218, Correspondence
- State Papers 78/232, Correspondence
- War Office 1/501, 543, 576, 605–7, 771, Correspondence
Francis, Dilys. 'The Mines and Quarries of Cape Breton Island during the
  French Regime, 1713–1760.' Unpublished report. November 1965

National Archives and Records Administration, Washington
German Naval Records 1919–45. Logs of U-boats
RG 24. Naval Logs
RG 45. Secretary of the Navy subject file, 1911–27
RG 80. Secretary of the Navy/Chief of Naval Operations
RG 313. CTF 24 Atlantic Fleet. U.S. Naval Forces in Newfoundland,
  1940–5

National Archives of Canada, Ottawa
MG 11, CO 217, CO 537, CO 889. Colonial Office Records
MG 12. War Office Records
National Map Collection
RG 7. Governor General's Office Records
RG 8. British Military Forces in Canada Records
RG 9. Department of Militia and Defence Records
RG 24. Department of National Defence, especially more recent accessions,
  including D10 (Royal Canadian Navy Atlantic Command) and records of par-
  ticular east coast bases, and Accession 83/4–167, consisting of Royal Canadian
  Navy Central Registry records, principally from 1943 to 1964
RG 25. Department of Foreign Affairs and International Trade Records
RG 28. Department of Munitions and Supply Records

National Personnel Records Centre, Ottawa
Service records

Naval Historical Center. Washington
Operational Archives. First World War Naval Intelligence Records. Second
  World War records of U.S. naval forces in Newfoundland, convoy records, and
  liaison with Canadian forces
Library. Typescript histories of Atlantic fleet and CTF 24 (Newfoundland)

North Sydney Historical Society, North Sydney, Nova Scotia
North Sydney Flight. Published by the U.S. Naval Air Station, North Sydney,
1 December 1918
Pitch. Published by RCAF Station, North Sydney.

Nova Scotia Archives and Records Management, Halifax
Cambridge Library Letter-books on the Nova Scotia Militia
MG 1. Richard Brown Papers
MG 12. British War Office. Royal Engineers Records (including RG 8, C series
from NA)

Books

Allison, David. *History of Nova Scotia.* 2 vols. Halifax: A.W. Bowen 1916.
Balcom, B.A. *The Cod Fishery of Isle Royale, 1713–58.* Ottawa: Parks Canada,
National Historic Parks and Sites Branch 1984
Beck, J. Murray. *Joseph Howe. Vol. 2: The Briton Becomes Canadian, 1848–1873.*
Montreal and Kingston: McGill-Queen's University Press 1983
– *Politics of Nova Scotia.* Vol. 1. Tantallon, NS: Four East Publications 1985
Beeby, Dean. *Cargo of Lies: The True Story of a Nazi Double Agent in Canada.* Tor-
onto: University of Toronto Press 1996
Behrens, C.B.A. *Merchant Shipping and the Demands of War.* London and Nendeln:
HMSO and Kraus Reprints 1978
Bickerton, James P. *Nova Scotia, Ottawa, and the Politics of Regional Development.*
Toronto: University of Toronto Press 1990
Bird, Will R. *No Retreating Footsteps: The Story of the North Nova Scotia Highlanders.*
Kentville, NS: Kentville Publishing Company n.d.
Black, Jeremy, and Philip Woodfine, eds. *The British Navy and the Use of Naval
Power in the Eighteenth Century.* Atlantic Heights, NJ: Humanities Press Interna-
tional 1989
Bourne, Kenneth. *Britain and the Balance of Power in North America, 1815–1908.*
Berkeley: University of California Press 1967
Boutilier, James A. ed. *RCN in Retrospect, 1910–1968.* Vancouver: University of
British Columbia Press 1982
Brebner, John Bartlett. *The Neutral Yankees of Nova Scotia.* Toronto: McClelland
and Stewart 1969
Bridle, P., ed. *Documents on Relations between Canada and Newfoundland.* Vol. 1:
1935–1949. Ottawa: Department of External Affairs 1974
Brière, Jean-François. *La pêche française en Amérique du Nord au XVIIIᵉ siècle.* N.p.:
Fides 1990
Brock, Jeffry V. *The Dark Broad Seas.* Vol. 1. Toronto: McClelland and Stewart
1981

Brown, Richard. *The Coal Fields and Coal Trade of the Island of Cape Breton.* London: Sampson Low, Marston, Low and Searle 1871
– *A History of the Island of Cape Breton.* London: Sampson Low, Son, and Marston 1869
Bruce, Harry. *Lifeline: The Story of the Atlantic Ferries and Coastal Boats.* Toronto: Macmillan 1977
Buckner, Philip A., and John G. Reid, eds. *The Atlantic Region to Confederation: A History.* Toronto: University of Toronto Press 1994
Cameron, James M. *Pictonians in Arms: A Military History of Pictou County, Nova Scotia.* New Glasgow: privately published 1969
Campbell, G.G., ed. *Ensign Prenties's Narrative: A Castaway on Cape Breton.* Toronto: Ryerson Press 1968
Canada. *Report of Admiral of the Fleet Viscount Jellicoe of Scapa on Naval Mission to the Dominion of Canada (November–December 1919).* Ottawa: King's Printer 1920
– *Report of the Royal Canadian Mounted Police.* Ottawa: King's Printer 1936–8
Charbonneau, André. *The Fortifications of Île Aux Noix.* Ottawa: Parks Canada 1994
Charlevoix, P.F.X. *History and General Description of New France.* Translated by J.M. Shea. Vol. 5. Chicago: Loyola University Press, 1871. First published as *Histoire et description générale de la Nouvelle-France* 1744
Clark, Andrew Hill. *Acadia: The Geography of Early Nova Scotia to 1760.* Madison: University of Wisconsin Press 1968
Clowes, William Laird. *The Royal Navy: A History from the Earliest Times to the Present.* Vol. 4. London: Sampson Low, Marston and Company 1899
Corkum, Hugh H. *On Both Sides of the Law.* Hantsport, NS: Lancelot Press 1989
Courtemanche, Régis A. *No Need of Glory: The British Navy in American Waters, 1860–1864.* Annapolis: Naval Institute Press 1977
Cunliffe, Marcus. *Soldiers and Civilians: The Martial Spirit in America, 1775–1865.* New York and London: The Free Press 1968
Cunningham, Hugh. *The Volunteer Force: A Social and Political History, 1859–1908.* Hamden: Shoestring Press 1975
Donovan, Kenneth, ed. *Cape Breton at 200: Historical Essays in Honour of the Island's Bicentennial.* Sydney, NS: UCCB Press 1985
Douglas, W.A.B. *The Official History of the Royal Canadian Air Force.* Vol. 2. *The Creation of a National Air Force:* Toronto: University of Toronto Press 1986
– ed. *The RCN in Transition, 1910–1985.* Vancouver: UBC Press 1988
Duguid, A. Fortescue. *Official History of the Canadian Forces, 1914–1919.* Ottawa: King's Printer 1938
Eayrs, James. *In Defence of Canada: Appeasement to Rearmament.* Toronto: University of Toronto Press 1965
– *In Defence of Canada: From the Great War to the Great Depression.* Toronto: University of Toronto Press 1964.

English, John. *The Canadian Army in Normandy: A Study in the Failure of High Command.* New York: Praeger 1991

Facey-Crowther, David. *The New Brunswick Militia, 1787–1867.* N.p.: New Brunswick Historical Society and New Ireland Press 1990

Fergusson, C. Bruce. *The Labour Movement in Nova Scotia before Confederation.* Halifax: Public Archives of Nova Scotia 1964

– ed. *Uniacke's Sketches of Cape Breton and Other Papers Relating to Cape Breton Island.* Halifax: Public Archives of Nova Scotia 1958

Fetherstonhaugh, R.C. *The Royal Canadian Regiment, 1883–1933.* Montreal: Gazette Printing 1981

Forbes, Archibald. *The 'Black Watch': The Record of an Historic Regiment.* London: Cassell 1896

Forbes, Ernest R. *Maritime Rights: The Maritime Rights Movement, 1919–1927.* Montreal and Kingston: McGill-Queen's University Press 1979

Fraser, Dan, ed. *CFS Sydney Jubilee Booklet, 1953–1978.* Sydney: CFS Sydney 1978

Gesner, Claribel. *Cape Breton Anthology.* Windsor, NS: Lancelot 1972

Graham, Gerald S. *Empire of the North Atlantic.* Toronto: University of Toronto Press 1958

– *Sea Power and British North America, 1783–1820.* Cambridge: Harvard University Press 1941

– ed. *The Walker Expedition to Quebec, 1711.* Toronto: The Champlain Society 1953

Gray, Edwyn A. *The Killing Time: The German U-Boats, 1914–1918.* New York: Charles Scribner's Sons 1972

Greenhous, Brereton. *Dragoon: The Centennial History of The Royal Canadian Dragoons, 1883–1983.* Ottawa: Guild of the Royal Canadian Dragoons 1983

– *The Official History of the Royal Canadian Air Force.* Vol. 3. *The Crucible of War, 1939–1945:* Toronto: University of Toronto Press, 1994

Greenough, John Joseph. *The Halifax Citadel, 1825–60: A Narrative and Structural History.* Ottawa: Parks Canada 1977

Hadley, Michael L. *U-Boats against Canada: German Submarines in Canadian Waters.* Montreal and Kingston: McGill-Queen's University Press 1985

Hadley, Michael L., and Roger Sarty. *Tin-Pots & Pirate Ships: Canadian Naval Forces and German Sea Raiders 1880–1918.* Montreal and Kingston: McGill-Queen's University Press 1991

Haliburton, T.C. *An Historical and Statistical Account of Nova Scotia.* Halifax: Joseph Howe 1829

Halpern, Paul G. *A Naval History of World War I.* Annapolis: Naval Institute Press 1994

Harris, Stephen J. *Canadian Brass: The Making of a Professional Army, 1860–1939.* Toronto: University of Toronto Press 1988

Harvey, D.C., ed. *Holland's Description of Cape Breton and Other Documents.* Halifax: Public Archives of Nova Scotia 1935

Hillmer, Norman, et al., eds. *A Country of Limitations: Canada and the World in 1939.* Ottawa: Canadian Committee for the History of the Second World War 1996

Hitsman, J. Mackay. *Safeguarding Canada, 1763–1871.* Toronto: University of Toronto Press 1968

Hornsby, Stephen J. *Nineteenth-Century Cape Breton.* Montreal and Kingston: McGill-Queen's University Press 1992

How, Douglas. *Night of the Caribou.* Hantsport, NS: Lancelot Press 1988

Hoyt, Edwin. *U-Boats Offshore.* New York: Stein and Day 1978

Hunt, M.S. *Nova Scotia's Part in the Great War.* Halifax: Nova Scotia Veteran Publishing 1920

Jackson, Elva E. *Fivescore and More.* North Sydney: privately published 1984

– *Windows on the Past: North Sydney, Nova Scotia.* Windsor, NS: Lancelot Press 1974

Jenkins, Brian. *Britain and the War for the Union.* 2 vols. Montreal and Kingston: McGill-Queen's University Press 1974–80

Jockel, Joseph T. *No Boundaries Upstairs: Canada, The United States and the Origins of North American Air Defence, 1945–1958.* Vancouver: University of British Columbia Press 1987

Kealy, J.D.F. and E.C. Russell. *A History of Canadian Naval Aviation, 1918–1962.* Ottawa: Department of National Defence 1967

Keegan, John. *The Price of Admiralty.* New York: Viking Penguin 1989

Kennedy, Paul M. *The Rise and Fall of British Naval Mastery.* London: Ashfield Press 1983

Kerry, A.J. and W.A. McDill. *History of the Corps of Royal Canadian Engineers.* Ottawa: Military Engineers Association of Canada 1962–6

Kingsley, F.A. *The Development of Radar Equipments for the Royal Navy, 1935–45.* Basingtoke: Macmillan 1995

Lamb, James B. *The Corvette Navy: True Stories from Canada's Atlantic War.* Toronto: Macmillan n.d.

– *On the Triangle Run.* Toronto: Macmillan 1986

Lawrence, Hal. *A Bloody War: One Man's Memories of the Canadian Navy, 1939–1945.* Toronto: Macmillan 1979

Laws, M.E.S. *Battery Records of the Royal Artillery, 1716–1859.* Woolwich: Royal Artillery Institute 1952

Lee, A.M. *Chatham: An Airfield History.* Fredericton: CFB Chatham 1989

MacKinnon, J.G. *Old Sydney*. Belleville: Mika Publishing 1973. First published 1918

MacLeod, Mary K. *Whisper In The Air: Marconi, The Canada Years 1902–1946*. Hantsport, NS: Lancelot Press 1992

MacNutt, W.S. *The Atlantic Provinces: The Emergence of Colonial Society, 1712–1857*. Toronto: McClelland and Stewart 1965

Macpherson, Ken, and John Burgess, *The Ships of Canada's Naval Forces, 1910–1981*. Toronto: Collins 1981

Martin, Ged, ed. *Britain and the Origins of Canadian Confederation, 1837–67*. Vancouver: UBC Press 1995

McKee, F.M. *The Armed Yachts of Canada*. Erin: Boston Mills Press 1983

McLennan, J.S. *Louisbourg: From Its Foundation to Its Fall, 1713–1758*. Halifax: The Book Room 1979. First published 1918

McLeod, Dr William McK. *Memoirs*. Sydney: privately published n.d.

McLin, Jon B. *Canada's Changing Defense Policy, 1957–1963*. Baltimore: Johns Hopkins University Press 1967

Middleton, Richard. *The Bells of Victory: The Pitt-Newcastle Ministry and the Conduct of the Seven Years' War, 1757–1762*. Cambridge: Cambridge University Press 1985

Midddleton, W.E. Knowles. *Radar Development in Canada: The Radio Branch of the National Research Council of Canada, 1939–1946*. Waterloo: Wilfrid Laurier University Press 1981

Milner, Marc. *North Atlantic Run: The Royal Canadian Navy and the Battle for the Convoys*. Toronto: University of Toronto Press 1985

Miquelon, Dale. *New France, 1701–1744: 'A Supplement to Europe.'* Toronto: McClelland and Stewart 1987

Molson, K.M. and H.A. Taylor. *Canadian Aircraft Since 1909*. Stittsville, Ont.: Canada's Wings 1982

Morgan, R.J., ed. *More Essays in Cape Breton History*. Windsor, NS: Lancelot Press 1977

Morison, Samuel Eliot. *The Battle of the Atlantic, September 1939–May 1943*. Boston: Little Brown 1947.

Morrison, Alex, and Ted Slaney. *The Breed of Manly Men: The History of the Cape Breton Highlanders*. Toronto: Canadian Institute of Strategic Studies 1994

Morton, Desmond. *Ministers and Generals: Politics and the Canadian Militia, 1868–1904*. Toronto: University of Toronto Press 1970

Mount, Graeme S. *Canada's Enemies: Spies and Spying in the Peaceable Kingdom*. Toronto: Dundurn Press 1993

Mowat, Farley. *The Grey Seas Under*. Toronto: McClelland and Stewart 1958

Murdoch, Beamish. *A History of Nova Scotia or Acadie*. Halifax: James Barnes, 1866

Neary, Steve. *The Enemy on Our Doorstep: The German Attacks at Bell Island, Newfoundland, 1942.* St John's: Jesperson Press 1994

Newton, Pam. *The Cape Breton Book of Days.* Sydney: UCCB Press 1984

Nicholson, G.W.L. *The Gunners of Canada: The History of the Royal Regiment of Canadian Artillery.* Toronto: McClelland and Stewart 1967–72

Nova Scotia. *Debates of the House of Assembly of the Province of Nova Scotia.* Halifax 1861

– *Journals and Proceedings of the House of Assembly of the Province of Nova Scotia.* Halifax 1860–1

– *The Statutes of Nova Scotia.* Halifax 1865–7

Penlington, Norman. *Canada and Imperialism, 1896–1899.* Toronto: University of Toronto Press 1965

Pichon, Thomas. *Genuine Letters and Memoirs, Relating to the Natural, Civil, and Commercial History of the Islands of Cape Breton, and Saint John.* London: J. Nourse 1760

Piers, Harry. *The Evolution of the Halifax Fortress, 1749–1928.* Halifax: Public Archives of Nova Scotia 1947

Porter, Whitworth. *History of the Corps of Royal Engineers.* London: Longmans Green 1889

Prim, Joseph, and Mike McCarthy. *Those in Peril: The U-Boat Menace to Allied Shipping in Newfoundland and Labrador Waters, World War I and World War II.* St John's: Jesperson Press 1995

Pryke, Kenneth G. *Nova Scotia and Confederation, 1864–1874.* Toronto: University of Toronto Press 1979

Public Archives of Canada. *Annual Report, 1895.* Ottawa: King's Printer 1896

Quigley, John Gordon. *A Century of Rifles, 1860–1960: The Halifax Rifles.* Halifax: William Macnab and Son 1960

Richmond, H.W. *The Navy in the War of 1739–48.* Cambridge: Cambridge University Press 1918–20

Roberts, Leslie. *Canada and the War at Sea.* Montreal: Alvah M. Betty 1944

Rohwer, Jurgen. *Axis Submarine Successes, 1939–1945.* Annapolis: Naval Institute Press 1983

Runyan, Timothy J. and Jan M. Copes, eds. *To Die Gallantly: The Battle of the Atlantic.* Boulder: Westview Press 1994

Sarty, Roger. *Coast Artillery, 1815–1914.* Bloomfield, Ont.: Museum Restoration Service 1988

– 'Entirely in the Hands of the Friendly Neighbour': The Canadian Armed Forces and the Defence of the Pacific Coast 1909–1939.* Victoria: Pacific and Maritime Strategic Studies Group 1995. Occasional Paper No. 5

– *The Maritime Defence of Canada.* Toronto: Canadian Institute of Strategic Studies 1996

Saul, Donovan T., ed. *Red Serge and Stetsons.* [London]: Horsdal and Schubart 1993

Schull, Joseph. *The Far Distant Ships: An Official Account of Canadian Naval Operations in the Second World War.* Ottawa: Queen's Printer 1961

Senior, Elinor Kyte. *Roots of the Canadian Army: Montreal District, 1846–1870.* Montreal: The Society of the Montreal Military and Maritime Museum 1981

Senior, Hereward. *The Last Invasion of Canada: The Fenian Raids, 1866–1870.* Toronto: Dundurn Press 1991

Sleigh, B.W.A. *Pine Forests and Hacmatack Clearings; or Travel, Life and Adventure in the British North American Provinces.* London: Richard Bentley 1853

Spettigue, Douglas. *The Friendly Force.* Toronto: Longmans, Green [1955]

Stacey, C.P. *Canada and the British Army, 1846–1871: A Study in the Practice of Responsible Government.* Rev. ed. Toronto: University of Toronto Press 1963

– *The Canadian Army, 1939–1945.* Ottawa: King's Printer 1948

– *Six Years of War: The Army in Canada, Britain and the Pacific.* Ottawa: Queen's Printer 1955

Sydney (City). *Annual Report.* Sydney, 1917–19

Taylor, C.J. *Negotiating the Past: The Making of Canada's National Historic Parks and Sites.* Montreal and Kingston: McGill-Queen's University Press 1990

Tennyson, Brian Douglas, ed. *Impressions of Cape Breton.* Sydney: UCCB Press 1986

Tucker, Gilbert. *The Naval Service of Canada: Its Official History.* 2 vols. Ottawa: King's Printer 1952

United Kingdom. Admiralty. *U-Boat War in the Atlantic, 1939–1945 (German Naval History Series).* London: Admiralty 1950–77

– Admiralty Historical Section. *Home Waters and the Atlantic: September, 1939–6 December 1941 (Naval Staff History Second World War).* London: Admiralty 1954–61

– Admiralty Naval Staff. *The Atlantic Ocean, 1914–1915 (Naval Staff Monographs [Historical]).* London: Admiralty 1923

– Admiralty Technical History Section. *The Atlantic Convoy System 1917–18 (The Technical History and Index: A Serial History of Technical Problems Dealt with by Admiralty Departments, vol. 3, pt. 14).* London: Admiralty 1919

Upton, L.F.S. *Micmacs and Colonists: Indian-White Relations in the Maritimes, 1713–1867.* Vancouver: University of British Columbia Press 1979

van der Vat, Dan. *The Atlantic Campaign: World War II's Great Struggle at Sea.* New York: Harper and Row 1988

Vernon, C.W. *Cape Breton, Canada, at the Beginning of the Twentieth Century.* Toronto: Nation 1903

Waite, P.B. *The Life and Times of Confederation, 1864–1867: Politics, Newspapers, and the Union of British North America.* Toronto: University of Toronto Press 1962

Watt, Frederick B. *In All Respects Ready.* Scarborough: Prentice-Hall 1985

Whitelaw, William Menzies. *The Maritimes and Canada before Confederation.* 2nd paperback ed. Toronto: Oxford University Press 1966

Wilkshire, Michael, ed. *A Gentleman in the Outports: Gobineau and Newfoundland.* Ottawa: Carleton University Press 1993. First published as Joseph Arthur de Gobineau, *Voyage à Terre-Neuve.* 1861

Williams, Alan F. *Father Baudoin's War: D'Iberville's Campaigns in Acadia and Newfoundland, 1696, 1697.* St John's: Memorial University of Newfoundland 1987

Winks, Robin W. *Canada and the United States: The Civil War Years.* Baltimore: Johns Hopkins University Press 1960

Wise, S.F. *The Official History of the Royal Canadian Air Force.* Vol. 1. *Canadian Airmen and the First World War.* Toronto: University of Toronto Press and Department of National Defence 1980

Young, Richard J. *Blockhouses in Canada, 1749–1841: A Comparative Report and Catalogue.* Ottawa: Parks Canada, Canadian Historic Parks and Sites Branch 1980. Occasional Papers in Archaeology and History, no. 23

Zimmerman, David. *The Great Naval Battle of Ottawa.* Toronto: University of Toronto Press 1989

Articles

Anonymous. 'Cape Bretoners in World War One.' *Cape Breton's Magazine*, no. 33, 1–27

– 'Caribou Sinking, & Grandmère: 1942.' *Cape Breton's Magazine*, no. 46, 37–49

– 'Coast Gunners End Era Here.' *Mail-Star* (Halifax), 1 April 1960

– '"Fortress Sydney": Manning the Guns on the CB Coast.' *Cape Breton's Magazine*, no. 14, 33–40

– 'Magnificent Moxham's Castle in Sydney Used as a Convalescent Hospital in WWI.' *Cape Breton Post*, 9 November 1985

– 'Recall Last Ship Sinking.' *Atlantic Advocate*, June 1972, 25–6

– 'The Sinking of the "Caribou" Ferry.' *Cape Breton's Magazine*, no. 10, 20–8

– 'Sydney Harbour in World War 2.' *Cape Breton's Magazine*, no. 13, 27–40

– 'With Frank E. Jackson at 99.' *Cape Breton's Magazine*, no. 34, unpaginated

– 'With Sword and Rifle.' *Morning Sun* (North Sydney), 1 October 1892

Billard, Athelia Caldwell. 'The "Home Front" Was a Reality for Canadians on the Sea Coast.' *Northside Weekly*, 3 July, 10 July 1990

Black, Jeremy. 'Naval Power and British Foreign Policy in the Age of Pitt the Elder.' *The British Navy and the Use of Naval Power in the Eighteenth Century*, edited by Jeremy Black and Philip Woodfine. Atlantic Highlands, NJ: Humanities Press International 1989, 91–107

Braidwood, Ken L. 'The U-boat in the Straits.' *Atlantic Advocate*, June 1963, 88–91

Buckner, Philip A. 'The 1860s: An End and a Beginning.' *The Atlantic Region to Confederation: A History*, edited by Philip A. Buckner and John G. Reid. Toronto: University of Toronto Press 1994

Cameron, James M. 'Fenian Times in Nova Scotia.' *Collections of the Nova Scotia Historical Society* 37 (1970), 103–52

Campbell, John. 'Blackouts Remembered.' *Cape Breton Post*, 5 November 1994

Chirgwin, W.L. 'Harbour Forts of 200 Years Ago Recalled.' *Cape Breton Post* (undated clipping, c. 1961)

– 'The 94th Argyll Highland Regiment.' *Cape Breton Post* (undated clipping [1958])

– 'The Sydney Mines Volunteer Rifles.' *Cape Breton Post*, 13 June 1959

Collins, Julie. 'Historical Group to Show Northside as a War Port.' *Cape Breton Post*, 30 January 1997

Crowley, Terry. 'Monuments to Empire: Atlantic Forts and Fortifications.' *Acadiensis* 10, no. 2 (Spring 1981), 167–72

Donovan, Kenneth. 'A Nominal List of Slaves and Their Owners in Île Royale, 1713–1760.' *Nova Scotia Historical Review* 16, no. 1 (1996), 151–62

– 'Slaves and Their Owners in Île Royale, 1713–1760.' *Acadiensis* 25, no. 1 (Autumn 1995), 3–32

Douglas W.A.B. 'The Nazi Weather Station in Labrador.' *Canadian Geographic Journal* 101 (December 1981–January 1982), 42–7

Eccles, W.J. 'Paul Marin de La Malgue.' *Dictionary of Canadian Biography*. Vol. 3. Toronto: University of Toronto Press 1974

Edwards, Frank. 'Farthest East.' *Maclean's*, 1 November 1941, 18–9, 37–41. Reprinted in *Impressions of Cape Breton*, edited by Brian Douglas Tennyson. Sydney: UCCB Press 1986

Edwards, Joseph Plimsoll. 'The Militia of Nova Scotia, 1749–1867.' *Collections of the Nova Scotia Historical Society* 17 (1913), 63–108

Frank, David. 'The Cape Breton Coal Industry and the Rise and Fall of the British Empire Steel Corporation.' *Acadiensis* 7, no. 1 (1977), 3–34

Graham, Gerald S. 'Sir Hovenden Walker.' *Dictionary of Canadian Biography*. Vol. 2. Toronto: University of Toronto Press 1969

Gwyn, Julian. 'The Royal Navy in North America, 1712–1776.' In *The British Navy*

and the Use of Naval Power in the Eighteenth Century, edited by Jeremy Black and Philip Woodfine. Atlantic Highlands, NJ: Humanities Press International 1989
- 'Sir Peter Warren.' *Dictionary of Canadian Biography.* Vol. 3. Toronto: University of Toronto Press 1974
- 'War and Economic Change: Louisbourg and the New England Economy in the 1740s.' *Mélanges d'histoires*, edited by Pierre Savard. Ottawa: University of Ottawa Press 1978, 114–31
Harris, Daniel G. 'Canadian Warship Construction, 1917–19: The Great Lakes and Upper St Lawrence River Areas.' *Mariner's Mirror* 75 (May 1989), 149–58
Hines, Greg. 'Survivor Helps Remember Sinking.' *Cape Breton Post*, 11 December 1993
Horton, Donald J. 'Antoine-Denis Raudot.' *Dictionary of Canadian Biography.* Vol. 2. Toronto: University of Toronto 1969
Jones, J.R. 'Limitations of British Sea Power in the French Wars, 1689–1815.' In *The British Navy and the Use of Naval Power in the Eighteenth Century*, edited by Jeremy Black and Philip Woodfine. Atlantic Highlands, NJ: Humanities Press International 1989, 33–90
Kennedy, Paul M. 'Imperial Cable Communications and Strategy, 1870–1914.' *English Historical Review* 86, no. 341 (October 1971), 728–52
Keyserlingk, Robert H. '"Agents within the Gates": The Search for Nazi Subversives in Canada during World War II.' *Canadian Historical Review* 66, no. 2 (1985), 211–39
Kitchen, Martin. 'The German Invasion of Canada in the First World War.' *International History Review* 7, no. 2 (May 1985), 245–60
Knox, Bruce. 'The Concept of Empire in the Mid-nineteenth Century: Idea in the Colonial Defence Inquiries of 1859–61.' *Journal of Imperial and Commonwealth History* 15 (May 1987), 243–63
Langhout, Rosemary. 'Alternative Opportunities: The Development of Shipping at Sydney Harbour, 1842–1889.' In *Cape Breton at 200*, edited by Ken Donovan. Sydney: UCCB Press 1985, 53–69
MacDougall, Hector. 'Fond Memories of Fort Petrie in Wartime.' *Cape Breton Post*, 20 December 1990
MacGillivray, Dan. 'Many Who Protected CB Coasts Died Overseas.' *Cape Breton Post*, 28 September 1990
Macgillivray, Don. 'Military Aid to the Civil Power: The Cape Breton Experience in the 1920s.' *Acadiensis* 3, no. 2 (Spring 1974), 45–64
MacKinnon, Colin. 'Old and New Sydney; Notes by Mr M'Kinnon.' *Sydney Daily Post*, 21 March 1919
Marsh, Noreen. 'Cape Breton Prospered While War Raged.' *Cape Breton Post*, 8 May 1990

McDougall, David J. 'The Origins and Growth of the Canadian Customs Preventive Service Fleet in the Maritime Provinces and Quebec, 1892–1932.' *Northern Mariner* 5 (October 1995), 37–57

Milner, Marc. 'Canada's Naval War.' *Acadiensis* 12, no. 2 (Spring 1983), 162–71

Mitchell, R.B. 'Sydney Harbour – the War Years, 1939–1945.' In *More Essays in Cape Breton History*, edited by R.J. Morgan. Windsor, NS: Lancelot Press 1977

Moogk, Peter N. 'Fortress Sydney: Manning the Guns on the Cape Breton Coast.' *Cape Breton's Magazine*, No. 33, unpaginated

– 'From Fortress Louisbourg to Fortress Sydney: Artillery and Gunners on Cape Breton, 1743–1964.' In *Cape Breton at 200*, edited by Kenneth Donovan. Sydney: UCCB Press 1985, 127–82

– 'Remembering Cape Breton's Gunners.' *Canadian Gunner* 13 (December 1977), 124–38

Moore, Christopher. 'The Other Louisbourg: Trade and Merchant Enterprise in Île Royale, 1713–58.' *Histoire sociale/Social History* 12 (May 1979), 79–96

Morgan, Robert J. 'David Mathews.' *Dictionary of Canadian Biography*. Vol. 4. Toronto: University of Toronto Press 1979

– 'George Robert Ainslie.' *Dictionary of Canadian Biography*. Vol. 7. Toronto: University of Toronto Press 1988

– 'James Ogilvie.' *Dictionary of Canadian Biography*. Vol. 5. Toronto: University of Toronto Press 1983

– 'John Despard.' *Dictionary of Canadian Biography*. Vol. 6. Toronto: University of Toronto Press 1987

– 'Nicholas Nepean.' *Dictionary of Canadian Biography*. Toronto: Vol. 6. University of Toronto Press 1987

– 'Richard Gibbons.' *Dictionary of Canadian Biography*. Vol. 4. Toronto: University of Toronto Press 1979

– 'Richard Stout.' *Dictionary of Canadian Biography*. Vol. 5. Toronto: University of Toronto Press 1983

– 'William Macarmick.' *Dictionary of Canadian Biography*. Vol. 5. Toronto: University of Toronto Press 1983

Morton, Desmond. 'Aid to the Civil Power: The Canadian Militia in Support of Social Order, 1867–1914.' *Canadian Historical Review* 51, no. 4 (December 1970), 407–25

Preston, Adrian. 'Canada and the Russian crisis of 1878: a proposed contingent for imperial defence.' *Dalhousie Review* 48, no. 1 (1968–9), 185–99

Rohwer, Jurgen. 'Special Intelligence und die Geleitzugsteuerung im Herbst 1941.' *Marine Rundschau* 11 (November 1978), 711–19

Rohwer, Jurgen, and Roger Sarty. 'Intelligence and the Air Forces in the Battle of the Atlantic, 1943–1945.' International Commission of Military History. *Acta* 13, no. 2 (1991), 135–61

Roy, R.H. 'Hard Luck Flotilla: The RCN's Atlantic Coast Patrol 1914–18.' In *The RCN in Transition, 1910–1985*, edited by W.A.B. Douglas. Vancouver: UBC Press 1988

– 'Morale in the Canadian Army in Canada during the Second World War.' *Canadian Defence Quarterly* 16 (Autumn 1986), 40–5

Sarty, Roger. 'The Limits of Ultra: The Schnorkel Boat Offensive against North America, November 1944–January 1945.' *Journal of Intelligence and National Security* 12 (April 1997), 44–68

Scobie, Maureen. 'Ingonish Native Gordon Hardy Recalls Night Rose Castle Torpedoed Off Newfoundland.' *Cape Breton Post*, 10 November 1993

Shipley, Robert. 'Lest We Forget: War Memorials in Disrepair.' *Heritage Canada* (August 1979), 27–8

Stanley, G.F.G. 'The Defence of the Maritime Provinces during the Wars of the French Revolution.' *Canadian Defence Quarterly* 14 (1936–1937), 437–47

– 'The Royal Nova Scotia Regiment, 1793–1802.' *Journal of the Royal Army Historical Society* 21 (1942), 157–70

Talman, J.J. 'A Secret Military Document, 1825.' *American Historical Review* 37 (January 1933), 295–300

Tennyson, Brian Douglas. 'Cape Breton in 1867.' *Nova Scotia Historical Quarterly* 6, no. 2 (June 1976) 193–206

– 'Early Fortifications on Sydney Harbour.' *Nova Scotia Historical Review* 15, no. 1 (1995), 1–32

– 'Economic Nationalism and Confederation: A Case Study in Cape Breton.' *Acadiensis* 2, no. 2 (1972), 39–53

Tennyson, Brian Douglas, and Roger Sarty. 'Sydney, Nova Scotia, and the U-boat War 1918.' *Canadian Military History* 7, no. 1 (Winter 1998), 29–41

White, Jay. '"Sleepless and Veiled Am I": An East Coast Canadian Port Revisited.' *Nova Scotia Historical Review* 5, no. 1 (1985), 15–29

Yorke, Howard K. 'A Saga of the *Caribou*.' *Nova Scotia Historical Review* 5, no. 1 (1985), 31–6

Zatsman, Julie. 'War Years in Sydney Recalled.' *Cape Breton Post*, 10 November 1989

Unpublished Works

Anonymous. 'Initial Environmental Evaluation of Victoria Park Construction and Post Construction Activities.' 2 vols. Sydney: Washburn & Gillis Associates Ltd 1995

Douglas, W.A.B. 'Halifax as an Element of Sea Power, 1749 to 1766.' MA thesis, Dalhousie University 1962

Evans, Roger A. 'The Army and Navy at Halifax in Peace-Time, 1783–1793.' MA thesis, Dalhousie University 1970

Mackinnon, C.S. 'The Imperial Fortresses in Canada: Halifax and Esquimalt, 1871–1906.' PhD thesis, University of Toronto 1965

McDonald, Ronald H. 'The Public Career of Major-General Sir Hastings Doyle, 1861–1873.' MA thesis, Dalhousie University 1969

Morgan, Robert. 'Orphan Outpost: Cape Breton Colony, 1784–1820.' PhD thesis, University of Ottawa 1972

Pariseau, Jean. 'Forces armées et maintien de l'ordre au Canada, 1867–1967: un siècle d'aide au pouvoir civil.' PhD thesis, Université Paul Valéry III 1981

Sarty, Roger. 'Local Boys and Redcoats: The Relations of the Militia in Nova Scotia and the British Garrison at Halifax, 1860–1906.' MA research paper, Duke University 1976

– 'Silent Sentry: A Military and Political History of Canadian Coast Defence, 1860–1945.' PhD thesis, University of Toronto 1983

Vincent, Elizabeth. 'The British Garrison at Sydney, Cape Breton Island, 1785–1854.' Ottawa: Historic Sites and Monuments Board of Canada, 1984

Interviews

Avery, G.E. Halifax, January 1973

Callahan, G.C. Isaac's Harbour, NS, 2 August 1979

Coffin, David. Sydney, 10 June 1994

Haley, Martin (by telephone). Halifax, 29 December 1971

Huntley, Alec. Sydney, 9 June 1994

MacDougall, Duncan. Donkin, NS, 11 May 1994

Partington, K.J.B. Halifax, 28 July 1972

Quann, John. Glace Bay, 12 May 1994

Robertson, G.B. Halifax, 9 August 1979

Slaven, Sydney. Sydney, 21 January 1997

Illustration credits

Index